Exodus

The Contextual Critical Commentary

The Contextual Critical Commentary (CCC) on the Bible offers students, scholars, and clergy an affordable and scholarly resource to inform the reading and interpretation of the books of the Bible. The CCC integrates contextual work that critically explores the historical, literary, and theological context of biblical books in relation to the ancient Near Eastern and Greco-Roman worlds of ancient Israel, Judah, and the early church. The historical context will provide a background for future contextual readings of these texts, their reception, and their interpretation within Judaism and Christianity. Finally, the ancient context and key turning points in reception history will inform the concerns of contemporary readings of biblical texts, suggesting ways that their past contexts can guide both scholarly readers and readers in faith communities today.

"With this noteworthy volume, Sweeney inaugurates the new Contextual Critical Commentary. Arguing that the narratives in Exodus derive from traditions of northern Israel, the author presents an innovative perspective: that the book is 'a typical Ancient Near Eastern creation narrative.' In addition, Sweeney cites numerous examples from the reception history of Exodus: in later biblical texts, Jewish and Christian traditions, and appropriations by artists. A rich resource for understanding the book of Exodus."

—**David L. Petersen**, Franklin N. Parker Professor Emeritus of Old Testament, Emory University

"In his commentary on Exodus, Marvin Sweeney, one of the most learned and versatile biblical scholars of our time, once again demonstrates his impressive ability to address the scriptural text on multiple levels and through multiple periods, from the earliest pre-literary traditions through contemporary applications across the globe. Every reader, whether agreeing with his conclusions and speculations or not, will come away from this book informed and enriched. I certainly did."

—**Jon D. Levenson**, author of *Israel's Day of Light and Joy: The Origin, Development, and Enduring Meaning of the Jewish Sabbath*

"The book of Exodus generates numerous questions on strange terms, exotic culture, and age-old legal documents: ancient Near Eastern backgrounds behind Moses's upbringing, features of manna and quail, philosophy behind the Ten Commandments plus 'lex talionis' vis-à-vis Jesus' Sermon on the Mount, protection rights for female members or resident aliens, whereabouts of the ark, and so on. Professor Sweeney presents lucid explanations on these topics through expertise on ancient sources, in-depth literary-theological interpretations, and reception history of Second Temple texts, New Testament, and rabbinic hermeneutics. This commentary is richly informative, enlightening, and inspiring with ethical and theological lessons for today's worshipping communities and law-abiding societies."

—**Hyun Chul Paul Kim**, Harold B. Williams Professor of Hebrew Bible, Methodist Theological School in Ohio

"Sweeney defines Exodus as 'Israel's independence narrative'—the story of the people delivered by YHWH, the Israelite God, who triumphed over the Egyptian Pharaoh. Studying the book both synchronically and diachronically, Sweeney integrates literary-history, historical, and comparative methodologies, and contributes important theological observations on Exodus, considering its early stratum to reflect Israelite-Ephraimitic religion. Scholars, students, and interested readers will each find this commentary compelling, realizing that reception history starts already within the Hebrew Bible itself."

—**Dalit Rom-Shiloni**, Professor, Department of Biblical Studies, Tel Aviv University

Exodus

The Contextual Critical Commentary

Marvin A. Sweeney
Claremont School of Theology

CASCADE *Books* • Eugene, Oregon

EXODUS

The Contextual Critical Commentary

Cascade Books
An Imprint of Wipf and Stock Publishers
199 W. 8th Ave., Suite 3
Eugene, OR 97401

www.wipfandstock.com

PAPERBACK ISBN: 978-1-6667-4066-0
HARDCOVER ISBN: 978-1-6667-4067-7
EBOOK ISBN: 978-1-6667-4068-4

Cataloguing-in-Publication data:

Names: Sweeney, Marvin A. (Marvin Alan), 1953– [author].

Title: Exodus / by Marvin A. Sweeney.

Description: Eugene, OR: Cascade Books, 2026 | Series: The Contextual Critical Commentary | Includes bibliographical references and index.

Identifiers: ISBN 978-1-6667-4066-0 (paperback) | ISBN 978-1-6667-4067-7 (hardcover) | ISBN 978-1-6667-4068-4 (ebook)

Subjects: LCSH: Bible.—Exodus—Commentaries. | Commentaries.

Classification: BS1245.3 S944 2026 (paperback) | BS1245.3 (ebook)

VERSION NUMBER 03/03/26

For

Mikhail Beizer, PhD,

and

Marc J. Slotnick, Esq.

Contents

III. DIVINE REVELATION AT MOUNT SINAI

Exodus 19:1—Numbers 2:34

Preface

I WOULD LIKE TO thank a number of people for their roles in the production of this volume. First is my lovely wife, Dr. Soo Jung Kim Sweeney, who is also a Hebrew Bible scholar, for her wisdom and support. Professor Hye-Kyung Park, head of the College of Theology and a member of the Contextual Critical Commentary Series editorial board, Chang Jung Christian University, Tainan, Taiwan, read a draft of this volume. My research associate, Rev. Hyunghee Kim, also read the draft of this manuscript. My commissioning editor at Cascade Books, Mr. Michael Thomson, played a major role in commissioning this volume and seeing it through the publication process. Dr. K. C. Hanson, editor in chief of Cascade Books and a former classmate in the PhD program in Hebrew Bible at the Claremont Graduate School, for his role in commissioning this volume. I am indebted to Dr. Robin Parry, who served as my editor on behalf of Cascade for the publication of this volume. His careful work, with that of Rebecca Abbott, my proofreader, saved me from many embarrassing errors. Any that remain are my own responsibility. I would also like to thank my research associate, Mr. Hyunghee Kim, PhD student in Hebrew Bible at the Claremont School of Theology, for preparing the indices.

This volume is dedicated to Mikhail Beizer, PhD, now of Jerusalem, Israel, and Marc J. Slotnick, Esq., a prominent attorney, now of Charleston, West Virginia, with gratitude and admiration. In March, 1987, Marc, then an undergraduate student at the University of Miami, and I, then assistant professor of religious studies at the University of Miami, were sent on a mission to the former Soviet Union, sponsored by the South Florida Council on Soviet Jewry and the University of Miami Hillel, to meet with Refuseniks in Moscow and Leningrad (now

St. Petersburg). Apart from brief visits to the Mexican border cities of Tijuana and Nogales and the Bahamian port city of Freeport, I had never been to a foreign country before.

Marc and I were trained by the South Florida Conference on Soviet Jewry and given lists of contacts in Moscow and Leningrad and supplies of books, medications, and other necessary items for the persons we were assigned to meet in both cities. In Moscow, we met with all of our assigned contacts and many more individuals, but near the end of our stay in Moscow, the Soviet authorities, who recognized all along what we were doing, stopped us to ask questions and let us know that they were watching before they released us. Upon our arrival in Leningrad, I spotted the officer who oversaw our interrogation in Moscow as we were walking out of the Leningrad train station, and we knew that we were being watched. But we also knew that the Soviet authorities would do little to us beyond expelling us from the country. Nevertheless, we recognized that our contacts might face greater dangers.

In Leningrad, we met our primary contact and guide, Mikhail Beizer, and we informed him of our situation, but he was accustomed to such harassment from the Soviet authorities, and made sure that we met all of our contacts and more. Upon our departure from Leningrad, we were followed by a black Zil sedan, apparently to make sure that we left the Soviet Union as we intended, but the Zil broke off its contact when we entered the Leningrad Airport gate. We faced no more difficulties on departure, and the entire plane burst into cheers and applause when we crossed the Soviet border over Poland on the first leg of our return flight to Germany.

All of our contacts and more were released by the Soviet authorities within a few months after our visit. I have lost contact with most of them, except for Beizer, who made Aliyah to Jerusalem, studied for his PhD, and taught at the Hebrew University of Jerusalem, where I served as a Yad ha-Nadiv Barechah Foundation Post-Doctoral Fellow in Jewish Studies in 1989–1990. I have travelled to Jerusalem frequently over the years, and I see Beizer and his family every chance I can. I have also kept contact with Marc through the years as he married a lady from Charleston, West Virginia, and has served as an attorney there for many years. My father, Jack H. Sweeney, was originally from Pax, West Virginia, and much of my father's family is located in Beckley, West Virginia, where my paternal grandparents, Walter Isaac Sweeney and Callie Beth Stanley Sweeney, and my uncle, Private Dock J. Sweeney, US Army, killed in action in Germany near the end of World War II, are buried. I have dedicated other works to my parents, my grandparents, and my aunts and uncles, including Uncle Dock.

During our time in Moscow and Leningrad, I lectured on Exodus to groups of Refuseniks with whom we met. Hence, my interest in Exodus is informed by my identities as a scholar and as a Jew and by my role in meeting so many Refuseniks in the former Soviet Union in 1987. In keeping with some circles in Judaism, the terms G-d and L-rd are employed in reference to the Deity.

I therefore dedicate this volume to Dr. Mikhail Beizer and Mr. Marc J. Slotnick, Esq., with gratitude for our friendship and pride in what we accomplished.

Salem, Oregon December 29, 2024
Hanukkah, 4th Day 28 Kislev, 5785

Abbreviations

1 Apol.	*First Apology*
AB	Anchor Bible, now Yale Anchor Bible
ABD	*Anchor Bible Dictionary.* Edited by David Noel Freedman. 6 vols. New York: Doubleday, 1992
AGJU	Arbeiten zur Geschichte des antiken Judentums und des Urchristentums
AIL	Ancient Israelite Literature
AnBib	Analecta Biblica
ANEM	Ancient Near Eastern Monographs
ANEP	*The Ancient Near East in Pictures Relating to the Old Testament.* Edited by James B. Pritchard. Princeton: Princeton University Press, 1969
ANET	*Ancient Near Eastern Texts Relating to the Old Testament.* Edited by James B. Pritchard. Princeton: Princeton University Press, 1969
Ant.	*Jewish Antiquities*
ASOR	American Schools of Oriental Research
ATANT	Abhandlungen zur Theologie des Alten und Neuen Testaments
BA	*Biblical Archaeologist*
BAR	*Biblical Archaeology Review*

BASOR	*Bulletin of the American Schools of Oriental Research*
BDB	Brown, Francis, S. R. Driver, and Charles A. Briggs. *A Hebrew and English Lexicon of the Old Testament*. Oxford: Clarendon, 1974
BEATAJ	Beiträge zur Erforschung des Alten Testaments und des antiken Judentum
BETL	Bibliotheca Ephemeridum Theologicarum Lovaniensium
Bib	*Biblica*
BibSem	The Biblical Seminar
BJS	Brown Judaic Studies
BKAT	Biblischer Kommentar, Altes Testament
BO	Berit Olam
B. Qam.	Baba Qamma
BZAW	Beihefte zur Zeitschrift für die alttestamentliche Wissenschaft
CBQ	*Catholic Biblical Quarterly*
CBQMS	Catholic Biblical Quarterly Monograph Series
CBS	Core Biblical Studies
CC	Continental Commentaries
ChrH	The Chronicler's History
ConBOT	Coniectanea Biblica: Old Testament Series
CRINT	Compendia Rerum Iudaicarum ad Novum Testamentum
CurBS	*Currents in Research: Biblical Studies*
DDD	*Dictionary of Deities and Demons in the Bible*. Edited by Karel van der Toorn et al. 2nd rev. ed. Grand Rapids: Eerdmans, 1999
De univ.	*De universo de rerum naturis*
Dial.	*Dialogus cum Tryphone*
DJD	Discoveries in the Judean Desert
DtrH	Deuteronomistic History

EBR	*Encyclopedia of the Bible and Its Reception*. Edited by Hans-Josef Klauck et al. Berlin: de Gruyter, 2009–
ECC	Eerdmans Critical Commentary
EncJud	*Encyclopedia Judaica*. Edited by Cecil Roth et al. 16 vols. Jerusalem: Keter, n.d.
Enarrat. Ps.	*Enarrationes in Psalmos*
FAT	Forschungen zum Alten Testament
Fest.	Festschrift
FOTL	Forms of the Old Testament Literature
FRLANT	Forschungen zur Religion und Literatur des Alten und Neuen Testaments
Fug.	*De fuga et inventione*
Git.	Gittin
GKC	*Gesenius' Hebrew Grammar.* Edited by Emil Kautzsch. Translated by Arther E. Cowley. 2nd ed. Oxford: Clarendon, 1910
Haer.	*Adversus haereses*
HALOT	*The Hebrew and Aramaic Lexicon of the Old Testament.* Ludwig Koehler, Walter Baumgartner, and Johann J. Stamm. Translated and edited under the supervision of Mervyn E. J. Richardson. 4 vols. Leiden: Brill, 1994–99
HAT	Handbuch zum Alten Testament
HCOT	Historical Commentary on the Old Testament
Her.	*Quis rerum divinarum heres sit*
Hist.	*Histories*
HKAT	Handkommentar zum Alten Testament
HR	*History of Religions*
HS	*Hebrew Studies*
HSM	Harvard Semitic Monographs
HUCA	*Hebrew Union College Annual*

Ḥul.	*Ḥullin*
IBT	Interpreting Biblical Texts
ICC	International Critical Commentary
IDB	*The Interpreter's Dictionary of the Bible*. Edited by George A. Buttrick. 4 vols. Nashville, Abingdon, 1962
IDBSup	*The Interpreter's Dictionary of the Bible: Supplementary Volume*. Edited by Keith Crim. Nashville: Abingdon, 1976
IECOT	International Exegetical Commentary on the Old Testament
IEJ	*Israel Exploration Journal*
JAOS	*Journal of the American Oriental Society*
JBL	*Journal of Biblical Literature*
JBT	*Jahrbuch für Biblische Theologie*
JPS	Jewish Publication Society
JR	*Journal of Religion*
JSJSup	Journal for the Study of Judaism Supplement Series
JSOT	*Journal for the Study of the Old Testament*
JSOTSup	Journal for the Study of the Old Testament Supplement Series
KAT	Kommentar zum Alten Testament
KTU	*Die keilalphabetischen Texte aus Ugarit*. Edited by Manfried Dietrich et al. Münster: Ugarit, 2013
LBT	Library of Biblical Theology
Leg.	*Legum allegoriae*
LHBOTS	The Library of Hebrew Bible/Old Testament Studies
LSJ	Liddell, Henry George, Robert Scott, Henry Stuart Jones. *A Greek-English Lexicon*. 9th ed. with revised supplement. Oxford: Clarendon, 1996
LXX	Septuagint
Menaḥ.	Menahot

Miqw.	Mikwaʾot
Mos.	*De vita Mosis*
MT	Masoretic Text
NCBC	New Cambridge Bible Commentary
NCeBC	New Century Bible Commentary
NEAEHL	*New Encyclopedia of Archaeological Excavations in the Holy Land.* Edited by Ephraim Stern. 4 vols.; Jerusalem: Israel Exploration Society & Carta, 1993
NICOT	New International Commentary on the Old Testament
NT	New Testament
OBO	Orbis Biblicus et Orientalis
OBT	Overtures to Biblical Theology
ʾOhal.	Ohalot
Orig. Hom. Jos.	*Origenis Homiliae in librum Josua*
OT	Old Testament
OTG	Old Testament Guides
OTL	Old Testament Library
Pesaḥ.	Pesahim
RBS	Resources for Biblical Study
Roš Haš.	Rosh ha-Shanah
ROT	Reading the Old Testament
Šabb.	Shabbat
SAC	Studies in Antiquity and Christianity
Sanh.	Sanhedrin
SBL	Society of Biblical Literature
SBLDS	Society of Biblical Literature Dissertation Series
SBLMS	Society of Biblical Literature Monograph Series
SBLStBL	Society of Biblical Literature Studies in Biblical Literature

SBS	Stuttgarter Bibelstudien
SBT	Studies in Biblical Theology
SBTS	Sources for Biblical and Theological Study
Šebu.	Shevuot
SOTSMS	Society for Old Testament Studies Monograph Series
Spec.	*De specialibus legibus*
Strom.	*Stromateis*
SymS	Symposium Series
TDNT	*Theological Dictionary of the New Testament*. Edited by Gerhard Kittel and Gerhard Friedrich. Translated by Geoffrey W. Bromiley. 10 vols. Grand Rapids: Eerdmans, 1964–76
TDOT	*Theological Dictionary of the Old Testament*. Edited by G. Johannes Botterweck et al. Translated by John T. Willis et al. 16 vols. Grand Rapids: Eerdmans, 1974–2021
TLZ	*Theologische Literaturzeitung*
TSAJ	Texte und Studien zum antiken Judentum
VTSup	Supplements to Vetus Testamentum
WBC	Word Biblical Commentary
WMANT	Wissenschaftliche Monographien zum Alten und Neuen Testament
YAB	Yale Anchor Bible
ZAW	*Zeitschrift für die alttestamentliche Wissenschaft*

Introduction

I. Synchronic Canonical-Literary Role of Exodus Within the Pentateuch

The book of Exodus is the second book of the Five Books of Moses, known as the Torah (Hebrew, *tôrâ*, "instruction") in Judaism and as the Law (Greek, *ho nomos*) or the Pentateuch (Greek, *ho pentateuchos*, lit., "the five cases [for holding papyrus scrolls]") in Christianity. The order of the books is consistent in both traditions.[1] In Judaism, the titles of the books are derived from the first Hebrew words of each book, *bĕrēʾšît*, "when [G-d] began," for Genesis; *wĕʾēlleh šĕmôt*, "and these are the names," for Exodus; *wayyiqrāʾ*, "and (YHWH) called," for Leviticus; *bĕmidbar*, "in the wilderness," for Numbers; and *ʾēlleh haddĕbārîm*, "these are the words," for Deuteronomy. In Christianity, the names of the books are based in Greek phraseology meant to characterize the contents of each book, including *Genesis*, "beginning"; *Exodus*, "going out"; *Leuitikon*, "concerning the Levites"; *Arithmoi*, "numbers"; and *Deuteronomion*, "second [repetition of the] law."

Although the Pentateuch is divided into five major books, the synchronic literary form of the Pentateuch displays a very distinctive narrative structure.[2] Within the synchronic narrative structure of the Pentateuch, Exodus recounts the enslavement of Israel in Egypt after Jacob and his sons (and their families) journeyed to Egypt to escape famine in the land of Canaan as recounted in Genesis 46–50 (see esp. Gen 46:1). Exodus is

1. For discussion of the canonical literary form of the Pentateuch, see Leiman, *Canonization*; Beckwith, *Old Testament Canon*; Trebolle Barrera, *Jewish Bible and Christian Bible*; Lim, *Formation of Jewish Canon*; Sweeney, *Pentateuch*.

2. For an overview discussion, see Sweeney, *Pentateuch*, xvii–xxix.

therefore subsumed structurally under the formal structure of the final Priestly edition of the Pentateuch, which is organized into a succession of passages introduced by the formula, "these are the generations of PN" (Hebrew, *ʾēlleh tôlĕdôt PN).*[3] Thus, Exodus is part of the textual component, Genesis 37:2—Numbers 2:34, "these are the generations of Jacob," which recounts the history of the twelve tribes of Israel. Within Genesis 37:2—Numbers 2:34, Genesis 37:2—45:28 recounts how Joseph came to Egypt, rose to power, and revealed himself to his brothers when they came to seek assistance from Egypt during a period of famine in Canaan.[4] Once Joseph revealed himself to his brothers in Genesis 37:2—45:28, the travel itinerary formula, introduced by a *waw*-imperfect form of the verb *wayyissaʿ*, "and he travelled," or *wayyisĕʿû*, "and they travelled," recounts the movements of the people of Israel as they journeyed first to Egypt in Genesis 46:1—Exodus 12:36, and then through a succession of sites as they journeyed from Egypt to Mount Sinai in the Sinai wilderness, including from the city of Rameses in Egypt to Sukkot in Exodus 12:37—13:19;

3. The use of the toledoth formula in the final Priestly edition of the Pentateuch was introduced by Cross, "Priestly Work." Unfortunately, Cross failed to note Numbers 3:1 within his analysis of the toledoth formula. See now Thomas, *These Are the Generations*; Sweeney, *Tanak*, 45–53; Sweeney, *Pentateuch*, xxvii–xxix.

4. The role of the travel itinerary formula, originally considered as the wilderness itinerary formula, was identified by Cross as a structural feature of the P-stratum of the Pentateuch ("Priestly Work") for the account of the exodus and wilderness narratives in Exodus–Numbers. But Cross failed to take proper account of the role of the travel itinerary formula in Genesis 11:2; 12:9; 20:1; and 46:1 in his discussion, and the present author likewise failed to note the role of these texts in earlier discussion due to having followed Cross. But as the present commentary demonstrates, there are reasons to identity the travel itinerary formula as a feature of the E-stratum composition of the Pentateuch, due in part to its failure to align with the structural role of the P-stratum toledoth formula and its affinities to northern-oriented texts in the underlying exodus narrative. Likewise, Genesis 11:2; 12:9; 20:1; and 46:1 are all considered J-stratum texts (see Campbell and O'Brien, *Sources of the Pentateuch*, 97–98, 99, 104, 129). But each of these texts appears to be associated with texts that display E-stratum characteristics. The tower of Babel passage in Genesis 11:1–9 presupposes Israel's understanding of Babel, which begins in the late ninth century BCE, as demonstrated by the discovery of cuneiform legal tablets from Hammurabi's law code dating to the Middle Bronze Age at Hazor (Horowitz et al., "Hazor 18"). Genesis 12:9 concludes Genesis 12:1–9, which recounts Abram's journey from Haran through Shechem, Beth El, and Ai, all of which are in northern Israel, indicating that the text originated as an E-stratum text that was reworked by the J-stratum. Genesis 20:1 introduces Genesis 20:1–18, which is generally considered to be an E-stratum text. Genesis 46:1 introduces Genesis 46:1–34, which recounts Jacob's relocation from Canaan to Egypt at the invitation of his son, Joseph, the ancestor of Ephraim and Manasseh, the two key power tribes of the Northern Kingdom of Israel, thereby indicating its E-stratum origins. For further discussion, see the following commentary.

from Sukkot to Etham in Exodus 13:20–22; from Etham to the Reed Sea in Exodus 14:1—15:21; from the Reed Sea to the Wilderness of Shur/Elim in Exodus 15:22–27; from Elim to the Wilderness of Sin in Exodus 16:1–36; from the Wilderness of Sin to Rephidim in Exodus 17:1—18:27; and from Rephidim to Mount Sinai in Exodus 19:1—Numbers 2:24. While Israel resides at Mount Sinai, the narrative comprises four major components, including the arrival at Mount Sinai in Exodus 19:1–2; the revelation from the mountain in Exodus 19:3—40:38; the revelation from the tabernacle in Leviticus 1:1—27:34; and the census and organization of the people around the tabernacle in Numbers 1:1—2:34.

Following the revelation at Sinai, the formula "and these are the generations of Aaron and Moses" in Numbers 3:1 introduces the history of Israel under the guidance of the Levites in Numbers 3:1—Deuteronomy 34:12. Numbers 3:1—Deuteronomy 34:12 includes a second set of travel itinerary formulas to recount the journey from Mount Sinai to the Jordan River in Moab, immediately prior to Israel's entry into the promised land of Israel as recounted in the book of Joshua.

II. The Generic Character of Exodus as a Creation Narrative

Although the book of Exodus is written as a narrative account of the departure of the people of Israel from Egypt and Egyptian slavery, the narrative is formulated as a typical ancient Near Eastern creation narrative.[5] Within the canonical context of the Pentateuch, the original creation narratives appear in Genesis 1–3; therefore, creation in the Exodus–Numbers and the Deuteronomy narratives appears a secondary stage of creation in which elements of creation emerge to function as the agents that G-d employs to free Israel from Egyptian slavery and lead them to the promised land of Israel.

The book of Exodus includes a variety of creation elements and references in its depiction of G-d's efforts to free Israel from Egypt and to begin the process of leading Israel to the promised land of Israel. The narrative begins in Exodus 1 with an account of the efforts of a new pharaoh, who did not know Joseph, to limit, subjugate, and enslave Israel due to his fear that Israel might successfully revolt against Egypt.

5. Sweeney, "Creation as Sacred Space"; see also Sweeney, "Creation as Active Agent." Cf. Levenson, *Sinai and Zion*; Levenson, *Creation and Persistence of Evil.*

Insofar as pharaoh is considered to be a god in ancient Egypt, the narrative signals a motif of divine combat between pharaoh, the god of Egypt, and YHWH, the G-d of Israel, to determine which one is the true deity and ruler of creation and human beings. Despite pharaoh's efforts to kill all the newborn males among Israel, the Hebrew midwives, Shiphrah and Puah, played key roles in thwarting the attempted Egyptian murder of Israelite male babies by claiming that the Hebrew mothers were so vigorous that, unlike Egyptian mothers, the Hebrew mothers gave birth to healthy boy babies before the midwives could arrive. Such a claim asserts that Hebrew women were far more fertile than Egyptian women, and therefore better able to give birth in a world of creation controlled by the Israelite G-d, YHWH.

When G-d self-revealed to Moses on Mount Sinai (Exodus 3), itself an element in the world of creation, another element of creation played a key role. The burning bush image, which metaphorically depicted the divine presence on Mount Sinai, is based on a bush native to the Sinai wilderness known as the *rubus sanctus*. The *rubus sanctus* blossoms with red flowers in the spring that cause it to resemble a bush on fire when viewed from a distance. G-d then spoke through the agency of this bush to commission Moses to lead Israel out of Egyptian bondage and to the land of Israel. When Moses and his brother, Aaron, confronted pharaoh and his magicians to release Israel from bondage in Exodus 5, they employed Aaron's rod, which turned into a snake—an element of creation that was recognized as a symbol of divine power, life, and fertility in ancient Egypt and throughout the ancient world—to demonstrate G-d's power over the Egyptian pharaoh, his magicians, and creation itself.

When the confrontation with pharaoh turned into a conflict to demonstrate who the true G-d of creation was (i.e., pharaoh or the G-d of Israel), G-d in Exodus 7–13 employed the ten plagues, nine of which were elements of creation, to demonstrate that the G-d of Israel is the true G-d of creation. The elements include the Nile turning to blood, which presupposes the annual spring floods of the Nile, which carry the rich brownish-red soil of the Ethiopian and Sudanese highlands in their waters to flood the Nile Valley of Egypt to give the land its fertility. This is followed by other plagues, which presuppose the effects of the annual Nile flood, viz., frogs, which are also carried by the waters; gnats, which appear as the frogs die and decompose as the waters recede; flies, which grow up from gnats; cattle disease, which results from the bites of flies; boils on human beings, which also result from insect bites; hail, which is a natural phenomenon of creation; locusts, another feature of natural creation; and darkness caused when the sirocco winds—known as the *ḥamsin* winds in Arabic, the *sharav* in Hebrew, and the Santa Ana winds in the American Southwest—block out the sun due to the dirt and debris carried by the sirocco during times of seasonal change, such as the spring, in the so-called Mediterranean climate. The tenth plague, the death of the firstborn, presupposes the early conceptualization of the Israelite priesthood in which firstborn sons are offered to G-d to assist the Aaronide priests at sanctuaries, and firstborn animals and agricultural firstfruits are offered to G-d at the celebration of Passover at the beginning of the spring agricultural season.[6]

When pharaoh reneges on his promise to let the people of Israel go, G-d thwarts pharaoh and the Egyptian army by using the Sea of Reeds to deliver Israel from the Egyptians and to defeat the Egyptian army in Exodus 14–15. These purposes are carried out when G-d causes the waters of the Reed Sea to divide, thereby causing dry land to emerge from the depths of the Reed Sea's waters, a clear motif of creation in which dry land emerges from the waters of chaos. The dry land enables Israel to escape from the Egyptian army. But when the Egyptian chariots attempt to pass through the Reed Sea to pursue Israel, G-d causes the waters of the Reed Sea to flood the dry land once again, thereby drowning the Egyptian army.

When Israel undertakes its journey from the Reed Sea to Mount Sinai in the Sinai wilderness in Exodus 16–18, elements of creation again play roles as the agents of G-d's efforts to sustain and deliver the people of Israel. When the people become hungry in the wilderness in Exodus 16, G-d supplies them with quail and manna, both of which are features of the natural environment of creation in the Sinai wilderness, to serve as food. When the people lack water in Exodus 17:1–8, G-d supplies them with water in the wilderness.

When G-d self-reveals to Israel in the Sinai wilderness, G-d does so at Mount Sinai—again, a natural feature of creation—to provide Israel with the instructions necessary to build a just and holy society in the promised land of Canaan. Those instructions culminate in G-d's instructions to build a wilderness tabernacle, which serves as a precursor to the Israelite sanctuaries, such as those at Gilgal, Shiloh, Beth El, Dan, and Jerusalem, which are understood in the ancient world to function as the

6. Cf. Sweeney, "Literary-Historical Dimensions of Intertextuality"; Sweeney, "Samuel's Institutional Identity."

holy centers of creation, insofar as they serve as the temples or houses of G-d, the deity who brought creation into being, employed creation to deliver Israel from Egyptian bondage, instructed Israel in its obligations to G-d, and led them through the wilderness to take possession of the promised land. And once G-d took up residence in the wilderness tabernacle, G-d continued to lead Israel through the wilderness, as recounted in Numbers and reiterated in the book of Deuteronomy.

With its narrative elements of divine revelation, victory over the forces of chaos (in this case, Egypt), the portrayal of G-d as the author of creation, the deliverance of Israel from threat, and the building of a sanctuary for G-d in recognition of G-d's efforts on behalf of Israel, and the granting the land of Israel to the people of Israel, the exodus narrative—and its continuing narration in Leviticus, Numbers, and Deuteronomy—functions as a *creation* narrative. As such, Exodus–Numbers and Deuteronomy is analogous to other ancient Near Eastern creation narratives, such as the Babylonian Enuma Elish, in which Marduk, the city god of Babylon, is the creator god, who defeats Tiamat, the chaos goddess of salt water, to bring about creation,[7] or the Ugaritic Baal Epic, in which Baal is the god who defends creation from Yamm, the chaos god of the sea.[8] Such creation narratives in antiquity function as independence narratives in ancient cultures, akin to the narratives of Independence Day, July 4, in the United States, to celebrate the defeat of enemies that threaten the nation in question and ensure its freedom from foreign oppression and subjugation.

III. The Diachronic Compositional History of Exodus

The field of pentateuchal studies has changed markedly with the recognition that the source theory of Julius Wellhausen, which stood as the foundation of reconstructions of pentateuchal compositional history for about a century, is flawed.[9] Whereas Wellhausen, later supported by Rad, argued that the J source of the Pentateuch had to be the earliest source, due in large measure to its depictions of face-to-face encounters between YHWH and humans,[10] later scholars have recognized the considerable

7. See *ANET* 60–72, 501–3; Dalley, *Myths from Mesopotamia*, 228–77.

8. ANET 129–42; Wyatt, *Religious Texts from Ugarit*, 34–114.

9. Sweeney, *Pentateuch*, xxvii–xxix.

10. Wellhausen, *Composition des Hexateuchs*; Rad, "Form-Critical Problem of Hexateuch."

influence of the Neo-Assyrian Empire as well as the interdependent character of the pentateuchal sources to be factors that point to their being strata rather than independent sources.[11] Indeed, Wellhausen's decision to recognize J's face-to-face encounters between YHWH and humans as foundational for the divine-human relationship was based in the theological viewpoint of Protestant Christianity, which saw prophecy, rather than priestly law and ritual, as representing the purest form of relationship between G-d and humanity. Rad's dating of J to the tenth century BCE, to coincide with the foundations of the Davidic monarchy, introduced an element of messianism into the equation, again based in the fundamental theological viewpoints of Protestant Christianity. Many scholars now consider the differentiation between the J-stratum and E-stratum texts as too difficult to establish, and so they settle for assessments that call for recognition of a pre-P JE-stratum of the Pentateuch.[12] Other scholars began to recognize that elements of P, such as the Priestly Instruction in Leviticus 1–16 or the Holiness Code in Leviticus 17–26, might date to the late monarchic period rather than to the time of Nehemiah and Ezra in the mid-Persian period.[13] Such a view recognizes that Israel and Judah had temples and priesthoods throughout their history, but they did not always have kings.

The recognition that the J-stratum dates to the late monarchic or early exilic period opens the way for the recognition that the E-stratum of the Pentateuch is the foundational stratum in a heavily modified understanding of Wellhausen's reconstruction. Such a conclusion makes eminent sense, especially because northern Israel—which was based especially in the Rachel tribes of Ephraim, Manasseh, and Benjamin in the northern hill country (now identified with the northern West Bank)—is closely identified with the E-stratum. Indeed, the E-stratum stands for the Ephraimitic stratum as much as it stands for the Elohistic stratum in that Ephraim was the true power tribe of the northern Israel from the pre-monarchic period through the early reigns of the House of Saul and the House of David prior to the revolt against Rehoboam following the death of Solomon. Even after

11. Thompson, *Historicity of Pentateuchal Narratives*; Van Seters, *Abraham in History*; H. Schmid, *Sogenannte J-hwist*; Levin, *J-hwist*.

12. Kratz, "Pentateuch in Current Research"; Carr, "Changes in Pentateuchal Criticism."

13. Knohl, *Sanctuary of Silence*; Milgrom, *Leviticus 17–22*, 1319–67; Carr, "Changes in Pentateuchal Criticism," 460–64; Stackert, *Rewriting the Torah*; Nihan, *From Priestly Torah to Pentateuch*.

the northern revolt against the House of David, northern Israel remained the more dominant kingdom, insofar as the Southern Kingdom of Judah became the vassal of the Northern Kingdom of Israel through the reigns of the House of Omri and the House of Jehu until the destruction of the Northern Kingdom by the Assyrian Empire in the latter half of the eighth century BCE. The E-stratum pentateuchal narratives, such as the Jacob narratives, the exodus narratives, and the wilderness narratives, were known to northern prophets, such as Hosea ben Beeri, who cited them in detail in Hosea 12–13,[14] and Jeremiah ben Hilkiah, a priest of the House of Ithamar ben Aaron, Eli, and Abiathar, who likewise cited E-stratum elements in Jeremiah 2 and 8:14,[15] and drew upon his family's history at Shiloh in his critique of Judah in Jeremiah 7. Amos of Tekoa, a Judean prophet who went to Beth El to assist in paying Judah's tribute to Israel, likewise cites the Covenant Code in Exodus 20–23, which would have first appeared in the E-stratum Sinai narrative, in his critique of the Northern Kingdom of Israel in Amos 2:6–16.[16]

Recognition of the E-stratum as the foundational stratum of the Pentateuch makes eminent sense, insofar as the E-stratum narrative would have been brought south to Judah by northern refugees following the Assyrian destruction of Samaria in 722–721 BCE. Once in Judah, the northern narratives of Abraham, Jacob, the exodus, and the wilderness period would have heavily influenced the composition of the Judean D- and J-strata of the Pentateuch in the late monarchic period as well as the later P-stratum elements from the late monarchic period through the Persian period. Evidence for such influence appears into the prophetic works of Amos of Tekoa (Amos 2:10–12), Isaiah ben Amoz (Isa 10:24–26), Micah of Moreshet (Mic 6:1–8), and Jeremiah ben Hilkiah (Jer 2:1–8), all of whom spoke in Judah in the aftermath of the destruction of northern Israel. Similar conclusions may be drawn concerning Ezekiel ben Buzi, a Zadokite priest of the Jerusalem temple who was exiled to Babylonia in 597 BCE with King Jehoiachin ben Jehoiakim of Judah following the failed first revolt against Babylonia (Ezek 20; cf. Ezek 12, 16).

There is no historical account of the exodus in Egyptian records. There are accounts of slaves who escaped Egyptian slavery by fleeing to

14. Sweeney, "Hosea's Reading of Pentateuchal Narratives"; Sweeney, *Twelve Prophets*, 1:1–144.

15. Cf. Numbers 5:11–31, see esp. v. 18.

16. Sweeney, *Twelve Prophets*, 1:214–18.

the Sinai wilderness, but there is no account of a Hebrew or Israelite nation that fled Egyptian captivity as described in the book of Exodus. It is clear, however, that Egypt ruled Canaan in the pre-Israelite period and that it influenced Israel and Judah heavily in the early monarch period. Near the end of the period of the Hyksos rule of Egypt, in which Canaanite-based dynasties ruled Egypt from roughly 1800 BCE through 1550 BCE, several Egyptian pharaohs, such as Ah-mose I (1570–1545 BCE) and Thut-mose III (1490–1496 BCE) led revolts against the Hyksos rulers that had dominated Egypt. These revolts overthrew Hyksos rule and then opened a period of Egyptian campaigns in Egypt that led to Egyptian rule of Canaan through the reign of Pharaoh Merneptah in 1224–1216 BCE.[17] Even after Canaan broke free from Egyptian rule, Egypt continued to exert considerable influence even at the outset of the reign of the House of David. Solomon's primary wife appears to have been the daughter of pharaoh, according to 1 Kings 3:1, and his administration appears to be constructed along Egyptian models.[18] Most telling is the depiction of Solomon as a pharaoh himself, who imposed state slavery on the people of northern Israel—but not on his own tribe of Judah—to carry out the labor that was necessary to build the Jerusalem temple and his royal palace.

Although 1 Kings 11 claims that Solomon's sins were based in his marriage to foreign women and his support for their gods, the account of the northern revolt against his son, Rehoboam, in 1 Kings 12 cites Solomon's harsh policies in governing the northern tribes.[19] When Rehoboam declared that his rule would be even harsher than that of his father, the northern tribes revolted and established their own kingdom under the rule of Jeroboam ben Nebat of the tribe of Ephraim. The campaign against Israel of Pharaoh Shoshenq I of Egypt (945–924 BCE), recounted in 1 Kings 14:25–28 as a campaign by Pharaoh Shishak against Jerusalem in the fifth year of King Rehoboam ben Solomon, was apparently an expedition to reestablish Egyptian control over Israel, as presented in Shoshenq's record, and perhaps Judah as well.[20] But by the early ninth century BCE, which saw the beginning of the reign of the House of Omri (ca. 876 BCE) through the end of the rule of the House of Jehu in the mid-eighth century BCE (ca. 745 BCE), northern Israel

17. See *ANET* 230–41, 554–55.

18. Sweeney, *1–2 Kings*, 62–172; Särkiö, *Weisheit und Macht Salomos.*

19. Sweeney, *1–2 Kings*, 162–72.

20. Sweeney, *1–2 Kings*, 187–89; Wilson, *Campaign of Pharaoh Shoshenq I.*

was the suzerain ruler of its vassal, southern Judah.[21] But interpreters must note that during the reign of the House of Jehu (842–815 BCE), beginning in the mid- to late ninth century BCE, northern Israel had submitted to the Assyrian Empire to protect itself against the threats posed to Israel by Aram.[22] It would appear that the exodus narratives were read in the late ninth through the mid-eighth centuries BCE as accounts of how Israel freed itself from Egyptian control, including the rule of the early House of David, which had apparently been allied with Egypt, at least during the reign of Solomon.

Indications of E-stratum narratives appear throughout the book of Exodus, although in many cases, the presumed E-stratum narratives have been overwritten by J-stratum or P-stratum writers. The prior discussion of Exodus as a creation narrative has already noted the motif of divine combat at the outset of the exodus to determine whether pharaoh, the god of Egypt, or YHWH, the G-d of Israel, will be recognized as the true G-d of creation and human beings. Given Egypt's role as Israel's suzerain ruler during the pre-monarchic period and the early period of the monarchy itself, northern Israel's own conflicted relationship with Egypt clearly provides a basis for its interest in writing and reading an early version of the Pentateuch, featuring the exodus and wilderness narratives in which YHWH, the G-d of Israel, will emerge as the victor and true G-d of creation. Indeed, the exodus narrative is Israel's independence narrative, which explains how YHWH delivered Israel from Egyptian control and oppression. Judah's narrative was different, insofar as the book of Samuel recounts how Judah became independent from Israelite control when David successfully revolted against the House of Saul, which ruled the northern tribes of Israel, and established Judean control of Israel, at least through the reign of Solomon.

The account of YHWH's revelation to Moses on Mount Sinai in Exodus 3–4 is a classic example of an E-stratum narrative in which YHWH begins to reveal the divine Name to Moses. It is based in the genre of the prophetic call narrative, which is especially important in northern Israel, insofar as priestly figures in the north are recognized as prophets, even though they carry out priestly functions. Examples include Samuel, who is called in 1 Samuel 3 to serve as YHWH's prophet while sleeping by the ark of the covenant in the Shiloh temple,

21. Sweeney, *1–2 Kings*, 205–372.

22. Sweeney, "Hosea's Reading of Pentateuchal Narratives"; Sweeney, *Twelve Prophets*, 1:1–144; ANEP 351–55; Page, "Stela of Adad Nirari III."

a ritual that indicates priestly ordination.[23] Elijah the Tishbite counters the efforts of the 450 prophets of Baal at Mount Carmel in 1 Kings 18 to bring about rain by building an altar to YHWH and pouring out water libations upon it in a ritual celebration of Sukkot (Tabernacles, Booths), which marks the beginning of the rainy season in Israel.[24] Elisha, Elijah's successor, plays music to accompany his prophetic oracle for the Israelite-led campaign against Moab in 2 Kings 3, thereby functioning as a priestly musician (cf. 1 Chron 25). Moses himself begins to learn YHWH's Name, which is not actually revealed until Exodus 6 in the Priestly narrative. It is noteworthy that northern Israelite law, exemplified in the Ten Commandments in Exodus 20, forbids taking YHWH's Name in vain, insofar as YHWH's Name is to be uttered in Judah only on Yom Kippur and only by the high priest (cf. Lev 16). YHWH's response to Moses in Exodus 3 is an example of an *idem per idem* rhetorical device, "I am who I am," Hebrew, *'ehyeh 'ăšer 'ehyeh*, which defines a thing in relation to itself and only hints at the divine Name by suggesting its association with a Hebrew verbal form *yihyeh*, that means "he is," i.e., that YHWH actually exists and serves as the true power in creation over against pharaoh and other gods. Such a response polemicizes against the Egyptian practice in which Egyptian priests utter the names of Egyptian gods to gain their power and use them to bless or curse whomever they might choose. It is only later in Exodus 6 that YHWH tells Moses that in the past YHWH was known as El (Shaddai), the name of the Canaanite creator god, but now YHWH will be known by the divine Name YHWH. Such an account suggests a change in the conceptualization of G-d in Israel from a Canaanite creator god to the Israelite G-d, YHWH. Indeed, the very name Israel, Hebrew, *yiśrā'ēl*, actually means "may El rule," which indicates Israel's religious evolution from a Canaanite nation to an Israelite nation in which El has been subsumed to YHWH's identity.

Several religious features of the exodus narrative further demonstrate elements of Israel's relationship with Egypt and features of northern Israelite identity.

Exodus 4:24–26 presents a brief account of Zipporah's circumcision of her husband, Moses, or her son, Gershom, when YHWH attacked them while they were on the road from the Sinai wilderness to Egypt.

23. Sweeney, "Samuel's Institutional Identity"; Sweeney, *1–2 Samuel*, 36–40.

24. Sweeney, "Prophets and Priests"; Sweeney, *1–2 Kings*, 216–34, 276–84.

Zipporah protected her family by taking a flint knife and circumcising her son, declaring, "You are a bridegroom of blood to me." Her statement might suggest Moses, insofar as he would have been her bridegroom, as there is no clear indication elsewhere in the exodus narrative that Moses had been circumcised. Alternatively, it could refer to her son, Gershom, insofar as her statement might indicate that he had reached the age of puberty and marriage or that the circumcision anticipated his marriage when he would eventually come of age. Circumcision is a well-known Egyptian practice that is depicted in a twenty-third-century BCE text in which a number of Egyptian young men were circumcised, presumably at the age of puberty and marriage.[25] The fact that Zipporah is the one who circumcises either Moses or Gershom indicates the importance of women in ritual actions, which is a feature of northern Israelite religion.[26]

The role of women in northern Israelite religion is illustrated by the role of Miriam, a woman of the tribe of Levi, in leading the women in liturgical song in Exodus 15:20–21; the role of Deborah, a woman of the tribe of Ephraim, in leading Israel in liturgical song following the victory of Sisera and his army in Judges 5; and the presence of women who are abused by Hophni and Phineas at the Shiloh sanctuary in 1 Samuel 2:22–26. The role of women in Israelite religion is also illustrated by the eighth-century BCE Kuntillet Ajrud inscriptions, which refer to "YHWH of Samaria and his Asherah," a reference to the Canaanite goddess of fertility, and depict what appears to be a woman playing music in the background as men dance with their genitals exposed.[27] David engages in a similar dance in 2 Samuel 6 when the ark was brought to Jerusalem shortly after he became king of Israel, although his rebuke of his primary wife, Michal bat Saul, is intended to deny her fertility rather than to ensure it.[28] David's predecessor, King Saul ben Kish, the first true king of northern Israel, who was unable to bring David and Judah under his control, likewise stripped off his clothing to engage in ecstatic prophecy, according to 1 Samuel 19:19–24 (cf. 1 Sam 10:9–13). The Canaanite background to such actions appears in the Ugaritic mythological text "The Gracious Gods" (*KTU* 1.23), which is considered a sacred marriage myth in which the Canaanite creator good, El, has relations with his two wives, Athirath and Rahmay, which

25. *ANET* 326.

26. Sweeney, "Israelite and Judean Religions."

27. B. Schmidt, "Kuntillet ʿAjrud."

28. Sweeney, *1–2 Samuel*, 216–22.

leads to the births of Shahar and Shalem (i.e., Dawn and Dusk) in the world of creation.[29] The role of the king in such a sexually explicit ritual is to emulate El's efforts at creation in the human world. Analogous mythology and rituals appear in the Sumerian sacred love songs, which celebrate the reunion of the Sumerian fertility god, Dumuzi, with his consort, the Sumerian fertility goddess, Inanna, to inaugurate new birth in creation at the beginning of the New Year.[30]

Another distinctively Israelite practice is the use of firstborn sons to the mother as assistants to the Aaronide priests at northern Israelite sanctuaries. The first nine plagues in Exodus are features of the natural world of creation, but the tenth plague, the death of the firstborn, is a unique type of plague that sees all the firstborn humans and cattle of Egypt killed by the angel of death in Exodus 11–13.[31] Although firstborn animals are offered to YHWH at the springtime Festival of Passover, firstborn sons are treated differently. According to the law code in Exodus 34:19–20, firstborn sons are to be redeemed and not sacrificed, but the means and purpose of such redemption are not specified. The issue becomes clear in 1 Samuel 1–3 when Hannah, the wife of Elkanah ben Jeroham of the tribe of Ephraim, finally gives birth to baby Samuel shortly after praying to YHWH for a son.[32] Once baby Samuel is weaned, he is sent to the Shiloh sanctuary in northern Israel, where he is raised under the supervision of the high priest, Eli. Samuel is called by YHWH to serve as a prophet while sleeping next to the ark in the holy of holies of the Shiloh sanctuary, an act that was an ordination ritual for priests and Levites in Exodus 29, Leviticus 8, and Numbers 8. It is striking that YHWH mentions to Moses three times in Numbers 3:5–20; 3:40–51; and 8:5–19 the need to replace the firstborn sons of Israel with the Levites as assistants to the sons of Aaron, who served as the priests of Israel and later Judah. YHWH's decision is apparently motivated by the failure of Aaron and the firstborn sons of Israel to prevent the people from worshipping the golden calf in Exodus 32–34 and the role of the Levites in

29. Wyatt, *Religious Texts from Ugarit*, 324–35.

30. Sefati, *Love Songs in Sumerian Literature*. Although ancient Babylon had a similar Akitu festival to celebrate the renewal of creation at the New Year, the Babylonian king did not have relations with a priestess of Marduk. Instead, she slapped him in the face to remind him that he served Marduk. The Sumerian king, however, did have relations with a priestess of En-Lil, the Sumerian god of the wind and head of the Sumerian pantheon.

31. Sweeney, "Literary-Historical Dimensions of Intertextuality."

32. Sweeney, "Samuel's Institutional Identity."

guarding the sanctity of YHWH by killing those who engaged in illicit worship. First Kings 12:25–33 recounts that Jeroboam ben Nebat, the first king of northern Israel following the revolt against the House of David, appointed priests who were not Levites to serve at the sanctuary of Beth El, where he erected golden calves like the one described in Exodus 32–34.[33] It is therefore noteworthy that Samuel, the firstborn of Hannah, served in a priestly capacity throughout his lifetime even though his father was from the tribe of Ephraim.[34] It is also noteworthy that Elijah and Elisha, both of whom are designated as prophets and "men of G-d," serve in priestly capacities even though there is never any indication that they are Levites. Elijah builds an altar for YHWH on Mount Carmel in 1 Kings 18 to celebrate Sukkot, which marks the onset of the rainy season in Israel.[35] He also has an encounter with YHWH in 1 Kings 19 in a cave on Mount Horeb, the alternative name in northern sources for Mount Sinai, much like Moses in Exodus 32–34.[36] Elisha plays music in 2 Kings 3 to accompany his oracle, an action that is reserved for temple priests in 1 Chronicles 25. Although Chronicles corrects the record by labelling prophets who served in priestly capacities as Levites, Samuel and Kings offer no such identification. The books of Samuel and Kings nevertheless make sure to identify Judean priests as Levites. Apparently, the use of firstborn sons to assist the priesthood is a feature of northern Israelite religion, but it does not appear in southern Judean practice.

Exodus 25–31 and 35–40 recount respectively YHWH's instructions to Moses concerning the building of the wilderness tabernacle and Israel's compliance with YHWH's instructions to build the wilderness tabernacle. Both of these narrative blocks are recognized as P-stratum compositions by most scholars due to their concern with temple and ritual matters. But Israel had temples throughout its history as portrayed in the Bible even though it did not always have a king. Insofar as the building of a temple typically appears as the concluding action of a creation narrative—to honor the god who defeated the deities of chaos and placed the world of creation and human beings into order—it would be striking if an early E-stratum creation narrative lacked any such account, especially since early, pre-monarchic Israel was known for its sanctuaries, such as Shiloh and Gilgal, as well as the foundational sanctuaries of

33. Sweeney, *1–2 Kings*, 172–82.

34. Sweeney, *1–2 Samuel*, 26–40.

35. Sweeney, *1–2 Kings*, 216–30.

36. Sweeney, *1–2 Kings*, 230–34.

the Northern Kingdom of Israel in Beth El and Dan. It makes sense that Bezalel ben Uri ben Hur of the tribe of Judah is designated as one of the architects who oversees the construction of the tabernacle in a P-stratum narrative. But the presence of Oholiab ben Ahisamach of the tribe of Dan as the second architect is puzzling (see Exod 31:1–11). The identification of Oholiab as a member of the tribe of Dan is particularly striking since Dan is the site of the northernmost temple of Israel established by King Jeroboam ben Nebat of northern Israel (but see Judg 17–18). There is no reason to challenge the current understanding that the present forms of Exodus 25–31 and 35–40 are P-stratum compositions, but the presence of Oholiab ben Ahisamach of Dan raises questions as to whether the current forms of these narratives were produced as redactional rewritings of an earlier narrative that featured Oholiab of Dan as the primary architect of the wilderness tabernacle. If such an underlying narrative once existed, it would have functioned as the culmination of the E-stratum composition of the book of Exodus.

In short, there are good reasons to speculate that an early E-stratum version of the book of Exodus once existed, but it is impossible to reconstruct such a version in what presumably would have been its totality. Readers will have to be satisfied with the features noted here that point to such a possibility.

Finally, it is also clear that J-stratum accounts, such as Exodus 32–34, and P-stratum accounts, such as Exodus 6, 25–31, and 35–40, appear in the exodus narrative and that both strata may have overwritten earlier E-stratum accounts. Such an understanding of the history of the composition of the book of Exodus demonstrates the importance attached to this foundational account of Israel's independence in Israel's early history and the adaptation of the exodus narrative to later historical periods, such as the Judean revolt against Assyria in 701 BCE, the potential for the restoration of Judean independence during the late-seventh-century reign of King Josiah ben Amon of Judah, the return of exiled Jews to Jerusalem and Judah from Babylonia in late sixth century BCE, the restoration of Nehemiah and Ezra in the late fifth to early fourth century BCE, and beyond.

IV. Theological Perspective: El/YHWH as an Immanent G-d in Creation

Readers of the Hebrew Bible are accustomed to distinguish sharply between the conceptualization of the gods in pre-Israelite Canaanite and other ancient Near Eastern cultures and the ultimately monotheistic traditions of Israel and Judah and beyond. Canaanite and other ancient Near Eastern traditions generally presuppose a divine pantheon in which one god or married pair of deities are viewed as the head of the pantheon and other gods are identified with the various elements of creation.[37] In Canaanite tradition, as known from the mythological texts of Ugarit and other textual traditions, El is the creator god and head of the Canaanite pantheon.[38] His acts of creation include marital relations with his two wives, Athirath and Rahmay, in the text known as "The Gracious Gods." Athirath, also known as Asherah or Astarte, is a mother goddess, who is also known for wisdom and her role as a hunter.[39] She is generally represented by a tree, which is known for producing fruit and introducing principles of wisdom in creation. Rahmay is also a mother goddess, whose name means "womb," "compassion," and "mercy." El's leading role in the Canaanite pantheon is known from the Deir Alla Inscription, a presumably Ammonite text from south Canaan attributed to the seer Balaam bar Beor, in which El instructs the goddess Ishtar to sew up the heavens so that they will become darkened as part of his plan to defeat an unnamed enemy, presumably Israel.[40] El has a daughter, Anat, whose name means "spring," a vaginal metaphor to symbolize the feminine character of the earth and its fertility.[41] Anat is the consort of Baal, who is identified as the god of storm, thunder, and lightning, and the union of Baal and Anat represents the onset of rain in the fall and the production of new human, animal, and plant life in the spring. Other deities include Yamm, the chaos god of the sea; Mot (Mawet) the god of the underworld to which all the dead go; Kothar wa-Khasis, a craftsman god; and others, such as Shahar, "dawn," and Shalem, "sunset," who represent some of the first features of creation.

37. For discussion of the development of Israelite religion from its Canaanite background, see esp. Smith, *Origins of Biblical Monotheism*; Day, *YHWH and the Gods*.

38. Kurtz, "El."

39. Merlo, "Asherah."

40. Sweeney, "Balaam in Intertextual Perspective."

41. Walls, "Anath."

Although El is the head of the Canaanite pantheon, he is an aging god who displays weaknesses. He is known to get heavily drunk, insofar as the Canaanite gods spend a great deal of their time feasting and drinking. El is portrayed as so drunk that he has to be helped to his home by other gods, and he soils himself before he makes it inside. A remedy for hangovers is included in the account of this drunken escapade, apparently for the benefit of its readers who might want to emulate their god. When El attempts to discipline his daughter, Anat, she threatens to make his gray beard run red with blood, and he frequently backs down as a result of her threats. Anat has her weaknesses as well. She is a warrior who spends a great deal of her time fighting Ugarit's enemies, perhaps to be identified as the Sea Peoples. When she returns from battle to her own home, she mistakes the furniture of the house for enemy warriors, and destroys much of her furnishings in a depiction of what must be considered as an ancient case of post-traumatic stress syndrome.[42] But she also plays a key role in rescuing her consort, Baal. Baal is also a warrior and an up-and-coming challenger to El's position as head of the Ugaritic pantheon. He defeats Yamm, the chaos god of the sea, but he is unable to defeat Mot (Mawet), the god of the underworld, and Baal consequently goes down to the underworld dead to mark the beginning of the hot and dry summer season when no rain falls on the land. Anat comes to his rescue, going down to the underworld and bringing the dead Baal back to life to mark the beginning of the rainy season in the fall.

Canaanite religion displays both transcendent and immanent characters of the divine, insofar as El is the transcendent god of creation, although he is heavily flawed, and the other gods and goddesses display immanent characteristics even by their identifications with various facets of creation as they assist El and sometimes compete for his transcendent position as head of the pantheon. Other sets of mythologies are known from other ancient Near Eastern cultures, including Egypt, the Hittite Empire, Aram, Assyria, Babylonia, and others, that present analogous sets of gods and goddesses and analogous rituals to those of Ugarit and its Canaanite culture, that display their own combinations of transcendence and immanence in their own deities.

Israel is a nation that emerges from Canaanite culture, but it evolves over time into a distinctive monotheistic culture that ultimately produces

42. I am indebted for this observation to my former student Dr. Pamela Nourse, a retired US Army surgeon, who has extensive experience in treating combat injuries and post-traumatic stress syndrome.

Judaism, especially when the kingdom of Judah plays a key role as Israel's primary heir in the aftermath of Israel's destruction by Assyria in 722–721 BCE. Insofar as the exodus narrative begins as an E-stratum narrative, composed in northern Israel during the ninth and eighth century BCE, it displays a combination of transcendent and immanent characteristics in its portrayal of G-d, apparently first known to be an expression of El and later known to be YHWH in the narrative. Thus, YHWH is first known in the E-stratum narrative as *ʾĕlōhîm*, "G-d," and later as YHWH following the account of the initial revelation of the divine Name in the E-stratum narrative of Exodus 3–4 and explained in the P-stratum narrative of Exodus 6. Thus, G-d/YHWH is presumed to be the creator G-d throughout the exodus narrative, although there is no clear creation narrative in the E-stratum text of Genesis 1–3. Perhaps Genesis 2:4—3:24 once presented an underlying E-stratum text, but in its present form Genesis 2:4—3:24 is a J-stratum text. Nevertheless, G-d/YHWH acts as the true creator in Exodus by employing newer elements of creation in the conflict with pharaoh to demonstrate that G-d/YHWH is the true G-d of creation. In this respect, G-d/YHWH emerges as the transcendent G-d in the exodus narrative.

But in keeping with earlier Canaanite religious tradition, G-d/YHWH functions largely as an immanent deity, insofar as G-d/YHWH is identified with the various elements of creation employed to demonstrate G-d/YHWH's role as the true G-d of creation. G-d/YHWH employs each element of creation as an agent in the effort to defeat pharaoh. Such an understanding of the elements of creation presuppose G-d/YHWH's direct interaction with the element of creation in question. G-d ensures the fertility of the Hebrew women in Exodus 1, leaving the midwives little to do as the Hebrew women give birth through their own efforts. G-d speaks to Moses through the agency of the burning bush, otherwise known as the *rubus sanctus*, which then becomes a key feature of creation in the Sinai wilderness. Such an action entails that G-d is embodied in the bush. G-d ensures that Aaron's rod turns into a snake and devours the rods of the Egyptian magicians, again ensuring the G-d is embodied in Aaron's rod as it transforms itself to carry out the divine purpose. G-d/YHWH is likewise embodied in the various elements of creation that visit the first nine plagues on Egypt. The presence of G-d/YHWH is embodied in the pillar of smoke and fire that leads Israel to the Reed Sea, ensures the sea's division to allow Israel to cross on dry land, closes the sea on the pursuing Egyptian chariots, and continues to lead Israel through the Sinai wilderness to Mount Sinai. And finally, G-d/YHWH is embodied in the cloud that covers Mount Sinai and the thunder and lightning that manifest themselves at the top of the mountain as G-d/YHWH reveals divine instruction to Israel.

Altogether, the combination of transcendent and immanent characteristics of G-d/YHWH in the exodus narrative appear to be developments out of the combination of transcendent and immanent characteristics of the Canaanite gods and goddesses that appear in Ugaritic literature and other texts known from Canaanite culture. The difference is that Exodus portrays only one G-d, identified with YHWH, whereas the Canaanite literature portrays multiple gods and goddesses.

V. The Reception History of the Exodus Narrative

With its focus on the exodus of the people of Israel from Egyptian bondage and the journey to the promised land of Israel, the book of Exodus has been highly influential in the development of Jewish thought, literature, and practice from antiquity through present times, and will undoubtedly continue to be, insofar as it expresses some of Judaism's most foundational motifs.[43]

Genesis 12:10–20, the account of Abram and Sarai's sojourn in Egypt, signals concern with the exodus when it states in v. 17 that the pharaoh of Egypt and his household suffered plagues due to his marriage with Sarai. Genesis 15:12–15 likewise anticipates the exodus when Abram goes into a deep sleep and YHWH tells him that his offspring will be enslaved in Egypt for four hundred years, but they will depart from Egypt with great wealth when YHWH punishes Egypt.

Deuteronomy, attributed to Moses, but written primarily in the late seventh century BCE, presents a revised account of the exodus and wilderness narratives as well as a revised understanding of the revelation of Torah at Sinai, apparently to support the efforts of King Josiah ben Amon of Judah to free Judah from Assyrian and Egyptian control and to reestablish Israel based on the covenant with YHWH, as expressed in the earlier northern Israelite traditions and the revised Deuteronomic tradition.[44]

43. For discussion, see Daube, *Exodus Pattern*.

44. See Sweeney, *King Josiah of Judah*, 137–69.

The prophets of the Hebrew Bible frequently cite the book of Exodus in their recounting of the exodus from Egypt, the revelation at Sinai, and the wilderness journey to the promised land of Israel.

One of the earliest examples is found in Hosea, a mid-eighth-century northern Israelite prophet, who cites elements of the pentateuchal narratives in Hosea 11–13.[45] These citations begin with a notation of Israel's rebellion against YHWH as a child after Egypt; Jacob's conflict with his fraternal twin brother, Esau; his wrestling with an angel; his experience of G-d at Beth El; his journey to Paddan-Aram to find a wife from his mother's family; his conclusion of treaty with his uncle, Laban, which established boundaries between Aram and Israel; his exodus from Egypt under the leadership of a prophet who remains unnamed; his rebellion against G-d in the wilderness; and G-d's guidance and provision of water in the wilderness, in addition to the citation in Hosea 4 of the Ten Commandments that introduce elements of the Covenant Code. Although some scholars argue that these citations are later additions to Hosea, the argument is based in an ill-founded reliance on an old Wellhausenian principle that prophecy is older and more authentic than priesthood and law and a failure to grasp the overriding concerns of the book of Hosea. Insofar as Jacob is the eponymous ancestor of the Northern Kingdom of Israel, these citations function as elements of Hosea's argument against the alliance of the House of Jehu with the Assyrian Empire against Aram, from which Israel's ancestors migrated to Canaan.

The exodus motif is also well known to Amos, a mid- to late-eighth-century Judean prophet, who was tasked with bringing portions of Judah's tribute to the Northern Kingdom of Israel due to Israel's status as suzerain over its vassal, Judah.[46] Following Amos's oracles against the nations, which repeatedly cite elements of northern Israel's Covenant Code in critique of Israel, Amos's oracular discourse in Amos 3 begins with a fundamental statement of principle: YHWH had brought Israel up from the land of Egypt in order to establish a special relationship with Israel that now functions as a foundation for YHWH's critique for Israel's alleged wrongdoing. Amos also cites in Amos 4:9–10 Israel's punishment by locusts and pestilence, as well as YHWH's capacities to bring darkness and floodwaters in Amos 5:7–9 as analogies to the plagues visited by YHWH on Egypt.

45. Sweeney, *Twelve Prophets*, 1:112–36.

46. Sweeney, *Twelve Prophets*, 1:214–24, 231–42.

Micah, a late-eighth-century prophet from Moreshet Gath on the Judean border with Philistia, likewise cites the exodus and wilderness traditions in his critique of both the northern Israel and the southern Judean dynasties, whose wrongheaded policies resulted in invasion that turned him, his family, and his neighbors into refugees who had to flee to Jerusalem to seek refuge from the Assyrian onslaught. Micah 6 recounts how YHWH brought Israel up from Egyptian bondage and sent Moses, Aaron, and Miriam to lead the people at the time of the exodus. He also cites Numbers 22–24, which recounts how Balak, the king of Moab, sent the Aramean prophet Balaam ben Beor to curse Israel, although Balaam could only speak praise of Israel due to YHWH's power.[47] Again, some interpreters argue that Micah 6 is a later addition to Micah, but that conclusion is motivated once again by ill-considered Wellhausenian presupposition and a failure to grasp the entirety of Micah's argument.

Haggai, one of the early-Persian-period prophets of the late sixth century BCE likewise cites the Reed Sea narrative of Exodus 14–15 in Haggai 2:20–23 to portray YHWH's intentions to overthrow the throne of the nations, i.e., the Persian Empire, as part of YHWH's efforts to restore the House of David.[48] He refers specifically to the appointment of Zerubbabel ben Shealtiel, apparently the grandson of King Jehoiachin ben Jehoiakim of Judah, as YHWH's signet ring, a metaphorical reference to his projected role as a Davidic king.

Malachi, apparently a Persian-period prophet from the fifth century BCE, is named after YHWH's messenger from Exodus 23:20–33, to call for Judah's adherence to YHWH's covenant, culminating in Malachi 3:22 to remember the Torah of Moses and Malachi 3:23–24 to anticipate the coming of the prophet Elijah, who is portrayed in terms similar to Moses, on the Day of YHWH.[49]

The late-eighth-century Judean prophet Isaiah ben Amoz refers repeatedly to the exodus and wilderness traditions in his attempts to call upon the House of David, Jerusalem, Judah, and Israel, to return to YHWH.[50] The pilgrimage of the nations to Zion and the invitation to Jacob to join them in Isaiah 2:2–5, perhaps a sixth-century text, appears to represent a development of the exodus motif for the revelation of Torah at Zion as an analogy to the revelation of Torah at Sinai. The portrayal of

47. Sweeney, *Twelve Prophets*, 2:395–405.

48. Sweeney, *Twelve Prophets*, 2:549–55.

49. Sweeney, *Twelve Prophets*, 2:744–50.

50. For the texts discussed here, see Sweeney, *Isaiah 1–39*, ad loc.

YHWH's outstretched hand and Assyria as the rod of YHWH's anger in the oracles of Isaiah 5–10 appear to be derived from the imagery of the Moses's hand and Aaron's rod that signal YHWH's punishment of Egypt in the plague narratives and Reed Sea episode of Exodus 5–15. The analogy is made explicit in Isaiah 10:24–26 as YHWH promises to relieve Zion from Assyria's oppression just as YHWH relieved Israel from Egyptian oppression. The portrayal of YHWH's redemption of Israel and Judah from Assyrian oppression in Isaiah 11:11–16, perhaps to be dated to the latter seventh century BCE, likewise establishes an analogy between the downfall of Assyria and the defeat of Egypt at Reed Sea. A similar scenario appears in Isaiah 27:12–13 that anticipates the redemption of Israel from Assyrian oppression like the redemption of Israel from Egyptian oppression so that Israel may return to Zion. The presentation of the songs of thanksgiving to YHWH for deliverance quotes extensively from the Song of the Sea in Exodus 15. The oracle against Egypt in Isaiah 31 concludes with an announcement of the downfall of Assyria.

The second half of the book of Isaiah in Isaiah 34–66, largely the product of later writers ranging from the late seventh through the fifth or fourth centuries BCE, is replete with references to the exodus narratives.[51] Isaiah 35, apparently the work of a sixth-century writer that some identify as Second Isaiah, draws heavily on the wilderness and exodus narratives to portray the return of Judean exiles to Zion. The account of YHWH's deliverance of Jerusalem and King Hezekiah from the Assyrian King Sennacherib 701 BCE in Isaiah 36–37 (cf. 2 Kgs 18–19; 2 Chron 32), generally considered to be a late-seventh-century composition updated in the sixth century BCE, is heavily influenced by the exodus narrative. The story of how YHWH sends the angel of death to kill 185,000 Assyrian soldiers is based on the model of the plague of the death of firstborn in Exodus 10–13. Isaiah 40–48, considered to be the work of Second Isaiah in the late sixth century BCE, is also heavily influenced by the exodus and wilderness narratives. It envisions a highway in the wilderness to bring the exiles home to Jerusalem in Isaiah 40:1–11, it calls for the exiles to journey through the wilderness and the sea in Isaiah 42:14—44:23 as part of YHWH's plan for the redemption of Israel, and it concludes in Isaiah 48:20–22 with a call for Israel to depart from Babylon. Isaiah 66, considered to the work of an early-Persian-period prophet, presents YHWH's declaration that "the

51. For the passages discussed here, see Sweeney, *Isaiah 1–39*, ad loc.; Sweeney, *Isaiah 40–66*, ad loc.

heavens are my throne and the earth is my footstool," in recognition of the role played by the ark of the covenant, the construction of which is portrayed in Exodus 25–31 and 35–40.

Jeremiah, a late-seventh- to early-sixth-century prophet and priest from the line of Ithamar ben Aaron, Eli, and Abiathar, is also very much concerned with the exodus and wilderness narratives. Jeremiah 2 portrays Israel in the wilderness as the bride of YHWH, who pursues other lovers, as represented in the wilderness tradition's narratives. Jeremiah 30–31 envisions the return of the exiles of Israel and Judah in a scenario analogous to the exodus from Egypt and the return to the land of Israel as represented in Exodus–Numbers. Jeremiah also calls consistently for the observance of YHWH's covenant in his famous temple sermon in Jeremiah 7:1—8:3 and throughout the book. Jeremiah is a prophet patterned upon the example of Moses, and his oracles draw heavily from Exodus–Numbers, and especially from Deuteronomy.

Ezekiel ben Buzi, a visionary prophet and Zadokite priest, who was exiled to Babylon together with King Jehoiachin in 597 BCE, is also influenced by the exodus narratives.[52] His departure for Babylon as presented in Ezekiel 12 is modelled on Israel's departure from Egypt. And YHWH's relationship with Jerusalem is based on the understanding that YHWH discovered Jerusalem as a baby in the wilderness, took her under protection, raised her, and ultimately married her, only to see her rebel in a manner analogous to the portrayal of Israel in the wilderness.

The historical narratives in Joshua, Samuel, Kings, Chronicles, and Ezra-Nehemiah also show aspects of dependence on or recognition of the Exodus–Numbers traditions. Joshua's final speech to Israel at Shechem in Joshua 24 recounts the exodus and wilderness narratives as part of its summation of Israel's earlier history. First Samuel 4–6 and 2 Samuel 6 portray the exile of the ark of the covenant from Israel due to the Philistine defeat of Israel and David's efforts to restore the ark to Jerusalem.[53] Likewise, David is forced to go into exile across the Jordan River when his son, Absalom, revolts against him in 2 Samuel 13–19, and he is forced to defeat Absalom in battle to return. Second Kings 18–19 presents an account of YHWH's deliverance of Jerusalem and Hezekiah from Sennacherib's invasion in a narrative that is very similar to Isaiah 36–37, although the Kings narrative is written to demonstrate some of Hezekiah's faults,

52. For the passage discussed here, see Sweeney, *Reading Ezekiel*, ad loc.

53. For discussion of passages in Samuel related to Exodus, see Kim Sweeney, "Exile and Kingship"; Sweeney, *1–2 Samuel*, ad loc.

where the Isaiah narrative tends to idealize Hezekiah.[54] Second Chronicles 32 presents a summarizing portrayal of Hezekiah's deliverance from Sennacherib, and 2 Chronicles 30 and 35 respectively present accounts of the celebration of Passover by Kings Hezekiah and Josiah to illustrate their piety. Ezra 9 draws heavily on the Isaian traditions of the exodus to portray Ezra's return to Jerusalem as an analogy of the return to Israel as a result of the exodus from Egypt, and Nehemiah 8–10 portrays Ezra's own revelation of Torah to Israel in Jerusalem.

The Psalms also frequently refer to the exodus and wilderness journey in their efforts to depict YHWH's acts on behalf of Israel and Israel's rebellion against YHWH. Examples appear in Psalms 66:5–7; 78:40–55; 80:8–14; 95:1–11; 99:6–8; 105:24–44; 106:6–46; 135:8–12; and 136:10–22.

The Christian New Testament likewise makes extensive use of the book of Exodus, particularly in its use of Passover motifs to depict the crucifixion of Jesus as a Passover offering to atone for the sins of humankind. The Synoptic Gospels, Matthew 26–28, Mark 14–16, and Luke 22–24, associate Jesus's betrayal by Judas, his arrest, trial, and crucifixion, and his resurrection on the following Sunday with the Passover holiday. The accounts include much vilification of the Jewish community of Jerusalem, including claims that the Sanhedrin met on Passover to consider Jesus's fate. Indeed, such a meeting would be impossible in Judaism in that such a meeting would be forbidden on Passover. Although Pontius Pilate is portrayed as a merciful procurator who offered the Jews a choice of persons to be crucified, the Jews are portrayed as insistent on crucifying Jesus and declare in Matthew 27:25, "His blood be on us and our children." Such an attempt at mercy is inconsistent with the account of Pontius Pilate's cruelty, in that Josephus reports that Pilate was summoned to Rome in 37 CE to answer for his role in the slaughter of rebellious Samaritans at the village of Tirathana, near Mount Gerizim (*Ant.* 18.4.1–2). Although the outcome of this summons is unclear due to the death of the Emperor Tiberius prior to Pilate's arrival in Rome, it is clear that Pilate never returned to Jerusalem to resume his office. John 18–21 presents a more historically plausible scenario in which the Sanhedrin did not meet on Passover. Nevertheless, when given the choice to free Jesus or Barabbas, the Jews chose Barabbas and let Jesus be crucified.

54. For passage in Kings, see Sweeney, *1–2 Kings*, ad loc.

Overall, Jesus is depicted as analogous to a Passover sacrifice that results in the forgiveness of sin.

Another reference to Exodus in the New Testament appears in Acts 6:8—8:1, which recounts the final sermon and martyrdom of Stephen. Stephen's summation of biblical history includes the account of the life of Moses and the exodus from Egypt in Acts 7:17–44, which focuses especially on Israel's sins in the wilderness. Revelation 8–9 and 15–16 draw heavily on the exodus narratives concerning the plagues unleashed against Egypt in their depiction of judgment against the world in the final days. Revelation 8–9 portrays the opening of the seventh year, which calls for judgment by the seven angels, and Revelation 15–16 portrays the pouring out of the seven bowls of the wrath of G-d in punishment of the earth for its sins.

The portrayal of Jesus as a Passover sacrifice, which results in the forgiveness of human sin for those who turn to him, is a fundamental postulate of Christian theology throughout the entire history of Christianity. The Christian observance of Easter, also known as Pascha in Orthodox Christianity, which celebrates the resurrection of Jesus, is based in part on the celebration of Passover in Jewish tradition. The portrayal of Jesus's crucifixion as a Passover sacrifice continues to play a key role in many contemporary movements of Christian thought, such as liberation theology, which envisions the liberation of oppressed minorities, e.g., Latino and working-class people;[55] people of African descent, particularly African American people whose ancestors suffered slavery in the United States prior to the American Civil War of 1861–1865 and face continued discrimination even today;[56] women in almost all cultures of the world;[57] and nations and peoples who have suffered colonial oppression, such as Korea, China, India, Africa, and other nations that have been colonized by Japan, major Western powers, and the United States.[58] The claims of Palestinians who argue that they suffer colonial oppression by Israel are particularly problematic, insofar as Palestinian Arabs claim possession of the land of Israel based in earlier Roman-Byzantine, Muslim, and Turkish colonization, whereas modern Israel is the heir of ancient Israel and Judah, which were granted the land in the eternal covenant of the Hebrew Bible. Insofar as ancient Near Eastern

55. Pixley, "Liberation Criticism."

56. J. Cone, *Black Theology of Liberation.*

57. Steinberg, "Feminist Criticism."

58. Yee, "Post-Colonial Biblical Criticism."

records, such as the Amarna Letters, indicate that the early habiru, i.e., Hebrews, merged with the Canaanites of the hill country of Israel and Judah, Israel emerges as the only indigenous nation in that land, due to its persistence in maintaining its identity even in nearly two thousand years of forced exile by the Romans and the continued enforcement of that exile by its subsequent colonizers until modern times.

Indeed, the book of Exodus is foundational to Judaism and Jewish thought as well. Exodus presents the narrative accounts of the exodus from Egypt, the beginning of the wilderness journey to the land of Israel, and the revelation of divine Torah at Mount Sinai.[59] Each of these events in Exodus stands as the basis for the celebration of the three major holidays of Judaism, viz., Pesach or Passover, Shavuot or Weeks, and Sukkot or Booths. Each of these holidays is rooted in Torah narrative, especially from Exodus, but also including Leviticus, Numbers, and Deuteronomy, as well as the major features of the agricultural year in the land of Israel.

Passover or Pesach celebrates the exodus from Egypt as a form of an ancient Israelite Independence Day. The exodus narrative is constructed as an explanation of the origins and much of the practice of Passover, including the offering of the Passover sacrifice, the eating of matzah or unleavened bread, the plagues, culminating in the death of the firstborn, which explains the origins of an early stages of Israelite priestly practice. Passover also explains the beginnings of the agricultural year. Celebrated for seven days in Israel and eight days in the diaspora beginning on the evening of the fourteenth day of the first month of Nisan, Passover marks the beginning of the springtime agricultural season as the winter rains dissipate and come to a close. This period of the early spring (late March or April) is when the firstborn of the flocks and herds are born and the firstfruits of the crops of grain are harvested. It is also understood politically as a time when ancient Israel was freed from Egyptian control and as a time when Jews began to return to the land of Israel at the conclusion of the Babylonian exile. Following the Roman destruction of the Second Temple in 70 CE and the Roman genocide against the Jewish people in the Bar Kochba Revolt of 132–135 CE, Passover is celebrated in Jewish homes with the Passover Seder, a dinner service in which the food served symbolizes various aspects of the Passover narrative and the midrashic retelling and interpretation of biblical texts concerning the Passover story. The Passover Seder service

59. For discussion of the holidays of Judaism, Passover, Shavuot, and Sukkot, see I. Klein, *Jewish Religious Practice*.

appears in the Passover Haggadah, parts of which are considered some of the earliest midrashic texts of rabbinic Judaism.[60]

Shavuot or Weeks is celebrated fifty days after the initial date of Passover in Sivan (late May or June), the third month of the Jewish calendar. It marks the beginning of the revelation of Torah at Mount Sinai in Exodus 19—Numbers 10, and it also marks the conclusion of the grain harvest toward the end of the spring season.

Sukkot or Booths is celebrated for a total of eight days in Israel or nine days in the diaspora beginning on the fifteenth day of Tishri (late September or early October), the seventh month of the year following Rosh ha-Shanah, the Jewish New Year, on 1–2 Nisan and Yom Kippur, the Day of Atonement, on the tenth of Tishri. Sukkot marks the period of wilderness wandering from Egypt to the land of Israel, and it also marks the conclusion of the fruit harvest, e.g., grapes, figs, olives, prior to the onset of the fall rains. Both occasions are symbolized by sukkot, temporary booths or dwellings that would have been employed by Israel during the wilderness period and by Israelite farmers who would live in sukkot/booths in their fields and orchards to ensure the harvest of as much of the fruit as possible, fruit that would otherwise be ruined by the onset of the rains.

The exodus from Egypt also plays a role in Kabbalistic thought, which focuses on Jewish esoteric teachings on how the infinite G-d is manifested in the finite world.[61] According to Lurianic Kabbalah, G-d's presence in the world is manifested through the ten Sefirot, the ten emanations of the divine personality that permeate all of creation, including the three mental Sefirot (i.e., Keter Elyon, the divine crown which expresses the divine will to create and act; Hochmah, divine theoretical wisdom; and Binah, divine understanding or practical knowledge); the three moral Sefirot (i.e., Hesed, Mercy or the capacity to give; Gevurah, Power, or Din, Judgment, the capacity to take or punish; and Tiferet, Beauty, the capacity to balance the prior two Sefirot); the three material Sefirot (i.e., Netzah, Endurance or Dynamism in the material world; Hod, Majesty or Stability in the material world,; and Yesod, Foundation, which holds the previous two Sefirot in balance); and finally Shekhinah, Divine Dwelling or Presence in the World, or Malchut, Divine

60. Glatzer, *Passover Haggadah*; Tabory, *JPS Commentary on Haggadah.*

61. Sweeney, *Jewish Mysticism*, 325–62.

Sovereignty in the World, which result when all ten Sefirot are working together as a balanced whole.

According to Lurianic Kabbalah, the infinite G-d desired companionship, and therefore created the finite world. But the process of creating the finite world was expressed metaphorically when G-d attempted to pour out the divine light of the infinite Sefirot or divine qualities into ten finite containers, each of which represented one of the Sefirot to be manifested in the finite world of creation. Seven of the containers—representing the moral and material Sefirot and the final Sefirah of Shekhinah—were unable to withstand the divine light that was poured into them. They therefore shattered, scattering the sparks of the divine moral and material presence throughout the world of creation, and leaving only the three mental Sefirot in their designated containers. According to Lurianic Kabbalah, this shattering of the vessels is known in Hebrew as Tzimtzum, G-d's contraction, withdrawal, or exodus from the finite world, leaving the world an imperfect or less than ideal place. It therefore becomes the task of the human being, who possesses the knowledge of good and evil as a result of Eve's interaction with the snake in the garden of Eden, to use their mental qualities to undertake the study and practice of divine Torah in an effort to gather the scattered sparks of the divine moral and material presence in the world, reassemble them, and thereby to restore the divine presence to create the ideal world of creation that G-d intended.

Modern movements of Judaism are all heavily influenced by Lurianic Kabbalah and its interest in reestablishing the divine presence in an ideal world of creation. These movements include: the notion that Jews should play a role in the world at large as part of the Haskalah or Jewish Enlightenment inaugurated by Moses Mendelssohn; Hassidic Judaism, inaugurated by Israel ben Eliezer, known as the Baal Shem Tov, which emphasizes the role of traditional Jewish spirituality in the lives of all Jews as way to interrelate with the divine presence in the world; Reform Judaism, inaugurated by Abraham Geiger and others, which envisions the modernization of Judaism in relation to contemporary times; and Zionism, the restoration of Jewish political independence as a model of an ideal Jewish society, inaugurated by Ahad Ha-Am (Asher Ginzberg) and Theodor Herzl.[62]

62. Sweeney, "Democratization of Messianism."

The book of Exodus has taken on additional importance in modern times in relation to the Soviet Jewry movement, which ultimately saw the release of over a million Jews from the former Soviet Union in the 1990s,[63] and Operation Moses and its successors, which saw the release of Ethiopian Jewry in 1985.

The exodus narrative comes to expression in film, literature, and art. Film presentations of the exodus appear in Cecil B. DeMille's 1956 film *The Ten Commandments*, starring Charlton Heston as Moses, Yul Brenner as Pharaoh Rameses, and Ann Baxter as Nefretiri. *The Prince of Egypt*, a 1998 animated film produced by Jeffrey Katzenberg, stars voice actors Val Kilmer as Moses and G-d, Ralph Fiennes as Pharaoh Rameses, Michelle Pfeifer as Zipporah, and Sandra Bullock as Miriam. A more recent film is *Exodus: Gods and Kings*, released in 2014, directed by Ridley Scott, and starring Christian Bale as Moses.

Leon Uris's 1958 novel *Exodus* links the biblical exodus to the establishment of the modern state of Israel in 1948 by portraying the efforts of Jews to travel to Mandate Palestine and fight for independence in the aftermath of World War II and the Shoah or Holocaust. The novel was the basis for Otto Preminger's 1960 film by the same name, starring Paul Newman as Ari Ben Canaan and Eva Marie Saint as Kitty Fremont. Pearl S. Buck's 1931 novel *The Good Earth* draws on the themes of the biblical exodus in its depiction of the life of Wang Lung and his wife, O-Lan, in the twentieth-century Chinese village of Ahnwei as they struggled to live in China in the period prior to the outbreak of World War II. The novel was the basis for the 1937 film of the same name, which was instrumental in raising American consciousness of China as a potential ally in the coming war against Japan.

Michelangelo's sculpture of Moses, commissioned by Pope Julius II for his tomb, was completed in 1513–1515 CE. The sculpture depicts Moses, seated and with horns on his forehead, apparently motivated by a misunderstanding of the term *qāran*, "radiated, shone," translated as Latin, *cornutam*, "horned," in the Vulgate in Exodus 34:30. The sculpture now resides in the San Pietro in Vincoli Church in Rome.[64]

63. Gilbert, *Jews of Hope*; Azbel, *Refusenik*.

64. Janson, *History of Art*, 357–70, esp. 359 and fig. 535.

Critical Contextual Commentary

Egyptian Oppression of the Sons of Israel—Exodus 1:1—2:10

Translation[1]

1:1 And these are the names of the sons of Israel who came
to Egypt with Jacob, each and his house they came. 2 Reuben,
Shimon, Levi, and Judah; 3 Issachar, Zebulun, and Benjamin;
4 Dan and Naphtali, Gad and Asher; 5 And all who came out
from the thigh of Jacob were seventy persons, and Joseph
was [already] in Egypt. 6 And Joseph died and all his brothers
and all that generation. 7 And the sons of Israel were fruitful and they swarmed and they multiplied and they become
very, very strong, and the land was filled with them.

8 And a new king who did not know Joseph arose over Egypt.
9 And he said to his people, "Behold, the people of the sons
of Israel are more numerous and stronger than us. 10 Come,
let us be smart about them, lest they multiply, and it will be
when you declare war, then they, indeed, they, will join those
who hate us, and they will fight against us, and prevail over
the land." 11 And they appointed over them taskmasters to

1. Note that I have translated the Hebrew text of Exodus with a view to enabling the reader to see something of the syntactical order and word usage of the Hebrew, even if the reader does not know Hebrew him- or herself.

oppress them with their forced slavery, and they built depot cities for pharaoh, Pithom and Rameses. [12] And just as they oppressed them, so they would multiply and so they would spread out, and they abhorred the sons of Israel. [13] And the Egyptians enslaved the sons of Israel with harshness. [14] And they embittered their lives with hard work, with mortar and with bricks, and with all the work in the field, with all their work which they imposed on them with harshness.

[15] And the king of Egypt said to the Hebrew midwives, the name of the first was Shiphrah and the name of the second was Puah, [16] and he said, "When you deliver the Hebrew women, and you look upon their birth stones, if it is a son, then you shall kill it, and if it is a daughter, then it shall live." [17] But the midwives revered G-d, and they did not do as the king of Egypt spoke to them, and they let the children live. [18] And the king of Egypt summoned the midwives, and he said to them, "Why have you done this thing, and you have let the children live?" [19] And the midwives said to pharaoh, "Because the Hebrew women are not like the Egyptian women, for they are vibrant before the midwives come to them, and they have [already] given birth." [20] And G-d treated the midwives well, and the people multiplied and they became very strong. [21] And it came to pass that the midwives feared G-d, and he made for them houses. [22] And pharaoh commanded all his people, saying, "Every son that is born, into the Nile you shall throw it, but daughter shall live."

2:1 And a man from the House of Levi went, and he married a daughter of Levi. [2] And the woman became pregnant, and she bore a son, and she saw that he was healthy, and she hid him for three months. [3] And when she was no longer able to hide him, then she took for him a basket of reeds, and she coated it with asphalt and pitch, and she placed the child in it, and she placed it in the reeds by the bank of the Nile. [4] And his sister stationed herself far away to know what would be done to him.

[5] And the daughter of pharaoh went down to bathe in the Nile, and her maids were walking beside the Nile, and she

saw the basket in the midst of the reeds, and she sent her maidservant, and she took it. [6] And she opened [it], and she saw the child, and behold, the boy was crying, and she felt sorry for him, and she said, "From the children of the Hebrews is this one." [7] And his sister said to the daughter of pharaoh, "Shall I go, and shall I summon for you a nursing woman from the Hebrews, and she can nurse this child for you?" [8] And the daughter of pharaoh said to her, "Go!" And the young woman went, and she summoned the mother of the child. [9] And she said to her, "Bring this child home, and nurse him for me, and I will give to you your wages." And the woman took the child, and she nursed it. [10] And the child grew up, and she brought him to the daughter of pharaoh, and he became a son to her, and she called his name Moses, and she said, "Because from the waters, you were drawn."

Commentary

Exodus 1:1—2:10 serves as a transitional text, which narrates the transition from the ancestral narratives of Genesis to the account of the exodus from Egypt and the wilderness journey to the promised land of Israel in Exodus–Numbers and Deuteronomy. From a synchronic literary perspective, it is part of the toledoth structure of the Pentateuch in which the toledoth formula, viz., "these are the generations of PN," and the like in Genesis and in Numbers 3:1–2 appears within the macrostructure of the Pentateuch.[2]

Exodus 1:1—2:10 functions together with Exodus 2:11—12:36 as a component of Genesis 37:2—Numbers 2:34, which presents the account of the generations of Jacob. Following the Joseph narratives in Genesis 37:2—50:26, which function as the first component of the account of the generations of Jacob, Exodus 1:1—2:10 is demarcated at the outset by the formula "and these are the names," which introduces "the sons of Israel" in Exodus 1:1–7 as the first major characters of the following narrative. Subsequent characters appear in Exodus 1:8–22, which introduces the pharaoh of Egypt and his interaction with other figures, such as the people of Egypt and the Israelite/Hebrew midwives. Exodus 2:1–10 then introduces Moses as the third major character of the narrative. All

2. Sweeney, *Pentateuch*, xvii–xxix, 29–40; Sweeney, *Tanak*, 45–53, 85–91.

three of these sub-units presuppose the same temporal framework, i.e., the time following the death of the prior pharaoh and the rise of a new pharaoh who did not know Joseph, as stated in Exodus 1:8. Each of these characters will play key roles in the account of Israel's exodus from Egypt and wilderness journey to the promised land of Israel in Exodus–Numbers and Deuteronomy. Exodus 2:11 marks the beginning of a new unit in the narrative insofar as it presents an account of Moses's actions in the days after he had grown up to adulthood.

Insofar as Exodus–Numbers and Deuteronomy functions as a typical ancient Near Eastern creation narrative, Exodus 1:1—2:10 introduces the sons of Israel, pharaoh, and Moses as major figures in the combat between YHWH and pharaoh for control of creation and the future of Israel.[3] Exodus 1:1—12:36 recounts the first state of the combat, set in Egypt at the city of Rameses. Subsequent textual units, each of which is introduced by the travel formula "and they journeyed [Hebrew, *wayissĕʿû*] from X to Y," and the like (cf. Exod 12:37) introduce the successive stages of the journey through the wilderness from Egypt to the promised land of Israel.

Exodus 1:1–7

Exodus 1:1–7 introduces the "sons of Israel," here portrayed as the descendants of Jacob, as the first of the major characters of the narrative. The sub-unit begins with the formula "and these are the names of the sons of Israel" (Hebrew, *wĕʾēlleh šĕmôt bĕnê yiśrāʾēl*). The introductory conjunctive *wĕ-*, "and," plays a key synchronic role in connecting the following Exodus narrative to the preceding Genesis narrative. The formula "these are the names of the sons of Israel" appears to be stylistically modelled on the toledoth formula, "and these are the generations of PN." The organization of the names is intentional. Schmidt declares that it is a "list," but it actually functions as more of a catalog, insofar as it organizes the sons of Israel by their birth mothers and not by the sequence of their birth.[4] Joseph is not included because he arrived in Egypt in the narrative long before Jacob and the rest of the family journeyed there. Reuben, Shimon, Levi, and Judah, grouped together in v. 2, were the first four sons born to Jacob's wife Leah. Issachar, Zebulun, and Benjamin, grouped together in v. 3, were

3. Sweeney, "Creation as Sacred Space."

4. W. Schmidt, *Exodus 1–6*, 9; cf. Knierim and Coats, *Numbers*, 341–42.

the later sons born to Jacob's two wives Leah (Issachar and Zebulun) and Rachel (Benjamin). Dan and Naphtali and Gad and Asher, grouped in pairs in v. 4, were the sons of the handmaidens, i.e., Bilhah (Rachel) and Zilpah (Leah), respectively. The proliferation of Jacob's descendants compares with the proliferation of life at the beginning of creation as depicted in Genesis 1:1—2:3.

Most scholars recognize Exodus 1:1–7 to be the product of the Priestly compositional stratum of the Pentateuch. So much of the language employed in this passage appears also in Priestly compositions, e.g., the style of the above-noted introductory formula in Exodus 1:1 and its correspondence to the toledoth formulas; the concern with listing genealogical information in vv. 2–6; and the language pertaining to Israel being fruitful, swarming, and multiplying in the land of Egypt in v. 7.[5] Consequently, Exodus 1:1–7 appears to have been a P-redactional composition designed to join the ancestral and the exodus–wilderness narratives diachronically during the Persian period.[6] This proposal raises issues, however, insofar as Hosea 12–13 cites both the Jacob narratives and the exodus–wilderness narratives. Specific citations include Jacob's conflict with Esau beginning in the womb; Jacob's wrestling with an angel (instead of a man) from Genesis 32; G-d's revelation to Jacob at Beth El; Jacob's guarding sheep for a wife from Genesis 29–31; and Jacob's and Laban's establishing their borders from Genesis 31, as well as an unnamed prophet, presumably Moses, leading Israel up from Egypt; Israel/Ephraim's rebellion in the wilderness; worship of Baal at Baal Peor in Numbers 25; worship of (golden) calves from Exodus 32; and the need for water in the wilderness in Numbers 20. Some attempt to argue that these references are later additions to Hosea, but such a position does not hold up, especially when one recognizes that Hosea's issue is recounting Israel's past history and sins as part of an argument to abandon its alliance with Assyria and to restore its relationship with Aram, where Jacob found his wives and made peace with Laban.[7] Nevertheless, it remains uncertain as to whether Hosea is citing these instances from a single united narrative or from two separate compositions that were later united. The fact that Hosea appears to mix the two sets of narratives (i.e., Jacob's actions and the exodus–wilderness

5. E.g., Dozeman, *Exodus*, 55–69.

6. K. Schmid, "So-Called Y-hwist."

7. E.g., Wöhrle, *Frühen Sammlungen*; cf. Sweeney, *Twelve Prophets*, 1:118–36.

motifs) together suggests that they come from a united tradition, but this observation must be considered tentative.

Exodus 1:8–22

Exodus 1:8–22 presents the pharaoh of Egypt as one of the principal characters of the exodus narrative, particularly because the pharaoh will be the primary opponent of G-d in the combat scenario of the creation narrative. The term pharaoh (Hebrew, *parʿōh*) is based on an Egyptian term that means "great house (of the royal court)," and it functions as the title for the king of Egypt.[8] The pharaoh is considered as a manifestation of the Egyptian god Horus, the falcon god of the sky who rules the day and whose eyes are the sun and the moon.[9] Consequently, the conflict between pharaoh and YHWH in the exodus narrative is a conflict between two deities for control of creation. The pharaoh acts in relation to two different characters to assert his rule in Exodus 1:8–22, i.e., Egypt in Exodus 1:8–14 and the Hebrew midwives in Exodus 1:15–22.

Pharaoh's interaction with Egypt begins with a notice that "a new king who did not know Joseph arose over Egypt." This statement facilitates the transition between Genesis and Exodus by establishing that things had changed for Israel in Egypt in that the very favorable relationship between Joseph and the pharaoh would not continue. The exodus narratives never identify the pharaoh in question, but interpreters frequently maintain that the new pharaoh must be Rameses II (1279–1212 BCE, the son of Seti I (1291–1279 BCE), largely because Rameses II was the most powerful monarch of the Nineteenth Egyptian Dynasty and because one of the store cities was constructed by the Hebrew slaves as Rameses, which Rameses II named after himself. Nevertheless, there is no historical attestation of an Israelite or Hebrew exodus from Egypt along the lines indicated in the book of Exodus during the reign of Rameses II or any other pharaoh of Egypt. As portrayed in the present text, the new pharaoh uses fear to persuade his people to take action against the Hebrews or Israelites in Egypt by claiming that they are growing more and more powerful and therefore pose a threat against Egypt itself. In the event of war, they might join Egypt's enemies and fight against Egypt, resulting in their ascendency over the land. The Hebrew phrase *wĕʿālâ min*

8. Redford, "Pharaoh."

9. Morenz, *Egyptian Religion*, 262–63.

hāʾāreṣ, literally, "and he shall go up over the land," can mean either "and (he will) prevail (i.e., gain ascendancy) over the land," as translated here, or "and he will go up out of the land," which would indicate an escape or exodus from Egypt as portrayed in the following narratives.

The result is the enslavement of the Hebrews in Egypt. It is well known that Egypt enslaved many Apiru/Habiru people in antiquity. The term Apiru (Egyptian pronunciation) or Habiru (Akkadian pronunciation) is an Akkadian term, *ḫabiru*, which refers to people who stand outside of settled civilizations or legal norms (i.e., "barbarians") or the like. The term is considered by many to be cognate with, Hebrew, *ʿibrî*, "Hebrew," although this hypothesis is not universally accepted.[10] The two cities on which the Hebrew slaves worked, Pithom and Rameses, are well known in ancient Egypt. Pithom, derived from an Egyptian term, *pr ʾtm*, which means "House/Temple of Atum," the primordial Egyptian creator god. Its location is disputed. Most scholars identify it with Tell el-Maskhuta in the eastern Delta region, although several other sites are also proposed.[11] Especially noteworthy is the fact that *pr ʾitm* only designates a known city in the Saite period, after 525 BCE, which suggests a very late composition for this text. The city, Rameses, is identified with Piramesse, "House of Rameses, the royal palace of Nineteenth and Twentieth Dynasty pharaohs located at Khatana-Qantir in the Northeast Delta on the east bank of the Pelusaic branch of the Nile. Although identified with Tanis or Avaris, capital cities of the Hyksos in the past, the issue was confused by the plundering of Piramesse by the pharaohs of the Twenty-First and Twenty-Second Dynasties to build their palaces at Tanis and Bubastis."[12] Both cities are called "depot cities," Hebrew, *miskĕnôt*, also translated as "store/garrison cities," because they were part of the defensive network of cities, in which garrisons were posted and supplies were stored, that were built to protect Egypt's eastern frontier.

Exodus 1:15–22 recounts the pharaoh's interaction with the Hebrew midwives, Hebrew, *mĕyallĕdōt*, i.e., women who were trained to assist in giving birth. Only two women are named: Shiphrah, "beautiful," and Puah, "sparkling girl."[13] Interpreters speculate that these two women

10. Lemche, "Ḫabiru/Ḫapiru."

11. Wei, "Pithom."

12. Wente, "Rameses."

13. Cognate with Ugaritic, *pġt*, "princess," the daughter of Danʾel, who went down to the underworld to recover her dead brother, Aqhat, in the Ugaritic Aghat Epic (Olmo Lete and Sanmartín, *Dictionary of Ugaritic Language*, 656; *HALOT* 3:918).

were the head mistresses of a guild of midwives, but the only evidence for such a claim appears in v. 21, which claims that G-d established "houses" for them. Their role in the narrative is to illustrate G-d's power to make the Hebrew/Israelite slaves thrive, and thereby to demonstrate G-d's power to defeat pharaoh and rule over creation.[14] Although instructed by pharaoh to kill any boy babies born to the Hebrews, the midwives refused to do so due to their own reverence (Hebrew, *wattîre'nā*, "and they feared") for G-d. Interpreters have struggled over the phrase "and you shall look upon the two stones," Hebrew, *ûrĕ'îten 'et hā'ābnāyim*, "and you will see the stones," in v. 16. Many interpret the phrase as a reference to observing the testicles, if the baby is a boy, but the phrase more likely refers to the two stones on which a woman sits while giving birth which give space for the baby to drop from her body. When asked by pharaoh to explain their failure to kill the baby boys at birth, Shiphrah and Puah claim that the Hebrew women are so vibrant (Hebrew, *ḥāyōt*, "living"), more so than the Egyptian women, that the babies are born before the midwives can reach them. Such a response underscores G-d's power in creation over pharaoh. Nevertheless, the response prompts pharaoh to take even more drastic action, viz., he commands that all male Hebrew babies are to be thrown into the Nile, thereby setting the stage for the rescue of baby Moses in Exodus 2:1–10.

Exodus 2:1–10

Exodus 2:1–10 introduces the character of Moses with an account of his birth.[15] The birth report genre is designed to introduce a character who will become a leading figure in a narrative with an account of the special circumstances of birth that signals the importance of the character's future. In the present instance, Moses's birth report narrative builds on the preceding narrative by illustrating how baby Moses was saved from the pharaoh's decree of death for newborn Israelite baby boys due to the efforts of his mother and his sister. The narrative points to Moses's capacity for leadership by showing how he was set adrift in the Nile by his mother, discovered by the daughter of pharaoh, and subsequently adopted into the Egyptian royal family where he would have been raised in a privileged

14. Held argues that protest, such as that of the slaves who cry out for help, is a manifestation of faith (*Judaism Is About Love*, 61–71).

15. See esp. Finlay, *Birth Report Genre*, esp. 230–38; cf. Coats, *Exodus 1–18*, 25–29.

environment that would have prepared him for a leading role. He is also portrayed as having a close connection to his Israelite mother. When the daughter of pharaoh discovers baby Moses and proposes to adopt him, Moses's sister, who had been watching over her brother's vessel the entire time, stated to the daughter of pharaoh that she could secure an Israelite wet nurse to feed the baby on behalf of the princess. Consequently, Moses's mother is hired to nurse him, which establishes a basis for Moses's understanding of his Israelite identity. Both Moses's mother and his sister remain unnamed here, but Jocheved is identified as Moses's mother in Exodus 6:20, and Miriam is identified as Aaron's sister in Exodus 15:20 and Moses's sister in Numbers 26:59.

Dozens of birth stories that portray the deliverance of future leaders from death or other threats appear throughout the world's literatures.[16] The most important for the Moses narrative is "The Legend of Sargon," which recounts the birth of King Sargon I of Akkad (2334–2279 BCE), the founder of the Akkadian Empire, which united much of Mesopotamia in the latter part of the third millennium BCE.[17] Sargon's birth legend presents a narrative with tantalizing similarities to the Moses birth narrative, although it also has its differences. Having been conceived by a priestess mother in secret, perhaps illegitimately, baby Sargon was placed in a basket of reeds sealed with bitumen and set adrift on the Euphrates River. He was found by Akki, the drawer of water, who raised him as his own son. Having gained the favor of the goddess Ishtar, Sargon rose to become king of the "black-headed people" (i.e., the Mesopotamian population) and he ruled for a period of time that is lost to us due to damage to the tablet.

Another noteworthy parallel is the account of the birth of King Cyrus of Persia (559–530 BCE), who founded the Achaemenid Persian Empire in the sixth century BCE. The account of his birth appears in Herodotus, *Hist.* 1.95–130. According to Herodotus, Astyages, king of Medea, had a dream in which water flowed from his daughter, Mandane, to fill all of Asia, and a second dream after her marriage to Cambyses I in which a vine grew from her that covered all Asia. Having been told by interpreters that his dream portended the birth of a grandson who would supplant him, Astyages ordered his servant, Harpagus, to kill baby Cyrus. Knowing that Astyages had no son to serve as his successor, Harpagus

16. See esp. Redford, "Literary Motif of Exposed Child"; Lewis, *Sargon Legend*.

17. For English translation, see *ANET* 119; see also Lewis, *Sargon Legend*, for a full study of the text.

arranged for a cowherd to substitute his stillborn son for the live Cyrus, and claimed that he had killed baby Cyrus by exposure. In the meantime, Cyrus grew up under the care of the cowherd and his wife. When Astyages discovered the ruse years later, he murdered the son of Harpagus in revenge, but Harpagus then took action to ensure that young Cyrus, who had proved to be a capable leader, would overthrow his grandfather and rule the combined Persian-Medean Empire in his place.

Having been raised in the palace of the pharaoh of Egypt, Moses was prepared to become an Egyptian leader, but having been nursed by his own mother, Moses was prepared to become an Israelite/Hebrew instead. Indeed, Moses's mixed identity is signaled by his name, "Moses," Hebrew, *mōšeh*. The name "Moses" is derived from an Egyptian term, *mś(u)* or *mesu*, respectively, "to be born," and "child," which is often transliterated as the second element (-Mose) in Egyptian names, e.g., Thut-Mose, "born/child of Thut," Ah-Moses, "born/child of Ah."[18] Lacking a deity's name, "Moses" signifies "born/child of ??" in Egyptian, which is in keeping with the Israelite prohibition against stating the Name of G-d (Exod 20:7). But the meaning ascribed to the name in Hebrew, i.e., the verb, *māšâ*, "to draw out," of the water in this case, indicates his Israelite/Hebrew identity.

The purpose of the narrative concerning Moses's birth in Exodus 2:1–10 thereby indicates both his capacity to lead, as indicated by adoption into the House of Pharaoh, and his identity as an Israelite, as indicated by the circumstances of his birth.

Most interpreters view Exodus 2:1–10 as an example of the J-stratum in the composition of the Pentateuch due to its concern to conceal the Name of YHWH and its presumed place in the narrative structure of J, although they concede that it is likely a reworking of an earlier E-stratum text.[19] Indeed, the absence of the divine Name in this narrative and the lack of concern for Judean issues indicates that Exodus 2:1–10 is an E-stratum narrative.

18. *HALOT* 2:642–43; cf. Davies, *Exodus 1–18*, 1:188; Meyers, *Exodus*, 44.

19. Campbell and O'Brien, *Sources of the Pentateuch*, 131–32, 261; cf. Utzschneider and Oswald, *Exodus 1–15*, 80–88.

Reception History

The enslavement of Israel by Egypt and the subsequent narratives of the exodus and wilderness journeys are well known in the Hebrew Bible and post-biblical Jewish and Christian literature and traditions.[20] Deuteronomy 26:5–10a recounts a liturgical statement, apparently made by Israelite farmers when they brought their tithes to the temple, that summarizes their ancestral journey to Egypt where Israel became a great nation, Israel's enslavement by Egypt, and YHWH's deliverance of Israel and guidance to the land of Israel where the farmer now presents the firstfruits of his harvest at the temple altar. Such a statement indicates that the exodus and wilderness traditions are an integral part of Israelite memory and identity, and it is repeated throughout other biblical books, such as Isaiah, which cites the exodus and wilderness traditions as models for YHWH's deliverance of Israel and Judah from Assyrian and Babylonian oppression (see, e.g., Isa 10:20–26; 36–37; 40–48; cf. Ezek 12; Hos 12–13).

Early Christian Scripture notes the enslavement of Israel in Acts 7:14–18 in which Stephen preaches a sermon that recounts the exodus and wilderness narratives as evidence of G-d's mercy for Israel.

Rabbinic tradition likewise recognizes Egyptian enslavement of Israel and the subsequent exodus and wilderness narratives as foundational for Jewish identity, particularly in the Passover Haggadah, which cites Deuteronomy 26 and a number of texts from Exodus as part of its study of G-d's deliverance of Israel from Egyptian and Roman oppression.[21] Midrashic texts emphasize that the enslavement of Israel was a slow and gradual process that began with Egyptians working beside Israelites, but as a result of Egyptian jealousy and fear of Israel, especially when Israel grew strong under divine care, they gradually deprived Israel of its property, rights, and ultimately its freedom.[22] The midwives, Shiphrah and Puah, were heroines in saving the lives of Israelite baby boys, and they were identified in Talmudic tradition (b. Sotah 11b) as Jocheved, the mother of Moses, and Miriam, the sister of Moses, to emphasize their care of baby Moses as well as Israelite baby boys in general. The early Protestant Reformer John Calvin, however, considered

20. See the extensive treatment of the reception history of Exodus in the articles, Berner, "Book of Exodus"; and Berner, "Exodus."

21. Tabory, *JPS Commentary on Haggadah.*

22. Ginzberg, *Legends*, 2:245–58.

the actions of the midwives to be sinful, insofar as they had lied to pharaoh, despite his view that G-d had rewarded their courage and piety. He thereby missed an important point of the narratives, which was to emphasize divine mercy and the overwhelming imperative on the part of the women to protect human life, even though it involved lying when the pharaoh was intent on murder.[23]

When pharaoh considered his plans to oppress Israel, he consulted his counsellors, Balaam the son of Beor, Reuel the Midianite, and Job the Uzite.[24] Balaam advised the pharaoh to take further counsel with the others because pharaoh's efforts to oppress Israel would have great consequences for Egypt and result in a son who would lead Israel out of bondage. Reuel advised the pharaoh not to oppress Israel, advice based on G-d's past actions of mercy on behalf of Abraham, Isaac, Jacob, and Joseph. Job advised pharaoh to do as he pleased, but he noted that G-d would act on Israel's behalf. He therefore advised pharaoh to throw the Israelite male babies into the Nile in order to wipe out Israel and prevent the defeat of Egypt. Pharaoh followed Job's advice, but pharaoh's actions nevertheless prompted G-d to act on Israel's behalf because no one can thwart divine purpose.

The daughter of pharaoh, named Bithiah in rabbinic tradition, pretended to be with child for some time before Jocheved returned Moses to her. As a toddler, Moses was renowned for his exceptional wisdom. When Bithiah informed her father, pharaoh, of Moses's wisdom, he embraced him as his own grandson. But when little Moses took the crown from upon pharaoh's head and placed it on his own, Balaam identified Moses as a Hebrew and proposed that he be killed. But when pharaoh called together his counselors to consider the matter, the angel Gabriel disguised himself as one of pharaoh's wise men. Gabriel proposed that a stone of onyx and a coal of fire be placed before Moses to see which he would take. If he chose the onyx, then Moses had acted deliberately to take the crown and should be killed, but if he took the coal, he had not acted deliberately. Moses took the coal and touched it to his lips, which burned his lips and tongue and left him speech impaired, but the act saved his life.[25]

23. Calvin, *Last Four Books*, 34–36, cited in Dozeman, "Exodus," 143.

24. Ginzberg, *Legends*, 2:254–56; cf. Baskin, *Pharaoh's Counsellors.*

25. Ginzberg, *Legends*, 2:262–76; quoting Exod. Rab. 1.26; Josephus, *Ant.* 2.9.6–7; Philo, *Mos.* 1.5.

The exodus narratives likewise factor prominently in examples of liberation theology in which the enslavement of Israel is read in relation to the oppression of Africans and African Americans; Latino cultures both in the United States and in Central and South America;[26] women in general;[27] nations that have been colonized by Western powers, such as many Asian, American, and African nations, among others;[28] and other oppressed minorities, particularly Jews under Christian and Muslim rule from antiquity through modern times.

The realities of African enslavement in the American colonies and the early United States through the American Civil War (1861–1865) are a particular case in point. Whereas the American North was quick to industrialize, the American South continued to base its economy on agricultural production of cotton and other crops, and continued to use enslaved blacks as forced labor to support a Southern upper class. Although the Civil War brought an end to slavery in the American South, the assassination of President Abraham Lincoln enabled Southerners to continue to exploit and suppress American Blacks by use of the Jim Crow laws to restrict the rights of African Americans and racist organizations, such as the Ku Klux Klan, to terrorize them. Efforts to restrict the rights of African Americans included the tacit cooperation of the federal and state governments to segregate the US military through World War II; to limit American higher education through restricted admissions standards; to place limitations on employment opportunities, housing, and provision of elementary and high school education; and to increase rates of imprisonment throughout American culture. The exodus narratives became the foundation for liberation theology in African American Christianity as African Americans looked to G-d for deliverance and to themselves for organization to combat their oppression in American society.

The American film industry has also begun to play an increasing role in bringing attention to the enslavement and suppression of Africans and African Americans with films such as *Amistad* (1997), *Django Unchained* (2013), and *Twelve Years a Slave* (2014), as well as portrayals of African American life in modern times with films such as *Do the Right Thing* (1989), *Malcolm X* (1993), *The Tuskegee Airmen* (1995), *Miracle at St. Anna* (2008), and *The Six Triple Eight* (2024), among others. The Gerald

26. Pixley, "Liberation Criticism."

27. Steinberg, "Feminist Criticism."

28. Yee, "Post-Colonial Biblical Criticism."

Ford class aircraft carrier, USS *Doris Miller*, currently under construction, is named for an African American US Navy mess steward stationed on the battleship USS *West Virginia* during the Japanese attack on Pearl Harbor on December 7, 1941. Miller was a hero who carried wounded sailors to safety and manned an anti-aircraft gun, shooting down as many as four to six Japanese aircraft during the attack, although only one was confirmed by the Navy. Miller was awarded the Navy Cross for his actions at Pearl Harbor, although he was nominated for the Congressional Medal of Honor. The CMH was denied to him by Secretary of the Navy Frank Knox, who believed that African Americans should not serve in any combat role. Miller was killed in action during the battle of Makin Island in November 1943, when his ship, the escort aircraft carrier USS *Liscome Bay*, was torpedoed and sunk by a Japanese submarine.

Although slavery was practiced throughout most of the American colonies, the increasing industrialization of the American northern states demonstrated that there was little need for slavery when free whites could be exploited with inadequate compensation and requirements to buy food and other necessities from company stores and to live in housing rented at exorbitant rates from their employers. The American labor movement, initially led especially by Jewish workers, such as Samuel Gompers (1850–1924), played a key role in addressing the needs of such workers, although the export of American blue-collar jobs continues to challenge American workers of all races.

Likewise, modern Zionism, the movement to reestablish an independent Jewish state in the land of Israel, is heavily inspired by the centuries of persecution in Christian and Muslim societies and by recognition of the national identity of Jews, as well as Jewish religious identity.[29] The story of the exodus also plays a key role in the deliverance of Soviet Jewry and Ethiopian Jewry in modern times.

29. Sharansky, *Defending Identity*; Hazony, *Jewish State*; Laquer, *History of Zionism*; Shapira, *Israel.*

Moses Flees to Midian After Killing an Egyptian Who Was Beating a Hebrew Slave—Exodus 2:11–22

Translation

2:11 And it came to pass in those days that Moses grew up,
and he went out to his brothers, and he saw their burdens,
and he saw an Egyptian man beating a Hebrew slave from
among his brothers. 12 And he turned this way and that, and
he saw that no one was around, and he killed the Egyptian,
and he hid him in the sand. 13 And he went out on the second
day, and behold, two Hebrew men were fighting, and he said
to the guilty one, "Why do you beat your neighbor?" 14 And
he said, "Who appointed you as ruler and judge over us? Will
you say to kill me as you killed the Egyptian?" And Moses
was afraid, and he said [to himself], "Indeed! This matter
is known!" 15 And pharaoh heard about this matter, and he
sought to kill Moses.

And Moses fled from before pharaoh, and he lived in the land
of Midian, and he stopped by a well. 16 And a priest of Midian
had seven daughters, and they came, and they drew water,
and they filled their troughs to water the sheep of their father. 17 And the shepherd came, and they drove them away,
but Moses arose, and he delivered them, and he watered their

sheep. [18] And they returned to Reuel, their father, and he said,
"Why have you hurried to come [home] today?" [19] And they
said, "An Egyptian man saved us from the hand of the shepherds, and he also surely drew water for us, and he watered
the sheep." [20] And he said to his daughters, "Where is he? Why
did you leave this man? Summon him, so he can eat bread
[with us]." [21] And Moses was willing to live with the man, and
he gave Zipporah, his daughter, to Moses [as a wife]. [22] And
she bore a son, and he called his name Gershom, for he said,
"I was an immigrant in a foreign land."

Commentary

Exodus 2:11–22 recounts Moses's flight to Midian after having saved the life of a Hebrew slave from an Egyptian man who was beating him to death. Like the preceding narrative in Exodus 2:1–10, Exodus 2:11–22 is concerned with Moses's qualifications for leadership and his identification with his own Israelite/Hebrew people, but the narrative is demarcated from the preceding by the temporal formula at the beginning of v. 11, "and it came to pass in those days that Moses grew up . . ." The temporal formula advances the plot of the narrative by indicating the passage of time, and the following temporal form at the outset of Exodus 2:23—4:31, "and it came to pass in those many days . . . ," marks the beginning of the next unit in the narrative concerning the revelation of YHWH to Moses at Mount Horeb/Sinai.

The first component of the narrative in Exodus 2:11–15a recounts Moses's actions in saving the life of a Hebrew slave. Many interpreters contend that Moses committed murder by killing the Egyptian, and some even assert the Egyptian's right to beat the Hebrew slave for some presumed failure to carry out his duties on behalf of the crown. But there is no indication that the Egyptian is a taskmaster as many presume; the text only identifies him as "an Egyptian man," Hebrew, *'îš miṣrî*, which indicates no specific authority, such as that of a taskmaster, an office, or any member of the royal house. Furthermore, the use of the verb *makkeh*, "striking, beating," indicates beating that potentially leads to death. There is a presumption of guilt on Moses's part in that he turns "this way and that" to see if anyone is looking before he strikes (Hebrew, *wayyak*, "and he struck," based on the same verb as the Egyptian's action). His burial of the Egyptian's body in the sand further accentuates his presumption of guilt. But the reader must understand that Moses's presumption of guilt represents an Egyptian perspective. Regardless of whether the Egyptian had any right as a taskmaster, official, or member of the royal house to beat the Hebrew slave, the language of the narrative presumes the right of an Egyptian to beat and potentially to kill a Hebrew slave. But this issue also accentuates Moses's identity as a Hebrew; indeed, in v. 11 the narrative twice mentions that the Hebrew slaves are his brothers. From the perspective of an Israelite or Hebrew reader, Moses just saved the life of the Hebrew slave. Unlike Egyptian society, in which Egyptians would refuse to eat with a Hebrew, even if he was someone highly ranked like Joseph (Gen 43:32; cf. Gen 46:34), or Babylonian society, which prescribes different treatment in Babylonian law for persons convicted of a crime based on their class, ancient Israelite society and law does not allow for discrimination against anyone based on class or even foreign origin (Exod 12:19, 40, 48; 20:10; 22:20; 23:9, 12).[1] Furthermore, in modern jurisprudence, a bystander who observes of crime is considered complicit, and one who aids and abets a crime is considered guilty of the crime in a court of law.[2] Moses's actions would be considered justified in ancient Israelite jurisprudence and likely in modern jurisprudence as well.

The reaction of the Hebrew men whom Moses stopped from fighting likewise presumes the setting of the narrative in Egypt and the presumption that Egyptian perspective prevails. The question posed by one of the Hebrew men to Moses—"Who appointed you as ruler and judge over us? Will you say to kill me as you killed the Egyptian?"—shows the disdain of the Hebrew man for Moses as well as his presumption that Moses had committed a crime in the perspective of Egyptian law. The following statements concerning Moses's fear and pharaoh's intention to execute Moses for the alleged crime confirm that Egyptian law prevails in this setting. But it also accentuates the difference with Israelite perspectives.

The second component of the narrative in Exodus 2:15b–22 recounts Moses's encounter with the daughters of Reuel, the priest of Midian, his acceptance in Reuel's house, and his marriage to Reuel's daughter

1. See Unterman, *Justice for All*; Weinfeld, *Social Justice*. For Hammurabi's law code, see *ANET* 163–80; Driver and Miles, *Babylonian Laws*, beginning already in the first legal paragraphs, which specify the class of the guilty party and the penalty for the crime, which differs according to the class of the perpetrator.

2. See Guiora, *Crime of Complicity*.

Zipporah. Midian refers to the region located south of Edom in the southern Aravah (Gen 36:35; Num 22:4, 7; Josh 15:61; Judg 6:3, 33; 1 Chr 1:46) and to the east of the Gulf of Aqabah on the Arabian peninsula (Exod 2:15; 3:1; 1 Kgs 11:18).[3] According to Genesis 25:2, the Midianites are descendants of Abraham and his wife Keturah. Despite the alleged kinship with the Midianites, there was hostility between Israel and Midian (Num 22:4, 7; 25:6, 14–15, 17; 31:2–3, 7–9; Josh 13:21; Judg 6–8; Isa 9:3; 10:26; Hab 3:7; Ps 83:10). The hostility is evident in Numbers 12 in which Miriam and Aaron condemn Moses for his marriage to a Cushite, i.e., Midianite, woman (see Hab 3:7), although YHWH defends Moses and punishes Miriam for her charges. Later, Numbers 25:6–18 condemns Israel for relationships with Midianite women, which lead to idolatry, although this concern appears to be Judean insofar as Phineas ben Eleazar ben Aaron, the ancestor of the Jerusalem-based Zadokite line of priests, is granted an eternal covenant of priesthood for his actions against those who consorted with Midian women. Although there were hostilities between Israel/Judah and Midian, it appears that those hostilities were eventually resolved insofar as the present narratives indicate that Israel learned of YHWH through a Midianite priest, Reuel. It is noteworthy that the Kuntillet Ajrud inscriptions posit a relationship between Midian and Israel in the Sinai, insofar as the site in the Sinai wilderness was apparently used by Israelite caravaners who left inscriptions devoted to the worship of YHWH of Samaria and his Asherah, presumably, YHWH's consort. Such a view of YHWH would have been considered as apostasy in Jerusalem, but may have had adherents in Samaria and elsewhere in northern Israel, given Israel's frequently Canaanite practice.[4] Such a view of Moses and his relationship with the Midianites suggests that Exodus 2:15b–22 is an E-stratum narrative.

Reuel, Hebrew, *rĕʿûʾēl*, which means "friend of El/G-d," appears to be a Canaanite theophoric names based on the name of the Canaanite creator god, El. The name was later adapted as an Israelite name for G-d (Exod 6:2–13). Reuel is one of the names for Moses's father-in-law, the priest of Midian (Exod 2:18; Num 10:29). He is also known as Jethro, the priest of Midian, in Exodus 3:1; 4:18; 18:1, 5, 10, 12; and as Hobab in Judges 4:11, although Hobab is called the son of Jethro in Numbers 10:29.[5] Each name signifies a different tradition about Moses's

3. Leuenberger, "Midian, Midianites."

4. B. Schmidt, "Kuntillet ʿAjrud."

5. Garrone, "Jethro."

father-in-law, viz., Reuel appears to be identified with the J-stratum of the Pentateuch, although the identification with the name of El suggests E; Jethro is identified with the E-stratum, although references to YHWH suggest J or P redaction; and Hobab is considered to be Jethro's son as noted in Numbers 10:29.[6] In short, J or P edited and reworked an earlier E narrative.

The encounter of Moses with the daughters of Reuel at a well in the wilderness represents a classic motif associated with an impending marriage, as exemplified by Jacob's encounter with Rachel at the well in Paddan-Aram in Genesis 29. Moses defends the daughters of Reuel from shepherds who attempted to encroach upon their water rights. When the daughters returned to their father, they described Moses excitedly as an Egyptian who protected them from the shepherds. As an Israelite, Moses would not necessarily have looked much different from upper-class Egyptians; his accented speech, manner of dress, and other characteristics would have given him away as an Egyptian. Reuel, for his part, made sure to invite Moses to stay for dinner and much more. He gave Moses his daughter, Zipporah (Hebrew, *ṣippōrâ*, "bird"), as a wife. Their son, Gershom, Hebrew, *gēršōm*, is here interpreted as "I was an immigrant in a foreign land," based on the meaning of, Hebrew, *gēr*, "resident alien, immigrant," and, Hebrew, *šām*, "there," to indicate the foreign land.

Reception History

Exodus 2:11–22 has an extensive history of reception that begins within the Bible itself and continues into modern times.

The account of the Egyptian man beating a Hebrew slave influences the oracles of the prophet Isaiah ben Amoz, who compares Assyria's oppression of Zion to Egypt's oppression of Israel in Isaiah 10:24–26. Isaiah calls upon the people of Zion (i.e., Jerusalem) to have no fear of Assyria, who strikes them with a rod and raises his staff over them as the Egyptians had done to Israel long before. Isaiah announces that YHWH will punish Assyria much as Egypt was punished with YHWH's rod, wielded by Moses at the Red Sea in the exodus narratives.

The New Testament also takes up the account of Moses's defense of a Hebrew slave beaten by an Egyptian in Acts 7:23–29 as part of Stephen's

6. See Campbell and O'Brien, *Sources of the Pentateuch*, 131–32, 186–87, respectively.

sermon in Acts 7. Stephen recounts how Moses at the age of forty went out to visit his people and saw one of them being wronged by an Egyptian. Moses defended his oppressed kinsman and killed the Egyptian, but when he learned that his own kinsmen questioned his actions, he fled to the land of Midian and fathered two sons. Hebrews 11:24–28 recounts how Moses's faith led him to consider suffering for Christ to be greater wealth than the treasures of Egypt, and so he fled Egypt for fear of the wrath of pharaoh and subsequently led the people out of Egypt.

Jewish midrashic tradition recounts how Moses went out among his people in Egypt and learned of their oppression by the Egyptians. Identifying himself with his people, he relieved the oppressed slaves by working in their place. The pharaoh was impressed with how Moses advanced his decree by example, and Moses was able to convince the pharaoh that one day of rest in each week (i.e., the Sabbath) would enable them to be better workers. An Egyptian taskmaster took advantage of a Hebrew named Dathan, and had relations with Dathan's wife while her husband worked as a slave. When Dathan caught the man leaving his wife, the Egyptian beat Dathan. Moses witnessed this abuse and after realizing that no one was about to stop this abuse, stepped in and killed the Egyptian by pronouncing the holy Name of G-d. When Dathan proved to be the man who rebuked Moses for killing the Egyptian, Moses escaped to the wilderness assisted by angels sent by G-d.[7]

As for Jethro, rabbinic midrash notes how he was a worshipper of idols as priest of Midian, but began to turn to G-d. Jethro's apostasy from the Midianite idols prompted animosity on the part of Midianite shepherds, who began to harass Jethro's daughters at the well. After proving to Jethro that he had been chosen by G-d by bringing his prospective father-in-law a rod of sapphire that G-d had given to Adam when he was expelled from Eden, Moses married Zipporah and fathered Gershom.[8]

The portrayal of the Egyptian man beating a Hebrew slave also factors into the African American experience of slavery in the United States.[9] Alex Haley recounts his ancestors' enslavement in America, beginning with his ancestor Kunta Kinte, a Mandinka warrior from the region of Gambia, who was kidnapped by slave traders and sold into slavery in Virginia. The account of Kunta Kinte's whipping is particularly poignant here in that it was carried out to force Kunta Kinte to abandon his identify as a

7. Ginzberg, *Legends*, 2:277–85.

8. Ginzberg, *Legends*, 2:289–95.

9. Haley, *Roots*.

free African warrior and adopt the identity of Toby, a slave on the Virginia plantation. The scene does not appear in the book, which makes only a passing reference to Kunta Kinte's name change to Toby.[10] But the 1977 television miniseries *Roots* turns the episode into a major scene in which Kunta Kinte, played by Levar Burton, is nearly whipped to death when the overseer, played by Vic Morrow, directs another slave to beat Kunta Kinte until he succumbs and accepts that his name is Toby. The scene is especially important because the brutality of the whipping is made very clear to the viewing audience, and it signifies the loss of Kunta Kinte's identity as a respected Muslim Mandika warrior from the region of Gambia to that of a slave, Toby, on a Virginia plantation, a man who has little control over his own life. The 2016 remake of the series made sure to include this scene, in which Malachi Kirby played Kunta Kinte, in an effort to update the series for a new generation of viewers.

The 1989 film *Glory*, starring Matthew Broderick as Colonel Robert Gould Shaw and Denzel Washington as Private Silas Trip, also portrays a whipping scene. The film recounts the formation and early combat history of the Fifty-Fourth Massachusetts Infantry Regiment, one of the first African American Union regiments commanded by white officers during the American Civil War. The account is based on the letters of Colonel Shaw, which he wrote to his parents until his death in battle at Fort Wagner, South Carolina, in July 1863. Private Trip, a former slave, deserts the regiment to find shoes, because Union Army Supply claimed that the needs of white regiments engaged in combat superseded the needs of the Fifty-Fourth. Trip was caught and brought back to the Fifty-Fourth for punishment by whipping. The scene underscored the racism of the Union Army during the Civil War, insofar as Trip suffered whipping as a Union soldier, due largely to the Union Army's negligence in supplying African American regiments with essential equipment, much as he had suffered whipping as a slave. In the end, Trip became a good combat soldier and died together with Colonel Shaw during the nearly successful assault by the Fifty-Fourth against Fort Wagner, South Carolina, which demonstrated that African American soldiers were indeed fit and well motivated for combat.

10. Haley, *Roots*, 214.

G-d's Revelation to Moses in the Burning Bush on Mount Horeb (Sinai)—Exodus 2:23—4:31

Translation

2:23 And it came to pass during those many days that the
king of Egypt died, and the sons of Israel were groaning from
the work, and they cried out, and their cry for help from the
work went up to G-d. And G-d heard their moaning, and G-d
remembered his covenant with Abraham and Isaac and Jacob. 25 And G-d saw the sons of Israel, and G-d knew.

3:1 And Moses was shepherding the sheep of Jethro, his father-in-law, the priest of Midian, and he guided the sheep to
the wilderness, and he came to the mountain of G-d at Horeb.
2 And an angel of YHWH appeared to him in the heart of a
fire from the midst of the bush, and he looked, and behold,
the bush was with fire, but the bush was not consumed. 3 And
Moses said, "I will turn aside so that I can see this great vision. Why does the bush not burn?"

4 And YHWH saw that he turned to see, and G-d called to
him from the midst of the bush, and he said, "Moses! Moses!"
And he said, "Here I am!" 5 And he said, "Do not come near
here. Remove your shoes from upon your feet for the place
upon which you are standing is holy ground." 6 And he said,
"I am the G-d of your father, the G-d of Abraham, the G-d of

Isaac, and the G-d of Jacob." And Moses hid his face for he was afraid from looking to G-d.

7 And YHWH said, "I have surely seen the oppression of my people who are in Egypt, and their outcry due to their oppressors have I heard, for I know their pains. 8 And I will go down to deliver them from the hand of the Egyptians and to bring them up from that land unto a good and broad land, unto a land flowing with milk and honey, unto the place of the Canaanites, and the Hittites, and the Amorites, and the Perizzites, and the Hivvites, and the Jebusites. 9 And now, behold, the outcry of the sons of Israel has come to me, and also I have seen the mistreatment by which the Egyptians inflict them. 10 And now, come, and I will send you to pharaoh, and bring out my people, the sons of Israel, from Egypt."

11 And then Moses said to G-d, "Who am I that I should go to pharaoh and that I should bring out the sons of Israel from Egypt?"

12 And he said, "Because I will be with you, and this will be the sign that I have sent you; when you bring out the people from Egypt, you will serve G-d upon this mountain."

13 And Moses said to G-d, "Behold, I come unto the sons of Israel, and I say to them, 'The G-d of your fathers has sent me to you,' and they say to me, 'What is his Name?' What do I say to them?"

14 And G-d said to Moses, "I am who I am," and he said, "Thus shall you say to the sons of Israel, 'I am has sent me unto you.'" 15 And G-d said further unto Moses, "Thus shall you say unto the sons of Israel, 'YHWH, the G-d of your fathers, the G-d of Abraham, the G-d of Isaac, and the G-d of Jacob has sent me to you.' This is my Name forever, and this is my remembrance from generation to generation.' 16 Go, and you shall gather the elders of Israel, and you shall say to them, 'YHWH, the G-d of your fathers, appeared to me, the G-d of Abraham, Isaac, and Jacob, saying, "I have surely recognized you and what was done to you in Egypt. 17 And I say, 'I will bring you up from the oppression of Egypt unto the land of

the Canaanites and the Hittites and the Amorites and the Hivvites and the Jebusites, unto a land flowing with milk and honey.' [18] And they will hear your voice, and you will come, you and the elders of Israel, unto the king of Egypt, and you will say unto him, 'YHWH, the G-d of the Hebrews, has encountered us, and now, we shall go, please, on a three-day journey into the wilderness, and we will make offerings to YHWH, our G-d.' [19] And I know that the king of Egypt will not allow you [to go] without a strong hand [to compel him]. [20] And I will send forth my hand, and I will strike the Egyptians with all my wonders which I will do in their midst, and after that, he will send you away. [21] And I will grant the favor of this people in the eyes of the Egyptians, and it will be that when you go, you will not go empty handed. [22] And a woman will ask her neighbor and the one who lodges in her house items of silver and items of gold and garments, and you will place them upon your sons and upon your daughters, and you shall strip the Egyptians."

4:1 And then Moses answered and said, "And if they don't believe me and they don't listen to my voice when they say, 'YHWH did not appear to you!'"

[2] And YHWH said to him, "What is this in your hand?" And said, "A rod." [3] And he said, "Throw it on the ground," and he threw it on the ground, and it became a snake, and Moses fled from before it. [4] And YHWH said to Moses, "Send forth your hand, and seize its tail." And he sent forth his hand, and he seized it, and it became a rod in his palm. [5] "In order that they would believe that YHWH, the G-d of their fathers, the G-d of Abraham, the G-d of Isaac, and the G-d of Jacob, appeared to you."

[6] And YHWH said to him further, "Place, please, your hand upon your chest," and he placed his hand upon his chest, and then he brought it out, and behold, his hand was leprous like snow. [7] And he said, "Return your hand unto your chest," and he returned his hand unto his chest, and he brought it out from his chest, and behold, it had returned like his [own] flesh. [8] "And if they do not believe you and they will not

listen to the first sign, then they will believe the later sign.
9 And if they do not believe these two signs and they do not
listen to your voice, then you shall take some water from the
Nile, and you shall pour it out on dry ground, and the water
that you have taken from the Nile shall become blood on the
dry ground."

10 But Moses said to YHWH, "By me, my L-rd, I am not a
man of words, yesterday, or three days ago or even since your
speaking to your servant, for I have a heavy mouth and a
heavy tongue."

11 And YHWH said to him, "Who grants speech to a human?
Or who makes him dumb or deaf or open [of eyes] or blind?
Is it not I, YHWH? 12 And now go, and I will be with your
mouth, and I will teach you what you will say."

13 And he said, "By me, my L-rd, send, please, by the hand [of
whomever] you will send."

14 And YHWH was very angry with Moses, and he said, "Is not
Aaron, your brother, the Levite? I know that he will surely
speak! And also, behold, he is coming out to meet you and
see you, and he is happy in his heart. 15 And you will speak
to him, and you will place the words in his mouth, and I will
be with your mouth and with his mouth, and I will teach you
what you will say. 16 And he shall speak for you to the people,
and he will be a spokesman for you, and you will be [like]
G-d to him. 17 And this rod you will take in your hand so that
you will make with it signs."

18 And Moses went, and he returned to Jeter [Jethro], his
father-in-law, and he said to him, "I will go, please, and I will
return to my brothers who are in Egypt, and I will see that
they are still living." And Jethro said to Moses, "Go in peace."

19 And YHWH said to Moses in Midian, "Go! Return to Egypt,
for all the men who were seeking your life are dead." 20 And
Moses took his wife and his sons, and mounted them upon
the ass, and he returned to the land of Egypt, and Moses took
the rod of G-d in his hand.

21 And YHWH said to Moses, "When you go to return to
Egypt, see all the miracles which I have placed in your hand,
and you shall do them before pharaoh, but I will harden his
heart so that he will not send away the people. 22 Then you
shall say to pharaoh, 'Thus says YHWH, "My son, my firstborn, is Israel! 23 And I say to you, Send off my people that
they may serve me, but you refuse to send them off! Behold,
I am going to kill your son, your firstborn!"'"

24 And it came to pass on the way at a lodging that YHWH
met him, and he sought to kill him. 25 And Tzipporah took a
flint, and she cut the foreskin of her son, and she touched his
feet, and she said, "For you are a bridegroom of blood to me!"
26 And he withdrew from him, then she said, "A bridegroom
of blood for circumcisions."

27 And YHWH said to Aaron, "Go to meet Moses in the wilderness," and he went, and he met him at the mountain of
G-d, and he kissed him. 28 And Moses told to Aaron all the
words of YHWH by which he sent him and all the signs that
he had commanded him. 29 And Moses and Aaron went, and
they gathered all the elders of the sons of Israel. 30 And Aaron
spoke all the words which YHWH spoke to Moses, and he
made signs in the sight of the people. 31 And the people believed, and they heard that YHWH had appointed the sons of
Israel and that he had seen their affliction, and they bowed
down and they worshipped.

Commentary

The account of G-d's revelation to Moses on Mount Horeb (Sinai) in Exodus 2:23—4:31 is demarcated at the outset by the temporal formula in Exodus 2:23, *wayĕhî bayyāmîm hārabbîm hāhēm*, "and it came to pass during those many days," which distinguishes the unit temporally from the preceding unit in Exodus 2:11–22. The temporal formula in Exodus 5:1, *wĕʾaḥar*, "and later," introduces the next major sub-unit of the text beginning in Exodus 5:1.

The internal structure of the text emphasizes a very new situation in which we learn that the pharaoh who sought to arrest and execute

Moses for killing the Egyptian has died. We also learn of Moses's movements while tending the sheep of his father-in-law, now identified as Jethro. It includes three major components in Exodus 2:23–25; 3:1—4:17; and 4:18–31.

The first major component of this text is the introductory statement in Exodus 2:23–25, which recounts the death of the former pharaoh, here simply identified as "the king of Egypt," the continuing suffering of sons of Israel due to the slavery imposed upon them by the Egyptians, and G-d's recognition of that suffering in relation to the covenant made with Israel's ancestors. The temporal introduction stresses that Moses lived in the wilderness with his father-in-law for a long time, but it does not specify the amount of time that had passed. It notes the death of the pharaoh without identifying him. Many interpreters speculate that the late pharaoh was Seti I (r. 1294/1290–1279 BCE), the second pharaoh of the Nineteenth Egyptian Dynasty, and that his successor would have been Rameses II (1279–1213 BCE), but it is clear that the narrative is not interested in the identity of the pharaoh in question. Instead, it focuses on G-d's recognition of the suffering of the people of Israel under Egyptian rule and the covenant that G-d had made with the ancestors of Israel to protect them. In the present, synchronic form of the text, G-d's covenant with Israel would have to be recognized as an eternal covenant (Gen 17), although diachronic scholarship identifies G-d's eternal covenant with Abraham as the product of the P-stratum of the Pentateuch, generally dated to the time of Nehemiah and Ezra in the Persian period. Nevertheless, G-d has a covenant with the ancestors in the earlier E and J strata of the Pentateuch (Gen 12, 15, 28; see also Deuteronomy). The tradition of G-d's covenant with Israel is known to the mid-eighth-century northern Israelite prophet Hosea ben Beeri (Hos 12), although some scholars argue that Hosea's understanding of the tradition does not entail a unified tradition that includes both a version of the ancestral history together with an account of the exodus and wilderness narratives. Nevertheless, Hosea knows them both despite the efforts of some to claim that his citation of pentateuchal traditions is a later addition to his book. The reference to G-d as Elohim in this passage suggests that it is an E-stratum text, and the following discussion will show that there is cause to view Exodus 3:1—4:17 as an originally E-stratum text that has been reworked by the J-stratum redaction.[1] The references to

1. N.b., most interpreters view Exodus 3–4 as primarily a J-stratum text, although they generally recognize some E elements within the J narrative. See Campbell and

G-d's covenant with the ancestors (i.e., Abraham, Isaac, and Jacob) may be the product of J redaction, but Hosea's references indicate that G-d's covenant with Jacob would have already been known to E. There is also reason to recognize that E would have known covenant traditions with Abraham, Isaac, and Joseph as well.

Under the terms of the covenant with Israel, G-d/YHWH is obligated to protect Israel, and Israel is obligated to accept only G-d/YHWH as its own deity. The notice here raises questions as to why it took so long for G-d to recognize Israel's situation. Nevertheless, Exodus 2:23–25 indicates that G-d does recognize the situation and it introduces the account by which G-d will reveal the divine self to Moses in order to commission him as the human agent who will act on G-d's behalf to free the people from Egyptian bondage and guide them to promised land of Israel.

The second major component of Exodus 2:23—4:31 appears in Exodus 3:1—4:17, introduced by the circumstantial phrase *ûmōšeh hāyâ rōʿeh ʾet-ṣōʾn yitrô*, "and Moses was shepherding the sheep of Jethro, his father-in-law," which recounts G-d's revelation to Moses at Mount Horeb (Sinai) and the subsequent dialogue between G-d (YHWH) and Moses concerning G-d's instructions to Moses and Moses's questions concerning his duties and the problems that he expects to encounter.

Exodus 3:1—4:17 begins with an introductory notice in Exodus 3:1 concerning Moses's shepherding the flock of his father-in-law, Jethro, and leading them into the wilderness to "the mountain of G-d," here identified as "Horeb" (Hebrew, *ḥōrēb*, "desolate wasteland"). In a synchronic reading of the text, this statement does little more than identify the circumstances of G-d's revelation to Moses, but in a diachronic reading of the text, it provides clues to the compositional history of the text. The name Jethro is typically identified with the J-stratum of the Pentateuch, particularly since Jethro praises YHWH in Exodus 18:10–12.[2] The name Reuel, mentioned in Exodus 2:18 and Numbers 10:29, which means "friend of G-d," would clearly presuppose E-stratum composition. The reference to the mountain of G-d as Horeb—and not Sinai—is generally identified with northern Israelite tradition in both the Tetrateuch and Deuteronomy, and therefore would presuppose E-stratum composition.

O'Brien, *Sources of the Pentateuch*, 132–35; Noth, *History of Pentateuchal Traditions*, 30, 34–35, 203.

2. Garrone, "Jethro."

Such a combination of references suggests that an early E-stratum text was reworked by J-stratum for the present form of the text.[3]

The account of G-d's revelation to Moses in Exodus 3:2–22 presents a number of key issues. The first is the imagery of the burning bush, which is initially portrayed as an angel or messenger of G-d through whom G-d speaks (cf. Gen 22:15). The use of angelic imagery is typical of E-stratum composition, but the imagery of the bush that burns and yet is not consumed is also key to understanding the imagery and interpretation of this text. The Hebrew term for bush is *sĕneh*, which also helps to explain the alternative name for the mountain of G-d as Sinai, Hebrew, *sînay*, which is employed in the J and P traditions and is actually derived from *sîn*, "Sin," the name of the wilderness between Elim and Sinai (Exod 16:1; 17:1; Num 33:11, 12). Nevertheless, the association with *sĕneh*, "bush," suggests a false etymology of "my bush," when the term would better refer to "my wilderness." But the importance of the bush is not limited to the name Sinai. It also points to G-d's association with the world of creation, beginning with the E-stratum, which aids in configuring the exodus and wilderness narratives as a creation text, which points to the creation of Israel and G-d's role as the true creator G-d. The imagery of the burning bush as a bush that burns but is not consumed is based on two types of bushes that grow in the Sinai wilderness, the *rubus sanctus* and the *cassia senna*. Sarna identifies the *rubus sanctus* as a prickly bush that grows by wadis and humid soil.[4] It produces a flower that resembles a small rose and raspberry-like fruit that is initially red but turns black when it ripens. The reddish imagery of the bush suggests a flaming presence when viewed from a distance. Sarna also points to the *cassia senna*, which Zohary identifies as the bush in question based only on linguistic criteria. The *cassia senna* grows in the Sinai and southern Israel to a height of about a meter, and it produces racemes of large yellow flowers, which produce many seeded pods.[5] In either case, the imagery of the bush identifies G-d with a bush that is presumably native to the Sinai region. The reference is also etiological insofar as interpreters identify the burning bush with the eternal lamp (Hebrew, *nēr tāmîd*) of the temple mentioned in Exodus 27:20–21 (cf. Lev 6:2–6; 1 Sam 3:3).

The following revelation by YHWH to Moses brings together both etiological elements as well as indications of an earlier northern setting.

3. Sweeney, *Pentateuch*, 36–37.

4. Sarna, *Exodus*, 14; Sarna, *Exploring Exodus*, 39.

5. Zohary, *Plants of the Bible*, 140–41.

G-d's call to Moses in Exodus 3:4, "Moses! Moses!," is reminiscent of G-d's call to Samuel in the northern Israelite Shiloh temple in 1 Samuel 3:10 and Abraham in Genesis 22:14, which likewise has northern Israelite E-stratum associations. G-d's instruction to remove his shoes on holy ground is etiological, insofar as it explains the origins of Israelite priestly practice to serve at the temple barefoot (cf. Josh 5:15).[6] G-d's self-identification as "the G-d of your father," etc., in Exodus 3:6 ties the narrative into the ancestral narratives of Genesis, thereby indicating the work of J-stratum redaction that was intended to unite the ancestral and exodus/wilderness traditions.

Norman Habel has argued convincingly that G-d's self-revelation to Moses in Exodus 3 is a classic example of the prophetic call narrative, although the vision report also plays a key role.[7] Such an identification is not simply an indication of genre; it also points to the northern origins of this narrative, insofar as northern priestly functionaries were frequently understood to be prophets, such as Samuel, Elijah, and Elisha, even though they carried out priestly functions.[8] Moses, too, is construed as a prophet here and in the book of Deuteronomy, insofar as the Levites are not commissioned for priestly service until Numbers 17–18. Moses's identity as a prophet here points to an earlier E-stratum layer beneath the present narrative.

Habel's analysis of the prophetic call narrative genre points to six basic elements, viz., 1) divine confrontation; 2) introductory word; 3) commission; 4) objection by the prophet; 5) reassurance; and 6) a sign. All of these elements are in the present narrative. The divine confrontation appears in the vision of the burning bush in vv. 2–3. The introductory word appears in G-d's address to Moses in v. 4. The commission appears in vv. 7–10 in which G-d notes Israel's suffering under the Egyptians and instructs Moses to go to Egypt to free his people. Moses's objection appears in v. 11. G-d's reassurance to Moses appears in v. 12a with G-d's statement "I will be with you," an example of the assistance formula.[9] The sign appears in v. 12, both as the statement of

6. Sarna notes that Exodus 28, 29, and Leviticus 8 include no mention of footwear for priestly attire (cf. Exod. Rab. 2.13; b. Sotah 40a) (*Exodus*, 14n16, 240).

7. Habel, "Call Narratives"; cf. Coats, *Exodus 1–18*, 34–42; Sweeney, *Isaiah 1–39*, 542–43. For the vision report, see Sweeney, *Isaiah 1–39*, 542.

8. Sweeney, "Samuel's Institutional Identity"; Sweeney, "Prophets and Priests"; cf. Sweeney, *1 and 2 Samuel*, ad loc.; Sweeney, *1 and 2 Kings*, ad loc.

9. Coats, *Exodus 1–18*, 40, 175.

the assurance formula and in G-d's statement that Moses and the people will worship G-d at this mountain.

A further element of the combination of northern ideology and etiology appears in Exodus 3:13–15 with the discussion of G-d's Name. When Moses asks G-d what he shall say when the people ask for the Name of the G-d of their ancestors, G-d's response is "I am who I am" (Hebrew, *'ehyeh 'ăšer 'ehyeh*). This statement of the holy Name of G-d has a number of dimensions. First, the formula itself is a known rhetorical device in Egyptian literature. It appears in the Egyptian "Instruction of Pharaoh Merikare," a Tenth Dynasty Egyptian pharaoh who ruled Egypt in 1075–1040 BCE, although it is clear that he did not have full control of the country.[10] The "Instruction of Pharaoh Merikare," however, dates only to the Eighteenth Dynasty (1550–1292 BCE) in the form of three papyrus manuscripts.[11] The Eighteenth Dynasty overthrew the Hyksos rulers of Egypt, but died out in its last years because its final two pharaohs failed to produce male heirs to the throne.[12] The work appears designed to instruct its readers in the proper exercise of strong leadership to control the country against threats. A key phrase in the text is lines 94–95, in which Merikare's father instructs him, "But as I live [95], and shall be what I am, when the bowmen were a sealed wall, I breached [their strongholds], I made Lower Egypt attack them, I captured their inhabitants, I seized their cattle, until the Asiatics abhorred Egypt."[13] The Egyptian statement is a form of the *idem per idem* rhetorical device, in which a subject is defined in relation to itself. In the Egyptian text, it functions as a statement of pharaonic power as a means to convince its readers to exercise pharaonic power to defeat the enemies of Egypt. Insofar as its statement does not disclose the Name of G-d in this text, it appears that it also functions as a statement of divine power to enable Moses to act as G-d's agent in freeing the people of Israel from Egyptian captivity. In the context of the northern E-stratum tradition, such a statement then functions only

10. Kuhrt, *Ancient Near East*, 1:154–61, esp. 156–58. The relevance of this text to Exodus is noted by Davies, who cites Alt, "Mitteilungen" (*Exodus 1–18*, 1:276); see also Herrmann, *Israel in Egypt*, 53, 80n5. Most other interpreters appear to be unaware of this reference.

11. Lichtheim, *Ancient Egyptian Literature*, 1:97–109; *ANET* 414–18; Simpson, *Literature of Ancient Egypt*, 180–92.

12. Kuhrt, *Ancient Near East*, 1:188–94.

13. Lichtheim, *Ancient Egyptian Literature*, 1:104; cf. Wilson, who translates "But as I live! I am while I am!" (*ANET* 416); Simpson, who translates, "But I lived! And while I existed . . ." (*Literature of Ancient Egypt*, 188).

as encouragement for Moses to rely on G-d's power when confronting pharaoh. In such an instance, G-d is defined only as G-d, not as YHWH, insofar as G-d continues to instruct Moses to tell the people that Ehyeh, "I am," has sent him to free them from Egyptian slavery.

But another dimension of this narrative emerges in Exodus 3:15 when G-d discloses the divine Name, YHWH, to Moses, and self-identifies as "the G-d of your fathers, the G-d of Abraham, the G-d of Isaac, and the G-d of Jacob." G-d then states that YHWH is the divine Name forever. At this point, the influence of J-stratum redaction comes into play to identify G-d as YHWH as the G-d of Israel's ancestors. In this instance, the *idem per idem*, "Ehyeh Asher Ehyeh, "I am who I am," functions differently to assert the holy character of the divine Name and to polemicize against the Egyptian practice of pronouncing divine names as a means to employ their power for the benefit of their allies and the defeat of their enemies. The *idem per idem* device defines a subject in relation to itself and thereby offers no understanding of what the subject of the statement might be; in this case, it does not state the divine Name, but instead employs a verbal phrase to interpret the meaning of the Name. The Hebrew verb *'ehyeh*, "I am," is based on the verb root, *hyh*, "to be," and it asserts divine existence without defining the character of G-d or the divine Name in any appreciable way.

The hesitation in announcing the divine Name is an important dimension of the narrative because it signals caution and the need to think before employing the holy Name of G-d. The use of the verb *'ehyeh* is key here because it suggests that the divine Name, YHWH, is a third-person singular imperfect form of the verb root, *hyh*, i.e., analogous to *yihyeh*, which means "he is," thereby indicating the existence and power of G-d. The Name, YHWH, spelled with *a* and *e* vowels, of course differs from this form of the verb, which indicates that this is not a semantic definition of the divine Name; rather it is an interpretative definition of the Name. The narrative avoids pronouncing the Name at first, which reinforces the sanctity of the Name that is not to be taken in vain, as stated in the Ten Commandments (Exod 20:7; cf. Deut 5:11; Lev 24:10–23). According to Jewish tradition, the holy divine Name is uttered only at Yom Kippur by the high priest in the Jerusalem temple when he enters the holy of holies of the temple to atone for the sins of the Jewish people. Such a stance in Exodus 3:1–15 is also important because it signals a polemic against the Egyptian practice of invoking divine names so that the person who states the name of an Egyptian god in the context of blessings and curses, such as those found in the Egyptian Execration Texts, can thereby employ the power of the god or goddess in question to bless or to curse an ally or an enemy.[14] The exodus narrative and Jewish tradition reject such a stance by maintaining that the sanctity and power of the divine Name are such that human beings are not allowed to utter it, with the previously mentioned exception of the high priest in the holy of holies of the Jerusalem temple on Yom Kippur.

Exodus 3:16–22 then specifies the divine commission to Moses to go to Egypt to announce to the people YHWH's intentions to free them from Egyptian bondage and to confront the pharaoh in order to demand that pharaoh allow the people to go on a three-day journey into the wilderness so that they might worship their G-d. As depicted in this segment, YHWH knows that pharaoh will refuse the demand, and it thereby enables the narrative to foreshadow the plagues that YHWH will release against Egypt to demonstrate divine power and thereby compel pharaoh to release the people. The narrative also signals the willingness of the people of Egypt to provide Israel with valuables and clothing, both as a demonstration of their recognition of the divine power of YHWH and as a form of compensation for Israel's enslavement configured as offerings to YHWH. Insofar as this paragraph identifies G-d as YHWH and the G-d of Israel's ancestors, it constitutes an example of J-stratum expansion that further interpreters the apparently underlying E-stratum narrative of G-d's revelation and commission to Moses in Exodus 3:1–15.

Exodus 4:1–17 then follows the initial revelation episode with a conversational sequence in which Moses raises a series of objections that he has to YHWH's commission, and YHWH's five responses to Moses's objections. This narrative appears to be part of the J-stratum expansion of the burning bush episode in that it elaborates upon Moses's objections to his divine commission stated in Exodus 3:11–12, 13–15. Such elaboration provides the J-stratum opportunity to introduce several elements of Moses's role as YHWH's servant in leading Israel from Egyptian bondage to the land of Israel.

The first objection and response appears in Exodus 4:1–5 in which Moses asks what he should do if the people do not believe that Moses has been commissioned by G-d to lead them from Egyptian bondage. YHWH responds by pointing to Moses's shepherd's staff, which is particularly important because the metaphor of a shepherd is frequently

14. Muhlestein, "Execration and Execration Texts"; Redford, *Egypt, Canaan, and Israel*, 87–97.

applied to kings and priests in the ancient world. YHWH informs Moses that he should cast his rod to the ground so that it will become a snake, which refers to the Egyptian practice of snake charming, that will demonstrate how Moses exercises miraculous power on YHWH's behalf. The rod then functions as a symbol of priestly identity and power (e.g., Num 17:16—18:32; Hos 4:12).

The second response appears in Exodus 4:6–8, in which YHWH afflicts Moses with leprosy, insofar as his hand becomes leprous like snow. Interpreters caution that biblical references to leprosy are not the equivalent of Hansen's disease, as Hansen's disease did not appear in the ancient Near East until the troops of Alexander the Great bought it back from India in the late fourth century BCE.[15] Again, the purpose is to demonstrate divine power as the basis for Moses's commission.

The third response appears in Exodus 4:9 in which YHWH instructs Moses to take some water from the Nile River and pour it on the ground where it will allegedly turn to blood. This action exemplifies the first of YHWH's ten plagues against Egypt (see Exod 7:14–24) in which YHWH turns the Nile River into blood. This plague is actually based in the seasonal cycle of the Nile when melting snow from the southern mountains of Ethiopia and Sudan wash red soil into the headwaters of the Nile, thereby giving the Nile waters the appearance of blood.[16] Nevertheless, this action symbolizes YHWH's power over creation.

The fourth response appears in Exodus 4:10–12 in which Moses objects that he is "heavy" (Hebrew, *kābēd*) of mouth and tongue, indicating that he does not speak adequately. Most interpreters conclude that Moses had some sort of a speech impediment, although it is typical for oracle diviners in the ancient world, particularly in Egypt, to speak unclearly or elliptically in the course of oracular divination, thereby requiring an interpreter to discern and articulate the meaning of the oracular prophet's speech.[17] YHWH responds to Moses's objection by stating that YHWH will be with Moses and instruct him on what to say, thereby confirming Moses's role as an oracular prophet of G-d.

But the fifth response appears in Exodus 4:13–17 when Moses presses G-d by demanding that YHWH choose someone else to speak on behalf of the divine, thereby angering YHWH against Moses and signaling a difficult relationship between the two that will ultimately

15. Hieke, "Leper, Leprosy."

16. Kade and Huddleston, "Nile."

17. Miosi, "Oracle."

culminate in YHWH's decision to ban Moses from the land of Israel (see Num 20). YHWH therefore proposes that Moses's older brother,[18] Aaron, serve as Moses's spokesman, thereby anticipating Aaron's future role as the ancestor of the priestly lines and Moses's role as a prophet who will serve as YHWH's spokesman with Aaron serving as the priestly interpreter of YHWH's words through Moses. Moses will then act metaphorically as G-d, which is also the case in northern prophets, such as Elijah, Elisha, and others, who are called "man of G-d," Hebrew, *'îš hā'ĕlōhîm* (see 1 Sam 9:6–10; Deut 33:1; Josh 14:6; 1 Kgs 13:1–31; 17:18–24; 2 Kgs 1:9–13; 4:7–42; 5:8–20; 8:2–11), because they speak on behalf of G-d.[19] YHWH's concluding statement to Moses indicates that his rod will serve as the symbol of his authority.

The third major sub-unit appears in Exodus 4:18–31 concerning Moses's return to his Jethro and his journey to Egypt together with YHWH's continuing instructions. Jethro is initially identified as "Jether" (Hebrew, *yeter*, "remainder, excess, preeminence"), which is apparently a variation of the name Jethro (Hebrew, *yitrô*, "his preeminence"). The reference to the rod of G-d in Exodus 4:20 suggests that this narrative originated as an E-stratum narrative, but the references to YHWH indicate that it has been revised and expanded by J. Upon returning to Jethro in Midian, Moses asks permission from his father-in-law to return to Egypt to see if all is well with his people, i.e., if they are still alive. Jethro readily agrees.

YHWH then instructs Moses to return to Egypt because those who sought to kill him are now dead. Moses then packs up his family, including both his wife and sons, who remain anonymous at this point. Moses's wife is Zipporah, but only one son, Gershom, has yet been identified (Exod 2:21–22). The second son must therefore be Eliezer (1 Chr 23:14–17). YHWH's instructions reiterate the concern with Moses's performing miraculous acts to demonstrate to the pharaoh (and to the people of Israel) that he acts on behalf of YHWH. But the narrative introduces YHWH's intentions to harden the heart of pharaoh so that pharaoh will refuse to let the people go. The purpose of this notice is to signal the coming confrontation between YHWH and pharaoh, thereby to demonstrate YHWH's power over both creation at large and pharaoh

18. Exodus 7:7 states that Aaron is eighty-three years old and Moses is eighty years old when they confront pharaoh; cf. Exodus 6:20, which names Aaron first and Moses second as the sons of Amran, indicating that Aaron is the older brother.

19. D. Petersen, *Roles of Israel's Prophets*, 40–50.

in particular. The notice also adds the motif of Israel as YHWH's firstborn son, which will become a major concern in the exodus narrative, insofar as the firstborn sons of Israel will be redeemed to serve YHWH (cf. Exod 34:19–20). The obligation of the firstborn of Israel is to serve as assistants to the sons of Aaron, who function as the priests of Israel.[20] By designating Israel as YHWH's firstborn, the narrative highlights Israel's religious role in relation to YHWH, and this role therefore serves as the basis for designating Israel as "a kingdom of priests and a holy nation" in Exodus 19:6. This task anticipates the designation of Israel as the chosen people of YHWH, although such a role does not give Israel special privileges. Rather, it entails special obligations to G-d (Deut 4). Because pharaoh will refuse to let Israel go, YHWH will then kill pharaoh's firstborn son. The motif raises moral questions concerning YHWH's treatment of pharaoh and Egypt at large, much as Isaiah 6 raises questions concerning YHWH's treatment of the people of Israel in the time of the prophet Isaiah ben Amoz.[21] Nevertheless, the motif is understood as a portrayal of YHWH's power and as an etiology concerning early northern Israel's practice of using firstborn sons to assist the priests in northern sanctuaries (1 Sam 1–3).

Exodus 4:24–26 provides a striking example of YHWH's capacity to punish and to restore, much like Genesis 32:23–33, which recounts Jacob's wrestling with a man understood to represent G-d. The Genesis narrative functions as an etiology for naming Jacob as Israel and for the Israelite practice of offering the thigh portion of a sacrifice to the priesthood. In the present instance, YHWH's attack appears to be motivated by concern with circumcision. Circumcision is the sign of the covenant between Abraham (Israel) and YHWH in Genesis 17. It is a known practice in ancient Egypt where it was reserved especially for Egyptian priests although it functions in relation to other nations in the vicinity of Israel and Judah as well (Jer 9:24–25).[22] Zipporah steps forward to stop YHWH's attack when she uses a flint knife to circumcise her son and declare that he is "a bridegroom of blood" to her. It is not clear why a son should be labelled as "a bridegroom" in relation to his mother. It is possible that the statement is meant to apply to Moses, insofar as

20. Sweeney, "Samuel's Institutional Identity"; Sweeney, "Literary-Historical Dimensions of Intertextuality."

21. Sweeney, *Reading the Bible After the Shoah*, 84–103.

22. See the text concerning the circumcision of prospective Egyptian priests in *ANET* 326.

it is not clear that he was ever circumcised while living in the palace of pharaoh. Alternatively, the statement may indicate that Gershom is now eligible for marriage as circumcision appears to be a puberty ritual among the priests in ancient Egypt as well as for Abraham's thirteen-year-old son, Ishmael, as noted in Genesis 17:13–27 and the men of Shechem in Genesis 34. In Judaism, baby boys are circumcised on the eighth day after birth.[23] In any case, Zipporah proves to be a righteous gentile, or perhaps even a convert, insofar as Jethro and Zipporah appear to be sources for Moses to learn about YHWH.

The narrative concludes in Exodus 4:27–31 with Moses's reunion with his brother, Aaron, in which he recounts to Aaron all that has transpired. A meeting with the elders of Israel then follows in which Aaron informs them as well. When Aaron performed the prescribed signs from YHWH before the people, i.e., the snake and perhaps the water of the Nile turning to blood, the people at large were convinced that Moses had indeed encountered YHWH.

Reception History

Reception history begins within the text of the Hebrew Bible itself. As noted in the above commentary, an earlier E-stratum narrative that emphasized divine revelation through a burning bush was expanded and elaborated upon by a J-stratum narrator. Whereas E employed the imager of the burning bush to convey G-d's statement "I am who I am," a phrase that is known in Egyptian literature to express the power of the pharaoh, the J-stratum uses this phrase to interpret the meaning of the holy Name of G-d (i.e., YHWH) as a verbal statement that means "He is/exists," in order to convey divine presence and power. The later J-stratum narrative in Exodus 4:1–17 elaborates upon YHWH's responses to Moses's objections in order to emphasize the signs (i.e., Moses's rod turning into a snake, leprosy, turning the waters of the Nile into blood, and Aaron's role in interpreting Moses's speech) as signs of divine power to prove to pharaoh and to Israel that G-d is indeed with Moses.

The medieval rabbinic midrashic historical work *Sefer ha-Yashar Shemot*, "The book of the correct [history]," written ca. 1000–1200 CE, recounts how Moses served as king of Ethiopia from the age of twenty-seven to the age of sixty-seven after he fled from Egypt and before he settled

23. See Olson et al., "Circumcision."

in with Jethro in Midian.[24] Following the death of their King Ḳiḳanos, the Ethiopians could find no one fit to serve as king except for Moses. Under Moses's leadership, Ethiopia enjoyed victory over its enemies, but he refused to have relations with his queen, Adoniah, because she was a descendant of Ham, the ancestor of the Canaanites. During his fortieth year, Adoniah announced that her son, Monarchos, apparently from a prior marriage, had grown up and should be king in place of Moses, since Moses was not Ethiopian. Moses then journeyed to Midian, where he encountered Jethro and his daughters. Prior to the arrival of Moses, Jethro gave up idolatry and turned to G-d, which provoked hostile relations with the other peoples in Midian (Mekilta Yitro 1.57a).[25]

Moses's rod was made from a tree that grew in the garden of Jethro which he used to test anyone who wished to marry Zipporah or his other daughters. The tree was actually the rod created on the first Sabbath evening, which G-d gave to Adam. When Moses requested Zipporah in marriage, Jethro told him to go to the garden and bring him the rod. At first, Jethro thought Moses to be a threat and threw him into a pit, but Zipporah took care of him until Moses could prove his worth to Jethro, who then gave him Zipporah as wife.[26]

When Moses saw the thornbush on Mount Horeb, the mountain moved closer to him so that G-d could speak with him. Although Moses was accompanied by other shepherds, only Moses saw the vision of G-d in the bush. When G-d saw Moses's distress over the suffering of Israel, G-d decided to speak to him in familiar tones, and chose the voice of Amran, the father of Moses, to speak to him. Because Moses was meek, G-d granted him a Heikhalot journey through the seven levels of heaven to appear before the throne of G-d. The angel of the presence of G-d, Metatron, the angelic form of Enoch ben Jared, guided Moses through the seven levels and explained their meaning to Moses. Moses refused to leave the heavens, and so G-d granted Moses the Torah. When Moses initially refused G-d's commission, G-d punished him by making him the Levite and his brother, Aaron, the priest; otherwise, Moses would have been the priest and Aaron would have been the Levite. Moses declined, saying that G-d should send one of the great Torah scholars of Judaism,

24. Ginzberg, *Legends*, 2:286–89.

25. Ginzberg, *Legends*, 2:289–91.

26. Ginzberg, *Legends*, 2:291–95, and the various midrashic sources, such as Shemot Rabbah, cited there.

but when Moses saw that all of the great Torah scholars cited him as the basis for their knowledge, he accepted G-d's commission.[27]

In Christianity, Stephen cites the divine revelation to Moses through the burning bush in his speech before the high priest prior to his martyrdom (Acts 6:8—8:1a; see esp. Acts 7:30–34). Jesus cites Exodus 3:6, "I am the G-d of your father, the G-d of Abraham, the G-d of Isaac, and the G-d of Jacob," in Mark 12:18–27 (cf. Luke 20:27–40) in his attempt to refute the Sadducean view of resurrection.[28] The church father Justin Martyr, as part of his polemics against Judaism, claims that Jesus Christ spoke to Moses through the burning bush in Exodus 3:5, because G-d the Father is the creator, whereas only G-d's Logos is manifested on earth (Justin, *1 Apol.* 63.3). Origen understands the removal of Moses shoes to signify the removal of the shoes from the feet of our soul to symbolize that we come before G-d and Jesus for cleansing (*Orig. Hom. Jos.* 6.3).[29] Various Roman Catholic interpreters understood the burning bush to symbolize Mary's virginity, in that she conceived through the fire of the holy spirit, although her virginity remained intact (e.g., Bridget of Sweden, *Sermo Angelicus* 3.15). Martin Luther objected to this interpretation because it abandoned historical interpretation in favor of arbitrary allegorical interpretation. Luther maintains that the burning bush symbolizes Christ, who remains divine even as he appears on earth to redeem human beings (*Predigten über das 2. Buch Mose*).[30] In modern times, the burning bush has come to symbolize the Presbyterian Church, and the linkage to divine liberation in African American Christianity.[31]

The burning bush episode is cited three times in the Qur'an. G-d self-identifies as Allah in Sura 20:10–48. G-d shows signs to Moses, viz., the rod and the serpent and the whitening of Moses's hand in Sura 27.7–12. A third Sura, 28.29–35, specifies that Moses was called by G-d from a bush. None of the Suras indicate the divine Name of G-d.[32]

G-d's encounter with Moses is featured in the first act of Arnold Schoenberg's unfinished opera *Moses und Aron* (1930–1932), although Schoenberg had Moses address the bush first.[33]

27. Ginzberg, *Legends*, 2:303–31.
28. Kensky, "Burning Bush."
29. Meiser, "Burning Bush."
30. Egger, "Burning Bush."
31. Kling, "Burning Bush."
32. Nickel, "Burning Bush."
33. N. Petersen, "Burning Bush."

In the 1998 animated musical drama *The Prince of Egypt*, producer Jeffrey Katzenberg and his staff attempted to portray G-d's voice emanating from the burning bush as a collection of many voices to emphasize the all-inclusive nature of the divine presence, but the technology did not allow for a satisfactory result. Ultimately, they settled on using the voice of Val Kilmer, who portrayed the voice of Moses in the film, to emphasize that each person hears the voice of G-d from their own perspective.[34]

34. Based on Katzenberg's discussion of the matter with the author, who served as one of the six hundred anonymous scholarly consultants, during the production of *The Prince of Egypt*.

The First Confrontation of Pharaoh by Moses and Aaron—Exodus 5:1—6:13

Translation

5:1 And afterward, Moses and Aaron came, and they said to
pharaoh, "Thus says YHWH, the G-d of Israel, 'Send off my
people, so they may celebrate for me in the wilderness!'"
2 And pharaoh said, "Who is YHWH, that I should listen
to his voice to send off Israel? I do not know YHWH, and
also Israel I will not send away!" 3 And they said, "The G-d
of the Hebrews has been proclaimed upon us! Let us go,
please, on a journey of three days in the wilderness, and let
us sacrifice to YHWH, our G-d, lest he afflict us with plague
or with sword." 4 And the king of Egypt said to them, "Why,
Moses and Aaron, do you divert the people from its work?
Get back to your labors!" 5 And pharaoh said, "Indeed, the
people of the land are now so many! And you would stop
them from their labors?"

6 And pharaoh commanded on that day the taskmasters and
his officers, saying, 7 "You shall not continue to give straw to
the people to fire the bricks as before. They shall go and they
shall cut straw for themselves. 8 But you shall require of them
the same number of bricks that they were making before. You
shall not diminish it, for they are slackers! Therefore, they
cry out, saying, 'Let us go! Let us sacrifice to our G-d!' 9 Let

the work be heavier upon the men, so they will do it, and
they will not look to false words!"

10 And the taskmasters of the people and its officers went
out, and they said to the people, saying, "Thus says pharaoh,
'I will not give you straw! 11 You! Go! Take for yourselves
straw from wherever you will find it, but your work will not
be diminished a bit." 12 And the people scattered throughout
the land of Egypt to cut stubble for straw. 13 And the taskmasters pressed them, saying, "Complete your work each
day, just as much as when there was straw!" 14 And the officers of the sons of Israel, whom the taskmasters of pharaoh
had placed over them, were beaten, saying, "Why did you
not complete your assignment to fire bricks as before, even
yesterday and today?"

15 And the officers of the sons of Israel came, and they cried
out to pharaoh, saying, "Why did you do this to your slaves?
16 Straw is not given to your slaves, but they tell us, 'Make
bricks!' And behold, your slaves are beaten, but your people
are wrong!" 17 And he said, "You are slackers! Slackers! Therefore you say, 'Let us go! Let us sacrifice to YHWH!' 18 And
now, get back to work! And straw will not be given to you, but
the same number of bricks you must provide!"

19 And the officers of the sons of Israel recognized that they
were in trouble, due to the statement "You shall not diminish from your bricks each day!" 20 And they met Moses and
Aaron, standing to meet them when they left pharaoh. 21 And
they said to them, "May YHWH see you, and may he judge
how you have made us loathsome in the eyes of pharaoh and
in the eyes of his servants to put a sword in their hand to kill
us." 22 And Moses returned to YHWH, and he said, "My L-rd,
why have you wronged this people? Why have you sent me?
23 Ever since I came to pharaoh to speak in your Name, he has
wronged this people! And you certainly have not delivered
your people!"

6:1 And YHWH said to Moses, "Now you will see what I will
do to pharaoh, for with a strong hand he shall send them away,
and with a strong hand he will expel them from his land."

2 And G-d spoke to Moses, and he said to him, "I am YHWH. 3 And I appeared to Abraham, to Isaac, and to Jacob as El Shaddai, but my Name, YHWH, I did not make known to them. 4 And I also established my covenant with them to give them the land of Canaan, the land of their sojourning in which they sojourned. 5 And I also heard the groaning of the sons of Israel, whom Egypt enslaved, and I remembered my covenant. 6 Therefore, say to the sons of Israel, 'I am YHWH, and I will bring you out from under the burdens of Egypt, and I will deliver you from their slavery, and I will redeem you with an outstretched arm and with great judgments. 7 And I will take you to myself as a people, and I will be G-d to you! And you will know that I am YHWH, your G-d, who brought you out from under the burdens of Egypt! 8 And I will bring you to the land that I swore to give to Abraham, to Isaac, and to Jacob, and I will give it to you as a possession. I am YHWH!'"

9 But when Moses spoke this to the sons of Israel, they did not listen to Moses due to shortage of spirit and hard labor. 10 And YHWH spoke to Moses, saying, 11 "Go! Speak to pharaoh, king of Egypt, that he should send away the sons of Israel from his land!" 12 And Moses spoke before YHWH, saying, "Behold, the sons of Israel did not listen to me, and how then will pharaoh listen to me, when I am uncircumcised of lips?" 13 And YHWH spoke to Moses and to Aaron, and he commanded them concerning the sons of Israel and pharaoh, king of Egypt, to send out the sons of Israel from the land of Egypt.

Commentary

Exodus 5:1—6:13 presents the account of the first confrontation of pharaoh by Moses and Aaron. Interpretation of this unit has suffered markedly by scholars who are committed exclusively to diachronic source criticism. Diachronic source criticism is designed to uncover the compositional history of a text—not its literary plot and character development—and to a large extent, source criticism has been relatively successful in this endeavor. But the result is questionable when it comes to the discernment of the synchronic literary structure of this narrative.

Most scholars judge Exodus 5:1–23 as the product of J- or JE-stratum of the Pentateuch, and Exodus 6:1–30 or expanded texts, such as Exodus 6:1—7:7 or the like, as P-stratum texts.[1] They therefore conclude that the literary structure comprises the first encounter as Exodus 5:1–23, the J-stratum text, followed by the second account of YHWH's self-revelation in Exodus 6:1—7:7 or the like.

But such a diachronic-based understanding of the text overlooks important dimensions of the narrative. Exodus 5:1–23 recounts the first encounter with pharaoh, but it ends with unanswered questions, viz., why did YHWH bring evil upon the people? Why did YHWH send Moses? And why did YHWH not deliver the people? And pharaoh's earlier question in Exodus 5:4, "Who is YHWH that I should listen to his voice to send Israel away? I do not know YHWH, and I will not send Israel away." Furthermore, such an understanding fails to explain adequately the presence of the genealogy in Exodus 6:14–30, which appears in the midst of YHWH's so-called second self-revelation. It also fails to note that YHWH's self-revelation in Exodus 6:1–13 is not simply self-revelation; rather, it is an account of YHWH's self-assertion of power and determination to free the people from pharaoh's control and to make clear to pharaoh exactly who YHWH is. In this respect, Exodus 6:1–13 begins to answer the questions posed in Exodus 5:1–23. Exodus 6:14 begins with a syntactically independent formula, "These are the heads of the house of their fathers," which is generically distinct and marks the beginning of an entirely new unit in the synchronic literary form of the narrative. Furthermore, Exodus 6:26–30 points to issues of its own, specifically, Moses's inability to speak due to his "uncircumcised lips." Such a problem prompts YHWH's response in Exodus 7:1 to make Moses like G-d to pharaoh and to appoint Aaron as Moses's prophet to make Moses's statements clear to pharaoh and to Israel.

Such considerations point to an entirely different structural understanding of this narrative. Exodus 5:1—6:13 constitutes the account of the first, failed confrontation of pharaoh by Moses and Aaron. Problems emerge in this account as indicated by the questions noted above, viz., pharaoh has no reason to listen to them because he does not know YHWH; YHWH does not intend to harm Israel, but instead, YHWH intends to free Israel; YHWH sent Moses for just such a purpose; and YHWH will indeed free the people. YHWH's statements in Exodus

1. For assessment of Exodus 5–6, see Campbell and O'Brien, *Sources of the Pentateuch*, 36–37, 135–36.

6:1–13 answer those questions with YHWH's assertions of self-identity and intent. The account of the first encounter with pharaoh in Exodus 5:1—6:13 builds a sense of drama in the narrative, and it thereby prepares the reader for what is to follow.

Exodus 6:14–30 then serves as an introduction to the second confrontation with pharaoh in Exodus 6:14—15:27. This narrative unit presents a full demonstration of YHWH's power in creation and over pharaoh in the accounts of Aaron's rod turning into a snake that devours the rods of pharaoh's magicians, the plagues, the division of the Reed Sea, the full defeat of pharaoh, and Israel's recognition of YHWH as its G-d. The first portion of the genealogy in Exodus 6:14–25 introduces the narrative with a focus on Aaron and Moses as members of the tribe of Levi, which will ultimately lead Israel from Egyptian bondage to the promised land of Israel in Exodus–Numbers. It thereby looks forward to Numbers 3:1, which begins the account of the leadership of Moses and Aaron in the wilderness according to the toledoth structure of Genesis–Numbers.[2] It also anticipates the appointment of Aaron and the tribe of Levi as the priestly tribe in Numbers 17:16—18:32, and ultimately, the role of Aaron's descendants through Eleazar and Phineas in Numbers 25, when Phineas is granted "the covenant of eternal priesthood" for his actions in countering Israel's apostasy with Midianite women at Baal Peor. Indeed, the line of Phineas ultimately becomes the Zadokite line of priests that serve in the Jerusalem temple.

Exodus 5:1—6:13 is demarcated initially by the temporal formula in Exodus 5:1, "And afterwards, Moses and Aaron came," which marks the beginning of the new narrative unit by noting the passage of time following the prior narrative in Exodus 3–4, which recounts YHWH's revelation to Moses. It continues with the narrative of the first confrontation of pharaoh, which concludes with accounts of YHWH's self-assertion of identity and determination to free Israel from Egyptian bondage. The genealogy in Exodus 6:14–25 introduces the next narrative unit concerned with YHWH's demonstration of power, defeat of pharaoh, and deliverance of Israel in Exodus 6:14—15:27. The subunit in Exodus 6:26–30 emphasizes the identity of Moses and Aaron as Levites, and it explains their respective roles in the narrative action that is to follow, viz., Moses will speak for G-d throughout the narrative, and Aaron will interpret Moses's words as prophet.

2. For discussion of the toledoth structure of the Pentateuch in Genesis–Numbers, see Sweeney, *Pentateuch*, i–xxix; Sweeney, *Tanak*, 55–167.

The first major sub-unit of Exodus 5:1—6:13 appears in Exodus 5:1–5, which introduces the narrative with the initial confrontation of pharaoh by Moses and Aaron. The text emphasizes pharaoh's refusal to listen to Moses and Aaron, which serves as a means to build up the drama of the encounter between YHWH and pharaoh in the narrative as a whole. Moses and Aaron begin with the emphatic demand of YHWH that pharaoh should send away the people of Israel. Their demand begins with the prophetic messenger formula, "Thus says YHWH, the G-d of Israel," which identifies YHWH as the source of the message and themselves as the messengers, spokespersons, or prophets of YHWH. Such a formula is typical of prophets in the Hebrew Bible and the ancient Near East at large, although the formula originates in the realm of international relations in which kings and other leaders send messengers to those with whom they wish to communicate. The demand that pharaoh should "send away" (Hebrew, *šallaḥ*) Israel, essentially means that pharaoh should release them without any expectation that they should return.

The demand to release Israel in order for them to travel on a three-day journey into the wilderness to celebrate a festival for YHWH signals the religious character of the demand, which is particularly important insofar as the pharaoh of Egypt is considered to be a god. The demand therefore throws down a gauntlet of challenge to pharaoh, who is presumed to recognize the power of another god and the right of that god to override pharaoh to take control of Israel. It is not a disingenuous ruse as some have charged; it is in fact a power statement on YHWH's behalf. The notion of a three-day journey presupposes the distance that one would have to travel in the Northern Kingdom of Israel to reach a sanctuary, whether Beth El or Dan or perhaps even others. Excavations at the Lisan Peninsula on the eastern shore of the Dead Sea have uncovered a wilderness sanctuary, dating to the Early Bronze Age (3300–2150 BCE), to which people would travel at specific times of the year to celebrate festivals to their god(s).[3] When the festival was concluded, the people would depart from the site to wherever they normally lived until they returned to celebrate the next festival. Nevertheless, there is no assurance of return in the demand made of pharaoh by YHWH and communicated by Moses and Aaron; it is instead a statement of YHWH's power, i.e., YHWH is the true G-d, not pharaoh.

3. Schaub, "Bab edh-Dhra"; Rast, "Bab edh-Dhra."

The drama of the confrontation is highlighted by pharaoh's response, "Who is YHWH that I should listen to his voice to send Israel away? I do not know YHWH, and also, I will not send Israel away!" Pharaoh continues with commands that the people of Israel should get back to work and that the people of Israel are too numerous as it is. Such an assertion points to pharaoh's interest in diminishing the numbers of Israel with hard labor. The confrontation is now set in that pharaoh refuses to accede to YHWH's demand. The narrative will now proceed as an example of divine combat to determine who really is the true G-d who controls the world of creation and intervenes in human affairs. The rest of the narrative in Exodus 5:1—15:27 is designed to answer pharaoh's question rather pointedly, viz., YHWH—not pharaoh—is the true G-d of creation, including both the natural features of creation and the human beings who live within it.

The second major sub-unit of Exodus 5:1—6:13 appears in Exodus 5:6—6:13, which presents the consequences of the first failed confrontation with pharaoh. The passage is introduced with the temporal formula "and pharaoh commanded on that day" (Hebrew, *bayyôm hahû'*). Although many understand the formula *bayyôm hahû'*, "in that day," as an eschatological formula, the present context and De Vries's meticulous study of the formula demonstrate that it is nothing more than a reference to a future time.[4] In the present case, it points to the consequences that followed immediately, i.e., on the same day, after the failed confrontation with pharaoh.

The account of the consequences appears in two distinct parts. The first is the account of the consequences for the Israelite slaves, their taskmasters, and the officers, caused by pharaoh's commands in Exodus 5:6–23. The second is the account of the consequences for pharaoh (and Egypt), caused by YHWH's assertion of self-identity and the announcement of YHWH's determination to employ divine power to defeat pharaoh and force the release of the Israelite slaves in Exodus 6:1–13.

The account of the consequences for the slaves, their taskmasters, and their officers in Exodus 5:6–23 includes five major components, each of which is defined by the focus on the principal speaker or actor. The first appears in Exodus 5:6–9, which recounts pharaoh's commands to the taskmasters and the officers concerning the provision of straw to the slaves. The command to discontinue the provision of straw to the slaves

4. De Vries, *Old Revelation to New*, 38–63.

entails an increase in their workload. Whereas the Egyptians provided the straw previously, the Israelite slaves must now provide the necessary straw for themselves in addition to their other tasks. Pharaoh's command is clearly intended as punishment for the slaves as a response to the demand of Moses and Aaron to release them to worship YHWH. It is intended as a power play to demonstrate to them that pharaoh—and not YHWH—is the true power in Egypt, and they will suffer consequences if they fail to recognize pharaoh's leading role.

Readers may also note the identity of those who supervise the work of the Israelite slaves. The taskmasters (Hebrew, *hannōgĕśîm*, lit., "the oppressors") refers to the Egyptian overseers who supervise the slave labor on behalf of pharaoh. Their officers (Hebrew, *šōṭĕrāyw*, lit., "his/its officers"), i.e., the officers of the people (Hebrew, *ʿam*, a singular noun), refers to the Israelite men who were selected by the Egyptians as the immediate overseers of the work under the supervision of the Egyptian taskmasters. The use of Israelite "officers" or overseers would ensure that the slaves worked under the immediate supervision of men with whom they could identify and who spoke their language. The purpose of such an appointment was to force the most work possible from the enslaved Israelites. The practice was employed by the Nazis in the death camps of World War II when they appointed "kapos," i.e., Jews to oversee the slave labors and activities of their fellow Jews.[5] The kapos may have believed that their actions would save their own lives, but the Nazis readily executed them as well as their charges when they were no longer useful to them.

The second component appears in Exodus 5:10–14, which recounts the announcement of the taskmasters and officers concerning the increase in workload and the punishment of the officers for failing to enforce pharaoh's will. This account illustrates the position of the Israelite officers who were appointed by the Egyptians to oversee the work of the slaves. The Egyptian taskmasters made the announcement of pharaoh's decree that the people would have to gather their own straw from now on without any reduction in the number of bricks that they must produce. Upon hearing this requirement, the people immediately scattered throughout the land of Egypt to find straw. The lack of pushback at this point suggests that the people were afraid to challenge the authority of the taskmasters, undoubtedly because punishment would result if they

5. Michman, "Kapo."

attempted to do so. When the people apparently failed to produce the required number of bricks due to the increase in their workload, the Israelite officers were beaten for their failure. Such an act points to the true role of the Israelite officers, i.e., they are the enforcers of pharaoh's decrees, and they are easily punished and presumably replaced.

The third component of the narrative appears in Exodus 5:15–19, which recounts the audience of the Israelite officers with the pharaoh to demand an explanation for the new requirement to provide their own straw and yet continue to produce the same quota of bricks. Such an act constitutes a direct challenge to the pharaoh's authority, particularly when they stated that they were beaten, but that the problem, i.e., the sin (Hebrew, *ḥaṭṭa't*), actually lay with pharaoh's own people. The officers were mistaken. The problem actually lay with pharaoh, who gave the order in the first place, but the Israelite officers apparently did not understand that. Pharaoh's response in such an instance is predictable. He charged the Israelites with laziness by claiming emphatically that they were "slackers, slackers!" (Hebrew, *nirpîm*, lit., "those who are relaxed, sunk") followed by a charge that their laziness at work was the reason they demanded time off to worship their god. Pharaoh's last statements were a command to get back to work and an emphatic assertion that no straw would be provided to the Israelite slaves. At this point, it is clear that the Israelite officers knew that things had gone bad as indicated in the order that they must continue to produce the same number of bricks despite the increase in their workload.

The fourth component of the narrative then follows immediately in Exodus 15:20–21 when the Israelite officers encounter Moses and Aaron, who are standing outside the pharaoh's throne room to wait for the results of their audience. Pharaoh's response achieved exactly what it was designed to achieve when the officers confronted Moses and Aaron and charged them with wrongdoing by giving the pharaoh a reason to punish them. They call upon YHWH to punish Moses and Aaron for giving pharaoh such cause. The issue in the eyes of the Israelite officers is no longer the wrongdoing of pharaoh; Moses and Aaron are to blame for the problem as far as they are concerned. This is a typical ploy of oppressors, i.e., to find a way to lay the blame for their oppression on those who would seek to free those who are oppressed.

This encounter leads to the final component of the passage in Exodus 5:22–23 in which Moses raises his questions to YHWH: Why did you bring evil upon the people? Why did you send me? These questions are followed by Moses's assertion that ever since YHWH sent him to pharaoh, things have gotten worse, and YHWH has not succeeded in freeing the people. Again, pharaoh's attempt to turn the people against Moses and Aaron—and now—Moses against YHWH, is working. Moses's confrontation with YHWH will demand YHWH's response.

YHWH's response to Moses's questions follows immediately in Exodus 6:1–13 with YHWH's self-identification and announcement that YHWH will indeed confront pharaoh with divine power to free the people of Israel from Egyptian bondage.

The account of the consequences for pharaoh (and Egypt) of the failed confrontation with pharaoh appears in Exodus 6:1–13. Exodus 6:1–13 is identified by most scholars as a P-stratum narrative.[6] Consequently, Exodus 6:1–13 is frequently identified as the beginning of a discrete P-narrative block that continues through Exodus 6:30 or 7:13, both of which conclude P passages. Such a conclusion is unjustified because it is based on diachronic grounds of composition and the presupposition that the pentateuchal texts are based on discrete sources that constitute their own literary units. Such a stance ignores the role that textual units play in plot and character development in the larger synchronic literary structure of a text, which is determined on synchronic literary grounds, not on diachronic compositional grounds. Interpreters have long observed that the pentateuchal sources are not discrete sources that must be read independently of each other; rather, they are literary strata that build upon the previous strata of material to elaborate upon issues that arise in the earlier texts and to build upon the literary plot structure and characterization to provide a more complete and coherent narrative.[7]

Exodus 6:1–13 does not begin a new major sub-unit in the larger exodus narrative, a conclusion proposed on the grounds that it is a P text and the previous material in Exodus 5:1–23 is identified as a J-stratum text. Rather, Exodus 6:1–13 develops the earlier narrative in Exodus 5 by stating the consequences for pharaoh (and Egypt) of the failed confrontation with pharaoh. Exodus 6:1–13 is simply a second account of YHWH's self-revelation to Moses (and Aaron). It is an account of YHWH's determination to punish pharaoh and Egypt for the refusal to release the Israelite slaves. It begins the process of answering the questions that Moses posed to YHWH in Exodus 5:22–23.

6. Campbell and O'Brien, *Sources of the Pentateuch*, 36–37, although v. 1 is J (see p. 136).

7. H. Schmid, *Sogenannte J-hwist*.

Exodus 6:1–13 comprises three components, each of which is defined by an account of a speech made by YHWH/G-d to Moses in Exodus 6:1, 2–9, and 11–13. In the case of the latter two units, a brief narrative portrays action by Moses, in the case of Exodus 6:9, and the interaction between YHWH and Moses, in Exodus 6:12–13, in the aftermath of their respective speeches.

Exodus 6:1 constitutes the first component of Exodus 6:1–13. It presents a brief account of YHWH's initial response to Moses to indicate that Moses will see what YHWH will do, i.e., YHWH will employ great divine power against pharaoh in order to compel him to release the Israelite slaves and expel them from his land. The use of the Hebrew verbal construction *yĕgārĕšēm*, literally, "he will drive them out," accentuates pharaoh's desire to be rid of the Israelites after suffering from YHWH's use of divine power.

Exodus 6:2–9 constitutes the second component of Exodus 6:1–13 with an account of G-d's (YHWH's) second speech to Moses in vv. 2–8 and a brief account of the people's refusal to listen to Moses due to their hard labor in v. 9. Although the narrative initially identifies YHWH as G-d, this is not an indication of E authorship. Rather, it is necessary because G-d will now self-identify as YHWH in a speech that identifies the G-d of the ancestors, previously known as El Shaddai, with YHWH. The speech employs the self-revelation formula—in this case, "I am YHWH"—as a means to assert YHWH's identity, power, and determination to deliver Israel from Egyptian bondage.[8] Following G-d's statement of self-revelation, G-d continues with statement that G-d had appeared to Abraham, Isaac, and Jacob as El Shaddai in P narratives (Gen 17:1; 28:3; 35:11; 43:14; 48:3). This is especially striking because the name El is the name of the Canaanite creator god, indicating that the narrative points to the earlier Canaanite identity of Israel (Hebrew, *yiśrāʾēl*, "may El rule"). The name El Shaddai is typically understood as "G-d Almighty," largely because Shaddai is often derived from the root, *šdd*, which means "to deal violently, devastate, ruin." But the name appears to be better derived from the root, *šdh*, which forms the basis for *šad*, "breast," dual form, *šaddayîm*, "breasts." Such a derivation would suggest that El Shaddai refers to a sustaining or nurturing deity, which is more in keeping with the Canaanite understanding of El.

8. Coats, *Exodus 1–18*, 56, 178; cf. Zimmerli, "Word of Divine Self-Manifestation."

The name El Shaddai is nevertheless taken as an Israelite name for G-d, especially because it is incorporated into the name for Israel, but its Canaanite origins are undeniable, especially since Israel was formed by assimilation of seminomadic Habiru (Akkadian, *ḫabiru*, *ḫapiru*, "stranger, barbarian") tribes, who merged with the Canaanite population of the land, particularly around Shechem, beginning in the fourteenth century BCE.[9] But by the late thirteenth century BCE, during the reign of Pharaoh Mernepthah (r. 1224–1216 BCE), the son of Rameses, Israel had emerged as an identifiable seminomadic nation that had joined a Canaanite coalition known as the Nine Bows to revolt against Egypt.[10]

The purpose of YHWH's self-identification is not only to assert YHWH's power and determination to compel pharaoh to release Israel from bondage. It is also intended to create an intertextual link between the exodus–wilderness narratives of Exodus–Numbers with ancestral narratives of Genesis 11–50. In the present case, the link is created by P redaction, although the citations of both ancestral and exodus narratives in Hosea 12 indicate that the link may have already been forged in earlier times. The link expresses the continuity of YHWH's covenant with the ancestors in Genesis and the Mosaic generation of Israel in the exodus–wilderness accounts. Indeed, the covenant formula in Exodus 6:7, "and I will take you to myself for a people, and I will be to you G-d," is an explicit statement of the covenant relationship between YHWH and Israel.[11]

The narrative is also designed to introduce the means of YHWH's divine power, expressed here with expressions such as *yad ḥăzāqâ*, literally, "a strong hand" (Exod 6:1); *zĕrôʿa nĕṭûyâ*, "outstretched arm" (Exod 6:6); and *mišpāṭîm gĕdōlîm*, "great judgments" (Exod 6:6). YHWH's power is intended to keep the covenant with Israel, and to bring Israel out from Egyptian bondage and into the land of Israel, which YHWH swore to give to Israel's ancestors as a possession.

The final verse of Exodus 6:2–9 recounts Moses's attempt to communicate YHWH's statements to the people, but they would not listen because their spirit had been curtailed by hard labor. Indeed, this statement introduces the motif of rebellion in the wilderness on the part of the people, who complain about the hardships they suffer and state their longing for the fleshpots of Egypt. Such an attitude is common among people who have been broken by slavery or other trials. In the case of

9. Durand, "Habiru, Hapiru."

10. *ANET* 376–78.

11. Rendtorff, *Bundesformel*.

the biblical narrative, such rebellion led YHWH to decide to let the slave generation die in the wilderness so that those who would enter the promised land of Israel would not know slavery (Num 13–14).

Exodus 6:10–13 constitutes the third component of Exodus 6:1–13 with an account of YHWH's third speech to Moses in which YHWH commands him to go (back) to pharaoh and tell him to send away the people of Israel from his land. Essentially, YHWH commands Moses to try again, but to do so in a more forceful manner and not to take no for an answer. This aspect becomes clear when Moses answers YHWH by asking, how can he expect pharaoh to listen to him when even the people of Israel will not listen? And at this point, he adds that he is a man of "uncircumcised lips," Hebrew, *ʿăral śĕpātāyim*. Moses's question is important, largely because he makes the point that he is not fully capable of persuading either pharaoh or the people. The expression "uncircumcised lips" has been understood to refer to a speech impediment, insofar as it metaphorically implies a foreskin on the lips of Moses that must be removed. Interpreters must recognize at this point that, although Moses is a Levite, he is not a priest. The Levites will be commissioned as priests only in Numbers 17:16—18:32. Moses has no official institutional identity that would prompt an Egyptian pharaoh, who has his own priesthood, to listen to a man like Moses. Likewise, the people of Israel do not yet have priests of their own. But Moses's lack of priestly status is not the only issue. He is an oracle diviner or prophet, both of which are known in the ancient world for speaking in metaphorically and frequently unintelligible manners (cf. Hos 12:11; 1 Kgs 19:12). Not only is Moses not a priest, who would be recognized in either Egypt or Israel at this point, he needs an interpreter. Consequently, YHWH speaks to both Moses and Aaron, who had been designated as Moses's spokesman in Exodus 4:10–17, so that Aaron can be in a position to explain what Moses has to say.

Reception History

Rabbinic midrash relates how pharaoh refused to see Moses and Aaron until all others who wished to show their respects to him had left.[12] His palace had four hundred entrances, one hundred on each side, and it was guarded by sixty thousand soldiers who were posted to keep Moses and Aaron out. But the angel Gabriel appeared, and brought them

12. Ginzberg, *Legends*, 2:331–41, and the midrashic sources cited there.

into the palace by a secret entrance. Pharaoh punished the guards and replaced them, but the next day, Gabriel brought Moses and Aaron in again. So pharaoh posted two fearsome lions at the gate, and no one would enter for fear of being torn to pieces. But when Moses raised his rods, the lions ran toward him and jumped around like dogs when they greet their masters. In the meantime, pharaoh was busy dictating messages to his seventy secretaries who worked in seventy languages. When the secretaries saw Moses and Aaron, they rose in awe because the two old men looked like great angels, tall like the cedars of Lebanon, their faces radiant like the sun, their eyes like the morning star, their beards like palm branches, and their mouths spitting fire when they spoke. All of the pharaoh's secretaries bowed down when Moses and Aaron entered the pharaoh's throne room.

When pharaoh asked for G-d's name, how many soldiers he commanded, how many countries he had conquered, etc., Moses and Aaron answered that G-d's power fills the whole world, that heaven is G-d's throne and earth is G-d's footstool, and that G-d sustains the entire world. Pharaoh searched the royal archives, but could find no mention of G-d. Aaron cast his rod upon the ground, turning it into a great serpent, but pharaoh dismissed the act because his own magicians could do the same. When Aaron's serpent devoured those of pharaoh's magicians, pharaoh's advisor, Balaam ben Bear, scoffed, and pharaoh still refused to believe that G-d had sent Moses and Aaron. And so he ordered that the Israelite slaves should gather their own straw, but continue to make the same quantity of bricks. When Dathan and Abiram upbraided Moses for causing more suffering by the people of Israel, Moses studied Genesis and saw in Genesis 15 that Israel would suffer under Egyptian oppression. G-d told Moses that he would see what G-d would do to pharaoh. G-d accused Moses of faithlessness, and spoke about how G-d appeared to the ancestors as El Shaddai, and they believed in G-d. And so G-d swore then to redeem Israel from Egyptian bondage and assigned Aaron to assist Moses in the redemption of Israel.

The demand that pharaoh release the people of Israel, i.e., "let my people go," resonates in later Jewish history as well. Before and during World War II, the Roosevelt administration did little to assist Jews who were trying to escape from Nazi Germany. In one case, a German passenger liner, the MS *St. Louis*, was denied permission in 1939 to disembark its passengers, primarily Jews seeking to escape Nazi Germany, in the United States. Canada and Cuba also denied passengers, with a few exceptions in the case of Cuba, the right to disembark in their respective ports. The *St. Louis* was forced to return to Europe, where it disembarked its passengers at Antwerp, at that time free from German control, although some 255 of the Jewish passengers eventually perished in the Shoah (Holocaust).[13]

Jews also suffered under the Soviet Union during the Cold War when restrictions were placed on Jewish cultural and religious observance. Many Jews attempted to emigrate from the USSR after the 1967 Six-Day War, but were officially denied emigration visas even though Soviet law allowed emigration to Israel beginning in 1971. Jews who were refused exit visas were popularly known as refuseniks, and their suffering under the Soviet government led to efforts sponsored by both Israel and the diaspora Jewish community, especially in the United States, to obtain their release.[14] Major leaders of the Soviet refusenik movement included figures such as Yuli Edelstein, Natan (Anatoly) Sharansky, Ida Nudel, Mark Azbel, Mikhail Beizer, and others.[15] With the impending collapse of the Soviet Union, most Jews were finally able to leave by 1990.[16]

A similar movement took place in the late twentieth and early twenty-first centuries to release the Beta Israel, Ethiopian Ge'ez for "the House of Israel," from Ethiopia. The Beta Israel is the Ethiopian Jewish community, which was also suppressed and treated as "falashas," i.e., "strangers," in Ethiopia. Some 120,000 Ethiopian Jews were repatriated from Ethiopia to Israel during this time. The Beta Israel were heavily compromised by Christian missionaries throughout their history, but they traced their origins to the visit of the Queen of Sheba to the court of King Solomon ben David of Israel as recounted in 1 Kings 10. The Israeli rabbinic authorities ruled that they were descendants of the tribe

13. For a study of American policy concerning Jews during World War II, see Wyman, *Abandonment of the Jews*.

14. For background, see Pinkus, *Jews of Soviet Union*; Azbel, *Refusenik*; Gilbert, *Jews of Hope*; Beizer, *Jews of St. Petersburg*.

15. See Sharansky, *Case for Democracy*; Sharansky, *Defending Identity*; Taratuta and Taratuta, *Cheerful Memories/Troubled Years*.

16. In March 1987, the author, then assistant professor of religious studies at the University of Miami, made a trip to the Soviet Union to meet with refuseniks in Moscow and Leningrad. My guide in Leningrad (St. Petersburg) was Mikhail Beizer, to whom this volume is dedicated. University of Miami student Mark Slotnick, now a prominent attorney in Charleston, WV, accompanied the author on this trip. The trip was sponsored by the South Florida Conference on Soviet Jewry and the University of Miami Hillel Jewish Student Center.

of Dan, and the Beta Israel now live as Jews in freedom in the land of Israel.[17]

Christianity also pays close attention to these chapters. Acts 13:13–52 recounts Paul's speech to the people in Antioch, and cites Exodus 6:1, 6 in Acts 13:17, where he refers to G-d's choice of the people of Israel and G-d's uplifted arm to lead them out of Egyptian bondage.

Exodus 5:1—6:13 also plays a key role in African American spirituals, most notably, the demand of Moses and Aaron speaking on behalf of G-d, "Let my people go!" The phrase plays a key role in the spiritual "Go Down, Moses." The lyrics are as follows:

> When Israel was in Egypt's land,
> Let my people go!
> Oppressed so hard they could not stand,
> Let my people go!
>
> Go down, Moses!
> Way down in Egypt's land,
> Tell old pharaoh,
> Let my people go!

Although the exodus event is portrayed as G-d's redemption of the Jewish people, African American slaves appropriated the theme for themselves and composed a spiritual of several more stanzas that culminate in Christ's redemption of oppressed people.[18]

17. Spector, *Operation Solomon*.

18. N. Petersen, "Exodus," esp. 8:507.

The Second Confrontation with Pharaoh: The Plagues as Demonstrations of Divine Power—Exodus 6:14—12:36

EXODUS 6:14—12:26 PRESENTS THE account of the second confrontation with pharaoh by Moses and Aaron in which YHWH's demonstrations of divine power were unleashed against pharaoh and all Egypt. This narrative block is demarcated at the outset in Exodus 6:14a by the syntactically independent naming formula "these are the heads of the house of their fathers," which introduces the following ancestral table in Exodus 6:14b–25. The ancestral table is a genealogical listing of the descendants of Reuben, Shimon, and Levi, with a special focus on the Levites that accounts for Moses and Aaron, insofar as they will lead the confrontation against pharaoh as the representatives of YHWH. At the synchronic literary level, this passage serves as an introduction to Exodus 6:14—12:26 as a whole, but it also looks forward to toledoth formula in Numbers 3:1, "and these are the generations of Aaron and Moses on the day that YHWH spoke with Moses at Mount Sinai," which serve as the macrostructural structural markers for the pentateuchal narrative as a whole.[1] Insofar as the toledoth formula in Numbers 3:1 introduces the account of Moses and Aaron's leadership of Israel during their wilderness journey from Sinai to the Jordan River and the land of Israel, Exodus 6:14—12:25 begins the account of the actions of Moses

1. See Sweeney, *Pentateuch*, xvii–xxix.

and Aaron on behalf of YHWH that led to pharaoh's release of the people of Israel from Egyptian bondage.

Exodus 6:26–30, which begins with the syntactically independent statements "It is Aaron and Moses to whom YHWH said, 'Bring out the sons of Israel from the land of Egypt, according to their hosts.' They were the ones who spoke to pharaoh, king of Egypt, to bring out the sons of Israel from Egypt. It was Moses and Aaron," introduces the account of the confrontation per se in Exodus 7:1—12:25. This statement identifies the Moses and Aaron mentioned in the genealogical table as the same Moses and Aaron who would lead YHWH's confrontation with pharaoh. Moses's appeal to YHWH concerning his impeded speech leads to the next sub-unit in Exodus 7:1–7 in which YHWH appoints Aaron as Moses's spokesman. The sequences of instructions by YHWH to Moses and Aaron concerning YHWH's successive demonstrations of power and the accounts of Moses and Aaron's compliance with YHWH's instruction then follow. They include YHWH's instructions to Aaron to turn his rod into a serpent that will swallow the rods/serpents of pharaoh's magicians in Exodus 7:8–13; the account of YHWH's turning the Nile to blood in Exodus 7:14–24; the account of the plague of frogs in Exodus 7:25—8:11; the account of the plague of dust, lice, and vermin in Exodus 8:12–15; the account of the plague of flies in Exodus 8:16–28; the account of the plague of cattle disease in Exodus 9:1–7; the account of the plague of boils on humans and animals in Exodus 9:8–12; the account of the plague of thunder and hail in Exodus 9:13–35; the account of the plague of locusts in Exodus 10:1–20; the account of the plague of darkness in Exodus 10:21–29; and the account of the plague of the killing of the firstborn with its associated instructions concerning the Passover offerings in Exodus 11:1—12:36.

The appearance of the itinerary formula in Exodus 12:37, "and the sons of Israel journeyed [Hebrew, *wayisᶜû*] from Rameses to Sukkoth," then introduces the account of the first stage of Israel's journey from Egyptian bondage in the city of Rameses to Sukkoth.

The Heads of the Ancestral Houses of Reuben, Shimon, and Levi —Exodus 6:14–25

Translation

[14] These are the heads of the house of their fathers.

The sons of Reuben, the firstborn of Israel: Enoch and Pallu, Hezron and Karmi. These are the families of Reuben.

[15] And the sons of Shimon: Jemuel and Jamin and Ohad and Jakin, and Zohar, and Saul, the son of a Canaanite woman. These are the families of Shimon.

[16] And these are the names of the sons of Levi according to their generations: Gershon and Kohath and Merari, and the years of the life of Levi were 137 years.

[17] The sons of Gershon: Livni and Shimei according to their families.

[18] And the sons of Kohath: Amran and Yizhar and Hebron and Uzziel. And the years of the life of Kohath were 133 years.

[19] And the sons of Merari: Mahli and Mushi.

These are the Levitical families according to their generations.

[20] And Amram took Jocheved, his aunt, to himself for a wife, and she bore to him Aaron and Moses. And the years of the life of Amran were 137 years.

[21] And the sons of Yizhar: Korah and Nepheg and Zichri.

[22] And the sons of Uzziel: Mishael and Elzaphan and Sitri.

[23] And Aaron took Elisheba bat Amminadab, the sister of Nahsohn, to himself for a wife, and she bore to him Nadab and Abihu, Elazar and Ithamar.

[24] And the sons of Korah: Asir and Elkanah and Abiasaph. These are the Korahite families.

[25] And Eleazar ben Aaron took for himself for a wife [one] from the daughters of Putiel, and she bore Phineas.

These are the heads of the Levitical fathers' houses according to their families.

Commentary

Exodus 6:14–30 presents a genealogy of the tribes of Reuben, Shimon, and Levi in order to introduce Moses and Aaron as members of the tribe of Levi who would lead Israel on behalf of YHWH from Egyptian bondage through the wilderness to the border of the promised land of Israel.[1] The genealogy agrees generally with the account of Jacob's initial blessings of his sons in Genesis 49:1–7 and the genealogy presented in 1 Chronicles 5:1—6:66, although it is hardly dependent upon either. Although it gives cursory accounts of the descendants of Reuben in Exodus 6:14b and Shimon in Exodus 6:15, the major focus of the genealogy appears in Exodus 6:16–25 with the detailed focus on the descendants of Levi, especially the descendants of Moses and Aaron, who will lead Israel from Egypt through the wilderness, first to Sinai and afterwards to the promised land of Israel. The passage is generally considered a P-stratum text, but the reference to Amram's wife, Jocheved, as the sister of his father in v. 20 raises questions about that assertion (see below).[2]

1. Coats, *Exodus 1–18*, 58–59, 161–62.
2. Campbell and O'Brien, *Sources of the Pentateuch*, 36–37.

Reuben and Shimon are Jacob's oldest sons, but both are disqualified from leadership. Genesis 35:22 (cf. Gen 49:4) states that Reuben, Jacob's firstborn, apparently had an incestuous relationship with Bilhah, Jacob's concubine through his wife Rachel (Gen 30:1–8). His sons are listed as Enoch, Pallu, Hezron, and Carmi in keeping with 1 Chronicles 5:3 and Genesis 46:9. Genesis 34 (cf. Gen 49:5–7) recounts how Shimon and Levi had disgraced Jacob by slaughtering the men of Shechem, contrary to their father's instructions, while the Shechemites were recovering from their circumcisions. Shimon apparently disappeared when the tribe was absorbed into Judah (Josh 19:9).[3] Shimon's sons are listed as Jemuel, Jamin, Ohad, Jachin, Zohar, and Saul, who is distinguished from the first king of Israel, Saul ben Kish, by noting that Shimon's son, Saul, was the son of a Canaanite woman, although such a marriage is forbidden by Exodus 34:11–16 (cf. Deut 7:1–11) due to fears that marriages to the Canaanites will lead the Israelites to worship foreign gods (cf. Judg 3:1–6). The sons of Shimon do not appear in 1 Chronicles 5:1—6:66, but they appear as listed here in Genesis 46:10. First Chronicles 4:24 gives an alternative listing as Nemuel, Jamin, Jarib, Zerah, and Shaul (Saul).

The genealogy of Levi is much more extensive. Levi's sons are identified as Gershon, Kohath, and Merari, which corresponds to 1 Chronicles 6:1; Genesis 46:11; Numbers 3:17; and Numbers 26:57. The sons of Gershon are identified as Libni and Shimei, which corresponds to 1 Chronicles 6:2, but Genesis 46 does not list the grandsons of Gershon. The sons of Kohath are Amram, Izhar, Hebron, and Uzziel, which corresponds to 1 Chronicles 6:3, but again, Genesis 46 lacks reference to his grandsons. Nevertheless, the present passage will focus on Kohath's grandsons through Amram, the father of Moses and Aaron. Merari's sons are listed as Mahli and Mushi, which corresponds to 1 Chronicles 6:3, but Genesis 46 lacks references to the grandsons.

Although 1 Chronicles 6:5–15 gives a detailed account of Levi's descendants, Exodus 6:20–25 focuses squarely on the descendants of Amram, the father of Moses and Aaron, in order to establish their roles in defining the primary priestly lines of Israel and Judah. Exodus 6:20 states that Amram married his father's sister, Jocheved, who bore Moses and Aaron. This is a very striking statement in that it violates the instructions given in Leviticus 18:12 and 20:19, which prohibit relations with the sister of one's father. Most interpreters maintain that

3. Davies, *Exodus 1–18*, 1:451.

Amram's marriage to Jocheved, the sister of his father, indicates a very early tradition that must have preceded the composition of the Holiness Code in Leviticus 17–26.[4] Insofar as some date the Holiness Code to as early as the eighth century BCE, the present passage would have to be earlier. Such a consideration would suggest the J-stratum. Note that Numbers 26:59 states that Jocheved is the daughter of Levi, who was born in Egypt. This would make her Amram's aunt and Kohath's sister. Insofar as Numbers 26 is a non-source text that would date prior to the Deuteronomistic History, it would presumably date to the late monarchic period from the late-eighth-century reign of Hezekiah through the seventh-century BCE reign of Josiah.[5]

The genealogy of Kohath's sons continues in Exodus 6:21 with the sons of Izhar, which include Korah, Nepheg, and Zichri, who are absent in 1 Chronicles 6:1–15; Numbers 26:57–62; and Genesis 46. Exodus 6:22 lists the sons of Uzziel as Mishael, Elzaphan, and Sithri, who are absent in 1 Chronicles 6:1–15; Numbers 26:57–62; and Genesis 46. It is noteworthy that these names appear to be Canaanite, in the case of Mishael and Elzaphan, both of which are theophoric names based on El (i.e., "who is what El is" in the case of Mishael and "El of the north" in the case of Elzaphan).

Exodus 6:23–25 then focuses on the sons of Aaron, who are born to him through his wife, Elisheba bat Amminadab. Elisheba is likewise a Canaanite theophoric name based on El (i.e., "El of oath"). Her father, Amminadab, is the son of Kohath according to 1 Chronicles 6:7, which would suggest that she is Aaron's aunt, insofar as her father, Amminadab, is also a son of Kohath like Aaron's father, Amram, according to 1 Chronicles 6:7, although Amminadab is listed separately from Kohath's other sons. But Elisheba is also listed as the sister of Nahshon. This resolves the problem insofar as Numbers 1:7 identifies Nahshon as the son of Amminadab, a member of the tribe of Judah, which means that Elisheba's father, Amminadab is a different, Judean man, from the Levite Amminadab ben Kohath. Aaron's sons are listed as Nadab, Abihu, Eleazar, and Ithamar in Exodus 6:23. Aaron's first two sons, Nadab and Abihu, die in Leviticus 10:1–7 when they offer strange, alien, or loathsome fire before YHWH, which YHWH had not commanded. It is noteworthy that the names Nadab ("[he is] noble, generous") and Abihu ("my

4. Sarna, *Exodus*, 34.

5. Campbell and O'Brien, *Sources of the Pentateuch*, 201n51.

father is he") correspond closely to the sons of Jeroboam ben Nabat, the first king of northern Israel. His sons are Nadab ("he is noble, generous") and Abijah ("my father is YHWH"). Insofar as Jeroboam is condemned in 1 Kings 12:25–33 and 13:1–34 for idolatry, particularly for the worship of golden calves (cf. Exod 32–34) and other issues, it appears that the correspondence in the names of the sons of Aaron and the sons of Jeroboam ben Nebat is deliberate.[6] Abijah ben Jeroboam died of illness in 1 Kings 14:1–20, apparently as a punishment for his father's actions. Nadab ben Jeroboam succeeded his father on the throne, but his reign lasted only for two years as he was overthrown and assassinated by Baasha ben Ahijah of the tribe of Issachar, apparently because he continued in the sins of his father, according to 1 Kings 15:25–31.

Aaron's other two sons, Eleazar and Ithamar, are particularly noteworthy as they become the ancestors of the two major priestly lines of the sons of Aaron. Eleazar succeeds his father as priest when Aaron dies in Numbers 20:22–29. Eleazar's son, Phineas, was granted the covenant of eternal priesthood in Numbers 25 for his actions in killing an Israelite man, Zimri ben Salu of the tribe of Shimon, and a Midianite woman, Cozbi bat Zur, who were apparently engaged in some sort of illicit religious practice that seems to have involved sexual relations. The priestly line of Phineas ben Eleazar ben Aaron would continue to become the line of Zadok, the primary priestly line of the Jerusalem temple from the time of Solomon and afterwards (1 Kgs 2:35; cf. 1 Chr 5:27–41; 6:34–45; 24:1–6). The line of Eleazar, Phineas, and later Zadok would supervise the Kohathites (Num 4:16–20), whereas the line of Ithamar was responsible for supervising the Gershonites and the Merarites (Num 4:21–49; cf. 1 Chr 24, where the Zadokite line is given greater responsibility due to their greater numbers). There is no full genealogy of the sons of Ithamar in the Hebrew Bible. First Chronicles 24:3 states that Ahimelech from the sons of Ithamar was selected to supervise the priestly orders. The reference to Ahimelech is analogous to the reference to Zadok from the sons of Eleazer in this passage because it indicates that they are later descendants from their respective lines. But the reference to Ahimelech is crucial for understanding the line of Ithamar. Ahimelech is the son of Ahitub and the father of Abiathar according to 1 Samuel 22:20–23. He is viewed as a great-grandson of Eli, the high priest at Shiloh, insofar as his father, Ahitub, is the brother of Ichabod ben Phineas ben Eli (1 Sam

6. For discussion of the texts in Kings, see Sweeney, *1–2 Kings*.

14:3).[7] Because Ahimelech is a descendant of Eli and a descendant of Ithamar (1 Chr 24:3), Eli is also a descendant of Ithamar. This means that Ahimelech's son, Abiathar, is also a descendant of the line of Ithamar. Ahimelech was the head of the priestly village of Nob in 1 Samuel 21–22, and he gave support to David, who was fleeing from Saul. When Saul discovered what Ahimelech had done, he ordered the execution of all the priests at Nob, and the order was carried out by Doeg the Edomite, one of Saul's officers.[8] Ahimelech's son, Abiathar, was the only member of the line to escape the massacre at Nob, and he continued to serve David as a priest, together with Zadok. His service as priest concluded early in the reign of Solomon, when Solomon banished Abiathar to the Benjaminite town of Anathoth, apparently because he supported Adonijah's claim to kingship (1 Kgs 2:26–27; cf. 1 Kgs 2:22). Because Jeremiah is a priest from the town of Anathoth, he is considered to be a member of the line of Ithamar, Eli, and Abiathar.

Exodus 6:24 identifies the sons of Korah as Assir, Elkanah, and Abiasasph, which corresponds to 1 Chronicles 6:7, which identifies these men as successive sons of Korah. The reason for the attention to the sons of Korah is because of Korah's role as a temple singer and musician in Psalms 42:1; 44:1; 45:1; 46:1; 47:1; 48:1; 49:1; 84:1; 85:1; 87:1; and 88:1, and because of Korah's role in the revolt against Moses and Aaron in Numbers 16:1–35.

Exodus 6:25 returns the focus to the line of Aaron by noting that his son, Eleazar, married a daughter of Putiel, and she bore him Phineas. Phineas, as noted above, was awarded the covenant of eternal priesthood in Numbers 25:13 for his role in ending the apostasy in Moab brought about by Zimri ben Salu of Shimon and Cozbi bat Zur of Midian.

The summary statement, "These are the heads of the Levitical father's houses according to their families," marks the conclusion of the genealogy in Exodus 6:14–25.

Reception History

The genealogy in Exodus 6:14–25 focuses on the line of the early history of the Levites, especially Moses and Aaron, who lead Israel out

7. Some argue that the reference to Ahijah as the son of Ahitub must actually refer to Ahimelech, but such a view is unnecessary because it does not exclude the role of Ahimelech as a brother to Ahijah (see Müller, "Ahimelech").

8. For discussion of the texts in Samuel, see Sweeney, *1–2 Samuel*.

of Egyptian bondage. Aaron ultimately becomes the ancestor of the Israelite priesthood, including the lines of Eleazar, Phineas, and later Zadok, which serves in the Jerusalem temple, and the line of Ithamar, Eli, and Abiathar, which serves in the Shiloh temple prior to the time of the Israelite monarchy, but is expelled from the Jerusalem temple to Anathoth early in the reign of Solomon. Although the line of Ithamar is clearly secondary, rabbinic tradition assigns it a particularly important role. According to the Babylonian Talmud, b. Megillah 14b, Rahab, the Canaanite harlot from Jericho who assisted Joshua's spies in Joshua 2, became a righteous gentile, converted to Judaism, and married Joshua ben Nun. Their descendants included a total of nine prophets. There was one female prophet, Huldah, who explained the significance of the book of Torah, apparently a form of Deuteronomy, that had been discovered in the Jerusalem temple in 2 Kings 22:14–20. And there were eight male prophets, including Neriah, Baruch, Seraiah, Maaseiah, Jeremiah, Hilkiah, Hanamel, and Shallum. Jeremiah and his father, Hilkiah, were also priests of the line of Ithamar, Eli, and Abiathar (Jer 1:1–3), who had been expelled from Jerusalem to Anathoth by King Solomon ben David (1 Kgs 2:26–27; cf. 1 Sam 2:27–36). But when King Josiah ben Amon of Judah invited the countryside priests of Judah to serve in the Jerusalem temple according to 2 Kings 23:8, Jeremiah was apparently among those that came to Jerusalem. Midrash Shemuel and Yalqut on Joshua 10 note that Rahav was also the ancestor of Ezekiel, who was a priest of the Jerusalem temple and therefore would have been descended from the line of Eleazar, Phineas, and Zadok.[9]

9. Seligssohn, "Rahab."

The Account of Moses and Aaron's Second Confrontation with Pharaoh: Divine Power —Exodus 6:26—12:36

EXODUS 6:26–30 MARKS THE beginning of a new sub-unit that recounts the manifestation of divine power against pharaoh and Egypt in the second confrontation with pharaoh led by Moses and Aaron in Exodus 6:26—12:26. Following the initial notice that Moses and Aaron were the same figures as those mentioned in the genealogy, Exodus 6:26–30 poses Moses's question to YHWH, "Behold, I am uncircumcised of lips, and how will pharaoh listen to me?" Exodus 7:1–7 answers his question when YHWH states that Moses will be like G-d to pharaoh and Aaron will be his prophet. The rest of the narrative proceeds with YHWH's instructions to Aaron to turn his rod into a serpent that will swallow the rods/serpents of pharaoh's magicians in Exodus 7:8–13; the account of YHWH's turning the Nile to blood in Exodus 7:14–24; the account of the plague of frogs in Exodus 7:25–8:11; the account of the plague of dust, lice, and vermin in Exodus 8:12–15; the account of the plague of flies in Exodus 8:16–28; the account of the plague of cattle disease in Exodus 9:1–7; the account of the plague of boils on humans and animals in Exodus 9:8–12; the account of the plague of thunder and hail in Exodus 9:13–35; the account of the plague of locusts in Exodus 10:1–20; the account of the plague of darkness in Exodus 10:21–29; and the account of the plague of the killing of the firstborn with its associated instructions concerning the Passover offerings in Exodus 11:1—12:36. The itinerary formula in Exodus 12:27, which notes Israel's journey from Rameses to Sukkoth, marks the beginning of the next major unit of the exodus narrative.

YHWH's Instructions to Moses Concerning How to Convince Pharaoh to Listen: Moses Will Be Like G-d to Pharaoh and Aaron Will Be His Prophet —Exodus 6:26—7:7

Translation

[26] It is Aaron and Moses to whom YHWH said, "Bring out the sons of Israel from the land of Egypt, according to their hosts. [27] They were the ones who spoke to pharaoh, king of Egypt, to bring out the sons of Israel from Egypt. It was Moses and Aaron. [28] And it happened on the day when YHWH spoke to Moses in the land of Egypt. [29] And YHWH spoke unto Moses, saying, "I am YHWH! Speak to pharaoh, king of Egypt, all that I spoke to you!" [30] And Moses said before YHWH, "Behold, I am uncircumcised of lips, and how will pharaoh listen to me?"

7:1 And YHWH said to Moses, "See, I have made you as G-d to pharaoh, and Aaron, your brother, will be your prophet. [2] You will speak all that I command you, and Aaron, your brother, will speak to pharaoh so that he will send away the sons of Israel from his land. [3] And I will harden the heart of pharaoh, and I will multiply my signs and my wonders in the land of Egypt. [4] But pharaoh will not listen to you, so I will set my hand against Egypt, and I will bring out my hosts, my people, the sons of Israel, from the land of Egypt with great judgments. [5] And the Egyptians will know that I am YHWH, when I extend my hand against Egypt, and I bring out the sons of Israel from your midst."

[6] And Moses and Aaron acted; just as YHWH commanded them, so they did. [7] And Moses was eighty-three years old, and Aaron was eighty years old when they spoke to pharaoh.

Commentary

Exodus 6:26—7:7 introduces the sequence of plague narratives in Exodus 6:26—12:36 with a narrative that identifies Aaron and Moses as the same figures whom YHWH commissioned to bring out the people of Israel from Egyptian slavery. The passage continues by instructing them on how they should convince pharaoh to release the people of Israel.

Exodus 6:26—7:7 comprises three basic components. The first in Exodus 6:26 is a syntactically independent statement that identifies Aaron and Moses as the ones whom YHWH commissioned to lead the people of Israel out of Egypt. The second is Exodus 6:27, another syntactically independent statement that builds upon the first by identifying Aaron and Moses as the ones who spoke with the pharaoh of Egypt in an effort to secure the release of the people of Israel in Egypt. The third is Exodus 6:28—7:7, which recounts the beginning of the discussion between YHWH and Moses in Exodus 6:28—7:7 concerning how Moses and his brother, Aaron, will convince pharaoh to listen to them and release the people of Israel. Following this sub-unit are the successive accounts through Exodus 12:36 of the plagues, here described as signs and wonders, that YHWH will employ to convince pharaoh to release the people of Israel.

Exodus 6:26 is formulated as an assertion that Aaron and Moses are the same figures whom YHWH commissioned to bring the people of Israel out from Egyptian bondage. The syntactically independent assertion begins with the masculine singular Hebrew pronoun, *hûʾ*, "he," in reference to Aaron, who was the primary focus of the genealogy of the descendants of Amram and his wife, Jocheved, in Exodus 6:20–25. Although the introductory pronoun is singular, the statement includes a reference to Moses as well, who was mentioned in Exodus 6:26, even though the genealogy did not specify his descendants. The purpose of the statement is to shift the focus specifically to Aaron and Moses as the agents of YHWH in obtaining the release of the people of Israel. The statement concludes with a notice that the people will go out "according to their hosts," Hebrew, *ʿal-ṣibʾōtām*, a military term that suggests that the tribes of Israel function as a military force employed by YHWH in holy war to defeat pharaoh and to march through the wilderness to the land of Canaan in order to conquer it.[1]

Exodus 6:27 then follows with a second syntactically independent statement concerning both Aaron and Moses. It begins with the masculine plural Hebrew pronoun, *hēm*, "they," to identify Aaron and Moses as the ones who spoke with pharaoh on behalf of YHWH to secure the release of the people of Israel. The statement concludes with a restatement of the singular assertion that appeared at the beginning of v. 26, "It [he] was Moses and Aaron," to ensure that the reader understands that both Aaron and Moses were intended by the initial statement in v. 26.

Exodus 6:28—7:7 then introduces the beginning of the extended conversation between YHWH and Moses that continues through the so-called plague narratives that conclude in Exodus 12:36.

The passage begins with a temporal formula in Exodus 6:28, "And it happened on the day that YHWH spoke to Moses in the land of Egypt." Although the Masoretic text understands this verse as a conclusion to the preceding statements in vv. 26–27, the verse actually functions as an introduction to the conversation between YHWH and Moses that follows beginning in v. 29. Exodus 6:29 presents an account of YHWH's speech to Moses in which YHWH first self-identifies, "I am YHWH," and then instructs Moses to speak to pharaoh all that YHWH has said to him up to this time, i.e., Moses is to demand that pharaoh release the people of Israel so that they may undertake a three-day journey to the wilderness to worship YHWH, their G-d. Moses, however, has reservations concerning YHWH's instruction, in that he is not convinced that pharaoh will listen to him due to his speech impairment. Moses describes his speech impairment with language that indicates that he is "uncircumcised of lips," drawing an analogy with the circumcision of the penis that is required of Jews from the time of Abraham (Gen 17) and

1. Roskop, *Wilderness Itineraries*.

that is also required of Egyptian priests.[2] Most interpreters understand this reference to indicate that Moses suffers some sort of defect in the lips or mouth that impairs his speech, but such a presumption misses the point of the statement. Circumcision of the penis is a ritual that symbolizes the sanctity of an Egyptian priest to serve his gods and that likewise symbolizes the sanctity of Jewish men to serve their G-d, YHWH. The use of this analogy to portray Moses's concerns about his ability to speak to pharaoh depends on the fact that Moses and Aaron are to serve as representatives of YHWH before pharaoh, who is considered a god in Egypt. In ancient Near Eastern practice, prophets who speak on behalf of deities are required to go through a mouth purification ritual in which water, oil, hot coals, or other devices are employed to purify the mouth of the would-be prophet so that he or she can embody the deity in question so that the deity can speak through them. Such mouth purification rituals are well known in ancient Mesopotamia, where *barû* priests undergo such mouth purification to speak on behalf of their respective gods.[3] The Hebrew Bible portrays such mouth purification in the vocation account of the prophet Isaiah ben Amoz, in Isaiah 6, in which Isaiah exclaims that he is a man of impure lips when he views the presence of YHWH in Isaiah 6:5. It is only when a seraph, a fiery angel of YHWH in the vision, purifies his lips with a hot coal from the altar of the Jerusalem temple that Isaiah is able to hear YHWH's speech and to answer him in the affirmative when YHWH asks, "Whom shall I send? Who will go for us?" in his efforts to find a prophet to speak on his behalf.[4] Moses and Aaron are to speak on behalf of YHWH, but it is not yet clear to Moses, even with the commissioning account in Exodus 3–4, that he and Aaron are properly prepared to speak on behalf of YHWH.

The account of YHWH's speech to Moses in Exodus 7:1–7 makes it clear that YHWH is indeed commissioning Moses and Aaron to speak on YHWH's behalf. The account of YHWH's response to Moses begins with statements of commission concerning both Moses and Aaron. YHWH commissions Moses to serve as "G-d" (Hebrew, *ʾĕlōhîm*) to pharaoh, and Aaron will serve as Moses's prophet. This commission is particularly indicative of the role of prophets in northern Israel, such as Elijah and Elisha, who are named in Hebrew *ʾîš hāʾĕlōhîm*, "man of

2. See *ANET* 326, a twenty-third-century BCE text, which portrays the experience of a young man awaiting his circumcision so that he might serve as an Egyptian priest.

3. Hurowitz, "Isaiah's Impure Lips"; see also Cryer, *Divination*.

4. In addition to Hurowitz, "Isaiah's Impure Lips," see Sweeney, *Isaiah 1–39*, 132–42.

G-d," insofar as they speak and act on behalf of G-d, much as an oracle diviner would do.[5] Elijah is not simply a prophet; his actions on Mount Carmel as portrayed in 1 Kings 18 show him to act as a priest as well in that he builds an altar and pours a water libation on it in keeping with the temple celebration of the Festival of Sukkot, which marks the beginning of the rainy season in Israel. Elisha, when asked to speak an oracle while on campaign against Moab with the king of Israel and his allies, calls for instrumental accompaniment so he can sing his oracle as required in temple service. Such figures were also known in Judah, such as the man of G-d from Judah who condemned King Jeroboam ben Nebat of Israel for officiating improperly at the Beth El altar in 1 Kings 13.[6] As Moses will function as "a man of G-d" to speak to pharaoh, he will speak to pharaoh on behalf of YHWH, and YHWH's statement here confirms that role. Insofar as ancient Near Eastern oracle diviners often spoke in symbolic language, Aaron's role is to serve as Moses's prophet in order to explain by speech or illustrate by action what Moses has to say. In the case of the present narrative, Aaron will illustrate Moses's speech to pharaoh by action when Moses calls upon Aaron to cast down his rod so that it will become a serpent in Exodus 7:8–18 and ultimately devour the rods of the Egyptian priests who attempt to perform the same action. Aaron employs his rod in subsequent plague narratives as well to carry out the actions for which Moses calls on behalf of YHWH.

But YHWH also makes clear the intention to harden (Hebrew, *qāšeh*) pharaoh's heart so that YHWH may perform the signs (Hebrew, *ʾōtōt*) and wonders (Hebrew, *mōptîm*) that will demonstrate that YHWH is the true G-d of creation and the true monarch of the world. The narrative does not generally refer to YHWH's actions as "plagues"; the Passover Haggadah has tended to emphasize the terminology of the ten plagues as a way to demonstrate both divine power and Jewish empathy for the suffering of the Egyptians.[7]

YHWH's actions are both noteworthy and problematic. They are noteworthy because they demonstrate that YHWH—and not pharaoh—is the true monarch of creation and the land of Egypt. Insofar as YHWH's signs and wonders entail new elements of creation in Egypt and Canaan, they function as means to demonstrate that YHWH is the true G-d of creation and thereby facilitate the role of the exodus

5. For discussion of Elijah and Elisha, see Sweeney, *1–2 Kings*, 207–361.

6. Sweeney, *1–2 Kings*, 172–82.

7. See Tabory, *JPS Commentary on Haggadah*, 44–45, 94–96.

narrative as a creation narrative. But they are also problematic in that they do not allow pharaoh to recognize YHWH, indicating that pharaoh and Egypt are punished without the opportunity to repent at the outset. Such a motif is crucial for demonstrating YHWH's power of pharaoh, and it presumes that pharaoh would not have repented anyway, but it undermines the principle of free will, i.e., the ability to choose between good and evil, with which all human beings are endowed from the time of Eve in the garden of Eden (Gen 3; cf. Isa 6).[8] Such a motif illustrates teleological moral reasoning, viz., the end justifies the means to achieve a righteous outcome, but it violates ontological moral reasoning, viz., the issue of whether an action is morally correct in and of itself. Essentially, YHWH sets up pharaoh to fail and suffer punishment for doing so without allowing him the chance to make the right choice from the outset. The Jewish observance of the Passover Seder notes this when the suffering of Egypt is recalled as part of the Seder ritual. By the end of the passage, YHWH refers to the actions against Egypt as "great judgments," Hebrew, *šĕpāṭîm gĕdōlîm*, to emphasize their punitive character in enslaving the people of Israel in the first place.

In the end, the purpose of YHWH's signs and wonders is to demonstrate to pharaoh, Egypt, and the people, exactly who YHWH is, i.e., the all-powerful ruler of both creation and human events. The use of the recognition or self-identification formula, "I am YHWH," is as a generic statement that identifies YHWH as the source of the signs and wonders performed against Egypt and as the true G-d of creation and human events.[9] YHWH's statements here confirm that Aaron and Moses will act as YHWH's agents in demonstrating YHWH's true identity. They further confirm YHWH's answer to Moses's question as to why pharaoh should listen, i.e., because YHWH's signs and wonders will demand pharaoh's attention and thereby force him to listen and to release the people of Israel from Egyptian bondage.

The final statement in v. 7 aids in clarifying an issue of chronology, i.e., Aaron is eighty-three years old and Moses is eighty years old when they begin their confrontation with pharaoh. Such a statement confirms that Aaron is the older brother of Moses.

8. Sweeney, *Reading the Bible After the Shoah*, 86–91.

9. See Zimmerli, *I Am YHWH*, esp. 1–28, 99–110.

RECEPTION HISTORY

Although the exodus narrative begins the account of YHWH's signs and wonders in Exodus 6:26—7:6 with the account of Aaron's rod turned into a crocodile, which swallows the rods/crocodiles of the Egyptian specialists, the Passover Haggadah refers to the ten plagues, Hebrew, *'eśer makkôt*, "the ten blows," by which G-d struck the Egyptians. The Passover Haggadah account of the plagues comes in a context in which Jews reflect on the suffering of the Egyptians as part of the celebration of freedom from Egyptian bondage.[10] The reference to the ten plagues comes at the end of the early rabbinic midrash on Deuteronomy 26:5–8, which refers to G-d's actions in freeing Israel from Egypt by a strong hand, an outstretched arm, great power, signs, and wonders. The interest in defining ten plagues is based in part on an early Tannaitic interest in identifying analogies with G-d's ten statements that appear in the narrative of the six days of creation in Mishnah tractate Pirke Avot, "The Chapters of the Fathers."[11]

In the New Testament, the account of Stephen's preaching and martyrdom in Acts 6:8–8:1a refers in Acts 7:36 to G-d's "signs and wonders" in the exodus from Egyptian bondage. And Paul's Letter to the Romans refers to G-d's hardening pharaoh's heart in Romans 9:18.

10. Tabory, *JPS Commentary on Haggadah*, 44–45, 95–96; Glatzer, *Passover Haggadah*, 40–43; Elias, *Haggadah*, 128–36.

11. See m. Avot 5, in Herford, *Ethics of the Talmud*, 124–31.

The Sign of Aaron's Staff as Serpent—Exodus 7:8–13

Translation

> 7:8 And YHWH said to Moses and to Aaron, saying, [9] "When pharaoh speaks to you, saying, 'Give for yourselves a wonder,' then you shall say to Aaron, 'Take your staff and cast [it] before pharaoh.' It will become a serpent."
>
> [10] And Moses and Aaron came to pharaoh, and they did just as YHWH commanded, and Aaron cast his staff before pharaoh and before his servants, and it became a serpent. [11] And pharaoh also called for wise men and for sorcerers, and the magicians of Egypt, even they, did likewise with their flaming spells. [12] And each man cast his staff, and they became serpents, but the staff of Aaron swallowed their staffs. [13] But the heart of pharaoh became even harder, and he did not listen to them, just as YHWH had spoken.

Commentary

Exodus 7:8–13 presents the first of YHWH's signs and wonders before pharaoh, viz., Aaron's rod will transform into a "serpent" (Hebrew, *tannin*), which will proceed to swallow the serpents created when pharaoh's servants cast down their rods in a similar manner. This episode is generally not considered one of the ten plagues, which in the Passover Haggadah begin with the plague of the water of the Nile turning to blood.[1] The present sign does not kill, injure, or afflict anyone; it is simply a demonstration of YHWH's divine power in creation and humanity. Exodus 4:1–5 envisions this sign as an act that produces a "snake" (Hebrew, *nāḥāš*), which calls to mind the well-known Egyptian practice of snake charming. And the following narrative in Exodus 7:14–24 concerning the waters of the Nile turned to blood refers to the rod that turned into a snake in Exodus 7:15. But the present narrative in Exodus 7:8–13 portrays Aaron's rod turning into a "serpent" (Hebrew, *tannin*) that will swallow the serpents produced when the Egyptian figures cast their own rods down.

Pharaoh's servants include references to "wise men," *ḥăkāmîm*, and "sorcerers," *mĕkaššĕpîm*, Hebrew terms that well describe the experts of a nation known for its wisdom and incantations. But the term *ḥarṭōm*, "magician," is apparently an Egyptian loanword that is used to describe the lector priests of Egypt, literate specialists who focused on liturgies and the interpretation of dreams, omens, and oracles, much like the *baru* priests of Mesopotamia.[2]

Many interpreters see the present reference to "serpents" as just another term for a snake, hence the translation "serpent." But the term *tannin* generally refers to some sort of water or sea monster, such as Leviathan, the seven-headed water dragon that appears in the waters of the sea (Isa 27:1), although it is noteworthy that the seven heads of Leviathan appear to symbolize the waters of the Nile Delta region from which the waters of the Nile empty out into the Mediterranean Sea (cf. Isa 11:15–16; 27:12–13). Such an understanding suggests that the *tannin*, "serpent," mentioned here must represent the Nile crocodile, which inhabits the Nile River all the way down to the Nile Delta. Nile crocodiles prefer fresh water, but unlike alligators, which appear in the southeastern United States and in China, crocodiles are able to live in seawater. It appears likely that the capacity for Aaron's *tannin* to swallow those of the Egyptians would suggest a crocodile rather than a snake. Such an understanding indicates that this passage is a P-stratum text that is intended to interpret and clarify the earlier J reference to Aaron's rod that becomes a snake in Exodus 4:1–5.[3] The present narrative would then contribute to

1. Tabory, *JPS Commentary on Haggadah*, 95.

2. *HALOT* 1:352–53; Redford, *Egypt, Canaan, and Israel*, 427–28; cf. Cryer, *Divination*.

3. Campbell and O'Brien, *Sources of the Pentateuch*, 36–37, 132–33.

the role of Exodus as a creation narrative, insofar as it explains the origins of crocodiles in the waters of the Nile River.

Reception History

The rabbinic midrash, Exodus Rabbah 9.6–7, recounts the encounter between Moses and Aaron, on the one hand, and pharaoh, on the other, in which Aaron's rod transformed into a serpent and swallowed the rods of the Egyptians. When pharaoh saw Aaron cast his rod down to become a serpent, he laughed and said that his merchants and even his wife could perform magical feats like that. When Aaron's serpent devoured the Egyptian serpents, Balaam ben Beor, an advisor to pharaoh, said that there was nothing unusual in that since animals normally devour each other, but when Aaron's wooden rod devoured the wooden rods of the Egyptians, pharaoh reflected on the matter. But he nevertheless refused to let Israel go, claiming that if Moses and Aaron had called for a thousand or two thousand Israelites to be released, he would have done, but he would never allow six hundred thousand to go free.[4]

4. Ginzberg, *Legends*, 2:335–36.

The Plague of Blood —Exodus 7:14–24

Translation

[14] And YHWH said to Moses, "The heart of pharaoh has become fixed; he refuses to send the people away. [15] Go to pharaoh in the morning [when] behold, he is going out to the water, and you shall stand to address him on the bank of the Nile, and the staff which had turned into a snake you shall take in your hand. [16] And you shall say to him, 'YHWH, the G-d of the Hebrews, has sent me to you, saying, "Send away my people so that they may serve me in the wilderness," but, behold, you did not listen until now. [17] Thus says YHWH, "By this you will know that I am YHWH!" Behold, I am striking with this staff, which is in my hand, the waters which are in the Nile, and they will be turned to blood. [18] And the fish which are in the Nile will die, and the Nile will stink, and the Egyptians will be sick of drinking from the Nile."'"

[19] And YHWH said to Moses, "Say to Aaron, 'Take your staff, and extend your hand over the waters of Egypt, over its rivers, over its streams, and over its ponds, and over every water source, and they will become blood, and blood will be in all the land of Egypt, and in [vessels of] wood and in [vessels of] stone.'" [20] And Moses and Aaron did just as YHWH had commanded, and he raised the staff, and he struck the waters which were in the Nile in the sight of pharaoh and in the sight of his servants, and all the waters which were in the

Nile were turned to blood. [21] And the fish which were in the Nile died, and the Nile stank, and the Egyptians were not able to drink water from the Nile, and the blood was in all the land of Egypt. [22] But the magicians of Egypt did the same with their fiery spells, then the heart of pharaoh became harder, and he did not listen to them just as YHWH had spoken. [23] And pharaoh turned, and he went to his palace, and he did not set his heart, also for this. [24] And all the Egyptians dug around the Nile [for] water to drink because they were not able to drink from the waters of the Nile.

Commentary

Exodus 7:14–24 recounts the plague of the waters of the Nile turning to blood, which appears as the first of the ten plagues in the Passover Haggadah.[1] This text appears to be an E-stratum text that has been overwritten by the J-stratum, much like Exodus 4, in that it reverts to understanding Aaron's rod that had previously turned into a snake rather than a serpent or crocodile. Again, this sign, wonder, or plague should be understood as presenting a creation motif. Although the imagery here is the waters of the Nile turned to blood, such imagery is metaphorical in that it refers to the natural phenomenon of the spring flooding of the waters of the Nile as snow melts in mountain sources of the Nile to the south in Sudan and Ethiopia. As the snows melt, the waters carry down the reddish soil of these southern regions, which gives to Nile waters the appearance of a brownish-red coloring suggestive of blood. As the waters surge and inundate the Nile flood plain, they spread the reddish mud from the south over the Nile Valley, thereby ensuring that Egypt will enjoy fertile soil for agriculture which will feed the Egyptian population. Indeed, it is well known that the Nile is the natural resource that facilitated the creation of Egyptian civilization. Until the construction of the Aswan Dam in 1956, Egypt was a food-producing nation. But with the construction of the Aswan Dam, much of the silt and mud carried by the Nile has settled behind the dam, which then leaves the Nile Valley downstream from Aswan without its rich soil. As a result of this problem and the growing population of Egypt, the country has now become a food-importing nation to satisfy its population's need for food.

1. Tabory, *JPS Commentary on Haggadah*, 95.

There is no evidence that the waters of the Nile killed the fish that lived in its waters; fishermen and natural predators, such as the Nile crocodiles, would have seen to their mortality. But the waters carried a great deal of natural water life that would die, and the spread of water over land would leave the land with a stench as dead wildlife and plant life decompose and produce mold and the various toxins that make the waters of the Nile dangerous drinking for those whose digestive systems are not acclimated to the water of Egypt (cf. Isa 19:5–10). Even today, foreigners visiting Egypt are advised to drink only purified bottled water and to avoid any other sources of water as well as fresh vegetables and fruit that would have been washed with water. Otherwise, dysentery is the likely result, and it can be dangerous; even Cambyses, the son of Cyrus the Great and the Achaemenid Persian monarch who initially conquered Egypt (r. 530–522 BCE), died from dysentery on his march home to Persia after having spent time in Egypt.

YHWH's oracle, introduced by the prophetic messenger formula in Exodus 7:17, makes it clear that YHWH is the source for the portrayal of the Nile turning to blood. In this respect, the narrative presents the origins of the Nile's annual spring flood in which the reddish waters brought down from the mountains of Sudan and Ethiopia provide the foundations for Egyptian agriculture and life—it is an act of creation by YHWH, the true G-d of creation as portrayed in the exodus narratives.

When the Egyptian specialists proved to be able to perform the same sign and wonder with their own staffs, pharaoh's heart hardened and he refused to release the people of Israel as demanded by YHWH, Moses, and Aaron. In the meantime, the metaphorical portrayal of the waters as blood affected all the water of Egypt, and it killed the fish, leaving the people without food to eat or water to drink. But pharaoh's hardened heart then sets the stage for the next plague in the following narrative.

Reception History

According to Exodus Rabbah 12.4 and 15.27, G-d apportioned the ten plagues so that three were given to Aaron, three to Moses, one to Moses and Aaron together, and the last three were for G-d alone. Aaron's plagues were related to earth and water, and they were intended as punishments for the burdens inflicted upon Israel by Egypt. The Nile turning to blood was in punishment for the Egyptians' forcing Israel to draw water for them and preventing Israel from using the mikveh, the bath for personal purification.[2]

2. Ginzberg, *Legends*, 2:341–43; see also Philo, *Mos.* 1.17.

The Plague of Frogs —Exodus 7:25—8:11

Translation

7:25 And seven days were fulfilled after YHWH struck the
Nile, 26 and YHWH said to Moses, "Go to pharaoh, and you
shall say to him, 'Thus says YHWH, "Send away my people so
that they may serve me, 27 and if you refuse to send [them]
away, behold, I am plaguing all your borders with frogs.
28 And the Nile will swarm [with] frogs, and they will go up,
and they will enter your palace, and your bedroom, and your
bed, and the house of your servants, and among your people,
and in your ovens, and in your kitchen vessels, 29 and among
you, and among your people, and among all your servants
shall the frogs come up."'"

8:1 And YHWH said to Moses, "Say to Aaron, 'Extend your
hand with your staff over the rivers, over the streams, and
over the ponds, and bring up the frogs over the land of
Egypt.'" 2 And Aaron extended his hand over the waters of
Egypt, and the frog came up, and it covered the land of Egypt.
3 And the lector priests likewise did their spells, and they
brought up the frogs over the land of Egypt.

4 And pharaoh summoned Moses and Aaron, and he said,
"Appeal to YHWH, and he will remove the frogs from me and
from my people, and I will release the people, and they will
sacrifice to YHWH." 5 And Moses said to pharaoh, "Glorify

yourself over me as to when I will appeal for you and for your servants and for your people to cut off the frogs from you and from your houses; only in the Nile shall they remain.” 6 And he said, “For tomorrow.” And [Moses] said, “As you say, in order that you may know that there is none like YHWH, our G-d. 7 And the frogs will depart from you and from your houses and from your servants and from your people; only in the Nile shall they remain.”

8 And Moses and Aaron went out from pharaoh, and Moses cried out to YHWH concerning the matter of the frogs, which he had set upon pharaoh. 9 And YHWH did as Moses said, and the frogs died from the houses, from the courtyards, and from the fields. 10 And they piled them up in heaps, and the land stank. 11 But pharaoh saw that there was relief, and he hardened his heart, and he did not listen to them, just as YHWH had spoken.

Commentary

The initial temporal formula indicates a seven-day passage of time from the plague of blood to the plague of frogs. The formula does not indicate a major literary sub-unit in the sequence of the plagues. Rather, the seven-day passage of time is due to the need to cleanse the land from the impurity of blood in analogy to the menstrual period of a woman as understood in priestly tradition (see Lev 15:19–30; cf. Lev 12:1–8; Isa 4:4–5).[1] In ancient Near Eastern mythology, land is metaphorically considered feminine due to its ability to produce new life. Land is therefore often conceptualized as a woman who is impregnated by the rain of the male heavens.

The plague of frogs then follows the seven-day period of impurity as YHWH’s next strike against Egypt for pharaoh’s refusal to release Israel. The appearance of frogs in Egypt is a natural occurrence in the aftermath of the spring flooding of the Nile River, insofar as the floodwaters will bring up multitudes of frogs and other unwelcome water life that will then inundate the land with the water. The portrayal of frogs invading the innermost quarters of the human inhabitants of the Nile Valley is not an imaginative literary invention; it is a regular and natural

1. Erbele-Küster, “Menstruation.”

occurrence in the region here portrayed as an act of YHWH. In the context of the Exodus creation, the plague of frogs is an act of YHWH's creation that originates as part of YHWH's use of signs and wonders to demonstrate that YHWH—and not pharaoh—is the true G-d of Egypt and the world of creation at large.

Insofar as Aaron is the one who signals the beginning of the plague by raising his rod over the waters, interpreters generally view this narrative as the product of a P redaction of an underlying J narrative.[2] Pharaoh initially relents, and Moses tells pharaoh to "glorify himself" by telling Moses when it would be appropriate to appeal to YHWH as pharaoh requested. Moses's move is an attempt to allow pharaoh an appropriate degree of honor or recognition in the hope that pharaoh will ultimately recognize YHWH, but once the plague was concluded, pharaoh reneged on his offer to release the people of Israel just as YHWH had declared that he would (cf. Exod 7:1–7). Although the present passage does not indicate that YHWH hardened pharaoh's heart, the reference to YHWH's declaration acknowledges YHWH's statement that YHWH would harden pharaoh's heart in each case. Such a reference suggests that the underlying narrative placed the blame on pharaoh for his own punishment, whereas the P redaction maintains that YHWH is in full control and has hardened pharaoh's heart.

Once again, the narrative indicates that the Nile River Valley stinks following the spring floods, but this time it is due to the rotting corpses of the frogs, not simply inundation of the Nile Valley by flood (cf. Exod 7:21).

Reception History

Exodus 7:25—8:11 recounts the second of the plagues assigned to Aaron, which are based in actions related to earth and water, i.e., the elements that composed of more or less solid parts from which corporeal entities are made.[3] When Aaron called for the frogs, at first only one appeared, in keeping with the singular reference to the frog in Exodus 8:2. The one frog then summoned the others, which then filled the entire land of Egypt. The frogs were able to pierce all metals and marble, so there was no way to keep them from entering every palace and house in the land to attack

2. Campbell and O'Brien, *Sources of the Pentateuch*, 38, 136.

3. Ginzberg, *Legends*, 2:341; Philo, *Mos.* 1.17; Exod. Rab. 12.4, 15, 27.

the Egyptians. They were even able to enter the ovens for baking bread to consume all the food of Egypt in accordance with the will of G-d. Because the frogs survived the ovens of Egypt, Daniel's later companions, Hannaniah, Mishael, and Azariah, were able to survive the fiery furnace. The appearance of frogs also settled a boundary dispute between Egypt and Ethiopia, as the frogs appeared only in Egyptian territory.[4]

The New Testament alludes to the plague of frogs in the apocalyptic scenario of Revelation 16:13 in which the sixth angel pours his bowl into the Euphrates River to unleash three demonic spirits like frogs which emerge from the mouth of the dragon prior to the great battle that will see the fall of Babylon.

4. Ginzberg, *Legends*, 349–51; Exod. Rab. 10.2–6; Dan 3.

The Plague of Gnats —Exodus 8:12–15

Translation

8:12 And YHWH said to Moses, "Say to Aaron, 'Extend your staff, and strike the dirt of the earth, and it will become gnats in all the land of Egypt.'" [13] And they did so, and Aaron extended his hand with his staff, and he struck the dirt of the land, and it became gnats against humans and against animals; all the dust of the land became gnats in all the land of Egypt. [14] And the magicians did so with their spells to expel the gnats, but they were not able, and the gnats were against humans and animals. [15] And the magicians said to pharaoh, "It is the finger of G-d," but pharaoh's heart was hard, and he did not listen to them, just as YHWH spoke.

Commentary

The account of the plague of gnats is again signaled when Aaron raises his rod over the dust of the land to produce the swarm of gnats. Again, Aaron's role in the plague indicates the P-stratum of composition.[1] Gnats are tiny, swarming insects that are generally considered part of the larger family of Nematocera, which includes the various species of flies, mosquitos, and many other related pests. Indeed, commentators from at least Rashi on have attempted to identify the Hebrew term, *kinnîm*, with lice, maggots, gnats, and other tiny undesirable

1. Campbell and O'Brien, *Sources of the Pentateuch*, 38.

insects.[2] "Vermin" is also employed as a translation due to its broad range, including insects, rodents, etc. Although the term is somewhat ambiguous, "gnats" appears to be the best translation insofar as gnats so frequently precede flies. The understanding of the term as gnats would then tie it in more closely with the natural conditions of the Nile River Valley following the annual spring flood and the rotting corpses of the frogs that had spread throughout the land.

Reception History

This is the last of Aaron's plagues. Rabbinic interpretation understands the gnats to be lice. Like gnats, lice are too small for the Egyptian lector priests and their demonic allies to reproduce. They therefore had to acknowledge that "it is the finger of G-d," i.e., the G-d of Israel did this, and they did not have power to replicate the act. The lector priests are able to perform their actions only when their feet are planted firmly on the ground, but lice covered the ground, preventing them from doing so.[3]

2. Rosenberg, *Exodus*, 1:105; "*kēn, kinnîm*," BDB 487–88; *HALOT* 2:483; LXX, *sknipes*, "an insect under the bark of trees" (LSJ 1612–13), although the term may be associated with fleas and gnats as well.

3. Ginzberg, *Legends*, 2:351–52; Exod. Rab. 10.7; 11.2; cf. Rosenberg, *Exodus*, 1:105.

The Plague of Flies —Exodus 8:16–28

Translation

8:16 And YHWH said to Moses, "Get up in the morning, and
stand before pharaoh when he comes out to the waters, and
you shall say to him, 'Thus says YHWH, "Release my people
that they may serve me! 17 For if you do not release my people,
behold, I am sending against you and against your servants
and against your people and against your houses swarms of
flies, and they will fill the houses of Egypt with swarms of
flies and also the ground which they are upon. 18 But I will set
apart on that day the land of Goshen upon which my people
stand so that no swarms of flies will be there, in order that
you will know that I am YHWH in the midst of the land.
19 And I will make a ransom between my people and between
your people; this sign will be tomorrow."'" 20 And YHWH did
so, and a heavy swarm of flies came to the house of pharaoh and the house of his servants and against all the land
of Egypt; the land was destroyed due to the swarms of flies.

21 And pharaoh called to Moses and Aaron, and he said, "Go!
Sacrifice to your G-d in the land." 22 And Moses said, "It is
not right to do so, because it is an abomination of Egypt if
we sacrifice to YHWH, our G-d. Behold, we will sacrifice an
abomination of Egypt before their eyes, and will they not
stone us? 23 We will go on a journey of three days in the wilderness, and we will sacrifice to YHWH, our G-d, just as he

said to us." 24 And pharaoh said, "I will release you, and you
will sacrifice to YHWH, your G-d, in the wilderness; only
you will not go very far. Appeal on my behalf." 25 And Moses
said, "Behold, I am going out from you, and I will appeal to
YHWH, that he will remove the swarm of flies from pharaoh,
from his servants, and from his people tomorrow; only pharaoh shall not again deceive so as not to release the people to
sacrifice to YHWH."

26 And Moses went out from pharaoh, and he appealed to
YHWH. 27 And YHWH did as Moses said, and he removed the
swarms of flies from pharaoh, from his servants, and from
his people; not one remained. 28 But pharaoh hardened his
heart again this time, and he did not release the people.

Commentary

Exodus 8:16–28 presents the account of the plague of flies against Egypt. In this case, Aaron is no longer the one who signals the onset of the plague; instead, Moses meets pharaoh as he is going out to the waters of the Nile, apparently to bathe, etc., in the morning. Moses threatens pharaoh, declaring that YHWH will release the next plague if pharaoh does not release the people of Israel. Consequently, interpreters view this account as a largely J-stratum narrative.[1]

The translation of the Hebrew term *ʿārōb* is again complicated. The term is derived from the root *ʿrb* I, which generally refers to a mixed company, which could refer to people (e.g., Exod 12:38), the warp, the threads that run lengthwise, in weaving that are woven together with the woof, the threads that run across (see Lev 13:48), a swarm of insects, such as stinging flies (cf. Pss 78:45; 105:31).[2] The ambiguity of the term prompts interpreters to understand it as a reference to a mixture of insects or other objectionable creatures. Again, flies appear to be the best choice, in consideration of the aftermath of the flooding of the Nile Valley, and the presence of rotting frog corpses and gnats.

The reference to the land of Goshen apparently indicates a specific district in Egypt where Hebrews were apparently segregated due to ancient Egyptian racism (cf. Gen 46:34). Most interpreters identify

1. Campbell and O'Brien, *Sources of the Pentateuch*, 137–38.

2. "*ʿārōb*," BDB 786; cf. *HALOT* 2:879.

Goshen with the Egyptian name *Gsm*, in lower Egypt, i.e., the Nile Delta region.[3] In this case, the segregation of Israel in Goshen enables YHWH to plague the Egyptians with flies, whereas Israel will remain unaffected by the plague. The use of the self-identification formula indicates that all will know that "I am YHWH." And the use of the Hebrew term *pĕdut*, here translated "ransom," ensures that the people of Israel will be considered both separate from Egypt and ransomed by YHWH from Egyptian captivity.

When pharaoh relents and tells Moses that the people may sacrifice to their G-d, Moses replies to pharaoh that such an act would make no sense in that the Egyptians would consider sacrifice to a foreign G-d, in this case YHWH, as an abomination, and would then attack the people of Israel with stones due to their intolerance of foreigners. Consequently, Moses reiterates his initial demand that the people of Israel be released for a three-day journey into the wilderness to sacrifice to YHWH. When pharaoh accepts Moses's proposal, he demands that Moses plead with YHWH on his behalf so that he will end the plague against Egypt. Moses accepts pharaoh's proposal, but warns him against acting deceitfully. Nevertheless, when the plague is lifted, pharaoh again hardens his own heart and reneges on his promise to release the people of Israel.

Reception History

The three plagues allotted to Moses proceed from air and fire, which are necessary for the proliferation of life.[4] Rabbinic interpretation understands the Hebrew word *ʿārōb*, in Exodus 8:17, to refer to a mixed horde of creatures,[5] which rabbinic midrash understands to include lions, bears, wolves, panthers, and many types of birds of prey.[6] The Septuagint, however, understands the term as *kunommuiēs*, "dog flies." The creatures attacked pharaoh first and then the Egyptians in general, but they made a distinction between the Egyptians and the Israelites so that the latter were not attacked. After the plague ended and pharaoh reneged on his promise to release Israel, the creatures killed by the Egyptians returned to life so that the Egyptians could not profit from the hides and meat of the dead corpses.

3. Römer, "Goshen."
4. Ginzberg, *Legends*, 2:341; Philo, *Mos.* 1.17; Exod. Rab. 12.4, 15, 27.
5. Rosenberg, *Exodus*, 1:106–7.
6. Ginzberg, *Legends*, 2:352–53; Exod. Rab. 11.2–3; 16.27.

The Plague of Cattle Disease —Exodus 9:1–7

Translation

9:1 And YHWH said to Moses, "Go to pharaoh, and you shall say to him, 'Thus says YHWH, G-d of the Hebrews, "Release my people so they may serve me," [2] for if you refuse to release [them] and you continue to hold them, [3] behold, the hand of YHWH will be against your livestock which are in the field, [that is,] against your horses, against your asses, against your camels, against your cattle, and against your sheep, as a very heavy plague! [4] And YHWH will distinguish between the livestock of Israel and the livestock of Egypt so that none will die from all that belongs to Israel. [5] And YHWH has set the time, saying, "Tomorrow, YHWH will do this thing in the land."'"

[6] And YHWH did this thing the next day, and all the livestock of Egypt died, but from the livestock of Israel, not one died. [7] And pharaoh sent, and behold, not even one from the livestock of Israel died, but the heart of pharaoh hardened, and he did not release the people.

Commentary

Exodus 9:1–7 recounts YHWH's plague of cattle disease against the Egyptian livestock. In this case, Moses is the figure who acts on behalf of YHWH to threaten pharaoh in the event that he does not release the people of Israel as demanded. The plague represents another dimension of the Nile River Valley ecosystem in that the prior plagues of biting gnats and flies would lead naturally to the transmission of disease, insofar as the swarming gnats and flies would have been feasting on the rotting corpses of the frogs and other river life that was left to die as the waters of the Nile receded. In this case, the narrative mentions livestock in general (Hebrew, *miqneh*), which would include cattle, sheep, goats, and other animals, here specified as horses, asses, camels, bovines, and sheep/goats. The distinction made between the cattle of the Egyptians and those of the Israelites is not likely based on the properties of the Nile ecosystem; rather it serves the interests of the narrative in which YHWH has promised to protect the people of Israel as part of the combat against pharaoh and Egypt. In the present instance, pharaoh's heart remains hardened—it is not said to be directly caused by YHWH—and he continues to refuse to release the people of Israel.

Reception History

According to Midrash ha-Gadol 2.68–69, the fourth plague, understood in rabbinic literature as a plague of many animals, had killed many Egyptian children. Because the children had tended to Egyptian herds and flocks, the Egyptians had to enlist Israelites to tend to their animals. As a result, the fifth plague then annihilated the Egyptian livestock.[1] Israelite livestock remained untouched. If an Israelite had a claim on an Egyptian animal, that animal was also spared.

1. Ginzberg, *Legends*, 2:354, esp. n190 (5:430–31).

The Plague of Boils —Exodus 9:8–12

Translation

9:8 And YHWH said to Moses and to Aaron, "Take for yourselves handfuls of kiln soot, and Moses will toss it toward
the heavens in the sight of pharaoh. 9 And it shall be dust
over all the land of Egypt, and it shall cause a skin inflammation breaking out as blisters on humans and animals in
all the land of Egypt."

10 And they took the kiln soot, and they stood before pharaoh, and Moses tossed it toward the heavens, and caused a
skin inflammation to break out as blisters on humans and
animals. 11 And the lector priests were not able to stand
before Moses due to the rash because the rash was on the
lector priests and on all Egypt. 12 But YHWH strengthened
the heart of pharaoh, and he did not listen to them, just as
YHWH said to Moses.

Commentary

Exodus 9:8–12 recounts the plague of a skin inflammation that affects both human beings and animals (Hebrew, *bĕhēmâ*, "animal," in general). Again, the outbreak of this inflammation is a product of the effects of the prior plagues that take place within the Nile ecosystem as the earlier plagues of frogs and their rotting corpses, gnats, flies, and cattle disease now begin to affect the human population of Egypt as well as the animal.

The specific identification of the disease is not given, but it is described as an inflammation, Hebrew, *šĕḥîn*, often translated as "boils," although the root, *šḥn*, means "to be warm, hot." The meaning, "warm, hot," then indicates that the condition is some sort of inflammation of the skin. The condition is further described as *pōrēaḥ ʾăbaʿbuʿōt*, "blisters breaking out," which indicates some sort of skin rash. The condition is tied to the ash of the kilns, which would be employed for the firing of bricks, and so the narrative suggests that the plague is imposed on the Egyptians in return for their forcing the Israelites to work as slaves. A major part of their duties is to make bricks for the construction of Egyptian buildings; the firing of mud bricks is a key part of the construction process. By throwing the ashes or soot to the sky, the narrative portrays the land covered with the dust or soot of working kilns.[1]

The Egyptian lector priests are unable to stand before pharaoh to demonstrate that they can perform the same feat due to their own infection with this particular inflammation, insofar as skin inflammations render a human unclean in Israelite thought (see Lev 13–14). Although the inflammations are often considered to be leprosy (see Lev 14), it is not clear that these inflammations are examples of Hansen's disease. Rather, they seem to presuppose a variety of inflammations that can affect the skin.[2] Again, the narrative demonstrates its interest in portraying YHWH's protection of Israel and affliction of Egypt in relation to the effects of the Nile Valley ecosystem.

Reception History

Exodus Rabbah 11.4–6 indicates that Moses and Aaron threw their handfuls of soot so high that they reached the divine throne. The handfuls of soot were sufficient to cover the entire land of Egypt, some four hundred square parasangs.[3]

Revelation 16 presents the seven angels who are ready to pour out their bowls of wrath upon the earth. According to Revelation 16:2, the first

1. The author worked as a foundry man at the Wagner Casting Company and the Mueller Iron Foundry, both in Decatur, Illinois, during the summers of 1972–74 to pay for his undergraduate education. The areas around foundries are typically covered in such soot.

2. Hieke, "Leper, Leprosy."

3. Ginzberg, *Legends*, 2:354. A parasang is an ancient Persian unit of distance, roughly equivalent to 3.5 to 4 miles.

angel poured his bowl upon the earth, which caused foul and painful sores on those who had the mark of the beast and worshipped his image.

The Plague of Hail and Fire —Exodus 9:13–35

Translation

9:13 And YHWH said to Moses, "Get up in the morning, and stand before pharaoh, and you shall say to him, 'Thus says YHWH, G-d of the Hebrews, "Release my people so they may serve me, 14 for this time I will release all my plagues unto your heart, and against your servants, and against your people so that you may know that there is none like me in all the land, 15 for now I have released my hand, and have stricken you and your people with pestilence, and you have been ruined from the earth. 16 But indeed because of this, I have left you standing to show you my power, and to recount my Name in all the land. 17 Yet you still exalt yourself over my people so as not to release them! 18 Behold, I will rain down at this time tomorrow a very heavy hail, the like of which has not happened in Egypt from the time of its foundation and until now. 19 And now, send orders, shelter your cattle and all that is yours in the field! (But as for) any human and animal which is found in the field and not gathered inside, shall die when the hail comes down upon them."'" 20 Whoever feared the word of YHWH from among the servants of pharaoh caused his servants and his livestock to flee inside, 21 but whoever did not pay attention to the word of YHWH left his servants and his livestock in the field.

22 And YHWH said to Moses, "Extend your hand against the
heavens so that there will be hail in all the land of Egypt,
against human and against animal, and against all the grass
of the field in the land of Egypt." 23 And Moses extended his
staff against the heavens, and YHWH gave thunder and hail,
and fire went down to the land, and YHWH rained down hail
upon the land of Egypt. 24 And there was hail, and fire was
flashing in the midst of very heavy hail, which was not like
anything in all the land of Egypt since it became a nation.
25 And the hail struck in all the land of Egypt all who were in
the field from human and until animal. And all the grass of
the field the hail struck, and every tree of the field was shattered. 26 Only in the land of Goshen where the sons of Israel
were was there no hail.

27 And pharaoh sent and called for Moses and for Aaron, and
he said to them, "I have sinned this time. YHWH is right,
and I and my people are wrong. 28 Plead to YHWH so that
there will be enough of G-d's thunder and hail, and I will
release you, and you will not continue to stay [here]." 29 And
Moses said to him, "As I go out of the city, I will spread out
my hands unto YHWH; the thunder will cease, and there
will no longer be hail, so that you will know that the land
belongs to YHWH. 30 But as for you and your servants, I
know that you do not yet fear YHWH the G-d. 31 But the flax
and the barley have been stricken, because the barley was
in spring ear, and the flax was in bud, 32 but the wheat and
the spelt were not stricken because they had not ripened."
33 And Moses went out from pharaoh in the city, and he
spread his hands out to YHWH, and the thunder and the
hail ceased, and the rain was not poured out on the land.
34 And pharaoh saw that the rain and hail and the thunder
had ceased, and he continued to sin, and his heart became
hard, both he and his servants. 35 And the heart of pharaoh
became strong, and he did not release the sons of Israel,
just as YHWH had said by the hand of Moses.

Commentary

Exodus 9:13–35 recounts the plague of hail and fire unleashed by YHWH against Egypt. In this case, YHWH's instructions in Exodus 9:13–21 are addressed to both Moses and Aaron. YHWH instructs them to use the prophetic messenger formula, "Thus says YHWH, the G-d of the Hebrews," to address pharaoh, and YHWH makes it very clear in the instructions that the purpose of this plague is to demonstrate to pharaoh and to Egypt YHWH's power and identity as the true G-d and creator of the land. In the present case, the plague is no longer tied specifically to the Nile River Valley ecosystem; rather, hail and fire are typical of the world of creation at large, although both tend to be rather unusual. Hail, of course, is a form of freezing rain, and the fire apparently presupposes lightning strikes that accompany precipitation. The combination of freezing cold and hot fire become elements in apocalyptic scenarios in which fire and ice emerge from below the throne of YHWH to portray YHWH's controls over both the elements and the extremes of temperature that are a part of creation (1 En. 14.13; cf. Dan 7:9, which portrays "a river of fire" emanating from beneath the divine throne). The imagery also anticipates the theophanic portrayal of Mount Sinai covered in rain clouds and sparking lightning (Exod 19:16). In this case, YHWH's instructions call upon the Egyptians to protect their slaves and animals by bringing them inside to protect them from the hail and fire, although the narrative makes it clear that not all of the Egyptians would follow these instructions. Such a portrayal is intended to portray the insolence of the Egyptians, their disbelief in YHWH, and their lack of concern for their slaves and animals.

Exodus 9:22–26 recounts Moses's compliance with YHWH's instructions to extend his hand toward the heavens to bring about the plague of hail and fire as an act of YHWH embodied in the person of Moses. The narrative emphasizes that the combination of hail and fire destroys the crops of the Egyptians, but it also emphasizes that YHWH protects the people of Israel so that no hail or fire falls on the land of Goshen where the people of Israel reside.

Exodus 9:27–35 recounts the audience of Moses and Aaron with pharaoh as a result of the plague of hail and fire. Pharaoh pleads with them to pray to YHWH to halt the plague, and his comments indicate that he now recognizes his own guilt, presumably in enslaving Israel and failing to recognize YHWH as the true G-d and creator of the world.

Moses's response to pharaoh clearly indicates that he does not believe the Egyptian monarch, but he states his intention to spread his hands out to call upon YHWH to stop the hail and fire. The image of the outspread hands of Moses is well known in the iconography of ancient Israel and in Judaism, insofar as it represents the imagery of a priest spreading out his hands to pray to YHWH on behalf of the people. Such an image appears in a cultic stele engraved with the outspread hands of a priest as part of a thirteenth-century BCE Canaanite shrine excavated at Hazor.[1] The narrative notes that the flax and barley had been ruined by the hail, insofar as both were just beginning to sprout in the early spring. But the narrative also notes that the wheat and the spelt, both of which are essential food grains, had not yet sprouted, and they therefore had been spared from the effects of the hail. The differentiation in the crops indicates YHWH's intention to show a combination of power and mercy in afflicting the Egyptians with this plague. Of course, after Moses appealed to YHWH to stop the hail and fire, pharaoh once again reneged on his pledge to release the Hebrew slaves, thereby necessitating the next plague as a further demonstration of YHWH's power.

Reception History

The image of Moses spreading his hands out as he prays to G-d is also associated with the priestly blessing in Numbers 6:22–27 when descendants of the Kohanim or priests extend their hands to give the priestly blessing to the congregation in traditional Orthodox congregations. In Reform, Reconstructionist, and other progressive congregations, the rabbi, cantor, or other officiant might perform this ritual. The priestly blessing may also be given on other occasions, such as Rosh ha-Shanah, Sukkot, Shemini Atzeret, Shavuot, and Pesach, depending upon the practices of the congregation in question.[2]

According to Revelation 8:6–7, when the seven angels were ready to blow their trumpets, the first angel blew his trumpet, which caused hail and fire mixed with blood to be hurled against the earth. One-third of the earth was burned up, a third of the trees were burned up, and all green grass was also burned. According to Revelation 11:19, when G-d's heavenly temple was opened, the ark of the covenant was

1. *ANEP* 871.
2. See Brichto et al., "Priestly Blessing."

seen together with flashes of lightning, peals of thunder, earthquake, and heavy hail. According to Revelation 16:17, when the seventh angel poured his bowl into the air, Rome, the great city, split into three parts and the cities of the nations fell. Huge hailstones, each weighing a talent (ca. one hundred pounds) dropped on people from heaven until they cursed G-d for the plague of hail.

The Plague of Locusts —Exodus 10:1–20

Translation

10:1 And YHWH said to Moses, "Go to pharaoh, for I have hardened his heart and the heart of his servants in order that I may set these, my signs, in his midst, [2] and in order that you may recount in the ears of your sons and the sons of your sons how I acted ruthlessly in Egypt and my signs that I set against them so that you will know that I am YHWH."

[3] And Moses and Aaron came to pharaoh, and they said to him, "Thus says YHWH, G-d of the Hebrew, 'How long will you refuse to humble yourself before me? Release my people that they may serve me! [4] For if you refuse to release my people, behold, I am bringing tomorrow locusts against your borders! [5] And they will cover the eye of the land so that it will be impossible to see the land, and they will devour the rest of the remnant that remains to you from the hail, and they shall devour every tree that sprouts for you from the field. [6] And they shall fill your houses and the houses of all your servants and the houses of all Egypt, which your ancestors and the ancestors of your ancestors have not seen from the day that they were [first] on the ground until this day!'" And they turned, and they went out from pharaoh.

[7] And the servants of pharaoh said to him, "How long will this be a trap for us? Release the men so that they may serve

YHWH, their G-d! Do you not yet know that Egypt has lost?"
8 And Moses and Aaron were returned to pharaoh, and he
said to them, "Go, serve YHWH, your G-d! Who all is going?"
9 And Moses said, "With our youths and with our elderly we
will go, with our sons and with our daughters, with our sheep
and with our cattle we will go, for it is a festival for YHWH
for us." 10 And he said to them, "May it be so that YHWH will
be with you when I release you and your children! It is obvious that evil is on your mind! 11 It will not be so! Let the men
go now and serve YHWH, for that is what you seek!" And
they were expelled from before pharaoh.

12 And YHWH said to Moses, "Extend your hand over the
land of Egypt with the locusts, and they will come up over
the land of Egypt, and they will devour all the grass of the
land, that is, all the hail has left." 13 And Moses extended his
staff over the land of Egypt, and YHWH drove the east wind
in the land all that day and all the night. When morning
came, the east wind had carried the locusts. 14 And locusts
went up over all the land of Egypt, and they settled heavily
in all the boundary of Egypt. Before this, there had never
been locusts like this, and after this, there will never be [lo-
custs] like this. 15 And they covered [the] eye of all the land,
and the land was dark, and they devoured all the grass of the
land and all the fruit of the trees that the hail had left, and
there remained nothing green in the trees and in the grass
of the field in all the land of Egypt.

16 And pharaoh hurried to summon Moses and Aaron, and
he said to them, "I have sinned to YHWH, your G-d, and to
you. 17 And now, forgive, please, my sin this time, and plead
to YHWH, your G-d, that he may remove only from upon me
this death." 18 And he went out from pharaoh, and he pleaded
to YHWH. 19 And YHWH reversed the very strong wind of
the sea, and it carried away the locusts, and it blew them into
the Sea of Reeds. Not one locust remained in all the boundary of Egypt. 20 But YHWH hardened the heart of pharaoh,
and he did not release the sons of Israel.

Commentary

Exodus 10:1–20 presents the account of the plague of locusts. Locusts are a natural feature of creation throughout much of the world, where they appear on a regular basis. Locusts were well known in ancient Egypt, particularly because they destroyed crops and thereby instigate famine among human populations (cf. Amos 7:1–3; Joel 1–2). Although some interpreters maintain that the plague of locusts and other plagues represent attempts to portray anti-creation, locusts are part of the Egyptian ecosystem. The present narrative represents an attempt to portray locusts as part of YHWH's efforts to engage in acts of creation beyond those of Genesis 1:1—2:3 during the course of the battle against pharaoh, considered to be a god in Egypt, to demonstrate that YHWH is the true G-d of creation and human events.[1]

The present narrative is largely a J-stratum composition, although it would also constitute a part of the final P-stratum edition of the final form of the pentateuchal text.[2] The narrative begins in Exodus 10:1–2 with a presentation of YHWH's instructions to Moses to go to pharaoh, although it states that YHWH has already hardened pharaoh's heart. Consequently, the narrative signals that the confrontation with pharaoh will be futile, but it defines the purpose of this motif as a means to demonstrate YHWH's identity and power to pharaoh, Egypt, and Israel itself, particularly the children of the Israelites who are to be taught this narrative so that they will know who YHWH is. Indeed, the recognition formula in v. 2, "so that you will know that I am YHWH," makes this purpose clear.[3]

Exodus 10:3–11 presents the account of the first audience with pharaoh on this matter and its results. Exodus 10:3–6 recounts the initial portion of the audience in which Moses and Aaron demand the release of the Israelite slaves. Their demand begins with an example of the prophetic messenger formula, "Thus says YHWH, the G-d of the Hebrews," to indicate that they speak on behalf of YHWH.[4] In making their demand, Moses and Aaron stress that pharaoh must "humble" himself before YHWH, which would indicate pharaoh's recognition of YHWH's power, identity, and role as the true G-d of creation, and thereby settle

1. Sweeney, "Creation as Sacred Space."
2. Campbell and O'Brien, *Sources of the Pentateuch*, 140.
3. Zimmerli, *I Am YHWH.*
4. Sweeney, *Isaiah 1–39*, 546.

the issue of releasing the Israelites to go on a three-day journey into the wilderness to serve YHWH. Should pharaoh refuse to do so, they threaten him with a plague of locusts that will cover the land of Egypt so thoroughly that no one will be able to see it; a plague that will result in the locusts devouring all the trees and other plant life that had survived the plague of hail. These threats are especially important for Egypt in that Amon-Re, the sun god, is the chief deity of Egypt, and the inability to see the land of Egypt entails the negation of the power of Amon-Re, who enlightens the land with sunlight, fertility, and wisdom every day, thereby ensuring the stability of creation with its produce that enables life, both human and animal, to live. Furthermore, the locusts will be so numerous that they will fill the houses of the Egyptians, including the house of pharaoh, and make their lives miserable.

The account of pharaoh's response to the demand of Moses and Aaron in Exodus 10:7–11 begins with a notice that pharaoh's servants already feel defeated by the power of YHWH. They ask, "How long will this be a trap for us?" and argue that pharaoh should release the Israelites to serve YHWH, insofar as Egypt has already lost the conflict with YHWH, as demonstrated in the prior plagues. Consequently, Moses and Aaron are summoned back to pharaoh, so that he may make a counteroffer. Pharaoh begins by stating that Israel may go, suggesting that he is conceding, but his follow-up question, "Who are the ones to go?," indicates a sly attempt to limit those who would be released in order to ensure that the people will return to Egypt and their status as slaves. Moses, in his response, insists that *all* the people—young and old, men, women, children, and their flocks and herds—must go to ensure the proper worship of YHWH for a festival (Hebrew, *ḥag*), generally understood as Sukkot, but in this case, the term anticipates the Festival of Passover (Hebrew, *pesaḥ*), which will commemorate Israel's release from Egyptian slavery (see esp. Exod 12–13). Pharaoh insists that Moses intends to deceive pharaoh if the children would go with them, because then they would not return to Egypt. He further insists that only the men can go to serve YHWH, thereby indicating that he will hold the old, the women, the children, and the herds and flocks hostage to ensure the return of the men. With that, pharaoh attempts to underscore his own power and authority by having Moses and Aaron expelled from his court.

Pharaoh's expulsion of Moses and Aaron sets up YHWH's next set of instructions to Moses to unleash the plague of locusts against Egypt, thereby setting up the heightened tension and drama of this particular episode. YHWH instructs Moses to hold out his hand over Egypt so that the plague of locusts will ensue and ensure that Egypt's plant life will be devoured. Moses complies with YHWH's instructions by holding out his staff in his hand, which then prompts YHWH to send the plague of locusts by means of "the east wind" (Hebrew, *rûaḥ qādîm*), the sirocco wind, known in Hebrew as the *sharav*, in Arabic as the *ḥamsin*, and in the American Southwest as the Santa Ana wind. The sirocco is caused during the turn of the dry and wet seasons when a high-pressure area forms over a desert region that lies to the east of a coastal region, thereby forcing hot desert air to reverse its normal west-to-east flow to an east-to-west flow. The result is high, dry winds that bring heat to the coastal area and fill the sky with dust and dirt that block out the sun and the moon, causing darkness during the day and a moon that appears bloodred at night.[5] The Septuagint translators, who would likely be based in Egypt and therefore more familiar with Egyptian patterns of locust plagues, render the Hebrew *rûaḥ qādîm*,"the east wind," in Greek as *ho anemos ho notos*, "the south wind," to indicate where locusts actually came from in the Egyptian ecosystem. The result was as previously stated by Moses; that is, the locusts covered the land of Egypt so that it could not be seen, and they devoured all the remaining plant life, leaving nothing for people and animals to eat.

Exodus 10:16–20 recounts pharaoh's subsequent summons of Moses and Aaron, and his confession that he had sinned before YHWH and before men. Having confessed his sin, he begs Moses and Aaron to plead to YHWH on his behalf to bring the plague to an end. Moses and Aaron comply with pharaoh's request, and YHWH then sends a west wind, which drives all the locusts into the Reed Sea, thereby freeing Egypt from the plague. But in keeping with YHWH's original statement in Exodus 10:1–2, v. 20 states that YHWH hardened pharaoh's heart once again. Pharaoh reneged on his promise to release the people of Israel, thereby setting up the circumstances of the next plague, darkness over all the land of Egypt.

Reception History

The motif of the locust plague appears again in Amos 7:1–3 in which locusts devour the crops of Judean farmers after the king's mowings,

5. See esp. Fitzgerald, *L-rd of East Wind*.

leaving them without food for the coming year. The motif of the locust plague also appears in Joel 1–2 where the armies that threaten Jerusalem are portrayed as locusts that devour everything before them.

The motif of instructing Israelite children about how YHWH unleashed the plagues against Egypt in Exodus 10:2 provides one of the textual bases for the four questions that are asked by children at the Passover Seder, the ritual meal that celebrates G-d's deliverance of Israel from Egyptian bondage. Exodus 10:2 appears to be the basic text that instructs fathers to explain the meaning of Passover to their sons. The Passover Haggadah speaks of four sons, each of whom is different, who ask about the meaning of the distinctive practices of the Passover Seder or meal.[6] The questions and answers of each son are based on a different text from the Torah or Pentateuch. The wise son who asks about the meaning of the ritual and its laws is based on Deuteronomy 6:20–24, which gives a detailed account of G-d's deliverance of Israel from Egyptian slavery in order to bring them to the promised land of Israel. The wicked son, who asks, "What does this service mean to you?," as if it has nothing to do with him, is based on Exodus 13:8, which calls upon the father to explain what G-d did "for me." The simple son, who asks, "What is this?," is based on Exodus 13:14, which simply states that G-d redeemed Israel with a mighty hand. And the son who is too young to know how to ask is based again on Exodus 13:8, which opens a midrashic discourse on what G-d did "for me" in redeeming Israel from Egyptian bondage that culminates in an exposition of Deuteronomy 26:5–8, concerning how G-d delivered our ancestor, a wandering Aramaean (Jacob) and brought his descendants to the land of Israel. This midrash is considered to be one of the oldest rabbinic midrashim known; Mishnah Pesahim 10.4 refers to it as the basis for the answer given to the son who asks his father about the rituals conducted at the Passover Seder.

In the New Testament, Revelation 9:3 refers to the plague of locusts that emerged when the fifth angel blew his trumpet and unleashed darkness and the locusts from the bottomless pit.

6. For discussion of the four sons in the Passover Seder, see Glatzer, *Passover Haggadah*, 20–41; Elias, *Haggadah*, 70–127; Tabory, *JPS Commentary on Haggadah*, 25–44.

The Plague of Darkness —Exodus 10:21–29

Translation

10:21 And YHWH said to Moses, "Extend your hand over the heavens so that there will be darkness over the land of Egypt, so that one must grope [in the] darkness." [22] And Moses extended his hand over the heavens, so that there was deep darkness over all the land of Egypt for three days. [23] And one man could not see another, and a man could not rise from his place for three days, but for all the sons of Israel, there was light in their dwellings.

[24] And pharaoh summoned Moses, and he said, "Go, serve YHWH, only your sheep and your cattle be detained. Also, your children may go with you." [25] But Moses said, "You, also, will give in our hand sacrifices and whole burnt offerings, and we will make them for YHWH, our G-d. [26] And, also, our livestock shall go with us; there shall not remain a hoof, for from it we must take to serve YHWH, our G-d. And we will not know how to serve YHWH until we come there." [27] And YHWH hardened the heart of pharaoh, and he was not willing to release them. [28] And pharaoh said to him, "Go away from me! Be careful that you will not again see my face, for on the day that you see my face, you will die!" [29] And Moses said, "So, you have spoken, not again to see your face."

Commentary

Exodus 10:21–29 presents an account of the plague of darkness. The account is generally considered to be a J-stratum narrative, but its shortened form suggests some influence from P as well as indications of an underlying E-stratum narrative.[1] The concern with darkness is especially important in relation to Egypt. It builds upon the preceding account of the locust plague, insofar as the locusts will cover the land so completely that it cannot be seen (Exod 10:15). It also polemicizes against Egypt's devotion to the sun god, Amon-Re and his variations, in an effort to demonstrate YHWH's superiority over both pharaoh, also considered a god, and Egypt's primary deity.

The account begins in Exodus 10:21–23 with the presentation of YHWH's instructions to Moses to extend his hand toward the heavens so that darkness will prevail over Egypt. The statement "so that one must grope [in the] darkness," Hebrew, *wĕyāmēš ḥōšek*, literally, "and he/one will cause to feel darkness," employs a Hiphil form of the verb root, *mšš*, to indicate groping in the dark. Verses 22–23 then present Moses's compliance with YHWH's instruction, which leaves people unable to see in the dark and therefore unable to move about for a period of three days. The three days of darkness are known in Demotic Egyptian literature, such as Setne Khamwas and Si-Osiere (Stene II), as an idiom for the work of a sorcerer who cursed Egypt with three days and three nights of darkness,[2] and in Mesopotamian literature, such as the Gilgamesh epic and the Atraḫasis epic, where darkness covered the land as the gods attacked to bring about the flood.[3] According to v. 23, the people could not see each other for three days, although the people of Israel continued to have light in their own dwellings.

Exodus 10:24–29 then presents pharaoh's second audience with Moses and Aaron in which he desperately pleads with them to appeal to YHWH to reverse the plague. Pharaoh acts treacherously here. His initial statement in v. 24 allows Israel to go to serve YHWH, but he qualifies this announcement by stipulating that Israel's livestock will be left behind, even though their children will be allowed to go. Moses will

1. See Campbell and O'Brien, *Sources of the Pentateuch*, 141; Childs, *Exodus*, 131.

2. Lichtheim, *Ancient Egyptian Literature*, 3:144.

3. Davies presents Gilgamesh 11:96–112 (*Exodus 1–18*, 1:672; see also *ANET* 94), and Lambert and Millard present Atraḫasis 3.4–14, in which a dark cloud prevented people from seeing each other (*Atraḫasi*, 92–95).

not put up with such treachery, and responds by stating that pharaoh must provide the Israelites with the livestock to be offered to YHWH; their own livestock will go with them because they will not know what must be offered to YHWH until they arrive at the place where the offerings will be made. Moses's statement presupposes that the offerings are determined only at the time when they are made to YHWH. Pharaoh is forced to accede to Moses's demand, and he petulantly orders Moses to get out, so that he will never see pharaoh's face again lest he be put to death. Moses angrily affirms pharaoh's statement by announcing that he will not see pharaoh's face again.

Reception History

In the New Testament, Revelation 16:10–11 refers to the fifth angel, who poured his bowl on the throne of the beast, which plunged the beast's throne into darkness and prompted the people to suffer from sores and to curse the G-d of heaven.

The Plague of the Death of the Firstborn—Exodus 11:1—12:36

Translation

11:1 And YHWH said to Moses, "One more plague I will bring upon pharaoh and upon Egypt. Afterward, he will release you from this [place]. When he releases you, he will surely drive you out entirely from this [place]. [2] Speak, please, in the ears of the people, so that they will request, each man from his neighbor and each woman from her neighbor vessels of silver and vessels of gold, [3] and YHWH has made a favorable impression for the people in the eyes of Egypt; moreover, the man, Moses, is very great in the land of Egypt, in the eyes of the servants of pharaoh and in the eyes of the people."

[4] And Moses said, "Thus says YHWH, 'At about midnight, I will go out in the midst of Egypt, [5] and every firstborn in the land of Egypt will die, from the firstborn of pharaoh who sits upon the throne to the firstborn of the maidservant who is behind the millstones, and all the firstborn of animals. [6] And there will be a great outcry in the land of Egypt, like it has never been and like it will never be again, [7] but for all the sons of Israel, a dog will not sharpen his tongue, for a man or an animal, so that you will know that YHWH has distinguished between Egypt and Israel. [8] And all your servants, these will come down to me, and they shall bow down to me, saying, "Get out! You and all the people who are at

your feet! And afterward, I will leave.""" And he left pharaoh in hot anger.

[9] And YHWH said to Moses, "Pharaoh will not listen to you
in order that my wonders will be many in the land of Egypt."
[10] And Moses and Aaron performed all these wonders before
pharaoh, but YHWH hardened the heart of pharaoh so that
he did not release the sons of Israel from his land.

12:1 And YHWH said to Moses and to Aaron in the land of
Egypt, saying, [2] "This month shall be for you the head of
the months, it is the first for you for the months of the year.
[3] Speak to the entire congregation of Israel, saying, 'On the
tenth of this month they shall take, each for themselves, a
lamb for the household of the father, a lamb for the household. [4] And if the household is too small for a lamb, then he
and his neighbor who is near to his household shall take,
in the calculation persons, each according to the amount he
would eat, you shall calculate for the lamb. [5] Your lamb must
be unblemished, a male, one year old, from the sheep and
from the goats you shall take.

[6] "'And there shall be for you a watch until the fourteenth
day of this month. All the assembly of the congregation of
Israel shall slaughter it between sunset and dark. [7] And they
shall take from the blood, and they shall place it upon the
two doorposts and upon the lintel upon the houses in which
they will eat it. [8] And they shall eat the meat in that night,
roasted by fire, and [with] unleavened bread together with
bitter herbs, they shall eat it. [9] You shall not eat from it raw
or boiled in water, but only roasted by fire, its head, together
with its legs, and its innards. [10] And you shall not leave [any-
thing] from it until morning, and whatever is left of it until
morning you shall burn with fire.

[11] "'And like this you shall eat it, your loins girded, your shoes
on your feet, and your staff in your hand, and you shall eat
it in haste. It is a Passover offering to YHWH. [12] And I shall
pass through in the land of Egypt on this night, and I shall
strike down every firstborn in the land of Egypt from human to animal, and against all the gods of Egypt I will pass

judgments. I am YHWH! 13 And the blood shall be a sign for you upon the houses where you are, and I will see the blood, and I will pass over you, and there shall not be among you a plague for destruction when I strike in the land of Egypt.

14 "'And this day shall be a remembrance for you, and you shall celebrate it as a festival for YHWH for your generations. [As] an eternal statute you shall celebrate it. 15 For seven days you shall eat unleavened bread; indeed, on the first day you shall remove leavened bread from your houses, because anyone who eats leavening, that person shall be cut off from Israel from the first day until the seventh day.

16 "'And on the first day there is a holy service, and on the seventh day, there is a holy service for you. No work shall you do on them. Indeed, whatever is to be eaten by each person, that alone shall be made for you. 17 And you shall observe [the Festival of] Unleavened Bread, for on that very day I brought you out with your hosts from the land of Egypt, and you shall observe that day for your generations [as] an eternal statute. 18 On the first [month], on the fourteenth day of the month in the evening, you shall eat unleavened bread until the twenty-first day of the month in the evening. 19 For seven days, unleavened bread shall not be found in your houses, for anyone who eats leavening, then that person shall be cut off from the congregation of Israel, whether resident alien or indigenous in the land. 20 No leavening shall you eat in all your dwelling places. You shall eat unleavened bread.'"

21 And Moses summoned all the elders of Israel, and he said to them, "Proceed and take for yourselves sheep for your families, and you shall slaughter the Passover offering. 22 And you shall take a bundle of hyssop, and you shall dip it in the blood, which is in the basin, and you shall smear it on the lintel and on the two doorposts from the blood that is in the basin, and you shall not go out, each from the door of his house, until morning. 23 And YHWH will pass by to plague Egypt, but he will see the blood upon the lintel and upon the two doorposts, and YHWH will pass over the door, and he will not allow the destroyer into your houses to plague [you].

24 And you shall observe this matter as statute for yourself forever. 25 And it will be that when you enter the land which YHWH will give to you just as he said, then you will observe this service. 26 And it shall be when your sons say to you, 'What is this service to you?' 27 then you shall say, 'It is a Passover sacrifice for YHWH when he passed over the houses of the sons of Israel in Egypt when he plagued Egypt, but our houses he delivered.'" And the people knelt and they bowed down. 28 And the sons of Israel went, and they did just as YHWH commanded Moses and Aaron, so they did.

29 And it came to pass in the middle of the night that YHWH struck down all the firstborn in the land of Egypt, from the firstborn of pharaoh who sits upon his throne to the firstborn of the captive who is in the house of the pit, and all the firstborn of [the] animals. 30 And pharaoh arose in that night, and all his servants, and all Egypt, for there was no house where there was no one dead. 31 And he summoned Moses and Aaron at night, and he said, "Arise, get out from the midst of my people, both you and the sons of Israel, and go! Serve YHWH as you have said. 32 Also your sheep and your cattle. Take [them], just as you have said, and you will even bless me."

33 And Egypt forced the people to hurry to release them from the land, because they said, "All of us are dead." 34 And the people carried their unfermented dough before it was leavened with their leavening, bound up in their cloaks on their shoulders, 35 and the sons of Israel acted according to the word of Moses, and they requested from Egypt vessels of silver and vessels of gold and garments. 36 And YHWH granted favor for the people in the eyes of the Egypt, and they asked them, and they despoiled Egypt.

Commentary

Exodus 11:1—12:36 presents the account of the tenth plague, the death of the firstborn sons of humans and animals in Egypt and the deliverance of the firstborn sons of Israel. The passage is demarcated at the outset in

Exodus 11:1 by the notice of YHWH's speech to Moses to announce the plague of the firstborn in Exodus 11:1–10, and it continues through the accounts of the instructions for the observance of the Festival of Passover in Exodus 12:1–28 and the fulfillment of the tenth plague in Exodus 12:29–36. The itinerary formula in Exodus 12:27, "and the sons of Israel travelled from Rameses to Sukkoth as six hundred thousand men on foot, apart from children," introduces the next major textual unit of the book of Exodus concerning the first stage of Israel's departure from Egypt.

Interpreters have been generally confused concerning the interrelationship of the accounts of the death of the firstborn in Exodus 11:1–10 and 12:29–36 and the instructions concerning the observance of the Festival of Passover in Exodus 12:1–28, largely because they view the plague of the firstborn as a separate concern from the instruction concerning Passover. For the most part, they ignore the structural role of the itinerary formulas in Genesis–Numbers, identified by F. M. Cross, which introduces the secondary narrative episodes within the larger narrative units defined by the toledoth ("generations") formula in the Pentateuch.[1] Thus, the toledoth formula in Genesis 37:2, "These are the generations of Jacob," introduces the major narrative account of Joseph and his twelve sons in Genesis 37:2—Numbers 2:34, which recounts how Joseph came to Egypt, followed by his father and brothers, to be enslaved by Egypt and delivered by YHWH. Within Genesis 37:2—Numbers 2:34, Joseph, his father, and his brothers arrived in Egypt in Genesis 37:2—50:26, were enslaved in the city of Rameses in Exodus 1:1—12:36, journeyed from Rameses to Sukkoth in Exodus 12:37—13:19, journeyed from Sukkoth to Etam in Exodus 13:20–22, from Etam to the Red (Reed) Sea in Exodus 14:1—15:21, from the Reed Sea to the Wilderness of Shur/Elim in Exodus 15:22–27, from Elim to the Wilderness of Sin in Exodus 16:1–36, from Sin to Rephidim in Exodus 17:1—18:27, and from Rephidim to Sinai in Exodus 19:1—Numbers 2:34. Following Israel's departure from Sinai, the narrative shifts to "the generations of Moses and Aaron" in Numbers 3:1—Deuteronomy 34:12, which includes its own set of itinerary formulas as Israel journeys from Sinai to Moab prior to entering the promised land of Israel in the book of Joshua.

Unfortunately, most interpreters have failed to consider the interrelationship between the firstborn and the instructions for observing Passover in Exodus 11:1—12:36, i.e., why should these two concerns

1. Cross, "Priestly Work"; see also Sweeney, *Pentateuch*, xvii–xxix, 1–27, 29–34; Sweeney, *Tanak*, 45–53.

be grouped together within one major narrative unit?[2] Most consider the combination to be the result of redactional or editorial activity by either J-stratum or P-stratum authors without explaining why an editor would want to associate these two seemingly different concerns. The death of the firstborn is the culmination or "crowning" episode of the plague narratives,[3] whereas the instructions concerning Passover constitute nothing more than ritual instruction. The two concerns were lumped together by editors who didn't think very much about what they were doing.

But the combination of concern with the firstborn and instruction concerning the observance of Passover is quite intentional.[4] Interpreters must ask: Why were the firstborn of Israel saved from the plague against Egypt? The fact of the matter is that the firstborn of Israel, including both the firstborn sons and the firstborn animals, were intended for ritual functions, i.e., the firstborn sons of Israel were intended to serve as holy leaders for their families in the celebration of holy festivals for YHWH, and the firstborn animals were to serve as the holy offerings to YHWH on those festivals.

The interrelationship between the firstborn sons of Israel and the firstborn animals of Israel is made clear in the laws stated in Exodus 22:28–29 and Exodus 34:19–20:

> Your fullness [produce] and your juice [grape and olive] you shall not withhold. The firstborn of your sons you shall give to me. Thus you shall do for your bull, for your sheep: seven days it shall be with its mother, on the eighth day, you shall give it to me. (Exod 22:28–29)

> All that breaks the womb is mine, and all your livestock that produce a male breaking [the womb], bull or lamb. But the breaking [of the womb] of an ass you shall redeem with a lamb, and if you do not redeem it, you shall break its neck. All the firstborn of your sons, you shall redeem. And you shall not appear before me empty handed. (Exod 34:19–20)

2. E.g., Coats, who defines the unit as Exodus 11:1—12:36, but does not ask about the interrelationship between the firstborn plague and the observance of Passover in the text (*Exodus 1–18*, 79–89).

3. E.g., Beer, *Exodus*, 45–59.

4. Sweeney, "Literary-Historical Dimensions of Intertexuality."

Both of these laws provide legal instruction on offerings due to YHWH. Exodus 22:28–29 is a legal instruction from the Covenant Code in Exodus 20–24, which apparently was the law code of the Northern Kingdom of Israel. It specifies what is due to YHWH, i.e., the first produce from the field and the first wine and oil from the fruit trees, the firstborn sons from the mother, and the firstborn cattle and sheep (and goats). The instruction does not state what to do with each of these firstfruits or firstborn. From the final statement of the instruction, one might assume that they are to be offered to YHWH. The firstfruits of produce and juice, whether wine or olive oil, and the firstborn of cattle and flock may be offered in whole to YHWH on the altar or eaten by the priesthood who serve YHWH. But the firstborn of human sons are not likely to be eaten. There is speculation that this law presupposes some earlier practice of child sacrifice, but there is no evidence that ancient Israel ever engaged in child sacrifice, although the Moabites are charged with such practice. If the firstborn sons of their mothers are to be given to YHWH, what will YHWH do with them?

Similar questions arise with Exodus 34:19–20, which appears to be a revised law code, perhaps written in Judah by the J-stratum authors, that helps to explain unclear elements of the Covenant Code. The firstborn of the cattle or flock may likewise be offered to YHWH to be sacrificed in whole on the altar or used to support the priests. The firstborn of an ass may be redeemed with a lamb, which likewise might be used as a sacrifice or to support the priests, and the firstborn son of a human mother may likewise be redeemed with a lamb to be used for the same purposes.

But the next question to be asked is, who are the priests? Interpreters assume that the tribe of Levites will serve as the priesthood of Israel, but from a narrative standpoint, this remains an open question. Yes, the Levites will serve as priests, but this service is not commissioned in the pentateuchal narrative until Numbers 17–18 when Aaron and the tribe of Levi are chosen to serve as YHWH's priests. Prior to that time, the narratives in Numbers 3:1–13, 40–51, and 8:5–19 have YHWH state three times that past practice had called for the firstborn sons of Israel to serve as priests to assist Aaron. In the future, however, the tribe of Levi would serve in this sacred role, which is then finalized in Numbers 17–18.

The major example of this role appears in Samuel ben Elkanah of the tribe of Ephraim as portrayed in 1 Samuel 1–3.[5] Elkanah had two

5. Sweeney, "Samuel's Institutional Identity"; Sweeney, *1–2 Samuel*, 26–40.

wives, Hannah and Peninah. Although he loved Hannah, she did not bear children, but Peninah bore many, causing tension in the family. When Hannah prayed to YHWH at the sanctuary at Shiloh in northern Israel, the high priest, Eli, thought she was drunk and reprimanded her. But YHWH heard her prayer and her vow to give her son to YHWH, and YHWH granted her a son, Samuel, as the first of many children. Although Samuel was born to an Ephraimite father, he was sent to Shiloh to be raised by Eli and to function as priest and prophet in Israel through 1 Samuel 28.

We may also note that northern Israelite prophets, such as Elijah and Elisha, also served in priestly capacities. Elijah built an altar to YHWH to celebrate Sukkot and the onset of rain in the fall as part of his confrontation with the prophets of Baal in 1 Kings 18 to demonstrate who was truly the G-d of Israel, and Elisha called for musical accompaniment, a function of temple priests, when he was asked to give oracles by the king of Israel while on campaign with the kings of Judah and Edom against Moab in 2 Kings 3.[6] Northern Israelite prophets tended to function in roles normally assigned to priests, and northern Israel's first king, Jeroboam ben Nebat, was charged with allowing non-Levites to serve as priests, along with other infractions in 1 Kings 12:25—13:34. Although Jeroboam ben Nebat appears to be an apostate king in the Kings narrative, it appears that he would have understood himself to be acting in accordance with YHWH's expectations, i.e., northern Israel had different sets of practices from southern Judah.[7] One of them was the use of firstborn sons in priestly roles, whereas Judah relied on the tribe of Levi.

In the end, the accounts of the plague of the firstborn in Exodus 11:1–10 and 12:29–36 encase the instructions concerning the observance of Passover in Exodus 12:1–28 to provide an editorial envelope to identify the firstborn sons of Israel, who are committed to YHWH's holy service in order to carry out the observance of Passover in ancient Israel. The prevalence of the use of firstborn sons as a form of priesthood is characteristic of northern Israel, and indicates a narrative that was originally composed as part of the E-stratum of the Pentateuch and updated by the J- and P-strata of the pentateuchal narrative.[8]

Interpreters have noted that the account of the plague against the firstborn in Exodus 11:1–10 is closely tied to the account of the plague of

6. Sweeney, "Prophets and Priests."

7. Sweeney, *1–2 Kings*, 172–82; Sweeney, *Reading the Bible After the Shoah*, 67–72.

8. Cf. Campbell and O'Brien, *Sources of the Pentateuch*, 39–40, 141–42.

darkness in Exodus 10:21–29, insofar as the death of the firstborn takes place at night. It is also evident from Exodus 11:8 that Moses had not yet departed from the court of pharaoh. The account stresses the increasingly tense relationship between Moses and pharaoh in that pharaoh had told Moses that he would never see pharaoh's face again lest he die, and Moses had angrily affirmed that statement in Exodus 10:29. The account of the firstborn also emphasizes that Moses's reputation had risen greatly among the Egyptians, apparently because YHWH was demonstrating greater power than pharaoh and thereby winning the battle between the two deities for control of the universe. The portrayal of YHWH's address to Moses in Exodus 11:1–3 indicates YHWH's instructions concerning the despoliation of the Egyptians. The combat motif is thereby accentuated by the fact that the Egyptians were well disposed to grant the request of the people of Israel for vessels of silver and gold. The translation of the Hebrew word *wayiš'ălû* as "and they shall borrow" or "and they shall request" does not accurately represent the transaction.[9] Interpreters who employ these translations sometimes characterize the transaction as robbery, but more recent semantic study of the verb indicates that it means "and they shall demand."[10] Such a meaning is consistent with the combat motif in that the people of Israel are configured as YHWH's army, and YHWH is then understood to assume the role of a victorious monarch in war who has defeated his adversary and demands tribute from him. Such practice was common in the ancient Near Eastern world, especially as demonstrated by the Assyrian *palu* campaigns of the eighth century BCE in which the Assyrian king would assemble his army following the reaping of the spring harvest to march through his empire in order to collect the annual tribute from his subjugated vassals.[11]

The account of Moses's announcement, apparently to pharaoh, in Exodus 11:4–8 is presented as prophetic messenger speech as indicated by the messenger formula, "Thus says YHWH," in v. 4.[12] The life setting of the messenger speech and formula apparently originates in diplomatic message exchange between kings, leaders, and nations, such as the communication of Abraham's senior servant, presumably Eliezer, with Laban ben Bethuel of Padan Aram to negotiate with him for his sister, Rebekah bat Bethuel, to become the wife of his son, Isaac.

9. "*rōḥab*," BDB 981–82.

10. *HALOT* 4:1371–74.

11. Tadmor, "Campaigns of Sargon II."

12. Sweeney, *Isaiah 1–39*, 524, 546.

Another key example is the role of the Rab Shakeh, "chief cupbearer," of Sennacherib, king of Assyria, who was sent to negotiate the surrender of Jerusalem with King Hezekiah ben Amoz of Judah in Isaiah 36–37 and 2 Kings 18–19. In the present narrative, Moses as prophet acts as the diplomatic messenger of YHWH, king of the universe.

Moses informs pharaoh that, during the middle of the night, YHWH will go out among the Egyptians to kill all the firstborn of Egypt, both human and animal, from the one who sits on the throne, i.e., pharaoh, to the maidservant who sits behind the millstones. This refers to the role of maidservants who are tasked with the grinding of grain in which wheat, barley, and other grain stalks are crushed by millstones, which roll over the grain, crushing the stalks, and thereby separating the chaff from the grain when the crushed stalks are cast up into the breeze, allowing the heavier grain to drop as the chaff blows away.[13] But YHWH's message through Moses also emphasizes that YHWH will protect Israel from the plague so that "a dog will not sharpen his tongue," an idiom which means "a dog will not utter a sound" in warning as YHWH approaches. The purpose of this action is to demonstrate to pharaoh and to all Egypt that YHWH has done this and that pharaoh and all Egypt will then bow in homage to YHWH to acknowledge YHWH as the true king of all creation. Such acknowledgment will then prompt them to bow down to YHWH and demand that YHWH and all who follow YHWH to depart from Egypt. In the end, Moses departs from pharaoh in hot anger.

The third account of YHWH's instructions to Moses and Aaron in Exodus 11:9–10 concerning the death of the firstborn reiterates YHWH's view that pharaoh will not listen to them, thereby enabling YHWH's wonders to be multiplied throughout the land of Egypt as YHWH hardens pharaoh's heart once again.

Exodus 12:1–28 presents the account of YHWH's instructions to Moses and Aaron concerning the observance of the Festivals of Passover and Matzot (Unleavened Bread), which constitutes the second major sub-unit of Exodus 11:1—12:36. The passage is generally considered to be a P-stratum composition, although J-stratum materials appear in Exodus 12:21–23, 27b.[14] The basis for this assessment is the appearance of language that apparently derives from the Holiness Code in Leviticus 16–26. A second set of instructions concerning the observance of

13. Toorn, "Mill, Millstones"; cf. Richardson, "Mill, Millstone," which depicts an Egyptian woman grinding grain behind a millstone; Davies, *Exodus 1–18*, 2:15.

14. Campbell and O'Brien, *Sources of the Pentateuch*, 39–40, 142.

Passover and Matzot will appear in Exodus 13:1–16. Although most see Exodus 13:1–16 as a non-source text, there are indications that it may be an E-stratum composition.[15]

The account of YHWH's instructions concerning the observance of Passover and Matzot appears in Exodus 12:1–20, and the account of Moses's instructions to the elders of the people appears in Exodus 12:21–27. A notice concerning the compliance of the people with both sets of instructions appears in Exodus 12:28.

The account of YHWH's instructions concerning the observance of Passover and Matzot begins with the narrative formula in v. 1, and then YHWH's instruction speech to Moses and Aaron follows in vv. 2–20.

The first part of YHWH's instruction speech in Exodus 12:2–15 focuses on the observance of Passover, insofar as they take up the Passover meat offerings and the treatment of their blood. The treatment of blood is a special concern of the Holiness Code in Leviticus 16–26, especially in Leviticus 16–17.

YHWH's instructions in Exodus 12:2–10 focus on the date and treatment of the Passover offering. The date is established in vv. 2–3 as the first month of the year, viz., the month of Nisan in later calendars, also known as the month of Aviv in earlier calendars. The observance begins on the tenth of the month, prior to the offering on the fourteenth of the month, so that a lamb (Hebrew, *śeh*), whether sheep or goat, may be selected and watched or guarded for three days to ensure that it qualifies as an unblemished animal that can be offered for the holiday. The animal selected will serve as the offering of an ancestral house, Hebrew, *bêt-ʾābōt*, literally, "house of the fathers," which is a term known from P-stratum texts from the Persian periods to refer to an extended family. The instructions advise that the animal selected should be sufficient to feed the ancestral house, but they are also aware that such a house may be too small to consume the entire animal in one night. Consequently, they advise smaller ancestral houses to combine with other smaller houses so that the animal will be sufficient for members of the extended family households.

The qualifications for the animal include that it be male, insofar as females produce new life; "without blemish," insofar as diseased or injured animals are not used for the Passover offering; that it be one year old, insofar as it is to be born at the outset of the year following the last

15. Campbell and O'Brien, *Sources of the Pentateuch*, 198.

Passover; and that it may be either a sheep or goat, insofar as both types of animals were herded by Israelite and Judean shepherds in antiquity. The slaughter of the sacrificial animals takes place "between the evening" (i.e., between sunset and the onset of full darkness) on the fourteenth day of the first month, which marks the beginning of the one-day observance of Passover. Because Passover is both a family household and temple celebration, some of the blood of the sacrificial animal will be smeared on the lintel and the two doorposts of the family house to symbolize YHWH's protection of Israel during the plague of the firstborn, insofar as YHWH will pass by such marked houses and go on to the Egyptian houses to slay the firstborn. The family then eats the Passover offering during the night in their home. The animal is to be roasted over the fire and eaten with matzot (unleavened bread) and bitter herbs, which are generally understood to be bitter-tasting vegetables, such as wild romaine lettuce, bitter radishes, and other bitter vegetation. The animal is not to be eaten raw or boiled, and it should be roasted over the fire with its head, legs, and entrails intact, in an effort to replicate how seminomadic desert-dwellers would have cooked meat. The family is expected to eat the entire animal during the night, but if anything is left over, it is to be burned in fire the next morning.

Exodus 12:11–13 specifies that the family members who eat the Passover offering be dressed for hurried travel, to symbolize the haste in which Israel departed Egypt, apparently for fear that pharaoh might renege on his promise to release them as he had done repeatedly before and in fact would do once again. The people are to travel with their loins girded, that is, some sort of pants or underclothing is to be worn beneath the outer cloak with a belt to hold everything in place. Shoes are to be worn; although sandals are the typical footwear of the time, other forms of footwear must be considered because it gets cold and wet in western Asia and northeastern Africa during the wintertime. And the people are to carry their staffs in their hands. Ezekiel dresses like this when he prepares to march off into exile, in order to symbolize that his exile to Babylonia is a reversal of the exodus from Egypt (Ezek 12).[16] YHWH reiterates the intention to slay the firstborn of Egypt, and YHWH's statements indicate the purpose to punish all the gods of Egypt, which of course would include pharaoh. The blood on the lintel and doorposts of the Israelite houses informs YHWH to pass by their

16. Sweeney, "Ezekiel's Conceptualization of the Exile"; Sweeney, *Reading Ezekiel*, 69–73.

houses and to move on to Egyptian houses instead, in accordance with the intention to strike down the firstborn of Egypt.

Exodus 12:14–15 reiterates the character of the full holiday, including both Pesach (Passover) and Matzot (Unleavened Bread). The specification of the seven-day observance of the holiday indicates that it functions as a New Year's festival much like Rosh ha-Shanah, Yom Kippur, and the seven-day observance of Sukkot in the seventh month of Tishri. YHWH's statements also indicate that the observance of the holiday is mandatory; anyone who neglects to observe the Passover and Matzot requirement to eat only unleavened bread for the required seven days will be cut off from Israel.

YHWH's instruction speech turns to the observance of the Festival of Matzot, "Unleavened Bread," in Exodus 12:16–20. Passover and Matzot are typically treated as two distinct but interrelated observances in the festival calendars in Leviticus 23:4–8 as well as in Deuteronomy 16:1–8 and Numbers 28:16–25. The Covenant Code in Exodus 23:15 mentions only Matzot. The revised J-stratum code in Exodus 34 refers to Matzot as a holiday in Exodus 34:18 as well as the firstborn in Exodus 34:19, but the Passover offering is mentioned only later in Exodus 34:25. YHWH's speech explains the significance of the festival in relation to the deliverance of Israel from Egypt, although it is noteworthy that YHWH describes Israel in military terms as "your hosts" (Hebrew, *ʾet-ṣibʾōtêkem*), in keeping with the motif of divine combat between YHWH and pharaoh in the exodus narrative and the understanding that Israel constitutes YHWH's army, much like that of an ancient Near Eastern suzerain king. In addition, YHWH states that the festival must be considered as "an eternal statute" (Hebrew, *ḥuqqat ʿôlām*), which would constitute the decree of a suzerain king who rules all of creation. YHWH's instructions specify the dates for Matzot as the fourteenth through the twenty-first days of the first month of the year, and they state that anyone who eats leavened bread during this period, whether they are resident alien or indigenous to Israel, will be cut off from the nation.

Exodus 12:21–27 presents Moses's instruction speech to the elders of Israel to comply with the instructions given to him by YHWH to observe Passover and Matzot. The instructions are basic in that they call upon the elders to take lambs for their families to be used as Passover offerings, specifically to use the blood of these lambs to smear upon the lintels and doorposts of their home to protect them during YHWH's plague against the firstborn of Egypt. The procedure for smearing blood is specified by instructing them to use a bunch of hyssop (Hebrew, *ʾēzôb*), an aromatic shrub of the mint family that was known for its healing properties, especially in relation to cough and stomach disorders. The hyssop is to be dipped in the blood of the Passover lamb that has been collected in a basin and then used to smear the blood on the lintel and doorposts of the house to signal to YHWH that it is an Israelite house. Moses then instructs the people not to go outside until morning, presuming that such an act would be lethal. In his description of YHWH's actions during the plague, Moses describes YHWH seeing the blood on the Israelite homes so that YHWH will pass by the house and not allow "the destroyer" (Hebrew, *hamašḥît*) to enter the home and to strike down a firstborn son there. This statement gives rise to the belief that "the destroyer" is an angel or demon that acts on behalf of YHWH (cf. Isa 37:36; 2 Kgs 19:35).

Moses's speech to the elders continues in Exodus 12:24–27 with a statement that this instruction is "an eternal statute" (Hebrew, *ḥoq-lěkā ûlěbāneykā ʿad-ʿôlām*, "a statute for you and for your sons until eternity"). Consequently, future generations are to be taught about the Passover ritual. When their sons ask, "What is this service to you?" the fathers are to explain how YHWH passed over the Israelite houses in Egypt and struck down the Egyptian firstborn, thereby saving Israel. The people bowed down to YHWH in response.

Exodus 12:28 concludes the accounts of the instruction speeches by YHWH and by Moses with a statement of Israel's compliance with the instructions.

Exodus 12:29–36 concludes the account of the plague of the firstborn with an account of how YHWH carried out the plague of the firstborn against Egypt. The result is an envelope literary structure in which accounts of the firstborn plague in Exodus 11:10 introduce the account of the observance of Passover in Exodus 12:1–28 and conclude it in Exodus 12:29–36. Most interpreters understand Exodus 12:29–36 to be a J-stratum composition, which presupposes the J-stratum revised law code in Exodus 34.[17] The redactional association between the plague of the firstborn and the observance of Passover and Matzot makes it clear that firstborn Israelites are offered to YHWH so that they may officiate in holy service at Passover and at other times.

Exodus 12:29–36 makes it clear that YHWH struck down the Egyptian firstborn at night, thereby prompting pharaoh to awake in the

17. Campbell and O'Brien, *Sources of the Pentateuch*, 142.

middle of the night together with all his servants and all the people of Egypt to recognize what had happened to mourn for their dead. In his anger, pharaoh summons Moses and Aaron and orders them to get out of Egypt to worship YHWH as they had previously stated that they would do and to take their flocks and herds with them. Pharaoh's final statement that perhaps Moses and Aaron would bless him acknowledges their power and that of YHWH.

The people of Egypt likewise strongly call for Israel to get out of Egypt because they now fear for their own lives. The Israelites apparently recognize the Egyptians' urgency in this matter and realize that their own lives might be at stake as well, not to mention the repeatedly demonstrated duplicity of pharaoh. Consequently, the Israelites take their unfermented dough, wrapped in cloaks on their shoulders, prepared to depart as soon as possible before the situation changes. Before they leave, however, the Israelites demand vessels of silver and gold from the Egyptians, who readily give them these items because they now recognize YHWH's power as the true sovereign of creation.

The travel itinerary formula in Exodus 12:37, "and the sons of Israel journeyed from Rameses to Sukkot," marks the beginning of a new narrative unit in Exodus 12:37—13:19.

Reception History

Motifs from the plague of the firstborn appear already in the prophetic literature of the Hebrew Bible. Prophetic texts, such as Isaiah 30, which anticipates a nighttime festival celebration in v. 29 that will result in YHWH's deliverance of Jerusalem/Zion from Egypt, and Jeremiah 9:20, which portrays death as a demon climbing through the window to kill babies outside and young men, illustrate aspects of YHWH's plague against the firstborn in Egypt. Likewise, the account of the destruction of 185,000 Assyrian troops from the invading army of King Sennacherib of Assyria in Isaiah 37:36 and 2 Kings 19:35 by YHWH's angel of death demonstrates the application of the Exodus motif of the plague of the firstborn to the later scenario of Sennacherib's invasion of Judah in 701 BCE.

The plague of the firstborn figures prominently as the tenth of the ten plagues unleashed against Egypt by G-d in the Passover Haggadah. During the Passover Seder, Jews spill ten drops of wine, one for each of the plagues, in recognition of the suffering of the Egyptians as portrayed in the exodus narrative. Indeed, the instruction for fathers to teach their sons the meaning of the distinctive Passover rituals, as portrayed in Exodus 12:24–27, also plays a role in the Passover Seder. In the portion of the Seder devoted to the four questions as to why this night is different from other nights, the parents answer the wicked child's question, which is quoted directly from Exodus 12:26, "What is this service to you?" (understood to mean "to you," and "not to us," insofar as the child sees no importance of this observance to him or her). The retelling of the G-d's deliverance of Israel from Egyptian bondage then proceeds in answer to the four questions asked by the children of the family.[18]

The Christian New Testament takes up the issue of the plague of the firstborn. The portrayal of Jesus's crucifixion and subsequent rising on the third day is based in large measure on the treatment of the Passover lamb in Exodus 12:1–10 in which the lamb is watched for three days and then offered to YHWH as part of the process to deliver Israel. The Gospel accounts of Jesus's crucifixion in Mark 14–16, Matthew 26–28, Luke 22–24, and John 18–20 envision Jesus's arrest and interrogation and a three-day period prior to his crucifixion during Passover and recognition that he had risen on the following Sunday morning (the first day of the week).

First Corinthians 5:7 cites the instruction concerning the clearing out of leaven for new unleavened bread in relation to the role of Christ as an expression of the sacrifice of the Passover lamb in Exodus 12:18–23. Hebrews 11:28 cites the Passover account of Exodus 12:12–13 concerning the smearing of blood on the doors of the Israelite homes so that the destroyer would pass by them as part of its recounting of G-d's saving actions and its exemplification of faith.

In American history, the motif of deliverance in the morning following a night of danger appears in "The Star-Spangled Banner," the national anthem of the United States of America. The lyrics to "The Star-Spangled Banner" were written by Francis Scott Key on the morning of September 14, 1814, during the War of 1812, following the overnight bombardment of Fort McHenry, which guarded Baltimore Harbor, on the night of September 13–14, 1814. Key and several associates who had come to the British to secure the release of Dr. William Beanes, who had been arrested by the British, were detained aboard a thirty-eight-gun frigate, HMS *Surprise*, because the Americans had overheard British

18. Tabory, *JPS Commentary on Haggadah*, 39–45; Glatzer, *Passover Haggadah*, 10–43; Elias, *Haggadah*, 70–135.

plans for the assault. Following the savage, but unsuccessful, bombardment of the fort by the Royal Navy, the fort lowered its tattered storm flag, which had been flown during the bombardment and survived, and raised the oversized fifteen-star and fifteen-stripe American flag that was employed for reveille every morning. The approximately one thousand–man American garrison suffered only four dead and twenty-four wounded. The morning raising of the American flag signaled that the American garrison was intact and prepared to repel the British invasion force. After witnessing the raising of the American flag, the British made their decision to withdraw, and Key wrote the poem "The Defense of Fort M'Henry," which would eventually become the lyrics for "The Star-Spangled Banner," on the back of an envelope. The British released Key and his party on September 16, 1814. "The Star-Spangled Banner" was officially adopted as the national anthem of the United States of America on March 3, 1931.

The lyrics of the first stanza of "The Star-Spangled Banner," with Scott's original punctuation and spelling, read as follows:

O say can you see by the dawn's early light,
What so proudly we hail'd at the twilight's last gleaming,
Whose broad stripes and bright stars through the perilous fight
O'er the ramparts we watched, were so gallantly streaming?
And the rocket's red glare, the bomb bursting in air,
Gave proof through the night that our flag was still there,
O say does that star-spangled banner yet wave,
O'er the land of the free and the home of the brave?

HMS *Surprise*, an earlier frigate, captured from the French, which served in the Royal Navy from 1796 to 1802, is featured in the 2003 film *Master and Commander*, starring Russell Crowe and Paul Bettany, and the twenty novels written by Patrick O'Brien concerning the Napoleonic wars.

The Journey from Rameses to Sukkot—Exodus 12:37—13:19

Translation

12:37 And the sons of Israel journeyed from Rameses to Sukkot, as about six hundred thousand men on foot, apart from the children. 38 And also a great mixed company went up with them, and sheep and cattle, very much livestock. 39 And they baked the dough that they brought out from Egypt as unleavened cakes for there was no leavening because they were driven out from Egypt, and they were not able to delay, and even a provision of food they did not make for themselves.

40 And the [time of] settlement that the sons of Israel stayed in Egypt was 430 years, 41 and it was at the end of 430 years, and it was on that same day [that] all the hosts of YHWH went out from Egypt. 42 It was a night of watching for YHWH to bring them out from the land of Egypt; it was that night of watching for YHWH for all the sons of Israel for their generations.

43 And YHWH said to Moses and Aaron, "This is the statute of the Passover offering, no foreigner shall eat it. 44 But any slave of a man bought with silver, and you have circumcised him, then he shall eat it. 45 A temporary resident alien and a hired man shall not eat it. 46 In one house it shall be eaten. You shall not bring any meat out from the house, and bone of it you shall not break. 47 All the congregation of Israel shall

do it. [48] And if a resident alien resides with you and makes
the Passover offering for YHWH, circumcise him and every
male, and then he will come near to do it, and he will be
indigenous to the land, but all who are uncircumcised shall
not eat it. [49] One instruction there shall be for the indigenous
and for the resident alien who resides in your midst."

[50] And all the sons of Israel did just as YHWH commanded
Moses and Aaron, so they did. [51] And it was on that same day
that YHWH brought out the sons of Israel from the land of
Egypt according to their hosts.

13:1 And YHWH spoke to Moses, saying, [2] "Sanctify to me
every firstborn; whatever breaks any womb among the sons
of Israel, human and animal, is mine."

[3] And Moses said to the people, "Remember this day, when
you came out from Egypt, from the house of slavery, because
with a strong hand YHWH brought you out from this, and no
leavening shall be eaten. [4] Today you go out in the month of
Aviv. [5] And it shall be that YHWH will bring you to the land
of the Canaanites and the Hittites and the Amorites and the
Hivvites and the Jebusites, which he swore to your fathers to
give to you, a land flowing with milk and honey, and you will
perform this service in this month.

[6] "Seven days you shall eat unleavened bread, and on the seventh day is a festival for YHWH. [7] Unleavened bread shall be
eaten for seven days, and no leavening will be seen for you,
and no yeast will be seen for you in all your borders. [8] And
you shall declare to your son in that day, saying, 'It is because
of this that YHWH did for me when I came out from Egypt.'

[9] "And this shall be to you for a sign upon your hand and for
remembrances between your eyes in order that the instruction of YHWH shall be in your mouth, for with a strong hand
YHWH brought you out from Egypt. [10] And you shall observe
this statute at its appointed time from days to days.

[11] "And it will be when YHWH brings you out to the land of
the Canaanites just as he swore to you and to your fathers
and he has given it to you, [12] then you shall transfer all that

breaks the womb to YHWH, and all that breaks, dropping a male, among your animals, is for YHWH. [13] And every breaking of an ass you shall redeem with a sheep, and if you do not redeem it, you shall break its neck, and every firstborn human among your sons you shall redeem. [14] And it shall be if your son asks you tomorrow, saying, 'What is this?' then you shall say to him, 'With a strong hand YHWH brought us out from Egypt, from the house of slavery, [15] and it was that pharaoh refused to release us, that YHWH killed every firstborn human and animal. Therefore, I sacrifice to YHWH every male that breaks the womb, but every firstborn of my sons, I redeem. [16] And it shall be a sign upon your hand and frontlets between your eyes for with a strong hand, YHWH brought us out from Egypt.'"

[17] And it was when pharaoh released the people, G-d did not lead them by the road to the land of the Philistines that was near, but G-d said, "Lest the people are sorry when they see war, and they return to Egypt." [18] And G-d turned the people to the road to the wilderness of the Reed Sea, and the sons of Israel went up armed from the land of Egypt. [19] And Moses took the bones of Joseph with him because he had surely made the sons of Israel swear, saying, "G-d will surely pay attention to you, and so you will bring up my bones with you from this [place]."

Commentary

Exodus 12:37—13:19 recounts Israel's journey from Rameses to Sukkot, and it includes further instruction on the celebration of Passover. The passage is demarcated at the outset in Exodus 12:37 by an example of the itinerary formula,[1] which notes Israel's journey from Rameses, one of the store cities of Egypt where the people were enslaved, to Sukkot, which is located in the eastern portion of Egypt where it provides access to the Sinai wilderness. Exodus 13:20 employs another example of the itinerary formula to recount Israel's journey from Sukkot to Etham, and it therefore introduces the next major unit of the narrative in Exodus 13:20—15:21.

1. Coats, *Exodus 1–18*, 164; Cross, "Priestly Work."

As noted above, Rameses is identified with Piramesse, i.e., Khatana-Qontir, located in the northeast Delta on the east bank of the Pelusaic arm of the Nile River.[2] Sukkot (Succoth) is also located in the northeastern Delta, where it is identified with Tell el-Maskhuta, located some fifteen kilometers west of modern Ismailiya, near Lake Timsah in the Wadi Tumilat. Scholars maintain that the Hebrew name Sukkot, "booths," may be a Hebrew rendition of the Egyptian name *Tjeku* (*tkw*), which is identified with Tell el-Mashuta.[3] The Egyptian papyrus Anastasi V states that an Egyptian officer in pursuit of runaway slaves travelled from the royal palace, presumed to be in Rameses, to Tjeku in one day.[4]

Exodus 12:37—13:19 appears to presuppose a full range of sources. Exodus 12:37–39 is generally identified as a J-stratum text,[5] whereas Exodus 12:40–51 is generally identified as a P-stratum text.[6] Exodus 13:1–16 is generally identified as a non-source text,[7] and Exodus 13:17–19 is generally identified as an E-stratum text.[8]

Exodus 12:37–39 focuses specifically on the journey from Rameses to Sukkot, and numbers the Israelites as about 600,000 men, without including the numbers of women, who remain unmentioned, and children. This figure corresponds generally to the exact figures, 603,550, excluding the Levites, in Numbers 1:46 (see Num 3–4 for the census of the Levites) and 601,730, given in Numbers 26:51. The approximate number given in Exodus 12:37 appears to presuppose the two exact numbers given in Numbers, which cannot be reconciled. Verse 38 notes that a mixed multitude of persons, apparently Egyptians and persons born of mixed marriages or relationships (cf. Lev 24:10–23), would result from the reality of such relationships in the ancient world and their affinities with the people of Israel.[9] Verse 39 focuses on the rushed departure of the people of Israel, which compelled them to take unleavened dough out of Egypt to support themselves rather than wait for leavened dough,

2. Wente, "Rameses."

3. J. Seely, "Succoth."

4. *ANET* 259.

5. Campbell and O'Brien, *Sources of the Pentateuch*, 142.

6. Campbell and O'Brien, *Sources of the Pentateuch*, 39–40.

7. Campbell and O'Brien, *Sources of the Pentateuch*, 198.

8. Campbell and O'Brien, *Sources of the Pentateuch*, 185.

9. Rabbinic tradition holds that one born to a Jewish mother is considered Jewish, because the father cannot always be identified. For discussion, see Schiffman, *Who Was a Jew?*

which would rise while baking. Pharaoh's past record of changing his mind is the source of the threat to Israel, and they were not going to wait around to see if pharaoh would change his mind once again. As the later confrontation at the Reed Sea indicates, he did indeed change his mind. We may note that this scenario then plays a key role in the practice of eating only matzah (i.e., unleavened bread) at Passover, and not leavened bread. It also explains the origins of Israelite and Judean sacrificial practice, which calls for the offering of unleavened bread at the temple altar (see Lev 2).

Exodus 12:40–42 then turns to the length of time, 430 years exactly, during which Israel lived in Egypt, presumably from the time that Jacob arrived in Egypt according to Genesis 46 until the exodus from Egyptian slavery as recounted in the present passage. The basis for such calculation remains uncertain, although a variety of methods for counting have been employed. Examples include analogies with Ezekiel's days of lying on his side for Israel and Judah in Ezekiel 4:4–8 or the time that Solomon's Temple stood from the fourth year of Solomon to the Babylonian destruction of the temple in the eleventh year of Zedekiah as portrayed in Kings.[10] Although the basis for the number is not entirely clear, it is characteristic of the interest in periodization apparent in the P-stratum of the Pentateuch. Insofar as YHWH stood watch over Israel during the night of Passover, future generations of Jews are obligated to keep watch by celebrating the Passover offering in biblical times and the Passover Seder in later times. It is noteworthy that the priestly families are also obligated to stand watch at the temple to protect its sanctity as portrayed in 1 Chronicles 24 (cf. Jer 7:1—8:3, which illustrates Jeremiah's role in keeping watch in the temple, and Pss 15 and 24, entrance liturgies, which illustrate the practice as well).

Exodus 12:43–49 presents YHWH's instruction speech to Moses and Aaron concerning the statute of the Passover offering as it applies to indigenous Israelites and foreigners of various types, presumably from "the mixed multitude" mentioned above. YHWH's first statement in v. 43 identifies this particular instruction as "a statute" (Hebrew, *ḥuqqâ*), which identifies it as a legal decree from YHWH in the role of king of creation and Israel. The statute is that no "foreigner" (Hebrew, *ben-nēkar*) may eat the Passover offering, which functions as the general principle at stake here. But the following verses, 44–49, then specify what this

10. Davies, *Exodus 1–18*, 2:122–23; Propp, *Exodus 1–18*, 415–16; Blenkinsopp, *Pentateuch*, 47–50.

general statute entails. Verse 44 specifies that any bought by an Israelite to serve as slave may eat from the Passover offering, if he has been circumcised, which would make him a convert to Judaism in antiquity. Verse 45 then takes up the cases of a *tôšāb*, a "temporary resident alien," or a *śākîr*, "hired man," neither of whom have been circumcised, which means that they have not converted to Judaism. Consequently, neither can eat the Passover offering. Verse 46 specifies that the meat of the Passover offering must be eaten only within one house; it cannot be taken outside to eat elsewhere. The verse also specifies that the bones cannot be broken, which would enable the Passover sacrifice to be divided and eaten among several houses, thereby undermining the previously stated law. Verse 47 specifies that the whole "congregation" of Israel is obligated to make the Passover offering, which means that the Passover offering is required of all Jews. Verse 48 specifies that a "resident alien" (Hebrew, *gēr*) who resides with Israel and has been circumcised, together with all the males of his family, will offer and eat the Passover offering because he and his family have converted to Judaism and therefore have become as indigenous Israelites or Jews. In rabbinic Hebrew, *gēr* refers to a convert. But the verse specifies that a man who has not been circumcised (i.e., who has not converted to Judaism) may not offer or eat the Passover offering. Verse 49 specifies that this instruction applies to both indigenous Israelites and to resident aliens who have been circumcised and therefore converted to Judaism. Because of the focus on circumcision as the criterion for defining a Jew (cf. Gen 17), most interpreters consider this to be the work of the P-stratum text, although we must note that the circumcision of the men of Shechem in Genesis 34 is considered to be a J-stratum text, and Jeremiah 9:24 recognizes the practice of circumcision in Judah and other surrounding nations as a standard practice in the late monarchic period. Both of these texts suggest that Exodus 12:43–49 could presuppose J-stratum composition.

Exodus 12:50 states Israel's compliance with YHWH's instruction to Moses concerning who might offer and eat the Passover offering, i.e., only Jews may do so, whether they are indigenous in that they were born Jewish or converted by circumcision.

Exodus 12:51 then summarizes the preceding by stating that on that day, YHWH freed Israel from Egypt. The use of military language (i.e., Hebrew, *ṣibʾōtām*, "their hosts") presupposes YHWH's role as king of creation and of Israel and Israel's role as YHWH's army in the combat against the pharaoh of Egypt.

Exodus 13:1–2 presents YHWH's instruction to Moses concerning the sanctification of every firstborn, human and animal, which breaks the womb of the mother. This is a statement similar to that which appears in the revised J-stratum law code of Exodus 34:19, although 34:19 lacks the following material (i.e., Exod 13:3–16), which provides instruction on how to observe the initial statement.

Exodus 13:3–16 follows with Moses's instruction speech to the people on how they are to observe the statement concerning the sanctification of the firstborn. Moses's speech replaces the instructions in Exodus 34:20 from the earlier J-stratum law code. Moses's instructions develop statements made in Deuteronomy 6:4–25, 11:18–23, and 16:1–4. Although Exodus 13:1–16 is generally considered to be a non-source text, the correlation with the texts from Exodus 34 and Deuteronomy suggests that Exodus 13:1–16 is actually a J-stratum text.

Following the speech formula at the beginning of Exodus 13:3aα1–4, "and Moses said to the people," Moses's instruction speech comprises two major sections in Exodus 13:3aα5–13 and 13:4–16.

The first portion of Moses's instruction speech in Exodus 13:3aα1–4 presents Moses's instruction to remember the date of the Passover celebration. His statement begins with the imperative command to "remember" the day that you went free from Egyptian bondage due to the strong hand of YHWH together with the injunction that no leavened bread should be eaten, in remembrance of YHWH's actions on behalf of Israel. Exodus 13:4–16 then provides more specific instruction on how to remember this fundamental command.

Exodus 13:4–5 begins with a syntactically independent statement in v. 4 that explains the significance of this day, "Today, you go out in the month of Aviv." Aviv, "spring," appears to be the name of the first month of the year in the older version of the Israelite calendar. Verse 5 then continues the statement of v. 4 with a conjunctive phrase, "and it shall be," which explains that YHWH is giving the land of the five Canaanite peoples, i.e., the Canaanites, the Hittites, the Amorites, the Hivvites, and the Jebusites, which he swore to give to Israel's ancestors as stated throughout Deuteronomy, particularly in the Deuteronomic texts named above. The final statement of the verse reiterates that this special service is rendered to YHWH by Israel in return for what YHWH did on their behalf.

Exodus 13:6–16 begins with a fundamental set of instructions that present two apodictic instructions concerning the eating of unleavened bread. The first instruction in v. 6 states that unleavened bread, matzah, will be eaten for seven days, and the seventh day, i.e., the concluding day of Matzot, will be a holiday much like the first day of Passover, Pesach. The second instruction, in v. 7, reiterates the first instruction to eat unleavened bread for seven days. These two basic instructions concerning the eating of matzah for seven days are then embellished by a syntactically linked instruction that the fathers are to explain to their sons the meaning of this special observance: "It is because of this that YHWH did for me when I went out from Egypt." This statement then functions as the response to the wicked son in the Passover Seder.[11]

Three paragraphs, each introduced by the conjunctive phrase "and it shall be," then follow in Exodus 13:9–10, 11–15, and 16 to explain different aspects of the service to be rendered to YHWH in return for YHWH's deliverance of Israel from Egyptian bondage and YHWH's oath to give Israel the land of Canaan as part of YHWH's covenant with Israel.

Exodus 13:9–10 focuses on binding YHWH's instructions concerning these matters as a sign on the hand and the forehead of the men of Israel. They anticipate the Jewish practice of binding tefillin, prayer phylacteries that contain key texts concerning G-d's covenant with the Jewish people in traditional rabbinic practice. In biblical texts, they are called "a sign" (Hebrew, *'ôt*) on your hand, and "remembrances" (Hebrew, *ṭôṭapōt*) between your eyes. These symbols appear to be derived from ancient Near Eastern practices of wearing armbands and headbands to signify the king or god to which a person adhered. In traditional Judaism, the square boxes of the tefillin, one for the head and one for the arm, contain miniature handwritten texts (including Exod 13:1–10; 13:11–16; Deut 6:4–9; 11:13–21).

Exodus 13:11–15 then focus on the instruction to sanctify every firstborn male that breaks the womb, whether human or animal, to YHWH. The instructions follow especially Exodus 34:19–20, although some elements of the vocabulary differ. The firstborn asses shall be redeemed with a sheep, likely because they were not kosher for eating. But the practice of sacrificing an ass to make a treaty is well known in the Akkadian idiom *ḫarim ḳatalim*, "to kill an ass," which means "to make a covenant/treaty."[12] Again, when the son asks about the meaning of this practice, the father answers with the statement "with a strong

11. Glatzer, *Passover Haggadah*, 26–27; Elias, *Haggadah*, 80–89; Tabory, *JPS Commentary on Haggadah*, 39–45.

12. Noth, "Old Testament Covenant-Making."

hand YHWH brought us out from Egypt, from the house of slavery." In the Passover Seder, this statement functions as the father's response to the simple son.[13] The response continues in v. 15 with the father's statement that YHWH killed the firstborn of Egypt due to pharaoh's refusal to release Israel; consequently, Jews observe the command to sanctify the firstborn due to YHWH's redemption of the firstborn of Israel. As explained above, the firstborn sons of Israel were redeemed so that they might function as assistants to the priests in observing the Passover ritual—and apparently others. As exemplified by Samuel in 1 Samuel 1–3, Samuel is the firstborn of Hannah, the wife of Elkanah the Ephraimite, in the early history of northern Israel, and it was only later that the firstborn sons were replaced by the Levites as indicated in the Numbers narrative, especially Numbers 3, 8, and 17–18.

Finally, Exodus 13:16 presents the instruction with a summary statement that these words will be a sign upon the hand and remembrances between the eyes to remind Jewish men that G-d brought us out of Egypt with a mighty hand.

Exodus 13:17–19 then concludes this sub-unit with an account of the route taken by Israel to depart from Egypt and the manner in which they travelled. Although the easiest route to take would have been the road that ran along Mediterranean coast of the Sinai Peninsula, Egypt had already built and fortified that road, making it impossible to use it to travel to Canaan. The coastal road, known in Egyptian sources as "the Way(s) of Horus," was already built by the early twelfth century BCE when the Sea Peoples unsuccessfully invaded Egypt.[14] Consequently, the road that led southeast into the Wilderness of Sinai, toward the location of the Red Sea, was the better choice as the Egyptians had virtually no presence in the region.[15] The notice in v. 18 that G-d led the people toward this route indicates that the passage is likely the work of the E-stratum author.

The notice in the second part of v. 18 that Israel "went up armed" (Hebrew, *ḥămušîm ʿālû*) presupposes that the people of Israel constituted the army of YHWH, the true king of creation. The Hebrew term *ḥămušîm*, "armed," is derived from the root, *ḥmš*, "five," which suggests that the people are organized into companies of fifty and therefore they

13. Glatzer, *Passover Haggadah*, 26–27; Elias, *Haggadah*, 80–89; Tabory, *JPS Commentary on Haggadah*, 39–45.

14. Davies, *Exodus 1–18*, 2:205–6.

15. Davies, *Exodus 1–18*, 2:206–7.

are arranged (and armed) for battle (cf. Exod 18:21, 25). The verb, *ʿālû*, "they went up," employs the common Hebrew idiom from antiquity to the present for travel to the land of Israel, viz., one always "goes up" to the land of Israel and the city of Jerusalem, and one "goes down" when one departs from either.[16]

Verse 19 concludes Exodus 13:17–19 with a notice that Moses took the bones of Joseph with him back to the land of Israel in keeping with the oath that Joseph secured from the people of Israel in Genesis 50:25. Insofar as the verse refers to G-d and interpreters view Genesis 50 as an E-stratum composition, v. 19 serves as further evidence that Exodus 13:17–19 is an E-stratum composition.[17]

Reception History

The references Exodus 13:8 and 13:14–15 to the father's obligation to teach his sons about G-d's actions on behalf of Israel at the time of the Exodus are featured in the Passover Haggadah. The father's statement in Exodus 13:8, "It is because of this that YHWH did for me when I came out from Egypt," functions as the answer to the question of the wicked son, "What is this service to you?" because the wicked son's question—directed "to you" and not to himself—indicates his self-exclusion from Judaism and the people of Israel. Consequently, the father's answer refers to G-d's actions in taking "me" out of Egypt. The father's instruction of the son in Exodus 13:14, "With a strong hand YHWH brought us out from Egypt, from the house of slavery," functions as the response to the simple son, who simply asks, "What is this?" Here, the father's response makes sure to include the son by stating that G-d brought "us" out of the land of Egypt so that the son will understand that he is included in G-d's deliverance of the people of Israel.[18]

The references to G-d's instruction to function as "a sign upon your hand and for remembrances between your eyes" in Exodus 13:9–10 and 13:16 provide the foundation for the traditional practice of Jewish men to pray during the week with tefillin tied upon their heads and upon their arms (see m. Menaḥ. 4.1; b. Menaḥ. 34a–37b; m. Miqw. 10.3). As

16. Alcalay, *Hebrew-English Dictionary*, 1899; cf. *HALOT* 2:828–29; "ʿ*ālâ*," BDB 748.

17. Campbell and O'Brien, *Sources of the Pentateuch*, 183.

18. Glatzer, *Passover Haggadah*, 26–27; Elias, *Haggadah*, 80–89; Tabory, *JPS Commentary on Haggadah*, 39–45.

noted above, they presuppose the ancient practice of using headbands and armbands to signify adherence to a deity or king. In Judaism, they signify adherence to G-d. There are two bands, one for the head and one for the weaker arm, that include a square leather box into which miniature manuscripts with the texts of Exodus 13:1–10; 13:11–16; Deuteronomy 6:4–9; and 11:13–21 inserted inside. The meaning of the Hebrew term *tĕpillîn* is "prayer phylacteries," which is derived from the Hebrew root *pll*, "to pray, intercede."[19] When putting on the tefillin for morning prayers during the week, one recites these texts, which speak about adherence to G-d and G-d's promise to grant the land of Israel to the people of Israel.[20]

Exodus 12:37—13:19 appears a number of times in the Christian New Testament. Acts 7:6 cites Exodus 12:40 in reference to the 400 years spent by Israel in Egyptian slavery as part of Stephen's sermon prior to his martyrdom, although Exodus 12:40 states that the period was 430 years. The prohibition against breaking the bones of the Passover offering in Exodus 12:46 appears in John 19:36, where it is applied to Jesus's crucifixion in which the Roman soldiers did not break his legs to see if he was dead as they did for the other crucified men. Luke 2:23 cites the references to the firstborn son in Exodus 12:2, 12, and 15 in reference to the account of how Joseph and Mary brought Jesus to Jerusalem to present him before G-d in fulfillment of the "law" of Moses. Luke 1:35 presupposes the reference to the dedication of the firstborn son to G-d in Exodus 13:12 in relation to the holiness of Jesus as "the son of G-d."

19. Alcalay, *Hebrew-English Dictionary*, 2828.
20. Rabinowitz, "Tefillin."

YHWH's Defeat of Pharaoh and Deliverance of Israel at the Sea of Reeds—Exodus 13:20—15:21

The account of YHWH's defeat of pharaoh and deliverance of Israel at the Sea of Reeds in Exodus 13:20—15:22 is demarcated at the outset by the itinerary formula in Exodus 13:2, "And they journeyed from Sukkot, and they camped at Etham at the edge of the wilderness," to indicate the initial movement of Israel from Sukkot to Etham. Although Exodus 14:1–2 indicates further movement to Pi-Haḥiram between Migdol and the Sea, this notice does not appear in the form of the itinerary formulas, which indicate structure within "the generations of Jacob" in Genesis 37:2—Numbers 2:34 as indicated above. The next formal example of the itinerary formula appears in Exodus 15:22, "And Moses caused Israel to journey from the Reed Sea, and they went out to the Wilderness of Shur," which marks the beginning of the next structural unit within the narrative.

The internal structure of Exodus 13:20—15:21 comprises two major components, each of which is defined by location, viz., the journey from Sukkot to Etham in Exodus 13:20–22, and the relocation to Pi-Haḥiroth in Exodus 14:1—15:21. Exodus 14:1—15:21 comprises two formal subunits, defined by the action portrayed in each viz., the narrative account of YHWH's confrontation of pharaoh at the Reed Sea in Exodus 14:1–31 and the account of the Song at the Sea in Exodus 15:1–21.

Reception History

The account of YHWH's confrontation with pharaoh at the Reed Sea is well known in later biblical and post-biblical traditions. Isaiah 11:15–16 (cf. Isa 27:12–13) alludes to it with its statement "And YHWH will dry up the tongue of the Sea of Egypt when he waves his hand over the river with his hot wind and strikes it into seven streams so that he enables travel with shoes, and it will be a highway for the remnant of his people who were left from Assyria just as it was for Israel on the day that he brought them up from the land of Egypt." In this case, the reference to "his [YHWH's] hot wind" (Hebrew, *ba ʿyām rûḥô*) refers to the sirocco, known as the east wind in the exodus narratives. Here, the confrontation at the sea of Egypt is applied to those Israelites left over from Assyrian oppression who will be delivered by YHWH.[1] Likewise, Deutero-Isaiah refers to the confrontation at the Reed Sea in Isaiah 42:14—44:23 (see esp. Isa 43:16—44:5) when YHWH self-identifies as the redeemer of Israel from Babylonian exile.[2]

It also appears in rabbinic literature, especially in the account of the four (rabbis) who attempted to enter Pardes in b. Ḥaggigah 14b where R. Akiba warns his colleagues not to say "Water! Water!" when they see "the stones of pure marble," a reference to the walls of water in the Reed Sea between which the Israelites cross on dry land in Exodus 14:22; 15:8. R. Akiba's reference presupposes the understanding that the image of the watery walls depicts the entrance gate of G-d's heavenly temple, and it indicates that textual statements, such as the reference to the water walls piled up in the sea, must be interpreted metaphorically, not literally, in this case as a motif in a Heikhalot ascent to heaven to appear before the throne of G-d.[3]

The confrontation at the Reed Sea also plays a role in the Christian New Testament. The reference to the hardening of pharaoh's heart in Exodus 14:4 and 17 appears in Romans 9:18 where it acknowledges G-d's will to show mercy or harden hearts as G-d chooses. The reference to the uplifted arms of the Israelites in Exodus 14:8 appears in Acts

1. See Sweeney, *Isaiah 1–39*, 196–211. Insofar as this passage dates to the seventh-century BCE reign of King Josiah ben Amon of Judah, it contradicts Van Seters's argument that the account of the Reed Sea was first attested only in Deutero-Isaiah. See below.

2. Sweeney, *Isaiah 40–66*, 81–108.

3. See Gruenwald, *Apocalyptic and Merkavah Mysticism*, 82–92; see also Sweeney, "Pardes Revisited"; Sweeney, *Jewish Mysticism*, 214–16.

13:17 where it instead refers to G-d's uplifted arm, which enabled Israel to depart from Egypt. Revelation 15:3–4 refers to the Song of Moses from Exodus 15:1–19 in portraying the Song of the Lamb to be sung with harps by those who had conquered the beast. Childs notes that early church fathers, including Origen, Tertullian, Ambrose, and Gregory of Nyssa, understood the crossing of the sea to be a precursor to Christian baptism, based especially in 1 Corinthians 10:1–2.[4]

The Song of the Sea also figures prominently in at least three major films about Israel's exodus from Egypt. *The Ten Commandments* (1956), directed by Cecil B. De Mille and starring Charlton Heston as Moses, Yul Brynner as Rameses II, Anne Baxter as Nefretiri, Edward G. Robinson as Dathan, and Yvonne De Carlo as Sephora (Zipporah), portrays the confrontation at the sea as a demonstration of G-d's power through the pillar of fire and the parting of the sea, although the film ends only after depicting rebellion in the wilderness and the appointment of Joshua to lead the people into the promised land. *The Prince of Egypt*, the 1998 animated film produced by Jeffrey Katzenberg and starring Val Kilmer as the voice of Moses, Ralph Fiennes as the voice of Rameses II, Michelle Pfeiffer as the voice of Tzipporah, and Sandra Bullock as the voice of Miriam, portrays the confrontation at the sea, beginning with the approach of the Israelites as they run to the sea singing the Song of Moses in Hebrew. The 2014 film *Exodus: Gods and Kings*, directed by Ridley Scott and starring Christian Bale as Moses, Joel Edgerton as Rameses II, Maria Valverde as Zipporah, and Sigourney Weaver as Tuya, the mother of Rameses II, portrays the parting of the sea when Moses throws his sword into the sea in despair.

It is also noteworthy that the biblical account of the exodus inspired the 1958 novel *Exodus*, by Leon Uris, as well as the 1960 film based on the novel, also called *Exodus*, directed by Otto Preminger and starring Paul Newman as Ari Ben Canaan and Eva Marie Saint as Kitty Fremont, both of which portrayed the founding of the modern state of Israel.

4. Childs, *Exodus*, 232–34.

The Journey from Sukkot to Etham—Exodus 13:20–22

Translation

13:20 And they journeyed from Sukkot, and they camped at Etham at the edge of the wilderness. 21 And YHWH was going before them by day in a pillar of cloud to lead them [on the] way and by night in a pillar of fire to illumine [the way] for them to go, day and night. 22 And the pillar of cloud by day and the pillar of fire by night did not depart [from] before the people.

Commentary

Exodus 13:20–22 presents the account of the journey from Sukkot to Etham. The location of Sukkot is uncertain (see also Exod 12:37; Num 33:5). The most likely location of Sukkot is identified with Tel el-Maskuta, located about fifteen kilometers west of modern Ismailiia and Lake Timsah in the Wadi Tumilat. As noted above in Exodus 12:37, Sukkot appears to be a Hebrew rendition of Egyptian Tjeku, *tkw*, which was located one day's travel from Rameses.[1] The location of Etham is unknown (see also Num 33:6–7), but it is presumed to be located on the eastern border of ancient Egypt between Lake Timsah and Bitter Lakes, north of Suez in the Wadi Tumilat. It is possibly to be identified with Pithom.[2]

1. J. Seely, "Succoth"; see also *ANET* 259.
2. Higgins, "Etham."

The portrayal of YHWH as a pillar of cloud and fire draws upon the imagery of the temple altar in operation with a pillar of smoke and fire ascending from the altar into the heavens when it spreads out to form a canopy of smoke and cloud (cf. Isa 4:5–6).[3] The imagery of deities portrayed as fire and smoke leading armies is known as early as the thirteenth century BCE in the Tukulti-Ninurta Epic in which the army of King Tukulti-Ninurta I of Assyria (1244–1208 BCE) is led by the gods, such as Assur, Enlil, and Adad, who kindle flame and send wind before the Assyrian army in battle against the Cassites.[4] In the present text, YHWH's portrayal in a pillar of cloud by day and fire by night is intended to signal YHWH's leadership and protection of Israel all day and all night.

This text is generally considered to be a J-stratum text,[5] although it appears to represent a J reworking of older E-stratum texts as indicated in Exodus 13:17–19 and features of Exodus 14 and 15. YHWH later sends a messenger or angel to lead the people in Exodus 14:19–20, a combined E- and J-stratum text (see also Exod 23:20–33, which is normally considered a non-source text, but the motif of an angel of G-d is generally considered to be an E-stratum characteristic).[6]

3. Sweeney, *Isaiah 1–39*, 105–12.

4. Mann, *Divine Presence and Guidance*, 35–42.

5. Campbell and O'Brien, *Sources of the Pentateuch*, 143.

6. Campbell and O'Brien, *Sources of the Pentateuch*, 199.

The Narrative Account of YHWH's Confrontation with Pharaoh at the Reed Sea —Exodus 14:1–31

Translation

14:1 And YHWH spoke to Moses, saying, [2] "Speak to the sons of Israel so that they will turn and camp before Pi-haḥirot between Migdol and the sea before Baal Zephon; before the sea you shall camp. [3] And pharaoh will say of the sons of Israel, 'They are confused in the land. The wilderness has closed upon them,' [4] and I will strengthen the heart of pharaoh, and he will pursue after them, and I will be glorified against pharaoh and against all his army, and Egypt will know that I am YHWH." And they did so.

[5] And it was told to the king of Egypt that the people had fled, and the heart of pharaoh and his servants was changed toward the people, and they said, "What is this that we have done? That we have released Israel from our slavery?" [6] And he harnessed his chariot, and he took his people with him, [7] and he took six hundred chosen chariots and all the chariots of Egypt and chariot commanders over each one. [8] And YHWH hardened the heart of pharaoh, king of Egypt, and he pursued after the sons of Israel and the sons of Israel were departing with hands held high. [9] And Egypt pursued

after them, and all the horse chariotry of pharaoh and his
horsemen and his army overtook them camping by sea by
Pi-haḥiroth before Baal Zephon.

10 And pharaoh came near, and the sons of Israel lifted up
their eyes, and behold, Egypt was traveling after them, and
they were very afraid, and the sons of Israel cried out to
YHWH, 11 and they said to Moses, "Was it due to the lack of
graves in Egypt that [you] took us here to die in the wilderness? What is this that you have done to us to bring us out
from Egypt? 12 Is this not the word that we spoke to you in
Egypt, saying, 'Leave us alone, and we will serve Egypt! For
serving Egypt is better for us than our dying in the wilderness!'" 13 And Moses said to the people, "Do not fear! Stand
fast, and see the deliverance of YHWH which he will do for
you today, for once you have seen the Egyptians today, you
will never again see them forever! 14 YHWH will fight for
you, and you will remain silent!"

15 And YHWH said to Moses, "Why do you cry out to me?
Speak to the sons of Israel so that they will travel on. 16 And
you, raise your staff and hold out your hand over the sea and
divide it, and the sons of Israel will enter into the midst of
the sea on dry land. 17 And I, behold I, will strengthen the
heart of Egypt, and they will enter after them, and I will be
glorified against pharaoh and against his whole army, against
his chariotry and against his horsemen! 19 And Egypt will
know that I am YHWH when I am glorified by pharaoh, by
his chariotry, and by his horsemen."

19 And the angel of G-d travelled, going before the camp of Israel, and it went from behind them, and the column of cloud
travelled from before them, and it stood behind them, 20 and
it came between the camp of Egypt and the camp of Israel,
and there was cloud and darkness, and it cursed the night,
and no one could come near to another all night. 21 And Moses extended his hand over the sea, and YHWH made the
sea go back with a strong east wind all night, and it made
the sea into dry land, and it divided the waters. 22 And the
sons of Israel went into the midst of the sea on dry land, and

the waters were a wall for them on the right and on the left.
23 And Egypt pursued, and they came after them, every horse
of pharaoh, his chariotry, and his horsemen, into the midst
of the sea. 24 And it was at the morning watch that YHWH
looked out to the camp of Egypt in the pillar of fire and
cloud, and he terrified the camp of Egypt. 25 And he bound
the wheel of his chariots so that they drove with heaviness,
and Egypt said, "Let me flee before Israel, for YHWH is fighting for them against Egypt!"

26 And YHWH said to Moses, "Extend your hand over the sea,
and the waters will return over Egypt, over his chariotry, and
over his horsemen." 27 And Moses extended his hand, and the
sea returned at the turn of morning to its steady flow, and
the Egyptians were fleeing its meeting [them], and YHWH
shook off Egypt into the midst of the sea. 28 And the waters
returned, and they covered the chariotry and the horsemen
of all the army of pharaoh which came after them in the sea.
Not even one remained among them. 29 And the sons of Israel
went on dry land in the midst of the sea, and the waters were
a wall for them to the right and to the left.

30 And YHWH delivered on that day Israel from the hand
of Egypt, and Israel saw Egypt dead on the shore of the sea.
31 And Israel saw the great hand that YHWH used against
Egypt, and the people feared YHWH, and they believed in
YHWH and in Moses, his servant.

Commentary

Exodus 14:1–31 presents the narrative account of YHWH's confrontation with pharaoh at the Reed Sea. The narrative displays a range of characteristics that indicate that it is an E-stratum text that has been reworked by both the J- and P-stratum editors.[1] It is a transitional text in the narrative in that it presents the successful culmination of YHWH's confrontation with pharaoh in Exodus 1–15, but it also points to the beginnings of the wilderness rebellion motif in which the people of Israel complain about YHWH and Moses's leadership. Ultimately, the people's complaining will

1. Campbell and O'Brien, *Sources of the Pentateuch*, 40–41, 143, 185–86.

prompt YHWH to destroy the slave generation in the wilderness (Num 1–14; cf. Exod 32–34) in action that appears to be correlated with concerns over the destruction of the Northern Kingdom of Israel.

The narrative comprises components, including: Exodus 14:1–4, which recounts the repositioning of Israel at Pi-Haḥiroth; Exodus 14:5–9, which recounts pharaoh's decision to pursue Israel; Exodus 14:10–14, which recounts Israel's fear of Egypt and distrust of Moses; Exodus 14:15–18, YHWH's instructions to Moses to confront pharaoh; Exodus 14:19–20, which recounts the repositioning of the angel of G-d to defend Israel; Exodus 14:21–25, which recounts Moses's actions to defend of Israel; Exodus 14:26–29, which recounts YHWH and Moses's defeat of the Egyptian army at the Reed Sea; and Exodus 14:30–31, which presents a summation of YHWH's deliverance of Israel.

Exodus 14:1–4 recounts the repositioning of Israel to Pi-Haḥiroth, located between Migdol and Sea before Baal Zephon (cf. Num 33:7–8). The location of Pi-Haḥiroth is uncertain, although it might be identified with Pa-Kherta, located along the eastern edge of the Nile Delta.[2] Migdol, perhaps identified with a Judean colony in Egypt mentioned in Jeremiah 44:1—46:14 and Ezekiel 29:10 and 30:6, was located along the Ways of Horus, the Egyptian road running along the Mediterranean coast from the Nile Delta to Canaan.[3] Migdol is identified with Tell Qadua, although the site moved to other locations in the fifth century BCE. The location of Baal Zephon remains uncertain, although the name appears to be derived from the name of a Canaanite god, Baal Zaphon, "Baal of the north."[4] The present text is generally understood to a represent J redaction, insofar as the location changes from Etham to Pi-Haḥiroth, although a synchronic reading of the text suggests a repositioning of Israel away from the Ways of Horus and its Egyptian garrisons to a safer route that will lead them into the southern Sinai.[5] Van Seters argues that the J redaction of this text must date to the late exilic period, based on his observation of the parallel between the crossing of the Reed Sea and the crossing of the Jordan River in Joshua 5 and the appearance of the crossing of the sea motif in Deutero-Isaiah (e.g., Isa 43:16–21). He overlooks the significance of the records of the Assyrian King Shalmaneser III, 859–824 BCE, who repeatedly crossed the Euphrates River

2. Redford, "Pi-Hahiroth."

3. Wilson-Wright, "Migdol."

4. Kurtz, "Baal Zephon."

5. Cf. Van Seters, *Life of Moses*, 128–49, esp. 128–29.

in unsuccessful attempts to conquer Aram and Israel, a fact that would have been known to the E-stratum authors.[6] The text indicates that the Israelites were confused about their route of departure, although the locations indicate an attempt to proceed north followed by a change in route to the south. Verse 4 indicates YHWH's intention to strengthen or harden the heart of pharaoh so that YHWH may be glorified by defeating him and the Egyptian army. Such a statement raises questions, insofar as YHWH eliminates pharaoh's free will so that he and his army will suffer punishment. The use of the self-revelation formula (see also recognition formula) indicates YHWH's intent to be recognized as the true sovereign of creation and humanity.[7] The final statement indicates Israel's compliance with YHWH's instructions.

Exodus 14:5–9 recounts pharaoh's decision to pursue Israel as a result of YHWH's "strengthening" his heart. The reaction of the pharaoh to the news of Israel's departure, "What is this that we have done? That we have released Israel from our slavery?," suggests surprise on the part of pharaoh, as if he had been in a trance. The reference to the six hundred picked chariots indicates a sort of royal guard, much like David's six hundred men who served as his personal guard (1 Sam 27:2; 30:9; 2 Sam 15:18). In addition to the royal guard, the rest of the Egyptian chariot corps also followed in pursuit. The chariots are described as having "a chariot commander" (Hebrew, *šālîš*, lit., "a third [man]"). The term refers to the third man of a chariot in addition to the driver and the man who handled the weapons, e.g., bow and arrows, spears, etc. In the battle of Kadesh in 1275 BCE between Pharaoh Rameses II of Egypt and King Muwatallis of Hatti by the Orontes River, the Hittites were known to have three-man chariots whereas the Egyptian chariots carried only two men. Insofar as the Egyptians were seriously mauled at Kadesh—even Rameses II himself was nearly killed—the Egyptians may have revised their chariot crews to include three men, but evidence is lacking. The third man served as a shield bearer in the Hittite chariots, and he would also have defended the rear of the chariot in close-quarter combat. Otherwise, he was in a position to take command of the chariot.[8] When the Egyptians approached Israel, the Israelites are described as "departing with hands held high," which apparently indicates their efforts to express

6. *ANET* 276–81. See also note above.

7. Coats, *Exodus 1–18*, 178.

8. Davies, *Exodus 1–18*, 1:234; Littauwer and Crouwell, "Chariots."

defiance against the Egyptians, likely analogous to those used today.[9] Such gestures would have angered the Egyptian soldiers and prompted them to pursue with all haste to slaughter the Israelites.

Exodus 14:10–14 recounts Israel's fear of the Egyptians and distrust of Moses. Their words to Moses are realistic in that they employ rhetorical questions to assert that he brought them to the sea to die because there were not enough graves in Egypt and that they would be better off as slaves in Egypt rather than dead by the sea.[10] Moses's response employs the reassurance formula, "Do not fear!" (Hebrew, *ʾal tîrāʾû*), as he advises them to stand fast and watch how YHWH will deliver them.[11]

Exodus 14:15–18 relates YHWH's instructions to Moses concerning how to respond to pharaoh's advance. YHWH's instructions begin with a rhetorical question, which asserts that Moses should not have to ask YHWH what to do. YHWH then instructs Moses to have the people advance against pharaoh while Moses holds his staff in his hand to divide the sea so that the people may cross on dry land. The imagery of dry land emerging in the midst of the sea is a clear example of a creation motif akin to Genesis 1:1—2:3, which signals that the exodus narrative also functions as a creation account.[12] The repetition of YHWH's intent to strengthen the heart of pharaoh so that YHWH will gain glory and the Egyptians will know that YHWH is the true king expresses the culmination of the creation epic in the exodus narratives.

Exodus 14:19–20 recounts the repositioning of the angel of G-d (Hebrew, *malʾak ʾĕlōqîm*), which presupposes the portrayal of YHWH embodied in the pillar of cloud by day and the pillar of fire by night noted above in Exodus 14:21–22. Here the image shifts to the angel of G-d, indicating the E-stratum origins of this narrative that have been reworked by the J- and P-redactors of the text. Both the use of *ʾĕlōqîm* in reference to G-d and the use of angelic imagery are characteristics of the E-stratum. The motif here builds upon the older Mesopotamian tradition, exemplified in the Tukullti-Ninurta Epic, in which the Mesopotamian gods position themselves before and behind the Assyrian army to guard it against enemy attack.[13]

9. Davies, *Exodus 1–18*, 1:235.

10. Sweeney, *Isaiah 1–39*, 537.

11. E. Conrad, *Fear Not Warrior*, 143–46; Sweeney, *Isaiah 1–39*, 547.

12. Sweeney, "Creation as Sacred Space"; cf. Cassuto, *Bible and Ancient Oriental Texts*, 80–102.

13. Mann, *Divine Presence and Guidance*, 35–42.

Exodus 14:21–25 recounts Moses's compliance with YHWH's instructions to defend Israel against the Egyptian assault. When Moses raises his hand with his staff over the sea, the east wind splits the waters to form walls on either side of the emerging dry land. The east wind once again refers to the sirocco wind, known in Hebrew as *sharav*, in Arabic as *ḥamsin*, and in the American Southwest as the Santa Ana winds.[14] The term "wall" (Hebrew, *ḥōmâ*) would then metaphorically portray the divided sea as a gateway into a fortified city, presumably YHWH's heavenly fortress or palace, where they would enjoy YHWH's protection. The reference to YHWH's "looking out" at "the morning watch" presupposes both YHWH's position in the pillar of fire and cloud (cf. Exod 13:21–22) and the priestly watches at the Jerusalem temple (cf. 1 Chron 24; Jer 7:1—8:3). The imagery of the "bound" (Hebrew, *wayyāsar*, "and he bound," derived from the verb root *ʾsr*)[15] wheels suggests that the chariot wheels were stuck in the mud of the Reed Sea, where swampy conditions would prevail to impede the movement of the Egyptian chariots, prompting the Egyptians to flee.[16]

Exodus 14:26–29 recounts the defeat of Egypt at the Reed Sea by YHWH and Moses. Upon YHWH's instruction, Moses holds out his hand with the staff so that the waters will close over the Egyptians. Although the Egyptians attempt to flee, YHWH throws them back into the water, apparently from YHWH's position in the pillar of cloud behind Israel. Pharaoh's entire army was drowned in the waters, but Israel walked in safety on dry ground between the walls that formed the metaphorical gate to YHWH's heavenly palace.

Exodus 14:30–31 concludes the narrative account of YHWH's defeat of pharaoh and Egypt at the sea with a summary statement of the action and a declaration that Israel saw what YHWH had done and therefore had faith in both YHWH and Moses. Although such a statement should signal the end of the doubts expressed in Exodus 14:10–14, the continuing appearances of the wilderness-rebellion motif in Exodus and Numbers will quickly emerge, beginning in Exodus 16.

14. Fitzgerald, *L-rd of East Wind*, 66–70.

15. Davies, *Exodus 1–18*, 1:238; although he notes that many read the verb as a conjugation of root *swr*, "and he removed."

16. Cf. the statement of the Philistines at the battle of Aphek in 1 Samuel 4:5–11, which makes reference to YHWH's actions against the Egyptians in Exodus.

The Song of the Sea —Exodus 15:1–21

Translation

15:1 The Moses and the sons of Israel sang this song to YHWH, and they said, saying,

I will sing to YHWH, for he is surely exalted!

Horse and its rider, he has cast into the sea!

2 My strength and anthem of YH, and he is my deliverance.

This is my G-d, and I will adorn him with praise; the G-d of my father, and I will exalt him!

3 YHWH is a man of war; YHWH is his Name!

4 The chariots of pharaoh and his army, he has cast into the sea!

And the best of his chariot commanders are sunk [in] the Sea of Reeds!

5 The deeps cover them; they have gone down into the depths like stone!

6 Your right hand, O YHWH, majestic in strength;

Your right hand, O YHWH, shatters the enemy!

[7] And in the greatness of your exaltation, you tear down your enemies!

You send out your burning wrath; it devours them like chaff!

[8] And in the snorting of your nostrils, the waters are piled up!

They stand like a heap of torrents; the deeps have frozen in the heart of the sea!

[9] The enemy said, "I will pursue; I will overtake!

I will divide spoil until my desire is filled!

I will draw my sword; my hand will possess them!"

[10] You blew with your wind; the sea covered them!

They sank like lead in the majestic waters!

[11] Who is like you among the gods, O YHWH?

Who is like you, majestic in holiness? Awesome in praise? Doing wonders?

[12] You extend your right hand; the earth swallows them!

[13] You lead in your fidelity this people whom you have redeemed!

You guide [them] in your strength to your holy abode!

[14] The peoples have heard; they tremble!

Pain has seized the inhabitants of Philistia!

[15] Then terrified are the chieftains of Edom;

The leaders of Moab, trembling seizes them;

Melted down are all the inhabitants of Canaan!

[16] Dread and fear fall upon them;

In the greatness of your arm, they are silent like stone;

Until your people pass, O YHWH; until this people which you acquired pass!

[17] You will bring them and you will plant them in the mountain of your own property;

The site for your dwelling which you have made, O YHWH!

The sanctuary, my L-rd, which your hands have established!

[18] YHWH will rule forever and ever!

[19] For the horses of pharaoh with his chariot and his horsemen entered the sea, and YHWH turned upon them the waters of the sea, whereas the sons of Israel walked on dry land in the midst of the sea.

[20] And Miriam the prophetess, the sister of Aaron, took the hand drum in her hand, and all the women went out after her
with hand drums and with dancing, [21] and Miriam to them,

"Sing to YHWH, for he is surely exalted!

Horse and its rider, he has cast into the sea!"

Commentary

The account of the Song of the Sea in Exodus is the culminating element of the Exodus creation and combat myth narratives, which recount YHWH's defeat of pharaoh and deliverance of Israel. The song appears in a narrative context, which comprises two major narrative components. The first appears in Exodus 15:1–19, which recounts the singing of the song by Moses and the sons of Israel by the Sea of Reeds following YHWH's defeat of pharaoh and the Egyptian army. Exodus 15:1–19 in turn comprises two major elements, viz., Exodus 15:1–18, which includes a narrative introduction to the singing of the song in Exodus 15:1a followed by the song itself in Exodus 15:1b–18. The second element of Exodus 15:1–19 appears in Exodus 15:19, which recounts a summary of the action at the sea, including YHWH's use of the sea to inundate and drown the Egyptian army and its horses in Exodus 15:19a and Israel's marching on dry ground in the midst of the sea in Exodus 15:19b. The second major element of the narrative in Exodus 15:1–21 appears in Exodus 15:20–21 in which Miriam, identified here as "the prophetess and the sister of Aaron," leads the women in dancing to the beat of their own hand drums and singing the Song of the Sea itself, here represented only by its verse analogous to Exodus 15:1b, as an antiphonal response to the singing of Moses and the men.

The genre of the Song of the Sea, fully represented in Exodus 15:1b–18, is the Song/Hymn of Praise.[1] The Song of Praise is one of the most basic of the psalmic genres, which is intended to give praise to a deserving party, typically YHWH, for some great act, in this case the defeat of pharaoh and Egypt and the deliverance of Israel. The Song of Praise includes two basic elements, viz., the summons to praise and the reason or basis for praise.[2] Interpreters have noted that Exodus 15:1b–18 is a complex piece of poetry that shows the influence of other generic elements,[3] such as the Thanksgiving Song,[4] Declarative Praise,[5] Enthronement Psalm,[6] Litany,[7] and Victory Psalm.[8]

The song per se in Exodus 15:1b–18 comprises three major elements, including the declaration of praises in Exodus 15:1b–3, in which the psalmist asserts the intent to praise YHWH and concludes with the statement of YHWH's Name; Exodus 15:4–12, which recounts the first basis for the psalmist's praise, viz., YHWH's defeat of pharaoh and the Egyptian army, thereby defending Israel; and Exodus 15:13–18, which recounts YHWH's guidance of Israel to YHWH's "holy abode" (v. 13) and "sanctuary" (v. 17), which remains unnamed, allowing the reader to imagine that it might range from Mount Sinai in the wilderness to any of the sanctuaries of Israel and Judah, especially Shiloh or Jerusalem, which served as the major sanctuaries, although it does not exclude other possibilities, such as Gilgal, Shechem, Beth El, Dan, Samaria, Beer Sheba, Arad, and others. Jon Levenson points to the correlation of Sinai and the Jerusalem temple, although readers must recognize that other sanctuaries, such as those just named, likely shared a similar ideology which identified them with Mount Sinai/Mount Horeb.[9]

The dating of the Song of the Sea remains contested with Continental scholars favoring later dates and North American and Israeli scholars

1. Coats, *Exodus 1–18*, 119–20, 162.
2. Coats, *Exodus 1–18*, 162; cf. Gerstenberger, *Psalms*, 16–19.
3. Coats, *Exodus 1–18*, 119–20; Childs, *Exodus*, 243–44.
4. Noth, *Exodus*, 123.
5. Westermann, *Praise and Lament*, 141.
6. Mowinckel, *Psalms in Israel's Worship*, 155.
7. Beer, *Exodus*, 79–84; Muilenberg, "Liturgy," esp. 238–50.
8. Cross and Freedman, *Ancient YHWistic Poetry*, 45–65.
9. Levenson, *Sinai and Zion*.

favoring early dates. The omission of the site for YHWH's "holy abode" and "sanctuary" leaves the questions open, but the focus on Philistia, Edom, Moab, and Canaan offers possibilities for consideration. Philistia, Edom, and Moab were subdued by a so-called "united" Israel early in Israel's history and again later by Judah at various points during the "late monarchic" period of Judah. Such a scenario likewise leaves the question open, but the reference to Canaan is intriguing. Most interpreters simply assume that Canaan is to be identified with the land that constituted Israel until the destruction of the Northern Kingdom of Israel by the Assyrians in 722–721 BCE. But Canaan comprises a much larger swath of land which includes the Phoenicians, who were allies of Israel during the early reigns of David in the tenth century BCE and Solomon and again during the reign of the House of Omri during much of the ninth century BCE. Although the Phoenicians would have allied with Judah sporadically during later periods, reference to the Phoenicians suggests an earlier date for the composition of the Song of the Sea, which would correspond to a major defeat of Egypt that would have left Canaan free, Israel/Judah the space to coalesce into definitive kingdoms, and Philistia, Edom, and Moab to emerge in their own right. Such a scenario best presupposes the aftermath of the reign of Pharaoh Merneptah of Egypt (1224–1216 BCE) who apparently attempted to subdue a coalition known as the Nine Bows, which included the coastal and interior cities of Canaan as well as Israel itself, albeit in seminomadic form. The Egyptians were forced to withdraw from Canaan following the reign of Merneptah, the early period of the formation of Israel. Consequently, the reference to the Philistines, the Edomites, and the Moabites would suggest a lengthy period dating to roughly 1200–800 BCE. The concerns with these nations indicate a setting in relation to the formation of northern Israel under the Saulide, Omride, and Jehu Dynasties as a more likely scenario for the composition of Exodus 15.

The liturgical participation of women, who dance, play hand drums, and sing in response to the men, would more likely presuppose the Northern Kingdom of Israel, which shows evidence of allowing women to play a more important role in the northern temples in contrast to the south, where the Jerusalem temple presents very little evidence of the role of women in its liturgy or other activities.[10]

10. Sweeney, "Israelite and Judean Religions."

The narrative introduction in Exodus 15:1a employs an unusual imperfect verbal form, *yāšîr*, "he will sing." The subjects of the verb include both Moses and the sons of Israel, even though the verb is a singular form, which indicates the leading role played by Moses in the singing by the entire mass of the sons of Israel. The imperfect verbal form indicates incomplete action, which suggests that it is to be understood as an ongoing act of singing on behalf of the sons of Israel long after Moses and the exodus generation of Israel are gone. The second verb, *wayyōʾmĕrû*, "and they said," is a *waw*-consecutive verbal form, which converts the imperfect verb into a perfect, indicating completed action, and thereby conveying the narrative of an event that has already been completed in the past. Similar usage of verbs appears in Ugaritic poetry to indicate action that is both ongoing and completed in the mythological perspective of the composition. The plural verb presupposes both Moses and the sons of Israel as its subject. Overall, the purpose of this formula is to introduce the song that follows in Exodus 15:1b–18.

Exodus 15:1b–3 constitutes the psalmist's declaration of praise of YHWH. The declaration begins with the lengthened cohortative form of the first-person singular imperfect verb *ʾāšîrāh*, "I will sing" or "let me sing," which declares the psalmist's intent to sing praises for YHWH.[11] Indeed, v. 1bα, "I will sing to YHWH, for he is surely exalted," is a compact form of the basic hymn or song of praise, which declares intent to praise together with the basis or reason for praise.[12] In this case, the reason for praise is stated emphatically with an absolute infinitive form preceding the base verb, *kî-gāʾōh gāʾā*, "for he is surely exalted," to indicate emphasis. Verse 1bβ, "horse and its rider he has cast into the sea," elaborates upon the basis for praise by explaining what exactly it was that YHWH did to earn the exaltation proclaimed by the psalmist.

Exodus 15:2 develops the basis for praise further by declaring that YHWH is the psalmist's strength and deliverance, employing the shortened form of the divine Name, YH, that so frequently appears in poetry and in theophoric names.[13] The reference to "[the] anthem of YH" might seem perplexing at first, insofar as *zimrat YH* would normally be translated as "the melody or music of YH," but the term actually functions as a depiction of YHWH covered with songs of praise much like a soldier might be covered with medals to celebrate his heroism in

11. GKC 48e.

12. Gerstenberger, *Psalms*, 16–19; cf. Coats, *Exodus 1–18*, 162.

13. "*yhwh*," BDB 219.

battle. The final element of this verse identifies YHWH as the psalmist's G-d, "This is my G-d," and the psalmist reiterates the intent to adorn YHWH with praise, thereby reinforcing the earlier metaphor of YH covered with praises. The parallel statement identifies YHWH as the G-d of the psalmist's father, and it again reiterates the psalmist's intent to exalt YHWH for what YHWH has done.

The final element of Exodus 15:1b–3 identifies YHWH by name and function as suits the purpose of the psalm, viz., "YHWH is a man of war; YHWH is his Name!" YHWH is a warrior (who has defeated pharaoh and thereby delivered Israel), and YHWH is the deity's Name.

Exodus 15:4–12 focuses on recounting the first basis for the psalmist's praise of YHWH, viz., YHWH has defeated pharaoh and the Egyptian army by casting the pharaoh's chariots, horses, and soldiers into the sea, thereby employing YHWH's power as the creator of the natural world to act among the human beings who inhabit that creation. Exodus 15:4–5 sets the theme of this section by announcing YHWH's use of the sea to defeat pharaoh's army, beginning with the basic statement in v. 4a, "The chariots of pharaoh and his army, he has cast into the sea!" followed by the parallel statement, "And the best of his chariot commanders are sunk the Sea of Reeds!" The parallel statement has two features that need explanation. First is the phrase *mibḥar šālišāyw*, literally, "the choice of his thirds," in which *mibḥar*, "choice," refers to the "best," and *šālišāyw*, "his thirds," refers to the third man in the crew of a chariot, whose function it was to serve as the chariot commander and to protect the other two crew members (i.e., the driver and the weapons handler) from attack from behind when the chariot plunged into a body of enemy foot soldiers.[14] Without the third man, the driver and the weapons handler would find themselves overwhelmed, dragged out of the chariot from behind, and killed. Curiously, Egyptian chariots of the twelfth century BCE typically carried a two-man crew, whereas Assyrian chariots of the ninth century BCE, the high point of the Northern Kingdom of Israel, typically carried a three-man crew, apparently due to hard lessons learned in combat. The reference to *yam-sûp*, "Sea of Reeds" or "Reed Sea," indicates that the sea in question is not the Red Sea, which is how the Greek text of the Septuagint reads the narrative, but a swampy region in the area now drained as the site for the present-day Suez Canal.[15] Finally, v. 5, "The deeps cover

14. Littauwer and Crouwell, "Chariots."

15. "*sûp*," BDB 693.

them; they have gone down into the depths like stone!" reiterates the role of divine combat and creation motifs insofar as Hebrew, *tĕhōmôt*, "deeps," is a plural form of the Akkadian *Tiamatu*, "Tiamat," the goddess of the deep, whom Marduk fights and defeats in the Babylonian creation epic, Enuma Elish. The defeat of the sea is also the concern of the Ugaritic Baal Cycle in which the Ugaritic god Baal defeats Yamm, the god of the sea, to bring order into the world.

Exodus 15:6–8 turns to a direct address to YHWH, first in v. 6 with recognition of YHWH's right hand (Hebrew, *yĕmînĕkā*, "your right hand"). The right hand is the presumed hand for wielding weapons, even though it ignores all of us who are left-handed, and it praises YHWH's right hand for its strength and its capacity to instill fear and trembling in enemies. The reference to the right hand would also recall YHWH's, Moses's, and Aaron's extended hands (with staff) throughout the plague narratives. Verse 7 then turns to YHWH's qualities and their metaphorical effects, viz., YHWH's exaltation (Hebrew, *gĕ'ōnĕkā*, "your exaltation"), as YHWH tears down enemies (Hebrew, *qāmeykā*, "those who stand against you"), and YHWH's burning wrath (Hebrew, *ḥărōnĕkā*), which devours them like chaff. Verse 8 continues with metaphorical depictions of YHWH's actions to defeat the enemy, beginning with a reference to the "snorting of nostrils" (Hebrew, *bĕrûaḥ 'apeykā*, "with the wind of your noses") by which the waters are heaped up, depicting the east wind blowing the waters of the Reed Sea thereby causing the waters to pile up like heaps of grain (Hebrew, *niṣṣābû kĕmô-nēd*, "they stand like a heap [of grain]") and to freeze (Hebrew, *qāpĕ'û*) so that they stand like frozen torrents in the heart of the sea. The imagery of the heaped-up waters of the Reed Sea and the congealed or frozen torrents suggests the imagery of the gates of YHWH's heavenly palace or fortress through which Israel passes to reach safety from the threat of pharaoh and the Egyptian army. The imagery is both tangible, due to the metaphors of heaps and frozen torrents, and non-tangible, due to the metaphor of water, which is likewise both tangible (when frozen) and non-tangible (when liquid and one's hand passes through it), and therefore provides a suitable metaphor for the heavenly palace of YHWH manifested in the tangible world of creation.

Exodus 15:9 portrays the statements of the enemy who state their intention to pursue, overtake, and divide spoil to fulfill their desire (Hebrew, *timlā'ēmô napšî*, "the filling of my life"), and to draw the sword (Hebrew, *'ārîq ḥarbî*, "I will uncover my sword") to kill Israel and take what they possess. Verse 10 then returns to direct address to YHWH to recount how YHWH blew at the sea with wind so that its waters covered the enemy, causing them to sink in the waters. Verse 11 then asks the question "Who is like you among the gods, O YHWH? Who is like you, majestic in holiness? Awesome in praise? Doing wonders?" which is adapted for use in the Kedushah of the Jewish prayer service. Finally, v. 12 returns to the initial theme of this section with its depiction of YHWH's right hand, which causes the earth to swallow up the enemy.

Exodus 15:13–18 then portrays the second major reason for praising YHWH, i.e., YHWH's deliverance of Israel to YHWH's holy dwelling in the sight of the nations that were closest to Israel. Again, this section begins with direct address to YHWH in v. 13, "You lead in your fidelity this people whom you have redeemed! You guide [them] in your strength to your holy abode!" The Hebrew term *ḥesed*, "fidelity," refers to YHWH's trustworthiness to keep the terms of the covenant with Israel in order to protect them from danger.[16] And YHWH's "holy abode" (Hebrew, *nĕwēh qōdšĕkā*) remains undefined so that it might refer to Mount Sinai in the context of the exodus narrative or to the later sanctuaries of Israel and Judah, such as Gilgal, Shiloh, Jerusalem, Beth El, Dan, Beer Sheba, and others. Verse 14 turns to the terror of the nations who witness what YHWH has done for the people of Israel; they tremble in pain (Hebrew, *ḥîl*, "labor pain") like that of a woman in childbirth. The nations named here—Philistia in v. 14, the chieftains of Edom, the leaders of Moab, and the inhabitants of Canaan in v. 15—all tremble in fear. They are the nations that border Israel and Judah, Philistia to the west, Edom to the southeast, Moab to the east across the Jordan River, and Canaan, perhaps to be identified with Phoenicia to the north, representing the four principal points of the compass during the Iron Age, ca. 1200–586 BCE when Israel and Judah flourished. Verse 16 reiterates the motif of YHWH's arm (Hebrew, *zĕrôʿăkā*), akin to YHWH's right hand noted in vv. 6 and 12 above, which renders the nations speechless like stone in dread and fear as the people of Israel and Judah pass by, led by YHWH. The people whom YHWH "acquired" (Hebrew, *qānîtā*) refers to Israel, the people with whom YHWH entered into a covenant to protect them and to grant them a land in return for their fidelity to YHWH as their G-d. Verse 17 emphasizes that YHWH will lead Israel and Judah to their own mountain (Hebrew, *har*), generally the site of a temple, their own

16. Glueck, *ḤESED*.

property, *naḥălâ*, literally, "inheritance," the site for their dwelling, i.e., the land of Israel, prepared for them by YHWH, and the sanctuary of YHWH, which YHWH's own hands have made. Again, that sanctuary (Hebrew, *miqdāš*) remains undefined in the narrative so that it might be Sinai, Gilgal, Shiloh, Jerusalem, and the others noted above. Verse 18 then concludes the song with the proclamation "YHWH will rule forever and ever!" (Hebrew, *YHWH yimlōk lĕʿōlām wāʿēd*) to underscore YHWH's role as the sovereign deity of the world of creation by virtue of the defeat of pharaoh, the deliverance of Israel, and the role of creator as recounted throughout the exodus and wilderness narratives.

Exodus 15:19 then provides a concluding narrative statement that employs explanatory *kî*, "for, because," to explain what took place at the Reed Sea as depicted in the Song of the Sea, viz., pharaoh's horses and chariots pursued Israel into the sea, which YHWH then turned back upon them as Israel marched to safety on dry ground. Such imagery provides a suitable narrative envelope together with Exodus 15:1a for the Song of the Sea in Exodus 15:1b–18, and it reinforces the imagery of an act of creation insofar as it portrays dry land emerging from the waters of the sea (cf. Gen 1:1—2:3).

Exodus 15:20–21 then follows with a brief narrative account of Miriam, here named for the first time in the exodus narrative and identified as a female prophet and sister of Aaron, who took up a hand drum and led the women of Israel in singing the Song of the Sea and dancing in celebration of YHWH's deliverance of Israel. The hand drum—Hebrew, *tōp*, an onomatopoeic name for the drum based upon the sound it makes when beaten with the hand—is a typical instrument employed by both women and men in the ancient and modern worlds. The citation of the first stanza of the Song of the Sea (cf. Exod 15:1b) simply indicates that the women sang the same song as the men led by Moses, but they did so separately—and perhaps antiphonally—as part of the liturgical celebration of YHWH's deliverance. The participation of women in liturgical life and temple service is indicative of northern Israel, but not so much of southern Judah. Examples include Miriam's role in leading the women in singing the Song of the Sea, which appears to presuppose a northern setting; Deborah's role in singing liturgical poetry as an Ephraimite prophet in Judges 5; and the roles played by women at the Shiloh temple in 1 Samuel 2 where they are abused by the high priest Eli's sons, Hophni and Phineas.[17]

Reception History

The reception history of the Song of the Sea in Exodus 15:1–21 begins within the Hebrew Bible itself, especially the book of Isaiah. The Exodus pattern is evident throughout the book.[18] With regard to the Song of the Sea, Isaiah 11:15–16 is especially noteworthy given its portrayal of YHWH's ban against the tongue of the Sea of Egypt and YHWH's waving the divine hand against the river (Nile) with YHWH's "hot wind," (Hebrew, *baʿyām rûḥô*, lit., "with the heat of his wind") to strike it into seven streams to allow for passage across the sea in shoes. YHWH's action against Egypt is then applied to the deliverance of the people from Assyria so that they might travel on a highway to return home to the land of Israel. The oracle apparently dates to the reign of King Josiah of Judah, who sought to restore the unity of Israel and Judah as the Assyrian Empire faced imminent collapse.[19]

The exodus motif also plays a key role in the second part of the book of Isaiah (Isa 34–66), which anticipates the return of Israelite and Judean exiles to Jerusalem and the land of Israel from Babylonian exile, especially in Isaiah 40–48. The Song of the Sea is conspicuous particularly in Isaiah 43:16–19, which portrays YHWH's deliverance of Israel by means of a road through the sea and a pathway through the mighty waters that will also see the destruction of chariots, horses, and a mighty army.[20]

When read in its final form, the book of Isaiah understands YHWH's deliverance from Babylonian exile to be analogous to YHWH's deliverance from Egyptian slavery at the time of the exodus from Egypt. But the final form of the book of Isaiah also understands King Cyrus of Persia to be YHWH's messiah and temple builder (Isa 44:21; 45:1), and it envisions the Davidic covenant to include *all* Israel, which is expected

17. Sweeney, "Israelite and Judean Religions."

18. Sweeney, *Isaiah 1–4*, 18–20.

19. Sweeney, *Isaiah 1–39*, 196–211.

20. Sweeney, *Isaiah 40–66*, 81–108.

to serve Cyrus and Achaemenid Persian Empire as the will of YHWH (Isa 55).[21]

The Song of the Sea also factors into the book of Haggai, an early Persian-period Judean prophet who called for the restoration of the Davidic Dynasty in the form of Zerubbabel ben Shealtiel, apparently the grandson of King Jehoiachin ben Jehoiakim, who was exiled to Babylonia in 597 BCE. Haggai's final oracle in Haggai 2:20–23 envisions Zerubbabel as YHWH's "signet ring," which entails that he will rule as king of Judah on YHWH's behalf in the classic understanding of the role of the Davidic king as YHWH's regent. When he is recognized as king, YHWH will shake the heavens and the earth to overturn the throne of the kingdoms (i.e., the Achaemenid Persian Empire) and destroy its horses and riders just as YHWH destroyed pharaoh's army at the Reed Sea in Exodus 14–15. Haggai's oracle presupposes the turmoil in the Persian Empire during the early reign of the Achaemenid King Darius I, who authorized the rebuilding of the Jerusalem temple in 520–515 BCE. Haggai understood the rebuilding of the temple to portend the restoration of the House of David. As part of the book of the Twelve Prophets, Haggai and the other prophets among the Twelve opposed the view of the book of Isaiah and called for the restoration of the House of David and the defeat of the Achaemenid Empire as the nations of the world would recognize YHWH as the true G-d, creator, and sovereign of the world of creation.[22]

The Song of the Sea is given special treatment in the writing of Torah scrolls and the reading of the passage in the synagogue worship service as part of the Torah portion *Bashalaḥ* (Exod 13:17—17:16) and on the seventh day of Passover, which is when the deliverance at the sea is believed to have taken place.[23] The Song of the Sea is written with a special pattern for the arrangement of the text which imitates the art of the bricklayer, who would stagger the layering of bricks when building a wall so that half of a brick would cover a whole brick and a whole brick would cover half of a brick.[24] In addition, the Song of the Sea would be chanted in the synagogue service with a special trope.

In Jewish mysticism, the depiction of the waters of the sea congealing to form a "heap" (Hebrew, *nēd*) and a frozen mass (Hebrew, *qāpĕʾû*,

21. Sweeney, *Isaiah 40–66*, 235–48.

22. Sweeney, *Twelve Prophets*, 2:549–55; Sweeney, "Swords into Plowshares."

23. Sarna, *Exodus*, 76–77.

24. Sarna, *Exodus*, 76, 247; citing b. Megillah 16b; y. Megillah 3.8 (74b); Sofrim 12.9.

"they [the waters of the deep] froze") in Exodus 15:8 is understood to have greater significance than the simple imagery of water itself. The tangible formation of the intangible waters is understood to refer to G-d's heavenly palace or temple, which Israel metaphorically enters when passing through the sea. The passage through the sea therefore depicts the Heikhalot journey to the heavenly throne to appear before G-d. In the case of the rabbinic Heikhalot Rabbati, Rabbi Nehuniah ben ha-Qana undertakes the journey to ask G-d why the temple was destroyed, Israel was exiled, and the Bar Kochba Revolt failed. G-d's answer was to confess that perhaps G-d had not acted "beautifully" (i.e., properly) in doing so, but that continued study of the issue in relation to Jewish tradition would be necessary to understand the matter fully as the revelation of divine Oral Torah was still ongoing.[25]

The New Testament cites the Song of Moses in Revelation 15:3 to mark the closely related episodes of the wrath of G-d in which those who had conquered the beast would sing the Song of Moses, the servant of G-d, and the Song of the Lamb. The song itself in Revelation 15:3–4 does not quote the Song of the Sea directly, but it quotes phrases from various Jewish Scriptures.

The early church fathers, such as Origen, Tertullian, and Ambrose, view the exodus from Egypt as an extended allegory, a type of baptism, in which crossing through the waters of the Reed Sea portends Christian baptism as a passage from sin into redemption (cf. 1 Cor 10).[26]

The Song of the Sea was also featured in *The Prince of Egypt*, the 1998 animated film, produced by Jeffrey Katzenburg et al., which portrayed the exodus story. As the Israelites were running toward the Reed Sea with the Egyptian chariots in pursuit, they sang the Song of the Sea in Hebrew.

Finally, Martin Luther King Jr. comments on the significance of the Song of the Sea: "The meaning of this story is not found in the drowning of the Egyptian soldiers, for no one should rejoice at the death or defeat of a human being. Rather the story symbolizes the death of evil, of human oppression and unjust exploitation."[27]

25. Gruenwald, *Apocalyptic and Merkavah Mysticism*, 82–92; Sweeney, "Pardes Revisited"; Sweeney, *Jewish Mysticism*, 214–16.

26. Childs, *Exodus*, 234–35.

27. Utzschneider and Oswald, *Exodus 1–15*, 333; quoting King, *Strength to Love*.

Journey from the Reed Sea to the Wilderness of Shur/Elim: Water in the Wilderness—Exodus 15:22–27

Translation

15:22 And Moses caused Israel to travel from the Reed Sea, and they went out into the Wilderness of Shur, and they went for three days in the wilderness, but they did not find water. [23] And they came to Marah, but they were not able to drink the waters from Marah because they were bitter; therefore, he called the place Marah. [24] And the people complained against Moses, saying, "What shall we drink?" [25] And he cried out to YHWH, and YHWH showed him some wood, and he cast [it] into the waters, and the waters became sweet. There he enacted for himself a statute and a law, and there he tested them. [26] And he said, "If you will surely listen to the voice of YHWH your G-d, and what is right in his eyes you will do and you give ear to his commandments and you observe all his statutes, [then] all the disease that I inflicted upon Egypt I will not inflict upon you, for I, YHWH, am your healer."

[27] And they came to Elim, and there were twelve springs of water and seventy palm trees, and they camped there by the waters.

Commentary

Exodus 15:22–27 is demarcated at the outset by an example of the itinerary formula, "And Moses caused Israel to travel [Hebrew, *wayyassaʿ*, 'and he caused to travel'] from the Reed Sea, and they went out into the Wilderness of Shur." The Wilderness of Shur would refer to the Sinai Desert located to the east of the Reed Sea as indicated by the meaning of the term, Shur, Hebrew, *šûr*, "wall," which is derived from Aramaic, *šûrāʾ*, "wall." The name is apparently derived from the fortifications built by Egypt to protect the approaches to its eastern borders with the Sinai wilderness.[1] Although some interpreters attempt to group v. 27 with the following account of the journey to the Wilderness of Sin, the absence of the itinerary formula in v. 27 indicates that v. 27 belongs structurally to vv. 22–26, despite the indication of the movement to Elim (Hebrew, *ʾêlimāh*, "to Elim"). Elim, "terebinths, palm trees," is generally identified with an oasis site called et-Tur, located in the far southwest of the Sinai Peninsula.[2] Exodus 15:22–27 therefore recounts Israel's movement south from the Reed Sea to the southern Sinai Peninsula as the first leg of Israel's journey following the encounter at the sea.

Exodus 15:22–27 comprises three major components. The first appears in Exodus 15:22–25a, which recounts the basic problem of the narrative, viz., the failure to find potable water following a three-day journey into the wilderness. The reference to the three-day journey apparently refers to the three-day journey proposed by Moses and Aaron to pharaoh, to enable Israel to travel into the wilderness so that they might worship YHWH. The absence of potable water is hardly surprising in the Sinai. When they came to a site called Marah (Hebrew, *mārâ*, "bitter") the water was unsurprisingly bitter and therefore undrinkable. The people complained (Hebrew, *wayyillōnû*, "and they complained/murmured") to Moses demanding to know what they will drink. Moses in turn appealed to YHWH. When YHWH showed Moses a piece of wood, Moses threw it into the water, which rendered the water sweet and drinkable, and the problem was solved. The narrative does not define what the tree or bush might be, but there are any number of plants growing in the Sinai wilderness, such as hyssop, which have medicinal qualities. An analogous narrative appears in 2 Kings 2:19–22, where the people of Jericho find that their water is undrinkable. When they appeal to Elisha, the northern

1. Davies, *Exodus 1–18*, 1:410–11.

2. Davies, *Exodus 1–18*, 1:416–17.

prophet and disciple of Elijah, he throws salt from a new plate into the water and purifies it.[3] Although the means by which the wood or the salt purified the water is not clear in either narrative, the point of each is power, viz., the power of YHWH to heal in Exodus 15:22–25a and the power of Elisha to heal in 2 Kings 2:19–22.

The second component appears in Exodus 15:25b–26 in which Moses enacts "a statute and a law" (Hebrew, *ḥōq ûmišpāṭ*) concerning the need for the people to listen to YHWH's commandments and statutes. There is a threat in Moses's statement in that he makes it clear that the people will become sick if they do not listen to YHWH, and he concludes his pronouncement with the statement "for I, YHWH, am your healer."

The third component of the narrative appears in Exodus 15:27, which recounts the movement of Israel to Elim, identified with the oasis at et-Tur in the southwestern Sinai Peninsula, as noted above. There, the people would find ample potable water.

Most interpreters recognize Exodus 15:22–27 as the beginning of the wilderness journey tradition for the very obvious reason that it marks the first stage of the wilderness journey following the deliverance of Israel at the Reed Sea in Exodus 15:21.[4] Indeed, Frank M. Cross Jr. argues that the wilderness journey narratives are marked by the use of the wilderness itinerary formulas, which employ *waw*-consecutive forms of the verb *nāsaʿ*, "to journey, travel," to signal movement from one location to another in the wilderness itinerary following the encounter at the Reed Sea. Cross maintains that the itinerary formulas are characteristic of the P-stratum of the Pentateuch.[5] Others have argued that the wilderness itineraries are a factor in the redactional joining of the Genesis and Exodus–Numbers narratives in the final form of the Pentateuch.[6] But with the growing recognition of the priority of the E-stratum in the composition of the Pentateuch and the late monarchic dating of the J-stratum, other possibilities emerge for understanding the interrelationship between Genesis and Exodus–Numbers in the composition of the final form of the Pentateuch. For one, the wilderness itineraries do not begin with Exodus 15:22; they begin in Genesis 46:1 when Jacob, identified as Israel, travelled first to Beer Sheba on his journey to Egypt to find relief from the famine that had engulfed Canaan. Indeed, G-d spoke to Jacob

3. Sweeney, *1–2 Kings*, 274–75.
4. E.g., Coats, *Rebellion in the Wilderness.*
5. Cross, "Priestly Work."
6. E.g., K. Schmid, "So-Called Y-hwist."

in a vision in Genesis 46:2–4 to promise to make him into a great nation in Egypt and to bring him back from Egypt. Further itinerary formulas appear in Exodus 12:37, as Israel journeyed from Rameses to Sukkot, and Exodus 13:20, as Israel journeyed from Sukkot to Etham as Israel fled before the Egyptian army to escape across the Reed Sea. Furthermore, Jacob journeys to Egypt at the invitation of Joseph, who is signaled at the very beginning of the exodus narrative in Exodus 1:8.

In short, the wilderness itineraries indicate a linkage between Genesis and Exodus that appears to overlap the toledoth formulas that constitute the primary structural markers of the final form of the P-stratum narrative of the Pentateuch. Although it is clear that some of the wilderness itinerary formulas introduce P-stratum narrative, such as the quail and manna narratives set in the Wilderness of Sin in Exodus 16:1–36, interpreters must ask if the wilderness itinerary formulas played a role in introducing E-stratum narratives that chronicled the journey from Egypt to Canaan. Most interpreters maintain that the wilderness narratives function as a means to portray the rebelliousness of northern Israel against YHWH in J, based especially on the role of the golden calf narrative in Exodus 32–34,[7] but the E-stratum would need to include an account of the wilderness journey as well, configured not so much as a rebellion against YHWH but as a means to secure support from YHWH during a very trying journey through the wilderness. Exodus 15:22–27, which portrays Israel's need for potable water in the wilderness and YHWH's actions to ensure that such water would be available, would be an example of such a narrative. The account has northern intertextual relationships, such as the account of Elisha's purification of the water by Jericho in 2 Kings 2:19–22.[8] In both Exodus 15:22–27 and 2 Kings 2:19–22, YHWH emerges as a healer and as a deliverer for the people of Israel. In both cases, YHWH also acts as a deity who functions as master of creation and makes modifications in the world of creation that will benefit YHWH's people, Israel.

Thus, Exodus 15:22–27 begins the wilderness journey narrative of Exodus–Numbers, but the wilderness itinerary formula indicates a tie into the narratives concerning Jacob and the discovery of his son, Joseph, that are instrumental in ensuring the move of the people of Israel to Egypt, which is where YHWH will forge them into a nation, save them

7. E.g., Coats, *Rebellion in the Wilderness.*

8. Sweeney, *1–2 Kings*, 274–75.

from famine, deliver them from Egyptian bondage, and lead them to the promised land of Israel where they will find a land of milk and honey, devoid of famine, as a result of their covenant with YHWH at Sinai.

Although most interpreters view Exodus 15:22–25a as a J-stratum text, Exodus 27 as a P-stratum text, and Exodus 15:25b–26 as a non-source text,[9] the simple plot sequence and resolution of Exodus 15:22–27, the portrayal of YHWH's protection of Israel in the wilderness, and the intertextual relationship with the Elisha narrative in 2 Kings 2:19–22 indicate that the passage derives from the E-stratum of the Pentateuch.

Reception History

The statement in Exodus 15:26, "for I, YHWH, am your healer," plays an important role in the Christian Science tradition, based on the teachings of Mary Baker Eddy (1821–1910), where it indicates that only G-d is the true healer.[10]

9. See Campbell and O'Brien, *Sources of the Pentateuch*, 143–44, 41, 198 respectively.

10. Baker Eddy, *Science and Health.*

Journey from Shur/Elim to the Wilderness of Sin: Quail and Manna—Exodus 16:1–36

Translation

16:1 And they travelled from Elim, and all the congregation of the sons of Israel came to the Wilderness of Sin, which is between Elim and Sinai, on the fifteenth day of the second month since their departure from the land of Egypt. 2 And all the congregation of the sons of Israel complained against Moses and against Aaron in the wilderness. 3 And the sons of Israel said to them, "Who would have appointed our death by the hand of YHWH in the land of Egypt, where we sat by pots of meat when we ate bread to fullness, but you brought us out to this wilderness to put to death this whole assembly by starvation!"

4 And YHWH said to Moses, "Behold, I will rain down for you bread from the heavens, and the people will go out and they will gather a daily portion on that day so that I will test them: Will they walk in my instruction or not? 5 And it will be on the sixth day when they ascertain what they will bring in, then it will be double what they would gather each day." 6 And Moses and Aaron said to all the sons of Israel, "In the evening you will know that YHWH brought you out from the land of Egypt. 7 And in the morning you will see the glory of YHWH when he hears your complaints against YHWH, and

what are we when you complain against us?" [8] And Moses
said, "When YHWH gives to you in the evening meat to eat
and bread in the morning to fullness, when YHWH hears
your complaints which you are complaining against him, and
what are we? Not against us are your complaints, but [they
are] against YHWH!"

[9] And Moses said to Aaron, "Say to all the congregation of
the sons of Israel, 'Come near before YHWH because he has
heard your complaints!'" [10] And when Aaron spoke to all the
congregation of the sons of Israel, they turned toward the
wilderness, and behold, the glory of YHWH appeared in a
cloud. [11] And YHWH spoke to Moses, saying, [12] "I have heard
the complaints of the sons of Israel. Speak to them, saying,
'Between the evenings you shall eat meat, and in the morning
you shall have your fill of bread, and you shall know that I
am YHWH, your G-d!'"

[13] And in the evening quail appeared, and they covered the
camp, and in the morning there was a falling of dew all around
the camp, [14] and the falling of dew came up, and behold, upon
the face of the wilderness was a fine flaky substance, fine
like frost upon the land. [15] And the sons of Israel saw [it],
and they said, each to the other, "What is it?" because they
did not know what it was. And Moses said to them, "It is the
bread which YHWH gave to you to eat. [16] This is the thing
that YHWH commanded you, 'Gather from it, according what
he can eat, an omer per each head [for] the number of your
persons, for each in his tent, you shall take.'"

[17] And the sons of Israel did so, and they gathered, some
much and some little. [18] And they measured by the omer, and
the one who gathered much had no excess, and the one who
gathered little had no lack; each according to his eating had
gathered. [19] And Moses said to them, "Do not cause any to remain until morning." [20] And they did not listen to Moses, and
people caused some from it to remain until morning, and
worms rose up, and it stank, and Moses was angry at them.

[21] And they gathered it every morning, each according to his
eating, and when the sun became hot, it would melt. [22] And

on the sixth day, they gathered a double amount of bread, two omers for each, and all the leaders of the congregation came, and they told Moses. 23 And he said to them, "It is what YHWH said, a Shabbaton, tomorrow is a holy Shabbat for YHWH. Whatever you bake, bake; whatever you boil, boil. And all that remains, set aside for yourselves to keep until morning." 24 And they set it aside until morning, just as Moses commanded, and it didn't stink, and there was no maggot in it. 25 And Moses said, "Eat it today because today is a Shabbat for YHWH; today you will not find it in the field. 26 Six days you shall gather, but on the seventh day is a Shabbat; there will not be [anything] on it."

27 But on the seventh day, some of the people went out to gather, but they did not find. 28 And YHWH said to Moses, "How long will you refuse to observe my commandments and my instructions? 29 See that YHWH has given to you the Shabbat! Therefore, he gives to you on the sixth day bread [for] two days. Remain, each, in his place. Do not go out, each from his place, on the seventh day!" 30 And the people rested on the seventh day.

31 And the House of Israel called its name mān. And it was like a seed of white coriander, and its taste was like flat cake with honey. 32 And Moses said, "This is the word which YHWH commanded, 'Fill the omer from it to keep for your generations in order that they will see the bread that I caused you to eat in the wilderness when I brought you out from the land of Egypt.'" 33 And Moses said to Aaron, "Take one jar, and place there a full omer of mān, and behold, it will be before YHWH for keeping for your generations." 34 Just as YHWH commanded Moses, Aaron placed it before the testimony for keeping. 35 And the sons of Israel ate the mān for forty years until they came to settled land; the mān they ate until the edge of the land of Canaan. 36 And an omer is one-tenth of an ephah.

Commentary

The account of Israel's journey from the Elim to the Wilderness of Sin in Exodus 16:1–36 is demarcated at the outset by the itinerary formula in Exodus 16:1, "And they travelled from Elim, and all the congregation of the sons of Israel came to the Wilderness of Sin." The narrative is concerned especially with Israel's complaints to YHWH for the lack of food and YHWH's provision of manna and quail to Israel as bread and meat. A special feature of this narrative is its focus on the role of Shabbat in the world of creation and its impact on the people's ability to gather manna and quail. The appearance of the itinerary formula in Exodus 17:1, which recounts Israel's journey from the Wilderness of Sin to Rephidim, demarcates the beginning of the next major sub-unit of the narrative.

The narrative comprises three major components. The first is the account of Israel's journey to the Wilderness of Sin and their complaining to Moses and Aaron concerning the lack of food in Exodus 16:1–3. The second is YHWH's speech to Moses in Exodus 16:4–8 concerning YHWH's intention to test whether or not the people will listen to YHWH's instruction and the speech by Moses and Aaron to Israel concerning YHWH's intention to provide them with meat and bread. The third is Exodus 16:9–36, which recounts in detail YHWH's provision of meat and bread to the people in the form of quail and manna and the refusal of some of the people to observe YHWH's instruction concerning the observance of the Shabbat. The basic purpose of the narrative is to demonstrate how YHWH, the master of creation, provides for the people's needs, but it also signals resistance on the part of the people to observe YHWH's instruction. Within the present context of the narrative shortly before the account of the revelation of YHWH's Torah on Mount Sinai, Exodus 16 points to the need for such revelation.

Exodus 16:1–3 recounts Israel's journey from Elim to the Wilderness of Sin and their complaints to Moses and Aaron concerning the need for food. The exact location of the Wilderness of Sin remains uncertain. According to the text, the Wilderness of Sin is located between Elim and Sinai. Although Elim is located in the southwestern Sinai Peninsula, the location of Sinai remains the subject of debate. Some identify the site with "Debbet er-Ramleh, close to Serabit el-Khadem," and others locate the site on "the coastal plain at el-Marḫa close to the mouth of the Wadi Sidri."[1] The date of Israel's arrival on the fifteenth of the second month following

1. See Davies, *Exodus 1–18*, 1:448–49, with bibliography.

the exodus from Egypt would be the fifteenth of Iyyar in the current Jewish calendar, which would anticipate Israel's arrival at Sinai on the third month, Sivan, of the Jewish calendar, as indicated in Exodus 19:1. The fifteenth day of Iyyar would be in May or possibly early June. The complaint of the people to Moses and Aaron constitutes a deliberate caricature of the people, who wish they had died in Egypt, where they claim that they sat before pots of meat and ate their fill of bread. As slaves, they would have had little opportunity to do much more than look at the pots of meat that were meant for consumption by the Egyptian, and their fill of bread would have been unleavened matzah, which would have been considered suitable for the feeding of slaves. Their charge that Moses and Aaron brought them to the wilderness to starve is patently absurd, especially when considered in relation to the account of YHWH's deliverance of Israel at the Reed Sea. Nevertheless, the caricature of the people accentuates their rebellious nature and builds dramatic tension for the portrayal of Israel's rebellions in the golden calf narrative of Exodus 32–34 and rebellion narratives of Numbers 11–25, most of which presuppose the alleged apostasy of the Northern Kingdom of Israel in later times.

The account of YHWH's speech to Moses concerning YHWH's intention to provide the people with food and to test their observance of YHWH's instructions followed by the speech of Moses and Aaron concerning YHWH's intentions in Exodus 16:4–8 signals the key issues that will emerge in the detailed account of the provision of food that follows.

The presentation of YHWH's speech in Exodus 16:4–5 portrays YHWH as "raining down" (Hebrew, *mamṭîr*) bread for the people from the heavens. This is a deliberate use of metaphor to emphasize that YHWH is the true G-d of creation and to demonstrate that it is YHWH—and not Baal, the Canaanite god of rain and fertility—who provides rain and food for the people. Such a portrayal actually targets northern Israel for its alleged devotion to Baal. The use of the Hebrew verb *wĕlāqĕṭû*, "and they will gather/glean," employs the verb used in the Holiness Code in Leviticus 19:9–10 and in Ruth 2:3, 7–8, 15–19 to portray the grain left for the poor to glean in priestly literature and the Persian-period Ruth narratives.[2] YHWH concludes the speech in v. 5 with a statement that indicates the intention to provide a double portion of food for the people on the sixth day so that they might observe the Shabbat on the seventh day. Such a concern is characteristic of the P-stratum of the Pentateuch,

2. See Cohn Eskenazi and Frymer-Kensky, *Ruth*, xvi–xix.

although it is noteworthy that concern with the Shabbat appears in the Covenant Code, especially in the laws concerned with leaving the fields fallow during every seventh year (Exod 23:10–11) and observance of the seventh day as Shabbat (Exod 23:12). There is no antecedent in the E-stratum for the observance of Shabbat, but it is clear that the Covenant Code presumes observance of Shabbat in the Northern Kingdom of Israel. The present narrative portrays observance of Shabbat as an integral feature of creation in the P-stratum of the Pentateuch.[3] Although it remains possible that the present narrative is based on an older E-stratum narrative, that stratum is now lost to us.

The following speech by Moses and Aaron to the people in Exodus 16:6–8 emphasizes that the people will know YHWH, based on YHWH's deliverance of Israel from Egypt, the appearance of YHWH's presence of "glory" (*kābôd*), and YHWH's provision of food for the people in the wilderness. The people's knowledge of YHWH is based on the self-revelation formula, "and they shall know that I am YHWH," which is characteristic of priestly literature in the Pentateuch and Ezekiel.[4] The use of the term "glory" to portray the presence of YHWH is also characteristic of priestly literature, and it appears at the conclusion of the book of Exodus when "the glory of YHWH" settles into the newly built and consecrated tabernacle in Exodus 40:33b–38. The imagery of the glory of YHWH is based on the imagery of the pillar of fire and smoke that accompanies and leads Israel out from Egypt to the Reed Sea and from the Reed Sea to Mount Sinai. Such imagery presupposes the imagery of the pillar of fire and cloud that rises from the altar of the temple during the ancient temple worship service (cf. Isa 4:5–6). The purpose of the speech is to inform the people that their complaints are not simply against Moses and Aaron; rather they are against YHWH, the master of creation, who provides them with meat and bread in the wilderness in response to their complaints.

Exodus 16:9–36 recounts YHWH's provision of quail and manna to the people together with the people's resistance to the observance of Shabbat. The sub-unit is demarcated at the outset by an account of Moses's instructions to Aaron to announce that YHWH has heard the people's complaint in v. 9, the appearance of "the glory of YHWH" in a cloud as Aaron spoke to the people in v. 10, and YHWH's speech to

3. Sweeney, "Shabbat."

4. Coats, *Exodus 1–18*, 178; Zimmerli, "I Am YHWH."

Moses in vv. 11–12 in which YHWH announces that the people will eat meat and bread so that they will know "that I am YHWH, your G-d." The exchange of speeches among Moses, Aaron, and YHWH, which announce the coming provision of food, is followed by an account of YHWH's provision of food to the people and their reaction to that provision in vv. 13–36.

The account of Moses's speech to Aaron in Exodus 16:9 functions simply to acknowledge that YHWH has heard the people's complaint and will presumably act to resolve it.

The account of the revelation of "the glory of YHWH" in a cloud as Aaron spoke to the people in Exodus 16:10 constitutes an announcement of YHWH's theophany.[5] Although this is a very brief example of the theophany announcement, its placement here is important to the narrative in that it illustrates YHWH's commitment to address the complaints of the people, thereby to demonstrate that YHWH is indeed the true G-d of creation and the true redeemer of Israel.

The account of YHWH's statement to Moses in Exodus 16:11–12 confirms YHWH's intentions to address the complaint of the people by ensuring that they have both meat and bread to eat. The appearance of the self-revelation formula, "and you shall know that I am YHWH, your G-d," confirms the narrative purpose to reveal YHWH as the true G-d of creation and redeemer of Israel.[6]

The following narrative in Exodus 16:13–36 recounts YHWH's provision of food, the condition that the people observe the Shabbat, the people's reaction, and Moses's statement of YHWH's command for the display of the omer before YHWH. The narrative comprises five major components in vv. 13–16, 17–21, 22–26, 27–30, and 31–36, based on the advancement of plot coupled with statements by Moses or YHWH concerning the understanding of each element of the plot development.

The first element in the plot appears in Exodus 16:13–16, which recounts YHWH's efforts to address the complaint of the people together with statements by the people and by Moses that explain YHWH's actions. The timing of the event is the evening, technically, the beginning of the Israelite and Jewish day when the evening worship service would take place in the temple. At this point, YHWH provides quail for the people to eat and the next morning YHWH provides a "fine, flaky

5. See Coats, *Exodus 1–18*, 173.

6. Coats, *Exodus 1–18*, 178.

substance," like dew on the ground. Both of these items are elements of creation in the Sinai wilderness. The quail appear during periods of migration between the northern areas of the Mediterranean basin and the southern reaches of Africa. When the birds are exhausted from their long flight, they are easy to catch. The "fine, flaky substance" appears to be a secretion from gum resin produced by several flowering trees found in the Sinai wilderness and elsewhere in the ancient Near East, such as Alhagi Maurorum, Tamarisk Gallica, or Fraxinus Ornus, or it may also result from an insect secretion linked to the resin of the above-named trees.[7] The substance is described in Numbers 11:7–9 as similar to coriander seed, bdellium in color. It may be ground between millstones, pounded in a mortar, boiled in a pot, or made into cakes, and it tasted like "cream of oil" (cf. Exod 16:31 below). The people did not know what it was, and so they asked, "What is it?" (Hebrew, *mān hû*, lit., "What is it?" or "It is manna"). Their question then becomes the basis for the name, *mān*, "manna." Moses explains to the people that the manna is food provided by YHWH, and each person should gather an omer of the substance, normally one-tenth of an ephah, which is here defined as the amount of food that each person needs to eat for each day.

Exodus 16:17–21 recounts the reaction of the people of Israel to the provision of manna with a focus on the principle that each person should receive as much as s/he could eat in one day. Each person gathered an omer, which proved to be as much or as little as one ate during the day. This segment of the narrative includes Moses's instructions not to leave the manna over night, but the people did not listen to Moses, only to find that worms appeared in the manna when it was left until morning. Their refusal to abide by his instructions angered Moses, and portended the growing conflict between Moses and YHWH, on the one hand, and the people, on the other, that would break out in Exodus 32–34 and Numbers 11–25. When the people left the manna until morning, it would decompose.

Exodus 16:22–26 follows with an account of the people's need to gather a double portion of manna on the sixth day (i.e., Friday), before the onset of the Shabbat on Friday night and during the day on Saturday, the seventh day of the week. The reason for the need to gather a double amount on Friday is that creation would rest on the Shabbat, and therefore no food would be provided on the seventh day. When the leaders

7. Slayton, "Manna"; see also Davies, *Exodus 1–18*, 1:455–58.

of the congregation informed Moses of the issue, he explained to them the principle of the Shabbat, i.e., they should gather and prepare enough manna for both Friday and the Shabbat; the manna would not produce worms or decompose insofar as the Shabbat is holy to YHWH.

Exodus 16:27–30 then recounts how some of the people ignored the instructions to gather a double amount of manna on Friday, and went out on the Shabbat to find some, but without success. YHWH's response, spoken to Moses, was to question how long the people would refuse to observe YHWH's commandments and instructions. This is a rhetorical question, which actually functions as a statement that they should observe YHWH's commands and instructions. YHWH reiterates the instructions to observe the Shabbat and that no one should leave their place on the Shabbat. Although the people rested (Hebrew, *wayyišbĕtû*) on the seventh day, this episode portrays the increasing tensions between the people, on the one side, and YHWH and Moses, on the other.

Exodus 16:31–36 closes the narrative with an account of Moses's instructions to Aaron to place an omer of manna in the tabernacle before YHWH to commemorate YHWH's provision of food for the people in the wilderness. The sub-unit begins with a description of manna, indicating that it was like coriander seed, white in color, and that it tasted like "flat cake with honey." Moses instructed Aaron to keep one omer of manna "for a watch for your generations" (Hebrew, *lĕmišmeret lĕdōrōtêkem*), i.e., to serve as a reminder of how YHWH supported Israel in the wilderness, and that it be placed before YHWH. Verse 34 specifies that Aaron placed it before "the testimony" (Hebrew, *lipnê hāʿēdut*), a term that is understood to refer to ark of the covenant where the tablets of the covenant would eventually be kept in the holy of holies of the tabernacle and the temple. Verse 35 notes that the people ate manna during their forty years in the wilderness up until the time that they came to the border of the land of Canaan, and v. 36 specifies that an omer is one-tenth of an ephah.

Reception History

YHWH's provision of meat and bread also appears in the Psalms. Psalm 78:17–39 recounts YHWH's provision of quail and manna in the context of Israel's failure to trust in YHWH in the wilderness. Psalm 78:23–24 refers YHWH's command to the heavens to rain manna down upon the people for food. Likewise, Psalm 105:40 recounts how YHWH brought quail for Israel to eat and satisfied them with bread from heaven.

The Christian New Testament refers to manna in John 6:22–59, which recounts Jesus's bread from heaven discourse.[8] The phrase "bread from heaven" (Greek, *artōn ek tou ouranou*) (John 6:31) appears throughout the discourse in John 6:31–33, 41–42, 50, 58, together with "bread of G-d" (Greek, *artos tou Theou*) (John 6:33) and "bread of life" (Greek, *ho artos tēs zōēs*) (John 6:35); and it culminates in John 6:51 with Jesus's statement "I am the living bread, which came down from heaven" (Greek, *egō eimi ho artos ho ek tou ouranou katabas*), all of which appear to presuppose the depictions of manna raining down from heaven in Exodus 16 and Psalms 78 and 105, as well as Jewish midrashic sources. Hebrews 9:4 portrays manna stored in a golden jar within the ark of the covenant together with the tablets of the covenant and Aaron's rod. And Revelation 2:17 refers to hidden manna as a gift from Christ. First Corinthians 10:3–4 presents Paul's depiction of manna as a spiritual food, like that of the Last Supper, and 2 Corinthians 8:15 refers to the adequate amount of manna collected in the Exodus 16 narrative.

Second Temple–period Jewish texts focus especially on manna as heavenly food. Josephus quotes Nehemiah 9:15 in referring to manna as "food/bread of heaven" in *Antiquities* 3.5.3. Fourth Ezra 1.19 refers to manna as "the bread of angels," and 2 Baruch 29.8; History of the Rechabites 13.2; and the Sibylline Oracles 7.146–49 consider manna to be the food of the messianic age. Joseph and Asenath 16.14 portrays an angel who gives Asenath a honeycomb produced in heaven as the food of angels and the elect produced in paradise. Philo considers manna to represent the logos or word of G-d, and considers it to be the food of prophecy (*Fug.* 137–39; *Her.* 79; *Leg.* 86).[9]

Manna appears throughout rabbinic sources. Most notably, it is viewed as food that stimulates Torah study in the wilderness to reinforce dependence on G-d and faith (Sifra Bamidbar 88; b. Yoma 76a). According to the Mekhilta de R. Ishmael 1.248–49, G-d provides manna in the wilderness to relieve Israel of the need to support itself so that it can focus on Torah study. According to the Mekhilta, Jeremiah presents this teaching to Israel, and Elijah will ultimately provide manna at the time of the final restoration.[10] Rabbi Saadiah Gaon viewed the provision of manna

8. Kobel, "Manna."

9. Moore, "Manna."

10. Wilfand, "Manna."

as the greatest of G-d's miracles on behalf of Israel, and R. Abraham Ibn Ezra, commenting on Exodus 16:5, lists the ten miraculous qualities of manna. The Zohar views manna as the vehicle by which divine wisdom is absorbed by the human body (Zohar 2.62b).[11]

Christianity generally equates manna with the Eucharist and the word of G-d, based especially on John 6 and 1 Corinthians 10:3. Ambrose and Augustine consider manna to prefigure the holy supper, and Aquinas identifies it with the Eucharist.[12]

Manna also appears in film. Steven Spielberg's film *Empire of the Sun* (1987) portrays the gratitude of the protagonist, Jamie, following the Japanese surrender when Red Cross food packets fall from the sky. His 1993 film *Schindler's List* portrays Schindler as Moses insofar as he saves his factory workers from starvation. When Schindler informs a Nazi officer that he wants his people, the officer responds, "Who are you? Moses?"[13]

11. Walfish, "Manna."
12. Mumme, "Manna."
13. Wong, "Manna."

Journey from the Wilderness of Sin to Rephidim: Water, Amalek, and Jethro—Exodus 17:1—18:27

Translation

17:1 And all the congregation of the sons of Israel travelled
from the Wilderness of Sin by segments at the command of
YHWH, and they camped in Rephidim, but there was no water for the people to drink. [2] And the people contended with
Moses, and they said, "Give us water, so we can drink!" And
Moses said to them, "Why do you contend with me? Why do
you test YHWH?" [3] And the people thirsted there for water,
and the people complained against Moses, and they said,
"Why is this that you brought us up from Egypt to die, me,
and my sons, and my cattle, from thirst?" [4] And Moses cried
out to YHWH, saying, "What shall I do for this people? In a
little while, they will stone me!" [5] And YHWH said to Moses,
"Pass before the people, and take with you some of the elders of Israel, and your staff with which you struck the Nile
take in your hand, and you shall go. [6] Behold, I am standing
before you there by the rock at Horeb, and you shall strike
the rock, and water will come out from it, and the people
will drink." And Moses did so before the eyes of the elders of
Israel. [7] And he called there the place Massah and Meribah
because of the contention of sons of Israel and because of
their testing YHWH, saying, "Is YHWH in our midst or not?"

17:8 And Amalek came, and he fought with Israel in Rephidim. 9 And Moses said to Joshua, "Choose for us men, and go out and fight with Amalek. Tomorrow, I will take a position on the top of the hill, and the rod of G-d [will be] in my hand." 10 And Joshua did just as Moses said to him to fight against Amalek. And Moses and Aaron and Hur went up to the top of the hill. 11 And when Moses raised his hand, Israel would overpower, and when Moses rested his hand, Amalek overpowered. 12 But the hands of Moses were heavy, so they took a stone, and they placed it under him, and he sat upon it, and Aaron and Hur supported with his hands, on one side and on the other, and his hands were firm until the setting of the sun. 13 And Joshua disabled Amalek with the sword. 14 And YHWH said to Moses, "Write this as a record in a book, and place it in the ears of Joshua that I will utterly erase the memory of Amalek from under the heavens." 15 And Moses built an altar, and he called its name "YHWH is my banner." 16 And he said, "Because the hand is above the throne of YH, there will be war for YHWH with Amalek from generation to generation."

18:1 And Jethro, priest of Midian and father-in-law of Moses, heard all that G-d had done for Moses and for Israel, his people, that YHWH brought out Israel from Egypt. 2 And Jethro, the father-in-law of Moses, took Zipporah, the wife of Moses, after he sent her away, 3 and her two sons, of whom the name of the first was Gershom, because he said I have been a resident alien in a foreign land, 4 and of whom the name of the other was Eliezer, because the G-d of my father was my help, and he delivered me from the sword of pharaoh. 5 And Jethro, the father-in-law of Moses, came with his sons and his wife to Moses in the wilderness where he was camping at the mountain of G-d. 6 And he said to Moses, "I, your father-in-law, have come to you, with your wife and her two sons." 7 And Moses went out to meet his father-in-law, and he bowed down, and he kissed him, and each asked the other about [his] welfare, and they came into the tent.

8 And Moses recounted to his father-in-law all that YHWH had done to pharaoh and to Egypt on behalf of Israel, all the

hardship that Egypt [had inflicted] on the way, and [how]
YHWH had delivered them. [9] And Jethro rejoiced over all the
good which YHWH did for Israel when he delivered him from
the hand of Egypt. [10] And Jethro said, "Blessed be YHWH,
who delivered you from the hand of Egypt and from the
hand of pharaoh when he delivered the people from under
the hand of Egypt. [11] Now I know that YHWH is greater than
all the gods due to the matter in which they acted insolently
against them." [12] And Jethro, the father-in-law of Moses, took
a whole burnt offering and sacrifices [of well-being] for G-d,
and Aaron and all the elders of Israel came to eat bread with
the father-in-law of Moses before G-d.

[13] And it was on the next day when Moses sat to judge the
people, and the people stood by Moses from the morning
until the evening. [14] And the father-in-law of Moses saw all
that he was doing for the people, and he said, "What is this
thing that you are doing for the people? Why are you sitting
alone, and all the people take a stand by you from the morning until the evening?" [15] And Moses said to his father-in-law,
"Because the people come to me to inquire of G-d. [16] When
they have an issue, it comes to me, and I judge between one
man and another, and I make known the statutes of G-d and
his instructions." [17] But the father-in-law of Moses said to
him, "The thing that you are doing is not good. [18] You will
surely wear out, both you and this people who are with you,
because the matter is too heavy for you. You are not able to
do it yourself. [19] Now, listen to my voice. I will counsel you,
and may G-d be with you. You are before G-d for the people,
and you bring [their] issues to G-d. [20] And you explain [to]
them the statutes and the instructions, and you inform them
[of] the path on which they shall walk and the action that
they are to do. [21] And you will see among all the people, capable men who revere G-d, men of truth who hate a bribe,
and you shall place over them officers of thousands, officers
of hundreds, officers of fifties, and officers of tens. [22] And
they shall judge the people all the time, and when there is a
major issue, they shall bring it to you, but every minor issue
they will judge. Lighten [your load] from upon yourself, and

they shall carry [it] with you. [23] If you do this thing, and G-d commands you [to do it], then you will be able to stand, and also all this people will go in peace unto its place."

[24] And Moses listened to the voice of his father-in-law, and he did all that he said. [25] And Moses chose capable men from all Israel, and he appointed them as heads over the people, officers of thousands, officers of hundreds, officers of fifties, and officers of tens. [26] And they judged the people all the time; a difficult issue they brought to Moses, but every minor issue they would judge. [27] And Moses sent his father-in-law away, and he went on his own to his land.

Commentary

Exodus 17:1—18:27 recounts Israel's journey from the Wilderness of Sin to Rephidim with a focus on the people's complaints concerning their need for water, the attack launched against Israel by the Amalekites, and the visit of Jethro, the father-in-law of Moses, who advised him on setting up the judicial system for the people of Israel.

The unit is demarcated at the outset by the itinerary formula in Exodus 17:1, and the combination of the temporal formula and the itinerary formula in Exodus 19:1–2 recounting Israel's travel from Rephidim to Sinai marks the beginning of a new unit in Exodus 19:1. Exodus 17:1—18:27 comprises three major sub-units constituted by the above-noted accounts concerning Israel's need for water in Exodus 17:1–7; Amalek's attack against Israel in Exodus 17:8–16; and Jethro's visit to Moses and Israel in Exodus 18:1–27. The first two accounts concerning water and Amalek are generally considered as J-stratum narratives with some E-stratum elements,[1] whereas the Jethro narrative is generally considered to be an E-stratum narrative.[2] Now that J is considered to be a late monarchic or early exilic stratum, the combined narrative would have to be considered an E-stratum narrative that has been reworked by J. When read together, the three sub-units of Exodus 17–18 address the various needs of the people of Israel in the wilderness, including water, defense from enemies, and the organization of a

1. Campbell and O'Brien, *Sources of the Pentateuch*, 144, 185.
2. Campbell and O'Brien, *Sources of the Pentateuch*, 185–86.

legal system of justice, each of which is resolved by YHWH or Jethro acting in conjunction with YHWH.

The first constituent sub-unit in Exodus 17:1–7 takes up Israel's need for water in the wilderness. They journey from the Wilderness of Sin, a location that remains unknown between Elim and Sinai. Those who posit a southern route for the people of Israel identify it with Debbet er-Ramleh or el-Markhah in the southwestern plain of the Sinai Peninsula. Those who posit a northern route for Israel place it in the vicinity of several mountains identified as Mount Sinai.[3] The location of Rephidim remains unknown and dependent upon the identification of Mount Sinai. Those who opt for a northern location place it in the Negev highlands, northern Sinai, or Midian, whereas those who opt for a southern location place it near Jebel Musa, with the Wadi Feiran as the most likely location.[4] This problem of water has already appeared in Exodus 15:22–27 in the Wilderness of Shur, but there the problem was that the water was undrinkable and had to be purified. In the present instance, the water has to be found. A similar narrative appears in Numbers 20, but in that case, the narrative addresses the need for priests, in this case, Moses and Aaron, to purify themselves in the aftermath of impurity caused by the burial of their sister, Miriam.[5]

The plot development of the present narrative concerning water portrays Israel as increasingly rebellious with their demands for water and their charge that Moses brought them to the wilderness in order to kill them and their livestock. He responds to their initial demand for water in v. 2 with impatience to exclaim, "Why do you contend [Hebrew, *māh tĕrîbûn*] with me? Why do you test [Hebrew, *māh-tĕnassûn*] YHWH?" The Hebrew verbs employed here lend themselves to the naming of the site in v. 7. Moses's reaction to the charges in v. 4 exhibits extreme frustration and fear; rather than answer them, he appears to be fed up, and he fears that they will stone him to death. He therefore turns to YHWH to demand to know, "What shall I do for this people? In a little while, they will stone me!"

YHWH's response to Moses in vv. 5–6—viz., that he should pass before the people with some of the elders of the people and the staff that he used to strike the Nile River in Egypt—is designed to show his presence among the people, his relationship with their leaders, and

3. D. Seely, "Sin, Wilderness of."

4. J. Seely, "Rephidim."

5. Sweeney, "Why Moses Was Barred."

his relationship with YHWH by virtue of his staff that he used to turn the Nile into blood in Exodus 7:19–29. In short, it is a reminder of the power of YHWH to deliver the people and YHWH's relationship with Moses and the leaders of Israel.

Exodus 17:7 then concludes the sub-unit by naming the site Massah and Maribah (Hebrew, *massāh ûmĕrîbāh*, "testing and contention"), as noted above in v. 2. The name is designed to recall the event at the site. Some speculate that this was a site for assembly and the resolution of dispute, but such a view must be considered speculative due to the absence of firm evidence. The underlying question of the narrative is expressed at the end of v. 7 when the people ask, "Is YHWH in our midst or not?" The narrative is designed to answer their question in the affirmative.

Exodus 17:8–16 constitutes the second component of Exodus 17:1—18:27. It recounts the attack by Amalek against Israel at Rephidim. Amalek are well known as the people who attacked Israel during the wilderness journey from Egypt to the promised land of Israel. The present narrative, which appears to be a J-stratum composition that reworked an underlying E-stratum account, would represent an early narrative concerning their attempts to destroy Israel. Amalek was the son of Elphaz and his concubine, Timna, and the grandson of Esau, according to Genesis 36:12, 16 (cf. 1 Chr 1:35). The Amalekites are therefore associated with Edomites and perhaps also Moab and Ammon. They are located in the Negev (Num 13:29). Other accounts of Amalek's attack against Israel in the wilderness specify that they were among the nations that attempted to eradicate Israel's name (Ps 83:5, 8) and that Amalek attacked the weak and vulnerable at the rear of the Israelite column. They are therefore considered as an enemy that sought to destroy Israel. Other texts (see 1 Sam 15) present YHWH's instruction to destroy the Amalekites for their crimes against Israel, and Esther posits that Haman, who plotted to destroy the entire Jewish people during the Persian period, is a descendant of Agag, the leader of the Amalekites in 1 Samuel 15 (Esth 3:1).[6]

The Amalekite attack takes place at Rephidim, which is derived from the Hebrew root *rpd*, which means "to spread out," apparently in reference to Moses's hands as portrayed in the narrative. When the Amalekites attack, Moses calls on Joshua, who is named for the first time in the pentateuchal narrative, to choose men to defend Israel

6. Lipton, "Amalek, Amalekites."

against the Amalekite attack. The details of Joshua's identity are not mentioned here, but they will appear later in the wilderness, Deuteronomy, Joshua, and Judges narratives (see e.g., Exod 24; Num 13–14; Deut 31; Joshua; Judg 1–2). Moses stations himself atop the hill located by Rephidim, with "the staff of G-d" (Hebrew, *maṭṭēh hā'ĕlōqîm*), which suggests the Elohistic origins of the narrative. Moses is accompanied by Aaron and Hur, who will hold his hands (with the rod of G-d) up when Moses gets tired; as long as Moses's hands are up, Israel prevails; when they are down, Amalek prevails. Aaron and Hur eventually had to find a stone on which Moses could sit, and this made it easier for them to hold up Moses's hands so that Israel, led by Joshua, would eventually defeat Amalek with the sword. This is the first time that Hur is mentioned in the Pentateuch; he also joins Moses, Aaron, Joshua, and the elders when they ascend to Mount Sinai in Exodus 24 to join in a festival meal with YHWH. Moses's stance, supported by Aaron and Hur, represents an embodiment of G-d that is characteristic of a "man of G-d" (Hebrew, *'îš hā'ĕlōqîm*), and is especially well known in northern Israel (e.g., Elijah, Elisha, and the blind prophet from Beth El).

YHWH's concluding statement to Moses in Exodus 17:14 instructs Moses to record the defeat of Amalek in order to remind Israel of what Amalek had done, so that the memory of Amalek would be utterly erased from under the heavens due to Amalek's attempt to destroy Israel. Moses built an altar at the site, and he named it *YHWH nissî*, "YHWH is my banner," which apparently presupposes Moses's raised hands with the staff of G-d to signify Israel's victory over Amalek at Rephidim. The Hebrew explanation of the name, *kî yād ʿal-kēs YH*, "because the hand is above the throne of YH [YHWH]," apparently symbolizes Moses's raised hand above the stone that represents the seat or throne of YHWH. The Hebrew term *kēs* is problematic because it is a hapax legomenon, i.e., the sole occurrence of the term. It is generally assumed to be a shortened form of *kissē'*, "seat, throne," derived from the root *ksh*, "to cover," hence "cover," which would be analogous to the mercy seat that will cover the ark of the covenant. The shortened form of the term was likely inspired by the similar form of the noun, *nēs*, "banner, ensign."[7] Note that the phrase also uses a shorted form of the divine Name, YH, in place of YHWH. The final declaration that "there will be war for YHWH with Amalek

7. Cf. Davies, *Exodus 1–18*, 1:534–36.

from generation to generation" signifies YHWH's eternal commitment to defend Israel against those who seek to destroy it.

Exodus 18:1–27 constitutes the third major narrative component of Exodus 17:1—18:27, which recounts Jethro's visit to Moses at Rephidim and the establishment of the Israelite judicial system. Although this narrative is generally treated as a separate unit within the larger literary structure of the text, the absence of an itinerary formula in Exodus 18:1 indicates that the events recounted here take place in Rephidim due to the presence of the itinerary formula in Exodus 17:1. Most interpreters consider Exodus 18:1–27 to be an E-stratum narrative, due largely to the repeated instances of *ʾĕlōhîm*, "G-d," in vv. 1, 4, 5, 12 (2x), 15, 16, 19 (3x), 21, and 23.[8] Nevertheless, the shift in Exodus 18:1 from *ʾĕlōhîm*, "G-d," to *yhwh*, "YHWH," suggests that Exodus 18 was originally composed as an E-stratum narrative, but that it was later overwritten as a J-stratum redaction. Other examples of the use of YHWH in the narrative appear in vv. 8 (2x), 9, 10, 11, and suggest that the account of YHWH's deliverance of Israel from Egypt in vv. 8–11 together with the reference in v. 1 constitute the major extent of J redaction of the passage. Most interpreters maintain that the judicial organization discussed here represents the efforts of King Jehoshaphat ben Asa of Judah (873–849 BCE) to enact judicial reform as discussed in 2 Chronicles 19. Although Jehoshaphat was king of Judah, which might suggest Judean redaction of the account in Exodus 18:13–26, he was also a vassal of King Ahab ben Omri of Israel (869–850 BCE); his son, King Ahaziah ben Ahab of Israel (850–849 BCE); and Ahab's second son, King Jehoram ben Ahab of Israel (849–842 BCE). If King Jehoshaphat of Judah did indeed enact judicial reform, he did so as a vassal of the House of Omri, apparently as the first Judean king to submit to northern Israel, according to 1 Kings 22:45, and the judicial reforms would have included all of northern Israel and southern Judah, which together comprised a territory that would require a better organized and stratified system of jurisprudence that would serve the needs of such an extensive territory. Most interpreters doubt the historicity of the account of Jehoshaphat's judicial reform as the product of the Chronicler.[9] It is noteworthy, however, that the combined territory of the Northern Kingdom of Israel and the Southern Kingdom of Judah would have required such a judicial system.

8. Campbell and O'Brien, *Sources of the Pentateuch*, 186–87.

9. See R. Klein, *2 Chronicles*, 272–74.

Exodus 18:1–27 comprises three major literary components, defined by the action that each component recounts. The first is the account of Jethro's arrival and Moses's reception of his father-in-law in Exodus 18:1–12; the second is the account of Jethro's advice to Moses concerning judicial reform in Exodus 18:13–26; and the third is the notice of Jethro's departure for his own land in Exodus 18:27.

The first component of the narrative in Exodus 18:1–12 recounts Jethro's arrival at Rephidim in vv. 1–7 and Moses's reception of his father-in-law in vv. 8–12.

Exodus 18:1–7 begins with a twofold notice of Jethro's arrival in v. 1. The verse is careful to identify Jethro as the priest of Midian and as Moses's father-in-law, identities that are emphasized throughout the entire narrative in Exodus 18. Jethro's identity as priest of Midian is crucial because it raises questions as to whether Jethro adheres to a foreign god, but his affirmation of YHWH in vv. 8–12 answers any questions as to where his loyalties lie. Nevertheless, it is not entirely clear as to what deity a Midianite priest might represent, especially since the account of Israel's apostasy at Baal Peor in Numbers 25 would suggest that the Midianites worshipped other gods, such as those of Moab. Furthermore, historical records, particularly the El Amarna tablets, indicate that Israel may have originated as seminomadic tribes, labelled as *habiru*, "barbarians," by Canaanite scribes writing to their Egyptian overlords in the mid-fourteenth century.[10] The Amarna tablets indicate that the Habiru allied with King Labayu of Shechem and his sons against other city states in Bronze Age Canaan, such as Jerusalem and Megiddo.[11] The Amarna letters and the question of Jethro's priesthood sparked an important conversation among scholars concerning the so-called Kenite hypothesis, as to whether Israel's devotion to YHWH began during their Bronze Age lives as seminomadic tribes that migrated into Canaan during the mid-second millennium BCE and assimilated into the Canaanite culture of Shechem and other regions prior to the emergence of the Israelite monarchies in the tenth century BCE and beyond.[12] Such a portrayal of Israel's origins and its relationship with YHWH is largely consistent with the view that Israel originated as Habiru seminomadic tribes that migrated into Canaan and assimilated into the Canaanite culture, particularly at Shechem,

10. Durand, "Habiru, Hapiru."

11. Mumford, "Amarna Letters."

12. For summation of the Kenite hypothesis, see esp. Vaux, *Early History of Israel*, 330–38.

which became an important center for Israel during its early history (see Gen 34; Deut 27; Josh 24; Judg 9; 1 Kgs 12).

As noted above, the shift from "G-d" to "YHWH" signals J redaction of an E-stratum narrative.

The next question appears beginning in v. 2, i.e., what is the reason for Jethro's visit? The passage indicates that Jethro is returning Moses's wife, here identified as Zipporah, and her two sons, Gershom and Eliezer. Zipporah and Gershom were already identified in Exodus 2:22, but Eliezer has not appeared until now. There has been extensive discussion as to whether or not Moses divorced Zipporah, arising from the statement that Jethro returned her "after he [Moses] sent her away" (Hebrew, *'aḥar šillûḥeyhā*), which rabbinic exegesis argued meant that Moses had divorced her.[13] But the fact that Jethro returned her and her sons to Moses—and Zipporah's actions in defending her family by circumcising her son, presumably Gershom, when YHWH attacked in Exodus 4:24–26—indicates that she is a righteous gentile, if not a convert herself. Some maintain that Moses married another wife, a Cushite woman identified in Numbers 12, but Midianites would have been considered as Cushites, apparently because of their dark skin and parallel reference to Midian and Cushan in Habakkuk 3:7. Others have argued that Moses sent the bride-price to Jethro for his marriage to Zipporah, but the fact that she had already borne two sons indicates that any financial arrangements for the marriage had already been concluded long ago. It seems best to recognize that Moses sent his wife and sons away prior to the confrontation with pharaoh to ensure their safety during the forthcoming conflict.[14] Now that the conflict with pharaoh was settled, Jethro could return his daughter and grandsons to his son-in-law.

Zipporah's name, *ṣippōrâ*, which means "[female] bird," is not explained. The explanation for Gershom's name, *gēršōm*, "I was a resident alien (Hebrew, *gēr*) in a foreign land," in which Hebrew *šām*, "there," is understood as a reference to the foreign land (Egypt, Midian), repeats the explanation given in Exodus 2:22. Eliezer's name (Hebrew, *'ĕlîʿezer*) is explained as "for the G-d of my father is my help," in which *'ĕlî*, "my G-d," is understood as "the G-d of my father," and *ʿezer*, "help," is understood in reference to "my help," *bĕʿezrî*. It is noteworthy that the name El, the name of the Canaanite creator god, appears as the first element of

13. Rosenberg, *Exodus*, 1:264–65; cf. Davies, *Exodus 1–18*, 1:557–58.

14. Davies, *Exodus 1–18*, 1:562.

Eliezer's name, although Exodus 6:2–3 identifies it as an earlier name of YHWH. It is not clear that Moses had seen Eliezer before, so this might have been the first time that he saw his second son.

The formalities of the relationship are made clear in vv. 6–7 in which Jethro announces his arrival. When Moses comes out to meet and greet his father-in-law, he bows down, which means face down on the ground, kisses him, inquires about his welfare, and invites Jethro into his tents. Such formalities are still observed in traditional Muslim societies and in traditional East Asian societies, among others.

The second component of Exodus 18:1–12 appears in Exodus 18:8–12, in which Moses recounts to Jethro YHWH's actions to deliver Israel from pharaoh and Egypt. The use of the divine Name, YHWH, in this sub-unit indicates J redaction of the earlier E-stratum narrative. Jethro responds to Moses's account by exclaiming, "Blessed be YHWH, who delivered you from the hand of Egypt and from the hand of pharaoh when he delivered the people from under the hand of Egypt. Now I know that YHWH is greater than all the gods due to the matter in which they acted insolently against them," in vv. 10–11. The phrase "due to the matter in which they acted insolently against them" (Hebrew, *kî baddābār ʾăšer zādû ʿălêhem*) has proved to be difficult for some interpreters, but it simply refers to Egypt's insolent actions against Israel in enslaving and otherwise oppressing them. Rabbinic tradition maintains that, with these statements, Jethro converts to Judaism or at least the worship of YHWH.[15] Although Jethro's statement indicates his acknowledgment of YHWH, his action in presenting "a whole burnt offering" (Hebrew, *ʿōlâ*) (see Lev 1) and "sacrifices [of well-being]" (Hebrew, *zĕbāḥîm*; see Lev 3), together with Moses, Aaron, and the elders of Israel, would constitute actions that suggest acknowledgment and possibly conversion. There is no indication of circumcision, which was required of the men of Shechem in Genesis 34, so the issue remains open. Some interpreters might be tempted to consider v. 12 to originate in P redaction, but whole burnt offerings and sacrifices of well-being are known from narratives concerning early Israelite history as well (e.g., 1 Sam 15:22; Amos 5:22, for the whole burnt offering; 1 Sam 2:12, 29; 3:14; 6:15; 9:12, 13; 15:12, 22; 16:3, 5, for sacrifices of well-being).[16] Whole burnt offerings are offered to honor G-d, and they are entirely burned on the altar (Lev 1),

15. See Lauterbach, *Mekilta de-Rabbi Ishmael*, 2:162–78, esp. 173–78; cf. Rosenberg, *Exodus*, 1:268–69.

16. Cf. Durham, *Exodus*, 245.

whereas well-being sacrifices are to be eaten by the priests and people at the temple (Lev 3). The phrase employed here, "to eat bread," is a common idiom for eating a meal, even though the meal includes meat and perhaps other foods. It is akin, for example, to Malay, *makan nasi*, "to eat rice," which also functions as an idiom for eating a meal.

Exodus 18:13–26 constitutes the second major sub-unit of Exodus 18:1–27 in which Jethro advises Moses on how to set up a tiered system of judges to handle the workload of judging the legal cases of the people of Israel. As noted above, the passage appears to presuppose the judicial reforms for Israel attributed to King Jehoshaphat ben Asa of Judah (873–849 BCE), who was a vassal of the Northern Kingdom of Israel ruled by the House of Omri. Jehoshaphat's actions are recounted in 2 Chronicles 19, which presupposes an attempt to establish a tiered court system for the kingdoms of northern Israel and southern Judah.

The account of Jethro's proposal to Moses in Exodus 18:13–26 comprises three major components. The first appears in Exodus 18:13–16 in which Jethro observes Moses's heavy workload and asks why Moses conducts legal affairs in this matter. The second appears in Exodus 18:17–23 in which Jethro makes his proposal for a tiered court system to Moses. And the third appears in Exodus 18:24–26 in which Moses complies with Jethro's proposal.

Exodus 18:13–16 recounts Jethro's observation of Moses's heavy workload in attempting to judge all the cases himself. Although Jethro's visit was initially intended to return Moses's wife, Zipporah, and her sons, Gershom and Eliezer, to Moses, Jethro apparently stays for a period of time and has the opportunity to observe his son-in-law at work. He observes Moses sitting to hear all the legal cases of the people of Israel and sees that Moses has to sit as a judge every day from morning until evening. Jethro concludes that Moses has taken on too heavy a workload, and so he informs his son-in-law that such practice is wrong in that it will leave both Moses and the people worn out unless Moses can find a way to bring on extra help to organize a better legal system that will enable Moses to handle his own workload more efficiently and enable the people to have their cases heard and decided in a far more timely fashion. When Jethro asks Moses why he acts as he does (i.e., alone) to hear the cases of Israel, Moses responds that the people come to him "to inquire of G-d" (Hebrew, *lidrōš ʾĕlōqîm*). This phrase indicates that Moses makes oracular inquiry of G-d. Insofar as Moses acts as G-d's representative or prophet for the people, Moses then makes the decision on how to resolve the legal case in question, and explains the basis on which his decision is made, i.e., on the basis of the "statutes of G-d and G-d's instructions" (Hebrew, *ʾet-ḥuqqê ʾĕlōhîm wĕʾet-tôrōtāyw*). It is not clear from this narrative how Moses knows the statutes and instructions of G-d, particularly because they have not yet been revealed publicly at Mount Sinai. But Moses's role in oracular inquiry would supply the presumed means by which Moses would know G-d's statutes and instructions so that he could make them known to the people.

Exodus 18:17–23 recounts Jethro's response to Moses. The first thing he tells his son-in-law is that he is acting incorrectly. By hearing all the legal cases of Israel himself, he has taken on too heavy a workload, which will only result in wearing out both Moses and the people. Moses is working far too hard, and he will burn out. The people do not have their cases heard and resolved in a timely manner, and they will also burn out and lose confidence in Moses's leadership. Jethro observes that, as a prophet of G-d, Moses represents the people before G-d. The people bring their cases to him, and Moses takes the cases to G-d, presumably through oracular inquiry. Upon receiving an answer from G-d, Moses informs the people how each case is resolved and what they must do, apparently based on G-d's instructions.

In order to make this a workable legal system, Moses must have assistance in hearing and deciding the cases. Consequently, Jethro advises Moses to seek out capable men from among the people, men of truth who hate bribes, to assist him. The verb employed here, *teḥĕzeh*, "you shall envision," presupposes Moses's role as a visionary prophet of G-d, although the verb itself means both to hear and to see in a vision, and thus it means "to perceive." The men that Moses is to search out are described as "capable men" (Hebrew, *ʾanšê ḥayil*, lit., "men of strength/ power") who "revere G-d" (Hebrew, *yirʾê ʾĕlōhîm*, lit., "fear G-d"); "men of truth" (Hebrew, *ʾanšê ʾemet*), which means that they are men of integrity; and "haters of a bribe" (Hebrew, *śōnĕʾê bāṣʿa*), which means that they will not take bribes in deciding legal cases.

Consequently, Jethro advises Moses to appoint them as "officers of thousands" (Hebrew, *śārê ʾălāpîm*), "officers of hundreds" (Hebrew, *śārê mēʾôt*), "officers of fifties" (Hebrew, *śārê ḥămiššîm*), "and officers of tens" (Hebrew, *wĕśārê ʿăśārōt*). These terms are generally used to name the hierarchy of officers in a military context, and Israel is described throughout the exodus and wilderness narratives as a military organization that departs from Egypt, travels through the wilderness, and ultimately conquers the land of Canaan.[17] Such language is employed to portray YHWH as a form of super-monarch, based on the metaphorical portrayals of Mesopotamian and Egyptian kings in the ancient world. But interpreters must recognize that these terms are inherently hierarchical, given the gradation of numbers over which each officer (Hebrew, *śar*) has authority. Note that Hebrew *śar* means, simply, "officer," and it may be used in a variety of contexts, military, administrative, governmental, judicial, etc. It is not inherently military, and in the present judicial context, it simply refers to the hierarchy of judges moving from the higher courts to the lower courts where legal cases originate and then move through the appeals system, depending on the outcome of the lower court decisions. Moses then becomes the judge of the highest court in that he makes all of the most difficult decisions, again based on his inquiry of G-d. Deuteronomy 16:18—17:13 describes a similar hierarchical court system, although it is made up of a combination of "judges" (Hebrew, *šōpĕṭîm*) and "officials" (Hebrew, *šōṭĕrîm*) that includes both Levitical priests and non-priests, apparently from the time of King Josiah ben Amon of Judah (640–609 BCE), but in the Exodus–Numbers narrative, the Levites have not yet been appointed as priests, and so they have no official role here (see Num 17–18). Although Moses is a Levite, he functions as a prophet and not as a priest.[18] Jethro makes it clear to Moses that G-d has commanded him to do this, so Moses cannot object even if he was inclined to do so. In the end, such an organization will make things much easier for Moses and for the people of Israel at large.

Exodus 18:24–26 recounts Moses's compliance with Jethro's proposal. This brief sub-unit simply states that Moses followed Jethro's instructions in setting up a hierarchically structured judicial system in which the lower courts would hear the legal cases of the people, appeals could be made through the higher courts, and Moses would represent the supreme judge to whom the most difficult cases would come.

Exodus 18:27 then functions as the third and final sub-unit of Exodus 18:1–27. It simply recounts Moses's action in sending Jethro home, followed by Jethro's departure for his own land.

17. See Knierim, "Exodus 18"; Roskop, *Wilderness Itineraries*.

18. See Stackert, *Prophet Like Moses*.

Reception History

Amalek represents the quintessential enemy of G-d and Judaism in rabbinic thought. Based on the biblical sources noted above, Amalek represents an enemy committed to the destruction of Israel/Judaism and the presence of G-d in the world. Exodus 17:8–16 presents YHWH's commitment to engage in war against Amalek for all generations. Deuteronomy 25:1–19 presents Amalek's commitment to Israel's destruction in the wilderness. First Samuel 15 represents YHWH's command to destroy Amalek. And the book of Esther illustrates what can happen if Amalek survives to attack Israel in later generations, in this case, in the form of Haman, portrayed as a descendant of Agag, the leader of the Amalekites in 1 Samuel 15.[19] Consequently, Israel/Judaism has the obligation to defend itself against the threat posed by Amalek, which entails the destruction of Amalek. In the Babylonian Talmud in b. Sanhedrin 20b, the destruction of Amalek is one of the three tasks required of Israel once it conquers the land of Israel. The other two are the establishment of the monarchy and the building of the temple.[20]

Throughout history, a number of enemies may be identified with Amalek, viz., the Seleucid Syrian Dynasty during the reign of Antiochus IV in 176–163 BCE, who proscribed Judaism; the Roman Empire under Hadrian, which committed genocide against the Jewish people in the Bar Kochba War (132–135 CE); the Nazis in World War II for their role in perpetrating the Shoah or Holocaust in 1939–1945; the former Soviet Union for its role in murdering Jews under Stalin and its later efforts to destroy Judaism until its collapse in 1991; and the Arab countries, which attacked Israel in an attempt to destroy it, beginning in 1948 and beyond. More recently, Iran and Hamas might be considered as candidates for Amalek, given their commitment to the destruction of the state of Israel. Dozeman mischaracterizes the issue when he cites misguided publications by Alistair Hunter and Nur Masalha to claim that West Bank Arabs are examples of Amalek to Israeli settlers. He erroneously portrays Amalek as a cipher for any enemy to suggest that Israel's goal is to exterminate West Bank Arabs.[21]

19. Sweeney, *Reading the Bible After the Shoah*, 219–22; Sweeney, "Absence of G-d."

20. Walfish, "Amalek, Amalekites."

21. Dozeman, "Exodus," 158.

Others point to Amalek as a manifestation of evil within ourselves based on the treatment of the subject in Kabbalistic and Hasidic thought.[22] Consideration of Lurianic Kabbalah, however, would recognize that the evil comes ultimately from G-d. According to Lurianic Kabbalah, the ten Sefirot or emanations of G-d appear both within G-d and within creation, including all human beings. Insofar as Hesed, divine mercy and fidelity (the capacity for good), are counterbalanced by Gevurah, divine judgment (the capacity for evil), Gevurah was released when Hesed prompted G-d to withdraw into the divine self to make room for the finite world of creation with which G-d desired a relationship, thereby disrupting the unity and sanctity of creation. Insofar as both Hesed and Gevurah infuse creation and all human beings, it is the task of the human, beginning with Jews, to restore the balance between Hesed and Gevurah within themselves to restore the unity and sanctity of all creation and the presence of G-d within creation. Insofar as Gevurah represents evil, it is identified with Amalek, and it appears within all humans as a force to be overcome and placed back into balance with Hesed.[23]

As noted in the commentary above, rabbinic tradition understands Jethro's blessing of YHWH and offerings to YHWH in Exodus 18:8–12 to constitute Jethro's conversion to Judaism and adherence to G-d. Rabbinic texts, especially b. Yebamot 46a–47a, specify the laws of conversion, which require circumcision for a male, immersion in the mikveh or Jewish ritual bath, and the witness of a three-man bet din, or Jewish ritual court.[24]

Stephen's sermon prior to his martyrdom in Acts 6:8—8:1a alludes to Exodus 18:3–4 in Acts 17:29 in noting that Moses went to Midian and had two sons. Patristic and medieval Christian interpreters, such as Cyril of Alexandria, Bede, and Nicholas of Lyra, considered Jethro's conversion to foreshadow conversion to Christianity. Later Christian interpreters, such as Calvin, Luther, and Zwingli, raised questions about the purity of Jethro's conversion.[25]

The name Jethro appears in modern American popular television culture in the situation comedy *The Beverly Hillbillies*, which ran from 1962 to 1971. The character of Jethro Bodine, played by Max Baer Jr.,

22. For a comprehensive treatment of Amalek in biblical and rabbinic thought, see Schochet, *Amalek*.

23. In addition to Schochet, *Amalek*, see also Sweeney, *Jewish Mysticism*, 325–62.

24. Roth et al., "Proselytes."

25. Childs, *Exodus*, 332–34.

is the dim-witted cousin of the family patriarch, Jed Clampett, whom Jethro addresses as "Uncle Jed." The series portrays the move of a hill family from the Ozark Mountains in southern Missouri to Beverly Hills, California, as a result of their accidental discovery of oil on their land which makes them fabulously rich. The purpose of the series is to get a good laugh by portraying the culture clash between the allegedly backwards "hillbilly" family and the allegedly "sophisticated" upper-class urban culture of Beverly Hills. The series deliberately underestimates the capabilities of hill people as the basis for their comedic premises.

Divine Revelation at Mount Sinai —Exodus 19:1—Numbers 2:34

EXODUS 19:1—NUMBERS 2:34 CONSTITUTE the account of divine revelation at Mount Sinai. Many scholars define the Sinai Pericope on diachronic grounds as the Priestly account of the revelation of divine Torah at Mount Sinai, but a synchronic reading of the narrative would have to recognize a more limited account due to the role of the toledoth formulas and the wilderness itinerary formulas in structuring the narrative.[1] Exodus 19:1—Numbers 2:34 is demarcated by the introductory wilderness itinerary formula in Exodus 19:1–2, which relates Israel's journey from Rephidim to the Wilderness of Sinai, and the introductory toledoth formula in Numbers 3:1 introduces the history of the guidance of Israel in the wilderness by Moses and Aaron.

Within Exodus 19:1—Numbers 2:34, issues of plot and theme define the constituent sub-units. Exodus 19:1–2 recounts the journey from Rephidim to the Wilderness of Sinai. Exodus 19:3—40:38 comprises the account of the revelation from the mountain. This account is comprised of a sequence of sub-units, including the account of YHWH's revelation at Sinai in Exodus 19:3–25; the account of the Covenant Code in Exodus 20:1—24:18; the account of the instructions to build the tabernacle, its equipment and furnishings, and related matters in Exodus 25:1—31:18; the account of Israel's apostasy with the golden calves in Exodus 32:1—34:35; and the account of Israel's compliance with YHWH's instructions to build the tabernacle in Exodus 35:1—40:39.

Leviticus 1–27 recounts YHWH's revelation of the laws of sacrifice and holiness in Leviticus 1–27. And Numbers 1:1—2:34 recounts

1. Sweeney, *Pentateuch*, xvii–xxix; 29–34; Sweeney, *Tanak*, 45–53, 85–122.

the census and organization of the people around the tabernacle as they prepare to depart from Mount Sinai.

YHWH's Revelation at Mount Sinai—Exodus 19:1–2, 3–25

Translation

19:1 In the third month of the departure of the people of Israel from the land of Egypt, on that day, they came to the Wilderness of Sinai. 2 And they had journeyed from Rephidim, and they came to the Wilderness of Sinai, and they encamped in the wilderness, and Israel camped there before the mountain.

3 And Moses went up to G-d, and YHWH called to him from the mountain, saying, "Thus you shall say to the House of Jacob, and you shall declare to the people of Israel, 4 'You have seen what I did to Egypt, how I lifted you up on the wings of eagles, and I brought you to me. 5 And now, if you listen carefully to my voice, and you observe my covenant, then you shall be to me more treasured from all the peoples, because all the earth is mine. 6 And you shall be to me a kingdom of priests and a holy nation.' These are the words that you will speak to the people of Israel."

7 And Moses came, and he called all the elders of the people, and he placed before them all these words, which YHWH commanded him. 8 And all the people answered together, and they said, "All that YHWH has spoken, we will do," and Moses returned the words of the people to YHWH. 9 And YHWH said to Moses, "Behold, I am coming to you in thick

cloud so that the people will hear my word with you, and
also in you they will trust forever," and Moses declared the
words of the people to YHWH. [10] And YHWH said to Moses,
"Go to the people, and you will sanctify them today and tomorrow, and they will wash their clothing, [11] and they shall
be ready on the third day, for on the third day YHWH will
come down in the sight of all the people on Mount Sinai,
[12] and you will set boundaries for the people all around, saying, 'Be careful not to go up on the mountain or to touch its
edge! Anyone who touches the mountain will sure die! [13] No
hand shall touch him, but he will certainly be stoned or shot,
whether animal or man, he shall not live.' During the Jubilee,
they shall go up on the mountain."

[14] And Moses went down from the mountain to the people,
and he sanctified the people, and they washed their clothing.
[15] And he said to the people, "Be ready for three days! Do not
approach a woman!"

[16] And it was on the third day, when it was morning, then
there was thunder and lightning and heavy cloud upon the
mountain, and the sound of the shofar was very strong, and
all the people who were in the camp trembled. [17] And Moses
brought out the people from the camp to meet G-d, and they
stood below the mountain.

[18] And Mount Sinai was entirely smoking because YHWH
came down upon it in fire, and its smoke went up like the
smoke of a kiln, and the entire mountain shook terribly.
[19] And the sound of the shofar continued to grow stronger.
Moses would speak, and G-d would answer him with voice.
[20] And YHWH came down upon Mount Sinai to the top of
the mountain, and YHWH called Moses to the top of the
mountain, and Moses went up. [21] And YHWH said to Moses,
"Go down, warn the people lest they break out to see YHWH,
so that many will fall. [22] And also the priests who come near
to YHWH shall be sanctified lest YHWH burst out against
them." [23] And Moses said to YHWH, "The people will not be
able to go up to Mount Sinai because you have warned us,
saying, 'Set boundaries on the mountain, and sanctify it.'"

[24] And YHWH said to him, "Go, go down, and then you shall
come up, you and Aaron with you, and the priests and the
people will not break out to go up to YHWH lest he burst out
against them." [25] And Moses went down to the people, and
he said to them:

Commentary

Exodus 19 serves as the introductory narrative of the revelation of YHWH and YHWH's Torah, "instruction," at Sinai in Exodus 19:1—Numbers 2:34.[1] It begins with the notice of Israel's entry into the Sinai wilderness and its journey from Rephidim to Sinai in Exodus 19:1–2, and the account of the revelation at Sinai then follows in Exodus 19:3—Numbers 2:34. Exodus 19:3–25 introduces the account of the revelation from the mountain in Exodus 19:3—40:38. Leviticus 1–27 recounts the revelation from the tabernacle, and Numbers 1:1—2:34 recounts the census of the people at Sinai prior to the account of the preparations for the journey from Sinai to the land of Israel under the leadership of Moses and Aaron.[2]

Exodus 19:1–25 comprises four major sub-units. The first is the initial notice concerning Israel's entry into the Wilderness of Sinai and its journey from Rephidim to Sinai. The second is the account of Moses's meeting with YHWH on Mount Sinai in Exodus 19:3–14, including his initial meeting with YHWH in Exodus 19:3–6, in which YHWH gives him his first set of instructions, and his intermediation between YHWH and the people in Exodus 19:7–14, in which Moses goes back and forth between YHWH and the people to convey YHWH's instructions and the people's response. The third is Exodus 19:15–24, in which Moses instructs the people in their proper conduct in preparation for the revelation of YHWH's presence in Exodus 19:15, and the revelation itself begins when YHWH comes down to the top of the mountain in Exodus 19:16–24. At this point, Moses once again moves between YHWH on the top of the mountain and the people at the bottom of the mountain to convey YHWH's further

1. The Hebrew word *tôrâ* is often translated into Greek as *nomos*, "law," in the LXX (followed by the NT), but it actually means "instruction," based on the Hiphil form of the root, *yrh*, "to guide."

2. For discussion of the formal literary structure of Exodus 19 within the larger context of the Pentateuch, see Sweeney, *Tanak*, 25–53, 96–106; Sweeney, *Pentateuch*, xxvii–xxix, 30–34, 44–52.

instructions to the people. Exodus 19:25 employs a speech formula that introduces YHWH's speech in Exodus 20:1–14.

Exodus 19:1–2

Exodus 19:1–2 is identifiable as the work of the Priestly redaction of the Pentateuch due to its formulaic character, although the wilderness itinerary formulas are subordinated to the P toledoth formula, which govern the structure of the Pentateuch as a whole.[3] The third month of the year is when the Festival of Shavuot (Weeks, Pentecost)—which celebrates the revelation of Torah at Sinai and the conclusion of the grain harvest in the land of Israel—is observed.[4] No specific day is given because the festival is set some fifty days or seven weeks (forty-nine days) following Pesach (Passover). The location is unknown, in part because it is associated with the location of Mount Sinai. The traditional location of Mount Sinai is generally identified with Jebel Musa near the southern tip of the Sinai Peninsula, where St. Catherine's Monastery is located.[5] Rephidim, located in the Wilderness of Sin, is then likely located by the Wadi Feiran, northwest of Jebel Musa in the southern Sinai Peninsula.[6] The location of the revelation at Mount Sinai builds upon mythological motifs that locate gods, such as the Canaanite creator god, El, on mountaintops together with the assertion that YHWH is the sovereign creator of the world.

Exodus 19:3–14

Exodus 19:3–14 recounts Moses's meetings with YHWH on Mount Sinai and his mediation between YHWH and the people.

The first component of the text is Exodus 19:3–6, which recounts Moses's first meeting with YHWH on Sinai in which YHWH instructs Moses in what he should say to the people of Israel, here identified as "the House of Jacob," a title that presupposes the twelve tribes of Jacob, based upon the accounts of the twelve sons of Jacob in Genesis 29–31. YHWH's speech to Israel is based on ancient international treaty language, such as

3. For source analysis of Exodus 19, see Campbell and O'Brien, *Sources of the Pentateuch*, 43, 145–46, 187–88, 198–99; Noth, *History of Pentateuchal Traditions*, 270.

4. Jacobs, "Shavuot."

5. Davies, "Sinai, Mount."

6. J. Seely, "Rephidim"; Beit Arieh, "Route Through Sinai."

the Hittite treaties or the Neo-Assyrian treaties between a suzerain monarch and his individual vassals.[7] Such treaties generally begin with an identification of the suzerain monarch, the gods who support him, and his powerful actions in the world, especially on behalf of the vassal king. In this case, YHWH instructs Moses to inform the people what YHWH has done on their behalf. YHWH's speech begins with the messenger formula, "Thus you shall say to the House of Jacob," which typically introduces prophetic speech, although it apparently originates in diplomatic speech in which a king or other leader sends a messenger to another king or party (Isa 36–37; Gen 24). The reference to what YHWH did to the Egyptians presupposes the plagues against Egypt and the splitting of the Red Sea. The reference to lifting the people up, "on the wings of eagles," presupposes the typical representation of Mesopotamian kings, flying through the heavens in a sun disk borne by eagles' wings; it is intended to represent YHWH as king,[8] but in this case, YHWH is king over the entire earth. A variation of the covenant formula, "And now, if you listen carefully to my voice, and you observe my covenant, then you shall be to me more treasured from all the peoples, because all the earth is mine.[9] And you shall be to me a kingdom of priests and a holy nation," appears in vv. 5–6, which indicates the fundamental terms of the relationship. The reference to Israel as "more treasured from all the peoples," is intended to recognize Israel's status as the chosen people of YHWH.[10] As Deuteronomy 7:6–8 explains, the chosen status of Israel does not entail special qualities; it entails the obligation to observe the commandments of YHWH. The following reference to Israel as "a kingdom of priests and a holy nation," signals Israel's obligations as the chosen people of YHWH, viz., to observe YHWH's commandments, which are not entirely incumbent on other nations, and thereby serve as representatives of the holy G-d, who rules over the entire earth.[11]

7. Hillers, *Covenant*; McCarthy, *Old Testament Covenant*; cf. Crouch, *Israel and the Assyrians*.

8. E.g., *ANEP* 536.

9. Rendtorff, *Bundesformel*, 28n36.

10. Kaminsky, *Yet I Loved Jacob*.

11. See the Laws of Noah in the Babylonian Talmud (b. Sanh 56–60), which maintain that other religious traditions may be considered as true religions if they follow seven basic stipulations: prohibition of idolatry, murder, theft, sexual promiscuity, blasphemy, eating meat from a live animal, and the requirement to have just laws. See Schwarzchild, "Noachide Laws."

The second component of this text is Exodus 19:7–14, which portrays Moses's role as meditator between YHWH and Israel as he goes down and up the mountain to deliver the messages and responses of each party. The elders of Israel serve as the representatives of Israel, apparently as the elders of each of the Israelite tribes. In 2 Samuel 5:1–3, the elders of northern Israel play the key role in inviting David to be king. As part of the negotiation, Israel agrees to do all that YHWH asks, and YHWH agrees to appear on the mountain in thick cloud so that the people may hear all of YHWH's requirements.

Most interpreters correctly argue that the imagery of YHWH's appearance on Sinai constitutes an example of a theophany, in which appearances by YHWH are expressed in mythological terms, such as the thick cloud, thunder, and lightning that appear in this text.[12] Such imagery is associated with mountains to express YHWH's highness in relation to the world of creation and the human beings that inhabit it. But this imagery is also replicated in the temples of YHWH, such as the *heikhal*, "palace," the central receiving hall of the Jerusalem temple that stands before the holy of holies, where the ark of the covenant, configured as YHWH's throne, stands.[13] Ten incense burners in the *heikhal* produce the imagery of smoke or thick cloud, ten menorahs or candelabras produce the imagery of lightning with their seventy burning lamps, and the noise of the heavy doors opening in their stone lintel sockets produces sound akin to the thunder of the theophany (see 1 Kgs 6–7; cf. Isa 6).[14]

The imagery of the holy temple, in which only the priests may enter, is accentuated by the requirement that boundaries be established around the mountain to prevent the people from crowding into the sacred site of the mountain where YHWH will appear. The death penalty for those who cross that sacred boundary indicates the seriousness with which the separation between the sacred and the profane is taken. (See Num 15–16, which portrays the deaths of Korah and his supporters, who violated the sanctity of the divine presence.) It is not clear, however, that anyone was ever executed for entering the temple.

12. Hiebert, "Theophany in the OT."

13. See Levenson, who demonstrates the interrelationship between Sinai and Zion, the site of the Jerusalem temple (*Sinai and Zion*).

14. For discussion of the features of the Jerusalem temple in 1 Kings 6–7, see Sweeney, *1–2 Kings*, 104–24; for discussion of the temple features in Isaiah 6, see Sweeney, *Isaiah 1–39*, 132–42; Sweeney, *Jewish Mysticism*, 132–35.

The third day following the beginning of the third month mentioned in Exodus 19:1 is the fiftieth day following the first day of Passover, which is when Leviticus 23:11 and Deuteronomy 16:9 stipulate that the counting of the omer, barley sheaf, is to be completed for the celebration of the Festival of Shavuot. The commandment for the people to wash their clothing signals that the people are to be pure (i.e., clean) for their appearance before YHWH. The commandment not to approach a woman entails that the men should not have sexual relations with women prior to their appearance before YHWH. The basis for this command is due to the emission of semen from the male body. Insofar as semen is a living substance that dies when it is emitted from the body, the dead substance renders the man impure.

Exodus 19:15–24

The third component of the text is Exodus 19:15–24, which recounts the initial revelation of YHWH before the people when YHWH comes down to the top of the mountain to speak at dawn on the third day. The timing of this revelation at dawn is intended to signal the time of the first morning service of the day, in this case, the first day of Shavuot, in the temple. The loud sounding of the shofar, made from a ram's horn, signals the onset of the revelation on the first observance of Shavuot. The passage continues the configuration of Mount Sinai as a temple site by portraying YHWH's descent to the top of the mountain in thick smoke, replicated by the ten incense burners of the temple, and Moses's ascent to the mountain to appear before YHWH, replicating the approach of the high priest before YHWH on the holiday. Additional correlations include the concerns with establishing boundaries around the mountain that the people do not cross and the purity of the priests who will appear before YHWH.

Exodus 19:25

The final segment of the chapter is Exodus 19:25, which recounts how Moses came down from atop the mountain to join the people and the speech formula, which introduces YHWH's first speech, the announcement of the Ten Commandments, in Exodus 20:1–14.

Reception History

Exodus 19 plays a very important role in Judaism because it recounts the revelation of YHWH's Torah, "instruction," at Mount Sinai, the foundation of Judaism's covenant relationship with G-d. Exodus 19 therefore recounts the first celebration of Shavuot, "Weeks" (known as "Pentecost" in Christian tradition), the festival that celebrates both the revelation of the Torah at Sinai and the conclusion of the grain harvest in the land of Israel. Although Exodus 19 dates the revelation to the third day of the third month, rabbinic tradition concludes that the holiday is to be celebrated on 6 Sivan, the fifty-first day following the first day of Passover (Targum Jonathan to Exod 19:6; b. Šabb. 86b; b. Pesaḥ. 86b; b. Yoma 4b; b. Ta`an 28b).[15] The rabbinic date is in keeping with Leviticus 23:15–21, which instructs the people to count seven weeks, culminating in fifty days, from the Shabbat, understood as the first day of Passover. Because Exodus 19 recounts the initial stages of YHWH's revelation of Torah to Israel, it is considered as a primary text that narrates the establishment of the covenant between YHWH and Judaism, i.e., Israel.

Exodus 19–20, including both the revelation at Sinai and the Ten Commandments, are read in the synagogue service as the Torah portion on the first day of Shavuot together with Ezekiel 1:1–28, which serves as the prophetic haftarah ("completion, interpretation") portion because both texts are concerned with the revelation of the divine presence of G-d in the world. The readings for the second day of Shavuot include Deuteronomy 14:22—16:17, which recounts the laws for observance of Pesach, Shavuot, and Sukkot, as the Torah portion and Habakkuk 2:20—3:19, which presents the Psalm of Habakkuk, which is again concerned with the revelation of the divine presence in the world. The book of Ruth is also read on Shavuot, both because it portrays Ruth as gathering the wheat harvest and because Ruth becomes a convert to Judaism (Ruth 1:16–17) and thereby enters the covenant revealed at Sinai.

Because of the focus on divine revelation, Shavuot is especially devoted to the study of Torah and associated texts concerned with revelation. All-night study sessions, called Tikkun Leil Shavuot, "study [lit., repair] of the night of Shavuot," are held on the first night of Shavuot, beginning in the sixteenth century under the leadership of R. Isaac Luria of Safed (1534–72), the primary founder of Lurianic Kabbalah.[16]

15. Sarna, *Exodus*, 15, 250.

16. See Sweeney, *Jewish Mysticism*, 325–62.

Exodus 19 serves as an important inspiration for the development of Jewish mysticism, particularly Kabbalah, which attempts to trace the process by which the divine presence of G-d is manifested in the soul of the human being as well as in the world at large. Kabbalist tradition posits that there are ten Sefirot, literally, "countings," understood as the ten emanations of the divine, in which the Ein Sof, the "Infinite" character of G-d, is manifested in the finite human being.[17] The ten Sefirot begin with the three mental emanations, including Keter Elyon, "Crown of the Most High," which refers to the will of G-d and humans to create; Hokhmah, "Wisdom," which refers to the divine and human capacity to conceptualize or plan; and Binah, "Understanding," which refers to the practical understanding of how to make a concept or plan into a reality. The three moral Sefirot include Hesed, "Mercy, Fidelity," which refers to the capacity to give to others; Gevurah, "Power," or Din, "Judgment," which refers to the capacity to take from others; and Tiferet, "Beauty," understood as a balancing principle in moral action between the capacity to give or show mercy and love and the capacity to take or punish. The three material Sefirot include Netzah, "Endurance" or "Dynamism," the principle of change or movement in the material world; Hod, "Majesty" or "Stability," the principle of constancy in the material world; and Yesod, "Foundation," which creates the balance between change and stability in the world of creation. Shekhinah, "Dwelling" or "Presence," portrays G-d's holy presence in the soul of the human being and the finite world at large.

Indeed, there were differences in the dating and conceptualization of Shavuot in antiquity. The Temple Scroll from Qumran, written as early as the third century BCE prior to the emergence of rabbinic Judaism, stipulates the celebration of three holidays, each counted off fifty days from the preceding holiday, to celebrate the firstfruits of wheat, wine, and oil (11QTem 18.10–23.2).[18]

Shavuot, understood as Pentecost in reference to the fifty-day period of counting for the observance of the holiday, also plays an important role in Christianity. The Four Gospels are fundamentally concerned with a new revelation of the divine in the form of Jesus Christ, and the book of Revelation is likewise concerned with the revelation of the heavenly throne of G-d and Jesus as the Lamb. Acts 2 presents a new understanding

17. Sweeney, *Jewish Mysticism*, 300–304.

18. Sweeney, "Sefirah at Qumran."

of Pentecost in which the apostles experienced a wind from heaven that filled each of them with the Holy Spirit and prompted them to speak in tongues. Peter would then quote Joel 2:28–32, in which G-d would pour the Holy Spirit upon all flesh to portend the revelation of Jesus the Nazarene as G-d's Messiah or Christ. And Paul would develop the concept of election into the principle of justification by faith, in which faith in the divine would become the basic criterion for those who would be deemed chosen by G-d (Rom 10:4, 12–13; Gal 3:28; 4:22–26; cf. Gen 15:6; cf. 1 Pet 2). Paul's polemic against Judaism in Galatians 4:22–26 identifies Hagar, "the slave woman," with the Sinai covenant and the "other woman" with his own audience. First Peter 2:9–10 reinterprets the treasured people of Exodus 19:6 to identify Christians as G-d's chosen race, a royal priesthood, and G-d's people.

Among the church fathers, Justin Martyr would develop Paul's principle of justification by faith and his polemics against the "old covenant" of Judaism (*Dial.*). Irenaeus (*Haer.* 4.5.1; 12.1–5, 13–16), Clement of Alexandria (*Strom.* 4.5.327), and Augustine (*Enarrat. Ps.* 104.7), in their efforts to polemicize against Judaism, would further develop the notion that faith and obedience were available to all human beings.

The Covenant Code: The Foundational Law Code of Israel—Exodus 20:1—24:18

THE ACCOUNT OF YHWH's proclamation of the Covenant Code as the foundational law code of ancient Israel appears in Exodus 20:1—24:18. The account is tied syntactically to the preceding narrative concerning YHWH's revelation at Sinai in Exodus 19:1–25 by the *waw*-consecutive speech formula in Exodus 20:1 that introduces the first segment of YHWH's speech in Exodus 20:1–14 concerning YHWH's announcement of the Ten Commandments. Exodus 20:1–14 therefore serves as YHWH's own introduction to the account of the announcement of the Covenant Code in Exodus 20:15—24:18.

The account of the announcement of the Covenant Code then comprises three major narrative sub-units. The first is the narrative introduction in Exodus 20:15–18 (Exod 20:18–21 in Christian Bibles) which recounts the reaction of the people of Israel to YHWH's announcement of the Ten Commandments as they prepare to hear the following announcement of the Covenant Code per se. This sub-unit does not begin with a *waw*-consecutive verbal formulation, which would continue the preceding narrative. Instead, it begins with a conjunctive *waw* formation, which indicates disjunction in the narrative, viz., "and all the people were seeing." The announcement of the Covenant Code then follows in Exodus 20:19—23:33, where the *waw*-consecutive speech formula in Exodus 20:19 (Exod 20:22 in Christian Bibles) introduces the whole as a speech by YHWH which is tied syntactically to the narrative introduction in Exodus 20:15–18. Following the speech formula in Exodus 20:19aα, the announcement of the Covenant Code comprises two major segments, the announcement of the altar law in Exodus 20:19aβ–23 (Exod 20:22aβ–26 in Christian Bibles) and the announcement of the laws and the statutes of the Covenant Code in Exodus 21:1—23:33.

The narrative concerning YHWH's meal with Moses, Aaron, Nadab and Abihu, and the seventy elders of Israel in Exodus 24:1–18 then concludes the account of the revelation of the Covenant Code in Exodus 20:1—24:18, and introduces the account of YHWH's instructions to Moses concerning the construction of the tabernacle and associated issues in Exodus 25–31.

Introduction: The Ten Commandments—Exodus 20:1–14

Translation

20:1 And G-d spoke all these words, saying,

[2] I am YHWH, your G-d, who brought you out from the land of Egypt, from the house of bondage. [3] You shall not have other gods before me.

[4] You shall not make for yourself a sculptured idol or any image which is in the heavens above or on the earth below or in the waters below the earth. [5] You shall not bow down to them and you shall not serve them, for I, YHWH your G-d, am a jealous G-d, punishing the iniquity of the fathers upon the sons upon the third generations and upon the fourth generations of those who hate me, [6] and showing fidelity to the thousandth generations to those who love me and to those who observe my commandments.

[7] You shall not raise the Name of YHWH, your G-d, fraudulently, for YHWH will not acquit the one who raises his Name fraudulently.

[8] Remember the day of Shabbat to sanctify it. [9] Six days you shall work, and you shall do all your labor, [10] but the seventh day is a Shabbat for YHWH, your G-d. You shall not do any labor, you, and your son and your daughter, your servant and your maidservant, and your animal, and your resident alien

who is in your gates, [11] for [in] six days YHWH made the heavens and the earth, the sea, and all that is in them, but he rested on the seventh day. Therefore, YHWH blessed the seventh day, and he sanctified it.

[12] Honor your father and your mother in order that your days shall be long upon the ground that YHWH, your G-d, is giving to you.

[13] You shall not murder. You shall not commit adultery. You shall not steal. You shall not testify against your neighbor falsely.

[14] You shall not covet the house of your neighbor; you shall not covet the wife of your neighbor, or his servant, or his maidservant, or his bull, or his ass, or anything that belongs to your neighbor.

Commentary

The account of YHWH's announcement of the Ten Commandments in Exodus 20:1–14 actually continues the narrative that commenced in Exodus 19, specifically, the account of the events on the third day in Exodus 19:16–25. Whereas Exodus 20:15–23 introduces the setting of the following revelation of the Covenant Code with a portrayal of the smoking mountain and the actions of the people at its base, Exodus 20:1–14 presents the account of YHWH's first speech in the revelation of the Covenant Code. The speech formula in v. 1aα introduces YHWH's speech, and the narrative voice in v. 15 marks the beginning of a new sub-unit in the narrative.

The account of YHWH's first speech in Exodus 20:1–14 functions as an introduction to the account of YHWH's following speech in Exodus 20:18—23:33. Exodus 20:1–14 presents one version of the Ten Commandments. The other version appears in Deuteronomy 5, especially vv. 6–18, which function as part of the introduction to the Deuteronomic law code in Deuteronomy 12–26. The Hebrew Bible does not refer to the Ten Commandments as Ten Commandments; rather it refers to the "Ten Words" (Hebrew, *ʿăśeret haddĕbārîm*) in Exodus 34:2 and Deuteronomy 4:13; 10:4. Some interpreters might consider the Ten Commandments to be an example of an ancient Israelite law code, especially because they appear as part of an account of a speech by YHWH that appears prior to the presentation of the Covenant Code in Exodus 20:18—23:33. Albrecht Alt, for example, considered them as examples of a uniquely Israelite legal form, which he labelled "apodictic law," i.e., laws that were formulated as legal pronouncements by an authority figure, such as a tribal leader from the time when the ancestors of Israel were seminomadic tribes living in the Arabian and Negev Deserts.[1] Close examination of the language of the Ten Commandments demonstrates that they cannot function as examples of Israelite law in that there is no instruction as to how they might be adjudicated in a court law. The prohibition "You shall not murder" in Exodus 20:13 clearly prohibits an act of murder, but there is no instruction as to what the courts might do in the event that someone commits murder. Indeed, the entirety of the Ten Commandments is composed in a similar fashion, as a set of commands and prohibitions that do not provide instruction concerning the legal resolution of a case in which the command or prohibition is somehow violated. It is also the case that the definition of the crime (i.e., what is murder) is also not addressed. Furthermore, such commands and prohibitions are not uniquely Israelite, as Alt contended. They appear prominently in ancient Near Eastern treaty texts, such as the seventh-century BCE treaties of the Assyrian King Esarhaddon (ruled 681–669 BCE), in which apodictic forms are employed to spell out the obligations of kingdoms that are allied with Assyria as subordinate vassals.[2]

The Ten Commandments in Exodus 20:1–14—and the alternative version in Deuteronomy 5—are not examples of ancient Israelite laws; rather, they are statements of the ideal principles that are addressed in Israelite law.[3] Detailed discussion of these ideal principles then appear in the presentation of the various laws of the Covenant Code in Exodus 20:15—23:33.

The composition of the Ten Commandments in Exodus 20:1–17 is generally presumed to be Elohistic, although there is actually little evidence to prove that they are the product of the E-stratum of the Pentateuch.[4] Nevertheless, Hosea 4:1–3 cites the prohibitions against false swearing, lying, murder, theft, and adultery, which suggests that this

1. Alt, "Origins of Israelite Law," esp. 151–71.

2. See Wiseman, *Vassal Treaties.*

3. See Sweeney, *King Josiah of Judah*, 137–69, esp. 142–50; cf. Braulik, *Deuteronomischen Gesetze*; Braulik, "Sequence of the Laws."

4. Campbell and O'Brien, *Sources of the Pentateuch*, 188–89.

mid-eighth-century northern prophet knew some version of the Ten Commandments, presumably the E-stratum version.[5] It is clear, however, that the present text has been edited by both the P- and J-strata of the Pentateuch. The rationale for the observance of Shabbat in Exodus 20:8–11 is described in relation to the creation of the world in six days with the seventh day reserved for the Shabbat in Genesis 1:1—2:3. And the punishment of those who engage in idolatry in Exodus 20:4-6 to the third and fourth generations as well as the fidelity shown to those who do observe YHWH's command to the thousandth generation is consistent with Deuteronomistic principles, which place the blame for the punishment of Israel and Judah on past kings (i.e., Jeroboam ben Nebat for Israel and Manasseh ben Hezekiah for Judah) and not on the later generations that actually suffered the punishment. Priestly theology holds that the generation that suffers punishment must be the one that committed the sins for which punishment is required (e.g., Ezek 18; 2 Chron 33–36).[6] Insofar as Exodus 20:4–6 articulates Deuteronomistic theology concerning the punishment for sin, it would appear to be the product of J-stratum redaction.

There is no agreement concerning the enumeration of the Ten Commandments, as they are read differently in Jewish and Christian interpretative traditions. Note that Exodus 20:2–14 presents the Ten Commandments in the Jewish Bible, whereas Christian Bibles renumber the Ten Commandments as Exodus 20:2–17.[7]

In Jewish tradition, the identification of YHWH as your G-d in v. 2 is understood to constitute the first commandment to recognize YHWH as G-d, and the prohibitions against having other gods and the making and worship of idols in vv. 3–6 together constitute the second. The prohibition against using the divine Name to swear fraudulently in v. 7 is the third commandment, and the command to remember the Shabbat in vv. 8–11 is the fourth. The command to honor parents in v. 12 is the fifth commandment, and the prohibitions against murder, adultery, stealing, and false witness in v. 13 constitute the sixth, seventh, eighth, and ninth commandments. The prohibition against coveting a neighbor's home, wife, slaves, and animals in v. 14 is the tenth

5. Sweeney, *Twelve Prophets*, 1:40–45.

6. See Sweeney, *Reading Ezekiel*, 92–99; Sweeney, "Question of Theodicy."

7. For discussion of the Ten Commandments in the Jewish Bible, see Sarna, *Exodus*, 107–17; for discussion of the Ten Commandments in the Christian Bible, see Dozeman, *Exodus*, 478–96.

commandment. Exodus 20:15–18 then presents the people's reaction to YHWH's announcement of the Ten Commandments.

In Christianity, the identification of YHWH as G-d in v. 2 functions as the self-introduction of G-d, and the prohibition against other gods in v. 3 functions as the first commandment. The prohibition against making and worshipping idols in vv. 4–6 functions as the second commandment, and the prohibition against using the divine Name to swear fraudulently in v. 7 is the third. The command to remember the Sabbath in vv. 8–11 is the fourth commandment, and the command to honor parents in v. 12 is the fifth. According to the Christian numbering of the verses, the prohibition against murder in v. 13 is the sixth commandment, the prohibition against adultery in v. 14 is the seventh commandment, the prohibition against stealing in v. 15 is the eighth commandment, the prohibition against false testimony is the ninth commandment, and the prohibition against coveting is the tenth commandment. Exodus 20:18–20 then presents the people's reaction to YHWH's announcement as the conclusion of this part of the narrative.

The account of YHWH's announcement of the Ten Commandments begins with the speech formula in Exodus 20:1 in which G-d (Hebrew, *'ĕlōhîm*) is identified as the speaker. The identification of Elohim as the speaker plays a key role in identifying Exodus 20:1–14 as an E-stratum text, although it is clear that P- and J-stratum redactors have reworked portions of the text.

The first commandment appears in Exodus 20:2, according to Jewish tradition. This verse identifies YHWH as the G-d of Israel, who redeemed the people of Israel from Egyptian bondage. This statement functions as a theological self-identification formula in which YHWH identifies the divine self as the G-d of Israel and the world at large who acts in the world of creation and human beings to achieve divine purpose.[8] This formula appears frequently in priestly literature, particularly in the book of Ezekiel, a Zadokite priest who was exiled to Babylon in 597 BCE, where he became a visionary prophet following Judah's first revolt against Babylon. The revolt was instigated by King Jehoiakim ben Josiah of Judah, who died of unknown causes when the Babylonian army appeared to besiege Jerusalem, leaving his eighteen-year-old son,

8. Zimmerli, "I Am YHWH"; Zimmerli, "Word of Divine Self-Manifestation."

Jehoiachin, to be exiled and his younger brother, Zedekiah, to be installed as king of Judah by the Babylonians.[9]

The first commandment is heavily influenced by ancient Near Eastern treaty texts. George Mendenhall pointed out the parallels between the Ten Commandments—and ancient Israelite law in general—with Hittite treaty texts of the Bronze Age.[10] Hittite treaty texts—and other ancient Near Eastern treaty texts, such as those of King Esarhaddon of Assyria—typically begin with a self-identification formula which identifies the suzerain king of the treaty who specifies the obligations of his vassals. The preamble of the treaty between the Hittite King Mursilis II (1321–1295 BCE) and his vassal, King Duppi-Tessub of the Amorites, introduces King Mursilis: "These are the words of the Sun Mursilis, the great king, the king of the Hatti land, the valiant, the favorite of the Storm-god, the son of Suppiluliumas, the great king, the king of the Hatti land, the valiant."[11] The preamble identifies Mursilis, son of Suppiluliumas, as the suzerain monarch, who will specify the terms by which King Duppi-Tessub of the Amorites will meet his obligations to the Hittite Empire. The identification of "YHWH, your G-d" plays a similar role in the Ten Commandments, which introduce the Covenant Code of Exodus 20:19—23:33 as the obligations of the people of Israel, for whom YHWH will serve as divine king.

Exodus 20:2 introduces YHWH as "your G-d," but it also specifies actions that YHWH has taken on behalf of Israel, viz., "who brought you out of the land of Egypt, from the house of bondage." This statement relates YHWH's statement of Israel's obligations to the actions that YHWH undertook to free Israel from Egyptian bondage in the exodus and early wilderness narratives in Exodus 1–18. Such a recounting of YHWH's actions on Israel's behalf corresponds to the second feature of ancient Near Eastern treaty texts, which Mendenhall labels "the Historical Prologue." The Historical Prologue of the treaty between Mursilis II and Duppi-Tessub recounts the actions of his own father

9. Zimmerli, "Knowledge of G-d"; Sweeney, "Ezekiel: Zadokite Priest."

10. Mendenhall, "Covenant Forms," esp. 32–36. For discussion, see McCarthy, *Treaty and Covenant*; McCarthy, *Old Testament Covenant*. Not all the elements that Mendenhall identified proved to be parallels with the Decalogue (e.g., witnesses by the gods), but the basic categories of the self-identification, the historical preamble, and the stipulations hold for the Decalogue, while the blessings and curses appear in other contexts (i.e., Lev 26 and Deut 28–30). The provision for public reading appears in Deuteronomy 31 and Nehemiah 8–10.

11. *ANET* 203–5.

and the father of Duppi-Tessub, who fought as allies against a common enemy. Insofar as Duppi-Tessub's father was a vassal of Mursilis's father, Mursilis makes a treaty with Duppi-Tessub to continue the suzerain-vassal alliance between the two kingdoms, based on what the Hittite Empire had done on behalf of the Amorite kingdom.[12]

In the case of the Jewish reading of Exodus 20:2, the appearance of the self-recognition form is read as a requirement that Israel recognize YHWH as its G-d, who led the nation out of Egyptian bondage. Indeed, the narrative of YHWH's role in leading Israel out of bondage is the primary concern of the narrative in Exodus 1–18.

The stipulations or obligations of the vassals then follow in ancient Near Eastern treaty forms. In many cases the stipulations appear in apodictic command and prohibitions forms.

The second command in the Jewish understanding of the Ten Commandments is the command in Exodus 20:3–6 that Israel will have no other gods before YHWH, and that they will not make nor worship idols that depict YHWH. In Christianity, this is understood as two different commands since Exodus 20:2 is not considered a command per se. The stipulation for Israel to recognize YHWH exclusively corresponds to stipulations in the ancient treaties that the vassal will recognize no other suzerain than the one named in the treaty. Such a requirement is intended to ensure that neither Israel nor the vassal will have any dual loyalties that will impede or overturn the required loyalty to YHWH or the suzerain named in the treaty. Polytheistic ancient nations might recognize other gods, but such gods were understood to be subordinate to the suzerain god of the treaty. But in the case of ancient Israel and Judah, no other gods could be recognized because of the concept that YHWH was the one and only true G-d or divine power in the world of creation or human events. Politically speaking, recognition of YHWH alone meant that Israel and Judah could not be subject to other nations and their gods, as YHWH alone had the right to defend the nation. Historical experience, however, would challenge that notion, especially when Israel and Judah were attacked and destroyed (Israel by Assyria in 724–721 BCE and Judah by Babylon in 588–586 BCE) or when Israel or Judah were compelled to ally with other nations for their own protection. The development of local autonomy on the part of nations subject to the Persian Empire, beginning in the reign of Cyrus of Persia, the Achaemenid king, enabled Judah

12. See *ANET* 203.

to accept protection while recognizing only YHWH as their G-d—and Cyrus as YHWH's choice as monarch and temple builder in Isaiah 44:28 and 45:1.[13] Nevertheless, early examples of local autonomy emerged under the rule of the Assyrians and, later, the Babylonians.[14]

The prohibition against manufacturing and worshipping idols has little to do with treaty texts, but it has much to do with the conceptualization of YHWH as the sovereign creator and master of human events. The portrayal of YHWH in any tangible form is prohibited in Judaism due to the fact that YHWH is to be understood as beyond human comprehension and limitation. Such views of YHWH become apparent in Ezekiel's visions in Ezekiel 1–3 and Second Isaiah's oracles in Isaiah 40–48. But they are also evident in depictions of divine presence that employ non-tangible imagery, such as depictions of YHWH metaphorically in relation to such images as fire, smoke, water, wind, etc., such as one might see in 2 Kings 19, Isaiah 6, Ezekiel 1–3; the exodus narratives themselves; and portrayals of the hands of a priest with palms raised toward the heavens and the thumbs and fingertips touching.[15] The purpose of the prohibition is to avoid any suggestion of tangible limitation in portrayals of the presence of YHWH, all the better to portray YHWH as the all-powerful and all-present G-d of creation and human events who surpasses any other gods, portrayed in tangible idols, or human kings.

The portrayal of YHWH's punishment imposed on the third and fourth generations of those who sin against YHWH and YHWH's fidelity extended to the thousandth generation of those who adhere to YHWH appears to presuppose the theology of punishment for sin and fidelity as expressed in the Deuteronomistic History (i.e., Joshua, Judges, Samuel, and Kings), which holds King Jeroboam ben Nebat accountable for the punishment of the Northern Kingdom of Israel some two hundred years following his reign and King Manasseh ben Hezekiah accountable for the destruction of Jerusalem some sixty years after his reign. Such a reference

13. Sweeney, "Reconceptualization of Davidic Covenant"; Sweeney, *Isaiah 40–66*, 108–57.

14. See Kuan, *Neo-Assyrian Historical Inscriptions*. The appointment of Gedaliah ben Ahikam ben Shaphan to function as governor of Judah by the Babylonians constitutes an example of local autonomy under Babylonian rule.

15. *ANEP* depicts a stele from thirteenth-century BCE Hazor with two hands raised in supplication toward a crescent with disk and two tassel-like circles, which apparently depicts the moon and the sun or a star. The stele appears in what is labelled as a Canaanite shrine, and it apparently represents a Canaanite precursor to the later-Israelite priestly benediction (fig. 871).

suggests editing of this commandment by the late monarchic period J-stratum author of the Pentateuch, who would have been familiar with an early version of Deuteronomy and the Deuteronomistic History.[16]

The third commandment in the Jewish understanding of the sequence is the prohibition against raising the Name of YHWH fraudulently in Exodus 20:7. This prohibition is generally understood as using the Name of YHWH to swear falsely in any kind of formal legal transaction, i.e., international treaty, business, family matter, etc. The purpose of the prohibition is to protect the integrity of the Name of YHWH—and therefore YHWH per se—in a public forum, insofar as YHWH must be recognized as the true sovereign creator of the universe and ruler in human events. To impugn YHWH's Name through fraudulent testimony would entail compromising YHWH's integrity or holiness and thereby rendering YHWH like any other false god that the nations might worship. Such an action would likewise impugn the integrity of the Israelite—or Judean—people themselves.

The fourth commandment in the Jewish sequence is the command to remember the Shabbat to ensure its sanctity. No other nation in the ancient world is known to have a concept of the seventh day as a holy day of rest, although Mesopotamian cultures observed *šappatum/šabbatum* periods of some ten days in the fall and the spring as days when human beings might be cursed by the gods if they engaged in any form of public activity. The Jewish concept is not understood punitively, but as a day of joy and celebration because it releases people to observe the Shabbat as a celebration of YHWH's act of creation in six days, thereby leaving the seventh day, Saturday, as a day of rest, worship, and reflection, without the usual demands of work related to making a living, etc. The command to "remember" (Hebrew, *zākôr*) the Shabbat is understood as a command to observe the Shabbat, although the use of *šāmôr*, "observe," makes this understanding more clear in keeping with the role of the Deuteronomic law code to interpret and expand upon the earlier Covenant Code in Exodus 20–24.[17] The command to "remember" entails "looking upon," "remembering," and "acting upon," in keeping with the Babylonian Talmud in b. Menaḥot 43b,[18] whereas the command to "observe," in this case, means to remember what YHWH did in creating the universe in six days so that humans could observe

16. Sweeney, "Question of Theodicy."

17. Cf. Levinson, *Deuteronomy*.

18. Cf. Sarna, *Exodus*, 13, on Exod 2:24.

the Shabbat on the seventh day. Deuteronomy 5:12 entails action in relation to the observance of the Shabbat per se.[19]

The rationale for the remembrance of the Shabbat is YHWH's act of creation during the six profane days of the week and YHWH's rest following the work of creation on the seventh day, Saturday. Most interpreters correctly conclude that this rationale is the product of P-stratum redaction due to its correspondence to the account of creation in Genesis 1:1—2:3, which is understood to be a P-stratum composition. It is not clear that an E-stratum account of the initial creation of the universe appears in the Pentateuch. If there was one, it was either rewritten by P or replaced entirely by the P-stratum composition. Nevertheless, it is clear that the exodus and wilderness narratives in Exodus and Numbers portray YHWH as a creator G-d, who uses elements of the natural world—in the burning bush narrative, the plague narratives, the account of the encounter at the Reed Sea, and the wilderness journey—as part of YHWH's actions to deliver Israel from Egyptian bondage and guide them to the promised land of Israel. In this way the text presents the redemption story as a divine act of creation.[20] It is clear that the Covenant Code includes laws that presuppose the role of the Shabbat in creation as a basis for legislation that will help to ensure support for the poor in Exodus 21:1–11; 23:10–12.[21] And it is also clear that Shabbat was known during the monarchic period, as references to Shabbat appear in: 2 Kings 4:23 concerning the ninth-century prophet Elisha; Hosea 2:11–15 concerning the mid-eighth-century northern Israelite prophet Hosea ben Beeri; Amos 8:4–7 concerning the eighth-century Judean prophet Amos of Tekoa, who addressed northern Israel; and Isaiah 1:10–17 concerning the late-eighth-century Jerusalemite prophet Isaiah ben Amoz.[22] These passages indicate that Shabbat was known and practiced in the monarchic period of Israel and Judah, and it therefore would have been part of the E-stratum edition of the Pentateuch.

The fifth commandment in Exodus 20:12 calls for honoring one's parents. Such a command is designed to ensure the protection of social structure, family relationships, and the ownership of property by the family in question. Indeed, the rationale for the command, "that your

19. Cf. Dozeman, *Exodus*, 488.

20. Cf. Sweeney "Creation as Sacred Space."

21. Sweeney, "Shabbat."

22. Dozeman, *Exodus*, 491; for discussion of each passage, see Sweeney, *1–2 Kings*, 290–91; Sweeney, *Twelve Prophets*, 1:32–33, 262–64; and Sweeney, *Isaiah 1–39*, 78–81.

days shall be long upon the ground that YHWH, your G-d, is giving to you," is intended to ensure long life and protection of land ownership on the part of the individual in question and his family.

The sixth commandment in v. 13 is a prohibition of murder (Hebrew, *lōʾ tirṣāḥ*), understood as the illegal killing of a human being. Although some interpret the command to prohibit killing in general, which would require the Hebrew prohibition, *lōʾ tiqṭōl*, "you shall not kill," the Hebrew prohibition used here, *lōʾ tirṣāḥ*, "you shall not murder," is explicit.

The seventh commandment in v. 13 (v. 14 in Christian Bibles) is a prohibition against adultery. Adultery here differs from the understanding of adultery in modern Western culture, where it involves sexual relations between two people, at least one of whom is married to another person. In ancient Israel and Judah—and the ancient Near East in general—adultery refers to a man who has sexual relations with a woman who is married to another man. The prohibition presumes a society in which polygamy is allowed, which entails that the man's marital status is largely irrelevant. But women are allowed to marry only one man at a time. The prohibition is therefore designed to protect the marriage relationship of ancient men by ensuring that their wives will not engage in relations with another man. It thereby protects the presumption that any children born to a man's wife will be the man's own and not those of another man. It thereby ensures that only his own sons will inherit his property and name after his death.

The eighth commandment in v. 13 (v. 15 in Christian Bibles) is the prohibition against stealing. The prohibition presumes the illegal taking of any property not rightly one's own from another person.

The ninth commandment in v. 13 (v. 16 in Christian Bibles) is the prohibition against testifying falsely against one's neighbor in a court of law. This prohibition is designed to protect the integrity of the ancient Israelite and Judean court systems by making false legal testimony against another person a crime. Such an act constitutes perjury in modern legal parlance, which is punishable by the court.

The tenth commandment in v. 14 (v. 17 in Christian Bibles) is the prohibition against coveting a neighbor's house, wife, male or female slave, animals, and anything else that might belong to one's neighbor. It is nearly impossible to determine if someone covets something that belongs to one's neighbor unless the person in question states that he covets his neighbor's wife or possessions or takes action to make that coveting clear, especially if it entails taking possession of the person or items in question. Like the prohibition against stealing, this command is intended to protect people against the actions of those who would attempt to take possession of their family members—beginning with the wife—and property by targeting the intent of the prospective thief who reveals his jealousy.

Reception History

The differences in the enumeration or versification of the text are discussed in the above commentary. The Ten Commandments are already cited by selected prophets in the Hebrew Bible. Hosea 4:1–3 cites the prohibitions against fraudulent testimony, lies, murder, theft, and adultery, as noted in the commentary above, apparently based upon the presumed Elohistic version of the proto-Pentateuch. Jeremiah cites the prohibitions against theft, murder, adultery, fraudulent swearing (presumably employing the Name of YHWH), and following other gods, presumably from the Deuteronomic law code, but possibly from the Elohistic version, in his famous temple sermon in Jeremiah 7:9. Deuteronomy 5 presents a presumably reworked version of the Ten Commandments that includes several variations, as noted in the commentary.[23] Leviticus 19 cites various elements of the Ten Commandments in its presentation of ritual and ethical instruction.[24]

According to the Babylonian Talmud, b. Makkot 24b, the first two commandments were stated directly by G-d to the people at Sinai, but the subsequent commandments were announced by Moses. Every person at Sinai believed that G-d had announced the commandments directly to him.[25] The announcements of the command to "remember" and to "observe" the Shabbat, together with all the other variations between Exodus 20 and Deuteronomy 5, entail that both versions of the Ten Commandments were announced simultaneously by YHWH to Israel at Mount Sinai, "which transcends the capacity of the human mouth to utter and the human ear to hear" (b. Šebu. 20b; b. Roš Haš. 27a). The Ten Commandments were originally part of the daily temple service, but the practice was discontinued due to the contentions of the minim, "sectarians," that

23. For commentary, see esp. Tigay, *Deuteronomy*, 61–72.

24. For commentary, see esp. Levine, *Leviticus*, 124–35.

25. For rabbinic Judaism's understanding of the Ten Commandments, see Rubens, "Decalogue."

the Ten Commandments constituted the entirety of the divine revelation (m. Tamid 5.1). The rabbinic position reinforces the view that the Ten Commandments function as an introduction to the larger body of law in Exodus–Numbers and Deuteronomy. The Ten Commandments are read, however, when they appear in the weekly Torah portions for Parashat Yitro (Exod 18:1—20:23), Parashat Va-Etḥannan (Deut 3:23—7:11), and the festival Torah portion for Shavuot (Exod 19:1—20:23).

Many modern synagogues display a visual rendition of the Ten Commandments above or by the ark, where the synagogues' Torah scrolls are stored when not in use.

The Christian New Testament cites the Ten Commandments frequently. Acts 4:24 (cf. 14:15) cites the reference to G-d's six-day creation of heaven and earth in Exodus 20:11 in its account of the arrest and release of Peter and John. Revelation 10:6 alludes to this verse in its account of the angel associated with the seventh trumpet. Revelation 14:7 again cites G-d's role in creation in its account of the three angels who will come on the day of judgment. Matthew 15:4 and Mark 7:10 cite the command to honor parents in Exodus 20:12 in their critique of the Pharisees and scribes for allegedly not honoring G-d. Paul cites Exodus 20:12 in Ephesians 6:2 when he calls on his audience to honor their parents. Matthew 19:18; Mark 10:19; and Luke 18:20 cite commandments concerning murder, adultery, theft, false witness, and honoring parents from Exodus 20:12–16 (according to the Christian versification of the commandments) in calling for observance of the command to love your neighbor as yourself and to sell possessions in order to follow Jesus. Matthew 5:21 cites the prohibition against murder in Exodus 20:13 in Jesus's teaching concerning the need to abandon anger. James 2:11 cites the prohibition against murder and adultery in Exodus 2:13, 14 (according to the Christian versification of the text) in its argument that to violate one aspect of law is equivalent to violating all of the law. Romans 13:9 cites the prohibitions against adultery, murder, theft, coveting, and other commandments in Exodus 20:13–17 (Christian versification) as part of Paul's argument to love your neighbor as yourself. Matthew 5:27 cites the prohibition against adultery in Exodus 20:14 (Christian versification) to argue that one commits adultery simply by looking at a woman with lust. Romans 7:7 cites the prohibition against coveting in Exodus 20:17 (Christian versification) as part of Paul's argument that the law alerted him to the sin of coveting.

Beginning with patristic interpretation, by such figures as Justin, Irenaeus, and Tertullian, Christianity developed the notion that the Ten Commandments represented Jewish law, but humanity in general was bound to observe only natural law.[26] Whereas Origen argued that the freedom of the spirit had comprised the observance of the entire law, Augustine argued that law was good for humanity but it had been killed by sin. Instead, the law of the spirit secured by faith became the basis for human freedom to engage in works of charity based in divine love. Martin Luther maintained that the Ten Commandments played a comprehensive role in human life in that they contain natural law. Although Luther contends that Jewish law has nothing to say to Christians, justification by faith opens a new life of freedom based on the fear, love, and trust of G-d above all else. Jean Calvin argued that the Ten Commandments pointed to the "third use" of the law, which must consider the goals for which law was revealed, i.e., how to achieve the ideals for which law was revealed in a life based on Christian faith and love.

More recently, modern America has seen an attempt by conservative Christians to argue that American law, beginning with the Declaration of Independence and the Constitution, is actually based on "Old Testament law," beginning with the Ten Commandments. Hence, sculptures or other representations of the Ten Commandments are placed in judicial settings, such as the Alabama Supreme Court, or governmental settings, such as the Texas or Arkansas state capitols. But such a view ignores the development of American jurisprudence, which is based on English common law in forty-nine states of the Union and the Napoleonic Code in Louisiana.

26. For Christianity's understanding of the Ten Commandments, see esp. Childs, *Exodus*, 431–37.

The Account of YHWH's Announcement of the Covenant Code—Exodus 20:15—24:11

THE ACCOUNT OF YHWH's announcement of the Covenant Code in Exodus 20:15—24:11 begins with a brief narrative introduction in Exodus 20:15–18. This text is demarcated at the outset by a conjunctive-*waw* participle construction—"And all the people were viewing the thunder"—that signals the beginning of a new unit by means of syntactical disruption but nevertheless indicates a syntactical join with the preceding text. The purpose of the brief narrative is to indicate the people's reaction to YHWH's announcement of the Ten Commandments in Exodus 20:1–14 and to prepare the reader for the following speech by YHWH in Exodus 20:19—23:33, in which YHWH will announce the Covenant Code.

The Covenant Code is presented as a speech by YHWH, introduced by the speech formula in Exodus 20:19aα, "And YHWH said to Moses." The speech proper then follows in Exodus 20:19aβ—23:33. It comprises two major portions. The first is YHWH's initial announcement concerning the construction of the altar in Exodus 20:19aβ–23, which is necessary because oracular inquiry of YHWH takes place in relation to the altar at which offerings are made to YHWH and from which YHWH responds.[1]

1. See 2 Kings 16:10–16, in which King Ahaz ben Hezekiah is required by King Tiglath-Pileser of Assyria to build a new altar at the temple. The old altar of bronze is then set aside for use by the Judean king to make inquiry (v. 15, Hebrew, *lĕbaqqēr*). Although some interpreters maintain that this verb is meant to indicate Ahaz's inquiry concerning what to do with the altar, the term is used for making inquiry of YHWH. See Sweeney, *1–2 Kings*, 379, 385.

The second portion of the Covenant Code appears in Exodus 21:1—23:33, which is introduced by its own superscription, "And these are the laws which you shall set before them," which is jointed syntactically by conjunctive-*waw* to Exodus 20:19–23. The superscription introduces the laws of the Covenant Code in Exodus 21:2—23:33.

Exodus 24:1–11 concludes the account of the revelation of the Covenant Code to Israel with the account of YHWH's sacred meal with Moses, Aaron, Nadab and Abihu, and the seventy elders of Israel on Mount Sinai to seal the covenant between YHWH and Israel. Exodus 24:12–18, which recounts how Moses will remain on the mountain alone for forty days and forty nights, constitutes the introduction to the account of YHWH's instructions to Moses concerning the building of the tabernacle and its fixtures and the conduct of its associated activities.[2]

David Wright demonstrates how the Covenant Code was written with the laws of Hammurabi as a compositional model, although the Covenant Code has modified Hammurabi's laws to account for characteristic Israelite concerns,[3] such as the influence of Shabbat patterns in the calculation of time, the absence of class distinctions in the treatment of criminals, and the concern to protect women and girls from sexual abuse. Wright argues that the Covenant Code was written during the late Assyrian period, ca. 740–640 BCE, on the basis of apparent Babylonian influence,[4] and Van Seters argues that the Covenant Code was composed during the Babylonian exile.[5] But Van Seters does not recognize Judah's relations with Babylon during the reign of Hezekiah, who allied with Merodach Baladan of Babylon in revolt against Assyria. And neither Wright nor Van Seters recognizes the discovery of cuneiform legal tablet fragments at Hazor during the Middle Bronze Age.[6] The Middle Bronze Age dating of the Hazor fragments, which also take up the treatment of slaves, make it possible to date the Covenant Code to the time of the Northern Kingdom of Israel when the E-stratum of the Pentateuch would have been written. The initial case in Exodus 21:2–11 specifies the term of service of a Hebrew slave as six years, with release to take place in the seventh year. This time period is based on

2. Cf. Dozeman, *Exodus*, 569–92.

3. D. Wright, *Investigating G-d's Law*. For the text, translation, and commentary of Hammurabi's law code, see Driver and Miles, *Babylonian Laws*; cf. *ANET* 163–80.

4. D. Wright, *Investigating G-d's Law*, 91–120.

5. Van Seters, *Law Book for Diaspora*.

6. Horowitz et al., "Hazor 18."

the Shabbat principle of time calculation in which six years of work are specified and the seventh year calls for release or rest. Indeed, Jacob's terms of service for his marriages to Rachel and Leah and the term of service for his flock is six years in each case, with release coming in the seventh year. The Jacob narrative in Genesis 25:19—35:29 is an E-stratum narrative that has been redacted into the overall Genesis narrative by the J-stratum and P-stratum writers.[7] It is also noteworthy that Hosea cites elements of the Ten Commandments from Exodus 20 in Hosea 4:1–3 and elements from the E-stratum ancestral history and the exodus–wilderness traditions in Hosea 12.[8] Likewise, the late-eighth-century prophet Amos of Tekoa cites cases from the Covenant Code in his accusations of wrongdoing against the Northern Kingdom of Israel in Amos 2:6–16.[9] All of these factors provide support for viewing the origins of the Covenant Code as an E-stratum composition.

It is noteworthy that the Covenant Code contains three types of legal formulations. The first is the casuistic or case law form that employs formulas based on the particles *kî*, "when/when," to address the primary statement of the case, and *'im* ("if"), to address specifications of the primary case in the protasis or statement of the facts of the case in the law prior to the resolution of the case in the apodosis of the law.[10] The second is a mixed form that employs a participial formation that describes the facts of the case in the protasis of the law prior to the statement of its resolution in the apodosis. Specifications continue to appear in clauses introduced by *'im*, "if." Alt had grouped these laws together with the case laws noted above, but others argue that these laws represent a combination of case law and apodictic forms, insofar as they sometimes use second-person address forms in the apodosis (e.g., Exod 21:12–14).[11] It is noteworthy that these types of laws appear in ancient Near Eastern suzerain vassal treaties from the Hittite Empire of the Bronze Age and also from the Neo-Assyrian Empire of the eighth and seventh centuries BCE. Finally, there is the third legal form, viz., the apodictic forms, basically commands and prohibitions, which Alt deemed were unique to Israel, and posited that they must have originated among the seminomadic tribal leaders (e.g., the *ḥabiru*) who would have issued authoritative statements of pre-Israelite

7. Sweeney, "Jacob Narratives."

8. Sweeney, *Twelve Prophets*, 1:1–144, esp. 43–45, 117–30.

9. Sweeney, *Twelve Prophets*, 1:189–276, esp. 214–18.

10. Alt, "Origins of Israelite Law."

11. E.g., Gilmer, *If–You Form*.

law. But these apodictic statements appear to be closely aligned with the apodoses of the mixed forms noted above.

Given the treaty background of such forms and the efforts to portray YHWH as the overruling king of kings, superior to the Neo-Assyrian, Neo-Babylonian, and Achaemenid kings of the ninth through the fourth centuries BCE, it would be best to maintain that these apodictic forms developed from ancient Near Eastern treaty forms that played a role in depicting YHWH as the overarching monarch who would issue such authoritative apodictic statements as part of the specifications for the obligations of the people of Israel and Judah bound to YHWH in covenant. The presence of mixed and apodictic forms that presuppose ancient Near Eastern suzerain-vassal treaties may represent expansions of an earlier version of the Covenant Code when Israel became an ally of the Aramean kingdom during the ninth-century BCE rule of the Omride Dynasty or when Israel became a vassal of the Jehu Dynasty during the late ninth century BCE. Such expansions would have been introduced in these periods in an effort to portray G-d/YHWH as the true G-d of Israel over against the gods of the Arameans or the Assyrians. The critique of northern Israel by prophets, such as Hosea and Amos, would have made this point very clear.

Translation

> **20:15** And all the people were viewing the thunder, and the lightning, and the sound of the shofar, and the mountain was smoking, and the people saw, and they trembled, and they stood far away. [16] And they said to Moses, "Speak—yourself—with us, and we will listen, but do not let G-d speak with us lest we die." [17] And Moses said to the people, "Do not fear, for in order to test you has G-d come and in order that the fear of him will be on your faces so that you will not sin." [18] And the people stood far away, and Moses approached the deep darkness where G-d was.

> **20:19** "Thus shall you say to the sons of Israel, 'You have seen that from the heavens I have spoken with you. [20] You shall not make with me gods of silver, and gods of gold you shall not make for yourselves. [21] An altar of earth you shall make for me, and you shall sacrifice upon it your whole burnt offerings

and your sacrifices of well-being, your sheep and your cattle, in every place where I cause my Name to be remembered, I will come to you and I will bless you. 22 And if an altar of stones you make for me, you shall not build them with cut stones; if you use your tool upon it, then you will profane it. 23 And you shall not go up on steps upon my altar, so that you will not reveal your nakedness upon it.'

21:1 And these are the laws that you will set before them. 2 When you acquire a Hebrew slave, six years he shall work, and in the seventh he will go out for free, without compensation. 3 If he comes by himself, by himself he shall go out. If he is the husband of a wife, then his wife will go with him. 4 If his master gives to him a wife, and the wife bears for him sons or daughters, then her children will belong to her master, and he will go out by himself. 5 But if the slave surely says, 'I love my master, my wife, and my sons. I will not go out free,' 6 then his master will bring him to G-d, and he shall bring him to the door or to the doorpost, and his master shall pierce his ear with an awl, and he shall serve him forever.

7 But when a man sells his daughter as a maidservant, she shall not go out like the going out of the male slaves. 8 If there is something wrong in the eyes of her master who designated her for himself, then he must redeem her. He may not designate her for sale to a foreign people by his acting treacherously with her. 9 And if for his son he designated her, according to the law of daughters he shall do with her. 10 If he takes another [wife] for himself, her food, her clothing, and her sexual rights he may not diminish. 11 And if these three things he does not do for her, then she will go out free without payment.

12 Whoever strikes a man so that he dies shall surely be put to death. 13 But when he does not lie in wait or G-d allowed his hand [to act], then I shall appoint you a place where you may flee. 14 But if a man lies in wait against his neighbor to kill him with cunning, from my altar you may take him to die.

15 And whoever strikes his father and his mother, he shall
surely be put to death, 16 and whoever steals a man and sells
him or he is found in his hand, he shall surely be put to death.

17 And whoever curses his father and his mother shall surely
be put to death.

18 And when men contend, and one man strikes his neighbor
with a stone or with a fist, and he does not die, but falls to
his bed, 19 if he rises and walks about outside upon his staff,
then the one who struck shall go unpunished; only [for] his
convalescence shall he pay so that he will surely recover.

20 And when a man strikes his slave or his maidservant
with a rod so that he dies under his hand, he must surely be
avenged. 21 But [if after] a day or two days he stands, he will
not be avenged, for its his money.

22 And if men struggle, and they hit a pregnant woman, and
her children come out, but there is no [other] harm, he [i.e.,
the one who hit her] shall surely be fined just as the husband
of the woman set upon him, and he shall give according to
the judges. 23 But if there is harm, then he shall give life in
place of life, 24 eye in place of eye, tooth in place of tooth,
hand in place of hand, foot in place of foot, 25 burn in place
of burn, wound in place of wound, bruise in place of bruise.

26 And if a man strikes the eye of his slave or the eye of his
maidservant, and he destroys it, for free he must send him
out in place of his eye, 27 and if the tooth of his servant or the
tooth of his maidservant he causes to fall, for free he must
send him out in place of his tooth.

28 And if a bull gores a man or a woman so that he dies, the
bull will surely be stoned, and its flesh shall not be eaten, but
the owner of the bull is unpunished. 29 But if a bull has gored
previously, and its owner was notified, but he did not watch
it, and it kills a man or a woman, the bull will be stoned,
and also its owner shall be killed. 30 If a ransom is set upon
him, then he shall pay the redemption of his life according to
what is set upon him. 31 Or [if] it gores a son or [if] it gores
a daughter, according to this law shall it be done to it. 32 If a

slave the bull gores or a maidservant, thirty shekels in silver
he will give to his [or her] [i.e., the slave's] master, and the
bull will be stoned.

33 And if a man opens a pit, or if a man digs a pit, and he does
not cover it, and a bull or an ass falls into it, 34 the owner of
the pit shall pay. [With] silver he shall compensate its master,
but the dead [animal] shall belong to him.

35 And if the bull of a man hits the bull of his neighbor and it
dies, then they shall sell the living bull, and they shall divide
its [price in] silver, and also the dead [bull] they shall divide.
36 Or [if] it is known that the bull had gored previously and
its owner did not watch it, then he shall surely pay a bull in
place of a bull, and the dead [bull] shall be his.

37 When a man steals a bull or a lamb and he slaughters it or
sells it, five cattle he shall pay in place of the bull and four
sheep in place of the lamb.

22:1 If in digging the thief is found, then he may be stricken
down; there is no bloodguilt for him. 2 If the sun has risen
upon him, there is bloodguilt for him. He shall surely compensate. If he has nothing [to pay compensation], then he
will be sold for his theft. 3 If there is surely found in his hand
anything from a bull to an ass to a sheep alive, he shall pay
double.

4 When a man causes [his cattle] to graze in a field or a vineyard, and he sends his cattle so that it grazes in the field of
another, then for the restoration of his field and the restoration of his vineyard he shall compensate.

5 When fire breaks out, and it finds thorns, and it consumes
stacked grain or standing grain or the field, the one who
started the fire shall surely compensate.

6 When a man gives to his neighbor silver or vessels to watch,
and it is stolen from the house of the man, if the thief is
found, he shall compensate double. 7 If the thief is not found,
then the owner of the house shall come near to G-d [to show]
that he did not send his hand against the property of his

neighbor. 8 Concerning any case of wrongdoing concerning a bull, concerning an ass, concerning a sheep, concerning a garment, concerning anything that is lost which he says, 'this is it,' unto G-d the two of them shall come. Whomever G-d declares guilty, he shall surely compensate double to his neighbor.

9 When a man gives to his neighbor an ass or a bull or a sheep or any animal to watch, and it dies, or it is injured or it is taken away without anyone seeing, 10 an oath of YHWH shall be between the two of them that he did not send his hand against the property of his neighbor. Then its owner shall take [his word], and he shall not compensate. 11 But if it was surely stolen from him, he shall compensate its owner. 12 If it was surely torn by an animal, he shall bring a witness of the tearing. He does not compensate.

13 And when a man asks from his neighbor and it is injured or it dies [and] its owner is not with it, he shall surely compensate. 14 If its owner is with it, he will not compensate. If it was hired, he comes with its hiring price.

15 And when a man seduces a virgin who is not betrothed, and he lies with her, he will surely pay her bride-price to become his wife. 16 If her father surely refuses to give her to him, he must weigh the money according to the bride-price for virgins.

17 A sorceress you shall not allow to live.

18 Anyone who lies with an animal shall surely die.

19 One who sacrifices to gods shall be banned, except to YHWH alone.

20 A resident alien you shall not mistreat, and you shall not oppress him, for you were resident aliens in the land of Egypt.

21 Any widow or orphan you shall not humiliate. 22 If you surely humiliate him, when he surely cries out to me, I will surely listen to his cry, 23 and my anger shall burn, and I will kill you with the sword so that your wives shall be widows and your sons shall be orphans. 24 If you lend money to my

people, to the poor among you, you shall not be a creditor to him; you shall not place upon him interest. 25 If you surely take in pledge the cloak of your neighbor, at the setting of the sun you will return it to him, 26 for his cloak is his only covering for his skin. In what would he lie down [to sleep]? And it shall be when he cries out to me, then I will hear, for I am gracious.

27 G-d you shall not denigrate, and a leader among your people you will not curse.

28 Your produce and your juice you shall not delay; the first-born of your sons you shall give to me. 29 So you shall do for your bull [and] for your sheep. Seven days it shall be with its mother. On the seventh day, you shall give it to me.

30 And holy people you shall be to me. And meat torn [by animals] in the field, you shall not eat; to the dog you shall throw it.

23:1 You shall not raise a false report.

You shall not lend your hand to the wicked to be a perjured witness.

2 You shall not be with the majority to do evil, and you shall not testify concerning a lawsuit to turn after the majority to turn aside [justice], 3 and [for] the poor you shall not show special favor in his lawsuit.

4 When you meet the bull of your enemy or his straying ass, you shall surely return it to him.

5 When you see the ass of someone who hates you lying under its burden and you would decline to set it free, you will surely set it free with him.

6 You will not turn aside the justice of your poor in his lawsuit.

7 From a false statement you must keep far, and the innocent and the righteous you must not murder, for I will not declare the wicked to be just, 8 and a bribe you will not take, for the bribe blinds those whose eyes are open, and it subverts the

words of the righteous, 9 and a resident alien you will not oppress since you know the life of the resident alien because you were resident aliens in the land of Egypt.

10 And for six years you shall sow your land and you shall gather your produce, 11 but in the seventh [year] you shall release it and you will leave it alone so that the poor of your people may eat, and whatever they leave, the animals of the field will eat. Thus you shall do for your vineyard and your olive tree.

12 For six days you shall do your work, but on the seventh day you shall stop so that your bull and your ass may rest, and the son of your maidservant and the resident alien may be refreshed. 13 And in all that I have said to you, you shall be observant, and the name of other gods you shall not invoke; it shall not be heard upon your mouth.

14 Three times you shall celebrate for me in the year. 15 The Festival of Unleavened Bread you shall observe. For seven days you shall eat unleavened bread just as I commanded you at the appointed time of the month of Aviv, because in it you went forth from Egypt, and there shall not appear before me anyone empty handed. 16 And the Festival of the Harvest of the Firstfruits of your labor, which you planted in the field, and the Festival of Ingathering at the close of the year when you gather your work from the field. 17 Three times in the year, all your men shall appear before me, the Lord, YHWH.

18 You shall not sacrifice with leavening the blood of my sacrifice, and you will not leave the fat of my festival offering until morning.

19 The first of the firstfruits of your land you shall bring to the House of YHWH, your G-d.

You shall not boil a kid in the milk of its mother.

20 Behold! I am sending an angel before you to guard you on the road and to bring you to the place that I have established. 21 Be careful before him, and listen to his voice. Do not rebel against him, for he will not forgive your rebellion because

my Name is within him, 22 for if you surely listen to his voice,
and you do all that I speak, then I will treat your enemies as
my enemy, and I will afflict those who afflict you.

23 When my angel goes before you, and he brings you to the
Amorites and the Hittites and the Perizzites and the Canaanites, the Hivvites, and the Jebusites, I will annihilate them.
24 You shall not bow down to their gods, and you shall not
serve them, and you will not do works, but you shall surely
tear down and surely shatter their pillars. 25 And you shall
serve YHWH, your G-d, and he will bless your bread and
your water, and I will remove sickness from your midst.
26 There shall be no miscarriage or barrenness in your land;
the number of your days I will fulfill.

27 My terror I will send before you, and I will confuse all the
people among whom you come, and will make all your enemies turn their neck to you. 28 And I will send the plague before you, and it will drive away the Hivvites, the Canaanites,
and the Hittites from before you. 29 I will not drive them out
from before you in one year lest the land become desolate,
and the animals of the field multiply against you. 30 Little by
little I will drive them out from before you until you become
fruitful and you take possession of the land. 31 And I will set
your border from the Sea of Reeds to the Sea of the Philistines and from the wilderness to the river for I will give into
your hand the inhabitants of the land, and you will drive
them out from before you. 32 You will not cut with them or
with their gods a covenant. 33 They will not live in your land
lest they cause you to sin against me, for you will surely serve
their gods for they will become a snare for you."

24:1 And to Moses, he said, "Go up to YHWH, you and Aaron,
Nadab and Abihu, and seventy from the elders of Israel, and
you shall bow down from afar. 2 And Moses alone shall approach to YHWH, but they shall not approach, and the people
shall not go up with him."

3 And Moses came, and he related to the people all the words
of YHWH and all the laws, and all the people answered in one
voice, and they said, "All the words that YHWH has spoken,

we will do." 4 And Moses wrote all the words of YHWH, and he arose early in the morning, and he built an altar below the mountain, and twelve pillars for the twelve tribes of Israel. 5 And he sent young men of the sons of Israel, and they sent up a whole burnt offering, and they sacrificed bulls as peace offerings to YHWH. 6 And Moses took half of the blood, and he placed it in basins, and half of the blood he sprinkled on the altar. 7 And he took the Book of the Covenant, and he read [it] in the ears of the people, and they said, "All that YHWH has spoken, we will do and we will listen." 8 And Moses took the blood, and he sprinkled [it] on the people, and he said, "Behold, the blood of the covenant which YHWH cut with you concerning all these words."

9 And Moses and Aaron, Nadab and Abihu, and seventy from the elders of Israel went up, 10 and they saw the G-d of Israel, and under his feet was the likeness of a pavement of sapphire, and it was like the sky itself for purity. 11 And against the nobles of the sons of Israel, he did not send forth his hand, and they envisioned G-d, and they ate, and they drank.

Commentary

Exodus 20:15–18

As noted above, Exodus 20:15–18 presents the reaction of the people of Israel to YHWH's announcement of the Ten Commandments as the first stage of YHWH's revelation of the Covenant Code. The passage indicates the continuing appearance of thunder, lightning, the sound of the shofar, and smoke on the mountain, which instills a sense of fear or awe on the part of the people. Indeed, these features presage the features of the Jerusalem temple during times of holy service (cf. Isa 6).[12] The passage thereby illustrates the proper comportment of the people at times of sacred service at the tabernacle and later at the temple. The people indicate their reluctance to have YHWH address them directly, and they therefore request that Moses stand before them to receive YHWH's address while they stand far away. This action sets the pattern for the representation of

12. For discussion of the imagery of the temple during a time of sacred service, see Sweeney, *Isaiah 1–39*, 132–42.

the people by a prophet, who will receive YHWH's communication. Although prophets appear to represent the people at sacred times, much as Elijah does during the altar service at Mount Carmel in 1 Kings 18,[13] this role is later taken over by the priests in the Jerusalem temple. The people swear that they will listen to what Moses hears directly from YHWH, but they claim that they are afraid to approach YHWH themselves for fear that they will die. Moses employs the reassurance formula, "Do not fear" (Hebrew, *ʾal-tîrāʾû*), to reassure the people that YHWH is only testing them so they do not commit sin.[14]

Exodus 21:1—23:33

Exodus 21:1—23:33 presents the specific law code of the Covenant Code. The term is based on Exodus 24:7, which recounts how "the Book of the Covenant" (Hebrew, *seper habbĕrît*) is read to the people by Moses in a ceremony that confirms ratification of the covenant. The Covenant Code begins with the superscription in Exodus 21:1, "And these are the laws [Hebrew, *hammišpāṭîm*] that you will set before them." The laws then follow in Exodus 21:2—23:33.

Exodus 21:2–11

Exodus 21:2–11 addresses cases that involve the personal status of human beings as slaves and the liabilities that are relevant in each case. The main case is introduced with the particle *kî* ("if/when") or the conjunctive particle *wĕkî* ("and if/when"). Specifications to the case are introduced with *ʾim* ("if") or *wĕʾim* ("and if").

The case in Exodus 21:2–11 takes up the laws concerning the treatment of Hebrew slaves. The first paragraph concerning the treatment of male slaves, introduced by the particle *kî* ("when"), appears in Exodus 21:2–6, and the second paragraph, introduced by the conjunctive particle *wĕkî* ("and when"), which concerns the treatment of female slaves, appears in Exodus 21:7–11. The term "slave" (Hebrew, *ʿebed*) refers to debt slaves, i.e., men who become slaves for a limited period of time to pay off a debt. They are not to be confused with the chattel slaves who were kidnapped from Africa and sold or born into perpetual slavery for

13. See Sweeney, *1–2 Kings*, 224–30.

14. Sweeney, *Isaiah 1–39*, 547.

the rest of their lives in the American colonies or the United States—and other locations—in the sixteenth to nineteenth centuries CE. The women, identified here as "maidservant" (Hebrew, *ʾāmâ*), were generally presumed to be married to the owner or some member of his family, and were therefore not released on the same terms as the men, except under specified circumstances. Wright has demonstrated that the Covenant Code debt slave laws are modelled on those of Hammurabi's law code (sect. 117, 119, 175, 282, 178, 148, 154–56, 148–49) in terms of form and general content, but they have been modified substantially to account for Israelite interests in the Shabbat principle of the term of service (i.e., six years of service with release in the seventh year) and concern for the protection of the women from sexual abuse.[15]

Male slaves were "acquired" (Hebrew, *tiqneh*, "[when] you acquire"), which could refer to purchase in the case of those acquired by a debt to be paid by a term of service, by inheritance in the case of the death of the original owner, or by other means. They are specified as "Hebrew" (*ʿibrî*), which indicates that they are Israelite or Judean. This law does not apply to foreign slaves, which are not addressed in the Covenant Code. They serve for a term of six years, and they are released in the seventh year, if they choose to go free. The time period is based on the Shabbat principle of six days of labor and the seventh day of release calculated in terms of years rather than days.[16] When they complete their term of service, they "go out for free, without compensation" (Hebrew, *yāṣāʾ laḥopšî ḥinnām*). The specification that they go "for free" entails that they are released without further compensation due to the owner, and the specification that they go out without compensation entails that they are given no funds or property with which to start their life of freedom anew. Four specifications, each introduced by the particle *ʾim* ("if") then follow. The first specification in v. 3a states that if a male slave comes in single (Hebrew, *bĕgappô*, lit., "with his body") and with nothing else, he will go free, without compensation, by himself. Some interpreters argue that *bĕgappô* means "with his skirt," i.e., with the clothing on his back, based on an Aramaic loanword, but this interpretation is generally rejected because a man's clothing is not likely to last for six years, and he is not likely to go free without any clothing at all. The second specification in v. 3b states that if the male slave is accompanied by his wife, she

15. D. Wright, *Investigating G-d's Law*, 123–53.

16. See Sweeney, "Shabbat."

will go out free, without compensation, with him. The third specification in v. 4 states that if his owner gives him a wife and she bears sons or daughters to him, the wife's children remain the property of the owner, and the male slave goes free, without compensation, alone. No specification is given for the wife as she becomes a factor in vv. 5–6 in which she apparently continues to belong to the owner. The fourth specification in vv. 5–6, introduced by *wĕʾim* ("and if"), states that if the male chooses to remain a slave for life, he may undergo a procedure in which he states that he loves his master, his wife, and his children, and therefore chooses not to go free without compensation. He is taken "to G-d" (Hebrew, *ʾel hāʾĕlōhîm*), which apparently refers to a sanctuary, to have his ear pierced at the doorpost of the sanctuary so that he may be fitted with an earring that will signal his status as a perpetual slave for life. Interpreters may note that this version of the slave law is formulated to encourage single men to become slaves for life. Because they are released without compensation, they have nothing to start their life anew, and they are therefore very likely to return to debt slavery without some outside support from their family or other resources. But even if they do have funding from some source, their marriage to a woman in slavery and the birth of children become additional factors in their decision to remain perpetual slaves, unless they have the means—or perhaps they may acquire them—to purchase the freedom of the wife and her children. Given the lack of compensation, this appears to be very unlikely. A revision of the slave law in Deuteronomy 15:1–18 ensures that male slaves are provided with compensation when they are set free, and women are released on the same terms as men.[17] Such a revision would have made it less likely that men or women would choose to remain slaves in perpetuity.

The laws concerning a female slave or "maidservant" (Hebrew, *ʾāmâ*) then follow in Exodus 21:7–11. The law is introduced by the conjunctive case law form, *wĕkî* ("and when"), and she is described as sold by her father, i.e., "when a man sells [Hebrew, *yimkōr*] his daughter as a maidservant." Single women are presumed to be married as a wife or more likely as a concubine for the master or for one of his sons, and so they does not go free on the same terms as the male slaves. Four specifications then follow. The first in v. 8, introduced by the particle *ʾim* ("if"), states that if the master finds something wrong with her, if he has designated her as his own wife, he may not redeem her to a foreign people.

17. Cf. Levinson, *Deuteronomy*.

Such a transaction on his part would be considered a case of treachery on the master's part in that the woman would be sold to foreigners and the case would therefore be considered a case of fraud. Such a redemption or sale is therefore forbidden by law. A second specification in v. 9, introduced by *wĕʾim* ("and if"), states that if the woman is designated as a wife for one of his sons then she will be treated "according to the law of daughters" (Hebrew, *kĕmišpat habbānôt*) and she is therefore a daughter-in-law and not a maidservant. The third specification follows in v. 10, introduced by the particle *ʾim* ("if"). As a wife, she therefore has legal rights that must be observed. If he—either the master or his son—marries another wife in addition to her, he may not diminish three things due to her as a wife: *šĕʾērāh*, "her flesh/meat," understood here as "her food"; *kĕsûtāh*, "her covering," understood as "her clothing"; and *ʿōnātāh*, "her cohabitation," understood as her marital rights to her own home and her sexual relations with her husband. This last right is key to her future in that it ensures that she has her own home—and therefore does not have to share a home with a rival wife (see 1 Sam 1)—and children who will support her in her old age when her husband is presumably dead. The fourth specification appears in v. 11, introduced by the conjunctive particle *wĕʾim* ("and if"). If her husband does not do these three things for her, then she goes out without compensation (Hebrew, *ḥinnām*). This clause also gives the owner an advantage because she is divorced, but without compensation, which leaves her in a difficult situation. She would presumably return to her father's house, and her father would have received payment when he originally sold her. But she is now an extra mouth to feed in a subsistence economy, or perhaps her father is already dead. Otherwise, she would have to marry another man or support herself, which would suggest that she might be considered as a prostitute (cf. Rahab in Josh 1:1). Again, the revised law in Deuteronomy 15:1–18 ensures that women are provided with a stipend when they go free, which presumably addresses this particular need.[18]

Exodus 21:12–32

Exodus 21:12–32 addresses cases of liability for manslaughter, murder, personal injury, and damage to property, caused by human beings or animals owned by human beings. The cases are introduced in some

18. Cf. Levinson, *Deuteronomy*.

instances by a participle, which introduces the action that is addressed in the case at hand, the syntactically independent particle *kî* ("if/when"), formulated in case law form, or the conjunctive particle *wĕkî* ("and if/when"). Specifications in any given case are introduced by *'im* ("if") or *wĕ'im* ("and if"), with the exception of Exodus 21:14, a specification that is introduced by *wĕkî* ("and if/when"), as it could also function as a main case. Nine cases appear in this section.

The first case appears in Exodus 21:12–14, which addresses the killing of one man by another. The section is demarcated at the outset by a syntactically independent participial statement in v. 12, *makkēh 'îš wāmēt môt yûmāt*, "whoever strikes a man so that he dies, shall surely be put to death," which sets the basic concern of the passage with the death of a man caused by the action of another. Verse 12 is formulated as a variation of the case law form, which substitutes the participial phrase "whoever strikes so that he dies" as the statement of the protasis or case, introduced by the particle *kî* ("if/when") followed by the apodosis or disposition of the case, "[he] shall surely be put to death." The use of the formula *môt yûmāt*, "he shall surely be put to death," is an example of the death penalty formula.[19] Verse 12 states the basic case of the section, i.e., anyone who strikes a man so that he dies will be put to death, to indicate the disposition of a case of murder or manslaughter. But the variations of this basic case then follow, each of which is introduced by the formula *wa'ăšer* ("but when") to introduce the case of a man who does not lie in wait, i.e., who does not kill intentionally, in v. 13, or *wĕkî* ("and if") to introduce the case of a man who does lie in wait, i.e., who does kill intentionally, in v. 14. In the case of a man who does not lie in wait but kills another man accidentally, the law allows for the perpetrator to flee to a designated place where he will be protected. Although the law does not specify this place, later texts specify Levitical cities or sanctuary sites to which one could flee to seek sanctuary from a charge of murder until a trial could be held that would decide the person's guilt or innocence in the matter (see Num 35; see also Josh 21; 1 Chron 6).[20] If the accused was found guilty of murder in a trial, he would be executed as specified in v. 14, but if he was acquitted as specified in v. 13 and still needed protection from the dead man's family, he could remain in the sanctuary city until the death of the priest who officiated there. It is noteworthy, however, that the second-person

19. Schulz, *Todesrecht*.

20. Lee-Sak, "Levitical Cities."

statement in v. 14, introduced by *wĕkî*, allows that a man who lies in wait to kill another by cunning (Hebrew, *ʿārĕmâ*) may be taken away from the altar of the sanctuary for execution. Such a situation applied to Solomon's orders to Benaiah to kill Joab in 1 Kings 2:26–35, even though he had taken refuge at the altar, for his murders of Abner ben Ner (2 Sam 3) and Amasa ben Jether (2 Sam 20).

The second case of this section appears in Exodus 21:15, introduced by the participial phrase *ûmakkēh*, "and whoever strikes," which specifies that anyone who strikes his father or his mother will be put to death. There are no exceptions or qualifications concerning this particular case.

The third case appears in Exodus 21:16, introduced by the participial phrase, *wĕgōnēb ʾîš*, "whoever steals a man" (i.e., kidnaps a man to sell him into slavery) will be put to death. Again, there is no qualification or exception to this law.

The fourth case appears in Exodus 21:17, introduced by the participial phrase *ûmĕqallēl*, "whoever curses" his father and his mother will be put to death. There is no qualification or exception.

The fifth case appears in Exodus 21:18–19, introduced by the formula *wĕkî* ("and if") in v. 18, with the following specification in v. 19, introduced by the formula *wĕʾim* ("and if"). The case involves a situation in which two men are quarreling and one strikes the other with a stone or with his fist so that he does not die, but must take to his bed to recover from the injury. Verse 19 specifies that if the injured man recovers, as indicated by his ability to rise from his bed and walk about supported by a cane, then the man who struck him is free from a manslaughter charge, but he is obligated to pay for the injured man's convalescence until he is able to recover completely.

The sixth case appears in Exodus 21:20–21. Verse 21 introduces the case with the case law form *wĕkî*, "and if" a man strikes his slave or his maidservant so that he (or she) dies, then the servant must be avenged. The penalty is not specified, although the prior laws would indicate that if he killed the servant intentionally, he would be guilty of murder, but if not, he would be guilty of only of manslaughter. But v. 19, introduced by the formula *ʾāk ʾim* ("but if"), specifies that if the injured servant is able to stand after a day or two, there is no need for restitution because the servant is the man's investment, i.e., he does not pay compensation because he has lost whatever work the servant was required to do and must therefore bear his loss.

The seventh case appears in Exodus 21:22–25, introduced by the formula *wĕkî* ("and if/when") in standard case law form, with a qualification, introduced by *wĕʾim* ("and if") in v. 23. The basic case takes up a situation in which two men are fighting and they hit a pregnant woman during the fight, causing her to lose her yet-unborn baby, but leaving her with no further harm or injury. In this case, the man who hit her will be required to pay a fine to the husband of the pregnant woman in whatever amount the husband may specify as approved by a court of law. Note that this case is not treated as murder or manslaughter because the baby is not yet born and therefore not treated as a full human being that can live independently of the mother's umbilical cord. But v. 23 qualifies this law by specifying that if there is additional harm to the mother, then the lex talionis applies, i.e., "the law of retaliation." Verses 23b–25 then specify "life in place of life, eye in place of eye," etc., suggesting that the same death or injury be inflicted on the person who caused the death or injury to the victim in this situation. The principle appears elsewhere in Deuteronomy 19:15–21 and Leviticus 24:10–23 and in the laws of Hammurabi, sect. 196–201.[21] When read literally, these laws call for the exact same death or injury to be inflicted upon the perpetrator, but subsequent rabbinic interpretation of the issue recognized that the law instead calls for financial compensation of the victim of such death or injury (see "Reception History" below).

The eighth case appears in Exodus 21:26–27, introduced by *wĕkî* ("and if/when") which specifies that a man who strikes the eye of his slave, whether male or female, and destroys it must set the slave free due to the destruction of the eye. The specification in v. 27, introduced by *wĕʾim* ("and if"), says that if the owner causes the tooth of a slave, whether male or female, to fall then the slave must also go free due to the destruction of the tooth.

The ninth case appears in Exodus 21:28–32, introduced by *wĕkî* ("and if/when"), which addresses the various situations in which a bull kills or injures someone by goring. Although many understand the animal featured here to be an ox, an ox is a neutered bull, and the goring that appears in this law appears more likely to be that of a bull that has not been neutered and is therefore more aggressive. The classic study of this case by Finkelstein recognizes that this set of laws provides a legal template for personal liability when one's property causes death or

21. D. Wright, *Inventing G-d's Law*, 179–206.

personal injury.[22] The basic case in v. 28 is introduced with the formula *wĕkî* ("and if/when") and the specifications for the case are introduced by *wĕ'im* ("and if") in v. 29, *'im* ("if") in vv. 30–31, and *'im* ("if") in v. 31. The basic case in v. 28 addresses a situation in which a bull gores a man or a woman, and he or she dies. In such an instance, the law calls for the bull to be stoned to death and its meat to remain uneaten. The owner of the bull is exempted from punishment, apparently because the bull was not known to gore before and therefore no extra precautions were deemed necessary. The first specification in v. 29 states that if the bull had been known to gore in the past and its owner had been notified of this behavior but did not take any precautions to watch and protect people, then the owner is liable for the death of anyone subsequently gored by the bull. In such a case, the owner will be stoned to death together with the bull. The second specification in vv. 30–31 allows the owner of the bull to save his life by paying a ransom (Hebrew, *kōper*) that will be set upon him, presumably by a court of law, and the bull will be stoned to death. If the victim of the bull is a child, either male or female, the same law will apply. The third specification in v. 32 calls for a fine of thirty shekels of silver to be paid to the master or a male slave or a female maidservant who might be gored by the bull. The bull will then be stoned to death. As Finkelstein points out, the same conditions would apply if another animal or property caused the death or injury of a person as specified in these laws.

Exodus 21:33—22:16

Exodus 21:33—22:16 addresses cases of property destruction or damage and the liabilities relevant in each case. Each of the cases is introduced in standard case law form by the particle *kî* ("if/when") or the conjunctive particle *wĕkî* ("and if/when"). Eight cases appear in this section.

The first case appears in Exodus 21:33–34, introduced by the conjunctive particle *wĕkî* ("and if/when"). This law addresses a case in which a man digs a pit and does not cover it, so that a bull or an ass falls into it and dies. The owner of the pit is then responsible for paying a fine in cash to the owner of the dead animal, but the owner of the pit keeps the carcass of the bull or ass. This law would presumably be applied to other instances

22. Finkelstein, *Ox That Gored*.

in which someone did work on a property and did not take precautions to prevent the death or injury of animals belonging to others.

The second case appears in Exodus 21:35–36, introduced by the conjunctive particle *wĕkî* ("and if/when"). This law addresses a case in which the bull of one man hits the bull of another man so that the second bull dies. The law specifies that they shall sell the living bull and divide its price in silver. But if the bull was known to gore previously and its owner was warned but did not take appropriate precautions, then the owner of the living bull is obligated to compensate the owner of the dead bull with another bull in its place. The law does not stipulate whether or not the goring bull could be given to the owner of the dead bull as compensation.

The third case appears in Exodus 21:37—22:3, introduced by the particle *kî* ("when"), which addresses situations of deliberate theft. The first clause in Exodus 21:37 states a basic principle concerning the theft of livestock, i.e., a bull or a lamb, which is slaughtered or sold. The clause states the basic principle of compensation to the owner of the animal, viz., five bulls for the stolen bull and four lambs for the stolen lamb. The statement would serve as template for compensation at the rate of five times the value of the bull, presumably because of its increased utility, and four times the value of the lamb, again considering its utility. The second clause, introduced by the particle *'im* ("if"), takes up the circumstances of the attempted theft. If the thief is killed while attempting to tunnel into the house at night, there is no bloodguilt for the owner of the house, who is attempting to protect his property from a threat, someone who is unidentified due to darkness. But the third clause, also introduced by the particle *'im*, specifies that if the thief is caught in daylight when it is possible to identify him, there is bloodguilt if he is killed by the owner of the house. Presumably, he should be restrained and brought to trial where the compensation specified in the first clause may be applied to him. If he lacks the means to compensate the owner, then he is to be sold into debt slavery for his crime. The fourth clause in v. 3, again introduced by *'im* ("if"), specifies that if a stolen animal, ranging from a bull to an ass to a lamb, is found alive in the thief's possession, then he compensates the owner at the standard rate of double the number or the value of the animals stolen. The presence of the ass in this sequence signals that other animals are included in the earlier valuation stated in Exodus 21:37, presumably at a rate determined by the court.

The fourth case appears in Exodus 22:4, introduced by the particle *kî* ("when"), addresses a situation when a man allows his livestock to graze on another man's property, whether it is a field or a vineyard. The man who allowed his livestock to graze is then liable for the damage to the property cause by his animals.

The fifth case in Exodus 22:5, again introduced by *kî* ("when"), addresses a situation in which a fire breaks out in the thorns (i.e., the underbrush) and destroys harvested produce that is piled up or stacked, standing produce, or the field itself. The person responsible for starting the fire is then responsible for compensating the owner of the property for the damages caused by the fire.

The sixth case in Exodus 22:6–8, introduced by *kî* ("when"), shifts from clear theft or damage to property to cases in which one person gives money or property to another for safekeeping and the money or property is then stolen from the second person's house. If the loss was caused by deliberate theft and the thief is caught, then the thief is obligated to compensate the owner of the money or property at the standard twofold rate. But Exodus 22:7–8 follows up with a clause, introduced by the particle *'im* ("if"), which discusses circumstances for consideration. The basic clause in v. 7 calls for the owner of the house from which the money or property was stolen to appear before "G-d" (Hebrew, *hā'ĕlōhîm*), apparently a reference to a court in which he will swear before G-d that he did not steal the property of the first person. Verse 8 then continues by addressing cases in which the missing money or property is found. In such a case, both parties must appear before "G-d," again a presumed reference to the court, where an investigation will be held. The court will then make a decision concerning the guilt or innocence of the parties involved. The party determined by the court to be guilty will then make restitution to the other party at the standard twofold rate.

The seventh, eighth, and ninth cases appear in Exodus 22:9–16 in which the first case in Exodus 22:9–12 is introduced by the particle *kî* ("when"). The eighth and ninth cases in Exodus 22:13–14 and 22:15–16, however, are joined to the seventh case by a conjunctive *waw* and the particle *kî*, i.e., *wĕkî* ("and when"), apparently because the three cases are understood to address a common set of issues.

The seventh case in Exodus 22:9–12 addresses a case in which one man gives an animal to a second man for safekeeping and the animal dies, is injured, or is stolen while in the second man's possession. Verse 9 specifies that the animal may be a bull, an ass, a sheep, or any other possible animal. Consequently, the case is concerned with liability. Verse 10 specifies that both men must appear in court to swear an oath that they are not attempting to defraud the other. When that oath is sworn, the original owner of the animal is required to accept his loss because the second man is not considered to be liable for the loss because he did nothing to cause the death, injury, or loss. Verse 11, introduced by *wĕ'im* ("and if"), specifies that if the animal was stolen from the second man, apparently by a third party, then the second man is liable for the loss because he had the responsibility to watch the animal and did not take appropriate precautions against theft. The second man is then required to make restitution to the first man. Verse 12, introduced by *'im* ("if"), specifies that if the animal was attacked and torn, i.e., killed or injured, by another animal, then the second man is required to bring evidence of the attack, i.e., the remains of the dead animal or the injured animal, to the court to prove that the death or injury was indeed caused by an animal's attack.

The eighth case appears in Exodus 22:13–14, introduced by the conjunctive particle *wĕkî* ("and when"). The case involves a man who requests (i.e., borrows) an animal from another man so that he may use the animal in some capacity. This case differs from Exodus 22:9–12, which deals with an animal owned by one man and watched or guarded by another, whereas the present case involves an animal that is borrowed for use. If the animal dies or suffers injury while the borrower uses the animal, and the owner is not present, then the man borrowing the animal must compensate its owner. But v. 14, introduced by *'im* ("if"), specifies that if the owner is present, then the borrower is not liable, presumably because the owner was in a position to supervise the use of his animal.

The ninth case appears in Exodus 22:15–16, again introduced by the conjunctive particle *wĕkî* ("and when"). The case addresses a situation in which a man has sexual relations with an unmarried virgin woman who is not engaged to be married. This case is tied to the previous two cases because it threatens a father's right to receive a bride-price for the marriage of his virgin daughter. She is not his property as the animals in the preceding cases were, but Israelite family law specifies that fathers of virgin daughters are entitled to collect a bride-price when the daughter is married.[23] Verse 15 states the basic concern of the case. It addresses the case of a man who seduces an unmarried virgin, who is not engaged to be married, and has sexual relations with her. He is therefore required to marry her and to pay the bride-price to her father. But v. 16, introduced

23. See Meyers, *Exodus*, 195–99.

by *'im* ("if"), stipulates that if the father refuses to allow his daughter to marry the man, the man must still pay the bride-price to the father. The law anticipates that the fact that the daughter is no longer a virgin may impede her chances of marriage to another man. It thereby ensures the father's right to collect the bride-price for his daughter.

Exodus 22:17–26

Exodus 22:17—23:26 then presents a series of apodictically formulated statements that are typical of treaty stipulations in the ancient Near Eastern world. Some are formulated as apodictic commands or prohibitions, which in some cases do not indicate a legal outcome for the case in the event that the command or prohibition is violated. Such apodictic statements indicate legal principles that inform ancient Israelite jurisprudence, but they are not adjudicable in court. Others employ the "if–you" apodictic forms, which do indicate a legal outcome.[24] These statements are adjudicable in court in that they state a general outcome, although the details of that outcome would have to be decided by the court.

Exodus 22:17 presents the first apodictic statement, which is a prohibition against allowing a sorceress to live. The prohibition presumably also functions as a command to execute anyone who functions as a sorceress (Hebrew, *mĕkaššēpâ*), which would refer to a woman who practices divination, trafficking with foreign deities or spirits, or engaging in magical practice. The probation would presumably function as a death sentence for anyone who engages in such practice, although the term does not define precisely what practices might be involved. The Holiness Code develops this prohibition with a prohibition against trafficking with ghosts and evil spirits in Leviticus 20:6 and 20:27.

Exodus 22:18 is an apodictic statement that prohibits sexual relations between a human being and an animal. In a pastoral society, the possibilities for such interaction are rampant, and it is unlikely that animals would testify against an offender. Presumably, anyone engaging in such action would be subject to prosecution. The purpose of such a prohibition would be to preserve the ideal order for sexual relations in the world of creation, viz., humans engage in sexual relations with other humans, and animals engage in sexual relations with other animals. The Holiness Code

24. Gilmer, *If–You Form*.

develops this statement with prohibitions against bestiality in Leviticus 18:23 and death sentences in Leviticus 20:15–16.

Exodus 22:19 is an apodictic statement that bans anyone from offering sacrifices to deities other than YHWH. The verb *ḥrm* ("to ban") entails expulsion from the people of Israel, which is generally understood to be a death penalty for both the offender and the offender's family. Such an example appears in the case of Achan, who was found to have stolen resources from Israel's spoils in the conquest of Canaan (see Josh 7). In his case, Achan's theft led to the deaths of thirty-six Israelite men in the initial assault against the Canaanite city of Ai. Once Achan and his family were executed and his property destroyed, Israel was able to conquer Ai, although they devised a more effective plan for defeating the men of Ai in Joshua 8. The purpose of the present command is to ensure the worship of YHWH alone. Worship of foreign deities is therefore forbidden.

Exodus 22:21–26 presents a lengthy paragraph that addresses the treatment of widows and orphans, resident aliens among the people of Israel, and indigenous Israelites, here portrayed as your "neighbor" (Hebrew, *rēʿa*) in v. 25. The paragraph begins in v. 21 with a prohibition against "humiliating" any widow or orphan. The Hebrew verb *ʿannâ*, "to humiliate," entails any act of oppression, whether economic or legal or acts of unwarranted violence or murder, rape, and other forms of sexual mistreatment. The prohibition of mistreating widows and orphans is based in a common principle of justice that was widespread throughout the ancient Near Eastern world,[25] and it later emerges as a fundamental principle of the laws in Deuteronomy. Unlike the prior apodictic legal statements in Exodus 22:17–20, Exodus 22:21–26 provides legal elaboration concerning the treatment of different classes of people in three sub-units, each of which is introduced by the particle *'im* ("if"), in vv. 22–23, 24, 25–26. The first sub-unit in vv. 22–23 elaborates upon the initial prohibition against humiliating widows and orphans in v. 21. It refers to the widows and orphans by employing third-person masculine singular pronouns, which would suggest that it addresses only orphans, but Hebrew generally employs masculine pronouns in reference to mixed groups of males and females. Verses 22–23 state that if an Israelite humiliates a widow or orphan, YHWH will surely hear "his" outcry, presumably whether the issue comes to court or not. In the event that such humiliation and outcry come about, YHWH will ensure the punishment

25. Fensham, "Widow, Orphan, and Poor."

of the guilty party. In this case, YHWH will ensure the death of the perpetrator by the sword, so that his wife and children will become widows and orphans themselves, who are therefore potentially subject to similar humiliation. Verse 24 addresses the case of a man who would lend money at interest to one of the poor among the people of Israel. Such an act is forbidden. Instead, a poor person who is in need would generally become a debt servant for the prescribed six-year period, as discussed in Exodus 21:2–11. As noted above, debt slavery calls for the debt slave to work for the creditor to produce crops, animals, or other forms of income. In such a case, the debtor becomes a partner, albeit without independent legal standing, with the creditor, and he is subject to release at the end of his six-year term of service, unless he chooses to remain a debt slave forever. Verses 25–26 then address the case of a man who pledges his outer garment, i.e., a cloak (Hebrew, *śimlâ*), as security while he works for the creditor to pay off a debt.[26] The creditor is forbidden to hold the cloak after sunset because the cloak is the debtor's only covering for when he sleeps at night. Should the creditor violate the prohibition, YHWH pledges that YHWH will hear the outcry of the debtor and presumably administer appropriate punishment, e.g., ensuring the loss of the creditor's cloak at night so that he will suffer as his debtor did.

Exodus 22:27–30

Exodus 22:27 prohibits sedition. It includes both the denigration (Hebrew verb *qll*, "to make light of," i.e., "to denigrate") and the cursing of a leader (Hebrew, *nāśîʾ*) among the people. The term *nāśîʾ* is typically employed for a tribal leader (e.g., Num 17:21). No penalty is prescribed, but it is likely to be a capital offense.

Exodus 22:28–29 address issues of taxation. It begins in v. 20a with a prohibition against delaying or withholding the produce (Hebrew, *mělēʾâ*, lit., "work," i.e., the produce or grain of the field) and the juice (Hebrew, *demʿa*, lit., "tear," i.e., the juice and oil produced from grapes, olives, and other fruits typically grown by ancient Israelite farmers). A command to give the firstborn of your sons to YHWH, here expressed in first-person form as the speaker of the command, follows in v. 28b. The command to give the firstborn to YHWH is understood as an offering

26. See the Yavneh-Yam ostracon, dated to the late seventh century BCE, in which a hired man, presumably Judean, demands the return of his cloak from his employer (*ANET* 568).

to YHWH, although the firstborn sons are not offered on the altar (see Gen 21). Rather, they are obligated to serve as priestly assistants to the sons of Aaron in the sanctuaries of Israel (see 1 Sam 1–3; see also Exod 34:19–20).[27] Apparently, the firstborn sons served in this role in northern Israel during its early history. Numbers 3:5–13; 3:40–51; and 8:13–19 present three speeches by YHWH to Moses in which YHWH instructs Moses to take the Levites to serve as priestly assistants to the priests in place of the firstborn sons, who had previously served in this capacity (see also Num 17–18 in which Aaron and the tribe of Levi are selected to serve as Israel's priests). Verse 29 then follows with a command to do the same with cattle (i.e., bulls) and the flocks (i.e., sheep and goats). The command entails that the firstborn (to the mother) of the cattle and flocks are to be given to YHWH. Unlike the firstborn sons of human mothers, the firstborn of cattle and flocks are intended for offerings to YHWH. Verse 29 specifies that the newborn animals remain with their mothers for seven days, and then they are presented as offerings to YHWH on the eighth day.

Exodus 22:30 presents a command that the people of YHWH are to be holy to YHWH in v. 30a. This command is specified in v. 30b by a prohibition against eating meat that has been killed by animals, i.e., an ancient form of roadkill. Such meat is not fit for human consumption, and it should instead be fed to the dogs. Verse 30a anticipates the outlook of the Holiness Code in Leviticus 17–26, which calls upon Israel to be a holy people (e.g., Lev 19:2), and v. 30b functions as an early form of the commands to keep kosher (see Lev 11; Deut 14).

Exodus 23:1–3

Exodus 23:1–3 presents a sequence of five prohibitions that provide instruction to judges concerning their proper conduct in judicial proceedings. Exodus 23:1a begins with a prohibition against admitting false reports as evidence in a trial. The prohibition does not define "a false report" (Hebrew, *šemaʿ šāw')* (cf. Exod 20:7). Presumably it forbids a judge to accept testimony that the judge knows to be false. But the criteria for such knowledge remain undefined. Deuteronomy 19:15–21 defines proper testimony in court as statements that are corroborated by more than one witness. Exodus 23:1b prohibits the court from accepting

27. Sweeney, "Samuel's Institutional Identity."

the testimony of a witness known to have perjured himself in order to render an evil (i.e., wrong) verdict in a case. Again, the criteria for such a prohibition are not defined, but the prohibition apparently expects that a thorough investigation, such as securing at least two witnesses to corroborate the testimony in course, would be expected. Exodus 23:2a prohibits a judge from siding with a majority to render judgment in court if there is evidence to the contrary. Again, the prohibition expects that evidence uncovered in a thorough investigation must be considered. Exodus 23:2b expands the point of v. 2a by employing a pun based on the root *nṭʿ*, "to turn aside," by prohibiting a witness from giving presumably false testimony, i.e., by turning aside (Hebrew, *linṭōt*) to follow the majority in order to overturn (Hebrew, *lĕhaṭṭōt*) justice in a court of law. The use of the pun apparently renders the principle as a legal proverb that will be easily memorized. Exodus 23:3 then concludes the sequence by specifying that the poor (Hebrew, *dāl*) are not to receive special consideration in court. The intent of such a prohibition is to ensure that justice is the only criterion in deciding court cases; the economic standing of the parties to the case, whether poor or rich, is not the deciding factor.

Exodus 23:4–5

Exodus 23:4–5 presents two commands that call upon individuals in Israelite society to render assistance to a neighbor who has problems with his animals, even if the neighbor is an enemy of the person in question or someone who hates him. Both commands are rendered as "if you" commands, which employ second-person masculine singular address language to state a condition or situation, introduced by the particle *kî* ("when/if"), followed by the resolution to the situation. The first command in Exodus 23:4 posits a situation in which a person encounters the bull or a stray ass belonging to someone whom he considers to be his enemy. The command requires him nevertheless to render assistance by returning the animal to its owner. Such a command would play a role in preventing people from deliberately turning loose the livestock of their enemies. Exodus 23:5 then follows with a command that specifies a situation in which a man encounters the ass of his enemy crouching down while loaded to carry a burden, apparently because the burden is too heavy or because it has been improperly loaded. The man is required to render assistance to his enemy in helping to get the ass moving again, likely by reloading the animal in such a way that it can carry the load. The command again employs a pun based on the verb root *ʿzb* ("to abandon/leave") to specify that the first man would likely decline to set the animal free (Hebrew, *mēʿăzōb lô*, lit., "from setting it free"). The command requires him to help his enemy "surely set free" (Hebrew, *ʿāzōb taʿăzōb*, lit., "you shall surely set free") the animal. Such a command would likely play a role in enabling enemies to overcome their mutual antipathy to cooperate in situations of trouble, thereby providing an opportunity to resolve enmities among the people.

Exodus 23:6

Exodus 23:6 prohibits the court from denying justice to the poor. This legal instruction complements Exodus 23:5, which prohibits the court from showing special favor to the poor. Again, the intent of these laws is to ensure that court decisions are based on justice, not on economic status.

Exodus 23:7–9

Exodus 23:7–9 presents a series of three legal commands or prohibitions, each of which is accompanied by a statement concerning the rationale for the law in question. Exodus 23:7 prohibits the acceptance of false statements by the court. Again, the definition of a false statement is not given, but Deuteronomy 19:15–21 later specifies that statements must be corroborated by at least two witnesses. The rationale for this law is to ensure that the court does not murder someone due to false testimony. The use of the prohibition *ʾal tahărōg*, "you shall not murder," is deliberate because the conviction of an innocent person based on a false statement is considered to be murder. A further rationale specifies that YHWH will not tolerate the wicked (i.e., the guilty) to be just (i.e., innocent). Exodus 23:8 prohibits the court from accepting a bribe (Hebrew, *šōḥad*) because bribes threaten the justice that is supposed to inform all court decisions. A bribe blinds judges to the truth, and it subverts (Hebrew, *wîsalēp*) the legal testimony of the righteous in court. Exodus 23:9 prohibits the oppression of a *gēr*, "a resident alien" (i.e., a foreigner who takes up residence in the land of Israel). The term would indicate an immigrant in modern legal parlance. In later rabbinic parlance, it indicates a convert to Judaism. The resident alien is to enjoy full legal rights while living in the land of Israel. The rationale for this law is that Israelites should understand the status of resident aliens because they were resident aliens in the land of Egypt, which imposed slavery upon them.

Exodus 23:10–13

Exodus 23:10–11 issues a command that Israelites are to let their land, their vineyards, and their olive orchards lie fallow every seventh year. They may plant seed in the fields, grapevines in the vineyards, and olive trees in the orchards, but in the seventh year, they do not plant and they do not harvest. The purpose of this practice is to enable the land to replenish itself naturally, which is assumed to happen when the land is not planted for the year, and to provide for the poor, who are able to come and harvest what grows naturally in order to feed themselves. Such a command indicates that the concept of a seven-day Shabbat cycle is operative in ancient Israel in which labor is conducted for six days, but the seventh day is a day of rest that allows humans and animals to refresh themselves (cf. Exod 23:12; 20:8–11).[28] In this case, the Shabbat principle is applied to the agricultural cycle so that the seventh year is a year of release (Hebrew, *tišmiṭenna*, "you shall release it," i.e., "you shall let it rest"). The verb root *šmṭ*, "to release," becomes the basis for the year of "release" (Hebrew, *šĕmiṭṭâ*) in Deuteronomy 15:1, 2, 9, and 31:10. It is doubtful that the entire land would have been on the same release schedule at this time. Such a practice would have rendered the purpose of this law (i.e., to feed the poor and the animals of the land) meaningless, because they would have been able to eat only in every seventh year. Rather, the seventh year would be calculated for each plot of land separately from the time that it was first planted. Such a practice would enable the poor to find food every year due to the different schedules employed for each tract of land.

Exodus 23:12–13 commands the observance of the seventh day as the Shabbat, i.e., the day of rest for each week on Saturday, the seventh day. Although the Shabbat principle is based upon the seven-day pattern of creation by YHWH in Genesis 1:1—2:3 in the P-stratum of the Pentateuch (cf. Exod 20:8–11), the appearance of this command in the E-stratum Covenant Code indicates that it was known in the Northern Kingdom of Israel in the ninth century BCE. The purpose of this legal

28. Sweeney, "Shabbat."

instruction is to ensure that people, including servants, resident aliens, and draft animals, such as bulls and asses, are able to rest for one day of the week and thereby be refreshed. Exodus 23:13a functions as a summary statement, formulated as a second-person masculine singular command, for this legal instruction by advising Israel to be observant of all YHWH's instructions. Exodus 23:13b then adds a prohibition, again formulated in the masculine plural, against invoking (Hebrew, *lō' tazkîrû*, lit., "you shall not cause to remember") the name of any other gods.

Exodus 23:14–19

Exodus 23:14–19 presents a festival calendar for the festivals and practices of ancient Israel's holiday year. Exodus 23:14 introduces the calendar with an introductory command, formulated in the second-person masculine singular, that the people will celebrate festivals three times in the year. The Hebrew term for "times" here is *rĕgālîm*, literally, "feet" or "footsteps," which some have understood as a reminder that ancient Israelites had to walk to the sanctuary. But the alternative term, *pĕʿāmîm*, means "strikes" or "footsteps," and it therefore appears to be a dialectical variation. Exodus 23:15 presents commands to celebrate the Festival of *Maṣṣôt*, "Unleavened Bread." Insofar as it does not mention *Pesaḥ*, "Passover," it appears to be an early rendition of the holiday that focuses on the harvest of the firstfruits of grain in the early spring (cf. Exod 34:18–20; Lev 23:4–8; Num 28:16–31; Deut 16:1–8). There is a reference to animal sacrifice in v. 18, but it does not appear to be central to the observance of Matzot as it is in later times when Pesaḥ emerges as the first day of the holiday followed by the seven days of Matzot. The duration of the festival is seven days, which once again applies the seven-day Shabbat time period to the celebration of the holiday. The designation of the month of Aviv (Hebrew, *hāʾābîb*, "the spring" or "the fresh [ears of barley]") appears to be an earlier Israelite name for the month, which may have originated in Canaanite times. It is the first month of the year, and in later times it is known as Nisan (Hebrew, *nîsān*) (Neh 2:1), a name apparently derived from the Babylonian calendar. No specific dates for the month of Aviv are given. Although the festival is a celebration of the first grain harvest, it is also tied to the exodus of Israel from Egypt. The statement "there shall not appear before me anyone empty handed" (Hebrew, *rêqām*) means that the people should appear before G-d at the temple with their firstfruit grain offerings in hand. Exodus 23:16 presents commands for two holidays. The first is the Festival of the Harvest (Hebrew, *haqqāṣîr*) of the Firstfruits of your labor, which is later known as Shavuot (Hebrew, *šābuʿōt*, "Weeks") (Exod 34:22; also known as "Pentecost"; cf. Exod 34:22; Lev 23:15–21; Num 28:26–31; Deut 16:9–12). The harvest festival marks the conclusion of the grain harvest. It is celebrated fifty days after the celebration of Passover (see, e.g., Lev 23:15–16, but again, no date for the celebration of the harvest festival is given in this text). The second is the Festival of "the Ingathering" (Hebrew, *hāʾāsip*), also known as Sukkot, "Booths" or "Tabernacles," which marks the conclusion of the fruit harvest (i.e., grapes, olives, figs, etc.) in the fall prior to the onset of the fall rainy season (Exod 34:22; Lev 23:33–36; Num 29:1–38; Deut 16:13). Although Sukkot is celebrated for seven days, with a concluding festival on the eighth day, no mention of the duration of the festival appears here. There is also no date, although the other calendars place it on the fifteenth day of the seventh month of the year, Tishri, following Rosh ha-Shanah, "New Year," and Yom Kippur, "the Day of Atonement." Exodus 23:17 reiterates the point that all Israelite men are to appear before YHWH at the Festivals of Harvest (Shavuot) and Ingathering (Sukkot), and they are not to appear empty handed, i.e., they must bring their offerings to YHWH.

Exodus 23:18 presents supplementary prohibitions concerning the observance of the three major festivals discussed above. The first prohibits the offering of leavening bread (Hebrew, *ḥāmēṣ*). Some interpreters presume that this prohibition applies only to Passover or Matzot, but Leviticus 2, especially vv. 4 and 11, makes it clear that all grain offerings presented at the temple altar are to be matzot or unleavened bread. The purpose of such an instruction is to ensure that all grain offerings are fresh. The second instruction prohibits the fat (Hebrew, *ḥēleb*) of the sacrificial animal from lying around until morning. Leviticus 3, especially vv. 9–11, 14–16, and 17, specifies that the fat of sacrificial animals is to be offered to YHWH at the altar as a fire offering.

Exodus 23:19 presents additional supplementary instructions concerning the offerings to be made to YHWH. The first is to specify that grain and fruit offerings to YHWH are to be from the firstfruits of the harvest. This command ensures that all grain and fruit offerings to YHWH will be fresh. The second instruction prohibits a kid (Hebrew, *gĕdî*, "baby goat") from being boiled in its mother's milk. Although the use of dairy products to cook meat is widely practiced, e.g., cheeseburgers, the use of a mother's milk to cook a baby goat violates the purpose for which mother's milk was created by G-d, viz., to nourish the young animal, not to serve as an element in its death and consumption. Although Cassuto points to an Ugaritic text (i.e., "The Gracious Gods," *KTU* 1.23, line 14) as an example of the Canaanite practice of cooking a young goat in milk, later interpreters have recognized that this text does not envision a young goat (Ugaritic, *gdy*) but instead refers to "coriander" (Ugaritic, *gd*) (cf. Hebrew, *gad*, "coriander," Exod 16:31; Num 11:7).[29] This instruction, together with Exodus 34:26 and Deuteronomy 14:21, provides the basis for the kosher dietary prohibition of eating meat together with milk products.

Exodus 23:20–33

Exodus 23:20–33 concludes the Covenant Code with discussion of the role that YHWH's "angel" (Hebrew, *mal'āk*, "messenger"/"angel"), also identified as YHWH's "terror" (Hebrew, *'ēmātî*, "my terror"), played in guiding Israel to the promised land and in driving out the Canaanite inhabitants of the land, who would otherwise serve as a "snare" to the people by prompting them to worship their foreign gods. The role of YHWH's "angel" and "terror" is derived from the ancient Near Eastern notion that when a nation goes to war, either in reality or in mythology, its army is led by a vanguard of deities, who constitute the first wave of attack against an enemy, instilling terror in the enemy ranks and thereby making it easier for the attacking army to overcome enemy resistance. Thomas W. Mann has studied this motif, and demonstrated how such portrayals of ancient Near Eastern vanguards, in Mesopotamian texts and iconography and in northwest Semitic texts, illustrate the role of the vanguard in the conceptualization and composition of biblical texts, such as: the Song of the Sea and the Reed Sea narrative (Exod 14–15); Exodus 33:7–11; Numbers 10–11; Habakkuk 3; Psalm 68; Judges 5; and other texts that depict YHWH in combat with enemy nations and the role of YHWH's own "vanguard" in defeating those nations.[30] The pattern applies here in Exodus 23:20–33 as well, although here YHWH's vanguard is YHWH's angel and terror, insofar as other deities cannot be portrayed in a text that has just warned against the worship of other gods (Exod 23:13). The reference to YHWH's angel likewise indicates that this is an

29. Cassuto, *Exodus*, 305; but see Wyatt, *Religious Texts from Ugarit*, 327–28n17.

30. Mann, *Divine Presence and Guidance*.

E-stratum text, insofar as representations of the divine presence, such as smoking firepots and burning torches (Gen 15), angels (Gen 22), or burning bushes (Exod 3) are characteristic of the E-stratum composition. The identity of the divine angel appears to be associated with a column of fire and smoke, based on the imagery of the temple altar in operation, and appears to represent the divine presence in the Reed Sea narratives in Exodus 14–15 and elsewhere, e.g., Exodus 40. The imagery of the altar in operation would indicate YHWH's presence to receive the offerings ascending to YHWH in the pillar of fire and smoke.

Exodus 23:20–22 introduces the narrative segment concerned with YHWH's angel and terror. This paragraph begins in Exodus 23:20 with YHWH's first-person statement that YHWH is sending an angel to guard Israel on the road and to bring Israel to "the place" (Hebrew, *hammāqôm*) that YHWH has established. The Hebrew term *hammāqôm*, "the place," is frequently employed to designate the site of YHWH's temple, although it is not always clear which temple is intended, e.g., Shiloh, Jerusalem, Beth El, Dan, or others (e.g., Gen 12:6; 13:3; 22:3, 4, 9, 14; 28:19; Deut 12:5; 14:23, 25, and many others).[31] Exodus 23:21–22 indicates that the angel speaks for YHWH and that the people must be careful to obey the angel to ensure that the angel will protect them. It is suggested that if they disobey the angel, the angel will punish them. Insofar as YHWH's Name is within the angel, the angel serves as an example of Name theology in which the presence of YHWH's Name signals the sanctity of the place or figure with which it is identified.[32] Although Name theology is especially identified with Deuteronomy and Deuteronomistic literature, Deuteronomy is formulated to appeal especially to the northern Israelite population, whom Josiah attempted to draw back to the rule of the House of David as part of his program of national restoration and reform.[33]

Exodus 23:23–26 then follows with YHWH's assertions of the intention to annihilate (Hebrew, *wĕhikḥadtîw*), "and I will annihilate him," i.e., the Canaanite nations, including the Amorites, Hittites, the Perizzites, the Canaanites, the Hivvites, and the Jebusites, who lived in the land of Israel prior to Israel. Although YHWH promised to annihilate the Canaanite nations, there is no evidence that such an annihilation ever took place. When Israel failed to destroy the Canaanite nations in Judges 1, YHWH swore to use them as a snare to justify punishing Israel throughout the

31. "*tĕqûpâ*," BDB 880.

32. See Mettinger, *Dethronement of Sabaoth*, 38–79.

33. Sweeney, *King Josiah of Judah*, 137–69.

Former Prophets or Deuteronomistic History (see Judg 3). Indeed, Joshua recounts the annihilation of the Canaanites in Joshua 1–12, but both Judges 1 and archeological evidence indicate that no such annihilation ever happened. Likewise, when David conquered Jerusalem, the Jebusite population was not destroyed; instead, it became the basis for the population of David's Jerusalem. It appears, instead, that the Canaanites were assimilated into the Israelite and Judean populations.[34] Exodus 23:24 prohibits the people of Israel from bowing down to the gods of these peoples, serving them, or doing their work, and it also calls upon them to destroy the religious installations, such as the pillars (Hebrew, *maṣṣēbōtêhem*, "their sacred pillars") of the Canaanite peoples mentioned here. The pillars apparently symbolized the presence of Canaanite gods, such as Baal. Exodus 23:25–26 then call upon the people to serve YHWH and thereby receive YHWH's blessings and protection, including plentiful food and water, the absence of sickness, the absence of miscarriages and barrenness among Israel's women, and a long life for all.

Exodus 23:27–33 then concludes the Covenant Code with an announcement of curses that will be inflicted on the Canaanite population of the land. YHWH's angel is here identified as YHWH's "terror," as noted above, all the better to accentuate YHWH's intention to drive out the Canaanite population of the land. Exodus 23:27 emphasizes the "vanguard" motif discussed above in which the angel will function like the ancient Near Eastern vanguard of the army to terrorize an enemy and facilitate their defeat. Exodus 23:28 emphasizes "the plague" (Hebrew, *haṣṣirʿâ*), sometimes translated as "the hornet," although the Canaanite god of plague, Dever, often finds a place in the vanguard to bring sickness and starvation on an enemy, which is a common feature of lengthy siege warfare (cf. 2 Kgs 6:24—7:20). Exodus 23:29–30 envisions a gradual process of driving out the Canaanites, which might suggest a long-drawn-out campaign against the Canaanites, or more realistically, a long process of assimilation of the Canaanites into Israelite and Judean society. Exodus 23:31 envisions that Israel will control a land that extends from the Red Sea (the Sea of Reeds) and the Mediterranean Sea (the Philistine Sea) to the south and the west as far as the wilderness (the Arabian Desert) and the river (the Euphrates River) to the east and the north. Such an extensive land is akin to that controlled by King Jeroboam ben Joash of Israel (786–746 BCE), who ruled a kingdom that

34. Sweeney, *King Josiah of Judah*, 33–177; J. Wright, *David, King of Israel*.

extended from LeBo Hamath in the north to the Sea of the Arabah at the height of northern Israelite power (2 Kgs 14:23–29). Exodus 23:32–33 concludes the Covenant Code with warnings that Israel is not to cut a covenant with the Canaanites or their gods. The rationale is that if the Canaanites continue to live in the land, they will cause Israel to sin by attracting them to worship their gods and thereby abandon YHWH. The Hebrew idiom "to cut a covenant" (Hebrew, *likrōt bĕrît*) presupposes ancient Near Eastern treaty ("covenant") rituals in which the parties to the treaty cut sacrificial animals in half (cf. Gen 15:17–21) so that the parties to the treaty can pass between them and state "may the same thing happen to me if I violate the terms of this covenant."[35]

Exodus 24:1–11

Exodus 24:1–11 closes the account of the Covenant Code in Exodus 20:1—24:11 with an account of the ratification of the covenant.[36] It is apparently an E-stratum text, although vv. 3–8 are generally considered non-source texts.[37] Moses led a major delegation from the people of Israel—including himself and Aaron; Aaron's sons, Nadab and Abihu; and seventy elders from Israel—up Mount Sinai to meet with YHWH, although only Moses would be allowed to approach YHWH directly. The ratification of the covenant would be followed by a sacred meal, which appears to be a festival celebration for the dedication of a new altar, although the meal appears intended to be based on known rituals for treaty or covenant ratification. Following the meal, Moses will ascend Mount Sinai (Exod 24:12–18) to record YHWH's instructions for building the wilderness tabernacle (Exod 25:1—31:18).

The delegation led by Moses to meet with YHWH for covenant ratification includes the leading figures of Israel in Exodus 24:1–2. Moses leads the people as the prophet of YHWH, although his role appears also to include his functions as a priest and as an ersatz monarch, much on the pattern of Joshua and Samuel in later times. The delegation includes Aaron, Moses's brother and the future high priest of Israel; Nadab

35. See the Sefire treaty, in which Matti'iel, a party to the treaty, states, "[As] this calf is cut up, thus Matti'el and his nobles will be cut up" (*ANET* 660). For discussion, see Sweeney, "Form Criticism."

36. See McCarthy, *Old Testament Covenant*, 10–34; McCarthy, *Treaty and Covenant*, 243–76.

37. Campbell and O'Brien, *Sources of the Pentateuch*, 189, 199.

and Abihu, Aaron's two older sons, who are presumed to succeed him as priests in Israel; and seventy elders of the people of Israel. All of these figures are closely identified with what will become the future Northern Kingdom of Israel. The sons of Aaron will eventually serve in the sanctuary at Shiloh culminating in the lifetime of Eli, the high priest among the sons of Aaron during the pre-monarchic period. Shiloh is located in the tribal territory of Ephraim, some eighteen and a half miles north of Jerusalem and ten miles north of Beth El.[38] In the pre-monarchic period it functioned as a central sanctuary of northern Israel, including primarily the tribes of Ephraim and Manasseh as well as Benjamin and others, although the Aaronide priesthood appears to have had some influence in Judah due to the sanctuary at Nob, immediately north of Jerusalem. Nadab and Abihu, Aaron's sons, have names that are very much like those of Nadab and Abijah, the sons of Jeroboam ben Nebat, the alleged first king of northern Israel. Nadab and Abihu would eventually die as punishment for offering strange fire (i.e., foreign incense) before YHWH in Leviticus 10. The seventy elders of Israel were an authoritative assembly of tribal or royal leaders, generally referred to as "the sons of the king," who advised monarchs in the northern tribes, particularly following the lifetime of the Manassite Judge, Gideon, and the northern Israelite kings of the House of Omri.[39] Comprised of the leading figures of Israel in the pentateuchal narrative, these figures would represent Israel, apparently understood in relation to the later Northern Kingdom of Israel, to ratify the covenant with YHWH.

Before ascending the mountain with the delegation of Israel's leaders, Moses recounts to the people all the words of the covenant that were just presented in Exodus 20–23. Once the people affirmed that they would observe the covenant in Exodus 24:3–4, Moses wrote down all the words of YHWH in the Covenant Code so that the people would have a record of what they needed to do while Moses and the Israelite delegation were away.

The formal covenant ratification appears in Exodus 24:5–8. The account begins with Moses setting up an altar at the base of Mount Sinai and twelve pillars (Hebrew, *maṣṣēbôt*, "uninscribed pillars") to represent the twelve tribes of Israel.[40] Joshua ordered a similar array of twelve Matzevot to be built in the Jordan River at the site where Israel crossed

38. Kempenski and Finkelstein, "Shiloh."

39. Fox, *In Service of King*, 43–53; cf. Sweeney, *Zephaniah*, 83–85.

40. Richelle, "Maṣṣēbâ, Maṣṣēbôt."

from Moab into Canaan in Joshua 4; they were later moved to the site of Gilgal, which remains unidentified in modern times. The twelve stones ideally represent the twelve-tribe federation of Israel. Moses then ordered the young men of Israel to present whole burnt offerings (Hebrew, *ʿōlōt*) (Lev 1) and "peace offerings" (Hebrew, *zĕbāḥîm šĕlāmîm*) (Lev 3) at the newly constructed altar. The whole burnt offering is burned in its entirety on the altar as an offering to YHWH, and the peace offerings, also known in English as "offerings of well-being," are to be eaten by the priests and people. They are both standard offerings at most festival occasions. Moses orders that the blood drained from the sacrificial animals be divided in half. One half was placed in basins and the other half was "sprinkled" or "thrown" (Hebrew, *zāraq*) against the altar, apparently to dedicate the altar. Moses then reads the Book of the Covenant to the people, who respond by stating, "We will do, and we shall listen," indicating that the people are eager to do what YHWH requires even before they hear the specifics. Moses then sprinkles or throws the blood in the basins upon the people. Most interpreters understand this action as a means to purify or sanctify the people involved in this holy ritual. The practice appears to derive from treaty making in the ancient Near Eastern world, insofar as the parties to a treaty would pass between the severed halves of sacrificial animals stating that the same thing should happen to them if they did not fulfill the terms of the treaty. In the present case, the blood sprinkled or thrown upon the people would signify their fate if they failed to observe the terms of the covenant.

The account of covenant ratification concludes with Exodus 24:9–11 in which Moses and the other representatives of Israel dined with YHWH, apparently in a festival meal. During the course of the meal, they had a vision of the presence of YHWH, here portrayed as YHWH's feet resting upon a pavement of sapphire, apparently a representation of the footstool of the heavenly throne of YHWH. YHWH states in Isaiah 66:1, "Heaven is my throne and earth is the footstool of my feet," apparently in reference to the ark of the covenant placed in the holy of holies of the Jerusalem temple. The ark of the covenant is repeatedly referred to in relation to "YHWH who is enthroned upon the cherubim" (see 1 Sam 4:4; 2 Sam 6:2; 2 Kgs 19:5; Isa 37:16; Pss 80:2; 99:1; 1 Chr 13:6), apparently in reference to the cherubim who are built atop the ark of the covenant, which is understood as the throne of YHWH. The ark is topped by a cover, presumably overlaid with lapis lazuli or sapphire to represent the heavens mentioned here or the firmament of the heavens that stand between the heavens above and the earth beneath in Genesis 2:12 (cf. Ezek 10:1; 1:26). Although YHWH can be a threatening presence to humans (cf. Isa 6), v. 11 indicates that YHWH takes no action against the Israelite delegation.

Reception History

Hosea 4:1–3 cites elements of the Ten Commandments that introduce the E-stratum Covenant Code as well as E-stratum narratives in Genesis concerning Jacob's wrestling with an angel and settling his boundaries with Laban as well as Exodus–Numbers narratives concerning a prophet (Moses) who led Israel out of Egypt and through the wilderness. But Amos's indictment of northern Israel in Amos 2:6–16 cites laws from the Covenant Code itself.[41] The charge in Amos 2:6 that Israel sold the righteous for silver and the poor for a pair of shoes presupposes the slave law in Exodus 21:2–11, which specifies the conditions under which men and women can be sold into debt slavery. Amos's statement also presupposes Exodus 23:6–8, which prohibits judges from taking bribes to rule against the poor in that the term "righteous" (Hebrew, *ṣaddîq*) is also used to refer to someone judged to be innocent in a court of law (Exod 23:7, 8; Deut 16:19; 1 Kgs 8:32). The charge in Amos 2:7 that father and son have relations with the same woman likewise presupposes the slave law concerning women in Exodus 21:7–11, which stipulates that a woman may be designated for marriage to the master or to his son, but not to both. The charge in Exodus 21:7 that such actions profane G-d's holy Name also presupposes Exodus 22:30, which stipulates that Israel will be a holy people to G-d. And G-d's statements in Amos 2:10 concerning the divine role in bringing the people out of Egypt and guiding them through the wilderness for forty years likewise cite the E-stratum exodus–wilderness narratives into which the Covenant Code is set.

The law in Exodus 21:14 concerning a man who lies in wait to kill another and stipulating that such a man may be taken away from the altar for execution plays a role in 1 Kings 2:28–35 (cf. 1 Kgs 2:5–6). First Kings 2:28–35 recounts how Solomon gives orders to take Joab from the altar where he had taken refuge so that he might be executed for lying in wait to murder Abner ben Ner and Amasa ben Jether.[42]

41. Sweeney, *Twelve Prophets*, 1:189–276, esp. 214–18.

42. Sweeney, *1–2 Kings*, 59–60, 69–70; although it is noteworthy that Joab had the right to kill Abner because Abner had killed Joab's brother, Abishai (2 Sam 3:6–39), and

The law concerning men who struggle and hit a pregnant woman, causing her to lose her unborn baby, plays a key role in defining the view of abortion in rabbinic Judaism.[43] Philo (*Spec.* 3.108), the Samaritan Targum, and many Karaite commentators call for the death penalty for one who performs an abortion. But rabbinic tradition sees the matter differently, especially because Exodus 21:22–23 calls for only a fine in the case of a miscarriage, construed to be an abortion. Abortion therefore is not considered murder unless the fetus is viable (Mekhilta de R. Ishmael, Nezikin 8.18; b. Sanh. 84b; b. Nid. 44b).[44] Consequently, m. Niddah 5.3 rules that one who kills a one-day-old child is culpable for murder. Abortion is therefore prohibited, but it is not considered murder (t. Sanh. 59a; b. Ḥul. 33a). If the fetus constitutes a danger to the mother's life, however, abortion may be permitted because the fetus is seen as an agent that pursues the mother in order to kill her (m. ʾOhal. 7.6). If, however, the greater part of the fetus has come out of the womb, e.g., the head or the feet, then the life of the fetus must be saved because one life does not take precedence over another (m. ʾOhal. 7.6; b. Sanh. 72b).

The law of talion, derived from Latin *talio*, "retaliation," concludes in Exodus 21:23–25 the law concerning the two men who struggle (see also Lev 24:17–22; Deut 19:19–21).[45] The law of talion calls for punishment that is equivalent to the harm caused to a victim by the perpetrator. Consequently, the law of talion as stated in Exodus 21:23–25 reads, "But if there is harm, then he shall give life in place of life, eye in place of eye, tooth in place of tooth, hand in place of hand, foot in place of foot, burn in place of burn, wound in place of wound, bruise in place of bruise." Most interpreters suggest that this law was interpreted literally in ancient Israel and Judah—and it is still interpreted literally in Islam. Josephus maintains that in ancient Rome, the victim had the right to claim monetary compensation in place of the literal application of the law of talion (*Ant.* 4.280). Rabbinic halakah, however, recognizes that the literal understanding of this law is not what G-d intended, especially because a blind victim cannot take a similar eye from a perpetrator who himself was not blind or a victim with crippled legs cannot take similar legs from a perpetrator who is not himself crippled. Consequently, rabbinic

Amasa was a traitor against David and deserved death for his treason (2 Sam 17:25). He also failed to stop Sheba when he revolted against David (2 Sam 20:1–22).

43. For discussion, see Elon, "Abortion"; Schiff, *Abortion in Judaism*.

44. Lauterbach, *Mekilta de-Rabbi Ishmael*, 3:63.

45. Cohn, "Talion."

halakah maintains that the law of talion calls for monetary compensation of a victim by the perpetrator of the crime (m. B. Qam. 8.1; b. B. Qam. 83a–84a). Although the monetary compensation was intended as a form of punishment against a perpetrator, it actually has the effect of not creating two injured parties who are not able to function in society. Rather, it enjoins upon the perpetrator a constructive activity, i.e., working and paying to restore to the victim—at least in part—what was taken from him or her by the perpetrator of the crime.

Laws from Exodus 21 appear in several instances in the Christian New Testament Gospels. The law in Exodus 21:12 concerning a man who strikes and kills another appears in Jesus's Sermon on the Mount in Matthew 5:21, where Jesus cites laws of murder as part of an effort to motivate people to resolve the underlying anger that causes murder by going to them in an attempt to settle the issue without murder. The law proscribing insult against a parent apparently stands in the background when Jesus calls upon those who insult a brother or a sister in Matthew 5:22–23 to resolve issues in a similar manner. It also appears in Mark 7:10 that an offering to atone for the insult is inadequate; instead, one must recognize that what comes out of one's own mouth is defiling and therefore people must examine their own intentions to overcome the evil that is within them. The lex talionis from Exodus 21:24–25 appears in Matthew 5:38 in which Jesus calls upon people to turn the other cheek when someone strikes them, apparently in an effort to change the ways of one who would do evil.

Acts 23:5 reports Paul's explanation for his insult to the high priest, Ananias, when he explains that he did not know that Ananias was the high priest. He then cites the probation in Exodus 22:27 against cursing a leader of the people. (Paul's failure to recognize the high priest appears rather strange.) The Synoptic Gospel narratives cite Exodus 23:20 together with Isaiah 40:3, "Behold! I am sending my messenger before you, who will prepare your way before you," to identify John the Baptist as the one who prepares for Jesus in Matthew 11:10; Mark 1:2; and Luke 7:27. Hebrews 9:20 cites Exodus 24:6–8 as part of its polemic against the practice of shedding and sprinkling blood as a process of purification. Matthew 26:28; Mark 14:24; Luke 22:20; and 1 Corinthians 11:25 cite Exodus 24:8 to identify the wine of the Passover Seder with the blood of Jesus to signify the new covenant of Christianity as expressed in Holy Communion. Hebrews 10:29 cites Exodus 24:8 as part of its polemic against those who spurn Jesus and therefore profane the blood of the covenant.

Patristic interpreters and later Christian theologians showed little interest in the specific laws of the Hebrew Bible, and focused instead on the concept of law itself.[46] Marcion rejects the laws of the Old Testament altogether as unnecessary for Christianity. The Epistle of Barnabas follows suit by claiming that the kosher dietary laws were intended to be understood "in the spirit," but an evil angel had caused the Jews to misunderstand these laws literally. But in the aftermath of the collapse of the Roman Empire, church theologians began to take an interest in forms of the laws instituted in the various nations of Christianity, drawing inspiration from the laws of the Old Testament, to replace the earlier focus on Roman canon law. Whereas Aquinas viewed Old Testament law simply as prefiguring Christ, Renaissance thinkers began to consider the Old Testament laws in relation to natural laws and humanism. By the seventeenth century, Calvinist thinkers, such as Piscator (d. 1625) argued that many laws in Exodus continued to have validity for contemporary Christians. The Puritans, who originated in England and emigrated to North America, developed codes of law for their colony that were heavily dependent on Old Testament law. The study by John Spencer, *De Legibus Hebraeeorum Ritualbus* (1685), which argued that Old Testament law was largely derivative from Egyptian law, was highly influential in stirring up debate over the role of law in Christian society, particularly because Spencer maintained that it pointed to the origins of monotheism. Early critical scholars, such as Michaelis, began to probe Old Testament law in an effort to reconstruct the history of its composition, which led ultimately to the critical source theory of Julius Wellhausen, which had considerable influence on modern biblical scholarship.[47]

The prohibition in Exodus 22:17 against allowing a sorceress to stand was behind the Salem witch trials in Salem, Massachusetts, from February 1692 through May 1693, in which some two hundred people were accused of witchcraft, and nineteen were executed by hanging.[48] Arthur Miller's 1953 play *The Crucible* employed the portrayal of the Salem witch trials as a literary device for the metaphorical portrayal of McCarthyism when the United States government persecuted persons suspected of Communist Party membership or sympathies.

46. See Childs, *Exodus*, 488–96, for the following.

47. Wellhausen, *Composition des Hexateuchs*; Nicholson, *Pentateuch*.

48. See, e.g., Burns and Geiss, *Trial of Witches*.

The Account of YHWH's Instructions to Moses on the Building of the Tabernacle and Its Fixtures and the Conduct of Its Associated Activities —Exodus 24:12—31:18

Following the account of YHWH's announcement of the Covenant Code in Exodus 20:1—24:11, which concludes with the account of the ratification of the Covenant Code in Exodus 24:1–11, Exodus 24:12—31:18 recounts YHWH's further instructions to Moses concerning the building of the wilderness tabernacle and its fixtures and the conduct of its associated activities in Exodus 24:12—31:18. Exodus 24:11–18 functions as an introduction to this major unit, insofar as it relates how Moses, accompanied only by Joshua, identified here as Moses's "servant" or "assistant," ascends to the top of Mount Sinai to receive instruction from YHWH. The elders of Israel, Aaron and Hur, and presumably Aaron's sons, Nadab and Abihu, are left behind to supervise the people of Israel at the foot of the mountain. The account of YHWH's instructions to Moses then follows in Exodus 25:1—31:17. The brief statement in Exodus 24:18 concerning the conclusion of YHWH's instruction speech to Moses and YHWH's giving the two tablets of the testimony (Hebrew, *hāʿēdut*) then closes the unit. The narrative then shifts to the golden calf narrative in Exodus 32:1—34:35.

Translation

24:12 And YHWH said to Moses, "Go up to me on the mountain, and stay there, and I will give to you the tablets of stone and the instruction and the commandment which I have written to teach them." [13] And Moses and Joshua, his assistant, rose, and Moses went up to the mountain of G-d. [14] And to the elders he said, "Wait for us in this [place] until we return to you, and, behold, Aaron and Hur are with you. Whoever has business may approach them."

[15] And Moses went up to the mountain, and the cloud covered the mountain. [16] And the glory of YHWH settled upon Mount Sinai, and the cloud covered it for six days, and he called to Moses on the seventh day from the midst of the cloud. [17] And the appearance of the glory of YHWH was like a consuming fire on top of the mountain to the eyes of the sons of Israel. [18] And Moses entered into the midst of the cloud, and he went up to the mountain, and Moses was on the mountain forty days and forty nights.

Commentary

Exodus 24:12–18 presents a narrative introduction to the account of YHWH's instruction to Moses concerning the building of the wilderness tabernacle and its fixtures and the conduct of its associated activities in Exodus 24:12—31:18.

The introductory narrative begins in Exodus 24:12–14 with a brief account of the departure of Moses, accompanied by his assistant (Hebrew, *mišārĕtô*, lit., "his minister"), from the foot of Mount Sinai, here identified as "the mountain of G-d" (Hebrew, *har hāʾĕlōhîm*). YHWH invites Moses to ascend the mountain so that YHWH may give Moses the stone tablets inscribed with YHWH's "instruction" (Hebrew, *hattôrâ*) and "commandment" (Hebrew, *hammiṣwâ*), with which he is to instruct the people. Moses leaves behind the elders of Israel, Aaron, and Hur (cf. Exod 17:10, 12), to supervise the people of Israel at the base of the mountain. No mention is made here of Aaron's sons, Nadab and Abihu, although they presumably also remained behind. The phrase "anyone who has business" (Hebrew, *mî-baʿal dĕbārîm*, "whoever is a master of words") refers to anyone who has words to speak with Israel's leadership.

Exodus 24:15–18 then recounts Moses's ascent to Mount Sinai to appear before "the glory of YHWH" (Hebrew, *kĕbôd-yhwh*), a characteristic P-stratum meme for the presence of YHWH, which identifies Exodus 24:15b–18 as a P-stratum text.[1] The delay of six days before Moses appears before YHWH on the seventh day appears to be derived from the priestly ordination ceremony in which prospective priests are incubated for seven days at the wilderness tent of meeting as part of their ordination as priests in Exodus 29 (see esp. Exod 29:35–38) and Leviticus 8 (see esp. Lev 10:33–35). Moses is not one of the sons of Aaron, but the narrative prescribes an incubation period of seven days before he can appear before the glory of YHWH. To the eyes of the people of Israel at the foot of the mountain, the glory of YHWH appears as "a consuming fire" at the top of the mountain. Moses then enters the cloud to complete his ascent of the mountain so that he may receive instruction from YHWH. Joshua is not mentioned here, but he presumably remains behind to wait for Moses.

Reception History

Rabbinic tradition posits that Joshua is one of the elders of Israel. Rashi considers Hur to be a son of Miriam, fathered by Caleb ben Jepunneh, insofar as Miriam is identified with Ephrath in 1 Chronicles 2:19, "and Caleb took for himself Ephrath" (see b. Sotah 11b).[2]

Second Corinthians 3:3 refers to the tablets of stone mentioned in Exodus 24:12 so that they might be contrasted with "the tablets of human hearts" (Greek, *plaxin kardiais sarkinais*, lit., "tablets of flesh hearts") to represent the spirit of the living G-d. Second Corinthians 3:18 posits that "all of us," apparently a reference to all the Christians in Corinth and throughout the world, may see the glory of the L-rd, here identified with the spirit of the L-rd in freedom as though it is reflected in a mirror. The expression apparently serves as a metaphor for seeing the reflection of the spirit of the L-rd in Jesus (cf. 2 Cor 4:6).

1. Campbell and O'Brien, *Sources of the Pentateuch*, 43.

2. Rosenberg, *Exodus*, 2:401.

The Account of YHWH's Instructions to Moses Concerning the Building of the Wilderness Tabernacle and Its Fixtures and the Conduct of Its Associated Activities—Exodus 25:1—31:18

Overview

EXODUS 25:1—31:18 RECOUNTS YHWH's instructions to Moses concerning the building of the wilderness tabernacle and its fixtures and the conduct of its associated activities. Following the narrative introduction in Exodus 24:12–18, the account of YHWH's instructions proceeds as a sequence of speech reports by YHWH to Moses in which YHWH reveals the various details of the construction.

The first speech by YHWH appears in Exodus 25:1—30:10. Following the YHWH speech formula in Exodus 25:1, Exodus 25:2—30:10 constitutes YHWH's instructions to Moses to announce to the people the various aspects of the building and the conduct of its activities. Knierim has demonstrated that the first instruction in Exodus 25:2–9 concerning the provision of building materials on the part of the people is distinct from the following sub-units which provide instruction concerning the actual building of the tabernacle and the conduct of its activities that follow in Exodus 25:10—30:10.[1] The sequence of instruc-

1. Knierim, "Conceptual Aspects in Exodus 25:1–9."

tion in Exodus 25:10—30:10 includes: construction of the ark in Exodus 25:2–22; construction of the table of the presence in Exodus 25:23–30; construction of the lampstand in Exodus 25:31–40; construction of the tabernacle in Exodus 26:1–37; construction of the altar in Exodus 27:1–8; construction of the courtyard of the tabernacle in Exodus 27:9–19; provision of the oil for the lamps in Exodus 27:20–21; production of the holy garments for Aaron and his sons in Exodus 28:1–43; ordination of Aaron and his sons as priests in Exodus 29:1–46; and construction of the incense altar in Exodus 30:1–10.

YHWH's second speech to Moses appears in Exodus 30:11–16, which takes up the census of the people and the tax that they must pay to support the tabernacle. YHWH's third speech, which addresses the construction of the laver for washing upon entering the tabernacle, appears in Exodus 30:17–21. YHWH's fourth speech appears in Exodus 30:22–33, and provides instruction concerning the spices that will be used for the incense and the anointing oil used in the tabernacle. YHWH's fifth speech, appearing in Exodus 30:34–37, addresses the manufacture of incense to be used in the tabernacle. YHWH's sixth speech appears in Exodus 31:1–11 and names the artisans, Bezalel ben Hur of the tribe of Judah and Oholiab ben Ahisamach of the tribe of Dan, who will oversee the construction of the tabernacle and its fixtures. And YHWH's seventh speech to Moses appears in Exodus 31:12–17 providing instruction concerning Shabbat as an eternal covenant that serves as the foundation for the holiness of the tabernacle based on YHWH's creation of the world in six days followed by a seventh day of rest.

Exodus 31:18 then provides the narrative conclusion to the account of YHWH's instructions concerning the construction of the tabernacle and its fixtures and the conduct of its activities in Exodus 24:12—31:18.

Insofar as YHWH is understood in the exodus narrative to be the true sovereign of creation and human events, the tabernacle is conceived to be YHWH's royal palace. It is built according to the pattern of the typical ancient Near Eastern three-room royal palace with an entry hall (Hebrew, *'ûlām*), a great reception hall (Hebrew, *hêkāl*), and a throne room (Hebrew, *dĕbîr*), where the ark of the covenant, understood to serve as the throne of YHWH, resides.[2] The various furnishings—i.e., the ark of the witness (covenant), the table of the presence, and the lampstand—are the furnishings of the ideal royal palace; the

2. Halpern, *First Historians*, 46–58.

priesthood is the idealized staff that would serve in a royal palace; and the offerings made at the temple are the idealized meals that would be served in a royal palace. The tabernacle serves as the model for the Israelite temples, such as the Jerusalem temple, and thereby functions as an idealized royal palace that is intended to overshadow the royal palaces of the ancient Near Eastern world.

Most interpreters follow Wellhausen in viewing Exodus 24:10—31:18 as the work of the Priestly stratum of the Pentateuch,[3] but Meyers correctly argues that there is reason to view the final form of this text as a work of Priestly redaction, which reworked earlier texts concerned with the northern Shiloh sanctuary into the present form of the P-stratum narrative.[4] Her considerations point to the need to consider that a northern Israelite E-stratum narrative underlies the present text, and that subsequent redaction has produced the present E-stratum text over time.

Reception History

The Torah does not include much in the way of specific instructions concerning the command to refrain from work on the Shabbat. Exodus 35:1–3 states that no fire should be kindled on the Shabbat day, but otherwise, there is no explicit instruction concerning work that is to be avoided on Shabbat. Mishnah Shabbat 7.2 consequently specified the thirty-nine categories of work that are to be avoided on Shabbat. The Mishnah passage apparently took its cue from the citation in Exodus 35:1–3, which appears within the compliance account for the building of the wilderness tabernacle. The Mishnah passage then presupposes the reasoning as to what activities would have been necessary to construct the wilderness tabernacle, and defines those thirty-nine categories of "work" (Hebrew, *ʿābôdâ*) that must be avoided to enable Jews to undertake the "service, work" (Hebrew, *ʿābôdâ*) necessary to observe Shabbat.

Ginzberg recounts a number of Talmudic and Midrashic texts that recount Moses's arrival at the top of Mount Sinai to receive instruction from G-d concerning the construction of the wilderness tabernacle, such as b. Shabbat 89a, b. Menaḥot 29b, b. Sanhedrin 111a–111b, and others.[5] His summation recounts that when Moses arrived in heaven,

3. Campbell and O'Brien, *Sources of the Pentateuch*, 43–52.

4. Meyers, *Exodus*, 219–26.

5. Ginzberg, *Legends*, 3:114–19, 6:nn249–72.

he found G-d providing crowns for the letters of the Torah, but he said nothing. When G-d asked him why he did not greet G-d properly, Moses responded with the proper greeting and asked G-d about the meaning of the crowns, which provide guidance on the meaning of the Torah. G-d's response indicated that R. Akiba ben Joseph, the great sage of rabbinic Judaism, would then be able to provide a multitude of teachings concerning the meaning of the Torah. When Moses asked to see this man, G-d brought Moses into R. Akiba's yeshivah classroom where they sat in the back with the beginning students. Moses could not understand the discussion. But when one of the students asked how R. Akiba knew the basis for his interpretation, R. Akiba responded that it was all based on the teachings given to Moses at Mount Sinai. Moses then asked to see R. Akiba's reward, and G-d showed him how R. Akiba was executed by the Romans by having his flesh torn from his body with iron combs. When Moses protested to G-d, G-d told him to be silent because this was G-d's decree. Moses then appealed to G-d to show mercy, but G-d reminded Moses that he had called for the punishment of sinners.

Moses spent forty days and nights studying Torah with G-d. By day they studied the Written Torah and by night they studied the Oral Torah. G-d showed Moses the seven levels of heaven, the angels dressed in violet (blue), the color of the sea, and the angels dressed in royal purple, crimson, and twisted linen, all the colors and fabrics that were to be embroidered into the lower curtains of the wilderness tabernacle. At the end of forty days and nights, G-d gave the Torah to Moses and enabled him to remember it all. When Moses returned to Israel at Sinai with the tablets of the Torah in hand, Satan demanded to know where the Torah was. G-d told him that it was with Moses. When Satan demanded the Torah from Moses, Moses responded with humility that he could not declare that the Torah was in his possession. G-d therefore declared that for his humility, Moses would be rewarded by having the Torah known as the Torah of Moses. At this point, G-d's divine radiance shined on Moses's face.

YHWH's Instructions to Moses Concerning the Manufacture of the Ark, the Table, and the Lampstand—Exodus 25:1–40

Translation

25:1 And YHWH spoke to Moses, saying, [2] Speak to the sons of Israel that they will take for me a contribution from every man whose heart impels him, "You shall take the contribution. [3] And this is the contribution which you shall take from yourselves: gold, and silver, and bronze, [4] blue, and purple, and crimson, and fine linen, and goat's hair, [5] and tanned skins of rams, and skins of dolphins, and acacia wood, [6] oil for lighting, spices for the oil of anointing, and for the incense of spices, [7] stones of onyx, and stones of setting for the ephod and for the breastpiece, [8] and they shall make for me a sanctuary and I will dwell among them. [9] According to all that I show you, the pattern of the tabernacle and the pattern of all its fixtures, and thus you shall you make.

[10] And they shall make an ark of acacia wood two and a half cubits long, and a cubit and a half wide, and a cubit and a half high. [11] And you shall overlay it with pure gold inside and outside you shall overlay it, and you shall make upon it a border of gold all around, [12] and you shall cast for it

four rings of gold, and you shall place upon its four feet, and two rings upon its first side, and two rings upon its second side. 13 And you shall make poles of acacia wood, and you shall overlay them with gold. 14 And you shall bring the poles into the rings upon the sides of the ark to carry the ark with them. 15 In the rings of the ark the poles will be; the poles shall not depart from it. 16 And you shall place into the ark [the tablets] of the testimony that I shall give to you.

17 And you shall make a cover of pure gold two and half cubits long and a cubit and a half wide, 18 and you shall make two cherubs; of hammered gold you shall make them at the two ends of the cover. 19 Make one cherub at one end and the other cherub at the other end of the cover; you shall make the cherubs upon its two ends. 20 And the cherubs shall be spreading out [their] wings above protecting the cover with their wings over the cover, and their faces shall be each to the other; unto the cover shall the faces of the cherubs be. 21 And you shall place the cover upon the ark above, and into the ark you shall place [the tablets of] the testimony, which I will give to you. 22 And I will meet you there, and I will speak with you above the cover from between the two cherubs, which are above the ark of the witness—all that I will command you concerning the sons of Israel.

23 And you shall make a table of acacia wood two cubits long and one cubit wide and a cubit and a half high. 24 And you shall overlay it with pure gold, and you shall make for it a border of gold all around. 25 And you shall make for it a frame, a handbreadth wide, around it, and you shall make a border of gold for a frame around [it]. 26 And you shall make for it four rings of gold, and you shall place the rings upon the four corners, which are at its four feet. 27 Next to the frame shall be the rings for the poles alone to carry the table. 28 And you shall make the poles of acacia wood, and you shall overlay them with gold, and you shall carry with them the table. 29 And you shall make its dishes and its spoons and its jars and its pitchers with which one pours out; of pure gold you shall make them. 30 And you shall place upon the table the bread of the presence before me always.

> 31 And you shall make a lampstand of pure gold; of hammered work you shall make the lampstand, its base and its shaft, its cups, its bulbs, and its blossoms from it shall be [the same]. 32 And six branches going out from its sides, three branches of the lampstand from its first side, and three branches of the lampstand from its second side. 33 Three cups, almond blossoms, on one shaft of the bulb and blossom, and three cups, thus for the six branches going out from the lampstand. 34 And on the lampstand are four cups, almond blossoms, its bulbs and its blossoms. 35 And a bulb under two branches from it, and a bulb under two branches from it, and a bulb under two branches from it for the six branches going out from the lampstand. 36 And their bulbs and their branches shall be entirely one, hammered work of pure gold. 37 And you shall make its seven lamps, and mount its lamps so that it shines from across its face. 38 And its tongs and its snuffers are pure gold. 39 And a talent of pure gold, one shall make it with all its utensils. 40 And look [carefully], and make [it] according to the pattern that you see on the mountain.

Commentary

Exodus 25:1

The YHWH speech formula in Exodus 25:1, "and YHWH spoke to Moses, saying," introduces the whole of Exodus 25:2—30:10 as YHWH's speech to Moses.[1] The first phrase of YHWH's speech, "speak to the sons of Israel," in Exodus 25:2aα identifies the speech as an instruction speech,[2] whereas the content of the speech in Exodus 25:2aβ—30:10 presents instruction concerning the construction of the tabernacle and its fixtures and the conduct of its activities. As noted above, Exodus 25:2–9 presents YHWH's speech to Moses concerning the need for Moses to instruct Israel to provide the construction materials for the tabernacle, whereas the rest of YHWH's instruction speech in Exodus 25:10—30:10 calls upon Moses to instruct Israel to build the tabernacle and its fixtures and to conduct the sacred activities of the tabernacle.[3]

1. Sweeney, *Isaiah 1–39*, 547.
2. Sweeney, *Isaiah 1–39*, 522.
3. Knierim, "Conceptual Aspects in Exodus 25:1–9."

Exodus 25:2–9

Exodus 25:2–9 presents YHWH's instruction speech to Moses concerning the need for the people of Israel to provide the materials necessary for building the tabernacle and its fixtures and conducting the holy activities of the tabernacle. Following YHWH's instruction to Moses to speak to the people in Exodus 25:2aα, the balance of this particular instruction appears in Exodus 25:2aβ–9. YHWH refers to the people's provision of materials as a *tĕrûmâ*, "contribution," which the people are to give as each man's "heart impels him" (Hebrew, *ʾăšer yiddĕbennû libbô*). The use of the verb *yiddĕbennû*, "it impels him," is based on the Hebrew verb root *ndb*, "to incite/impel," which also stands as the basis for the noun *nĕdābâ*, "a freewill offering" to YHWH, as described in Exodus 35:29. A freewill offering is generally made to the central sanctuary to give thanks to YHWH for some action or blessing on the individual's or the community's behalf.[4] In the present case, the people of Israel would give freewill offerings in thanks to YHWH for delivering them from Egyptian bondage and guiding them through the wilderness to Mount Sinai (Horeb) and revealing to them divine instruction. Such offerings may take any form—whole burnt offerings, offerings of well-being, etc.—although they are to be distinguished from vows, which entail a sense of obligation (cf. Lev 22:23). In the present case, the contribution of freewill offerings indicates that the tabernacle, which will function as YHWH's holy sanctuary in the wilderness and serve as the model for sanctuaries in the land of Israel, is wholly voluntary on the part of the people as a means to acknowledge what YHWH has done, is doing, and will do for them.

The items provided by the people include the raw materials necessary for building the tabernacle and its fixtures and conducting the activities of the sanctuary. The first items mentioned are valuable metals—including gold, silver, and bronze—for casting or overlaying the various furnishings of the tabernacle (e.g., the ark, the table of the presence, and the lampstand) as well as the utensils used in the tabernacle. A second group of items includes dyed fabrics, including blue, purple, scarlet materials, as well as linens and goat's hair for the production of sacred clothing for the priests or draperies and other textiles that will adorn the tabernacle to identify it as the house of YHWH. A third group of items includes tanned ram's skins, dolphin skins, and acacia wood that will be used to construct the walls of the tabernacle as well as the courtyard

4. J. Conrad, "*ndb*."

walls, and the various fixtures, such as the ark and the table of the presence. A fourth set of items includes the various olive oils for lighting and anointing, spices, and incense for the fragrances to be experienced in the tabernacle. Finally, the fifth set of items includes the precious stones, onyx and others, that will be used to construct the ephod and the breastpiece to be worn by the high priest. All of these items will be used to construct the tabernacle, based on the pattern (Hebrew, *tabnît*, apparently a small model used in the ancient world for the construction of buildings, monuments, etc.) that YHWH shows to Moses.

Exodus 25:10–22

Exodus 25:10–22 presents YHWH's instructions concerning "the ark of the witness" (Hebrew, *ʾărōn hā ʿēdut*), sometimes translated as "the ark of the testimony" or "the ark of the pact."[5] Insofar as Hebrew *ʿēdut* is derived from the root *ʿwd*, "to call as a witness," it seems best to translate the expression as "the ark of the witness." The reference to the witness would then refer to the witness of the covenant between YHWH and Israel, particularly because the witness to the covenant in the form of the two tablets of the covenant will be deposited into the ark (see Exod 25:16, 21; 34:29). The expression "the ark of the witness" may also be understood to refer to the witness of the presence of YHWH Sebaʾot, G-d of Israel, insofar as YHWH's presence above the ark is acknowledged by the phrase *yhwh (ṣĕbāʾôt) yōšēb hakkĕrûbîm*, "YHWH (Sebaʾôt), who is enthroned (above/upon) the cherubim" (1 Sam 4:4; 2 Sam 6:2; 1 Chr 13:6; cf. 2 Sam 22:11; 2 Kgs 19:15; Isa 37:16; Pss 18:11; 80:2; 99:1) in reference to the understanding that the ark serves as YHWH's throne—or at least the footstool for YHWH's heavenly throne (see Isa 66:1). The imagery of cherubim guarding the throne of YHWH is due to common ancient Near Eastern understandings of cherubim who are positioned at the sides of royal thrones to guard them from attack or beside palace doors or city gates for the same purpose.[6] Ancient seminomadic peoples in the Near East were known to carry arks,

5. *HALOT* 2:790–91; Exod 25:21 NJPS.

6. See the photos of the sarcophagus of King Ahiram (Hiram) of Tyre, which depicts him on his throne, guarded by cherubim on either side (*ANEP* 456, 458) and the gates of the palace of Ashurnasirpal at Nimrod, which guard the gates of cities (e.g., ANEP 456–57).

representing the presence of their gods as they travelled from place to place,[7] and vassal nations were known to have images of their gods carried on thrones, e.g., to appear before their suzerain deities, such as Assur of Assyria or Marduk of Babylon.[8]

The ark of the witness is constructed as a wooden chest, made of acacia wood (Hebrew, *šiṭṭîm*), a genus now identified as Vachellia or Faidherbia.[9] The measurements of the ark appear as 2.5 cubits long, 1.5 cubits wide, and 1.5 cubits high. The standard cubit measures approximately 17.5 inches, which would produce measurements of 43.75 inches long, 26.25 inches wide, and 26.25 inches high. The royal cubit is approximately 20.5 inches, which would produce measurements of 51.25 inches long, 30.75 inches wide, and 30.75 inches high.[10] The entire structure is to be overlaid with hammered gold and gold framework moldings throughout, due to its ideal role as the throne or footstool of YHWH. First Kings 14:25–28 recounts that Pharaoh Shishak of Egypt, apparently identified as Pharaoh Shoshenq, subjugated Jerusalem in the fifth year of King Rehoboam ben Solomon (ca. 917 BCE), and stripped the temple of its gold, forcing Rehoboam to replace the gold with bronze. Although Pharaoh Shoshenq of Egypt (r. 945–924 BCE) did raid Israel and Judah, his list of tributary cities does not include Jerusalem, and the Egyptian chronology does not match the biblical chronology.[11] Four rings are to be built on the four feet at the corners of the chest to enable the placement of acacia rods, overlaid with gold, so that the ark might be carried. The poles are not to be removed from the rings, and (two tablets) of the witness to the covenant are to be deposited inside.

A cover (Hebrew, *kappōret*) for the ark is to be constructed of pure gold, 2.5 cubits long and 1.5 cubits wide. No depth is given. The Hebrew term *kappōret* is derived from the root *kpr*, which means "to cover," although the root is also used in reference to the atonement (i.e., covering) for wrongdoing. Two cherubim made of hammered gold—no reference is made to their substructure—are to be made to place atop the two ends of the ark. The cherubim face each other with wings outstretched and touching the wings of the other. As noted above, their function is to guard the

7. Grintz, "Ark of the Covenant."

8. See *ANEP* 538.

9. Zohary, *Plants of the Bible*, 116.

10. For calculations of the length of the cubit, see Dever, "Weights and Measurements," 1210.

11. *ANET* 263–64; Redford, *Egypt, Canaan, and Israel*, 312–15.

throne of YHWH Seba'ot. When the Jerusalem temple is completed, two additional cherubim are constructed inside the *d'bîr* or holy of holies of the temple where the ark resides, for a total of four cherubim (cf. Ezek 1). The cover is to be placed on top of the ark, which suggests that the ark itself is indeed the footstool of YHWH's throne, as depicted in Isaiah 66:1, and that YHWH sits invisibly enthroned above the cover of the ark and its cherubs. The two tablets of the "witness" to the covenant are placed within the ark. The instruction concludes with a statement that the ark of the witness is the place from which YHWH will appear and issue commands or instructions to the people of Israel, presumably through Moses and the priests and prophets who will follow him.

Exodus 25:23–30

Exodus 25:23–30 presents instructions for building "the table" (Hebrew, *šulḥān*) to be placed before the ark of the witness (i.e., the throne of YHWH) in the wilderness tabernacle and later in the temple. The purpose of the table is to place "the bread of the presence" (Hebrew, *leḥem pānîm*, see Exod 25:30) before YHWH as a symbolic, idealized meal. The table is to be 2 cubits long, 1 cubit wide, and 1.5 cubits high. Using the standard cubit, the table would be 35 inches high, 17.5 inches wide, and 25.75 inches high. Using the royal cubit, the dimensions would be 41.20 inches long, 17.5 inches wide, and 30.9 inches high. The table is overlaid with pure gold, and a rim will be built as a frame around its surface, one handbreadth (Hebrew, *ṭōpaḥ*), about 3 inches, wide.[12] Again, four rings are to be built on each of its four feet so that acacia-wood poles overlaid with gold can be used to carry it. A collection of dishes, spoons, jars, and pitchers, all made of pure gold, shall be cast to serve and consume food and drink. The above-noted bread of the presence is to be placed before YHWH at all times, to be replaced on a weekly basis.

Exodus 25:31–40

Exodus 25:31–40 presents YHWH's instructions to Moses concerning the manufacture of the menorah or lampstand (Hebrew, *mĕnōrâ*). Together with the ark of the witness, i.e., the throne or footstool and the table, the lampstand completes the furnishings of the interior of the

12. Dever, "Weights and Measures," 1210.

wilderness tabernacle and the temples that will be built in the land of Israel. From a practical standpoint, the lampstand is a necessity, insofar as the interior of the tabernacle or temple will not be well lighted, and the lampstand provides that light in the symbolic interior of YHWH's house. The wilderness tabernacle/temple lampstand differs from the Hanukkah menorah in that the former has only seven branches for lamps, whereas the Hanukkah menorah has nine. In both cases, the central lamp would be used to light the other lamps of the lampstand. The reason for the difference is that the tabernacle/temple menorah symbolizes the six days of creation and the seventh day of Shabbat, in which the seventh lamp provides the foundation for the other six, whereas the Hanukkah menorah symbolizes the eight days of Hanukkah plus the Shamash, which also serves as a foundation for the other eight lamps in that it is used to light them. An additional understanding is that temple fixtures are not to be replicated following the destruction of the temple.

The structure of the tabernacle/temple lampstand is the image of a tree, which in biblical literature would symbolize the trees of the garden of Eden, i.e., the tree of life and death and the tree of the knowledge of good and evil. It is striking, however, that the tree imagery would also represent the presence of the Canaanite mother goddess, Asherah, who is symbolized by a flourishing fruit tree to represent fertility. Such trees were apparently features of Canaanite sanctuaries, together with a pillar or *maṣṣēbâ*, perhaps a phallic-inspired symbol to represent the presence of Baal, the male god of rain and fertility. The imagery suggests that elements of Canaanite iconography were retained and re-signified in ancient Israel's and Judah's development from their Canaanite roots. It is noteworthy, then, that the blooming flower imagery also plays a role in the selection of Aaron and the Levites as YHWH's priesthood in Numbers 17–18, in that the selection is signified when Aaron's rod blossoms as almond flowers. A blossoming flower cap, described as a pomegranate blossom, has been discovered in excavations of pre-Israelite Jerusalem.[13] The ceramic piece is designed so that it can serve as the cap of a priestly rod. Unfortunately, there are problems with this artifact in that its provenance is uncertain and it was later used to forge an inscription, which reads, "Holy to YHWH."

13. Avigad, "Inscribed Pomegranate."

The instructions for the manufacture of the lampstand call for a work of hammered pure gold.[14] It is to be made in two pieces, i.e., its base (Hebrew, *yĕrēkāh*, lit., "its thigh") for support and its shaft or stem (Hebrew, *qānāh*, lit., "its reed"). The stem is to be made as one piece of hammered gold with six branches (Hebrew, *qānîim*, "reeds"). The shaft and branches are to be topped with flowered constructions, including "its cups" (Hebrew, *gĕbîʿehâ*, "its cups/bowls"), "its bulbs" (Hebrew, *kaptōreyhā*, "its capitals/bulbs"), and "its blossoms" (Hebrew, *pĕrāḥeyhā*, "its blossoms/flowers"). The reference to "cups" indicates the need for olive oil to fuel the lamps that burn due to wicks soaked in oil, and the reference to "capitals" indicates an architectural feature atop pillars that is oftentimes cut to resemble the bulbs of blossoming flowers. Here, the imagery is designed to depict the blossoming flowers on a fruit tree.

The arrangement of the structure includes the central shaft with the cups, bulbs, and blossoms atop.[15] Three pairs of branches extend from the central shaft from top to bottom to represent the branches of a tree, each with a blossoming flower constructed of cups, bulbs, and blossoms on top. There are four cups to each blossoming flower, designed to resemble flower petals, but shaped as cups so that they can hold the necessary olive oil to serve as fuel.[16] The lampstand is designed so that it gives light to the front. It associated implements—viz. "its tongs" (Hebrew, *malqāḥeyhā*) and "its snuffers" (Hebrew, *maḥtōteyhā*)—are also to be made of pure gold. The lampstand will require "a talent" (Hebrew, *kikkār*, lit., "a round [of gold]"), which is equivalent to a range from 67.3 pounds in the Light Standard measure, to 134.6 pounds in the Heavy Standard measure.[17] It was common to use architectural models for construction projects in the ancient world, but the "pattern" (Hebrew, *tabnît*) shown to Moses remains known only to G-d.

Reception History

According to the rabbinic midrashic work Numbers Rabbah 2.9, the ark travelled two thousand cubits ahead of Israel in the wilderness so that the people could go there on the Shabbat to pray. When the ark

14. For full discussion, see Meyers, *Tabernacle Menorah*.

15. Meyers, *Tabernacle Menorah*, figs. 43, 60.

16. Meyers, *Tabernacle Menorah*, figs. 21, 22.

17. Dever, "Weights and Measures," 1206.

was set down in the wilderness, fire came out from between the cherubs to destroy snakes, scorpions, thorns, and Israel's enemies according to Midrash Tanḥuma, Va-Yakhel 7.[18]

The ultimate fate of the ark remains uncertain. First Esdras 1.54 states that the Babylonians carried off all the holy vessels, chests, and stores of the temple to Babylonia, and Daniel 5 recounts how Belshazzar gave a great banquet in which the vessels of the temple were brought out for his guests to use in eating and drinking. Some maintain that the ark was hidden in the Second Temple storage rooms for wood beneath the pavement of the temple courts.[19] Talmudic tradition in b. Yoma 53b and y. Sheqalim 6.1, 49c holds that King Josiah of Judah hid the ark and its utensils so that it would not be taken to Babylonia. Maimonides states in Yadaim Hilkhot Beit ha-Beḥirah 4.1 that Solomon built a secret storage space in the Temple Mount that Josiah used to hide the ark. Second Maccabees 2:4 states that Jeremiah hid the ark in a cave on the mountain from which Moses viewed the land of Israel before his death. Ethiopian tradition maintains in the *Kebra Nagast*, "The Glory of the Kings," 13, 51–52, 87, that the Queen of Sheba brought the ark back to Ethiopia together with Manyelek (Manelek), her son by Solomon, when she returned to Aksum (Axum), the capital of the Ethiopian kingdom, from her visit to Jerusalem.[20]

Exodus 25:40 is cited in Acts 7:44 in Stephen's final sermon prior to his martyrdom in the Christian New Testament. Exodus 25:40 is also cited in Hebrews 8:5 as part of the polemic that characterizes Jesus as the mediator of a covenant better than that of Moses.

The wilderness ark of the witness served as a model or inspiration for the building of an ark, i.e., "the holy ark" (Hebrew, *ʾărôn haqqōdeš*, derived from 2 Chr 35:3), which serves as the receptacle for the storage of the Torah scrolls in Jewish synagogues. In Ashkenazi synagogues, i.e., those representing the European traditions of Judaism, the ark was usually built along the eastern wall of the synagogue, insofar as Jerusalem was located to the east, whereas Babylonian synagogues located the ark along the western wall, again so that the congregation would face Jerusalem.[21]

18. Freedman, "Ark of the Covenant."

19. Freedman, "Ark of the Covenant."

20. Budge, *Queen of Sheba*, xiii, 17, 75–78, 147–50.

21. Sanders, "Ark," 3:459.

The ark is featured in Stephen Spielberg's 1981 action film *Raiders of the Lost Ark*, starring Harrison Ford as Indiana Jones, a fictional archeologist who travels to Egypt to save the biblical ark of the covenant from the Nazis prior to World War II, who want to use it for their purposes to dominate the world.

YHWH's Instructions to Moses Concerning the Construction of the Tabernacle and Its Courts —Exodus 26:1–37

Translation

26:1 And [for] the tabernacle you shall make ten curtains [of] twisted linen, and blue and purple and scarlet worm [with] two cherubim, the work of an artisan, you shall make
them. [2] The length of each curtain shall be twenty-eight cubits and the width shall be four cubits for each curtain, the
same measure for each of the curtains. [3] Five of the curtains shall be joined, each to the other, and five [other] curtains
shall be joined, each to the other. [4] And you shall make loops of blue on the edge of the curtain from the end of the first joined set, and so you shall make [loops of blue] on the edge
of the second joined set. [5] Fifty loops you shall make on the first curtain, and fifty loops you shall make on edge of the second curtain, which is joined as a set to the loops of the
first curtain, each to the other. [6] And you shall make fifty hooks of gold, and you shall join the curtains, each to the other, with the hooks, and the tabernacle shall become one.

[7] And you shall make curtains of goats' hair for the tent above the tabernacle; eleven curtains you shall make them.
[8] The length of each curtains shall be thirty cubits, and the

width four cubits for each curtain, one measure for the
eleven curtains. 9 And you shall join five curtains alone, and
the [other] six curtains alone, and you shall double over the
sixth curtain before the front of the tent. 10 And you shall
make fifty loops upon the edge of the outermost curtain of
the joined set, and fifty loops on the edge of the second curtain on the joined set. 11 And you shall make fifty hooks of
bronze, and you shall insert the hooks into the loops, and you
shall join the tent, and it shall be one. 12 And the excess that
hangs over the curtains of the tent, half of the curtain that
hangs over shall be excess over the back of the tent. 13 And
the cubit from each end shall be overhang for the length of
the curtains of the tent. It shall be excess over the sides of the
tent from one to the other to cover it. 14 And you shall make
a covering for the tent of tanned rams' skins and a covering
of dolphin skins above.

15 And you shall make the planks for the tabernacle of acacia
wood standing upright. 16 Ten cubits shall be the length of
each plank, and a cubit and a half shall be the width of each
plank. 17 Two brackets shall be on each plank, parallel, each
to the other, thus you shall make them for each of the planks
of the tabernacle. 18 And you shall make the planks for the
tabernacle twenty planks for the side facing the south. 19 And
forty bases of silver you shall make under the twenty planks,
two bases under each plank, for the two brackets and two
bases under each plank for its two brackets. 20 And for the
second palisade of the tabernacle, on the north side, twenty
planks. 21 And their forty bases of silver, two bases under
each plank and two bases under each plank. 22 And for the innermost part of the tabernacle to the west, you shall make six
planks. 23 And two planks you shall make for the two corner
posts of the tabernacle in the innermost space. 24 And they
shall be matching twins below, and together they shall be
matching upon its top to one ring; so it shall be for the two
of them, for the two corner posts. 25 And there shall be eight
planks and their bases of silver, sixteen bases, two bases under each plank and two bases under each plank.

[26] And you shall make bars of acacia wood, five for the planks on the one side of the tabernacle, [27] and five bars for the second side of the tabernacle, and five bars for the planks of the innermost side of the tabernacle to the west. [28] And the middle bar in the midst of the planks passing through from end to end, [29] and the planks you shall overlay with gold, and the rings you shall make of gold as housings for the bars, and you shall overlay the bars with gold. [30] And you shall raise up the tabernacle according to the specification that you were shown on the mountain.

[31] And you shall make a curtain of blue and purple and scarlet worm and twisted linen, the work of an artisan, who shall make it with cherubim. [32] And you shall place it upon the four columns of acacia wood overlaid with gold, and hooks of gold upon four bases of silver. [33] And you shall place the curtain under the hooks, and you shall bring in there behind the curtain the ark of the witness so that the curtain will distinguish for you between the holy [sanctuary] and the holy of holies. [34] And you shall place the cover upon the ark of the witness in the holy of holies. [35] And you shall place the table outside the curtain and lampstand opposite the table by the south side of the tabernacle, and the table you shall place by the north side.

[36] And you shall make a screen for the entrance of the tent of blue and purple and scarlet worm and twisted linen, a work of embroidery. [37] And you shall make for the screen five columns of acacia wood, and you shall overlay them with gold and their brackets will be gold, and you shall cast for them five bases of bronze.

Commentary

Exodus 26:1–37 presents YHWH's instructions to Moses concerning the construction of the tabernacle tent, which will house the ark of the witness, the table, and the lampstand. It is designed as an adaptation of the typical ancient Near Eastern three-room temple structure, which is based on the typical structure of a royal palace.[1] Whereas the palace/temple structure includes three rooms—the *'ûlām*, "porch, entryway"; the *hêkāl*, "reception hall"; and the *dĕbîr*, "throne room/holy of holies"—the tabernacle includes only the *hêkāl*, where the table and the lampstand are placed, and the *dĕbîr*, where the ark of the witness, which serves as YHWH's throne or footstool, is placed. Insofar as the eastern end of the tabernacle is left open with a screen mounted on five columns, it serves as an alternative to the *'ûlām*.

The tabernacle structure comprises a number of essential components, which give the structure the shape and dimensions that illustrate its analogy to the structure of the Jerusalem temple as described in 1 Kings 6 and 2 Chronicles 3, adapted to a tent structure. The tabernacle structure is defined by its planks, each of which is ten cubits high and one and one-half cubits wide. Twenty planks placed side by side form the north and south sides of the tabernacle structure, each side of which measures thirty cubits long and ten cubits high. The west side of the structure is constructed from six planks placed side by side, each of which again measures ten cubits high and one and one-half cubits wide, and two additional corner planks, which results in the west side measuring twelve cubits wide and ten cubits high. The east side, which is left open by the absence of planking, would be the same width. The resulting structure is then thirty cubits long by ten cubits high, whereas the dimensions of the Jerusalem temple are sixty cubits long and twenty cubits high, including the *hêkāl*, measuring forty cubits long, and the *dĕbîr*, measuring twenty cubits wide (1 Kgs 6:14–22; 2 Chr 3:1–17; n.b., the Chronicler measures the *'ûlām* as twenty cubits long). The *'ûlām* adds an additional ten cubits in length and twenty cubits in width, according to 1 Kings 6:14, and twenty cubits in length (and width) and one hundred twenty cubits in height, according to 2 Chronicles 3:1–17. Altogether, the tabernacle, excluding the measure of the *'ûlām*, is approximately one-half the size of the Jerusalem temple in terms of length, width, and height. The major differences are the width of the structure, which is short by one cubit in the tabernacle to be considered as one-half the dimension of the temple width, and questions concerning the measure of the *'ûlām* in 2 Chronicles 3.

The components of the tabernacle structure include the following.

1. Halpern, *First Historians*, 46–58.

Exodus 26:1–6

Exodus 26:1–6 presents the construction and dimensions of the lower or under course of curtains for the tabernacle. The lower curtains of the structure include ten curtains, five each joined together. Each assemblage includes five twenty-eight-cubit curtains joined together to be hung over the ten-cubit planks (see below, vv. 15–30) by twenty cubits (five curtains, each of which is four cubits wide) for a total of forty cubits. Such an arrangement would call for each assemblage to be draped over the planks on both the south and north sides of the tabernacle structure. This would then account for the nine and one-half cubit width of the structure (eight planks, each measuring ten by one and one-half cubits) and height of both the south and north walls of planks, again measuring ten cubits high and one and one-half cubits wide. Two assemblages of five curtains would be employed, totaling forty ncubits in length, and would cover the outer sides of the planks and the middle width of twelve cubits between them. This would allow the embroidery of the lower curtains to be viewed along the top width of the structure. The text does not state whether or not there is a gap between the planks. Without a gap the planks aligned one against the other would measure thirty cubits in length, leaving ten cubits to drape over the planks that form the west wall of the tabernacle. The lower curtains are woven from dyed wool in blue, purple, and crimson by a skilled artisan to produce a multicolored embroidered design. The cloths are joined by adding fifty loops of blue at the end of each cloth assemblage and hooks of gold on the other end of the assemblage to hold the two major assemblages together as they serve as the inner ceiling of the structure. The thirty cubits per side and twelve cubits width of the full assemblage is approximately one-half the size of the Jerusalem temple, in which the combined *hêkāl* and *dĕbîr* would measure sixty cubits in length and twenty cubits in width (see 1 Kgs 6:11–22).

Exodus 26:7–14

The upper curtains hang down and overlap the lower curtains. Eleven upper curtains are to be manufactured from goat's hair, which provides better protection from the elements than the wool lower curtains. Each segment is to be thirty cubits in length and four cubits wide. Five lengths of curtain will be joined together to produce an assemblage of twenty cubits by thirty cubits, and a second set of six curtains will be joined together to produce an assemblage of twenty-four cubits by thirty cubits. The reason for the difference is that the sixth curtain of the second assemblage will be used as a covering for the eastern entrance of the tabernacle; it will be folded open when the tabernacle is open, and it can cover the entrance when the tabernacle is closed. It is unclear whether the sixth assemblage is folded over the top of the structure or to the side. Fifty loops will be added to the end of each assemblage, and fifty hooks of bronze will be made to hold the entire assemblage together. The two assemblages are then draped over the lower set of curtains, but the extra two cubits in their thirty-cubit length allow them to cover the lower curtains entirely. Two coverings of unspecified measure, one of tanned rams' skins and the other of dolphin skins, provide even greater protections from the elements insofar as they protect the two sets of lower and upper coverings.

Exodus 26:15–30

Exodus 26:15–25 recounts YHWH's instructions to Moses concerning the construction of the supporting "planks" (Hebrew, *qĕrāšîm*, sometimes translated, "frames") for the tabernacle structure. Each plank is to measure ten cubits high and one and one-half cubits wide with two brackets extending down from the bottom of the plank/frame. The brackets are to fit into the silver bases that will support the planks, enabling them to stand upright. There will be two silver bases for each plank. A total of twenty planks and forty silver bases are to be made for the south side of the tabernacle structure, with another twenty planks and forty silver bases for the north wall. Six planks and twelve bases will then form the west wall of the tabernacle structure. The reason for translating *qĕrāšîm* as "frames" (i.e., open structures) is to allow the woolen lower curtains to be visible from the inside of the tabernacle structure. But this is unnecessary as the blue, purple, and crimson embroidery is likely meant to represent the heavens, clouds, and stars/planets above, and these need to be visible only on the interior ceiling of the structure. No mention is made as to how the planks are to be placed next to each other, viz., whether or not there is a gap between each plank. If there is no gap, then the total length for each of the south and north walls would be thirty cubits, which would mean that the total forty cubits in length for the ten upper curtain assemblages would require them to be draped over the west and east sides of the tabernacle structure. The lack of a gap would then leave ten cubits of upper curtain assemblages, which would be exactly the length necessary to drape over the west wall. If there is a half-cubit gap between each plank, then the structure would accommodate the entire forty-cubit length of the ten curtain assemblages. The absence of a gap for the eight planks and sixteen silver bases of the west wall (n.b., six planks plus two corner planks, each with two silver bases; the east opening would then be the same size, but it would lack planks and silver bases) would allow only twelve cubits in width. The matching rings on the corner planks at both the bottom and the top would allow for the insertion of poles (see vv. 26–30 below) to hold the planks of the structure together. But if there is a half-cubit gap between the planks, the width would be sixteen cubits. The absence of gaps between the *qĕrāšîm* appears to be the preferred arrangement because it enables the west wall of the tabernacle to be covered.

Exodus 26:26–30 then recounts YHWH's instructions to Moses concerning the construction of the poles that will be used to hold the planks of the tabernacle structure together.

Five bars are to be constructed for each of the south and north walls of the tabernacle, and five bars are to be constructed for the west wall as well. No measure is given for the lengths of the bars; presumably the measures of the walls themselves determine the lengths. This would call for one bar for assemblages of eight planks along the tops and bottoms of the south and north sides, with the fifth bar to serve as the center bar for each wall. The west wall calls for five bars for the eight planks that form the west wall of the tabernacle. It is possible that the five bars—four along the top and bottom and one as the center bar for the structure—required for the west wall indicate a need for double reinforcement of the west wall. A center bar runs from end to end for each of the walls along the south, west, and north sides of the structure. All the planks are to be overlaid with gold, and rings of gold are to be fashioned to accommodate the bars. The bars themselves are also to be overlaid with gold.

As noted above, YHWH apparently shows Moses a pattern or model of the tabernacle structure to explain its structure and assembly, but the text provides no additional clue as to how this model looks.

Exodus 26:31–35

Exodus 26:31–35 presents YHWH's instructions to Moses concerning the manufacture of the "curtain" (Hebrew, *pārōket*) that will divide the "holy of holies," on the west side of the interior of the tabernacle where the ark of the witness will be placed, from the "holy" area, i.e., reception hall where the table and the lampstand will be placed. The curtain will be made like the lower curtain assemblages that will be visible inside the structure, i.e., blue, purple, and crimson wool, and twisted linen, with cherubim embroidered within. The dyed wool and twisted linen likely represent the heavens, clouds, and planets and stars where YHWH resides. The cherubim indicate the heavenly creatures that guard and convey YHWH in the heavens. The curtain is to be hung on four columns of acacia wood overlaid with gold. Each column has four "hooks" (Hebrew, *wāwêhem*, "their hooks," lit., "their *waws*," insofar as the Hebrew letter *waw* looks like a hook). The difference in language from the earlier planks and their brackets indicates a different type of structure, i.e., planks to form a wall versus columns on which to hang a curtain. With the curtain in place, the ark of the witness, with its cover placed on top, may be then carried behind the curtain to replicate the *d'bîr* or "holy of holies" of the future temple. The table may then be placed on the south side of the "holy," representing the *hêkāl*, "the palace" or "reception hall" of the temple, and the lampstand may be placed on the north side of the "holy."

Exodus 26:36–37

Exodus 26:36–37 recounts YHWH's instructions to Moses concerning the manufacture of the screen that will stand at the eastern entrance of the tabernacle. It is again woven from blue, purple, crimson wool, and twisted linen, albeit without cherubim, to represent the heavens where YHWH resides, apparently as seen by the people on earth, who stand outside of the *hêkāl*, "the palace" or "reception hall." Five columns of acacia wood and their hooks, overlaid with gold, are to be inserted into five bases of bronze for support. The reason for the bronze bases is that the screen and its supports will be visible to the people on earth, whereas the priests will enter the tabernacle where the bases for the planks and the columns are made from gold to represent the greater sanctity of the presence of YHWH. The screen is then to be hung from the five columns to mark the eastern entrance to the tabernacle.

The Account of YHWH's Instructions to Moses Concerning the Altar, the Courtyard, and the Provision of Pure Olive Oil for Lighting the Wilderness Tabernacle—Exodus 27:1–21

Translation

27:1 And you shall make the altar of acacia wood, five cubits
long and five cubits wide—square shall be the altar—and
three cubits [shall be) its height. [2] And you shall make its
horns upon its four corners—from it shall be its horns—and
you shall overlay it [with) bronze. [3] And you shall make its
pots for its ash, and its shovels, and its bowls, and its forks,
and its spatulas; for all its utensils, you shall make [them of)
bronze. [4] And you shall make for it a grating work of mesh
of bronze, and you shall make upon on the mesh four rings
of bronze upon its four edges. [5] And you shall place it under
the grating of the altar below, and the mesh shall be unto half
of the altar. [6] And you shall make poles for the altar, poles of
acacia wood, and you shall overlay them with bronze. [7] And
there shall be brought its poles into the rings, and the poles
shall be on the two sides of the altar when carrying it. [8] Of

hollow boards you shall make it just as [it] was shown to you on the mountain, thus you shall make [it].

9 And you shall make the courtyard of the tabernacle. On the south side hangings for the courtyard of fine twisted linen one hundred cubits long for one side. 10 And twenty columns and their twenty bases of bronze and the hooks of the columns and their bands of silver. 11 And thus for the north side in length hangings, one hundred cubits long, and its twenty columns and their twenty bases of bronze, and the hooks of the columns, and their bands of silver. 12 And the width of the courtyard for the west side, hangings, fifty cubits, their ten columns, and their ten bases. 13 And the width of the courtyard on the side facing east, hangings, fifty cubits, 14 and fifteen cubits of hangings on the side, their three columns, and their three bases. 15 And on the second side, fifteen hangings, their three columns, and their three bases. 16 And for the gate of the courtyard, a screen of twenty cubits, blue, and purple, and crimson yarn, and fine twisted linen, a work of an embroiderer, their four columns, and their four bases.

17 All the columns of the courtyard round about shall be banded with silver, and their silver hooks, and their bronze bases.

18 The length of the courtyard shall be one hundred cubits by the cubit, and the width fifty cubits by the fifty [cubits), and the height five cubits of fine twisted linen, and their columns, and their bases of bronze. 19 For all the utensils of the tabernacle in all its work, and all its pegs, and all the bronze pegs of the courtyard.

20 And you shall command the sons of Israel, and they shall take to you pure beaten olive oil for light to ignite the eternal lamp. 21 In the tent of meeting outside the curtain which is over the witness, Aaron and his sons shall arrange it from evening until morning before YHWH as an eternal statute for their generations from the sons of Israel.

Commentary

Exodus 27:1–8

Exodus 27:1–8 recounts YHWH's instructions to Moses concerning the construction of the tabernacle altar. Insofar as the tabernacle anticipates the role of the temple as the sacred palace and residence of YHWH, the altar functions as an idealized form of holy kitchen to send up food offerings, particularly meat, to YHWH. The offerings then constitute an idealized form of holy meals for YHWH, which YHWH does not need or consume, but they give appropriate honor and recognition to YHWH as the true sovereign of creation and humankind.

The altar is to be built from acacia-wood planks overlaid with bronze. Its dimensions are five cubits by five cubits so that it forms a perfect square, appropriate to its role as the center of the universe at the junction of all four primary directions. Its height is three cubits. Horns are to be constructed on each of its four corners and overlaid with bronze so that each horn appears as one piece with the rest of the altar. The horns again represent the four cardinal directions of creation, but their character is otherwise widely misunderstood. The Hebrew term for horns is *qĕrānôt*, which is generally understood as physical horns that project from the altar, but the term also refers to rays of light that project from the skin of Moses's face when he descends from Mount Sinai with the tables of the witness in Exodus 34:29–35 in the aftermath of the golden calf episode. In this case, the "horns" represent the radiance of Moses's face as a result of his encounter with YHWH. The horns of the altar would then represent a similar representation of radiance, insofar as the altar is the site of the sacrificial fire that sends offerings up to YHWH.

A number of necessary utensils and features that support the role of the altar are also included in YHWH's instructions. Pots, shovels, bowls, forks, and spatulas, all made from bronze, will be used to prepare the altar offerings and carry away the remaining ash once the offering is complete. A mesh grating made of bronze will also be cast to be placed in the midst so that the grating forms a ledge for the altar, and the mesh, which extends halfway down within the altar, can serve as a base for the placement of the wood and offerings that are to be burned on the altar. Four rings built into the mesh facilitate its transport with poles of acacia wood overlaid with bronze. The altar structure is to be hollow, apparently to enable the fire to burn properly, and the structure should again follow the pattern shown by YHWH to Moses on Mount Sinai.

Exodus 27:9–19

Exodus 27:9–19 recounts YHWH's instructions to Moses concerning the construction of the tabernacle courtyard, Hebrew, *ḥāṣēr*, "court, enclosure." Like the walls of the tabernacle itself, the courtyard walls are to be constructed of fine twisted linen–embroidered hangings, dyed blue, purple, and crimson. The south side and north side courtyard walls will be one hundred cubits long, with twenty columns on each side for support. The columns are presumably made of acacia wood overlaid with bronze, although this is not stated in this passage. Each column will be provided with a base of bronze, and the "hooks," Hebrew, *wāwîm*, are to be made of silver. Each column will likewise be provided with bands of silver.

The width of the courtyard will be fifty cubits. The west wall will include the embroidered hangings, dyed in blue, purple, and crimson fine twisted linen, and ten columns, their bronze bases, their silver hooks for insertion, and the silver bands for the columns, as described above. The courtyard side facing east will also be fifty cubits wide. Because the east includes the entrance to the court year, there will be only fifteen cubits of hangings, again embroidered with fine twisted linen and dyed with blue, purple, and crimson, on the two sides of the entrance. Each side will call for three columns, their bronze bases, their silver hooks, and their silver bands. Such a measure leaves an entrance gate, twenty cubits wide. The entrance gate will be covered by a "screen," Hebrew, *māsāk*, again made as a work of embroidered fine twisted linen and dyed in blue, purple, and crimson. The screen will be supported by four columns and four bases, with their bronze bases, silver hooks, and silver bands.

Verses 18–19 present a summary statement concerning the construction and purpose of the court year. Again, the courtyard will be one hundred cubits long and fifty cubits wide, but the text adds that the height of the courtyard will be five cubits. The hangings will be made of fine twisted linen. The bases for the column, the utensils of the tabernacle manufactured for its "service," Hebrew, *ʿăbōdătô*, literally, "its work," and all the "pegs," Hebrew, *yĕtēdōtāyw*, apparently a reference to the various brackets and hooks used to hold the tabernacle and courtyard structures together, will be made of bronze. This last statement apparently does not refer to those fixtures that will be made of silver.

Exodus 27:20–21

Exodus 27:20–21 recounts YHWH's instructions to Moses concerning the provision of pure olive oil for lighting the lamps of the tabernacle and the role of Aaron and his sons in setting up the lamps and lighting them. The oil for the lamps is to be "pure, beaten olive oil," Hebrew, *šemen zayit zāk kātît*, i.e., olive oil that has been thoroughly processed so that no impurities that might produce dark smoke remain. The oil is to be provided by the people of Israel for use in the "eternal lamp," Hebrew, *nēr tāmîd*, which apparently represents the eternal presence of YHWH in the tabernacle. Aaron and his sons are responsible for making the arrangement for the eternal lamp to stand in the tent of meeting before the curtain that conceals the holy of holies where the ark of the witness is to be placed. They would also be responsible for making sure that the lamp is provided with oil so that it will burn properly all night long. The provision of the eternal lamp is considered as an "eternal statute," Hebrew, *ḥuqqat ʿôlăm*, for all the generations of Israel.

Reception History

Acts 7:44 cites Exodus 27:21, as part of Stephen's final sermon in the Christian New Testament. The citation refers to YHWH's instructions to Moses to build the wilderness tabernacle according to the pattern shown to him at Sinai.

The instruction to provide an eternal lamp, Hebrew, *nēr tāmîd*, for the tabernacle and temple continues throughout the history of Judaism in the provision of the *nēr tāmîd* as a prominent feature of Jewish synagogues. It is usually hung, suspended from the ceiling, before the synagogue ark, where the Torah scrolls are stored. In ancient synagogues, it was frequently placed in a niche in the western wall of the synagogue to commemorate the placement of the menorah or lampstand in the wilderness tabernacle.[1]

1. Editor, "Ner Tamid."

The Account of YHWH's Instructions to Moses Concerning the Tailoring of Priestly Vestments for Aaron and His Sons —Exodus 28:1–43

Translation

28:1 And you shall bring near to you Aaron, your brother, and his sons with him from the midst of the sons of Israel for his service as a priest for me, Aaron, Nadab and Abihu, Eleazar and Ithamar, the sons of Aaron. 2 And you shall make holy garments for Aaron, your brother, for glory and for beauty. 3 And you shall speak to all who are wise of heart, whom I have filled with the spirit of wisdom, to consecrate him for his service as a priest to me. 4 And these are the garments that they shall make: a breastpiece, an ephod, an outer robe, an embroidered inner tunic, a turban, and a sash; and they shall make holy garments for Aaron, your brother, and for his sons for his service as priests for me. 5 And they shall take the gold, and the blue, and the purple, and the crimson yarn, and the fine linen.

6 And they shall make the ephod of gold, blue and purple, crimson yarn, and fine twisted linen, the work of a craftsman. 7 Two shoulder pieces will be joined to it, onto its two

ends and joined. 8 And the intricate band that is upon it
shall be from it like its work, gold, blue and purple and
crimson yarn, and fine twisted linen. 9 And you shall take
the two stones of carnelian, and you shall engrave upon
them the names of the sons of Israel, 10 six of their names
upon the one stone, and the six remaining [names] upon
the second stone, according to their birth. 11 A work of an
engraver, a stone with the engravings of a seal, you shall
engrave the two stones according to the names of the sons
of Israel, [with] inlaid borders of gold you shall make them.
12 And you shall place the two stones on the shoulders of the
ephod as stones of remembrance for the sons of Israel, and
Aaron shall carry their names before YHWH upon his two
shoulders for a remembrance.

13 And you shall make frames of gold, 14 and two chains of
pure gold, braided you shall make them, a work of woven
cords, and you shall place the chains of woven cords upon
the frames.

15 And you shall make the breastpiece of justice, a work of a
craftsman like the work of the ephod you shall make it, gold,
blue and purple and crimson yarn, and fine twisted linen
you shall make it. 16 Square it shall be, doubled, a finger its
length and a finger its breadth, 17 and you shall fill in it a
filling of stone, four rows stone. A row of red, topaz, and emerald shall be the first row. 18 And the second row, turquoise,
sapphire, and diamond. 19 And the third row, amber, agate,
and amethyst. 20 And the fourth row, beryl, carnelian, and
jasper, framed in gold in their fillings. 21 And the stones will
be according to the names of the sons of Israel, twelve, upon
their names, engravings of a seal, each upon its name they
shall be, for the twelve tribes.

22 And you shall make upon the breastpiece braided chains,
a work of woven cords of pure gold. 23 And you shall make
upon the breastpiece two rings of gold, and you shall place
the two rings upon the two ends of the breastpiece. 24 And
you shall place the two woven cords of gold upon the two
rings onto the shoulders of the breastpiece. 25 And the two

ends of the two woven cords you shall place upon the two
frames, and you shall place [them] upon the shoulders of
the ephod onto its front. 26 And you shall make two rings
of gold, and you shall place them upon the two ends of the
breastpiece upon its lip, which is across the inside of the
breastpiece. 27 And you shall make two rings of gold, and you
shall place them upon the two shoulders of the ephod below
its front, near its seam above the intricate band. 28 And they
shall bind the breastpiece from its rings to the rings of the
ephod with a blue cord above the intricate band of the ephod,
and the breastpiece shall not be loosened from the ephod.
29 And Aaron shall carry the names of the sons of Israel on
the breastpiece of justice, upon his heart, when he comes to
the sanctuary for remembrance before YHWH always. 30 And
you shall place into the breastpiece of justice the urim and
the thummim, and they shall be upon the heart of Aaron
when he comes before YHWH, and Aaron shall carry the justice of the sons of Israel upon his heart before YHWH always.

31 And you shall make the outer robe of the ephod entirely of
blue. 32 And the opening for his head shall be in its middle; a
lip shall be for its opening all around, a work of weaving, like
the opening of armor it shall be for him that will not be torn.
33 And you shall make upon its edges pomegranates of blue
and purple and crimson yarn upon its edges round about,
and bells of gold in their midst all around. 34 A bell of gold
and a pomegranate, a bell of gold and a pomegranate upon
the edges of the outer robe all around. 35 And it shall be on
Aaron while he serves, and its sound shall be heard when he
comes into the sanctuary before YHWH and when he goes
out so that he will not die.

36 And you shall make a blossoming frontlet of pure gold,
and you shall engrave upon it the seal engravings, Holy to
YHWH. 37 And you shall place it on a cord of blue, and it
shall be on the turban, on the front of the turban it shall be.
38 And it shall be on the forehead of Aaron, and Aaron shall
carry the iniquity of the holy things, which the sons of Israel
will sanctify for all the gifts of their holy things, and it shall
be on his forehead always for their acceptance before YHWH.

39 And you shall weave the tunic of fine linen, and you shall
make the turban of fine linen, and a sash you shall make as
embroidered work.

40 And for the sons of Aaron you shall make tunics, and you
shall make for them sashes, and turbans you shall make for
them for glory and for beauty. 41 And you shall dress them,
Aaron, your brother and his sons with him, and you shall
anoint them, and you shall fill their hand, and you shall sanctify them, and they will serve as priests for me.

42 And you shall make for them linen pants to cover the
naked flesh from the loins and to the thighs they shall be.
43 And they shall be upon Aaron and upon his sons when
they come into the tent of meeting or when they approach
the altar to serve in the sanctuary so that they will not carry
iniquity and die. [It is] an eternal statute for him and for his
seed after him.

Commentary

Exodus 28:1–43 recounts YHWH's instructions to Moses concerning the tailoring of priestly garments for Aaron and his sons to be used when they officiate in holy service at the wilderness tabernacle and the temples of Israel. Insofar as the wilderness tabernacle and the later temples are conceptualized as idealized royal houses or palaces for YHWH, the use of priestly garments by the priests would be inspired by the garments presumably worn by the staff that served in the royal palaces of the House of David in Jerusalem and the palaces of the various dynasties that ruled the Northern Kingdom of Israel. The nature of the garments worn by palace staff remains unknown, although it is possible to point to some of the official roles of staff in the palace, such as the official who was designated to oversee the palace (Hebrew, *ʾăšer ʿal habbāyit*, lit., "who is over the house"). Examples would include Shebna, who holds this title in Isaiah 22:15, and Eliakim ben Hilkiah, who is authorized to wear a tunic and sash due to his service on behalf of the government in Isaiah 22:20–21.[1]

1. For discussion of the office "[he] who is over the house," see Fox, *In Service of King*, 81–96.

Exodus 28:1–5 introduces the passage with YHWH's instruction that Moses should bring near Aaron and his sons—i.e., Nadab, Abihu, Eleazar, and Ithamar—to serve as priests for YHWH. It is noteworthy that Nadab and Abihu have names very similar to the names of the sons of Jeroboam ben Nebat, the first king of northern Israel following the revolt of the northern tribes against the House of David (1 Kgs 14:1, 20). Jeroboam ben Nebat is condemned in the book of Kings as the monarch who initiated the sins of all the kings of northern Israel, which resulted in YHWH's decision to destroy northern Israel in 2 Kings 17. Insofar as Aaron allows Israel to commit sins analogous to those of Israel in the golden calf narrative of Exodus 32–34 (cf. 1 Kgs 12:25–33), Aaron's actions are seen as a critique of northern practice under Jeroboam.[2] Aaron's sons, Nadab and Abihu, are then put to death in Leviticus 10:1–7 for offering foreign fire before YHWH in the wilderness tabernacle, a practice that is considered idolatrous. The account in Leviticus 10 is intended to emphasize the need to observe YHWH's instructions concerning holy practice in the sanctuary on the part of the priesthood. YHWH's instructions include the need to train skilled artisans in the tailoring of the holy garments. The garments will include the breastpiece, the ephod, the outer robe, the embroidered tunic, the turban, and the sash. Materials from which these holy garments are to be made include blue, purple, and crimson yarn, fine linen, and gold.

Exodus 28:6–13 presents YHWH's instructions for the tailoring of the ephod (Hebrew, *ʾēpōd*), a device that is used for oracular inquiry of YHWH.[3] The term ephod appears to be derived from Egyptian *ifd*, which refers to a special type of linen (cf. Ugaritic, *ʾpd*, and Akkadian, *epattu*). The ephod is sometimes mistaken as a gold object based on the description of the ephod made by Gideon in Judges 8:27, presumed to be made from the gold taken from the Midianites in Judges 8:28, but the Hebrew text of Judges 8:27 makes no reference to the gold.[4] Otherwise, the ephod is described as a linen garment (1 Sam 2:18; 14:3; 22:18), e.g., worn by David as he danced before the ark in 2 Samuel 6:14. Insofar as the ephod described here in Exodus 28:6–13 is idealized, it is made with gold and precious jewels, but this may not be the case in other examples in Israelite or foreign practice. The ephod described here in Exodus 28:6–13 is idealized because it is understood to be employed

2. Sweeney, *Reading the Bible After Shoah*, 67–72.

3. Blischke, "Ephod."

4. Cf. Sasson, *Judges 1–12*, 366–68; contra Smith and Bloch-Smith, *Judges 1*, 568–70.

before YHWH in YHWH's sanctuary. The ephod is tailored from a combination of wool dyed blue, purple, and crimson, and fine twisted linen. The two shoulder pieces indicate a garment that is designed to support the weight of the gold and precious stones that will be included in its tailoring. The shoulders of the garment will feature two carnelian stones, a precious stone known for its red color, inlaid in the garment on the shoulders. The two stones are engraved with the names of the twelve tribes of Israel in the order of their birth. The first six, presumably Reuben, Shimon, Levi, Judah, Dan, and Naphtali, given the order in Genesis 30:1–8, on one, and Gad, Asher, Issachar, Zebulun, Joseph, and Benjamin, given the order in Genesis 30:9–24; 35:16–22, on the other stone. The two stones are to be inlaid with gold to highlight the names and aid in holding the stones in place, and affixed to the garment with settings of gold by expert artisans. The braided gold chains are then affixed to the shoulders of the ephod to support the breastpiece.

Exodus 28:14–30 presents the instructions for the tailoring of the breastpiece of justice (Hebrew, *ḥōšen mišpāṭ*). The breastpiece is also made from a combination of wool dyed blue, purple, and crimson, fine twisted linen, and gold. It is inlaid with four rows of three stones each in which each different precious stone is engraved successively with the name of one of the tribes of Israel. The inclusion of the names suggests the symbolism of the breastpiece as a device that indicates the "justice" or "law" underlying the union of the twelve tribes of Israel under YHWH. The engraved names are inlaid with gold, and the stones are set in the breastpiece with settings of gold. There is no certainty concerning the meanings of the names of the precious stones, but the variation in stones suggests a colorful display of the names of the twelve tribes of Israel. The breastpiece is affixed with golden, braided chains, woven cords, and rings to function as a harness for the breastpiece which facilitates its attachment to the ephod. The urim and thummim, apparently the divinatory devices that enable oracular inquiry of YHWH, are affixed to the breastpiece, apparently in relation to the two frames described above for the ephod. The meaning of the terms "urim" and "thummim" (Hebrew, *ʾet hāʾûrîm wĕʾet hattummîm*) is uncertain. Some derive it from the presumed roots of the two terms *ʾwr*, "light, instruction," and *twm*, "whole, complete," to refer to "true light, instruction," or the like as suggested by renditions in the Aramaic Targums, the Greek Septuagint, and the Latin Vulgate.[5] The placement of the breastpiece over the heart of the high priest suggests that he keep the tribes of Israel, justice, and true teaching in mind at all times.

Exodus 28:31–35 presents YHWH's instruction concerning the tailoring of the outer robe (Hebrew, *mĕʿîl*), which functions as a sort of overcoat for the priestly garments. It is made entirely of blue cloth, and appears to function as an overtunic, insofar as it has an opening in the middle for the head of the high priest, and it therefore folds over his front and back. Presumably, the ephod and breastpiece will be placed over the robe for visibility, and the robe will cover the tunic. The opening for the head will be reinforced with a woven lip that will function like armor to keep the garment from wear and tear as it will undergo frequent use. The alternating golden bells and pomegranates are both decorative and functional. The pomegranates symbolize the fruit of the garden of Eden, especially because the high priest represents Adam attempting to return to the garden, represented by the holy of holies of the sanctuary. The golden bells represent the ideal beauty of the gold, and their tingling produces musical sound as the high priest walks about in the performance of his duties. The bells also announce his presence in the sanctuary so that he does not die when he appears before YHWH.

Exodus 28:36–38 presents instruction concerning the blossoming frontlet (Hebrew, *ṣîṣ*, lit., "blossom"). The blossoming frontlet symbolizes the selection of Aaron and the tribe of Levi by YHWH to serve as priests in Numbers 17–18 when Aaron's rod blossoms to indicate YHWH's choice. It is to be made of pure gold and affixed to the front of Aaron's turban. It is further inscribed with the phrase "Holy to YHWH" (Hebrew, *qōdeš laYHWH*) to signify the status of high priest. The statement that Aaron—and after him, his sons—will bear the iniquity of the holy things, which the sons of Israel will sanctify as gifts in YHWH's sanctuary, reiterates the language of Numbers 18:1 in which YHWH states that Aaron and his sons will bear the iniquity of the sanctuary in their roles as the holy priests of the sanctuary.

Exodus 28:39 presents YHWH's instruction concerning the tailoring of the tunic and the turban from fine linen and the sash made of embroidered work.

Exodus 28:40–41 presents YHWH's instruction concerning the tailoring of tunics, sashes, and turbans for the sons of Aaron for their

5. Greenberg, "Urim."

"glory" (Hebrew, *kābôd*) and their "beauty" (Hebrew, *tip'eret*), although the high priest is still distinguished by the ephod and the breastpiece. The instruction to dress Aaron and his sons in the holy garments discussed in Exodus 28, followed by their anointing with fragrant olive oil, facilitates their service as priests in YHWH's sanctuary. The phrase "to fill their hand" is idiomatic for ordaining them as priests, insofar as they are entitled to eat from the various offerings intended for the support of the priesthood.

Exodus 28:42–43 presents YHWH's instruction to tailor linen pants that cover the loins down to the knees, and it concludes the instruction concerning the priestly garments. The placement of this instruction at the end of the passage may indicate that it was added after the initial composition of Exodus 28 to ensure that the priests would not be exposed during priestly service at the altar, as noted in Exodus 20:23 (see also 2 Sam 6:16–23). The statement that this instruction is an "eternal statute" (Hebrew, *ḥuqqat ʿôlām*) may signify its secondary status and ensure that it is considered to be authoritative.

Reception History

Revelation 21:12 cites Exodus 28:21 as part of its efforts to conceptualize the twelve jewels on the breastpiece of the high priest as a symbol for the new Jerusalem, which has twelve gates, each of which is inscribed with the name of one of the twelve tribes of Israel.

The Account of YHWH's Instructions to Moses Concerning the Ordination of Aaron and His Sons as Priests—Exodus 29:1–46

Translation

29:1 And this is what you shall do to them to sanctify them
to serve as priests to me. Take one bull of the cattle and two
rams without blemish, [2] and unleavened bread, and unleavened challah mixed with oil, and unleavened wafers anointed
with oil—of fine wheat flour you shall make them. [3] And you
shall place them in one basket, and you shall bring them
near in the basket together with the bull and the two rams.
[4] And Aaron and his sons you shall bring near to the entrance of the tent of meeting, and you shall wash them with
water. [5] And you shall take the garments, and you shall dress
Aaron with the tunic and the outer robe of the ephod, and
the ephod, and the breastpiece, and you shall strap on him
the bejeweled ephod. [6] And you shall place the turban upon
his head, and you shall place the holy crown upon the turban.
[7] And you shall take the anointing oil, and you shall pour it
upon his head, and you shall anoint him. [8] And his sons you
shall bring near, and you shall dress them in tunics, [9] and you
shall gird them with sashes, [both] Aaron and his sons, and
you shall bind for them turbans, and they shall have priestly
status as an eternal statute.

And you shall fill the hand of [i.e., ordain] Aaron and the hand of his sons. 10 And you shall bring near the bull before the tent of meeting, and Aaron and his sons shall lay their hands upon the head of the bull. 11 And you shall slaughter the bull before YHWH at the entrance of the tent of meeting. 12 And you shall take some of the blood of the bull, and you shall place it upon the horns of the altar with your finger, and all the rest of the blood you shall pour out upon the base of the altar. 13 And you shall take all the fat that covers the entrails and the appendage upon the liver, and two kidneys and the fat which is upon them, and you shall burn [them on] the altar. 14 And the meat of the bull and its skin and its waste you shall burn with fire outside the camp; it is a sin offering.

15 And the first ram you shall take, and Aaron and his sons shall lay their hands upon the head of the ram, 16 and you shall slaughter the ram, and you shall take its blood, and you shall pour it upon the altar all around. 17 And the ram you shall cut up to its pieces, and you shall wash its entrails and its legs, and you shall put them together with its pieces and its head. 18 And you shall burn the entire ram upon the altar. It is a whole burnt offering for YHWH, a pleasing odor, a fire offering for YHWH.

19 And you shall take the second ram, and Aaron and his sons shall lay their hands upon the head of the ram, 20 and you shall slaughter the ram, and you shall take some of its blood, and you shall place it upon the lobe of the right ear of Aaron and upon the lobe of the [right] ear of his sons and upon the thumb of their right hand and upon the big toe of their right foot, and you shall pour the [rest of the] blood upon the altar round about. 21 And you shall take some of the blood which is upon the altar and some of the anointing oil, and you shall pour [it] upon Aaron and upon his garments and upon his sons and upon the garments of his sons with him, and he and his garments shall be holy, and his sons and the garments of his sons with him.

22 And you shall take from the ram the fat tail and the fat that covers the entrails and the appendage of the liver and

the two kidneys and the fat that is upon them and the right
thigh, for it is the ram of ordination. [23] And one square of
bread and one challah of bread with oil and one wafer from
the basket of unleavened bread which is before YHWH.
[24] And you shall place all of it upon the palms of Aaron and
upon the palms of his sons, and you shall wave them as an
elevation offering before YHWH. [25] And you shall take them
from their hand, and you shall burn [them] together with
the whole burnt offering for a pleasing odor before YHWH;
it is a fire offering for YHWH.

[26] And you shall take the breast from the ordination ram
which is for Aaron and from that which is for his sons. [27] And
you shall sanctify the breast of the elevation offering and
the thigh of the gift offering which was waved and which
was raised from the ram of ordination, from that which is
for Aaron and from that which is for his sons. [28] And it shall
be for Aaron and for his sons for an eternal statute from the
sons of Israel because it is a gift offering and a gift offering
for YHWH from the sons of Israel from their sacrifices of
well-being, their gift offerings for YHWH.

[29] And the holy garments that are for Aaron shall be for his
sons after him, for anointing in them and for their ordination. [30] Seven days shall the priest, who serves in his place
from his sons who shall enter the tent of meeting to serve in
the sanctuary, wear them.

[31] And the ram of ordination you shall take, and you shall
cook its meat in the place of the sanctuary. [32] And Aaron and
his sons shall eat the meat of the ram and the bread that is
in the basket at the entrance of the tent of meeting. [33] And
they shall eat those things with which atonement was made
for them in order to fill their hand [i.e., to ordain them] and
to sanctify them, but a foreigner shall not eat [from them]
because they are holy. [34] And if there is left anything from
the meat of ordination or from the bread until morning,
then you shall burn the remainder with fire; it shall not be
eaten because it is holy.

35 And you shall do for Aaron and for his sons like this according to all that I have commanded you; for seven days
you shall ordain them. 36 And a sin offering bull you shall
make for each day for atonement, and you shall make a sin
offering for the altar when you make atonement on it, and
you shall anoint it to sanctify it. 37 For seven days you shall
make atonement upon the altar and you shall sanctify it,
and the altar shall be a holy of holies; all who touch the
altar shall be holy.

38 And this is what you shall do upon the altar: two-year-old
sheep for each continuously. 39 The first sheep you shall make
with the cattle, and the second sheep you shall make at dusk.
40 And a tenth measure of fine flour mixed with a quarter hin
of beaten oil, and a libation of a quarter hin of wine for each
sheep. 41 And the second lamb you shall make at twilight, like
the grain offering of the cattle and like its libation you shall
make it for a pleasing odor, a fire offering for YHWH. 42 A
continuous whole burnt offering for your generations at the
entrance of the tent of meeting before YHWH, where I will
meet with you to speak with you there.

43 And I will meet there with the sons of Israel, and it will
be sanctified by my glory. 44 And I will sanctify the tent of
meeting and the altar, and Aaron and his sons I will sanctify
to serve as priests for me. 45 And I will dwell in the midst
of the sons of Israel, and I will be G-d for them. 46 And they
will know that I am YHWH, their G-d, who brought them out
from the land of Egypt so that I would dwell in their midst. I
am YHWH, their G-d.

Commentary

Exodus 29:1–46 presents the account of YHWH's instructions to Moses concerning the ordination of Aaron and his sons as priests. Although Exodus 35–40 constitutes the account of the compliance by Moses and Israel with YHWH's instructions, the account concerning the ordination of Aaron and his sons in Exodus 40:12–15 is a relatively perfunctory statement in which the ordination is to take place on the first day of the first month of the year (Exod 40:2). The full account of the compliance of Moses and Israel with this instruction appears in Leviticus 8, which overlaps extensively with Exodus 39.[1] Insofar as the present form of Exodus 25–31 and 35–40 is the product of the P-stratum of the Pentateuch, this would suggest that Leviticus 8 was a pre-existing text. Such a conclusion does not preclude an earlier version of Exodus 25–31 and 35–40 underlying the present form of the text.[2]

Exodus 29 displays a very logical and well-ordered formal structure. It begins in Exodus 29:1–9a with an introductory overview discussion of the ordination procedure. The overview begins with the statement "and this is what you shall do to them to sanctify them to serve as priests to me," followed by a summation of the various topics to be treated in the following sub-units. It is noteworthy that the passage mentions only Aaron and his sons who are to serve as priests. The role of the tribe of Levi as a whole will not be addressed until the book of Numbers, where YHWH states three times the intention to ordain the Levites as a whole as helpers to the Aaronide priesthood in place of the firstborn sons of Israel (Num 3:5–13, 40–51; 8:5–20). The ordination of the Levites is discussed in Numbers 8, and their formal selection as assistants to Aaron and his sons is recounted in Numbers 17–18. Exodus 29:1–9a introduces the offering of the bull and the two rams together with the grain offering, the washing of Aaron and his sons, their dressing in holy garments, their anointing, and their service as priests as an eternal statute.

The washing of Aaron and his sons is intended to ensure their metaphorical purity to serve at the altar, and it is reinforced by their anointing, insofar as olive oil, often scented with spices, was the preferred cleansing agent of the time. The statement that their priesthood is "an eternal statute" (Hebrew, *ḥuqqat ʿôlām*), although it may originally have been understood as "a statute of creation," insofar as the Hebrew word *ʿôlām* originally referred to the creation of the world. In such a case, the Aaronic priesthood would have been understood to continue throughout the period in which the temple in which they would serve, i.e., Shiloh and later Jerusalem, would stand. Such a concept presupposed the understanding that an ancient temple represented the holy center of creation, which would continue as long as the temple in question stood. But the concept would have developed into an eternal statute with the

1. Cf. Houtman, *Exodus*, 3:524–53.

2. Cf. Koch, who attempts to establish a model for the tradition-historical composition of Exodus 25–40, albeit on very different grounds (*Priesterschrift*).

presumed destruction of the Shiloh sanctuary and the transfer of the Aaronide priesthood to the Jerusalem temple and its successors, i.e., the Second Temple and the presumed Third Temple portrayed in Ezekiel 40–48, which is yet to come.

Exodus 29:9b–14 discusses the initial bull and its role in sanctifying the altar. The passage is demarcated at the outset in Exodus 29:9b by the instruction "and you shall fill the hand Aaron and the hand of his sons." The idiom "and you shall fill the hand of Aaron" (Hebrew, *ûmillēʾtā yad-ʾahărōn*) refers to the ordination of Aaron (and his sons), insofar as their service as holy priests entails "filling their hands" with the ordination ram and the "sacrifices of well-being" (Lev 3) as their due in return for their service as priests. Such provision enables the priests to devote their time to the holy activities of the tent of meeting and later the temple; their support from the offerings of the people enables them to forego their own work at providing food for themselves. The passage then discusses the slaughter of the bull at the entrance of the tent of meeting and the use of its blood to sanctify the horns and the base of the altar. By laying their hands on the bull, they metaphorically sanctify the bull for sacrifice by symbolically endowing the bull with their own holy status as priests. Insofar as the altar stands before the entrance to the tent of meeting, all the people can witness their offering of the consecration as only the priests are authorized to enter the tent of meeting itself. The entrails of the bull are then burned on the altar, and the rest of the bull is burned outside the camp as "a sin offering" (Hebrew, *ḥaṭṭaʾt*) to YHWH (Lev 4:1–26).

Exodus 29:15–18 discusses the offering of the first ram as a whole burnt offering. Again, Aaron and his sons metaphorically sanctify the ram by laying their hands upon it. The blood of the ram is used to sanctify the altar, and the ram is cut into pieces in relation to the major joints of its body. The ram is then offered as "a whole burnt offering" (Hebrew, *ʿōlâ*) (Lev 1) to YHWH. YHWH clearly does not need to eat food, and so that whole burnt offering functions as a symbolic offering of food to YHWH.

Exodus 29:19–28 discusses the offering of the second ram as the ram of ordination (Exod 29:22), including its various components: viz., the use of the blood drawn from the ram to sanctify and Aaron and his sons in Exodus 29:19–21; the presentation of the right thigh of the ram and the various elements of the entrails as part of the whole burnt offering to YHWH in Exodus 29:22–25; and the presentation of the breast of the ram as "an elevation offering" (Hebrew, *tĕnûpâ*) to Aaron and his sons in Exodus 29:26–28, from which they will present "a gift offering" (*tĕrûmâ*) to YHWH. The Hebrew term *tĕnûpâ*, "elevation offering," is based on the verb root *nwp*, which means "to elevate/wave/shake" (cf. Isa 10:32),[3] and the *tĕrûmâ*, "gift offering," is based on the root *rwm*, which means "to be high/exalted/rise."[4]

The first component of this instruction appears in Exodus 29:19–21, which calls for the second ram to be offered to sanctify Aaron and his sons as priests. Just as sacrificial blood was used to sanctify the altar, so the blood of the second ram will be used to sanctify Aaron and his sons. Blood from the ram is daubed upon the right earlobe of Aaron and his sons, and also upon the thumb of their right hand and the big toe of their right foot. These are parts of the body that protrude—and so they are especially visible, and the focus on the right side apparently presupposes the right side as the ideal side of the human body. The rest of the blood is then poured upon the altar and the holy garments of Aaron and his sons to sanctify them as well.

Exodus 29:29–30 discusses the use of the holy garments by the sons of Aaron after his lifetime. This sub-unit presents a relatively brief statement that the holy garments tailored for Aaron will pass on to his sons who succeed him as priests, once they undergo the seven-day ordination period discussed in Exodus 29 and Leviticus 8. The statement would presumably envision the tailoring of new holy garments to replace those that had worn out or become otherwise damaged and therefore unusable.

Exodus 29:31–34 presents instruction concerning the cooking and consumption of the ram of ordination by Aaron and his sons when they are ordained. The sub-unit indicates that those of the House of Aaron who are ordained to serve as holy priests are eligible to eat the meat of the ram of ordination and the bread made from the grain offerings that accompany it. Foreigners may not eat meat from the ram of ordination. Any meat or bread that remains until morning will be burned, presumably because decomposition will render it unfit for holy consumption.

Exodus 29:35–37 discusses the seven-day process of priestly ordination, including the presentation of a bull as a sin offering on each of the days to consecrate the altar. A bull from the herd is to be offered as a sin offering for those undergoing ordination and for the altar on each of

3. "*nûp*," BDB 631–32.

4. "*rûm tĕrûmâ*," BDB 926–27, 929.

the seven days of the ordination process. The sin offerings thereby play a role in the sanctification of the ordination candidates and the altar to establish their holy character as a result of their sacred involvement in the shedding of blood at the altar.

Finally, Exodus 29:38–46 discusses the daily offering of two rams as whole burn offerings, one at the morning service and one at the evening service, as the basis for YHWH's meeting with Israel through the agency of Aaron and his sons for all time. The sub-unit specifies that two sheep, each of which is one year old, are to be offered every day, one in the morning and one at dusk. They are to be accompanied by grain offerings, i.e., a tenth of a measure of fine flour mixed with a quarter hin of beaten oil, and a libation offering of a quarter hin of wine for each sheep. Both offerings are understood to constitute a whole burnt offering for YHWH, here described as a pleasing odor and fire offering to YHWH, and they are expected to continue forever, as long as the tent of meeting or the subsequent sanctuaries stand.

The purpose of these offerings is to honor YHWH's presence in the world of creation. Exodus 29:42–46 specifies that YHWH will meet with the people of Israel through the agency of the Aaronide priests at the sanctuary site. Verse 42 names the offerings as "a continuous whole burnt offering for your generations" (Hebrew, *ʿōlat tāmîd lĕdōrōtêkem*) and it specifies that the offerings will be made at the entrance of the tent of meeting, where the altar is expected to stand for both the tent of meeting and subsequent temples. The presence of YHWH, here described as YHWH's "glory" (Hebrew, *kābôd*), will sanctify the sanctuary.

Verses 43–46 then summarize the tent of meeting as YHWH's place to meet with Israel and to sanctify both the tent of meeting and the priests of the House of Aaron. The tent of meeting and the subsequent temples thereby become the place where YHWH dwells among the sons of Israel in the world of creation. Verse 45b then follows with a statement drawn from the covenant formula, "and I will be G-d for them."[5] Verse 46 concludes with a statement of the "self-introduction" formula, also known as the prophetic proof saying, "I am YHWH," in which YHWH states the deliverance of Israel from Egypt as proof that YHWH has acted on Israel's behalf and therefore establishes YHWH's identity as Israel's G-d.[6]

5. Rendtorff, *Bundesformel*, esp. 48, 61, 63, 92, 93.

6. Hals, *Ezekiel*, 362–63; Sweeney, *Isaiah 40–66*, 403; Zimmerli, "I Am YHWH"; Zimmerli, "Word of Divine Self-Manifestation."

Reception History

Ephesians 5:2 cites Exodus 29:18 in an effort to depict Christ's crucifixion as an act of love in which Jesus was understood to serve as a fragrant offering to G-d. Paul cites Exodus 29:18 to characterize the gifts received from Epaphroditus metaphorically as "a fragrant offering, a sacrifice acceptable and pleasing to G-d," in Philippians 4:18.

In rabbinic tradition, the laying on of hands is employed as a term (Hebrew, *sĕmîkâ*) for the ordination of rabbis.[7]

7. Jastrow, *Dictionary*, 2:1000.

The Account of YHWH's Instructions to Moses Concerning the Construction of the Incense Altar, the Census of Israel, the Basin for Washing, the Anointing Oil, and the Incense —Exodus 30:1–37

Translation

30:1 And you shall make an altar [for] burning incense; of
acacia wood you shall make it. [2] A cubit long and a cubit
wide; square it shall be, and two cubits high; from it shall its
horns be. [3] And you shall overlay it with pure gold, its top
and its sides round about, and its horns, and you shall make
for it a border of gold round about. [4] And two rings of gold
you shall make for it; from under its border upon its two
side supports you shall make upon its two sides, and it shall
be for housings for poles with which to carry it. [5] And you
shall make the poles of acacia wood, and you shall overlay
them with wood.

[6] And you shall place it before the curtain that is over the ark
of the witness before the cover that is over the witness, where
I will meet with you. [7] And Aaron shall burn upon it incense

of spices every morning when he prepares the lamps he shall burn it. 8 And when Aaron lights the lamps at dusk he shall burn it, a continual incense offering before YHWH for your generations. 9 You shall not light upon it foreign incense or a whole burnt offering or a grain offering, and a libation you shall not pour out upon it. 10 And Aaron shall atone upon its horns once a year; from the blood of the sin offering of atonement once a year he shall make atonement upon it for your generations. It is a holy of holies for YHWH.

11 And YHWH spoke to Moses saying, 12 When you raise the head of the sons of Israel for their mustering, then each of them shall give a payment for his life to YHWH when mustering them, so there will not be among them a plague when mustering them. 13 This is what all those who enter upon the musters shall give: half a shekel by the shekel of the sanctuary, twenty gerahs per shekel, half a shekel as a gift to YHWH. 14 All who enter upon the muster, from twenty years old and above, shall give a gift to YHWH. 15 The rich shall not give more, and the poor shall not give less than half a shekel to give a gift for YHWH to atone for their lives. 16 And you shall take the money of atonement from the sons of Israel, and you shall give it for the work of the tent of meeting, and it shall be for the sons of Israel for a remembrance before YHWH to atone for their lives.

17 And YHWH spoke to Moses saying, 18 And you shall make a basin of bronze and a stand of bronze for washing, and you shall place it between the ten of meeting and the altar, and you shall place there water. 19 And Aaron and his sons shall wash from it their hands and their feet. 20 When they come into the tent of meeting, they shall wash with water so that they will not die, or when they approach the altar to serve, to burn a fire offering to YHWH. 21 And they shall wash their hands and their feet so they will not die, and it shall be for them an eternal statute for him and for his seed for their generations.

22 And YHWH spoke to Moses saying, 23 And you, take for yourself top spices, flowing myrrh, five hundred; fragrant

cinnamon, half, two hundred and fifty; fragrant cane, two
hundred and fifty; 24 and cassia, five hundred by the shekel
of the sanctuary; and pure olive oil, a hin. 25 And you shall
make it into holy anointing oil, a mixture of ingredients, a
blended work; holy anointing oil it shall be. 26 And you shall
anoint with it the tent of meeting and the ark of the witness.
27 And the table and all its equipment, and the lampstand and
its equipment, and the alter of incense. 28 And the altar of the
whole burnt offering and all of its equipment, and the basin
and its stand. 29 And you shall sanctify it, and they shall be
holy of holies; all who touch it shall be holy. 30 And Aaron
and his sons you shall anoint, and you shall sanctify them to
serve as priests for me.

31 And unto the sons of Israel you shall speak, saying, Holy
anointing oil this shall be to me for your generations. 32 Upon
human flesh it shall not be anointed, and in its measures you
shall not make anything like it; holy it is, holy it shall be to
you. 33 Whoever mixes anything like it, and whoever places
some of it upon a foreigner shall be cut off from his people.

34 And YHWH said to Moses, Take for yourself spices, stacte
and onycha and galbanum spices, and pure frankincense,
part by part it shall be. 35 And you shall make it into incense,
a mixture, a work of mixing, salted, pure, holy. 36 And you
shall pulverize from it fine powder, and you shall place some
of it before the witness in the tent of meeting where I will
meet you. Holy of holies it shall be to you. 37 And the incense
that you shall make, according to its measures, you shall
not make for yourselves; holy it shall be for you, for YHWH.
38 And anyone who makes like it to smell with it, then he
shall be cut off from his people.

Commentary

Exodus 30:1–37 recounts YHWH's instructions to Moses concerning the construction or production of the incense altar, the census of Israel, the basin for washing, the anointing oil, and the incense. Some interpreters consider this to be a supplementary section to the basic account of

YHWH's instructions to Moses, although the passage takes up a number of smaller items, supplies, and procedures that are necessary for the operation of the tent of meeting and the later temples of Israel.[1]

The first sub-unit of this text appears in Exodus 30:1–10, which presents YHWH's instruction to Moses concerning the construction and placement of the incense altar. The purpose of the incense altar is to produce the unique smell of a special recipe for incense that will metaphorically represent YHWH's presence in the sanctuary. The altar will be built of acacia wood, a cubit square on top and two cubits high, overlaid with gold, and with four horns protruding from the top to represent rays or beams of light or smoke proceeding out to the four cardinal directions of creation. Again, gold rings are to be fitted, which will be used to fit poles with which to carry the altar. The placement of the incense altar will be in the central area of the tent of meeting, corresponding to the *heikhal* of the temple, before the cover that will shield the holy of holies where the ark of the witness is to be placed. It therefore is placed before the location of the metaphorical throne of YHWH from which YHWH will meet with Israel through the agency of the priest in the sanctuary. Aaron and the succeeding priests will light the incense altar prior to the morning and evening services as a continuous incense offering to YHWH for all time. No foreign incense, i.e., incense produced from a different recipe (see vv. 34–37 below) will be offered in the sanctuaries with the whole burnt offerings, grain offerings, or libations. Leviticus 10:1–7, in an effort to demonstrate the importance of observing this instruction, recounts how Aaron's first two sons, Nadab and Abihu, died for offering foreign incense before YHWH. Aaron and his sons are to purify the incense altar once a year with blood to atone for the potential defilement of the sanctuary, perhaps on Yom Kippur, the Day of Atonement.

Exodus 30:11–16 recounts YHWH's instructions to Moses concerning the census of Israel. The census of Israel is conducted in part to assess the people for the temple tax to be paid annually to support the temple—or in this case, the tent of meeting—thereby to prevent the people from suffering punishment. Leviticus 27:1–8 discusses the temple tax, and 2 Samuel 24 recounts the consequences of failing to pay a temple tax prior to the census of the people in the time of David. All men from age twenty and above are obligated to the pay the half-shekel temple tax on an annual basis. The half shekel is valued, apparently in common with

1. Meyers, *Exodus*, 250.

the Egyptian weight system, at twenty gerahs, and a shekel weighs approximately 16.667 grams for the common shekel and 16.74 grams for the royal shekel, according to Mesopotamian weights.[2] Everyone, regardless of their wealth, is obligated to pay the same tax.

Exodus 30:17–21 recounts YHWH's instructions to Moses for the construction of the basin for washing in the tent of meeting. The basin and its stand are to be cast from bronze, but the instructions give no size. It is to be placed between the entrance to the tent of meeting and the sacrificial altar located before the entrance. The purpose is so that the priests may wash their hands and feet with water when offering sacrifices at the altar.

Exodus 30:22–33 presents YHWH's instructions to Moses concerning the mixing of anointing oil. Anointing oil is made from a mixture of a hin (0.46 liter)[3] of pure olive oil mixed with spices, including five hundred shekels of flowing myrrh, two hundred and fifty shekels of fragrant cinnamon, two hundred and fifty shekels of fragrant cane, and five hundred shekels of cassia. The ingredients are to be blended and used to anoint the tent of meeting, the ark of the witness, and all of the equipment associated with them, apparently to ensure their divine odor. Anyone coming into contact with these items, i.e., Aaron and his sons, must be sanctified by anointing as well. No one is to use this special mixture of anointing oil for themselves. To do so will result in the offending party to be cut off from the people.

Finally, Exodus 30:34–37 presents YHWH's instructions for the production of incense from a mixture of spices, including stacte, onycha, galbanum spices, and pure frankincense. The spices are apparently to be used in equal parts, pulverized into fine dust, and salted. Again, anyone using this formula for personal reasons will be cut off from the people. Note also Numbers 16–17, in which Korah, Dothan, Abiram, and their followers revolted against Moses and Aaron when they presented their fire pans filled with incense, in an effort to challenge their authority. When YHWH rejected their offering, the earth opened up and swallowed them, sending them on their way to Sheol.

2. Dever, "Weight and Measures," esp. 1206.

3. Dever, "Weights and Measures," 1210–11.

The Account of YHWH's Instructions to Moses Concerning the Appointment of the Artisans to Oversee the Construction of the Tent of Meeting and the Observance of Shabbat —Exodus 31:1–18

Translation

31:1 And YHWH spoke to Moses, saying, [2] See, I have called upon the name of Bezalel ben Uri ben Hur of the tribe of Judah [3] and I have filled him with the spirit of G-d, with wisdom, and with understanding, and knowledge in all work, [4] to conceive plans for work in gold and in silver and in bronze, [5] and to cut stone for settings, and in the cutting of wood in all work. [6] And I, behold, I, have placed with him Oholiab ben Ahisamach of the tribe of Dan, and in the heart of all who are wise of heart I have given wisdom so that they may do all that I have commanded, [7] the tent of meeting, and the ark of the witness, and the covering that is upon it, and all the equipment of the tent, [8] and the table and its equipment, and the pure lampstand and all of its equipment, and the incense altar, [9] and the altar of the burnt offering and all of its equipment, and the basin and its stand, [10] and the braided garments, and the holy garments for Aaron, the priest, and the garments of his sons to serve as priests, [11] and the anointing oil, and the incense of spices for the sanctuary; according to all that I have commanded you, they shall do.

[12] And YHWH said to Moses, saying, [13] And you, speak to the sons of Israel, saying, Indeed, my Shabbats you shall observe for it is a sign between me and between you for your generations that I, YHWH, sanctify you. [14] And you shall observe the Shabbat for it is holy to you. Whoever profanes it shall surely die, for all who do work on it, that person shall be cut off from the midst of his people. [15] Six days shall work be done, but on the seventh day is a holy Shabbat Shabbaton for YHWH; all who do work on the Shabbat day shall surely die. [16] And the sons of Israel shall observe the Shabbat, to do the Shabbat for their generations as an eternal covenant. [17] Between me and between the sons of Israel it is an eternal sign, for in six days YHWH made the heavens and the earth, but on the seventh day, he stopped, and he was refreshed.

[18] And he gave to Moses when he finished speaking with him on Mount Sinai two tablets of the witness, tablets of stone inscribed with the finger of G-d.

Commentary

Exodus 31:1–18 recounts YHWH's instructions to Moses concerning the appointment of the artisans to oversee the construction of the tent of meeting and the observance of Shabbat. The passage comprises three major sub-units, viz., the account of YHWH's instructions to Moses concerning the appointment of the artisans, i.e., Bezalel ben Uri ben Hur of the tribe of Judah and Oholiab ben Ahisamach of the tribe of Dan, in Exodus 31:1–11; the account of YHWH's instructions concerning the observance of Shabbat in Exodus 31:12–17; and a concluding statement concerning YHWH's instructions to Moses on Mount Sinai in Exodus 31:18.

YHWH's instructions to Moses to appoint Bezalel ben Uri ben Hur of the tribe of Judah and Oholiab ben Ahisamach of the tribe of Dan have important implications for understanding the narrative, both in relation to its presumed final P-stratum form and its postulated E-stratum origins. The reference to Bezalel ben Uri ben Hur of the tribe of Judah points clearly to the P-stratum character of the present form of the text, insofar as it features a Judean tribal member as the leading artisan in the construction of the wilderness tent of meeting (see also Exod 35:30; 36:1–2; 37:1; 38:22; 1 Chr 2:20; 2 Chr 1:5).[1] Bezalel's grandfather, Hur, is also mentioned prominently in two earlier J-stratum narratives, viz., the account of Moses's ascent to Mount Sinai alone in which Aaron and Hur are left to administer the people of Israel in Exodus 24:12–14[2] and the account of the war with Amalek in Exodus 17:8–16.[3] Hur's presence in these J-stratum narratives points to a development in the character of Hur as a Judean figure who is then tapped in the P-stratum narrative as the ancestor of Bezalel. But the inclusion of Oholiab ben Ahisamach of the tribe of Dan is especially interesting. He appears only in P-stratum texts, including Exodus 31:6; 35:34; 36:1–2; and 38:23, which apart from the present text appear in Exodus 35–40 to depict Israel's compliance with the instructions given to Moses by YHWH in Exodus 25–30. Such an interest in an artisan from the tribe of Dan clearly serves the P-stratum agenda to include all the tribes of Israel within the larger Israelite nation, but it also points to the potential northern origins of the narrative in a postulated E-stratum account of YHWH's instructions concerning the building of the tent of meeting in Exodus 25–30 and Israel's compliance with those instructions in Exodus 35–40.

Exodus 31:12–17 recounts YHWH's instructions to Moses concerning Israel's observance of the Shabbat as an eternal covenant (Hebrew, *bĕrît ʿôlâm*) and a "sign" (Hebrew, *ʾôt*) between YHWH and Israel. Consequently, the observance of the Shabbat emerges as the key observance of ancient Israel and Judaism. Interpreters generally view this passage as a P-stratum composition,[4] and many subsequently argue that observance of the Shabbat is a late development in the history of Judaism, beginning in the time of Nehemiah and Ezra (Neh 13:19–22). But the discussion above has already noted the inclusion of laws concerning agriculture and treatment of the poor in the Covenant Code in Exodus 23:1–12, which, in addition to calling for the observance of Shabbat, employs the

1. Campbell and O'Brien, *Sources of the Pentateuch*, 53–61.
2. Campbell and O'Brien, *Sources of the Pentateuch*, 146.
3. Campbell and O'Brien, *Sources of the Pentateuch*, 144–45.
4. Campbell and O'Brien, *Sources of the Pentateuch*, 52.

principle of Shabbat to call for fields to lie fallow every seventh year so that the poor might collect grain.[5] The release of Hebrew slaves also presupposes the Shabbat principle, insofar as it stipulates the release of a Hebrew slave following seven years of service, unless he chooses to remain a slave. The inclusion of these laws in the Covenant Code, which originates in northern Israel during the late ninth and early eighth centuries BCE, points to the observance of Shabbat in the Northern Kingdom of Israel and the recognition of this principle in the northern Israelite Covenant Code. Such an appearance indicates the origins of Shabbat observance in northern Israel and the development of the concept in relation to the compositional history of the Pentateuch from the initial E-stratum through the P-stratum of the Pentateuch.[6]

Following the narrative tag in v. 12 that introduces YHWH's speech to Moses in vv. 12–17, v. 12 opens YHWH's speech with the basic instruction, directed to Israel, to observe the Shabbat as a "sign" between YHWH and Israel "for your generations" (Hebrew, *lĕdōrōtêkem*), a term that is understood to entail eternal observance. A form of the prophetic proof saying or recognition formula, "because I am YHWH who sanctifies you," follows to indicate YHWH as the source of this particular instruction.[7] The following verses then develop the concept. Verse 14 identifies the Shabbat as "holy" (Hebrew, *qōdeš*), and it employs the death sentence formula to specify that anyone who profanes the Shabbat by doing work on it "shall be put to death" (Hebrew, *môt yûmāt*) and be "cut off" from his people.[8]

Verse 15 reiterates the instruction to observe the Shabbat, based on early forms of the instructions that appear in the Covenant Code in Exodus 20:8–11 and 23:12, albeit lacking the death sentence formula. Verse 16 then restates the instruction that the sons of Israel shall observe the Shabbat "for their generations," and then specifies that this instruction is a *bĕrît ʿôlâm*. Although *bĕrît ʿôlâm* is generally understood as "eternal covenant" in the P-stratum of the Pentateuch, the Hebrew term *ʿôlâm* also means "world," especially in rabbinic Hebrew, Aramaic, Syriac, and other Semitic languages.[9] The term *bĕrît ʿôlâm*, "covenant of the world/

5. Sweeney, "Shabbat."

6. Sweeney, "Laws of Slavery."

7. Hals, *Ezekiel*, 362–63; Sweeney, *Isaiah 40–66*, 403; Zimmerli, "I Am YHWH"; Zimmerli, "Word of Divine Self-Manifestation."

8. Knierim and Coats, *Numbers*, 364; Schulz, *Todesrecht*.

9. "☒*ôlām*," BDB 761.

creation," therefore can be applied to the duration of creation, which is tied to the duration of a sanctuary in the ancient world, such as the temple of Marduk in Babylon or the temple of Baal in Ugarit, both of which are built as a result of Marduk's and Baal's defeat of chaos figures (i.e., Tiamat and Yamm, respectively). Interpreters should also note how the *bĕrît ʿôlâm* is broken in Isaiah 24:5, thereby resulting in the desolation of creation in Isaiah 24:1–23, and creation is renewed in Ezekiel 47 when the temple of YHWH is rebuilt, thereby resulting in the renewal of creation, particularly the Dead Sea. Insofar as the Exodus–Numbers narrative functions as a creation narrative, the reference here to a *bĕrît ʿôlâm* indicates a covenant of the world/creation due to the building of the wilderness tabernacle and the subsequent temples that will follow in Gilgal, Shiloh, Beth El, Dan, Arad, Beer Sheba, Jerusalem, and elsewhere where people will recognize YHWH's acts of creation, both in the natural world and in the creation of the nation, Israel, and in leading Israel to the promised land.[10] Such an understanding ties the *bĕrît ʿôlâm* to the E-stratum narrative of the exodus and wilderness traditions, which emphasize YHWH's acts of creation.

Verse 17 continues the reiteration of the Shabbat motif by tying it to the P-stratum narrative of YHWH's creation in Genesis 1:1—2:3 as well as to the above-noted references from the northern Israelite Covenant Code.

Finally, Exodus 31:18 closes the narrative of YHWH's instruction to Moses in Exodus 25–31 with a notice of YHWH's giving Moses the two tablets of the witness, "written with the finger of G-d" (Hebrew, *kĕtubîm bĕʾeṣbaʿ ʾĕlōhîm*). The reference to "G-d" suggests the influence of the E-stratum composition, which presumably underlies the current form of this text. Exodus 31:18 then forms an editorial envelope with Exodus 24:12–18, which introduces the account of YHWH's instructions to Moses on Mount Sinai in Exodus 25–31.

Reception History

Exodus 31:16–17, "And the sons of Israel shall observe the Shabbat, to do the Shabbat for their generations as an eternal covenant. Between me and between the sons of Israel it is an eternal sign, for in six days YHWH made the heavens and the earth, but on the seventh day, he stopped, and

10. See also Sweeney, "Creation as Sacred Space."

he was refreshed," was added to the Shabbat morning Amidah, "standing," prayer, which stands as the centerpiece of the prayer service. The passage was added during the Talmudic period after the Ten Commandments were removed from the service to counter assertions that only the Ten Commandments were important.[11] The passage is also traditionally sung at the Kiddush, or Shabbat morning lunch, that follows the morning Shabbat service, either at home or in the synagogue.[12]

11. Donin, *To Pray as a Jew*, 114; Idelsohn, *Jewish Liturgy*, 136.
12. Millgrom, *Jewish Worship*, 299.

The Golden Calf Narrative —Exodus 32:1—34:35

Overview

EXODUS 32–34 APPEARS BETWEEN the account of YHWH's instruction to Moses concerning the building of the wilderness tabernacle in Exodus 25–31 and the account of Israel's compliance with YHWH's instructions in Exodus 35–40. It recounts the golden calf incident in which Israel, frustrated in waiting for Moses to come down from Mount Sinai, abandons its adherence to YHWH and commences to worship the golden calf.

Although both Exodus 25–31 and 35–40 are P-stratum narratives in their current form, Exodus 32–34 is largely a J-stratum narrative, albeit with hints of E-stratum material underlying its present form.[1] Earlier understandings of pentateuchal source criticism would have viewed J as the earliest source of the Pentateuch, but recognition of the J-stratum as a late monarchy period text in recent years opens the way to see Exodus 32–34 as a critique of the Northern Kingdom of Israel and its building of golden calf images at Dan and Beth El. It is clear that the golden calves are not actually worshipped as gods as the narrative contends. The golden calves actually functioned as mounts, in keeping with typical ancient Near Eastern practice, upon which YHWH was understood to be invisibly mounted. Such practice would have been analogous to the role played by the ark of the witness/covenant, which was understood to represent YHWH's throne, upon which YHWH was invisibly seated, in the Jerusalem temple. Southern Judean scribes would have portrayed

1. Campbell and O'Brien, *Sources of the Pentateuch*, 146–49, 189–90, 199.

them as such during the late monarchic period in an effort to explain the destruction and exile of the Northern Kingdom of Israel in 722–721 BCE. In order to accomplish such an agenda, the narrative draws upon and frequently reworks earlier narratives, such as: the Covenant Code in Exodus 20–24; the law prohibiting intermarriage with the Canaanite nations in Deuteronomy 7:1–6; the critique of King Jeroboam ben Nebat of northern Israel in 1 Kings 12:25—13:34; and the account of YHWH's revelation to Elijah at Mount Horeb in 1 Kings 19.[2]

In addition to attempting to explain the destruction and exile of the Northern Kingdom of Israel, Exodus 32–34 explains Aaron's need for assistance in his future role as high priest, the role of the Levites as the holy assistants of the sons of Aaron in place of the earlier practice of commissioning the firstborn sons of Israel, and Moses's own close relationship with YHWH as the premier prophet or oracle diviner.

Translation

> 32:1 And the people saw that Moses delayed to come down
> from the mountain, and the people assembled against Aaron,
> and they said to him, "Get up! Make for us gods that will go
> before us, for this Moses—the man who brought us up from
> the land of Egypt—we do not know what has become of him."
> [2] And Aaron said them, "Tear off the rings of gold that are in
> the ears of your women, your sons, and your daughters, and
> bring them to me." [3] And all the people tore off the rings of
> gold that were in their ears, and they brought them to Aaron.
> [4] And he took [it] from their hand, and he fashioned it with
> an engraving tool and he made it [into] a molten calf, and
> they said, "These are your gods, O Israel, who brought you
> up from the land of Egypt." [5] And Aaron saw, and he built an
> altar before it, and Aaron proclaimed and said, "A festival for
> YHWH tomorrow!" [6] And they arose early the next day, and
> they offered whole burnt offerings, and they brought near
> sacrifices of well-being, and the people sat down to eat and
> drink, and they arose to celebrate.

2. Sweeney, "Wilderness Traditions"; Sweeney, *Reading the Bible After the Shoah*, 52–62. See also Sweeney, *Pentateuch*, xvii–xxix, 50–52; Sweeney, *1–2 Kings*, 172–82; 216–34; Anderson, who emphasizes the role of the final P redaction in its attempt to argue that the covenant may be restored in the Persian period ("Tablets of Testimony").

[7] And YHWH spoke to Moses, "Go down, for your people whom you brought up from the land of Egypt have acted corruptly. [8] They have turned away quickly from the path that I commanded them. They have made for themselves a molten calf, and they have bowed down to it, and they have sacrificed to it, and they have said, 'These are your gods, O Israel, who brought you up from the land of Egypt.'" [9] And YHWH [also] said to Moses, "I have seen this people, and behold, it is [a] stiff-necked people! [10] And now, leave me alone so that my anger shall blaze out against them and finish them, and I will make you into a great nation." [11] And Moses appealed to YHWH, his G-d, and he said, "Why, YHWH, would your anger blaze out against your people whom you brought out from the land of Egypt with great strength and a strong hand? [12] Why should the Egyptians say, 'With evil intent he brought them out to kill them in the mountains and to finish them from upon the face of the land? Turn back from your blazing anger and cancel the evil for your people. [13] Remember Abraham, Isaac, and Israel, your servants, to whom you swore by yourself, and you spoke to them, 'I will multiply your seed like the stars of the heavens, and all this land which I said, I will give [it] to your seed so that they will inherit [it] forever.'" [14] And YHWH cancelled the evil which he spoke to do to his people.

[15] And Moses turned, and he went down from the mountain, and the two tablets of the witness were in his hand, tablets written on both sides, on one side and the other they were written. [16] And the tablets were the work of G-d, and the writing was the writing of G-d, inscribed on the tablets. [17] And Joshua heard the sound of the people in its shouting, and he said to Moses, "The sound of war is in the camp!" [18] And he said, "There is no sound of singing in victory, and there is no sound of singing of defeat! It is the sound of singing that I do not know!"

[19] And when he drew near to the camp, and he saw the calf and the dancing, the anger of Moses blazed out, and he cast down from his hands the tablets, and he shattered them at the foot of the mountain. [20] And he took the calf, which they had made, and he burned it, and he ground it to dust, and

he scattered it upon the face of the waters, and he made the sons of Israel drink [it].

21 And Moses said to Aaron, "What has this people done to you that you brought upon it great sin?" 22 And Aaron said, "Let not the anger of my lord blaze forth! You know this people, that it is inclined to evil! 23 And they said to me, 'Make for us gods that will go before us because this Moses—the man who brought us up from the land of Egypt—we do not know what has become of him.' 24 And I said to them, 'Whoever has gold, tear it off!' And they gave it to me, and I cast it into the fire, and this calf came out."

25 And Moses saw the people, that they were beyond control, because Aaron let them go out of control to be an object of derision among those who stood against them. 26 And Moses stood by the gate of the camp, and he said, "Whoever is for YHWH, [come] to me!" And all the sons of Levi were gathered to him. 27 And he said to them, "Thus says YHWH, the G-d of Israel, 'Each man, put on his sword on thigh! Pass through and back, from gate to gate in the camp, and kill, each his brother, and each his neighbor, and each his kin!'" 28 And the sons of Levi did as Moses spoke, and there fell from the people on that day about three thousand men. 29 And Moses said, "Commission yourselves today to YHWH, for each of you is against his son and his brother, to give upon yourselves a blessing today."

30 And on the next day, Moses said to the people, "You have sinned a great sin! And now, I will go up to YHWH. Perhaps I will be able to atone for your sin." 31 And Moses returned to YHWH, and he said, "Ah, now! This people has sinned a great sin! And they have made for themselves gods of gold. 32 And now, if you will pardon their sin, [good], but if not, erase me, please, from your account which you have written." 33 And YHWH said to Moses, "Whoever has sinned to me, I will erase from my account. 34 But now, go, lead the people to where I spoke to you. Behold, my angel will go before you, but on the day of my punishment, I will punish them for their sin."

35 And YHWH plagued the people because of what they did with the calf that Aaron made.

33:1 And YHWH spoke to Moses, "Go, go up from this [place], you and the people whom you brought up from the land of Egypt to the land that I swore to Abraham, to Isaac, and to Jacob, saying, 'To your seed, I will give it.' 2 And I will send before you an angel, and I will drive out the Canaanites, the Amorites and the Hittites, and the Perizzites, the Hivvites, and the Jebusites, 3 unto a land flowing with milk and honey, but I will not go up in your midst, for a people of stiff neck are you, lest I destroy you on the road." 4 And the people heard this evil word, and they mourned, and each man would not put his ornaments upon himself. 5 And YHWH said to Moses, "Say to the sons of Israel, 'You are a stiff-necked people. [For] one moment I would go up in your midst, and I would destroy you. So now, put down your ornaments from upon you so that I can know what I will do with you." 6 And the sons of Israel stripped themselves of their ornaments from [their time at] Mount Horeb.

7 And Moses would take the tent, and he would set it up for himself outside of the camp, far away from the camp, and he would call it the tent of meeting, and all those seeking YHWH would go out to the tent of meeting, which was outside of the camp. 8 And it would be when Moses went out to the tent, all the people would rise, and they would stand, each at the entrance to his tent, and they would look after Moses until his entering the tent. 9 And it would be when Moses entered the tent, the pillar of cloud would go down, and it would stand at the entrance to the tent, and he would speak with Moses. 10 And all the people saw the pillar of cloud standing at the entrance of the tent, and all the people would rise, and they would bow down, each at the entrance of his [own] tent. 11 And YHWH would speak to Moses face-to-face, just as a man would speak to his neighbor, and he would return to the camp, and his guard, Joshua ben Nun, a young man, would not depart from the midst of the tent.

12 And Moses said to YHWH, "See, you say to me, 'Bring this people up,' but you do not let me know where you will send my people, and you said, 'I know you by name, and you have found favor in my eyes.' 13 And now, if, please, I have found favor in your eyes, let me know, please, your ways, so that I will know you in order that I will find favor in your eyes, and see that your people is this nation." 14 And he said, "My presence [lit., face] will go, and I will give you rest." 15 And he said to him, "If your presence [lit., face] is not going, do not bring us up from this [place]. 16 And how shall it be known where [we are going] if I and your people have found favor in your eyes? Is it not when you go with us, that we are distinguished, I and your people, from all the people on the face of the earth?" 17 And YHWH said to Moses, "Even this thing that you have spoken, I will do, for you have found favor in my eyes, and I know you by name." 18 And he said, "Show me, please, your glory." 19 And he said, "I will cause to pass by all my goodness before your face, and I will proclaim in the Name of YHWH before you, and I will be gracious to whom I will be gracious, and I will be merciful to whom I will be merciful." 20 And he said, "You will not be able to see my face, for the human will not see my face and live." 21 And YHWH said, "Behold, a place by me, and you will stand upon the rock, 22 and it will be when my glory passes by, then I will place you in a crevice of the rock, and I will make my palm cover you over until I pass, 23 and I will remove my palm, and you will see my back, but my face you will not see."

34:1 And YHWH said to Moses, "Cut for yourself two tablets of stone like the first ones, so that I will write upon the tablets the words that were on the first tablets which you shattered. 2 And be ready in the morning, and you will come up in the morning to Mount Sinai, and you will stand before me there upon the top of the mountain. 3 And no one shall go up with you, and also no one will be seen in all the mountain, even sheep and cattle shall not graze at the front of that mountain."

4 And Moses cut two tablets of stone like the first ones, and Moses got up early in the morning, and he went up to Mount

Sinai just as YHWH commanded him, and he took in his hand two tablets of stone. 5 And YHWH came down in the cloud, and he stood with him there, and he called out in the Name of YHWH. 6 And YHWH passed before his face, and he called out, "YHWH, YHWH, a G-d merciful and gracious, long [i.e., slow] on anger and abundant fidelity and truth, 7 guarding fidelity for thousands, pardoning iniquity and rebellion and sin, but surely he does not acquit, punishing the iniquity of the fathers upon sons and upon sons of sons upon the third and fourth generations."

8 And Moses quickly knelt down to the earth and prostrated himself, 9 and he said, "If, please, I have found grace in your eyes, my L-rd, go, please, my L-rd, in our midst because it is a stiff-necked people, and you shall pardon our iniquity and our sin, and you shall inherit us."

10 And he said, "Behold, I am cutting a covenant. Before all your people I will make wonders that have not been created in all the earth and among all the nations, and all the people in whose midst. You will see the work of YHWH, because wondrous is that which I do with you. 11 Observe for yourself that which I command you today. Behold, I am driving out from before you the Amorites and the Canaanites and the Hittites and the Perizzites and the Hivvites and the Jebusites. 12 Be careful for yourself lest you cut a covenant for the inhabitant of the land upon which you come, lest there be a trap in your midst. 13 For their altars you shall tear down, and their pillars you shall shatter, and their Asherim you shall cut down, 14 for you shall not prostrate yourself to another god, for YHWH, whose name is jealous, is a jealous G-d, 15 lest you cut a covenant for the inhabitant of the land, and whore after their gods, and sacrifice to their gods, and call for yourself, and you eat from his sacrifice, 16 and you take from his daughters for your sons, and his daughters will whore after their gods, and they will cause your sons to whore after their gods.

17 Molten gods you shall not make for yourself.

18 The Festival of Unleavened Bread you shall observe. For seven days, you shall eat unleavened bread just as I have

commanded you, for the appointed time in the month of Aviv because in the month of Aviv you went out from Egypt.

19 All that breaks the womb is mine, and all your cattle that are remembered with a breaking [of the womb], bull or sheep. 20 And the breaking of an ass you shall redeem with a sheep, but if you do not redeem it, you shall break its neck. All the firstborn of your sons you shall redeem, and they shall not appear before me empty handed.

21 Six days you shall work, but on the seventh day you shall cease; in plowing and in harvest you shall cease.

22 And the Festival of Weeks you shall make for yourself, the firstfruits of the harvest of wheat, and the Festival of the Ingathering at the turn of the year. 23 Three times in the year shall all your males appear before the L-rd, YHWH, G-d of Israel, 24 for I will dispossess nations from before you, and I will extend your borders, and no one will covet your land when you go up to see the face of YHWH, your G-d, three times in the year.

25 You shall not slaughter with leavening the blood of my sacrifice, and the sacrifice of the Festival of Passover shall not remain until morning.

26 The first of the firstfruits of your land you shall bring to the house of YHWH, your G-d."

27 And YHWH said to Moses, "Write for yourself these words, because according to these words I have cut with you a covenant and with Israel."

28 And he was there with YHWH forty days and forty nights. Bread he did not eat, and water he did not drink, and he wrote upon the tablets the words of the covenant, the Ten Words.

29 And Moses came down from Mount Sinai, and the two tablets of the witness were in the hand of Moses when he came down from the mountain, but Moses did not know that the skin of his face had become radiant when he spoken with him. 30 And Aaron and all the sons of Israel saw Moses, and behold, the skin of his face had become radiant, and they were

afraid to come near to him. [31] And Moses called out to them,
and Aaron and all the chieftains in the assembly returned to
him, and Moses spoke to them. [32] And afterwards, all the sons
of Israel came near, and he commanded them all that YHWH
had spoken with him on Mount Sinai. [33] And Moses finished
speaking with them, and he placed upon his face a veil.

[34] And when Moses came before YHWH to speak with him,
he removed the veil until he departed, and he departed and
he spoke to the sons of Israel that which he was commanded.
[35] And the sons of Israel saw the face of Moses, that the skin
of the face of Moses had become radiant, and Moses restored
the veil upon his face until he came to speak with him.

Commentary

The golden calf narrative begins in Exodus 32:1–6 with the apostasy of the people of Israel at Mount Sinai, by constructing a golden calf as an idol for worship in place of YHWH.[3] The apostasy is instigated when Moses remains on the mountain for a very long time, here signaled by the use of the verb *bōšēš*, generally translated as "he [Moses] delayed," although the verb means "to shame" or "to put to shame." As the people grew impatient with Moses's delay, they express fear or frustration about what happened to Moses and speak of him derisively (i.e., "for this Moses—the man who brought us up from the land of Egypt—we do not know what has become of him") and demand that Aaron make a god for them who will lead them in the wilderness. Aaron's characterization is very curious here; he functions as a holy man and leader who serves YHWH, but he does not argue with them and immediately acts to fulfill their demand. His command, that the people "tear off" (Hebrew, *pārĕqû*) their golden earrings, presumably acquired from the Egyptians when Israel departed from Egypt, suggests some harm or injury to be caused to the Israelite women, sons, and daughters. Aaron takes a metalworking tool, fashions the gold into a molten golden calf, and declares to the people, "These are your gods, O Israel, who brought you up from the land of Egypt."

3. For discussion, see esp. Sweeney, *Reading the Bible After the Shoah*, 52–57, 67–72; Sweeney, *1–2 Kings*, 172–82.

These are remarkable actions on Aaron's part because they relate intertextually with the account of the apostasies of Jeroboam ben Nebat, the first king of the Northern Kingdom of Israel following the revolt of the north against Solomon's son, Rehoboam, in 1 Kings 12:25–33. One of Jeroboam's first acts was to make two golden calves, one each for the northern sanctuaries at Beth El and Dan, declaring in nearly identical language in 1 Kings 12:28, "Behold, your gods, O Israel, who brought you up from the land of Israel." Although Jeroboam allegedly committed other acts of apostasy (1 Kgs 12:25—13:34), the construction of the golden calves, allegedly as idols for Israel's worship, symbolizes the charges of apostasy against northern Israel that appear throughout the book of Kings and justifies the destruction and exile of northern Israel by Assyria in 2 Kings 17. It should be noted, however, that the Kings narrative is the product of Judean efforts to discredit the Northern Kingdom and explain its destruction as the result of its apostasy against YHWH. The concluding notice in Exodus 32:6 indicates that the people ate, drank, and rose to celebrate, much like they did at Shiloh in 1 Samuel 1. Here is noteworthy that the verb "to celebrate" (Hebrew, *lĕṣaḥēq*) also has sexual connotations, such as those indicated in Genesis 26:8 or the Benjaminite seizure of brides at the Shiloh sanctuary in Judges 21:15–24.

It is also noteworthy that the construction of a golden calf is not inherently an act of apostasy. Gods in the ancient Near East were typically portrayed as mounted on bulls, lions, and other animals,[4] which functioned somewhat like the ark of the covenant in ancient Judah, which served as a throne for YHWH, both in the wilderness tabernacle or tent of meeting and in the Jerusalem temple (1 Sam 4:4; 2 Sam 6:2; 2 Kgs 19:15; Isa 37:16; Pss 80:2; 99:1; 1 Chr 13:6). The portrayals of Jeroboam's apostasy—and Israel's apostasy in the wilderness—is the product of Judean polemic against northern Israel in both instances that is intended to condemn northern Israel and motivate southern Judah to adhere to YHWH alone. Insofar as the priestly house of Aaron originally served in the Shiloh sanctuary of northern Israel, according to 1 Samuel 1–3 and 4, the placement of the golden calf narrative between the account of YHWH's instructions to Moses to build the wilderness tent of meeting and all of its fixtures in Exodus 25–31 and the account of Israel's compliance with YHWH's instructions in Exodus 35–40 is a deliberate effort to represent the shift of the House of Aaron from Shiloh in Israel's early

4. See *ANEP* 470–74, 479, 500–501, 522, 526, 534, 537.

history to Jerusalem, beginning with David's move to Jerusalem in 2 Samuel 5 and following. A further issue would be to demonstrate that Aaron does in fact need assistance, and the narrative will ultimately portray the Levites as the zealous assistants of Aaron and his sons, thereby justifying the displacement of the firstborn sons of Israel as Aaron's assistants in Numbers 3, 8, and 17–18. First Kings 12:31 charges that King Jeroboam appointed priests who were not from the tribe of Levi, which would account for the practice of appointing firstborn sons of Israel in northern sanctuaries, whereas David and later Solomon made sure to appoint priests from the sons of Zadok, a descendant of Aaron, and later Levites as the priestly assistants to the sons of Aaron in Jerusalem. The book of Chronicles ensures that all priests who came to Jerusalem were identified as Levites, even if Samuel–Kings identified them otherwise.

Exodus 32:7–8 and 32:9–14 then introduce a series of conversations between YHWH and Moses in which they discuss the responses to the golden calf episode. The first conversation in Exodus 32:7–8 merely presents YHWH's notice to Moses about the idolatrous actions of the people of Israel with regard to the golden calf in which it repeats the language of v. 4 to emphasize once again the intertextual relationship between the present narrative and the account of Jeroboam's apostasy in 1 Kings 12:31–33.

Exodus 32:9–14 then presents a very important conversation between YHWH and Moses in which YHWH notes the stiff-necked character of Israel, and proposes to Moses that Israel will be destroyed so that YHWH can make Moses into a great nation to replace them. Moses objects to YHWH's plan, thereby showing his own commitment to YHWH's covenant and his willingness to sacrifice himself should YHWH reject his objections. Moses reminds YHWH that YHWH made a covenant with Israel, and that any attempt to destroy Israel on YHWH's part would discredit YHWH in the view of the nations of the world, most notably Egypt. Such a comment reiterates the fact that YHWH's actions against Egypt (i.e., the Ten Plagues) demonstrated YHWH's power to Egypt and signaled that YHWH was the true G-d of creation and human life. But YHWH's proposed destruction of Israel in the wilderness would completely discredit YHWH in the eyes of the Egyptians—not to mention other nations—and undermine everything that YHWH had achieved in Exodus 1–15 and beyond. Moses also brings up YHWH's promises to the ancestors, Abraham, Isaac, and Jacob, about making their offspring as numerous as the stars of the heavens and about granting their descendants the land of Israel as an inheritance forever. Upon hearing Moses's reminders of YHWH's own obligations in the covenant with Israel, YHWH recognizes that Moses is correct, and YHWH therefore cancels the punishment.

Exodus 32:15–35 then recounts Moses's confrontation with Aaron and the people of Israel. The first segment of this textual sub-unit in Exodus 32:15–18 recounts Moses's descent from the mountain together with Joshua, who apparently had been left waiting outside of the cloud that Moses entered in Exodus 24:12–18. Upon approaching the Israelite camp, Joshua exclaimed that he heard the sound of war, but Moses explained that it was not the sound of war. Moses's comment in v. 18 begins with statements that it is neither the sound of "singing of strength [in battle]" (Hebrew, *ʿănôt gĕbûrâ*) nor the sound of "singing in weakness/prostration [in battle]" (Hebrew *ʿănôt ḥălûšâ*), i.e., it is neither the sound of victory nor defeat. Rather, it is the sound of "singing about deliverance from danger" (Hebrew, *ʿannôt*) that Moses hears. Although the verb, *ʿnh* IV, means "to sing," the rarely used Piel or intensive form of the verb means "to sing sweetly in relief," following deliverance from danger by G-d, in this case, the golden calf (cf. Isa 27:2; Ps 88:1).[5] The people think they are in danger, and they sing to the golden calf to call upon it as a god who will lead them out of danger in the wilderness.

Exodus 32:19–20 then portrays Moses's raging anger as he approaches the Israelite camp and sees what is going on. He throws the two tablets of the covenant down, shattering them. Moses then takes the golden calf, burns it, grinds it to dust, and then throws the dust into the water and makes the people drink it. This procedure is also employed by King Josiah when he burned down the shrine at Beth El, ground it to dust, and burned down the Asherah. The purpose of these actions is not only to destroy the offending object. The procedure is based on the instruction concerning the treatment of a woman suspected by her husband of having relations with another man in Numbers 5:11–31.[6] The husband takes her to the sanctuary, where the priest will make a grain offering to YHWH for her alleged transgression. The priest will then take sacred water in a clay vessel, mix dust from the floor of the sanctuary into the water, bare the woman's head, make her swear that no man other than her husband has had relations with her, offer the

5. "⊠*ānâ*," BDB 777.

6. For discussion of the instruction concerning Sotah, i.e., a woman suspected of adultery in Numbers 5:11–31, see esp. Milgrom, *Numbers*, 37–43.

grain offering to YHWH, and then make her drink the water with the dust mixed in. If she is innocent, nothing will happen to her, but if she is guilty, she will suffer pains and illness in her abdomen and thighs. The use of this procedure in Exodus 32 presumes that Israel is metaphorically the bride of YHWH and that by pursuing other gods, Israel has betrayed her husband, YHWH (cf. Hos 1–3; Jer 2; Ezek 16).[7] Moses employs this instruction to determine if the people of Israel have in fact committed metaphorical adultery against YHWH.

Exodus 32:21–24 presents Moses's interrogation of Aaron as to what happened. His question to Aaron presumes that the people were somehow guilty of causing Aaron to commit this great sin. Aaron's response, however, is outrageous, insofar as he takes no responsibility for the creation of the golden calf. Aaron's first statement reiterates the people's demand that Aaron make a god to lead them out of the wilderness, and it repeats their derisive language about Moses from v. 1. But rather than argue with the people that worship of a god other than YHWH might be wrong, Aaron simply accedes to their demand, orders them to tear off their golden earrings, throws the gold into the fire, and states remarkably that "this calf came out." He takes no responsibility for using metalworking tools to fashion the calf nor for his announcement to the people that "these are your gods, O Israel, who brought you up from the land of Egypt" in v. 4. Aaron's failure to take responsibility here displays a lack of character and commitment to his role as priest. Such a deficiency lays the groundwork for the much later decision by YHWH in Numbers 3, 8, and 17–18 to replace the firstborn sons as assistants to the sons of Aaron with the Levites, who will emerge as those zealous for YHWH in the following segment.

Exodus 32:25–29 presents the account of Moses's call for those who are for YHWH to come forward and the response of the Levites. Moses sees that the Israelites are out of control, which employs the terms *pāruʿa*, literally, "let loose/let go," and *parʿōh*, "loose/gone." The form is a deliberate pun on the Hebrew form of the noun *parʿōh*, "pharaoh," the standard Egyptian term, *pr-ʿo*, for the Egyptian king.[8] The pun is intended to suggest that the Israelites are still under the control of pharaoh, king of Egypt. Moses calls for support with the statement "Whoever is for YHWH, [come] to me" (Hebrew, *mî lyhwh, ʾēlāy*, lit., "Who is for YHWH,

7. See Baumann, *Love and Violence.*

8. "*parʿōh*," BDB 829.

to me!"). The Levites respond to Moses's call, and Moses instructs them to take up swords and kill anyone, including brothers, neighbors, and kin, throughout the camp, presumably those who have worshipped the golden calf. Three thousand Israelites die that day, although interpreters have not been able to explain why this particular number appears in the narrative. Moses's final statement to the Levites in v. 29 calls upon the Levites to "commission yourselves today to YHWH, for each of you is against his son and his brother, to give upon yourselves a blessing today." The language employed for commissioning yourselves in Hebrew is *mil'û yedkem*, literally, "fill your hand," which is the idiom for the commissioning or ordination of priests (cf. Exod 29:41). The use of this term anticipates the consecration of the Levites as priestly assistants to the sons of Aaron in Numbers 3, 8, and 17–18. It is striking, however, that Ezekiel does not accept the role of the Levites as having adhered to YHWH. In Ezekiel 44:9–24, YHWH maintains that only the Levitical priests of the line of Zadok have adhered to YHWH, whereas the other lines of Levitical priests have gone astray after their "fetishes," i.e., "turds," in Ezekiel's characteristically colorful language (cf. Ezek 8–11).[9]

Exodus 32:30 marks the beginning of the second major unit of Exodus 32–34 in which the narrative shifts from an account of Israel's sin in worshipping the golden calf in Exodus 32:1–29 to an account of the restoration of the covenant in Exodus 32:30—34:35. The use of the term "restoration" is crucial. Insofar as the covenant was a *bĕrît ʿôlām*, an "eternal covenant" (see Gen 17:7, 13, 18, 19; Exod 31:16), it cannot be broken, as some biblical texts (e.g., Isa 24:5) and interpreters might presume.[10] It can be violated, however, and that is what is at stake in the present passage. Consequently, the covenant is restored after having been violated, but not broken.

Exodus 32:30–35 recounts Moses's charge that the people of Israel have committed "a great sin" (Hebrew, *ḥaṭṭāʾâ gĕdōlâ*) against YHWH and his attempt to get YHWH to forgive them for what they have done. Moses therefore goes back up to YHWH, presumably on Mount Sinai, and he appeals to YHWH to forgive their sin. Such an attempt entails the role of the priest at Yom Kippur (Lev 16). Moses's appeal includes a request to "erase me from your record that you have written" (Hebrew, *mĕḥēnî nāʾ missiprĕkā ʾăšer kātābtā*), which entails that YHWH should

9. See also my commentary on Ezekiel 44 and 8–11, Sweeney, *Reading Ezekiel*, 52–70, 211–220.

10. Sweeney, "*Berit Olam*."

kill him and thereby remove him from the record of those who will live. In rabbinic thought, G-d records the fate of all human beings for the coming year on Yom Kippur. YHWH, however, refuses Moses's request and states instead the intention to "erase" only those who have sinned against YHWH. YHWH's final statement on the matter in v. 34 instructs Moses to lead the people where I told you to lead them, i.e., on to the promised land of Israel, and that "my angel" (Hebrew, *mal'ākî*) will go before you on the journey. (The term *mal'ākî*, "my angel," later becomes the name of the twelfth prophetic composition in the book of the Twelve Prophets.) YHWH then states a point made in Exodus 34:6–7, viz., that YHWH will visit punishment on those who commit sins. Interpreters must recognize, however, that this principle includes punishment on the descendants of those who commit sins as well, as stated in Exodus 20:5–6 and 34:6–7. Verse 35 then recounts YHWH's plague on the people for what they did with the calf that Aaron made. Such a statement does not condemn the making of the calf *per se*, insofar as the calf should be construed as a mount for YHWH, analogous to the role of the ark of the covenant as a throne for YHWH. The sin committed by the people is their worship of the golden calf as a god in place of YHWH.

Exodus 33:1–6 recounts YHWH's speech to Moses in which YHWH instructs Moses to lead the people to the land that YHWH swore to give to their ancestors, Abraham, Isaac, and Jacob. YHWH reiterates the statement made to the ancestors, "to your seed, I will give it," which refers to YHWH's statements in various J-stratum texts in Genesis (12:7; 13:15; 24:17; 26:3, 4; 28:13). In return, YHWH will send an angel before Israel to drive out six Canaanite nations, viz., the Canaanites, the Amorites, the Hittites, the Perizzites, the Hivvites, and the Jebusites. Exodus 23:23 presents a similar statement by YHWH in which YHWH states the intention to drive out the same nations that are mentioned in Exodus 23:23 near the end of the Covenant Code. They are not the same as those mentioned in Deuteronomy 7:15, which names seven nations, the six mentioned in the present text, plus the Girgashites, who do not appear in Exodus 33:16. The references to the J-stratum texts in the promise of the land to the ancestors and the E-stratum text in the promise to send an angel to drive out the six Canaanite nations indicates a J-stratum reflection upon and development of the E-stratum understanding of YHWH's leadership of Israel in the wilderness (E-stratum) and YHWH's promise to grant the land to the ancestors (J-stratum). YHWH's rationale for sending an angel to lead Israel presupposes the imagery of the pillar of fire and smoke mentioned in Exodus 13:21–22 and 14:19–20, both E-stratum texts in which YHWH appears within the pillar of cloud and fire. YHWH is therefore distinguished from the "angel," which covers and protects YHWH. The protections run two ways, viz., YHWH is protected from profanation by Israel and the rest of creation, and Israel is protected from destruction by contact with YHWH, a concern that is reiterated here in vv. 3 and 4–6. The people mourn, in part because they believe that they are being punished for apostasy, which is true in part. But direct contact with YHWH entails destruction in any case due to YHWH's holiness and the profane state of the people. The people therefore forego wearing ornamentation to express their mourning and their profane state, although the priests will wear ornamentation when they serve YHWH in the tent of meeting and later in the temples (Exod 28).

Exodus 33:7–11 presents problems to interpreters because they are uncertain what to do with a passage that recalls Moses's face-to-face meetings with YHWH in the tent of meeting, positioned outside of the Israelite camp. The passage appears to contradict a later statement in Exodus 33:17–23 that no human, including Moses, can see the face of YHWH and live. It also continues to employ the imagery of the pillar of cloud that protects YHWH and stands outside the tent of meeting while YHWH and Moses talk face-to-face. Interpreters are correct to speculate that Exodus 33:7–11 is an E-stratum text that has been incorporated into the J-stratum narrative of Exodus 32–34, but they miss the importance of the narrative. In its present position, Exodus 33:7–11 recounts Moses's past experience of meeting with YHWH face-to-face, but in the aftermath of the golden calf episode, YHWH's relationship with Israel has changed. YHWH will no longer meet face-to-face with Moses, despite YHWH's favor granted to Moses and YHWH's self-revelation to Moses discussed in this passage. Now that YHWH's anger, previously unleashed against Egypt, has been unleashed against Israel due to the sin of the golden calf, the potential for such a threat is apparent from here on. Indeed, the narratives concerning the wilderness murmuring tradition in Numbers 10–25 make that threat abundantly clear, even against Miriam, Aaron, and even Moses, as illustrated in Numbers 12 and 20. In the aftermath of the sin of the golden calf, Moses will no longer speak face-to-face with G-d as had been done before; now Moses will see YHWH's back, but not YHWH's face. Such a situation is apparent in prophetic visionary texts, such as Isaiah 6; Jeremiah 1; and Ezekiel 1–3, in which Isaiah, Jeremiah, and Ezekiel respectively see YHWH, but not YHWH's face. It is striking that Moses returns to the camp after speaking with YHWH, but Joshua, Moses's close companion and later his successor, would remain in the tent. Joshua is not a priest, but apart from the sons of Aaron and the firstborn sons, no Levitical priesthood has yet been designated (see Num 17–18 for the designation of the Levites as the holy assistants to the sons of Aaron). By remaining in the tent of meeting, presumably to guard its sanctity, Joshua sets the pattern for the priestly watches who will later guard the temple (see 1 Chron 24).

Exodus 33:12–16 presents the continued conversation between YHWH and Moses in which Moses will ask for permission to better know YHWH and YHWH's plans for Israel. Such a request entails greater self-revelation on the part of YHWH to Moses, and it builds upon YHWH's stated grace that YHWH grants to Moses (vv. 12–13). YHWH therefore informs Moses that YHWH will lead the people, a concept that is already apparent in the imagery of the pillar of cloud and fire in which YHWH's presence is protected from contact with the profane world of creation, but it clarifies YHWH's presence at the head of Israel despite the efforts to conceal and protect that presence in the E-stratum conceptualization of the role of the pillar of fire and smoke. Moses's argumentation to convince YHWH to do so is to demonstrate YHWH's close relationship to the people, despite the tension created by the sin of the people in worshipping the golden calf. Such a close relationship thereby distinguished Israel as YHWH's "chosen" people, as articulated in later texts (e.g., Exod 19:4–6; Deut 7:6–11; 14:2; Isa 44:1; 55:1–13; Ezek 20, esp. vv. 5–6).[11]

Exodus 33:17–23 presents YHWH's agreement with Moses's proposal and the conditions that YHWH stipulated. YHWH states the intention to pass before Moses, with all of YHWH's "goodness" displayed. YHWH's "goodness" apparently portrays YHWH's fidelity to the covenant. YHWH's *idem per idem* statements—"and I will be gracious to whom I will be gracious [Hebrew, *wĕḥanōtî ʾet ʾăšer ʾāḥōn*] and I will be merciful to whom I will be merciful [Hebrew, *wĕriḥamtî ʾet ʾăšer ʾăraḥēm*]"—echo YHWH's statement to Moses at the burning bush in Exodus 3:14 when Moses asked for YHWH's Name, "I am who I am." Such a correspondence indicates the interest in the J-stratum text in Exodus 33:17–23 to reflect upon the E-stratum text in Exodus 3. But YHWH states conditions, viz., Moses will take his stance on a rock, and YHWH will place Moses in a cleft in the rock and protect Moses by

11. See also Kaminsky, *Yet I Loved Jacob*.

covering him with the divine palm. YHWH will then pass by Moses, but Moses will be able to see only YHWH's back, not YHWH's face.

Exodus 34:1–9 recounts YHWH's initiation of the restoration of the covenant between YHWH and Israel in the aftermath of the golden calf episode. The account begins with a presentation of YHWH's instructions to Moses to cut two tablets of stone like the first one and to inscribe the tablets with the words that were on the first set. Although Exodus 34:28 suggests that these words were the Ten Commandments, the current narrative indicates that the tablets would include a revised set of laws based on the earlier northern Israelite Covenant Code in Exodus 20–23. In the earlier version, the Ten Commandments in Exodus 20 functioned as an introductory statement of legal principles that informed the following set of laws presented in Exodus 21–23. It would appear that the Ten Commandments, presupposed in Exodus 34:28, would play a similar role in relation to the more detailed and revised set of laws presented here in Exodus 34:10–26. Because the Ten Commandments in Exodus 20 would not be revised for the present context—as they were in Deuteronomy 5, where they introduced the Deuteronomic Code in Deuteronomy 12–26—there was no need to restate them here. YHWH's instructions to Moses require him to ascend the mountain alone and to stand before YHWH to write at YHWH's dictation. No other persons nor even cattle or sheep are allowed on the mountain, apparently due to YHWH's holiness, which would present a threat to anyone other than Moses, who had received special recognition by YHWH in Exodus 33:17–23.

Exodus 34:4–9 recounts Moses's compliance with YHWH's instructions and YHWH's self-revelation to Moses.[12] YHWH comes down to the mountain in typical form, encased in the pillar of cloud, again to protect YHWH's holiness and those whom YHWH might encounter. YHWH's self-revelation is not limited to the self-revelation or proof saying formula; rather, it provides a full description of YHWH's character spoken by YHWH, in which YHWH discloses the basic characteristics of fidelity and mercy on the one hand, and capacity for justice and punishment on the other. The reason for such a disclosure is to explain why the punishment that followed the people's sin in worshipping the golden calf had to be explained. YHWH's covenant with Israel, expressed to the ancestors in Genesis and in YHWH's acts against Egypt in Exodus, had focused on YHWH's actions to protect Israel from threat by other

12. Hals, *Ezekiel*, 362–63; Sweeney, *Isaiah 40–66*, 403; Zimmerli, "I Am YHWH"; Zimmerli, "Word of Divine Self-Manifestation."

nations, most notably Egypt. But whereas the people—or more properly, the reader of Genesis and Exodus—might presume that YHWH was an entirely gracious, merciful, and beneficent G-d, YHWH's self-revelation to Moses makes it clear that YHWH is capable and willing to punish wrongdoing as well. In the aftermath of the destruction of the Northern Kingdom of Israel by the Assyrian Empire in 722–721 BCE, such an explanation would have been necessary to justify YHWH's failure to protect the Northern Kingdom of Israel as a statement in the promises to the ancestors in Genesis and to the people of Israel in Exodus. The principle here is that YHWH could not be wrong; the fault must lie with the people of northern Israel for engaging in the worship of other gods, forbidden by YHWH in the covenant. Such a portrayal raises questions concerning the presence and integrity of YHWH just as they do in the aftermath of the modern experience of the Shoah or Holocaust in which some six million Jews were murdered by Nazi Germany and its sympathizers in World War II. Modern interpreters of the Shoah have faced more difficulties in answering such questions than those of the past, although the situations are analogous. But biblical interpreters must recognize that the then-current attempt to justify the destruction of northern Israel by appealing to charges that northern Israel had sinned by worshipping the golden calf—especially when the golden calf is caricatured as an idolatrous god rather than as a simple mount for an invisibly mounted YHWH upon it, much like the ark of the covenant—is just as inadequate as contemporary attempts to justify the Shoah by charging modern Jews with sin. The modern experience of the Shoah was an example of state-sponsored murder; the destruction of northern Israel was an example of state-sponsored warfare against a revolting vassal. In both cases, YHWH or G-d was unable or unwilling to come to the rescue. Whereas the biblical authors tried to claim that northern Israel sinned against YHWH, later generations have found that such an explanation is inadequate.

YHWH's self-revelation to Moses begins with YHWH standing by Moses in v. 5, proclaiming the divine Name, and then passing by Moses while making a detailed statement of YHWH's fidelity and mercy on the one hand and justice on the other. YHWH's statement thereby becomes an explanation of the values represented by the divine Name, YHWH. The first part of YHWH's statement focuses on YHWH's fidelity, mercy, and compassion. The statement of the thirteen qualities here informs Maimonides's statement of faith in the late twelfth to early thirteenth century CE.

Following the dual statement of YHWH's Name, the first set of nine qualities in vv. 6–7a focuses on YHWH as "a G-d merciful and gracious, long on anger and abundant fidelity and truth, guarding fidelity for thousands, pardoning iniquity and rebellion and sin." The term G-d (Hebrew, *ʾēl*), "El," is the name of the Canaanite creator god, which illustrates the continuity between Israel and ancient Canaan, i.e., Israel (Hebrew, *yiśrāʾēl*)—whose name means "may El (G-d) rule"—is an indigenous nation that developed from earlier Canaanite culture. The term "merciful" (Hebrew, *raḥûm*) is derived from the noun *reḥem*, "womb," to assert compassion as an expression of a mother's love. The term "gracious" (Hebrew, *ḥanûn*) refers to favor, i.e., YHWH's capacity to show favor to those with whom YHWH is in relationship. The phrase "long on anger" (Hebrew, *ʾerek ʾapayim*, lit., "long of face") expresses YHWH's ability to be slow to anger, which would result in a change of facial expression when viewing the one with whom YHWH would become angry. The phrase "abundant fidelity" (Hebrew, *rab ḥesed*), often misunderstood as abundant mercy or the like, employs the term for "fidelity" (*ḥesed*) to underscore YHWH's reliability in a relationship. And the term "truth" (Hebrew, *ʾemet*) underscores YHWH's integrity, i.e., YHWH does not lie or deceive. The statement "guarding fidelity for thousands" (Hebrew, *nōṣēr ḥesed lāʾălāpîm*) reiterates the point made earlier about YHWH's fidelity. The phrase "pardoning iniquity and rebellion and sin" (Hebrew, *nōśēʾ ʿāwōn wāpešaʿ wĕḥaṭṭāʾâ*) emphasizes YHWH's compassion and mercy, insofar as YHWH is willing to forgive (Hebrew, *nōśēʾ*, lit., "lift") three types of wrongdoing: "iniquity" (Hebrew, *ʿāwōn*), "rebellion" (Hebrew, *pešaʿ*), and "sin"(Hebrew, *ḥaṭṭāʾâ*).

The second set of four qualities in v. 7b emphasizes YHWH's capacity for justice. The first is an emphatic statement, formulated with an infinitive absolute form of the verb that doubles the Piel form of verb *nqh* to indicate emphasis, "but surely he does not acquit" (Hebrew, *wĕnaqqēh lōʾ yĕnaqqeh*), i.e., indicating that YHWH does not acquit someone guilty of a crime when it is clear that they have committed the crime. The punishment of iniquity (Hebrew, *pōqēd ʿāwōn*, lit., "visiting iniquity") entails the punishment of three generations, viz., the fathers, the sons, and the sons of sons, thereby representing three acts of punishment.

Having heard YHWH's recitation of characteristics that define the divine Name, Moses bows down in vv. 8–9 to request that YHWH travel with the people of Israel, despite their "stiff-necked" or stubborn character, and pardon their iniquity and sins, as stated by YHWH in vv. 6–7, and take them as YHWH's own inheritance (Hebrew, *ûnĕḥaltānû*, "and you shall inherit us," an idiomatic way of asking YHWH to restore the covenant).

YHWH's response to Moses's request follows in Exodus 34:10–26 in which YHWH states the intention to conclude a covenant with Israel in v. 10, and then lays out a law code, which draws upon and revises stipulations from the Covenant Code in Exodus 20–23. In v. 10, YHWH states, "Behold, I am cutting a covenant," a typical Hebrew idiom for making a covenant or treaty that presupposes a ratification ritual in which the parties to the covenant or treaty walk between the severed halves of sacrificial animals while stating, "May the same happen to me," if they do not abide by the terms of the treaty.[13] YHWH then swears to perform wonders on behalf of Israel like those in the Exodus plague narratives.

The law code, which presents the stipulations of the covenant that Israel must follow, appears in Exodus 34:11–26.

The first stipulation appears in Exodus 34:11–16, which requires the people of Israel not to establish relationships, either treaties (covenants) or marriages with six Canaanite nations, viz., the Amorites, the Canaanites, the Hittites, the Perizzites, the Hivvites, and the Jebusites, who inhabited the land of Canaan prior to Israel and whom YHWH is driving out. There is no indication that YHWH actually succeeded in driving these peoples out; there was no war against the Canaanites like that described in Joshua 1–12, which saw the Canaanite people ejected from the land. Rather, archeological and textual evidence indicates that the Canaanite peoples remained in the land, and they were eventually assimilated into Israel. There was war, but it was between the Israelite/Canaanite peoples who lived in the hill country of Israel and Judah, now identified with the so-called West Bank, and the Philistine peoples who inhabited the coastal plain. The Philistines were a combination of the Sea Peoples, who migrated from Greek islands along the coast of Asia Minor and down the coast of the eastern Mediterranean until they were defeated by the Egyptians in 1196 BCE and then settled in the coastal areas from Yaffo south through the Gaza Strip to assimilate into the coastal Canaanite population to form the five-city Philistine coalition, including Ashdod, Ashkelon, Gaza, Gath, and Ekron. Israel eventually defeated the Philistines, who ultimately disappeared over time in the Persian period and beyond. The reason for the prohibition against treaties and marriages with the Canaanite peoples is that such relationships

13. See, e.g., Gen 15:7–20; Sweeney, "Form Criticism"; Sefire Treaty IA, *ANET* 660.

would result in Israelite and Judean worship of the Canaanite gods and goddesses, resulting in assimilation of Israel into Canaanite culture. The present stipulation draws upon the earlier Covenant Code law in Exodus 23:23–33, which names the six Canaanite people named here as well as the similar law in Deuteronomy 7:1–6, which names the Girgashites together with the six other Canaanite nations. The law formulated here in Exodus 34:11–16 is a highly edited version that shortens and reorganizes the original Covenant Code text to make its points clear. It requires Israel to tear down their altars; shatter their pillars, which appear to be phallic-inspired representations of the Canaanite fertility god, Baal; and cut down their Asherim, sacred, fruit-bearing trees, which represent one of the Canaanite fertility goddesses, Asherah. An example of such a sanctuary has been excavated at Arad, located in the Negev wilderness. Like the sanctuary at Beth El, portrayed in Genesis 28, the Arad sanctuary had a stone pillar to represent Baal; any trees that represented Asherah would have been long gone. Marriage with these Canaanite peoples is also forbidden as such marriages would put pressure on Israelites to adopt the Canaanite religious practices and thereby compromise their unique relationship with YHWH, which constituted the foundation for their identity as Israelites and Judeans, who adhered only to YHWH, the G-d of Israel. Adherence to other gods was often portrayed in sexual terms, i.e., "to whore after" their gods, insofar as Israel and Jerusalem were often portrayed as brides of YHWH, who abandoned their metaphorical husband, YHWH, to pursue other lovers, i.e., gods (Hos 1–3; Jer 2; Ezek 16).

The second stipulation is to prohibit the manufacture of molten gods, i.e., idols made of metal. It is noteworthy that this prohibition appears near the beginning of the revised law code, insofar as the golden calf was a molten idol. There is no such prohibition in the Covenant Code per se, but the Ten Commandments do prohibit the manufacture of a carved image of a god and any likeness of anything in heaven or on earth that would represent a foreign deity to which one might offer worship in Exodus 20:4–6. Because this was an issue in the golden calf episode, the new law code placed this prohibition right after the prohibition against establishing relationships with the Canaanite nations that would lure Israel away from adherence to YHWH.

Exodus 34:18–26 presents the laws concerning the observance of the holy days in the Israelite-Judean festival calendar. It reorganizes, expands, and clarifies the earlier Covenant Code calendar in Exodus

23:14–19 in an effort to update the earlier commands concerning the observance of the holidays.

The first set of commands in Exodus 34:18–20 takes up the observance of the Festival of Matzot, "Unleavened Bread," which is associated with the observance of Passover. Exodus 34:18 presents an imperative instruction to observe Matzot for a seven-day period. There is no mention of Passover at this point, but Matzot is the seven-day festival that follows Passover in other calendars (Deut 16:1–8; Num 28:16–25; Lev 23:4–8). The reference to the month of Aviv, "spring," which also appears in Exodus 23:15, is the older name for the first month of the year in the Jewish calendar, later known as Nisan. Like the Covenant Code, this passage mentions only Matzot, and it specifies that the festival starts at the appointed time of the month, elsewhere stated to be the fifteenth day of the first month in Numbers 28:17 and Leviticus 23:5, one day after the celebration of Passover on the fourteenth day of the first month. Observance of Matzot call for the eating of unleavened bread, understood to be slave food, because Israel departed from Egypt at this time in the month of Aviv. Exodus 34:19–20 addresses an issue that does not appear in the Covenant Code, the dedication of the firstborn to YHWH. The language of the instruction, Hebrew, *kol peṭer reḥem*, "all that breaks the womb," makes it clear that the instruction refers to the firstborn of the mother. The issue appears in the plague narrative itself in Exodus 13, which explains the purpose of the tenth plague concerning the death of the firstborn in Exodus 11–12. The role of the firstborn in Israel is to be understood as an offering to YHWH from the livestock, viz., cattle and sheep, although the firstborn of an ass is to be redeemed with a sheep. If the ass is not redeemed, its neck is to be broken. The ass was the preferred animal for sacrifice in Mesopotamian cultures, as witnessed by the Akkadian idiom for making a covenant, *ḫayarum ḳatālum birît*, "to slay an ass in between," which is known at Mari in Mesopotamia and Shechem in the land of Israel.[14] In the case of a firstborn son, the son is to be dedicated to YHWH as a sacred assistant to the sons of Aaron in YHWH's temples, as exemplified by the case of Samuel, the firstborn son to his mother, Hannah, and Ephraimite father, Elkanah, who was sent to the Shiloh temple, where he assisted the high priest Eli and his sons and was later called by YHWH to serve as a prophet (1 Sam 1–3).[15] The state-

14. Noth, "Old Testament Covenant-Making," esp. 112–13.

15. Sweeney, "Samuel's Institutional Identity."

ment "and they shall not appear before me empty handed," which also appears in Exodus 23:15, again indicates that Israelite men are obligated to bring their offerings to YHWH at the festivals of the agricultural year, beginning with Passover/Matzot.

Exodus 34:21 specifies the requirement to cease work on the Shabbat. It specifies six days of labor followed by a seventh day when work ceases, specifically, plowing and harvesting, which would take place throughout the agricultural year in which the three festivals are observed. An analogous command appears in the Covenant Code in Exodus 23:12, which specifies that one's animals, servants, and resident aliens are enabled to rest on the Shabbat as well.

Exodus 23:22–24 provides additional instruction on the observance of the Festival of Shavuot, "Weeks," which celebrates the completion of the wheat harvest in the spring, generally around late May to early June, and the Festival of the Asiph, the ingathering of the fruit harvest, later known as Sukkot, "Booths, Tabernacles," in which Israelite farmers live in sukkot, "booths, temporary huts," so that they might remain out in the fields and orchards to complete the fruit harvest prior to the onset of the fall rains, which would ruin them. Instruction for the observance of the harvest and ingathering festivals appears in the Covenant Code in Exodus 23:16. The command that all Israelite males appear before YHWH three times per year—i.e., at the three major holidays: Matzot (Pesach), Shavuot, and Asiph (Sukkot)—appears in vv. 23–24 as a means to ensure that YHWH will drive out the nations who would covet Israel's land. An analogous command appears in the Covenant Code in Exodus 23:14, where it reinforces the notion that festival observance is the time to bring required offerings to YHWH. Here in Exodus 34, it functions as a means to ensure Israel's possession of the land.

Exodus 34:25–26 returns to instruction concerning the Festival of Pesach, in this case with reference to the treatment of the Passover offering and the obligation to bring offerings to YHWH from the firstfruits of the land. In the first instance, v. 26 specifies that no blood sacrifice be offered with leavened bread; unleavened bread, matzot, is required, in part due to the combination of Pesach, in which the meat offering is made, and Matzot, in which the unleavened bread is specified. In this case, the matzot is understood to be drawn from the offerings of the firstfruits of the land; hence, the matzot will not be leavened as the firstfruits of grain would not have had the time to become leavened and rise. Furthermore, the Passover offering may not be left until morning. Such a requirement ensures that Israel would have only fresh meat on Pesach. Any meat left over is presumably burned. These commands concerning meat have their counterpart in Exodus 23:18. Verse 26 specifies that Israelite men are to bring the firstfruits of the land to YHWH's temple. Such a command covers the offerings of all three festivals, meat and unleavened bread for Pesach and Matzot; wheat for Shavuot; and fruit (e.g., grapes, figs, and olives) for Asiph/Sukkot. An analogous command appears in Exodus 23:19.

Exodus 34:27–28 concludes the account of YHWH's instructions concerning the revised law code in Exodus 34:10–26 with a concluding instruction by YHWH to Moses in v. 27 to write down these words so that they might serve as the basis for the covenant between YHWH and Israel. Exodus 34:28 then concludes the entire narration of YHWH's instructions to Moses in Exodus 24:12—34:28 with a closing statement concerning the forty days and forty nights that Moses spent on Mount Sinai recording YHWH's instructions for Israel as the basis for the covenant between YHWH and Israel. During this time, Moses ate no food nor drank water due to his focused concentration on the task. Such a statement perhaps presupposes YHWH's support of Elijah in 1 Kings 19:5–9, in which Elijah ate and drank sufficient food and water to sustain his journey to Mount Horeb and his encounter with YHWH there.

Exodus 34:29–35 recounts Moses's descent from Mount Sinai and his return to Israel with the new tablets of the witness in his possession. The passage indicates that Moses has been transformed as a result of his encounter with YHWH, insofar as the skin of his face radiates light. The radiance of Moses's face employs the Hebrew verb *qāran*, "to radiate, shine." Because the noun form of the root appears as Hebrew *qeren*, "horn," some interpreters have mistakenly presumed that Moses had horns on his head. Such an interpretation constitutes a gross misrepresentation of the text, insofar as the Hebrew word *qeren* indicates rays of light shining forth from Moses's face. Aaron and the Israelites do not understand what this radiance might mean, and so they are afraid to approach him. But after Aaron and tribal chieftains spoke with Moses about the matter, they apparently understood the significance of Moses's shining face, viz., Moses's encounter with the holy G-d, YHWH, had sanctified Moses with the light of the divine presence. Consequently, Moses was compelled to wear a "veil" (Hebrew, *masweh*) to separate the holiness that had transformed Moses into a holy, perhaps angel-like man, from the common or profane nature of the other Israelites.

The Hebrew term *masweh*, "veil," appears only in the present context in the Hebrew Bible. The veil apparently functions much like the curtain that covers the entrance to the holy of holies of the wilderness tabernacle, where the ark of the witness will reside to represent the throne and presence of YHWH. According to Exodus 33:7–11, Moses would enter the tent of meeting to speak directly with YHWH. The veil over Moses's face apparently functions much like the curtain that covers the entrance to the holy of holies in that both the curtain and the veil differentiate between the "commonness" of the people and the holiness of YHWH in the case of the curtain and the holiness of Moses in the case of the veil, and both thereby provide a boundary between these most holy figures and the less holy or even profane character of others. In this manner, the curtain and the veil protect the holiness of YHWH and Moses respectively. The veil apparently signifies the role of an Israelite oracle diviner, who speaks directly to G-d and does not need a veil to do so due to his holy character and task. But when an oracle diviner, in this case, Moses, emerges from his encounter with G-d, he must wear a veil to protect the people from the danger of encounter with the Holy One of Israel.

Reception History

The narrative of the golden calf in Exodus 32–34 receives extensive attention in the history of reception.

Second Temple and Hellenistic Judaism see several major interpreters engaging this text.[16] The Septuagint version of the narrative attributes the statement "These are your gods, O Israel, who brought you out from the land of Egypt" to Aaron and not to Israel as in the Masoretic Hebrew text. The LXX also maintains that Aaron made offerings to the golden calf. Philo treated the incident in detail in *De vita Mosis* 2.161–73, 270–74 and in other works. He was especially concerned that Israel worshipped an animal, and he is portrayed as especially stubborn. He also presents Moses as more knowledgeable in understanding Israel's actions and G-d as less angry in reacting to Israel and in proposing to make a new nation out of Moses. Josephus omits the golden calf episode altogether in *Antiquities* 3.5.7, although he hints that Israel feared that Moses had been victimized by wild animals. Pseudo-Philo in

16. Suomala, "Golden Calf: Second Temple"; Suomala, *Moses and G-d in Dialogue*.

Liber antiquitatum biblicarum focuses on Israel's moral failings, and he portrays Aaron as acting out of fear for his own safety.

Rabbinic Judaism considers worship of the golden calf to represent Israel's quintessential sin, and it focuses on three primary aspects: "the nature and gravity of sin"; "punishment and consequences"; and "the potential for forgiveness and atonement."[17] Rabbi Ulla compares the golden calf sin to a bride who commits adultery in her bridal canopy (b. Šabb. 88b; b. Git. 36b). Rabbi Judah bar Simon, in Leviticus Rabbah, maintains that Israel intentionally committed idolatry. Concern with consequences appears in Sifra Numbers 1.10.2–3 and Mekhilta de R. Ishmael, which suggest Israel's loss of control over the wilderness tabernacle and their own immortality. Concern with forgiveness and atonement appears in m. Megillah 4.10, which calls for Moses's critique of Aaron's actions to be read publicly only in Aramaic. Other passages indicate an attempt to defend Aaron, e.g., Exodus Rabbah 42.

Rashi attempts to defend Israel by arguing that Egyptian magicians actually made the gold calf.[18] Judah ha-Levi defends the nobility of Israel when questioned by the Khazar king in the Kuzari. Rashi's grandson, R. Samuel ben Meir, defends Israel by claiming that they would never have been so foolish, and argues that G-d was testing them. Abraham ibn Ezra suggests that the golden calf was a "channel for divine power."

Modern Jewish thinkers tend to develop earlier rabbinic positions.[19] Moses Mendelssohn follows Judah ha-Levi and Abraham ibn Ezra in arguing that Israel did not intend idolatry. Franz Rosenzweig asserts that Israel did not believe that the golden calf was a god. Rabbi Nahman of Bratslav maintains that Israel's sin was to abandon Moses, an example of a Hasidic zaddik or righteous leader. The present author argues that the narrative must be read as an example of Judean polemic against northern Israel in an effort to explain the destruction and exile of the Northern Kingdom of Israel.[20]

The recitation of YHWH's attributes in Exodus 34:6–7 appears also in Numbers 14:18–19, where Moses pleads with YHWH to forgive Israel in the spies narrative. The portion of Exodus 34:6–7 concerned with YHWH's mercy also appears in Jonah 3:9, in which the

17. Suomala, "Golden Calf: Rabbinic Judaism"; Ginzberg, *Legends*, 3:120–48; Smolar and Aberbach, "Golden Calf Episode."

18. Lindqvist, "Golden Calf."

19. Flatto, "Golden Calf."

20. Sweeney, *Reading the Bible After the Shoah*, 52–72.

king of Nineveh quotes Exodus 34:6–7 to suggest that perhaps G-d will show mercy on Nineveh due to the repentance of its people.[21] Exodus 34:6–7 also appears in Nahum 1:3, where the portions concerned with YHWH's justice appear to indicate that YHWH will punish those who deserve punishment.[22]

Christianity focuses especially on Israel's sin as a means to justify the emergence of Christianity. Stephen's sermon in Acts 7:40–42 condemns Israel for idolatry (see also Acts 7:51–53), although the sermon ignores the context of an eternal covenant as stated in Exodus 31. Paul's First Letter to the Corinthians likewise charges Israel with idolatry (cf. Rom 9:15). Second Corinthians 3:7–18 argues that Christ's glory will be greater than that of Moses, insofar as Moses's veil conceals the glory of G-d. The Epistle to Barnabas 4.6–8; 14.1–3 holds that the covenant with Israel was entirely abrogated, although later commentators, such as John Calvin, argued that the covenant was only temporarily suspended.[23] Works such as Justin's *Dial.* 20.3 and Apostolic Constitutions 6.20.6 argued that the ritual law of the second set of tablets was intended as punishment. Later writers, such as Ephraem Syrus (*Sermons* 3.421) and Rabanus Maurus (*De univ.* 7) read the golden calf episode as a precursor to Jewish rejection of Jesus. Modern Christian theologians, such as Karl Barth, argued that the golden calf episode represented human pride in general.

The golden calf episode is featured in Cecil B. DeMille's film *The Ten Commandments* (1956), which builds upon the reference to Israel's eating, drinking, and rising to play in Exodus 32:6, portraying it as a riotous orgy.[24] The dance was also featured in Arnold Schoenberg's unfinished opera, *Moses und Aron.*[25] The light beams emanating from Moses's face in Exodus 34:29–35 are erroneously portrayed as horns in Michelangelo's 1513–1515 marble sculpture of Moses.[26]

21. Sweeney, *Twelve Prophets*, 1:326–27.

22. Sweeney, *Twelve Prophets*, 2:428–29.

23. Holder, "Golden Calf."

24. Shepherd, "Golden Calf."

25. N. Petersen, "Golden Calf."

26. Bertman, "Antisemitic Origin."

Account of Israel's Compliance with YHWH's Instruction to Build the Wilderness Tabernacle and Associated Fixtures —Exodus 35:1—40:38

Overview

The account of Israel's compliance with YHWH's instruction to build the wilderness tabernacle and its associated fixtures in Exodus 35:1—40:38 displays a clear formal literary structure of five major components as follows:

I. The account of Moses's initial assembly of Israel and Israel's response concerning the building of the wilderness tabernacle

Exodus 35:1—36:7

II. The account of the construction of the tabernacle

Exodus 36:8–38

III. The account of the construction of the ark, the furnishings of the tabernacle, and the courtyard of the tabernacle

Exodus 37:1—38:20

IV. The account of the summation of the construction of the tabernacle, its furnishings, its equipment, and the holy garments for the priests

Exodus 38:21—39:31

V. The account of the completion of the wilderness tabernacle and YHWH's entrance into the sanctuary

Exodus 39:32—40:38

Account of Moses's Initial Assembly of Israel and Israel's Response Concerning the Building of the Wilderness Tabernacle —Exodus 35:1—36:7

Translation

35:1 And Moses assembled all the congregation of the sons of Israel, and he said to them, 2 "These are the things that YHWH has commanded [you] to do. Six days shall work be done, but on the seventh day, there shall be for you a holy Shabbat of Shabbat observance for YHWH. All who do work on it shall be put to death. 3 You shall not kindle a fire in all your settlements on the day of the Shabbat."

4 And Moses said to all the congregation of the sons of Israel, saying, "This is the thing that YHWH has commanded, saying, 5 'Take from yourselves a gift offering for YHWH. Anyone whose heart is willing shall bring it as a gift offering of YHWH, gold and silver and bronze, 6 and blue and purple and crimson yarn, and fine linen, and goats' hair, 7 and tanned rams' skins and dolphins' skins and acacia wood, 8 and oil for lighting and spices for anointing oil and sweet-smelling incense 9 and stones of beryl and stones of settings for the ephod and for the breastpiece.

10 "And all who are wise of heart among you shall come, and they shall do all that YHWH has commanded, 11 the tabernacle, its tent and its cover, its hooks and its planks, its bars, its posts and its bases, 12 the ark and its poles, the cover and the curtain of the screen, 13 the table and its poles and all its vessels and the bread of the presence 14 and the lampstand of the light and its vessels and its lamps and the oil of the lighting 15 and the altar of incense and its poles and the oil of anointing and the sweet-smelling incense and the screen of the entrance for the entrance of the tabernacle, 16 the altar of the whole burnt offering and the bronze grating that goes with it, its poles and all its vessels, and the washbasin and its stand, 17 the curtains of the court, its stands and its bases, and the screen of the gate of the court, 18 the pegs of the tabernacle and the pegs of the court and their cords, 19 the braided garments for service in the sanctuary, the holy garments for Aaron, the priest, and the garments of his sons to serve as priests."

20 And all the congregation of the sons of Israel went out from before Moses, 21 and everyone whose heart motivated him and everyone whose spirit was willing came; they brought the gift offering of YHWH for the work of the tent of meeting and for all its service and for its holy garments. 22 And the men came together with the women. All willing of heart brought brooch and earring and ring and necklace, all items of gold, and everyone who would make an elevation offering of gold to YHWH. 23 And everyone who had blue and purple and crimson yarn and fine linen and goats' hair and tanned rams' skins and dolphins' skins brought [them]. 24 All who would make a gift offering of silver or bronze brought the gift offering of YHWH, and all who had acacia wood for all the work of the service brought [them]. 25 And every woman wise of heart with her hands spun, and they brought what they had spun, the blue and the purple and crimson yarn and the fine linen, 26 and all the women whose heart motivated them with wisdom spun the goats' hair, 27 and the chieftains brought the stones of beryl and the stones of setting for the ephod and the breastpiece, 28 and the spices and the oil for

lighting and the oil of anointing and the sweet-smelling incense. 29 Every man and woman whose heart motivated them to bring for all the work that YHWH commanded to do by the hand of Moses, the sons of Israel brought willingly for YHWH.

30 And Moses said to the sons of Israel, "See! YHWH has called on the name of Bezalel ben Uri ben Hur of the tribe of Judah, 31 and he has filled him with the spirit of G-d, with wisdom, with understanding, and with knowledge, and in all work. 32 and to make designs to manufacture in gold and in silver and in bronze, 33 and to cut stone for setting and in cutting wood to do any work of design, 34 and to teach he has given his heart. He and Oholiab ben Ahisamach of the tribe of Dan, 35 he has filled them with the wisdom of the heart to do all the work, caring and designing and embroidering in blue and in purple and in scarlet yarn and in fine linen and weaving works of all types and planning designs.

36:1 "And Bezalel and Oholiab and everyone wise of heart to whom YHWH has given wisdom and understanding in them to know how to do all the work of the service of the sanctuary shall do all that YHWH has commanded."

2 And Moses called to Bezalel and to Oholiab and to every man wise of heart whom YHWH gave wisdom in his heart; all whose heart carried him to approach to the work to do it. 3 And they took from before Moses all the gift offering that the sons of Israel brought for the work of the service of the sanctuary to do it, they still brought to him freewill offerings every morning. 4 And all the wise ones who were doing all the work of the sanctuary came, each from the work which he was doing, 5 and they said to Moses, saying, "The people are bringing more too much for the service of the work which YHWH commanded to do." 6 And Moses commanded, and they caused the message to pass in the camp, saying, "No man nor woman shall do any more work for the gift offering of the sanctuary," and the people stopped bringing [anything]. 7 And the work was sufficient for all the work to do and more.

Commentary

The account of Moses's initial assembly of Israel and Israel's response concerning the building of the tabernacle in Exodus 35:1—36:7 begins in Exodus 35:1–3 with an account of Moses's assembly of Israel and his first speech concerning Israel's role in constructing the wilderness tabernacle. Following the assembly and speech formula in Exodus 35:1a, Exodus 35:1b–3 follows with Moses's speech concerning Israel's obligation to observe the Shabbat as YHWH had commanded. The initial instruction to observe the Shabbat makes an important point in the final version of the Priestly pentateuchal narrative. The temple, which the wilderness tabernacle prefigures, is considered in Israelite and Judean thought to be the holy center of creation in that it is understood to be the home of YHWH, the sovereign G-d of creation.[1] Similar understandings appear throughout the ancient Near East, e.g., in the Babylonian Enuma Elish, in which Marduk defeats Tiamat, establishes creation, and receives the Entemenankhi temple as his home or the Ugaritic Baal cycle in which Baal defeats Yamm, ensures the continuity of creation, and receives his own temple in Ugarit for doing so.[2]

The placement of the instruction to observe Shabbat at the head of the compliance narrative is analogous to the placement of the creation account in Genesis 1:1—2:3 at the head of the entire pentateuchal narrative in the Priestly stratum of the Pentateuch, viz., it recounts the foundation of creation and portrays the wilderness tabernacle as the holy center of creation. Likewise, the initial E-stratum of the Pentateuch portrays YHWH's actions to deliver Israel from Egyptian bondage and to guide them from Egypt through the wilderness to the promised land as an act of creation in which YHWH defeats the Egyptian pharaoh, employs elements of creation to do so, and receives the wilderness tabernacle as a temporary home that anticipates the eventual establishment of temples in Gilgal, Shiloh, Jerusalem, Beth El, Dan, and elsewhere.

It is striking that Moses's rehearsal of YHWH's instructions begins with the statement in Exodus 35:2a that "six days shall work be done, but on the seventh day, there shall be for you a holy Shabbat of Shabbat observance for YHWH." This statement repeats similar statements in the Ten Commandments, in Exodus 20:9–10, and in the Covenant Code in Exodus 23:12, which states the Shabbat principle for work and

1. Levenson, *Sinai and Zion*; Levenson, "Temple and the World."

2. Sweeney, "Creation as Sacred Space."

holy observance as an epistemological foundation for the understanding of YHWH's creation in Israel and Judah.[3] The following statement in Exodus 35:2b, "All who do work on it shall be put to death," employs a version of the death penalty formula (Hebrew, *yûmāt*, "[he] shall be put to death") to underscore the importance of this command as a foundational principle of YHWH's creation.[4] The final statement in Exodus 35:3, "You shall not kindle a fire in all your settlements on the day of the Shabbat," is one of the few examples of what work is to be prohibited on the Shabbat. The absence of much instruction on what work is to be avoided on the Shabbat prompted the rabbis of the Mishnah to infer that all the work necessary to build the wilderness tabernacle would constitute the thirty-nine categories of work that were prohibited on the day of the Shabbat (m. Šabb. 7.2).

The account of Moses's second speech to Israel in Exodus 35:4–19 presents YHWH's instruction that anyone among Israel who is so motivated should bring or prepare the materials necessary for the construction of the wilderness tabernacle and its associated equipment. The introductory speech formula appears in Exodus 35:4a and the instruction speech proper appears in Exodus 35:4b–19. The narrative employs the phrase *kōl nĕdîb libbô*, "anyone whose heart is willing," to emphasize that the people do this willingly, insofar as the materials are classified as a *tĕrûmâ lyhwh*, "gift offering for YHWH" (Exod 30:14; Num 15:19–21; Deut 12:6–11; Ezek 45:13)[5] or as a *nĕdābâ*, "freewill offering" (Exod 35:29; Lev 7:15; Num 15:3; 29:39; Deut 16:10).[6]

Exodus 35:5–9 calls for those willing to bring raw materials for the construction of the tabernacle, viz., gold, silver, bronze; blue, purple, and crimson yarn; fine linen and goats' hair; tanned rams' skins, dolphins' skins, and acacia wood; oil for lighting and sweet-smelling incense; and beryl and setting stones for the ephod and breastpiece. Exodus 35:10–19 calls for skilled persons who are willing to prepare items that must be manufactured: viz., for the tabernacle, its tent and covering; its hooks and planks; its bars, posts, bases; the ark, its poles, cover, and the curtain of the screen; the table, its poles, vessels, and the bread of the presence; the lampstand and its light, vessels, lamps, and oil for lighting; the incense altar and its poles, anointing oil, and sweet-smelling incense; the screen

3. Sweeney, "Shabbat."

4. Schulz, *Todesrecht*.

5. *HALOT* 4:1788–90; Wächter et al., "*tĕrûmâ*."

6. *HALOT* 2:671–72; J. Conrad, "*ndb*."

for the entrance of the tabernacle; the altar of the whole burnt offering, its bronze grating, poles, and its vessels; the washbasin and its stand; the curtains of the court and its stands, bases, and the screen of the gate of the court; the pegs of the tabernacle, the pegs of the court, and their cords; and the braided garments for service in the sanctuary, the holy garments for Aaron, and the garments of his sons to serve as priests.

Exodus 35:20–29 recounts Israel's compliance with the instruction communicated by Moses in Exodus 35:10–19. The passage once again emphasizes that the people brought or made these items of their own free will, and it emphasizes that men and women both brought items or used their special skills to manufacture the necessary items and that the chieftains of the tribes brought the precious stones for the ephod and breastpiece of Aaron. Exodus 35:19 emphasizes that all of these items were brought or made as a *nĕdābâ lyhwh*, "a freewill offering for YHWH."

Exodus 35:30—36:1 presents Moses's instruction speech in which he announces YHWH's choice of Bezalel ben Uri ben Hur of the tribe of Judah and Oholiab ben Ahisamach of the tribe of Dan to plan the designs and oversee the skilled work of manufacturing the specialized items necessary for the building of the wilderness tabernacle. Although Bezalel of Judah is emphasized in keeping with the interests of the Priestly stratum of the Pentateuch, Oholiab of Dan is also mentioned, perhaps in keeping with the interests of the foundational E-stratum of this narrative.

Exodus 36:2–7 recounts the willingness and generosity of the people in bringing freely all the materials and more for the construction of the wilderness tabernacle. Moses summoned Bezalel, Oholiab, and all the skilled people to take the materials brought by the people for the work. But even after they had taken the materials freely given for the work, the people kept bringing more and more every morning so that there was more than was necessary to complete the work. Consequently, Moses had to issue an order that was passed throughout the camp that the people should stop bringing additional materials. The people complied with Moses's order, but their willingness to bring so much material for the construction of the tabernacle demonstrated their willingness and enthusiasm to build the tabernacle for YHWH. When read in relation to the golden calf episode in Exodus 32–34, Exodus 35:1—36:7 demonstrates the loyalty of the people to YHWH in contrast to those who worshipped the golden calf.

Reception History

The Torah or Pentateuch makes a number of statements prohibiting work on the Shabbat, which appear in the Ten Commandments (Exod 20:8–11; Deut 5:12–15); the Covenant Code (Exod 23:12); the revision of the Covenant Code (Exod 34:21); the Holiness Code (Lev 23:3); and other texts (e.g., Gen 2:1–3). Because Exodus 35:2–3 is one of the few texts in which guidance is offered as to how work might be defined, the Tannaitic rabbis reasoned that the construction of the wilderness tabernacle itself must be employed to determine what categories of activity must define what work is prohibited on the Shabbat. They reasoned that all activities necessary to build the wilderness tabernacle must define work that is prohibited on the Shabbat, and they established a list of thirty-nine activities that were necessary for the construction of the tabernacle and that therefore were to be prohibited on Shabbat. The list appears in m. Shabbat 7.2.[7]

The commandment in Exodus 35:3, "You shall not kindle a fire in all your settlements on the day of the Shabbat," is understood to refer to kindling a fire on the Shabbat, based on the Hebrew prohibition, *lōʾ tĕbaʿărû*. Consequently, rabbinic Judaism maintains that a fire kindled prior to the onset of the Shabbat can continue to burn throughout the Shabbat day. Therefore, lights, heating, and electrical appliances that are turned on prior to Shabbat can continue to operate during the Shabbat, although they may not be turned off until the Shabbat has concluded. The Karaite sect of Judaism, which rejected rabbinic Oral Torah and opted instead to observe only the Written Torah as the basis for Jewish observance, read the prohibition *lōʾ tĕbaʿărû* to mean, "You shall not burn a fire in all your settlements on the day of the Shabbat." Consequently, Karaite households would remain unlighted and unheated on the Shabbat.[8]

7. Greenberg, "Sabbath"; Jacobs, "Sabbath."

8. Nemoy, *Karaite Anthology*, 17–18.

Account of the Construction of the Tabernacle—Exodus 36:8–38

Translation

36:8 And everyone who is wise of heart in doing the work
made the tabernacle, ten curtains of fine linen embroidered
with blue and purple and crimson yarn [with] cherubs as a
designer work they made them. [9] The length of each curtain
was twenty-eight cubits, and the width was four cubits for
each curtain, the same measure for all the curtains. [10] And
he joined five curtains, each to the other, and the other five
curtains he joined each to the other. [11] And he made loops
of blue on the edge of each curtain from the end of the assembly, [and] so he did on the edge of the end curtain in
the second assembly. [12] Fifty loops he made on each curtain,
and fifty loops he made on the end of the curtain which
was in the second assembly; opposite were the loops, each
to the other. [13] And he made fifty gold hooks, and he joined
the curtains, each to the other, with the hooks so that they
became one tabernacle.

[14] And he made curtains of goats' hair for the tent over the
tabernacle, eleven curtains he made them. [15] The length of
each curtain was thirty cubits, and four cubits was the width
of each curtain, one measure for the eleven curtains. [16] And
he joined the five curtains separately and six curtains separately, [17] and he made fifty loops on the edge of the outer
curtain in the assembly, and fifty loops he made on the edge

of the second joined curtain. 18 And he made fifty hooks of
bronze to join the tent to become one. 19 And made a covering for the tent of tanned rams' skins and a covering of the
skins of dolphins above.

20 And he made the boards for the tabernacle of standing
acacia wood. 21 Ten cubits was the length of the board, and
a cubit and a half was the width of each board. 22 Two clasps
for each board binding each to the other, so he made for each
of the boards of the tabernacle. 23 And he made the boards
for the tabernacle for the side facing the south. 24 And forty
bases of silver he made under the twenty boards, two bases
under each board for its two supports and their two bases
under each board for its two supports. 25 And for the second
wall of the tabernacle, for the north side, he made twenty
boards. 26 And their forty bases of silver, two bases under
each and every board. 27 And for the innermost side of the
tabernacle on the west, he made six boards. 28 And two boards
he made for the corners of the tabernacle in the innermost
part. 29 And they were double below, and they were joined
together as pairs at the top into one ring, so he made for the
two of them, for the two corners. 30 And there were eight
boards and their bases of silver, sixteen bases, two bases under each board.

31 And he made bars of acacia wood, five for each wall of the
tabernacle. 32 And five bars for the second wall of the tabernacle, and five bars for the boards of the innermost side of the
tabernacle to the west. 33 And he made the middle bar to pass
through in the midst of the boards from one end to the other.
34 And the boards he overlaid with gold, and their rings he
made of gold as housings for the bars he overlaid with gold.

35 And he made the curtain of blue and purple and crimson
yarn, and fine embroidered linen, a designer work, he made
it with cherubim. 36 And he made for it four columns of acacia wood, and he overlaid them with gold, and their hooks
were gold, and they cast for them four bases of silver.

37 And he made a screen for the door of the tent of blue and
purple and crimson yarn, and fine embroidered linen, a work

of embroidery. [38] And its five columns, and their hooks, and he overlaid their tops and their connecting bands of gold, and their five bases of bronze.

Commentary

Exodus 36:8–38 recounts the construction of the wilderness tabernacle. The passage attributes construction to "everyone who is wise of heart" (Hebrew, *kōl ḥăkam-lēb*), which is formulated as a masculine singular noun phrase, even when women are presumed to be the expert artisans who undertake the work of constructing the tabernacle (cf. Exod 35:25–26). Consequently, the verbs employed to portray the acts of work necessary to construct the tabernacle appear as masculine singular forms throughout this passage.

Exodus 36:8–13 describes the first set of items to be made, i.e., the ten curtains that will be sewn together to cover the walls of the tabernacle structure. Each curtain is embroidered in blue, purple, and crimson, with fine linen, and includes cherub designs. Each curtain measures twenty-eight cubits in length and four cubits in width. The ten curtains are joined together lengthwise in two assemblies of five, with fifty loops on the outermost curtain of each, fastened by an equal number of gold hooks, that enable the two assemblies to be joined into one piece that covers the walls of the tabernacle round about.

Exodus 36:14–19 describes the eleven curtains made of goats' hair that will form the covering tent that will overlie the top of the tabernacle structure. Each curtain measures thirty cubits in length and four cubits in width. They are joined together in two assemblies, one of five curtains and the other of six curtains. The sixth curtain of the second set will be folded back to allow the entrance of the tabernacle to remain open, and it will be used to close the entrance when necessary. Again, fifty loops are provided at the end of each assembly and fastened by bronze hooks to form one enclosure over the embroidered curtains described above. A second covering of tanned rams' skins forms the tent, and a third covering of dolphins' skins overlies the covering of rams' skins. The double layer enables maximal protection against rain and other elements.

Exodus 36:20–30 describes the boards and their fixtures that are constructed to form the walls of the tabernacle covered by the three sets of curtains described above. The boards are cut from acacia wood and stand upright. Each board is ten cubits high and a cubit and a half wide. Each board is fitted with two clasps that bind the boards together into a wall, and two supports along the bottom that fit into the two bases of silver for each board. The south and north walls of the tabernacle are formed with a wall of twenty boards each, to be covered with the three sets of curtains described above. The innermost side of the tabernacle to the west is formed by six boards, plus an additional two boards that form the two corners of the wall. The innermost side of the tabernacle is described metaphorically as "the two thighs" (Hebrew, *yarkātāyim*) to suggest the intimate nature of the relationship between YHWH, often understood to be the groom, and Israel or Jerusalem, often understood as the bride in a marital relationship (cf. Isa 54; Jer 2; Ezek 16; Hos 1–3; Zeph 3:14–20).[1] Such a relationship is then envisioned in the metaphorical interpretation of the Song of Songs.[2] The two corner pieces are formed like the other boards with two supports for their two silver bases, but the top of each board is formed with a ring on top to facilitate the placement of the curtain for the holy of holies where the ark of the witness will reside.

Exodus 36:31–34 describes the center bars that are constructed. Five bars each are to be placed in the middle of the board assemblies to stabilize the southern, western, and northern walls of the tabernacle. The bars are to be made of acacia wood and overlaid with gold. The boards and the rings for the bars are also to be overlaid with gold.

Exodus 36:35–36 describes the formation of the curtain (Hebrew, *pārōket*) for the inner sanctuary to be embroidered with blue, purple, and crimson yarn and fine linen, with a cherub design. The curtain will have four boards made of acacia wood for support. These boards will be overlaid with gold, and their hooks will be cast from gold. Their four bases will be cast from silver.

Exodus 36:37–38 describes the screen (Hebrew, *māsāk*) that will cover the entrance to the tabernacle. It will be embroidered from blue, purple, and crimson yarn, and fine linen, with five columns and hooks. The columns are overlaid on top with gold, and their hooks and connecting bands are also made of gold. Their five bases are made of bronze.

1. Baumann, *Love and Violence*.
2. Sweeney, *Jewish Mysticism*, 354–63.

The Construction of the Ark, the Furnishings of the Tabernacle, and the Courtyard of the Tabernacle —Exodus 37:1—38:20

Translation

37:1 And Bezalel made the ark of acacia wood, two and one-half cubits its length, one and one-half cubits its width, and one and one-half cubits its height. [2] And he overlaid it with pure gold, inside and outside, and he made for it a border of gold round about. [3] And he cast for it four rings of gold upon its four feet, and two rings each were on its first side and two rings were on its second side. [4] And he made poles of acacia wood, and he overlaid them with gold. [5] And he put the poles into the rings upon the sides of the ark to carry the ark.

[6] And he made a cover of pure gold, two and one-half cubits its length and one and one-half cubits its width. [7] And he made two cherubim of gold, hammered work he made them on the two ends of the cover. [8] One cherub on one end and the other cherub on the other end of the cover; he made the cherubs on its two ends. [9] And the cherubs were spreading out their wings above, overshadowing with their wings the cover, while their faces were each to the other, facing the cover.

[10] And he made the table of acacia wood, two cubits its length and one cubit its width and one and one-half cubits

its height. [11] And he cast it of pure gold, and he made for it a
border of gold round about. [12] And he made for it a frame of
a handsbreadth round about, and he made a border of gold
for its frame round about. [13] And he cast for it four rings of
gold, and he placed the rings upon the four corners, which
were for its four feet, [14] beside the frame were the rings holding the poles to carry the table. [15] And he made the poles of
acacia wood, and he overlaid them with gold to carry the
table. [16] And he made the vessels that were upon the table,
with its dishes and its bowls and its libation vessels and its
jars, which were used for pouring out, of pure gold.

[17] And he made the lampstand of pure gold, hammered he
made the lampstand, its base [thigh] and its shaft [stem], its
cups, its bulbs, and its flowers, which come from it. [18] And
six stems from its sides, three stems of the lampstand from
its first side, and three stems of the lampstand from its second side. [19] Three cups shaped like almond blossoms on each
stem, bulb, and flower, and three cups shaped like almond
blossoms on each stem, bulb, and flower, for the six stems going out from the lampstand. [20] And on the lampstand are four
cups shaped like almond blossoms, its bulbs, and its flowers.
[21] And a bulb under two stems [coming out] from it, and a
bulb under the two stems coming out from it, and a bulb
under the two stems coming out from it, for [a total of] six
stems coming out from it. [22] And their bulbs and their stems
[coming out] from it were entirely one hammered work of
pure gold. [23] And he made its seven lamps and its tongs, and
its snuffers [were] of pure gold. [24] [From] a brick [talent] of
pure gold he made it and all its vessels.

[25] And he made the incense altar of acacia wood, a cubit is
its length, and a cubit is its width, squared, and two cubits
is its height, and from it were its horns. [26] And he overlaid it
with pure gold, its top [roof] and its sides round about, and
its horns, and he made for it a border of gold round about.
[27] And two rings of gold he made for it, under its border for
its two walls, that is, on its two sides housing the poles with
which to carry it. [28] And he made the poles of acacia wood,

and he overlaid them with gold. [29] And he made the holy anointing oil and the incense of pure spices, a blended work.

38:1 And he made the altar of the whole burnt offering of acacia wood, five cubits was its length, and five cubits was its width, squared, and three cubits was its height. [2] And he made its horns on its four corners; from it were its horns. And he overlaid it with bronze. [3] And he made all the vessels of the altar, the pots, and the spatulas, and the bowls, and the forks, and the snuffers, all the vessels he made of bronze. [4] And he made for the altar a grating, a meshwork of bronze under its rim below its middle. [5] And he cast four rings on the four edges of the bronze grating that would hold the poles. [6] And he made the poles of acacia wood, and he overlaid them with bronze. [7] And he placed the poles into the rings upon the sides of the altar with which to carry it. Hollow he made it.

[8] And he made the washbasin of bronze and its base of bronze with the mirrors of the women who served at the tent of meeting.

[9] And he made the courtyard enclosure. On the south side the curtains of the courtyard enclosure of fine embroidered linen, one hundred cubits. [10] Their twenty columns and their twenty bases were bronze, and the hooks of the columns and their connecting bands were silver.

[11] And on the north side, one hundred cubits. Their twenty columns and their twenty bases were bronze. The hooks of the columns and their connecting bands were silver.

[12] And on the west side were curtains, fifty cubits. Their ten columns and their ten bases, the hooks of the columns and their connecting bands were silver.

[13] And on the side facing the east, fifty cubits. [14] Curtains, fifteen cubits to the shoulder side. Their columns, three, and their bases, three, [15] and to the second shoulder side, on each side of the gate of the courtyard enclosure, were curtains, fifteen cubits, their three columns and their three bases.

16 All the curtains of the courtyard enclosure round about
were of fine embroidered linen, 17 and their bases for the
columns were bronze, the hooks of the columns and the connecting bands were silver for all the columns of the courtyard enclosure. 18 And the screen of the gate of the courtyard
enclosure was of embroidered work, blue and purple and
crimson yarn, and fine embroidered linen, and [it was]
twenty cubits long, and its height by width was five cubits
beside the curtains of the courtyard enclosure. 19 And their
four columns and their four bases were bronze, their hooks
were silver, and the overlay of their tops and their connecting bands were silver, 20 and all the pegs of the tabernacle for
the courtyard enclosure, round about, were bronze.

Commentary

Exodus 37:1—38:20 recounts the construction of the ark, the furnishings of the tabernacle, and the courtyard enclosure of the entire sanctuary. Although many interpreters devote little attention to this section based on the claim that it largely replicates material from Exodus 25–27, it presents a very different organization for the material, which enables interpreters to better understand the layout of the tabernacle complex, which anticipates the layout of ancient Israelite and Judean temples in general.

The first item to be constructed is the ark of the witness in Exodus 37:1–9, which is to be set in the holy of holies of the tabernacle on the west side. Bezalel is identified as the craftsman who constructed the ark from acacia wood overlaid with pure gold, inside and outside. There is a gold border or molding round about the ark, and four rings at each of the lower ends of the ark to facilitate carrying the ark with acacia-wood poles overlaid with gold. The cover of the ark is made of pure gold, two and one-half cubits in length and one and one-half cubits in width, with two cherubim of hammered gold, a cherub on each end of the cover, one facing the other, with their wings spread above. The purpose of the cherubim is to guard the ark, insofar as the ark is understood to constitute a throne above which YHWH is seated (1 Sam 4:1; 2 Sam 6:2; 1 Chr 13:6; cf. 2 Kgs 19:15; Isa 37:16; Pss 80:2; 99:1).

Exodus 37:10–16 recounts the construction of the table of acacia wood, overlaid with pure gold, two cubits long, one cubit wide, and one and one-half cubits high. It is to be set before the holy of holies inside the tabernacle. Again, a border or molding is constructed round about, and a frame with its own border is also constructed. Four rings are attached to its four legs, again to facilitate carrying the table with poles of acacia wood overlaid with gold. The various vessels, cast in pure gold, to be used with the table, include its dishes, its bowls, its libation vessels, and its jars. The purpose of the table is to set an idealized symbolic meal consisting of two loaves of challah or braided bread, together with its various plates, bowls, jars, etc., before YHWH.

Exodus 37:17–24 recounts the construction of the lampstand from pure, hammered gold, to be set before the holy of holies of the tabernacle. The lampstand is constructed after the pattern of a seven-branched tree that brings light into the world. Such a pattern suggests an ancient representation of the tree of knowledge set in the garden of Eden from which Eve ate and thereby brought the knowledge of good and evil to humanity (Gen 3:1–7; cf. Prov 8–9), although in the present form of the Genesis 3 narrative, Adam and Eve are expelled from the garden of Eden for disobeying YHWH. It is possible that the imagery of the lampstand as a tree of knowledge is rooted in older Canaanite ideology in which a goddess, such as Asherah or perhaps Hathor, was symbolized by a tree and known for both fertility and knowledge.[1] It is noteworthy that the Kuntillet Ajrud inscription, a caravan site associated with northern Israelite trade in the Sinai wilderness, depicts YHWH of Samaria and his Asherah.[2] The construction of the lampstand includes a base, its shaft or trunk, and its bulbs and flowers which extend from its seven branches, apparently a reference to the seven days of creation.[3] Such trees also appear in Assyrian mythology to symbolize the wisdom of the ideal man, i.e., the Assyrian king sent by the gods to earth from the heavens.[4] The bulbs and flowers are associated with cups shaped like almond blossoms, which are symbolic of the Aaronic or Levitical priesthood in that the Levites were chosen as YHWH's priestly tribe when Aaron's rod blossomed in the form of an almond blossom (Num 17:16—18:32; cf. Jer

1. Merlo, "Asherah"; Goler, "Hathor."

2. B. Schmidt, "Kuntillet ʿAjrud."

3. Meyers, *Tabernacle Menorah.*

4. Widengren, *King and Tree of Life.*

1:11–12). The various vessels that were used in relation to the lampstand (i.e., its tongs and its snuffers) were also made of pure gold.

Exodus 37:25–29 recounts the construction of the incense altar of acacia wood overlaid with pure gold, a cubit in length and a cubit in width, squared, and two cubits in height. The incense altar is to be set inside the tabernacle before the holy of holies. The four horns built into the altar represent rays of incense smoke that spread to all the cardinal directions of the world of creation. The incense altar is constructed with a border or molding round about, with two rings on each side to hold the bars of acacia wood overlaid with gold used to carry the altar. A brief comment at the end of the passage notes the manufacture of anointing oil for the priests and the lampstand and sweet-smelling incense as blended works for use in the tabernacle.

Exodus 38:1–8 recounts the construction of the altar of whole burnt offerings, to be placed outside the tabernacle before its entrance. The altar is to be built of acacia wood overlaid with bronze. It is five cubits in length, five cubits in width, squared, and three cubits in height, with four horns protruding from each of its four corners to represent rays of light or smoke from the fire that emanates out to all four cardinal directions of the world of creation. The vessels employed at the altar, including its pots, spatulas, bowls, forks, and snuffers, are also made of bronze. The grating is a meshwork placed on a rim halfway down inside the hollow altar, apparently as a base for placing the wood necessary for the fires that will consume the offerings. Four rings are placed on the four edges of the bronze grating to facilitate carrying the structure with acacia-wood poles overlaid with bronze.

Exodus 38:8 recounts the construction of the bronze washbasin to be placed by the altar of whole burnt offerings. It is made from the bronze mirrors donated by the women who served at the tent of meeting. The use of mirrors to construct the basin would aid in explaining the reflective qualities of the temple fixtures that apparently allow for the reflection of the lights of the temple lampstand in Ezekiel's vision, based on temple imagery, in which he sees divine eyes on the wheels or rings of YHWH's ark of the covenant that bears YHWH through the heavens.[5] Women are known to have served in northern sanctuaries, such as Shiloh, apparently to assist in the cooking of sacrificial meat (1 Sam 2:12–17). Likewise, northern Israelite women, such as Miriam

5. Sweeney, "Ezekiel's Debate with Isaiah"; Sweeney, *Reading Ezekiel*, 24–34.

(Exod 15:20–21) and Deborah (Judg 5), apparently played roles as liturgical singers in northern Israel.[6] There is no clear evidence that they served as temple prostitutes, apart from polemics by southern Judean writers. The reference to women serving at the tabernacle here may indicate the possibility that an earlier version of this narrative had its origins in the E-stratum of the Pentateuch.

Exodus 38:9–20 recounts the construction of the tabernacle courtyard or enclosure that surrounds the tabernacle structure and its outer fixtures. The tabernacle courtyard enclosure measures one hundred cubits on its south and north sides and fifty cubits on its west and east sides. It is made of embroidered linen curtains supported by columns made of bronze with bases and hooks also made of bronze and silver connecting bands. Twenty columns with their bases, hooks, and connecting stands support the curtains on the north and south sides, and ten columns, with their bases, hooks, and connecting bands, on the west side. The east side is constructed differently because it includes a twenty-cubit entrance flanked on either side by fifteen-cubit curtains, supported by three columns on each side, with their bases, hooks, and connecting bands. The screen of the courtyard enclosure is made of embroidered fine linen with blue, purple, and crimson yarn, twenty cubits in length and five cubits in height, and supported by four bronze columns with silver tops and their bronze bases, silver hooks and connecting bands. All the pegs used to support the courtyard enclosure structure are made of bronze.

6. Sweeney, "Israelite and Judean Religions"; see also Everhart, "Serving Women."

Summation of the Construction of the Tabernacle, Its Furnishings, Its Equipment, and the Holy Garments for the Priests —Exodus 38:21—39:31

Translation

38:21 These are the inventories of the tabernacle, the taber-
nacle of the witness, which was authorized by the mouth of
Moses, the service of the Levites by the hand of Ithamar ben
Aaron, the priest.

[22] And Bezalel ben Uri ben Hur of the tribe of Judah did all
that YHWH commanded Moses. [23] And with him was Oholiab
ben Ahisamach of the tribe of Dan, engraver and designer
and embroiderer in blue and in purple and in crimson yarn
and in fine linen.

[24] All the gold that was made for the work in all the work of
the sanctuary, and the gold was an elevation offering, twenty-nine bricks [lit., talents] and 730 shekels by the shekel
of the sanctuary. [25] And the silver of those appointed from
the congregation was one hundred bricks [lit., talents] and
1,775 shekels by the shekel of the sanctuary. [26] A division
for each head of half a shekel by the shekel of the sanctuary
for all who were authorized, from the age of twenty years

and above for the 603,550 persons. [27] And the one hundred bricks [lit., talents] of silver were for casting the bases of the sanctuary and the bases of the curtain, one hundred bases for one hundred bricks [lit., talents], a brick [lit., talent] for each base. [28] And the 1,775 [bricks/talents] he made for hooks for the columns, and he overlaid their heads and he banded them together.

[29] And the bronze of the elevation offering was seventy bricks [lit., talents] and 2,400 shekels. [30] And he made with it the bases of the entrance of the tent of meeting and the bronze altar and the bronze grating that was for it and all the vessels of the altar, [31] and all the bases of the courtyard enclosure, round about, and the bases of the gate of the courtyard enclosure, and all the pegs of the tabernacle, and all the pegs of the courtyard round about.

39:1 And from the blue and the purple and the crimson yarn they made the braided garments for serving in the sanctuary, and they made the holy garments that were for Aaron just as YHWH had commanded Moses.

[2] And they made the ephod of gold, blue and purple and crimson yarn, and fine embroidered linen. [3] And they hammered the plates of gold, and they cut threads to make within the blue and within the purple and within the crimson yarn and within the fine linen a designer work. [4] Shoulder pieces they made for it, joining [them] upon its two joined ends.
[5] And the design of its ephod which was [to be] upon him was [one piece] from it like the work of gold, blue and purple and crimson yarn, and embroidered fine linen, just as YHWH commanded Moses.

[6] And they made the stones of beryl framed with overlays of gold, engraved with seal engravings according to the names of the sons of Israel. [7] And he placed them upon the shoulder pieces of the ephod [as] stones of remembrance for the sons of Israel, just as YHWH commanded Moses.

[8] And he made the breastpiece as a designer work like the work of the ephod, gold, blue and purple and crimson yarn,

and fine embroidered linen. [9] It was square; doubled they made the breastpiece, a handbreadth was its length and a handbreadth was its width, doubled. [10] And they filled in it four columns of stone, a column of carnelian, chrysolite, and emerald was the first column. [11] And the second column was carbuncle, sapphire, and diamond. [12] And the third column was amber, agate, and amethyst. [13] And the fourth column was yellow jasper, beryl, and jasper, framed, overlaid with gold in their fillings. [14] And the stones were according to the names of the sons of Israel; behold, twelve upon their names, [as] seal engravings, each above its name for the twelve tribes.

[15] And they made upon the breastpiece twisted chains, a work of cords, of pure gold. [16] And they made two overlays of gold and two rings of gold, and they placed the two rings upon the two ends of the breastpiece. [17] And they placed the two cords of gold through the two rings upon the end of the breastpiece, [18] and the two ends of the two cords they placed upon the two overlays, and they placed them upon the shoulder pieces of the ephod upon its front side. [19] And they made two rings of gold, and they placed [them] upon the two ends of the breastpiece, upon its folds [lit., lips] across the ephod inside. [20] And they made two rings of gold, and placed them upon the two shoulder pieces of the ephod, below its front side by its seam above the design of the ephod. [21] And they bound the breastpiece from its rings to the rings of the ephod [with] a thread of blue to be upon the design of the ephod so that the breastpiece would not move away from upon the ephod, just as YHWH commanded Moses.

[22] And they made the robe of the ephod as a work of weaving, entirely of blue. [23] And the opening of the robe within it was like the opening of a corset with a lip for its opening round about that will not tear. [24] And they made upon the hems of the robe pomegranates of blue and purple and crimson yarn, embroidered. [25] And they made its bells of pure gold, and they placed the bells in the midst of the pomegranates upon the hems of the robe round about within the pomegranates. [26] A bell and a pomegranate and a bell and a pomegranate

were upon the hems of the robe round about to serve, just as YHWH commanded Moses.

[27] And they made the tunics of fine linen, a woven work, for
Aaron and for his sons, [28] and the headdress was fine linen,
and the crowns of the turbans were fine linen, and the white
linen pants were of fine embroidered linen, [29] and the sash
was of fine embroidered linen, and blue and purple and crimson yarn, a work of embroidery, just as YHWH commanded Moses.

[30] And the made the blossom of the holy crown of pure gold,
and they wrote upon it, an engraved seal, "Holy to YHWH,"
[31] and they placed upon him a thread of blue to place upon
the headdress above, just as YHWH commanded Moses.

Commentary

Exodus 38:21–31 recounts the raw materials necessary for the construction of the tabernacle, its furnishings, and its equipment.

The passage begins in Exodus 38:21–23 with a superscription, which identifies the following as the inventory of the tabernacle (Hebrew, *pěqûdê hammiškān*, "the visitations/musterings/expenses of the tabernacle"). The verse makes sure to identify the tabernacle as "the tabernacle of the witness" to ensure the exact specification of its record and it follows with a further specification that the requisition for the following materials was made by Moses to support the work of the Levites under the supervision of Ithamar ben Aaron, the priest. The superscription identifies the following as an official document. Exodus 38:22–23 continues with a statement that Bezalel ben Uri ben Hur of the tribe of Judah and Oholiab ben Ahisamach, an engraver, designer, and embroiderer of the tribe of Dan, had carried out and overseen the work.

Exodus 38:24–31 then provides an accounting for all the metals used in the construction of the tabernacle, its furnishings, and its equipment. All of the metal is identified as an elevation offering (Hebrew, *tĕnûpâ*) given by the people for the construction of the tabernacle.

The gold employed in the project totaled twenty-nine bricks (talents) and 730 shekels according to the weight of the shekel recognized in the sanctuary.

The silver employed totaled one hundred bricks (talents) and 1,775 shekels, again, according to the weight of the shekel recognized in the sanctuary. This amount is calculated to be the equivalent of half a shekel for each male person (lit., *gulgōlet*, "skull, head") aged twenty years and older—numbering 603,550 men of the Israelite population at the time. The hundred talents of silver were used for casting the bases of the sanctuary and the curtains, and the remaining 1,730 shekels of silver were used to cast the hooks for the posts, the tops of the posts, and the bands that held the posts together.

The bronze from the elevation offering of the people totaled seventy bricks (talents) and 2,400 shekels. The bronze was used to cast the bases for the entrance of the tent of meeting, the bronze altar, its grating, its vessels, the bases of the courtyard enclosure, and all the pegs of the tabernacle and the courtyard enclosure.

Although many interpreters treat Exodus 39:1–31 as discrete unit within the larger formal structure of Exodus 35–40, the introductory wording of Exodus 39:1, "And from [Hebrew, *ûmin*] the blue and the purple and the crimson yarn they made the braided garments for serving in the sanctuary," indicates that it is a separate sub-unit within Exodus 38:21—39:31, which recounts the construction of the tabernacle, its furnishings, its equipment, and the priestly garments. Exodus 39:1 introduces Exodus 39:1–31 with a general statement concerning the production of the priestly garments, all of which use blue, purple, and crimson yarn in one form or another. Overall, Exodus 39:1–31 depicts the priestly garments from the standpoint of one who would view Aaron or his sons dressed in the garments, beginning with the outer garments and moving inward through the visible layers.[1]

Exodus 39:2–7 recounts the production of the ephod. The ephod is generally portrayed as a garment made of white linen (e.g., 1 Sam 2:18; 22:18) or as an item made of gold and employed in the oracular inquiry of YHWH (e.g., Judg 8:27; 1 Sam 23:6). The differentiation in descriptions suggests that two different items, one of linen and one of gold, were employed in antiquity.[2] The linen ephod appears to be akin to the Egyptian linen ephod (Egyptian, *ifd*; cf. Ugaritic, *'pd*; Akkadian, *epattu*), whereas the gold ephod is akin to an object used for divine inquiry, perhaps the urim and thummim that are carried in the ephod

1. For visual depictions of the priestly garments, based on the understanding of Rashi, see Arnovitz, *Exodus/Shemot*, 215–22.

2. Cf. Blischke, "Ephod."

(Judg 17:6; 18:14, 17, 18, 20; Hos 3:4; cf. esp. Exod 28:28–30). Insofar as the ephod in Exodus 28:28–30 is associated with the urim and thummim, the present understanding of the ephod appears to represent a combination of the two conceptualizations. The ephod is made of a combination of gold, blue, purple, and crimson yarn, and embroidered linen. It is worn over the breastpiece, with attached shoulder pieces made from braided chains of gold. The ephod may symbolize an ancient pouch in which the urim and thummim were carried.

Exodus 39:8–21 recounts the manufacture of the breastpiece. It is made of blue, purple, and crimson yarn, and fine embroidered linen. The description emphasizes the twelve tribes of Israel, each represented by a unique precious stone. The breastpiece is embellished with gold trim in the form of braided gold chains and additional set stones on the shoulder of the garment, including gold rings that facilitate the attachment of the ephod upon the breastpiece.

Exodus 39:22–26 recounts the production of the Aaron's robe. It is woven work, entirely blue in color. The portrayal of a corset-like lip suggests an opening above on the chest that would accommodate the breastpiece and the ephod. The hems of the garment include woven pomegranates of blue, purple, and crimson yarn interspersed with golden bells that would provide musical ringing as Aaron or the high priest would move about in the sanctuary.

Exodus 39:27–29 recounts the additional items of clothing for Aaron and his sons. Verse 27 portrays the tunics worn by Aaron and his sons, in the case of Aaron, under the blue robe described above. Verse 28 describes the white linen turbans, with their crowns, and the white linen pants or breeches worn by Aaron and his sons. Verse 29 describes the linen sash, embroidered with blue, purple, and crimson yarn.

Exodus 39:30–31 describes the golden "holy crown" (Hebrew, *nēzer haqqōdeš*) worn by Aaron. It is embellished with a "blossom" (Hebrew, *ṣîṣ*), apparently a metaphorical reminder of Aaron's blossoming rod in Numbers 17–18 (cf. Jer 1:11–12), which indicated YHWH's choice of Aaron and the tribe of Levi to serve as priests in the sanctuary. The "blossom" is inscribed with the Hebrew phrase *qōdeš lyhwh*, "Holy to YHWH," to indicate Aaron's status as YHWH's high priest in the sanctuary. The crown is secured to Aaron's headdress by a blue woven thread or cord.

The Account of the Completion of the Wilderness Tabernacle and YHWH's Entrance into the Sanctuary—Exodus 39:32—40:38

Translation

39:32 And all the work of the tabernacle of the tent of meeting was completed, and the sons of Israel did according to all that YHWH commanded Moses, so they did.

33 And they brought the tabernacle to Moses with the tent and
all of its vessels, its hooks, its boards, its bars, its columns,
and its bases, 34 and the covering of tanned rams' skins, and
the covering of dolphin skins, and the curtain of the screen,
35 the ark of the witness and its poles, and its cover, 36 the
table, all of its vessels, and the bread of the presence, 37 the
pure lampstand, its lamps, lamps of the arrangement, and
all its vessels, and the lighting oil, 38 and the altar of gold,
and the anointing oil, and the sweet-smelling incense, and
the screen for the entrance of the tent, 39 the bronze altar,
and the bronze grating for it, its poles, and all its vessels, the
basin and its stand, 40 the curtains of the courtyard enclosure, its columns and its bases, and the screen for the gate
of the courtyard enclosure, its cords and its pegs, and all the
vessels of the service of the tabernacle for the tent of meeting, 41 the braided garments for service in the sanctuary, the

holy garments for Aaron, the priest, and the garments for his sons to serve as priests, 42 according to all that YHWH commanded Moses, so the sons of Israel did all the service. 43 And Moses saw all the work, and behold, they did it just as YHWH commanded, so they did it, and Moses blessed them.

40:1 And YHWH spoke to Moses, saying, 2 "On the first month, on the first day of the month, you shall set up the tabernacle of the tent of meeting. 3 And you shall place there the ark of the witness, and you shall screen the ark with the curtain. 4 And you shall bring the table, and you shall arrange its arrangement, and you shall bring the lampstand, and you shall light up its lamps. 5 And you shall place the altar of gold for incense before the ark of the witness, and you shall place the screen at the entrance to the tabernacle.

6 "And you shall place the altar of the whole burnt offering before the entrance of the tabernacle of the tent of meeting. 7 And you shall place the basin between the tent of meeting and the altar, and you shall place there water. 8 And you shall place the courtyard enclosure all around, and you shall place the screen for the courtyard enclosure.

9 "And you shall take the anointing oil, and you shall anoint the tabernacle and all that is in it, and you shall sanctify it, and all of its vessels, and it shall be holy. 10 And you shall anoint the altar of the whole burnt offering, and the altar shall be holy of holies. 11 And you shall anoint the altar and its stand, and you shall sanctify it.

12 "And you shall bring near Aaron and his sons to the entrance of the tent of meeting, and you shall wash them with water. 13 And you shall dress Aaron with the holy garments, and you shall anoint him, and you shall sanctify him, and he shall serve as priest to me. 14 And his sons you shall bring near, and you shall dress them in tunics. 15 And you shall anoint them just as you anointed their father, and they shall serve as priests to me. Their anointing will be for them an eternal priesthood for their generations."

[16] And Moses did according to all that YHWH commanded
him, so he did.

[17] And it came to pass in the first month, in the second year,
on the first of the month, that the tabernacle was established.
[18] And Moses established the tabernacle, and he placed its
bases, and he placed its boards, and he placed its bars, and
he set up its columns. [19] And he spread out the tent over the
tabernacle, and he placed the cover of the tent upon it above,
just as YHWH commanded Moses.

[20] And he took the witness, and he placed [it] into the ark,
and he placed the poles upon the ark, and he placed the
cover above upon the ark. [21] And he brought the ark into the
tabernacle, and he placed the curtain of the screen, and he
screened the ark of the witness, just as YHWH commanded
Moses.

[22] And he placed the table in the tent of meeting upon the
innermost part of the tabernacle north, outside the curtain.
[23] And he arranged upon it an arrangement of bread before
YHWH just as YHWH commanded Moses. [24] And he placed
the lampstand in the tent of meeting, opposite the table,
upon the south side of the tabernacle. [25] And he lit up the
lamps before YHWH, just as YHWH commanded Moses.

[26] And he placed the golden altar in the tent of meeting before the curtain. [27] And he burned upon it sweet-smelling
incense, just as YHWH commanded Moses.

[28] And he placed the screen at the entrance of the tabernacle,
[29] and the altar of the whole burnt offering he placed at the
entrance of the tabernacle of the tent of meeting, and he offered up the whole burnt offering and the grain offering, just
as YHWH commanded Moses.

[30] And he placed the basin between the tent of meeting and
the altar, and he placed there water for washing. [31] And Moses and Aaron and his sons washed from it their hands and
their feet, [32] when they came into the tent of meeting and
when they came near to the altar they washed just as YHWH
commanded Moses. [33] And he established the courtyard

enclosure round about the tabernacle and the altar, and he placed the screen at the gate of the courtyard enclosure.

And Moses finished the work. [34] And the cloud covered the tent of meeting, and the glory of YHWH filled the tabernacle. [35] And Moses was not able to enter the tent of meeting because the cloud resided upon it, and the glory of YHWH filled the tabernacle. [36] And when the cloud went up from upon the tabernacle, the sons of Israel journeyed in all their journeys. [37] And if the cloud was not lifted up, then they did not journey until the cloud was lifted up, [38] because the cloud of YHWH was upon the tabernacle by day, and a fire would be on it at night to the eyes of all the House of Israel in all of their journeys.

Commentary

Exodus 39:32—40:38 recounts the completion of the wilderness tabernacle and YHWH's entrance into the sanctuary.

The account begins in Exodus 39:32–43 with a narrative that announces the completion of the work on the tabernacle and how the people of Israel brought the various elements of the tabernacle complex to Moses. A major concern in this passage is to assert that Israel completed the work exactly as YHWH had instructed Moses. Once the integrity of the work has been certified, Moses then blesses the people in an act that demonstrates his—and YHWH's—approval.

Michael Fishbane builds on the earlier work of Martin Buber to demonstrate that there is a major intertextual link between Exodus 39:32–43 and the account of creation in Genesis 1:1—2:3.[1] Language from Genesis 1:31; 2:1; 2:2; and 2:3 correlates with Exodus 39:32; 39:43; and 40:33, which indicates an interest in correlating the completion and blessing of humanity and creation in Genesis 1:1—2:4a with the completion and blessing of Israel and the wilderness tabernacle in Exodus 39:32—40:38. Indeed, such a correlation between creation and temple qua tabernacle underlies the work of Jon Levenson,[2] and the entire

1. Fishbane, "Genesis 1:1—2:4a"; cf. Buber and Rosenzweig, *Schrift und ihre Verdeutschung*, 39ff.

2. Levenson, "Temple and the World"; Levenson, *Sinai and Zion*.

narrative of the exodus–wilderness narratives in Exodus–Numbers, which underlies the present commentary.[3]

Exodus 40:1–16 then follows with an account of YHWH's instructions to Moses to set up and to sanctify the tabernacle, to dress and to ordain the priests on the first day of the first month, and to recount Moses's compliance with YHWH's instructions. The dating of YHWH's instruction to the first day of the first month presupposes an older, apparently solar-based calendar that appears to be of Canaanite origin, which was later replaced by a lunar calendar of Babylonian and Persian origin.[4] Although many scholars view this notice as a P-stratum statement, the interest in correlating the completion of the wilderness tabernacle and the tent of meeting with the first month of the Israelite calendar results in a correlation with the celebration of Passover and Matzot, which also take place in the first month of the year, beginning on the fourteenth day of the month. Such an interest is in keeping with the theological and liturgical outlook of the Northern Kingdom of Israel as represented in the E-stratum narrative of the exodus–wilderness traditions. Although the present form of the narrative may well represent the final P-stratum of the Pentateuch, the interest in correlating the completion of the tabernacle with Passover may signal an underlying E-stratum narrative that has been edited and reformulated by P.[5]

Exodus 40:17–38 then concludes the narrative with an account of how Moses completed the work of setting up the wilderness tabernacle, with the ark of the witness inside in vv. 17–33a, thereby enabling YHWH to take up residence in the newly created wilderness sanctuary in vv. 33b–38. The initial date presented in v. 17, viz., "the first month, in the second year, on the first of the month," indicates that it took Moses a year to set up the tabernacle and that he did so by himself. Again, the narrative emphasizes that Moses did everything in accordance with the instructions given to him by YHWH. It is careful to emphasize that Moses, Aaron, and Aaron's sons washed their hands and feet at the basin as they approached the altar, in keeping with the requirements of priestly purity in undertaking the duties of the tabernacle qua temple.

Once Moses finished the work, vv. 34–38 recount how "the glory of YHWH" entered the tabernacle, metaphorically represented as the

3. See also Sweeney, "Creation as Sacred Space."

4. Cf. Berner, "Calendar."

5. Cf. Sweeney, *Pentateuch*, xvii–xxix.

cloud that had covered Mount Sinai from the very beginning of the Sinai revelation in Exodus 19. According to v. 35, Moses is not able to enter the wilderness tabernacle while the cloud is upon it, presumably because he is not to serve as a priest in the tabernacle in the same manner as Aaron and Aaron's sons. Verses 36–38 then depict the movement of the tabernacle, i.e., when the cloud representing the presence of the glory of YHWH departs from the tabernacle, the tabernacle and the sons of Israel would be able to undertake the next stage in their journey through the wilderness to the promised land of Israel. Verse 38 correlates the cloud of the glory of YHWH with the pillar of smoke by day and the pillar of fire by night that led Israel out of Egypt to the Reed Sea in Exodus 14–15 and beyond. It also correlates the journeys of Israel with the wilderness itinerary formulas, based on the verb *wayissĕʿû*, which Cross identifies as a feature of the P-stratum narrative of the Pentateuch.[6] But this formula first appears in Genesis 46:1, which is identified by Noth as a part of the E-stratum narrative and Campbell and O'Brien as part of the J-stratum narrative closely associated with E.[7] Insofar as the toledoth formulas of the Pentateuch begin with creation in Genesis 2:4 and continue through Numbers 3:1, which introduces the wilderness journey as recounted in Numbers and Deuteronomy, it seems better to view the wilderness itinerary formula as an E-stratum feature, insofar as it introduces Jacob's and Israel's journey to Egypt and back again to the promised land of Israel, thereby highlighting a special concern of northern Israel's apparent view of its own origins and the role of the exodus narrative itself as a creation narrative.

Reception History

The New Testament book of Revelation 15:2–8 views the wilderness tabernacle as a harbinger of divine judgment from which seven angels robed in pure bright linen will emerge to bring seven plagues in the form of seven bowls filled with the wrath of G-d to be poured out upon the earth in Revelation 16:1–21. These plagues will ultimately bring about the fall of Babylon in Revelation 17:1—18:24.

6. Cross, "Priestly Work."

7. Noth, *History of Pentateuchal Traditions*, 211–13, 266; Campbell and O'Brien, *Sources of the Pentateuch*, 129, 181.

In her analysis of the wilderness tradition in relation to rabbinic interpretation, Rachel Adelman draws upon a model of the wilderness tabernacle as "a locomotive model of G-d's presence," offered by Benjamin Sommer, to depict the tabernacle as an expression of an imminent theology of G-d, which offers a mode of revelation and interrelationship with G-d that facilitates atonement for the sin of the golden calf from Exodus 32–34 and other sins that might be committed by Israel. She sees Exodus 25–40 as "a deep critique of Zion theology, which depicts the center of G-d's revelation as fixed to one particular place."[8] Such an understanding of the divine presence in the world lends itself well to the situation faced by Jews in the aftermath of the destruction of the First Temple in 587 BCE as well as after the destruction of the Second Temple in 70 CE.

Finally, the use of the verb *šākan*, "to dwell," in Exodus 40:35 as well as in the root of the term *miškān*, "dwelling, tabernacle," influences the concept of the divine Shekhinah (Hebrew, *šĕkînâ*, "presence," lit., "dwelling"), which is employed in rabbinic Hebrew to portray the divine presence in the temple and the world at large. The term functions especially well in Kabbalistic texts to portray the divine presence in the world as the culmination of the ten Sefirot, the "ten emanations [of G-d]," within human beings and the world at large that will ultimately see the sanctification of the world as the goal of creation.[9]

8. Adelman, "Wings of Desire."; cf. Sommer, *Bodies of G-d*, 80–108.

9. Sweeney, *Jewish Mysticism*, esp. 285–362.

Appendix

Exodus in the Synchronic Literary Structure of the Pentateuch

History of Creation/Formation of People Israel

I. **CREATION** of Heaven and Earth	Gen 1:1—2:3
II. **HUMAN** Origins	Gen 2:4—4:26
III. **HUMAN** Development/Problems	Gen 5:1—6:8
IV. **NOAH** and the Flood	Gen 6:9—9:29
V. **SPREAD** of Humans over the Earth	Gen 10:1—11:9
VI. **HISTORY** of the Semites	Gen 11:10–26
VII. **HISTORY** of Abraham (Isaac)	Gen 11:27—25:11
VIII. **HISTORY** of Ishmael	Gen 25:12–18
IX. **HISTORY** of Jacob (Isaac)	Gen 25:19—35:29
X. **HISTORY** of Esau	Gen 36:1—37:1
XI. **HISTORY** of the Twelve Tribes of Israel	Gen 37:2—Num 2:34
A. Joseph and his brothers in Egypt: Israel's journey to Egypt	Gen 37:2—50:26
B. Deliverance of Israel from Egyptian bondage: Rameses	Exod 1:1—12:36
1. The birth of Moses: These are the names	Exod 1:1—2:10

a. Tabulation of the tribes of Israel	Exod 1:1–5
b. Fertility of Israel following death of Joseph	Exod 1:6–7
c. Imposition of slavery on Israel by new pharaoh	Exod 1:8–14
d. Failure of pharaoh's attempt to use midwives to kill male Israelite babies	Exod 1:15–22
e. Birth and rescue of Moses	Exod 2:1–10
2. Moses's flight to Midian: And it came to pass in those days	Exod 2:11–22
a. Moses's flight to Midian after killing Egyptian taskmaster	Exod 2:11–15
b. Moses's marriage to Zipporah bat Reuel, priest of Midian	Exod 2:16–22
3. YHWH's commission of Moses: And it came to pass in those many days	Exod 2:23—4:31
a. Introduction concerning Egypt's oppression of Israel	Exod 2:23–25
b. Commission narrative proper	Exod 3:1—4:17
c. Moses's return to father-in-law to seek permission to leave	Exod 4:18
d. YHWH's instructions to Moses concerning encounter with pharaoh in Egypt	Exod 4:19–23
e. Circumcision of Moses/Gershom by Zipporah	Exod 4:24–26
f. Aaron joins Moses	Exod 4:27–31
4. Moses and Aaron's encounter with pharaoh: And afterward	Exod 5:1—12:36
a. Initial encounter with pharaoh: Snakes	Exod 5:1—6:13
b. Tabulation of the tribes of Israel culminating in Aaron and Moses	Exod 6:14–30
c. Plague narrative	Exod 7:1—12:36
1) First round: Initial encounter with pharaoh; snakes and Nile turned to blood	Exod 7:1–24
2) Second round: Frogs	Exod 7:25—8:11
3) Third round: Lice and vermin	Exod 8:12–15
4) Fourth round: Insects	Exod 8:16–28
5) Fifth round: Cattle disease	Exod 9:1–7

6) Sixth round: Boils	Exod 9:8–12
7) Seventh round: Thunder and hail	Exod 9:13–35
8) Eighth round: Locusts	Exod 10:1–20
9) Ninth round: Darkness	Exod 10:21–29
10) Tenth round: Death of the firstborn	Exod 11:1—12:36
a) YHWH's instruction concerning plague/ Moses's response	Exod 11:1–8
i. YHWH's instruction	Exod 11:1–3
ii. Moses's response: Convey instruction to Israel	Exod 11:4–8
b) YHWH's instruction concerning observance of Passover/Moses's response	Exod 12:1–28
i. YHWH's instruction	Exod 12:1–20
ii. Moses's response: Convey instruction to Israel	Exod 12:21–28
c) YHWH strikes Egypt/Egypt releases Israel	Exod 12:29–36
i. YHWH strikes Egypt	Exod 12:29
ii. Egypt's/pharaoh's response: Release Israel	Exod 12:30–36
C. From Rameses to Sukkot: Consecration of firstborn	Exod 12:37—13:19
1. Israel's departure from Rameses/Egypt	Exod 12:37–42
a. Departure proper	Exod 12:37–39
b. Summation of sojourn in Egypt	Exod 12:40–42
2. YHWH's instruction concerning Passover offering and Israel's compliance	Exod 12:43–5
a. YHWH's instruction	Exod 12:43–49
b. Israel's compliance	Exod 12:50
3. Summation of YHWH's action: Exodus from Egypt	Exod 12:51
4. YHWH's instruction concerning firstborn	Exod 13:1–2
5. Moses's instruction to Israel concerning observance of Passover and firstborn upon entry into the land of the Canaanites	Exod 13:3–16

6. Concerning Israel's journey	Exod 13:17–19
a. Journey by way of Reed Sea	Exod 13:17–18a
b. Israel is armed	Exod 13:18b
c. Moses carries bones of Joseph	Exod 13:19
D. From Sukkot to Etam: Pillar of fire and cloud	Exod 13:20–22
1. Itinerary formula	Exod 13:20
2. Concerning pillar of fire and cloud	Exod 13:21–22
E. From Etam to the Sea (Pihahirot/Baal Zephon): Deliverance at sea	Exod 14:1—15:21
1. YHWH's deliverance of Israel at the Sea of Reeds	Exod 14:1–31
2. Israel's song of praise for YHWH at the Sea	Exod 15:1–21
a. By Moses and the men	Exod 15:1–19
b. By Miriam and the women	Exod 15:20–21
F. From Reed Sea to Wilderness of Shur/Elim: Water in wilderness	Exod 15:22–27
1. Itinerary formula: From Reed Sea to Shur	Exod 15:22
2. Concerning purification of water at Marah	Exod 15:23–26
3. Arrival at Elim with twelve springs and seventy trees	Exod 15:27
G. From Elim to Wilderness of Sin: Quails and manna	Exod 16:1–36
1. Itinerary formula	Exod 16:1
2. Narrative concerning provision of manna in the wilderness	Exod 16:2–36
H. From Sin to Rephidim: Amalek and Jethro	Exod 17:1—18:27
1. Itinerary formula	Exod 17:1a
2. Narrative concerning provision of water	Exod 17:1b–7
3. Narrative concerning defense against Amalek	Exod 17:8–16
4. Narrative concerning Jethro's visit	Exod 18:1–27
a. Moses's reception of Jethro	Exod 18:1–12
b. Jethro's advice to Moses concerning judicial system	Exod 18:13–26
1) Jethro's advice	Exod 18:13–23

2) Moses's compliance	Exod 18:24–26
c. Jethro's departure	Exod 18:27
I. From Rephidim to Sinai: Revelation of Torah	Exod 19:1—Num 10:10
1. Introduction: Arrival at Sinai on the first (?) day of the third month	Exod 19:1–2
2. Revelation from mountain: Ten Commandments; Covenant Code; building of the tabernacle	Exod 19:3—40:38
a. The account of YHWH's initial revelation at Sinai	Exod 19:3–25
1) Moses's intermediation between YHWH and Israel	Exod 19:3–15
2) YHWH's descent to Mt. Sinai on the third day	Exod 19:16–25
b. YHWH's first instruction speech to Israel from Mt. Sinai: Ten Commandments: principles of Israelite law	Exod 20:1–18
1) YHWH's speech proper	Exod 20:1–14
2) Moses's reassurance of people	Exod 20:15–18
c. YHWH's second instruction speech to Israel from Mt. Sinai: Covenant Code: foundational law code of Israel	Exod 20:19—23:33
1) Construction of altar	Exod 20:19–23
2) Covenant Code proper	Exod 21:1—23:33
i. Superscription	Exod 21:1
ii. Covenant Code laws	Exod 21:2—23:33
aa. Treatment of human beings	Exod 21:2–36
bb. Theft	Exod 21:37—22:3
cc. Liability re. cattle	Exod 22:4
dd. Liability re. fire	Exod 22:5
ee. Liability re. theft	Exod 22:6–8
ff. Liability re. custodianship	Exod 22:9—23:3
gg. Responsibility conc. property of enemy	Exod 23:4

hh. Responsibility conc. just and holy treatment of animals, people, and land	Exod 23:5–19
ii. Concluding parenesis to adhere to YHWH	Exod 23:20–33
d. YHWH's summons to Moses for further instruction	Exod 24:1–18
1) YHWH's first summons to Moses, Aaron, et al. and the response	Exod 24:1–11
i. First summons proper to Moses, Aaron, et al.	Exod 24:1–2
ii. Response by Moses, Aaron, et al.	Exod 24:3–11
aa. Moses obtains Israel's agreement to observe YHWH's covenant	Exod 24:3–9
i) Moses obtains consent proper	Exod 24:3
ii) Moses records covenant and officiates over offerings to affirm covenant	Exod 24:4–9
bb. Moses, Aaron, et al. see presence of G-d	Exod 24:10–11
2) YHWH's second summons to Moses to receive tablets, Torah, and commandments and the response	Exod 24:12–18
i. Second summons proper to Moses	Exod 24:12
ii. Response: Moses ascends for forty days while Aaron et al. remain behind	Exod 24:13–18
e. Account of YHWH's instruction speeches to Moses on Mt. Sinai	Exod 25:1—31:18
1) YHWH's first speech: Instruction concerning construction of tabernacle, furnishings, and consecration of priesthood	Exod 25:1–30:10
i. Introductory YHWH speech formula	Exod 25:1
ii. YHWH instruction speech proper	Exod 25:2—30:10
aa. Introduction: Instruction to speak to the people conc. construction of tabernacle, etc.	Exod 25:2
bb. Conc. what the people shall bring: *Terumah*/gift	Exod 25:3–7

cc. Conc. what the people shall do	Exod 25:8—30:10
i) Programmatic statement: Build the tabernacle	Exod 25:8–9
(aa) Programmatic statement proper	Exod 25:8
(bb) Specification: Build as shown	Exod 25:9
ii) Enumeration of tasks	Exod 25:10—30:10
(aa) Furnishings	Exod 25:10–40
aa.i. Ark	Exod 25:10–16
aa.ii. *Kaporet*/cover for the ark	Exod 25:17–22
aa.iii. Table for bread of divine presence	Exod 25:23–30
aa.iv. *Menorot*/candlabra	Exod 25:31–40
(bb) *Mishkan*/tabernacle	Exod 26:1—27:19
bb.i. Cloths for the enclosures	Exod 26:1–6
bb.ii. Cloths for tent covering	Exod 26:7–14
bb.iii. Planks for enclosure	Exod 26:15–25
bb.iv Bars for enclosure	Exod 26:26–30
bb.v. *Paroket*/curtain for holy of holies	Exod 26:31–35
bb.vi. Screen for entrance	Exod 26:36
bb.vii. Posts for screen	Exod 26:37
bb.viii. Altar	Exod 27:1–8
bb.ix. Enclosure	Exod 27:9–19
(cc) Oil for lamps	Exod 27:20–21
(dd) Consecration of Aaron and sons for service at the altar as priests	Exod 28:1—30:10
dd.i. Preparation of Aaron and sons for role as priests: priestly garments	Exod 28:1–43
dd.ii. Consecration of Aaron and sons as priests	Exod 29:1–37

dd.iii. Preparation and function of the altar	Exod 30:1–10
2) YHWH's second speech: Census of the people	Exod 30:11–16
3) YHWH's third speech: Laver for purification	Exod 30:17–21
4) YHWH's fourth speech: Anointing oil	Exod 30:22–33
5) YHWH's fifth speech: Incense	Exod 30:34–38
6) YHWH's sixth speech: Commission of Bezalel ben Uri ben Hur of the tribe of Judah to perform the work	Exod 31:1–11
7) YHWH's seventh and concluding speech: Observance of Shabbat as eternal covenant	Exod 31:12–17
8) Concluding statement conc. YHWH's giving tablets of covenant to Moses upon completion of instruction	Exod 31:18
f. Account of the golden calf episode: Disruption and restoration of relationship between YHWH and Israel	Exod 32:1—34:35
1) YHWH's punishment of Israel for idolatry	Exod 32:1–29
i. Israel's construction and worship of golden calf	Exod 32:1–6
ii. YHWH's first speech to Moses conc. people's worship of golden calf	Exod 32:7–8
iii. Moses's confrontation with YHWH over plans to destroy Israel and make him a great nation	Exod 32:9–14
aa. YHWH's second speech to Moses conc. plans to destroy Israel and make him a great nation	Exod 32:9–10
bb. Moses's speech challenging YHWH's plans as contrary to YHWH's integrity and covenant	Exod 32:11–13
cc. YHWH's reconsideration of plans	Exod 32:14
iv. Moses's confrontation with Israel conc. idolatry with golden calf: purge of Israel	Exod 32:15–29
aa. Moses descends from the mountain with Joshua	Exod 32:15–18

bb. Moses destroys tablets of covenant and golden calf	Exod 32:19–20
cc. Moses's confrontation with Aaron	Exod 32:21–24
i) Moses's speech to Aaron: Why?	Exod 32:21
ii) Aaron's response: People are responsible	Exod 32:22–24
dd. Moses's summons to those who are for YHWH and Levites's response: Purge people of idolators	Exod 32:25–29
2) Moses's intercession with YHWH to restore relationship with Israel	Exod 32:30—34:35
aa. Moses's announcement to people conc. intercession	Exod 32:30
bb. First encounter with YHWH: Results in angel to lead people due to danger of divine presence	Exod 32:31—33:6
i) Moses's intercession: Forgive sin of people	Exod 32:31–32
ii) YHWH's first response: Refusal to forgive guilty	Exod 32:33–35
(aa) YHWH's response conc. refusal	Exod 32:33–34
(bb) YHWH's plague against people for calf	Exod 32:35
iii) YHWH's second response: Will keep covenant to grant land, but angel will lead due to danger of divine presence	Exod 33:1–3
iv) People's reaction: Dismay and decline to wear finery (holy garments for worship)	Exod 33:4
v) YHWH's affirmation: Leave off finery until decision is made	Exod 33:5
vi) People's compliance: No finery, no worship	Exod 33:6
cc. Second encounter with YHWH: Results in renewed covenant	Exod 33:7—34:28
i) Moses's appearance before YHWH in tent of meeting	Exod 33:7–11

ii) Dialog between Moses and YHWH on how to reestablish relationship	Exod 33:12—34:3
(aa) Moses to YHWH: How shall we proceed?	Exod 33:12–13
(bb) YHWH to Moses: I will lead and settle on/favor you	Exod 33:14
(cc) Moses to YHWH: How do we know that people are favored?	Exod 33:15–16
(dd) YHWH to Moses: I will do it/ show favor to people	Exod 33:17
(ee) Moses to YHWH: Let me see divine presence	Exod 33:18
(ff) YHWH to Moses: four statements	Exod 33:19—34:3
ff.i. 1st: I will pass before you, proclaim name, and show grace to nation	Exod 33:19
ff.ii. 2nd: You cannot see my face	Exod 33:20
ff.iii. 3rd: Stand in cleft in rock so to see my back	Exod 33:21–23
ff.iv. 4th: Carve two tablets of stone and come up to Mt. Sinai	Exod 34:1–3
iii) Moses's compliance with YHWH's instruction: Carve two tablets and come up to Mt. Sinai	Exod 34:4
iv) YHWH's appearance to Moses: proclamation of divine name, statement of compassion and justice	Exod 34:5–7
v) Moses's response: Bow and appeal for divine presence in Israel	Exod 34:8–9
vi) YHWH's instructions to Moses: restore covenant with renewed Covenant Code	Exod 34:10–26
vii) YHWH's further instruction to Moses: Write commands as basis for YHWH's covenant with Israel	Exod 34:27

viii) Moses's compliance: Remains forty days to write covenant without food or water	Exod 34:28
dd. Moses's return to Israel from Sinai with renewed covenant	Exod 34:29–35
i) Moses returns to Israel from Sinai with covenant and beaming face	Exod 34:29–31
ii) Moses instructs Israel in covenant and puts on veil	Exod 34:32–33
iii) Moses's mediation between YHWH and Israel with use of veil	Exod 34:34–35
3) Israel's compliance: Building of tabernacle for divine presence	Exod 35–40
3. Revelation from tabernacle: Laws of sacrifice and holiness code	Lev 1–27
4. Census and organization of people around tabernacle	Num 1:1—2:34
XII. **HISTORY** of Israel Under the Guidance of the Levites	Num 3:1—Deut 34:12
A. Sanctification of the people led by the Levites	Num 3:1—10:10
B. From Sinai to Wilderness of Paran/Kibroth Hattaavah: Rebellion in the wilderness	Num 10:11—11:35a
C. From Kibroth Hattaavah to Hazeroth	Num 11:35a–12:15
D. From Hazeroth to the Wilderness of Paran	Num 12:16—19:22
E. From Paran to Wilderness of Zin/Kadesh: Water from rock	Num 20:1–21
F. From Zin/Kadesh to Mount Hor: Death of Aaron	Num 20:22—21:3
G. From Mt. Hor to Edom/Moab: Defeat of Sihon and Og	Num 21:4–35
H. Arrival at Moab: Balaam; census and organization of people	Num 22:1—36:13
I. Moses's final address to Israel: Repetition of the Torah	Deut 1:1—34:12

Bibliography

I. Commentaries on the Book of Exodus

Arnovitz, David, et al. *Exodus/Shemot*. The Koren Tanakh of the Land of Israel. Jerusalem: Koren, 2020.

Beer, Georg. *Exodus*. HAT 3. Tübingen: Mohr Siebeck, 1939.

Cassuto, U. *A Commentary on the Book of Exodus*. Translated by I. Abrahams. Jerusalem: Magnes, 1967.

Childs, Brevard S. *The Book of Exodus: A Critical, Theological Commentary*. OTL. Philadelphia: Westminster, 1974.

Clements, Ronald E. *Exodus*. Cambridge Bible Commentary. Cambridge: Cambridge University Press, 1972.

Coats, George W. *Exodus 1–18*. FOTL 2A. Grand Rapids: Eerdmans, 1990.

Davies, G. I. *Exodus 1–18*. 2 vols. ICC. London: T&T Clark, 2020.

Dozeman, Thomas B. *Exodus*. ECC. Grand Rapids: Eerdmans, 2009.

———. "Exodus." In *The Old Testament and the Apocrypha: Fortress Commentary on the Bible*, edited by Gale A. Yee et al., 137–78. Minneapolis: Fortress, 2014.

Durham, John I. *Exodus*. WBC 3. Grand Rapids: Zondervan, 1987.

Greenberg, Moshe. *Understanding Exodus*. New York: Behrman, 1969.

Houtman, Cornelis. *Exodus*. 4 vols. HCOT. Leuven: Peeters, 1993–2002.

Meyers, Carol. *Exodus*. NCBC. Cambridge: Cambridge University Press, 2005.

Noth, Martin. *Exodus: A Commentary*. Translated by J. W. Bowden. OTL. Philadelphia: Westminster, 1962.

Propp, William H. C. *Exodus 1–18*. AB 2. New York: Doubleday, 1999.

———. *Exodus 19–40*. AB 2A. New York: Doubleday, 2006.

Rosenberg, A. J. *The Book of Exodus*. 2 vols. Judaica Books of the Bible. New York: Judaica, 1995, 1997.

Sarna, Nahum M. *Exodus*. JPS Torah Commentary. Philadelphia: JPS, 5751/1991.

Schmidt, Werner H. *Exodus 1–6*. BKAT 2/1. Neukirchen-Vluyn, Germ.: Neukirchen, 1988.

———. *Exodus 7,1—15,21*. BKAT 2/2. Göttingen: Vandenhoeck & Ruprecht, 2019.

Smith, Mark S. *Exodus*. New Collegeville Bible Commentary. Collegeville, MN: Liturgical, 2011.

Utzschneider, Helmut, and Wolfgang Oswald. *Exodus*. IECOT. Stuttgart: Kohlhammer, 2023.

———. *Exodus 1–15*. Translated by P. Sumpter. IECOT. Stuttgart: Kohlhammer, 2015.

II. Studies on Exodus

Alt, Albrecht. "Mitteilungen. 1. Ein Ägyptische Gegenstuck zu Ex 3,14." *ZAW* 58 (1940–41) 159–60.

Beit Arieh, I. "The Route Through Sinai—Why South?" *BAR* 14 (1988) 28–37.

Berner, Christoph. "The Book of Exodus." *EBR* 8:428–64.

———. "The Exodus." *EBR* 8:464–512.

Beyerlin, Walter. *Origins and History of the Oldest Sinaitic Traditions*. Translated by S. Rudman. Oxford: Blackwell, 1961.

Bills, Nathan. *A Theology of Justice in Exodus*. Siphrut 26. University Park, PA: Eisenbrauns, 2020.

Davies, G. I. *Exodus 1–18*. 2 vols. ICC. London: T&T Clark, 2020.

Dozeman, Thomas B. *G-d on the Mountain*. SBLMS 37. Atlanta: Scholars, 1989.

———, ed. *Methods for Exodus*. Methods in Biblical Interpretation. Cambridge: Cambridge University Press, 2010.

Egger, Christoph. "Burning Bush. IV. Christianity. B. Latin Patristics, Medieval Times and Reformation Era." *EBR* 4:667–70.

Everhart, Janet S. "Serving Women and Their Mirrors: A Feminist Reading of Exodus 38:8b." *CBQ* 66 (2004) 44–54.

Finkelstein, J. J. *The Ox That Gored*. Philadelphia: American Philosophical Society, 1981.

Flatto, David C. "The Golden Calf: Modern Judaism." *EBR* 10:536–39.

Halbe, Jörn. *Das Privilegrecht Jahwes Ex 34,10–26*. FRLANT 114. Göttingen: Vandenhoeck & Ruprecht, 1975.

Herrmann, Siegfried. *Israel in Egypt*. Translated by M. Kohl. SBT 2/27. Naperville, IL: Allenson, 1973.

Holder, Arthur. "The Golden Calf: Christianity." *EBR* 10:539–40.

Kensky, Meira Z. "Burning Bush. III. New Testament." *EBR* 4:663–65.

Kling, David W. "Burning Bush. IV. Christianity. C. Modern Europe and America." *EBR* 4:670–72.

Knierim, Rolf P. "Conceptual Aspects in Exodus 25:1–9." In *Pomegranates and Golden Bells: Studies in Biblical, Jewish, and Near Eastern Ritual Law and Literature in Honor of Jacob Milgrom*, edited by David P. Wright et al., 113–23. Winona Lake, IN: Eisenbrauns, 1995.

———. "Exodus 18 und die Neuordnung des Mosaischen Gerichtsbarkeit." *ZAW* 73 (1961) 146–71.

Koch, Klaus. *Der Priesterschrift von Exodus 25 bis Levitikus 16: Eine überlieferungsgeschichtliche und literarkritische Untersuchung*. FRLANT 71. Göttingen: Vandenhoeck & Ruprecht, 1959.

Lindqvist, Pekka. "The Golden Calf: Medieval Judaism." *EBR* 10:534–36.

Meiser, Martin. "Burning Bush. IV. Christianity. A. Greek Patristics and Orthodox Churches." *EBR* 4:665–67.

Meyers, Carol L. *The Tabernacle Menorah: A Synthetic Study of a Symbol from the Biblical Cult*. ASOR Dissertation Series 2. Missoula, MT: Scholars, 1976.

Moberly, R. W. L. *At the Mountain of G-d: Story and Theology in Exodus 32–34*. JSOTSup 22. Sheffield: JSOT, 1983.

Nickel, Gordon. "Burning Bush. V. Islam." *EBR* 4:672–74.

Paul, Shalom M. *Studies in the Book of the Covenant in the Light of Cuneiform and Biblical Law*. VTSup 18. Leiden: Brill, 1970.

Petersen, Nils Holger. "Burning Bush. VIII. Music." *EBR* 4:676.

———. "The Exodus. VII.B. Music. Christian." *EBR* 8:507–11.

———. "The Golden Calf: Music." *EBR* 10:545.

Pixley, Jorge. "Liberation Criticism." In *Methods for Exodus*, edited by Thomas B. Dozeman, 131–62.

Römer, Thomas. "Goshen." *EBR* 10:671–72.

Sarna, Nahum M. *Understanding Exodus: The Heritage of Biblical Israel*. New York: Schocken, 1986.

Shepherd, David. "The Golden Calf: Film." *EBR* 10:545–46.

Smith, Mark S. *The Pilgrimage Pattern in Exodus*. JSOTSup 239. Sheffield: Sheffield Academic, 1997.

Smolar, Levi, and Moses Aberbach. "The Golden Calf Episode in Post-Biblical Literature." *HUCA* 39 (1968) 91–115.

Sweeney, Marvin A. "Creation as Sacred Space in the Exodus Narratives." In *Visions of the Holy*, 297–306.

———. "The Literary-Historical Dimensions of Intertextuality in Exodus–Numbers." In *Visions of the Holy*, 273–84.

———. "Moses' Encounter with G-d and G-d's Encounter with Moses: A Reading of the Moses Narratives in Conversation with Emmanuel Levinas." In *Visions of the Holy*, 307–24.

———. *Visions of the Holy: Studies in Biblical Theology and Literature*. RBS 105. Atlanta: SBL, 2023.

———. "The Wilderness Traditions of the Pentateuch: A Reassessment of Their Function and Intent in Relation to Exodus." In *Visions of the Holy*, 285–96.

Steinberg, Naomi. "Feminist Criticism." In *Methods for Exodus*, edited by Thomas B. Dozeman, 163–92.

Suomala, Karla. "Golden Calf: Rabbinic Judaism." *EBR* 10:532–34.

———. "Golden Calf: Second Temple and Hellenistic Judaism." *EBR* 10:530–32.

———. *Moses and G-d in Dialogue: Exodus 32–34 in Post-Biblical Literature*. SBLStBL 61. Bern: Lang, 2004.

Van Seters, John. *A Law Book for the Diaspora: Revision in the Study of the Covenant Code*. Oxford: Oxford University Press, 2003.

———. *The Life of Moses: The Y-hwist as Historian in Exodus–Numbers*. Louisville: Westminster John Knox, 1994.

Wright, David P. *Inventing G-d's Law: How the Covenant Code of the Bible Used and Revised the Laws of Hammurabi*. Oxford: Oxford University Press, 2009.

Yee, Gale A. "Post-Colonial Biblical Criticism." In *Methods for Exodus*, edited by Thomas B. Dozeman, 193–233.

III. Other Relevant Studies

Adelman, Rachel. "Wings of Desire: Theophany Between the Cherubim Above the Ark's Cover." In *Texts, Readers, and Their Worlds*, edited by Soo Kim Sweeney et al., 61–78. Vol. 2 of *Theology of the Hebrew Bible*. RBS 107. Atlanta: SBL, 2024.

Alcalay, Reuben. *The Complete Hebrew-English Dictionary*. Jerusalem: Masada, 1987.

Alt, Albrecht. "The Origins of Israelite Law." In *Essays on Old Testament History and Religion*, translated by R. A. Wilson, 101–71. Garden City, NY: Doubleday, 1967.

Anderson, Craig Evan. "The Tablets of Testimony and the Reversal of Outcome in the Golden Calf Narrative." *HS* 50 (2009) 41–65.

Aurelius, Erik. *Der Fürbitter Israels: Eine Studie zum Mosesbild in Alten Testament*. ConBOT 27. Stockholm: Almqvist & Wiksell, 1988.

Avigad, Nahman. "The Inscribed Pomegranate from 'the House of the L-rd.'" In *Ancient Jerusalem Revealed*, edited by H. Geva, 128–37. Jerusalem: Israel Exploration Society, 1994.

Azbel, Mark Ya. *Refusenik: Trapped in the Soviet Union*. Boston: Houghton Mifflin, 1981.

Baker Eddy, Mary. *Science and Health with Key to the Scriptures*. Boston: Christian Scientist, 1875.

Bertman, Stephen. "The Antisemitic Origin of Michelangelo's Horned Moses." *Shofar* 9 (2009) 95–106.

Baskin, Judith R. *Pharaoh's Counsellors: Job, Jethro, and Balaam in Rabbinic and Patristic Tradition*. BJS 47. Chico: Scholars, 1983.

Baumann, Gerlinde. *Love and Violence: Marriage as Metaphor for the Relationship Between YHWH and Israel in the Prophetic Books*. Translated by Linda M. Maloney. Collegeville, MN: Liturgical, 2003.

Beckwith, Roger T. *The Old Testament Canon of the New Testament Church: And its Background in Early Judaism*. Grand Rapids: Eerdmans, 1985.

Berner, Christoph. "Calendar: II. Hebrew Bible/Old Testament." *EBR* 4:784–79.

Beizer, Mikhail. *The Jews of St. Petersburg: Excursions Through a Noble Past*. Philadelphia: JPS, 5749/1989.

Blenkinsopp, Joseph. *The Pentateuch: An Introduction to the First Five Books of the Bible*. New York: Doubleday, 1992.

Blischke, Marieke V. "Ephod." *EBR* 7:1020–22.

Blum, Erhard. *Studien zur Komposition des Pentateuch*. BZAW 189. Berlin: de Gruyter, 1990.

Boecker, Hans Jochen. *Redeformen des Rechtlebens im Alten Testament*. 2nd ed. WMANT 14. Neukirchen-Vluyn, Germ.: Neukirchen, 1970.

Braulik, Georg. *Die deuteronomischen Geseteze und der Dekalog: Studien zum Aufbau von Deuteronomium 12–26*. SBS 145. Stuttgart: Katholisches Bibelwerk, 1991.

———. "The Sequence of the Laws in Deuteronomy 12–26 and in the Decalogue." In *A Song of Power and the Power of Song: Essays on the Book of Deuteronomy*, edited by David L. Christensen, 313–35. Sources for Biblical and Theological Study, Old Testament 3. Winona Lake, IN: Eisenbrauns, 1993.

Brichto, Herbert Chanan, et al. "Priestly Blessing." *EncJud* 13:1060–63.

Buber, Martin, and Franz Rosenzweig. *Die Schrift und ihre Verdeutschung*. Berlin: Schocken, 1936.

Buck, Pearl S. *The Good Earth*. New York: Washington Square, 1958.

Budge, E. A. Wallis. *The Queen of Sheba and Her Only Son Menyelek: Also Known as Kebra Nagast (The Glory of the Kings)*. Repr., Chicago: Frontline and Lorne, 2000. First published 1922.

Burns, Ivan, and Gilbert Geiss. *Trial of Witches: A Seventeenth-Century Prosecution*. London: Routledge, 1997.

Calvin, John. *Commentaries on the Last Four Books of Moses: Arranged in the Form of a Harmony*. Translated by Charles William Bingham. Vol. 1. Grand Rapids: Eerdmans, 1950.

Campbell, Antony F., and Mark A. O'Brien. *Sources of the Pentateuch: Texts, Introduction, and Annotations*. Minneapolis: Fortress, 1993.

Carr, David M. "Changes in Pentateuchal Criticism." In *The Twentieth Century—from Modernism to Post-Modernism*, edited by Magne Sæbø, 433–66. Vol. III/2 of *Hebrew Bible Old Testament: The History of Its Interpretation*. Göttingen: Vandenhoeck & Ruprecht, 2015.

Cassuto, Umberto. *Bible and Ancient Oriental Texts*. Translated by I. Abrahams. Vol. 2 of *Biblical and Oriental Studies*. Jerusalem: Magnes, 1975.

Clements, R. E. *G-d and Temple: The Presence of G-d in Israel's Worship*. Philadelphia: Fortress, 1965.

Coats, George W. *Moses: Heroic Man, Man of G-d*. JSOTSup 57. Sheffield: JSOT, 1988.

———. *Rebellion in the Wilderness: The Murmuring Motif in the Wilderness Traditions of the Old Testament*. Nashville: Abingdon, 1968.

Cohn Eskenazi, Tamara, and Tikvah Frymer-Kensky. *Ruth*. JPS Bible Commentary. Philadelphia: JPS, 5771/2011.

Cohn, Haim Harmann. "Talion." *EncJud* 15:741–42.

Cone, James H. *A Black Theology of Liberation*. New York: Orbis, 1970.

Conrad, Edgar W. *Fear Not Warrior: A Study of* 'al tîrā' *Pericopes in the Hebrew Scriptures*. BJS 75. Chico: Scholars, 1985.

Conrad, J. "*ndb*." *TDOT* 9:219–26.

Cross, Frank Moore. *Canaanite Myth and Hebrew Epic: Essays in the History of the Religion of Israel*. Cambridge, MA: Harvard University Press, 1973.

———. "The Priestly Work." In *Canaanite Myth and Hebrew Epic*, 291–325.

Cross, Frank Moore, Jr., and David Noel Freedman. *Studies in Ancient YHWistic Poetry*. SBLDS 21. Missoula, MT: Scholars, 1975.

Crouch, C. L. *Israel and the Assyrians: Deuteronomy, the Succession Treaty of Esarhaddon, and the Nature of Subversion*. ANEM 8. Atlanta: SBL, 2014.

Cryer, Frederick H. *Divination in Ancient Israel and Its Near Eastern Environment: A Socio-Historical Investigation*. JSOTSup 142. Sheffield: JSOT, 1994.

Dalley, Stephanie. *Myths from Mesopotamia: Creation, the Flood, Gilgamesh, and Others*. Oxford: Oxford University Press, 1991.

Daube, David. *The Exodus Pattern in the Bible*. London: Faber and Faber, 1963.

Davies, G. I. "Sinai, Mount." *ABD* 6:47–49.

Day, John. *YHWH and the Gods and Goddesses of Canaan*. JSOTSup 265. Sheffield: JSOT, 2000.

Dever, William G. "Weights and Measurements." In *HarperCollins Bible Dictionary*, edited by Paul J. Achtemeier, 1206–11. Rev. ed. San Francisco: HarperSanFrancisco, 1996.

De Vries, Simon J. *From Old Revelation to New: A Tradition-Historical and Redaction-Critical Study of Temporal Transitions in Prophetic Prediction*. Grand Rapids: Eerdmans, 1995.

Donin, Hayim HaLevy. *To Pray as a Jew: A Guide to the Prayer Book and the Synagogue Service*. New York: Basic, 1980.

Dozeman, Thomas B., et al., eds. *The Pentateuch*. FAT 78. Tübingen: Mohr Siebeck, 2011.

Driver, S. R., and John C. Miles, eds. and trans. *The Babylonian Laws*. 2 vols. Oxford: Clarendon, 1955.

Durand, Jean-Marie. "Habiru, Hapiru." *EBR* 10:1053–56.

Editor [Cecil Roth et al.]. "Ner Tamid." *EncJud* 12:965.

Elias, Joseph. *The Haggadah: Passover Haggadah with Translation and a New Commentary based on Talmudic and Midrashic Sources*. Art Scroll Mesorah. Brooklyn: Mesorah, 1982.

Elon, Menachem. "Abortion." *EncJud* 1:98–101.

Erbele-Küster, Dorothea. "Menstruation, I. Hebrew Bible/Old Testament." *EBR* 18:661–63.

Fensham, F. C. "Widow, Orphan, and Poor in Ancient Near Eastern Legal and Wisdom Literature." *JNES* 21 (1962) 129–39.

Finlay, Timothy D. *The Birth Report Genre in the Hebrew Bible*. FAT 2/12. Tübingen: Mohr Siebeck, 2005.

Fishbane, Michael. "Genesis 1:1—2:4a: The Creation." In *Text and Texture: Close Readings of Selected Biblical Texts*, 3–16. New York: Schocken, 1979.

Fitzgerald, Aloysius. *The L-rd of the East Wind*. CBQMS 34. Washington, DC: Catholic Biblical Association of America, 2002.

Fox, Nili Sachar. *In the Service of the King: Officialdom in Ancient Israel and Judah*. Cincinnati: Hebrew Union College Press, 2000.

Freedman, Harry. "Ark of the Covenant. In the Aggadah." *EncJud* 3:465–66.

Frevel, Christian. *Desert Transformations*. FAT 137. Tübingen: Mohr Siebeck 2020.

Garrone, Daniele. "Jethro." *EBR* 14:139–41.

Gerstenberger, Erhard S. *Psalms, Part 1, with an Introduction to Cultic Poetry*. FOTL 14. Grand Rapids: Eerdmans, 1988.

Gert, Jan C., et al., eds. *The Formation of the Pentateuch*. FAT 111. Tübingen: Mohr Siebeck, 2016.

Gilbert, Martin. *The Jews of Hope: The Plight of Soviet Jews Today*. New York: Viking, 1985.

Gilmer, Harry W. *The If-You Form in Israelite Law*. SBLDS 15. Missoula, MT: Scholars, 1969.

Ginzberg, Louis. *The Legends of the Jews*. 7 vols. Philadelphia: JPS, 5727–30/1967–69.

Glatzer, Nahum N., ed. *The Passover Haggadah*. New York: Schocken, 1969.

Glueck, Nelson. *ḤESED in the Bible*. Translated by A. Gottschaulk. Cincinnati: Hebrew Union College Press, 1967.

Goler, Ogden. "Hathor." *EBR* 11:408–10.

Greenberg, Moshe. "Sabbath. In the Bible." *EncJud* 14:557–62.

———. "Urim." *EncJud* 16:7–9.

Grintz, Yehoshua M. "Ark of the Covenant." *EncJud* 3:459–65.

Gruenwald, Ithamar. *Apocalyptic and Merkavah Mysticism*. AGJU 14. Leiden: Brill, 1980.

Guiora, Amos N. *The Crime of Complicity: The Bystander in the Holocaust*. Chicago: Ankerwycke, 2017.

Habel, Norman. "The Form and Significance of the Call Narratives." *ZAW* 77 (1965) 297–333.

Haley, Alex. *Roots: The Saga of an American Family*. Garden City, NY: Doubleday, 1976.

Halpern, Baruch. *The First Historians: The Hebrew Bible and History*. San Francisco: Harper and Row, 1988.

Hals, Ronald M. *Ezekiel*. FOTL 19. Grand Rapids: Eerdmans, 1989.

Hartenstein, Friedhelm, and Konrad Schmid, eds. *Farewell to the Priestly Writing? The Current State of the Debate*. Translated by Wesley Crouser et al. AIL 38. Atlanta: SBL, 2022.

Hazony, Yoram. *The Jewish State: The Struggle for Israel's Soul*. New York: Basic, 2000.

Held, Shai. *Judaism Is About Love: Recovering the Heart of Jewish Life*. New York: Farrar, Straus and Giroux, 2024.

Herford, R. Travers. *The Ethics of the Talmud: Sayings of the Fathers*. New York: Schocken, 1962.

Hiebert, Theodore. "Theophany in the OT." *ABD* 6:505–11.

Hieke, Thomas. "Leper, Leprosy." *EBR* 16:143–47.

Higgins, Ryan. "Etham." *EBR* 8:94–95.

Hillers, Delbert R. *Covenant: The History of a Biblical Idea*. Baltimore: Johns Hopkins University Press, 1969.

Horowitz, Wayne, et al. "Hazor 18: Fragments of a Cuneiform Law Collection at Hazor." *IEJ* 62 (2012) 158–76.

Hurowitz, Victor Avigdor. *I Have Built You an Exalted House: Temple Building in the Bible in the Light of Mesopotamian Semitic Writings*. JSOTSup 115. Sheffield: JSOT, 1992.

———. "Isaiah's Impure Lips and Their Purification in Light of Akkadian Sources." *HUCA* 60 (1989) 39–89.

Idelsohn, A. Z. *Jewish Liturgy and Its Development*. New York: Schocken, 1972.

Jacobs, Louis. "Sabbath: In Rabbinic Literature." *EncJud* 14:562–64.

———. "Shavuot." *EncJud* 14:1319–22.

Janson, H. W. *History of Art*. Englewood Cliffs, NJ: Prentice-Hall, 1965.

Jastrow, Marcus. *A Dictionary of the Targumim, the Talmud Babli and Yerushalmi, and the Midrashic Literature*. 2 vols. Repr., Brooklyn: Shalom, 1967.

Kade, Robert, and John Huddleston. "Nile." *EBR* 21:460–64.

Kaminsky, Joel S. *Yet I Loved Jacob: Reclaiming the Biblical Concept of Election*. Nashville: Abingdon, 2007.

Kempenski, Aharon, and Israel Finkelstein. "Shiloh." *NEAEHL* 4 (1993) 1364–70.

Kim Sweeney, Soo J. "Exile and Kingship: Exploring YHWH's and David's Sojourns in Samuel Through the Lens of Tzimtzum." Paper to be presented at a symposium on Samuel as Novel, Doshisha University, Kyoto, Japan, forthcoming.

King, Martin Luther, Jr. *Strength to Love*. New York: Harper and Row, 1963.

Kiuchi, N. *The Purification Offering in the Priestly Literature: Its Meaning and Functions*. JSOTSup 56. Sheffield: JSOT, 1987.

Klein, Isaac. *A Guide to Jewish Religious Practice*. New York: Jewish Theological Seminary of America Press, 1979.

Klein, Ralph W. *2 Chronicles*. Hermeneia. Minneapolis: Fortress, 2012.

Knierim, Rolf P., and George W. Coats. *Numbers*. FOTL 4. Grand Rapids: Eerdmans, 2005.

Knohl, Israel. *The Sanctuary of Silence: The Priestly Torah and the Holiness School*. Minneapolis: Fortress, 1995.

Kobel, Esther. "Manna. New Testament." *EBR* 17:774–75.

Kratz, Reinhard G. "The Pentateuch in Current Research." In *The Pentateuch*, edited by Thomas B. Dozeman et al., 31–61.

Kuan, Jeffrey Kah-Jin. *Neo-Assyrian Historical Inscriptions and Syria-Palestine*. Hong Kong: Alliance Bible Seminary, 1995.

Kuhrt, Amélie. *The Ancient Near East, c. 3000–330 BC*. 2 vols. London: Routledge, 1995.

Kurtz, Paul Michael. "Baal Zephon." *EBR* 3:230–31.

———. "El." *EBR* 7:560–63.

Laquer, Walter. *A History of Zionism*. New York: Schocken, 1976.

Lauterbach, Jacob Z., ed. *Mekilta de-Rabbi Ishmael*. 3 vols. Repr., Philadelphia: JPS, 1976. First published 1933–35.

Lee-Sak, Yitzhak. "Levitical Cities." *EBR* 16:356–59.

Leiman, Sid Z. *The Canonization of Hebrew Scripture: The Talmudic and Midrashic Evidence*. Repr., New Haven: Connecticut Academy of Arts and Sciences Press, 1991. First published 1976.

Lemche, Nils Peter. "Ḫabiru/Ḫapiru." *ABD* 3:6–10.

Leuenberger, Martin. "Midian, Midianites." *EBR* 18:1211–13.

Levenson, Jon D. *Creation and the Persistence of Evil: The Jewish Drama of Divine Impotence*. San Francisco: Harper and Row, 1988.

———. *Sinai and Zion: An Entry into the Jewish Bible*. Minneapolis: Winston, 1985.

———. "The Temple and the World." *JR* 64 (1984) 275–98.

Levin, Christoph. *Der J-hwist*. FRLANT 157. Göttingen: Vandenhoeck & Ruprecht, 1993.

Levine, Baruch. *Leviticus*. JPS Torah Commentary. Philadelphia: JPS, 5749/1989.

Levinson, Bernard M. *Deuteronomy and the Hermeneutics of Legal Innovation*. Oxford: Oxford University Press, 1997.

Lewis, Brian. *The Sargon Legend: A Study of the Akkadian Text and the Tale of the Hero Who Was Exposed at Birth*. ASOR Dissertation Series 4. Cambridge: American Schools of Oriental Research, 1980.

Lichtheim, Miriam. *Ancient Egyptian Literature*. 3 vols. Berkeley: University of California Press, 1975–80.

Liedke, Gerhard. *Gestalt und Bezeichnung alttestamentlicher Rechtsätze*. WMANT 39. Neukirchen-Vluyn, Germ.: Neukirchen, 1971.

Lim, Timothy H. *The Formation of the Jewish Canon*. New Haven, CT: Yale University Press, 2013.

Lipton, Diana. "Amalek, Amalekites." *EBR* 1:918–21.

Littauwer, Mary Aiken, and J. H. Crouwell. "Chariots." *ABD* 1:888–92.

Mann, Thomas W. *Divine Presence and Guidance in Israelite Traditions: The Typology of Exaltation*. Baltimore: Johns Hopkins University Press, 1977.

McCarthy, Dennis J. *Old Testament Covenant: A Survey of Current Opinion*. Atlanta: John Knox, 1972.

———. *Treaty and Covenant*. AnBib 21A. Rome: Biblical Institute, 1978.

Mendenhall, George. "Covenant Forms in Israelite Tradition." In *The Biblical Archaeologist Reader* 3, edited by Edward F. Campbell Jr. and David Noel Freedman, 25–53. Garden City, NY: Anchor Doubleday, 1970.

Merlo, Paolo. "Asherah." *EBR* 2:975–80.

Mettinger, Tryggve N. D. *The Dethronement of Sabaoth: Studies in the Shem and Kabod Theologies*. ConBOT 18. Lund: Gleerup, 1982.

Michman, Joseph. "Kapo." *EncJud* 10:754–55.

Milgrom, Jacob. *Leviticus 17–22*. AB 3A. New York: Doubleday, 2000.

———. *Numbers*. JPS Torah Commentary. Philadelphia: JPS, 5750/1990.

Millgrom, Abraham. *Jewish Worship*. Philadelphia: JPS, 5732/1971.

Miller, Arthur. *The Crucible, a Play in Four Acts*. New York: Penguin, 2003.

Miosi, Frank T. "Oracle. Ancient Egypt." *ABD* 5:29–30.

Moore, Stewart. "Manna. Judaism. Second Temple and Hellenistic Judaism." *EBR* 17:775–76.

Morenz, Siegfried. *Egyptian Religion*. Translated by Ann E. Keep. Ithaca, NY: Cornell University Press, 1973.

Mowinckel, Sigmund. *The Psalms in Israel's Worship*. Translated by D. R. Ap-Thomas. Nashville: Abingdon, 1962.

Muhlestein, Kerry. "Execration and Execration Texts." *EBR* 8:376–78.

Muilenberg, James. "A Liturgy of the Triumphs of YHWH." In *Studia Biblica et Semitica T. C. Vriezen Dedicata*, edited by W. C. van Unnik and A. S. van der Woude, 233–51. Wageningen, Neth.: Veenman en Zonen, 1966.

Müller, Monika C. "Ahimelech." *EBR* 1:652–56.

Mumford, Gregory. "Amarna Letters." *EBR* 1:936–41.

Mumme, Jonathan. "Manna. Christianity." *EBR* 17:782–83.

Nemoy, Leon. *Karaite Anthology*. Yale Judaica Series 7. New Haven, CT: Yale University Press, 1952.

Nicholson, Ernest. *The Pentateuch in the Twentieth Century: The Legacy of Julius Wellhausen*. Oxford: Oxford University Press, 1998.

Nihan, Christoph. *From Priestly Torah to Pentateuch: A Study in the Composition of the Book of Leviticus*. FAT 25. Tübingen: Mohr Siebeck, 2007.

Noth, Martin. *A History of Pentateuchal Traditions*. Translated by B. W. Anderson. Englewood Cliffs, NJ: Prentice-Hall, 1972.

———. "Old Testament Covenant-Making in the Light of a Text from Mari." In "*The Laws in the Pentateuch" and Other Studies*, translated by D. R. Ap-Thomas, 108–17. Edinburgh: Oliver and Boyd, 1967.

Olmo Lete, G. del, and J. Sanmartín. *A Dictionary of the Ugaritic Language in the Alphabetic Tradition*. Edited and translated by W. G. E. Watson. Leiden: Brill, 2015.

Olson, Dennis T., et al. "Circumcision." *EBR* 5:324–26.

Page, S. "A Stela of Adad Nirari III and Nergal-ereš from Tell al-Rimah." *Iraq* 30 (1968) 139–53.

Petersen, David L. *The Roles of Israel's Prophets*. JSOTSup 17. Sheffield: JSOT, 1981

Pinkus, Benjamin. *The Jews of the Soviet Union: The History of a National Minority*. Cambridge: Cambridge University Press, 1988.

Pixley, Jorge. "Liberation Criticism." In *Methods for Exodus*, edited by Thomas B. Dozeman, 131–62.

Rabinowitz, Louis Isaac. "Tefillin." *EncJud* 15:898–904.

Rad, Gerhard von. "The Form-Critical Problem of the Hexateuch." In "*The Problem of the Hexateuch" and Other Essays*, translated by E. W. Trueman Dicken, 1–78. London: SCM, 1984.

Rast, Walter E. "Bab edh-Dhra." *ABD* 1:559–61.

Redford, Donald B. *Egypt, Canaan, and Israel in Ancient Times*. Princeton: Princeton University Press, 1992.

———. "The Literary Motif of the Exposed Child." *Numen* 14 (1967) 209–28.

———. "Pharaoh." *ABD* 5:288–89.

———. "Pi-Hahiroth." *ABD* 5:371.

Rendtorff, Rolf. *Die "Bundesformel": Eine exegetische-theologishe Untersuchung.* SBS 160. Stuttgart: Katholisches Bibelwerk, 1995.

Richardson, H. N. "Mill, Millstone." *IDB* 3:380–81.

Richelle, Matthieu. "Maṣṣēbâ, Maṣṣēbôt." *EBR* 18:37–41.

Roskop, Angela R. *The Wilderness Itineraries: Genre, Geography, and the Growth of the Torah.* Winona Lake, IN: Eisenbrauns, 2011.

Roth, C., et al. "Proselytes." *EncJud* 13:1182–93.

Rubens, Alfred. "Decalogue. In Rabbinical Literature." *EncJud* 5:1446–47.

Sanders, Ira E. "Ark." *EncJud* 3:450–59.

Särkiö, Pekka. *Die Weisheit und Macht Salomos in der Israelitischen Historiographie: Eine traditions- und redaktionskritische Untersuchung über 1 Kön 3–5 und 9–11.* Göttingen: Vandenhoeck & Ruprecht, 1994.

Sasson, Jack. *Judges 1–12.* YAB 6D. New Haven, CT: Yale University Press, 2014.

Schaub, R. Thomas. "Bab edh-Dhra." *NEAEHL* 1 (1993) 130–36.

Schiff, David. *Abortion in Judaism.* New York: Cambridge University Press, 2002.

Schiffman, Lawrence H. *Who Was a Jew? Rabbinic and Halakhic Perspectives on the Jewish-Christian Schism.* Hoboken, NJ: Schocken, 1985.

Schmid, Hans Heinrich. *Die sogenannte J-hwist: Beobachtungen und Fragen zur Pentateuchforschung.* Zurich: Theologisch, 1976.

Schmid, Konrad. "The So-Called Y-hwist and the Literary Gap Between Genesis and Exodus." In *A Farewell to the Y-hwist? The Composition of the Pentateuch in Recent European Interpretation*, edited by Thomas B. Dozeman and Konrad Schmid, 29–50. SymS 34. Atlanta: SBL, 2006.

Schmidt, Brian B. "Kuntillet ʿAjrud." *EBR* 15:493–97.

Schochet, Elijah J. *Amalek: The Enemy from Within.* Los Angeles: Mimetav, 1991.

Schulz, Hermann. *Das Todesrecht im Alten Testament.* BZAW 114. Berlin: Töpelmann, 1969.

Schwarzchild, Steven S. "Noachide Laws." *EncJud* 12:1189–90.

Seely, David R. "Sin, Wilderness of." *ABD* 6:47.

Seely, Jo Ann H. "Rephidim." *ABD* 5:677–68.

———. "Succoth." *ABD* 6:217–18.

Sefati, Yitzchak. *Love Songs in Sumerian Literatuere.* Bar-Ilan Studies in Near Eastern Languages and Cultures. Ramat Gan, Israel: Bar-Ilan University Press, 1998.

Seligssohn, Max. "Rahab." *EncJud* 10:309.

Shapira, Anita. *Israel: A History.* Translated by A. Berris. Waltham, MA: Brandeis University Press, 2012.

Sharansky, Natan. *The Case for Democracy: The Power of Freedom to Overcome Tyranny and Terror.* New York: Public Affairs, 2004.

———. *Defending Identity: Its Indispensable Role in Protecting Democracy.* New York: Public Affairs, 2008.

Simpson, William Kelly. *The Literature of Ancient Egypt.* New Haven, CT: Yale University Press, 1973.

Slayton, Joel C. "Manna." *ABD* 4:511.

Smith, Mark S. *The Origins of Biblical Monotheism: Israel's Polytheistic Background and the Ugaritic Texts.* Oxford: Oxford University Press, 2001.

Smith, Mark S., and Elisabeth Bloch-Smith. *Judges 1.* Hermeneia. Minneapolis: Fortress, 2021.

Sommer, Benjamin. *The Bodies of G-d and the World of Ancient Israel.* New York: Cambridge University Press, 2009.

Spector, Stephen. *Operation Solomon: The Daring Rescue of the Ethiopian Jews*. Oxford: Oxford University Press, 2007.

Stackert, Jeffrey. *A Prophet Like Moses: Prophecy, Law, and Israelite Religion*. Oxford: Oxford University Press, 2014.

———. *Rewriting the Torah: Literary Revision in Deuteronomy and the Holiness Legislation*. FAT 52. Tübingen: Mohr Siebeck, 2007.

Steinberg, Naomi. "Feminist Criticism." In *Methods for Exodus*, edited by Thomas B. Dizeman, 163–92.

Sweeney, Marvin A. *1–2 Kings: A Commentary*. OTL. Louisville: Westminster John Knox, 2007.

———. *1–2 Samuel*. NCBC. Cambridge: Cambridge University Press, 2023.

———. "Absence of G-d and Human Responsibility in the Book of Esther." In *Visions of the Holy*, 701–12.

———. "Balaam in Intertextual Perspective." In *Visions of the Holy*, 337–57.

———. "*Berit Olam*, the Eternal Covenant: Is the Eternal Covenant Really Conditional?" In *Visions of the Holy*, 93–106.

———. "Creation as Active Agent in the Exodus–Wilderness Narratives." In *From Creation to Eschaton: Biblical and Theological Explorations in Honor of J. Richard Middleton*. Eugene, OR: Cascade, forthcoming.

———. "The Democratization of Messianism in Modern Jewish Thought." In *Visions of the Holy*, 189–205.

———. "Ezekiel: Zadokite Priest and Visionary Prophet of the Exile." In *Form and Intertextuality in Prophetic and Apocalyptic Literature*, 125–43.

———. "Ezekiel's Conceptualization of the Exile in Intertextual Perspective." In *Visions of the Holy*, 605–24.

———. "Ezekiel's Debate with Isaiah." In *Reading Prophetic Books*, 185–202.

———. *Form and Intertextuality in Prophetic and Apocalyptic Literature*. FAT 45. Tübingen: Mohr Siebeck, 2005.

———. "Form Criticism." In *Visions of the Holy*, 251–72.

———. "Hosea's Reading of the Pentateuchal Narratives: A Window for the Foundational E-Stratum." In *The Formation of the Pentateuch*, edited by J. C. Gertz et al., 851–71. FAT 111. Tübingen: Mohr Siebeck, 2016.

———. *Isaiah 1–4 and the Post-Exilic Understanding of the Isaianic Tradition*. BZAW 171. Berlin: de Gruyter, 1988.

———. *Isaiah 1–39, with an Introduction to Prophetic Literature*. FOTL 16. Grand Rapids: Eerdmans, 1996.

———. *Isaiah 40–66*. FOTL. Grand Rapids: Eerdmans, 2016.

———. "Israelite and Judean Religions." In *The Cambridge History of Religions in the Ancient World*, edited by M. R. Salzman and M. A. Sweeney, 1:151–73. Cambridge: Cambridge University Press, 2013.

———. "The Jacob Narratives: An Ephraimite Text?" In *Visions of the Holy*, 227–49.

———. *Jewish Mysticism: From Ancient Times Through Today*. Grand Rapids: Eerdmans, 2020.

———. *King Josiah of Judah: The Lost Messiah of Israel*. New York: Oxford University Press, 2001.

———. "The Laws of Slavery in Exodus, Deuteronomy, and Leviticus: Witness to a Living Legal System." Forthcoming in a yet-to-be-titled volume edited by Soo J. Kim Sweeney et al. on slavery in the Bible.

———. "Pardes Revisited Once Again: A Reassessment of the Rabbinic Legend of the Four Who Entered Pardes." In *Form and Intertextuality*, 269–82.

———. *The Pentateuch*. CBS. Nashville: Abingdon, 2017.

———. "Prophets and Priests in the Deuteronomistic History." In *Visions of the Holy*, 489–502.

———. "The Question of Theodicy in the Historical Books: Contrasting Views Concerning the Destruction of Jerusalem in the Deuteronomistic History and the Chronicler's History." In *Visions of the Holy*, 665–78.

———. *Reading Ezekiel: A Literary and Theological Commentary*. ROT. Macon, GA: Smyth and Helwys, 2013.

———. *Reading the Hebrew Bible After the Shoah: Engaging Holocaust Theology*. Minneapolis: Fortress, 2008.

———. *Reading Prophetic Books*. FAT 89. Tübingen: Mohr Siebeck, 2014.

———. "The Reconceptualization of the Davidic Covenant in Isaiah." In *Reading Prophetic Books*, 94–113.

———. "Samuel's Institutional Identity in the Deuteronomistic History." In *Visions of the Holy*, 409–20.

———. "Sefirah at Qumran: Aspects of the Counting Formulas for the First-Fruits Festivals of the Temple Scroll." In *Reading Prophetic Books*, 337–45.

———. "Shabbat: An Epistemological Principle for Holiness, Sustainability, and Justice in the Pentateuch." In *Visions of the Holy*, 209–26.

———. "Swords into Plowshares or Plowshares into Swords? Isaiah and the Twelve in Intertextual Perspective on Zion." In *Visions of the Holy*, 517–31.

———. *Tanak: A Theological and Critical Introduction to the Jewish Bible*. Minneapolis: Fortress, 2012.

———. *The Twelve Prophets*. Edited by David W. Cotter. 2 vols. Berit Olam: Studies in Hebrew Narrative & Poetry. Collegeville, MN: Liturgical, 2000.

———. *Visions of the Holy: Studies in Biblical Theology and Literature*. RBS 105. Atlanta: SBL, 2023.

———. "Why Moses Was Barred from the Land of Israel: A Reassessment of Numbers 20 in Literary Context." In *Visions of the Holy*, 325–35.

———. *Zephaniah*. Hermeneia. Minneapolis: Fortress, 2003.

Tabory, Joseph. *JPS Commentary on the Haggadah: Historical Introduction, Translations, and Commentary*. Philadelphia: JPS, 5768/2008.

Tadmor, H. "The Campaigns of Sargon II of Assur: A Chronological-Historical Study." *Journal of Cuneiform Studies* 12 (1958) 20–40, 77–100.

Taratuta, Aba, and Ida Taratuta. *Cheerful Memories/Troubled Years: A Story of a Refusenik's Family in Leningrad and Their Struggle for Immigration to Israel*. Boston: Academic Studies 2019.

Thomas, Matthew A. *These Are the Generations: Identity, Covenant, and the Toledoth Formulae*. London: T&T Clark, 2011.

Thompson, Thomas L. *The Historicity of the Pentateuchal Narratives*. BZAW 133. Berlin: de Gruyter, 1974.

Tigay, Jeffrey. *Deuteronomy*. JPS Torah Commentary. Philadelphia: JPS, 5756/1996.

Toorn, Karel van der. "Mill, Millstones." *ABD* 4:831–32.

Trebolle Barrera, Julio. *The Jewish Bible and the Christian Bible: An Introduction to the History of the Bible*. Translated by W. G. E. Watson. Leiden: Brill, 1998.

Unterman, Jeremiah. *Justice for All: How the Jewish Bible Revolutionized Ethics.* Philadelphia: JPS, 2017.

Uris, Leon. *Exodus.* Garden City, NY: Doubleday, 1958.

Vaux, Roland de. *The Early History of Israel.* Translated by D. Smith. Philadelphia: Westminster, 1978.

Van Seters, John. *Abraham in History and Tradition.* New Haven, CT: Yale University Press, 1975.

Wächter, L., et al. "*tĕrûmâ.*" *TDOT* 15:770–77.

Walfish, Barry Dov. "Amalek, Amalekites." *EBR* 1:921–26.

———. "Manna. Medieval Judaism." *EBR* 17:778–80.

Walls, Neal H. "Anath." *EBR* 1:1093–96.

Watts, James W., ed. *Persia and Torah: The Theory of Imperial Authorization of the Pentateuch.* SymS 17. Atlanta: SBL, 2001.

Wei, Tom F. "Pithom." *ABD* 5:376–77.

Weinfeld, Moshe. *Social Justice in Ancient Israel and in the Ancient Near East.* Minneapolis: Fortress, 1995.

Wellhausen, Julius. *Die Composition des Hexateuchs und der historischen Bücher des Alten Testaments.* Berlin: Reimer, 1889.

Wente, Edward F. "Rameses." *ABD* 5:617–18.

Westermann, Claus. *Praise and Lament in the Psalms.* Translated by K. R. Crim and R. N. Soulen. Atlanta: John Knox, 1981.

Widengren, Geo. *The King and the Tree of Life in Ancient Near Eastern Religion.* Uppsala: Almqvist & Wiksells, 1951.

Wilfand, Yael. "Manna. Rabbinic Judaism." *EBR* 17:776–78.

Wilson, Kevin A. *The Campaign of Pharaoh Shoshenq I into Palestine.* FAT 2/9. Tübingen: Mohr Siebeck, 2005.

Wilson-Wright, Aren M. "Migdol." *EBR* 19:63–64.

Wiseman, D. J. *The Vassal Treaties of Esarhaddon.* London: British School of Archaeology in Iraq, 1958.

Wöhrle, Jakob. *Die frühen Sammlungen des Zwölfprophetenbuchs: Entstehung und Komposition.* BZAW 360. Berlin: de Gruyter, 2006.

Wong, Stephanie. "Manna. Film." *EBR* 17:790–92.

Wright, Jacob L. *David, King of Israel, and Caleb in Biblical Memory.* Cambridge: Cambridge University Press, 2014.

Wyatt, N. *Religious Texts from Ugarit: The Words of Ilimilku and His Colleagues.* Sheffield: Sheffield Academic, 1998.

Wyman, David S. *The Abandonment of the Jews: America and the Holocaust, 1941–1945.* New York: Pantheon, 1984.

Yee, Gale A. "Post-Colonial Biblical Criticism." In *Methods for Exodus*, edited by Thomas B. Dozeman, 193–233.

Zimmerli, Walther. *I Am YHWH.* Translated by D. W. Stott. Atlanta: John Knox, 1982.

———. "I Am YHWH." In *I Am YHWH*, 1–28.

———. "Knowledge of G-d According to the Book of Ezekiel." In *I Am YHWH*, 29–98.

———. "The Word of Divine Self-Manifestation (Proof-Saying): A Prophetic Genre." In *I Am YHWH*, 99–110.

Zohary, Michael. *Plants of the Bible.* Cambridge: Cambridge University Press, 1982.

Author Index

Scripture Index

Genesis *(continued)*

Exodus

Exodus *(continued)*

Exodus *(continued)*

Exodus *(continued)*

Leviticus

Numbers

Deuteronomy

Joshua

Joshua *(continued)*

Judges

Ruth

1 Samuel

2 Samuel

1 Kings

2 Kings

1 Chronicles

2 Chronicles

Ezra

Nehemiah

Esther

Psalms

Proverbs

Isaiah

Jeremiah

Ezekiel

Daniel

Hosea

Joel

Amos

Ancient Sources Index

www.ingramcontent.com/pod-product-compliance
Lightning Source LLC
LaVergne TN
LVHW041053080826
845145LV00007B/1558
* 9 7 8 1 6 6 6 7 4 0 6 6 0 *